ASHGATE
RESEARCH
COMPANION

THE ASHGATE RESEARCH COMPANION TO COSMOPOLITANISM

ASHGATE
RESEARCH
COMPANION

The *Ashgate Research Companions* are designed to offer scholars and graduate students a comprehensive and authoritative state-of-the-art review of current research in a particular area. The companions' editors bring together a team of respected and experienced experts to write chapters on the key issues in their speciality, providing a comprehensive reference to the field.

The Ashgate Research Companion to Cosmopolitanism

Edited by

MARIA ROVISCO
York St John University, UK

MAGDALENA NOWICKA
*Max Planck Institute for the Study of
Religious and Ethnic Diversity, Germany*

ASHGATE

© Maria Rovisco and Magdalena Nowicka 2011

All rights reserved. No part of this publication may be reproduced, stored in a retrieval system or transmitted in any form or by any means, electronic, mechanical, photocopying, recording or otherwise without the prior permission of the publisher.

Maria Rovisco and Magdalena Nowicka have asserted their right under the Copyright, Designs and Patents Act, 1988, to be identified as the editors of this work.

Published by
Ashgate Publishing Limited
Wey Court East
Union Road
Farnham
Surrey GU9 7PT
England

Ashgate Publishing Company
Suite 420
101 Cherry Street
Burlington,
VT 05401-4405
USA

www.ashgate.com

British Library Cataloguing in Publication Data
The Ashgate research companion to cosmopolitanism.
  1. Cosmopolitanism.
  I. Research companion to cosmopolitanism II. Rovisco,
  Maria. III. Nowicka, Magdalena.
  306-dc22

Library of Congress Cataloging-in-Publication Data
The Ashgate research companion to cosmopolitanism / [edited] by Maria Rovisco and Magdalena Nowicka.
    p. cm.
  Includes bibliographical references and index.
  ISBN 978-0-7546-7799-4 (hardback) -- ISBN 978-0-7546-9556-1 (ebook) 1. Cosmopolitanism. I. Rovisco, Maria. II. Nowicka, Magdalena.
  JZ1308.A73 2011
  306--dc23

2011024620

ISBN 9780754677994 (hbk)
ISBN 9780754695561 (ebk)

Printed and bound in Great Britain by the
MPG Books Group, UK

Contents

List of Contributors ix
Acknowledgements xi

    Introduction 1
    Maria Rovisco and Magdalena Nowicka

Part I Cultural Cosmopolitanism

1   Cosmopolitan Sociology: Outline of a Paradigm Shift 17
    Ulrich Beck

2   Cosmopolitanism and Consumption 33
    Jennie Germann Molz

3   Cosmopolitan Openness 53
    Zlatko Skrbiš and Ian Woodward

4   Mega-events and Cosmopolitanism:
    Observations on Expos and European Culture in Modernity 69
    Maurice Roche

5   The Cosmopolitan City 87
    Christina Horvath

6   Paradoxes of Postcolonial Vernacular Cosmopolitanism in
    South Asia and the Diaspora 107
    Pnina Werbner

7   Diaspora and Cosmopolitanism 125
    Vinay Dharwadker

Part II Political Cosmopolitanism

8   Cosmopolitanism and Natural Law: Rethinking Kant 147
    Robert Fine

9	Cosmopolitanism, Democracy and the Global Order *David Held*	163
10	Cosmopolitanism and the Struggle for Global Justice *Gillian Brock*	179
11	Cosmopolitan Memory and Human Rights *Daniel Levy and Natan Sznaider*	195
12	The Cosmopolitical *Pheng Cheah*	211
13	Hermeneutic Cosmopolitanism, or: Toward a Cosmopolitan Public Sphere *Hans-Herbert Kögler*	225
14	Cosmopolitan Citizenship *Nick Stevenson*	243
15	Cosmopolitan Borders: Bordering as Connectivity *Anthony Cooper and Chris Rumford*	261

Part III Debates

16	Critical Cosmopolitanism *Fuyuki Kurasawa*	279
17	From Cosmos to Globe: Relating Cosmopolitanism, Globalization and Globality *David Inglis and Roland Robertson*	295
18	Cosmopolitanism and Postcolonial Critique *Gurminder K. Bhambra*	313
19	Border Thinking, Decolonial Cosmopolitanism and Dialogues Among Civilizations *Walter D. Mignolo*	329
20	Cosmopolitanism and Mobilities *Mimi Sheller*	349
21	Cosmopolitanism and Feminism *Niamh Reilly*	367

| 22 | Cosmopolitanism and the Humanist Myopia
Harry Kunneman and Caroline Suransky | 387 |
| 23 | The Capabilities Approach and Ethical Cosmopolitanism:
The Challenge of Political Liberalism
Martha Nussbaum | 403 |

Index   *411*

List of Contributors

Ulrich Beck, University of Munich/LSE
Gurminder K. Bhambra, University of Warwick
Gillian Brock, University of Auckland
Pheng Cheah, University of California at Berkeley
Anthony Cooper, Royal Holloway, University of London
Vinay Dharwadker, University of Wisconsin
Robert Fine, University of Warwick
David Held, London School of Economics
Christina Horvarth, Oxford Brookes University
David Inglis, University of Aberdeen
Hans-Herbert Kögler, University of North Florida
Harry Kunneman, University of Humanist Studies – Utrecht
Fuyuki Kurasawa, York University, Toronto
Daniel Levy, Stony Brook University
Walter D. Mignolo, Duke University
Jennie Germann Molz, College of the Holy Cross
Martha Nussbaum, University of Chicago
Niamh Reilly, National University of Ireland – Galway
Roland Robertson, University of Aberdeen
Maurice Roche, University of Sheffield
Chris Rumford, Royal Holloway, University of London
Mimi Sheller, Drexel University
Caroline Suransky, University of Humanist Studies – Utrecht
Zlatko Skrbiš, University of Queensland
Nick Stevenson, University of Nottingham
Natan Sznaider, Academic College of Tel-Aviv – Yaffo
Pnina Werbner, University of Keele
Ian Woodward, Griffith University

Acknowledgements

We would like to thank Claire Jarvis our commissioning editor at Ashgate for inviting us to embark on this project and her support throughout the process. We wish to also thank Steven Vertovec, who from the beginning has been an enthusiastic supporter of the ideas behind this book, for his advice and suggestions at various stages of the project. Thanks are also due to Ulrich Beck for his insightful comments and suggestions during the initial stages of the project. We are indebted to our two superb Editorial Assistants, Bettina Voigt, at the Max Planck Institute for the Study of Religious and Ethnic Diversity in Göttingen, Germany, and Vanessa Simmons, at York St John University, United Kingdom, who worked tirelessly in the preparation of this manuscript.

We could have not completed this project without the supportive and stimulating environment provided by our academic institutions. At the Max Planck Institute for the Study of Religious and Ethnic Diversity, Magdalena Nowicka is thankful to Steven Vertovec for granting her time for completing this project work. At York St John University, Maria Rovisco would like to thank Julie Raby and the members of the Research Committee at the Faculty of Arts, for providing her funding for teaching relief. Finally, we would like to give special thanks to all the contributors. We could not have wished for a more enthusiastic and engaged set of scholars.

Introduction

Maria Rovisco and Magdalena Nowicka

Almost 10 years after the publication of *Conceiving Cosmopolitanism* (Vertovec and Cohen 2002), the enthusiasm for cosmopolitanism as a concept that has the potential to be socially and politically transformative has not waned. On the contrary, there is hardly any social or cultural theorist that has not in one way or another critically engaged with the notion. In order to circumvent the problem of the evanescent and slippery meanings of cosmopolitanism and the mutations of the term in a rapidly expanding literature, Vertovec and Cohen proposed a typology for six characterizations of cosmopolitanism that could be readily used by scholars from different disciplines. These are:

1. cosmopolitanism as a socio-cultural condition;
2. a kind of philosophy or worldview;
3. a political project towards building transnational institutions;
4. a political project for recognizing multiple identities;
5. an attitudinal or dispositional orientation; and
6. a mode of practice or competence.

The volume soon became a work of reference for the voluminous amount of research that has explored the multiple facets of cosmopolitanism as a descriptive social category that opposes cosmopolitans to locals or nationals, and as a normative concept concerned with struggles for global justice and the making of a new world order.

Vertovec and Cohen (2002: 21) were understandably cautious in conceding that 'there is little description or analysis of how contemporary cosmopolitan philosophies, political projects, outlooks or practices can be formed, instilled or bolstered'. In contrast, the so-called 'cosmopolitan turn' (Robins 2006: 19) across the social sciences and the humanities offers evidence of a now growing body of research that uses cosmopolitanism as a grounded category (Skrbiš et al. 2004, Skrbiš and Woodward 2007) – something that people do rather than a purely abstract idea (see Pollock et al. 2000). Cosmopolitanism emerges more and more as a key analytical tool to study a variety of outlooks, processes and ethico-political practices that are observable in a variety of social and political contexts

(Nowicka and Rovisco 2009). This renewed interest on cosmopolitanism in empirically-grounded research goes in tandem with Beck and Sznaider's (2006) call for an epistemological shift in the ways we grasp and study the social and political realities of the current global condition. In this sense, cosmopolitanism has become the notion for a new methodological approach or research programme – 'methodological cosmopolitanism' – which sheds the research lens that takes the national frame as the given unit of analysis (see also Chernilo 2006). The new cosmopolitan research agenda forcefully endorses the view that emerging cosmopolitan conditions (or cosmopolitanization in Beck and Sznaider's words), whether apparent in identity outlooks, lifestyles, political projects, and transnational ethico-political practices, are typically linked to the dynamics of the social and political processes as well as the material conditions that make up the current global condition of connectivity. Not surprisingly, negotiations of difference via empathetic engagements with other cultures and value-systems, issues of self-transformation, and mobilities of various kinds are processes very much at the heart of the new empirical research programme (Nowicka and Kaweh 2009, Robertson 2010, Nava 2007). Beck's (2004) call for the social sciences to equip themselves with a grammar that is capable of questioning exclusionary and categorical dichotomies (East/West, local/global, internal/external, us/them) has to be understood as an attempt to map and explain 'new' cultural phenomena – such as cultural hybridization, economic globalization, and conditions of intensified mobility and connectedness – in a global world. Yet, this vision of cosmopolitanism as a condition of the present that is mostly encountered in the Western world vis-à-vis a past understood as less cosmopolitan is giving way to more nuanced and historically-rooted understandings of both past and present cosmopolitanisms (Holton 2009, Jansen 2009, Delanty 2009). There is, in fact, increasing recognition in the literature that current processes of transnational contact, travel and migration that enabled intensified patterns of cultural exchange, new ways of co-existence and cosmopolitan affiliations are not wholly unprecedented (Euben 2006, Rovisco 2010).

It is against this background that *The Ashgate Research Companion to Cosmopolitanism* attempts to map new directions within a vastly expanding research agenda. It is possible to identify two main shifts of direction in the literature:

1. A shift from a theoretical concern with defining and mapping the multiple facets and meanings of the concept to a focus on cosmopolitanism as grounded category – which pertains to work developed primarily (but not exclusively) in the disciplines of sociology, anthropology and cultural studies. Rather than asking 'what is cosmopolitanism?' and 'who are the cosmopolitans?' this new research agenda probes instead how forms of 'lived cosmopolitanism' are experienced by different groups and individuals in the micro-scale of everyday life interactions in concrete times and places. There is here an attempt to go beyond the tendency to treat cosmopolitanism as a descriptive concept to label and distinguish between cosmopolitans and

non-cosmopolitans. A shift of analytical focus that brings into closer scrutiny issues of agency, class location and power structures is now shaping inquiries into what makes certain cross-cultural engagements and practices, but no others, cosmopolitan. Notably, issues of human agency and power relations are now at the heart of a more forceful call – especially from scholars working from a postcolonial standpoint – for cosmopolitan approaches to be sensitive to the plurality of modes and histories that enable cosmopolitan identities, memories and discourses in both Western and non-Western historical contexts (Pollock et al. 2000: 584). This is apparent in the emerging body of scholarship that critically engages the Eurocentric underpinnings of cosmopolitanism while calling for the recognition of multiple cosmopolitanisms (Holton 2009, Delanty 2009, Krossa 2009, Bhambra 2010, Euben 2006, Mignolo 2000).

2. The other important shift in the research agenda is a shift from purely understanding cosmopolitanism as an ethico-political ideal that is underpinned by legally-bound forms of supranational and transnational governance (Held 1995, Archibugi et al. 1998, Habermas 2001), to considerations of cosmopolitanism as a moral politics that is articulated in ordinary ways of thinking and acting of those agents that are active at the grassroots level in a range of transnational informal networks (Cheah 2006, Kurasawa 2007, Kögler 2005, Tarrow 2005). This new research direction – which cuts across the fields of international relations, political science and political philosophy – brings forth a more robust theorization of critical cosmopolitanism as reconstructive critique of alternative perspectives and concrete practices 'from below' that are underpinned by cosmopolitan principles (Chapter 16, this volume). In this new understanding, cosmopolitanism is not necessarily seen as a project of global governance that exists beyond the state form. In fact, the citizenship and the territoriality of the state are now seen as capable of renewal not only by optimizing the conditions that enable meaningful cosmopolitan experiences (Kendall et al. 2009), but also by facilitating adherence to cosmopolitan principles by a range of state and non-state actors. This is visible, for example, in the possibility of modes of action in negotiations between states (Vandenberghe, forthcoming) and the contribution of bottom-up resistance and legal innovation taking place around the world to the resilience of domination within and across state borders (Santos and Rodriguez-Garavito 2005).

The Aims and Structure of this Volume

The aim of *The Ashgate Research Companion to Cosmopolitanism* is to provide readers with a comprehensive and authoritative state-of-the-art review of current research on the topic of cosmopolitanism across the social sciences and the humanities. Although it would be tempting to provide an appraisal of the most current and up-to-date definitions of the term from within different disciplines, especially given the many hyphenated variations of cosmopolitanism ('vernacular', 'discrepant', 'rooted', 'subaltern', etc.), our approach to the content of this volume is one that commences by bringing together mainstream discussions with the newest thinking (Parts I and II) and goes on to cover contestations of the term from within a range of disciplinary traditions (Part III). Although we lament the lack of contributions originating from non-Western academic contexts, our choice of chapters and contributors inevitably reflects a concentration of scholarly work that has emerged from Anglo-Saxon academic contexts.

It is important to emphasize that the chapters are not strictly organized in terms of disciplinary boundaries and concerns. Part I deals with themes and issues that pertain to the disciplines of sociology, anthropology and cultural studies and are typically encountered within the strand of cultural cosmopolitanism approaches, while Part II focuses on debates and issues that are typically of concern for IR scholars and political scientists writing within the tradition of political cosmopolitanism. However, Part III (Debates) engages major debates and controversies on the topic and deliberately eschews any bland consensus to instead foreground the key arguments and lively intellectual discussions in play across disciplinary divisions.

While the volume showcases a range of theoretical and methodological approaches, not every discipline is thoroughly represented in this volume. This is hardly surprising when we consider how the literature on cosmopolitanism involves cross-fertilization among a multitude of disciplines across the social sciences and the humanities. In fact, scholars working on a given field often adopt conceptual approaches and reflect upon key developments and treatments of the notion of cosmopolitanism originating in other disciplinary fields. Ultimately, our aim has been to attain a selection of chapters that reflects how traditional disciplinary divisions shaped the literature without turning a blind eye to instances of dialogue and cross-fertilization between disciplines.

Finally, while the volume reflects a range of conceptual and methodological approaches that are representative of the major schools of thought – namely, 'political cosmopolitanism', 'cultural cosmopolitanism' and 'moral cosmopolitanism' – it is worth emphasizing that the issues and themes that are typically encountered in moral cosmopolitanism approaches – such as the anthropological and sociological strands in Kant's cosmopolitanism (Muthu 2003, Kleingeld 2007, 2009) – have received less direct attention in this book. This is, in part, because moral cosmopolitanism – as a philosophical perspective concerned with the moral equality of all human beings and emphasizing loyalty to the community of humankind as a whole – has shaped and informed both cultural and political cosmopolitanism approaches. Hence, it is not surprising moral cosmopolitanism approaches – especially, references to Kant's cosmopolitanism and Nussbaum's ethical cosmopolitanism – resurface throughout many of the contributions included in this volume, especially in parts II and III.

By including chapters by both world-renowned and newer scholars, we also envisaged to solicit contributions that shed light on the newest thinking and reconstructive critiques of the term. We believe that *The Ashgate Research Companion to Cosmopolitanism* breaks new ground in the way it captures cutting-edge debates in the literature, especially by bringing into light perspectives on feminist cosmopolitanism, postcolonial critique and cosmopolitanism, and the growing prominence of critical cosmopolitanism approaches.

Part I is concerned with exploring how cosmopolitanism as a practice and a cultural phenomenon that is observable in social life can be understood vis-à-vis issues of agency, class location, ethnicity and power relations. The chapters included in Part I illustrate some of the main directions that cultural cosmopolitanism has taken in the fields of sociology, anthropology and cultural studies. Cultural cosmopolitanism perspectives typically use an empirically-grounded approach to look at cosmopolitanism as something that people do and is 'in the making' (Pollock 2000: 593) and, as such, offer a corrective to the rather more abstract treatments of the notion within both political and moral cosmopolitanism perspectives. Part I opens with Beck's proposition for a paradigm shift in sociology towards a social scientific research programme that sheds away the paradigm of methodological nationalism. Positing 'cosmopolitanism' as a social scientific research programme, Beck purports that in order to respond adequately to conditions of heightened global interconnectivity the social sciences must resort to the cosmopolitan outlook ('methodological cosmopolitanism') to develop new concepts and research questions for empirical research.

Research into cosmopolitanism has, in fact, developed in recent years into a fully-fledged programme of theoretically informed empirical analysis (Holton 2009: 16–17). This research programme is consistent with the above-mentioned shift towards a more robust investigation of forms of lived cosmopolitanism vis-à-vis a range of cultural phenomena and socio-historical processes (e.g. cultural melange, mobilities of people and ideas, cross-cultural engagements, diasporas, transnational networks of professionals) that make up both past and current conditions of global interconnectedness. It is against this backdrop that cultural cosmopolitanism perspectives typically propose an empirically-grounded approach to study and understand a particular mode of being in a world that is said to be 'cosmopolitan'.

The set of contributions included in Part I is representative of a body of work that is indebted to Hannerz's (1990) influential definition of the cosmopolitan as someone who is endowed with a state of mind, or a perspective, that requires particular intellectual and cognitive capacities. Yet, each contribution also attempts in its own right to overcome some of the limitations of Hannerz's approach by moving beyond the tendency to see cosmopolitanism purely as a social category to qualify a particular kind of group – the 'cosmopolitans' – as opposed to, say, 'locals', 'nationals', 'transnational workers' or 'tourists'. What Hannerz had in mind with his attempt to categorize cosmopolitans vis-à-vis other types of social groups was a highly intellectualized, Western and elite characterization of cosmopolitanism whose limitations are currently widely acknowledged in the literature. And even though understandings of cosmopolitanism as a characteristic of the global elites are still entrenched in the literature (Calhoun 2002, Harvey 2008, Jones 2007), the focus of the debate has shifted to more grounded characterizations of cosmopolitanism as a more pervasive condition in a global world. Part I is primarily concerned with how cosmopolitanism is understood as an outlook, competence, aesthetic stance or a consumption practice that is observable within a variety of Western and non-Western socio-historical settings. Overcoming some of ethnocentric biases that have blighted the literature, Part I illuminates how particular social structural changes and conditions can both optimize and constrain the possibility of cosmopolitan practices, identities and imaginaries in the past as well as in the current conditions of global interconnectedness. Examining certain discursive frames (Roche, Horvarth, Dharwadker) and actual practices of consumption (Werbner, Molz, Skrbiš and Woodward) vis-à-vis the social structural changes (e.g. patterns of mobility of things, ideas and people, creolization, the rise of the modern state, gentrification and urban development) that enable mundane expressions of cosmopolitanism, the contributions to Part I document the latest developments in cultural cosmopolitanism approaches. The chapters by Dharwadker and Horvarth show how cosmopolitanism is often used interchangeably with notions of transnationalism, postcolonialism, diaspora and hybridity in a range of contemporary scholarly and political discourses. But whereas Horvarth is primarily interested in investigating how competing notions of the cosmopolitan, transnational, multicultural and postcolonial city shape and inform representations of cultural difference in contemporary urban discourses, Dharwadker's contribution shows how the emergence of cosmopolitanism as a major interdisciplinary field has relied on the appropriation of discursive frames that are commonly used by postcolonial scholars and cultural critics to characterize cultural phenomena such as diaspora and hybridity. Using the Jewish diaspora and the Indian labor diaspora and their socio-cultural processes as empirical examples, his chapter goes on to argue that the equation between cosmopolitanism and hybridity poses a number of conceptual and analytical problems. Thus while the cosmopolitan subject is culturally ambidextrous, and easily switches codes between the distinct cultures in which she feels at home, hybridity or creolization do not necessarily result in the cultural ambidexterity that defines cosmopolitanism. Hence, the hybrid or creole subject ultimately inhabits a single culture of her own, which emerges in the intermingling of two prior cultures. By mixing up the codes of these different cultures, the creole subject feels she is no longer fully at home in either culture in its unmixed form.

Like Horvarth and Dharwadker, Roche focuses on certain discursive frames in order to argue that Europe's mega-events offer a springboard for the maintenance and renewal of cosmopolitan ideas and experiences. Using a socio-historical approach and a sociological lens, the chapter locates the emergence of mega-events, such as Expos, in the historical context of the rise of the modern nation-state as this developed in tandem with more complex patterns of trade, cultural exchange and international cooperation between Europe and other parts of the world. Importantly, Roche's contribution usefully illuminates how since the nineteenth-century Expos were, paradoxically, vehicles for the anti-cosmopolitan ideologies of nationalism and imperialism as much as carriers of ideologies and discourses that contain and promote cosmopolitan values, imaginaries and actual cosmopolitan experiences.

Introduction

The chapter contributions by Skrbiš and Woodward, Molz and Werbner use a sociological and – in Werbner's case – an anthropological lens to argue how actual practices of mundane consumption can both facilitate and constrain forms of ordinary cosmopolitanism in conditions of greater mobility and cultural mix in a global world. Werbner's study of the South Asian diaspora of vernacular cultural consumption shares some features of Skrbiš and Woodward's and Molz's chapters, arguing that cultural consumption is an important vehicle of cosmopolitan experiences. Yet, Werbner's contribution is slightly different in terms of its ethnographic focus on popular aesthetic consumption in the Indian Subcontinent and its global diaspora as a form of vernacular cosmopolitanism. In contrast, the chapters by Skrbiš and Woodward and Molz are more specifically concerned with conceptualizing different forms of cultural consumption vis-à-vis certain material and socio-structural conditions. Their chapters draw on a number of empirical examples to distinguish between practices of consumption that are conducive to an authentic and reflexive cosmopolitanism – which translates into deeper forms of cross-cultural engagement connoting self-reflexivity, social learning and an ethico-political orientation – and certain forms of cosmopolitan consumption in which cultural openness involves little more than a positive engagement with aesthetic and sensual differences and a desire for cultural novelty. However, while Molz offers a more nuanced account of different types of cultural consumption, Skrbiš and Woodward's chapter is more specifically concerned with an exploration of contemporary cosmopolitan openness as an analytical and conceptual tool to understand everyday experiences of cultural consumption vis-à-vis certain social structural conditions. Interestingly, both chapters illuminate how the appreciation of cultural difference, which characterizes more superficial and less reflexive forms of cosmopolitan consumption, end up reproducing a range of symbolic and material inequalities and, as such, sit uneasily with the cosmopolitan ethics.

Taken all together, the contributions to Part I illustrate a shift from a primarily theoretical concern with the tension between elite cosmopolitanism (Calhoun 2002) and ordinary and vernacular forms of cosmopolitanism (Bhabha 1996, Werbner 1999, Lamont and Aksartova 2002, Nava 2002, 2007), towards a more robust and grounded investigation of the connection between cosmopolitanism as a historically-grounded practice and actual relations and structures of domination. Many of the chapters included in Part I are, in fact, wary of the dangers of 'thin' cultural cosmopolitanism approaches that tend to conflate certain cultural phenomena that are typical of the current global condition – such as hybridity and 'mix-and-match' cultural fusion in a more interconnected world – with mundane and everyday expressions of cosmopolitanism. The problem with these 'thin' cultural cosmopolitanism approaches is that they often remain oblivious of the hierarchies of power and material conditions underpinning certain cross-cultural engagements (Gilbert and Lo 2007: 8–9).

Part II covers those themes – human rights, democracy, global justice and citizenship – that are typically encountered in the writings of scholars working within the tradition of political cosmopolitanism. It considers two distinct theoretical strands within the tradition:

1. how cosmopolitan principles and ideas have been theorized in relation to the formation of legal and political frameworks of world governance in the context of processes globalization; and
2. how a 'cosmopolitanism from below' is articulated in the concrete ethico-political practices and ordinary ways of thinking of situated agents who are involved, at the grassroots level, in a range of transnational social movements, global protest movements and informal networks of activists.

These two strands of scholarship in political cosmopolitanism approaches often stand in tension with each other. While the advocates of cosmopolitan democracy (Held 2003, Archibugi et al. 1998) argue that legal arrangements operated by international and supranational structures (e.g. the United Nations, the European Union) are replacing the nation-state unit in addressing global challenges and problems (e.g. poverty, environmental threats, climate change, terrorism), those concerned with theorizing a 'cosmopolitanism from below' (Cheah 1998, Kurasawa 2004, 2007, Santos and Rodriguez-Garavito 2005) are critical precisely of the ways in which such forms of global governance 'from above' – by operating only at the elite level – fail to consider of political agency at the grassroots level. In a nutshell, Part II offers a springboard to understand how the theorization and study of cosmopolitan forms of governance moved from considering individuals purely as abstract subjects (Nash 2006) to a more nuanced and thorough consideration of how cosmopolitan principles are applied or interpreted by situated agents within and across a range of political arrangements (local, national, transnational).

Part II begins with Fine's contribution that goes on to reassert the significance of Kant's cosmopolitan thinking for contemporary debates in political cosmopolitanism, while also setting out to offer a reappraisal of the legacies of Kant's eighteenth-century vision of cosmopolitanism vis-à-vis the framework of modern natural law. The contributions by Held, Brock and Levy and Sznaider deal with the core themes and issues that make up mainstream scholarship within the strand of political cosmopolitanism. In this context, cosmopolitanism is a normative concept used to refer to forms of belonging and modes of citizenship which involve affiliation to political structures beyond the nation-state. Held's and Brock's chapters are, therefore, representative of a classical line of research in political philosophy that considers cosmopolitanism as a moral and political outlook. The underlying assumption here is that cosmopolitan principles and ideals – e.g. human rights, global justice, universal democratic principles, worldliness – ought to be legally enforced in global institutional structures. Such institutional arrangements not only override the nation-state system, but also treat people as equals regardless of any particularist attachments (say, to nation, religion). In a slightly different vein, Levy and Sznaider go on to argue that developments in the human rights regime led not so much to a decline of the nation-state sovereignty but rather to its internal transformation. The key argument in Levy and Sznaider's contribution is that since it has become widely accepted that human rights are based on historical experiences and memories of catastrophes that are not confined to specifically national experiences, states are

INTRODUCTION

now able to commit to a set of contemporary human rights norms that limit their sovereignty. One of the implications of this minimalist version of cosmopolitanism is that the human rights regime, although implying that each person is treated as a subject of equal moral concern, does not require major changes in the ways in which national citizens actually live and act towards distant others in their situated contexts (Benhabib 2002).

The chapters by Cheah, Kögler, Stevenson, and Cooper and Rumford take a rather different approach in directing research lenses to the ways in which ordinary individuals embrace and enact cosmopolitan principles in their situated contexts. In this sense, this set of contributors is more seriously concerned with micro-level forms of political and cultural agency, especially the ways in which cosmopolitan principles and ideas inform forms of public discourse, deliberation and contestation being, therefore, capable of challenging established power structures. Cheah's chapter argues that cosmopolitanism can be conceived as a moral politics (the 'cosmopolitical') that is capable of generating forms of cosmopolitan citizenship, consciousness and solidarity (i.e. a feeling of belonging to a shared world) that are generated and sustained within a range of non-state centred institutional structures. Yet, Cheah's key point is that cosmopolitan principles, which are embedded in various laws, formal rules and organizational structures, have so far failed to generate a genuine mass-based cosmopolitan consciousness. He is particularly critical of Habermas' (2001) vision of a cosmopolitan public sphere that in his view remains oblivious of the neoliberal drive of global capitalism, especially with regards to the imbalance in power relations created by an allegedly cosmopolitan North (which constitutes the model for a cosmopolitan public sphere) that is sustained by the global exploitation of a postcolonial South. Cheah's negative critique of the cosmopolitan project of global governance and its neoliberal underpinnings contrasts with Cooper and Rumford's as well as Kögler's more positive approaches to actual cosmopolitan experiences that are generated by 'real life' situated agents in various forms of ethico-political practice and public discourse. Highly indebted to Habermas' theory of discourse ethics, Kögler's proposal for a hermeneutic cosmopolitanism posits that the capabilities of cosmopolitan dialogue (self-reflexivity, empathy towards others, empathetic perspective-taking, critical engagement of generally accepted beliefs and notions) can be realized within the confines of transnational public communication. He suggests, for example, that new media (e.g. the Internet) and critical reportages broadcasted by transnational television channels can make the perils and power struggles of distant others more accessible and intelligible on a global scale. Thus the hermeneutic idea of a cosmopolitan public sphere is primarily based on the ways in which agents engage in serious public dialogue – emphatically aimed at understanding the other – outside the boundary of the nation-state, and without the legal and institutional guarantees of more formalized global institutional structures.

Cooper and Rumford's and Stevenson's chapters are in agreement with Kögler's with regards to the way in which socially situated cosmopolitan practices are not entirely ruled by either national or global structures of governance. But whereas Stevenson's contribution is primarily concerned with theorizing the political agency of concrete individuals and groups who are publicly engaged in the contestation of neoliberal forms of globalization in the European setting vis-à-vis an emerging cosmopolitan civil society, Cooper and Rumford draw on two case studies to propose a new conceptualization of borders as key sites whereby genuine cosmopolitan experiences enable various forms of contact and connectivity with others and the world. By looking at the activity of ordinary individuals in the making, shifting or dismantling borders, Cooper and Rumford argue that this borderwork can be quintessentially cosmopolitan as everyday life encounters with borders activate negotiations of difference and cross-cultural engagements that are no longer entirely imposed from above (e.g. nation-state, the EU).

Part III explores emerging debates involving a reconstructive critique of the notion of cosmopolitanism from a variety of critical perspectives (e.g. feminist, postcolonial, humanist). Cutting across disciplinary divisions, what the various chapters included in Part III have in common is a serious attempt to debate some of the limitations of cosmopolitanism both as an abstract idea of European provenance and an exclusionary social category that is markedly Western, male and elitist. As such, each chapter goes on to set out the terms in which a reconstructed notion of cosmopolitanism can be usefully employed as an analytical and critical tool to understand changes in the social and political world. Kurasawa's chapter traces the genesis of critical cosmopolitanism as a normative and socio-historically informed approach that offers not only a theoretical critique of other cosmopolitan perspectives, but also a range of theoretical paradigms (neo-Kantian, Levinasian, neo-Marxist). Kurasawa's contribution is illuminating in the way it explains how under the auspices of critical theory cosmopolitanism shifted from being understood purely as descriptive notion for a mode of being, an abstract notion or a normative project of global governance, towards a more fully-fledged and grounded project of universal emancipation for situated agents.

The chapters by Bhambra and Inglis and Robertson bring to the fore the historical grounding of cosmopolitanism while critically engaging overtly presentist and Eurocentric understandings of cosmopolitan practices, ideas and processes vis-à-vis understandings of the global. Whereas Inglis and Robertson make a case for cosmopolitan political theory to be linked to the historical dynamics of the political, social, economic and cultural facets of globalization and globality – if it is to avoid being narrowly-defined in terms of abstract philosophical commitments – Bhambra embarks on a forceful critique of the inadequacy of Beck's and Sznaider's (2006) cosmopolitan paradigm as a critical and analytical tool to explain the global as a multicultural world. Through the lens of postcolonial critique, she goes on to deconstruct the Eurocentric underpinnings of Beck's and Sznaider's cosmopolitan approach while calling for a provincialized cosmopolitanism that is capable of including postcolonial and decolonial voices and perspectives. Similarly to Bhambra, Sheller's contribution offers a strong critique of Beck's cosmopolitan realism via a discussion of both the tensions and interconnections between 'cosmopolitanism' and 'mobilities' as two distinct paradigms of research aiming at studying conditions of greater global interconnectedness and social complexity.

Sheller's key argument is that the material turn in mobilities research, with its emphasis on discourse, the non-human and forms of knowledge construction, has enabled the mobilities paradigm to offer a more robust critical analysis of structures of domination that is lacking in the cosmopolitan perspective. In her view, the latter remains strongly informed by a primarily theoretical concern with issues of reflexivity, human agency and politics in a shared global world.

The chapters by Kunneman and Suransky, Mignolo, and Reilly are primarily concerned with conceptualizing cosmopolitanism as a progressive and emancipatory notion through the lens of different critical perspectives, respectively, critical humanism, critical border thinking and feminism. Breaking new ground in the literature, Reilly's chapter points not only at how the leading proponents of cosmopolitanism have failed to bring into view the gendered power dynamics at play in forms of neoliberal globalization, but also at a lack of feminist approaches to issues of cosmopolitan democracy and citizenship. Against the gender blindness of mainstream political cosmopolitan scholarship, Reilly goes on to offer an account of cosmopolitan feminism as an emancipatory political practice that represents an attempt to theorize global feminism and transnational advocacy, especially in relation to feminist analyses of the global women's human rights movement. Part III concludes with a contribution by Nussbaum who challenges common readings of her work by explaining why her capabilities approach – as a political doctrine – should not be conflated with the comprehensive ethical doctrine of ethical cosmopolitanism. Highlighting that she has written relatively little on the latter, Nussbaum is particularly wary of how her capabilities approach – on which she has written extensively – is often misrepresented as a form of cosmopolitanism.

As editors, our hope is that readers will get a sense not only of how a major concentration of study on cosmopolitanism originated from within particular disciplinary traditions, but also of how major debates and critiques of the term are, in practice, interdisciplinary and, therefore, of concern for scholars pursuing a range of theoretical orientations and empirical analyses.

Bibliography

Appiah, K. A. 2006. *Cosmopolitanism: Ethics in a World of Strangers*. London: Allen.

Archibugi, D., Held, D. and Kohler, M. (eds). 1998. *Re-Imagining Political Community – Studies in Cosmopolitan Democracy*. Cambridge: Polity Press.

Beck, U. 2004. Cosmopolitan Realism: On the Distinction between Cosmopolitanism in Philosophy and the Social Sciences. *Global Networks*, 4(2), 131–56.

Beck, U. and Sznaider, N. 2006. Unpacking Cosmopolitanism for the Social Sciences: A Research Agenda. *British Journal of Sociology*, 57(1), 1–23.

Benhabib, S. 2002. *The Claims of Culture: Equality and Diversity in the Global Era*. Princeton: Princeton University Press.

Bhabha, H. 1996. Unsatisfied: Notes on Vernacular Cosmopolitanism, in *Text and Nation*, edited by L. Garcia-Moreno and P. Pfeiffer. Columbia: Camden House.

Bhambra, G. 2010. Sociology after Postcolonialism: Provincialized Cosmopolitanism and Connected Sociologies, in *Decolonizing European Sociology: Trans-disciplinary Approaches*, edited by M. Boatcă and S. Costa. Aldershot: Ashgate.

Calhoun, C. 2002. The Class Consciousness of Frequent Travelers: Towards a Critique of Actually Existing Cosmopolitanism. *The South Atlantic Quarterly*, 101(4), 869–97.

Cheah, P. 1998. Introduction Part II: The Cosmopolitical, in *Cosmopolitics: Thinking and Feeling Beyond the Nation*, edited by P. Cheah and B. Robbins. Minneapolis: University of Minnesota Press, 20–41.

Cheah, P. 2006. Cosmopolitanism. *Theory, Culture & Society*, 23(2–3), 486–96.

Chernilo, D. 2006. Social Theory's Methodological Nationalism. Myth and Reality. *European Journal of Social Theory*, 9(1), 5–22.

Delanty, G. 2009. *The Cosmopolitan Imagination: The Renewal of Critical Social Theory*. Cambridge: Cambridge University Press.

Euben, R. 2006. *Journeys to the Other Shore: Muslim and Western Travelers in Search of Knowledge*. Princeton: Princeton University Press.

Gilbert, H. and Lo, J. 2007. *Performance and Cosmopolitics: Cross-Cultural Transactions in Australasia*. Basingstoke: Palgrave.

Habermas, J. 2001. *The Postnational Constellation – Political Essays*. Cambridge: Polity Press.

Hannerz, U. 1990. Cosmopolitans and Locals in World Culture, in *Global Culture*, edited by M. Featherstone. London: Sage, 237–51.

Harvey, D. 2008. *Cosmopolitanism and the Geographies of Freedom*. New York: Columbia University Press.

Held, D. 1995. *Democracy and the Global Order: From the Modern State to Cosmopolitan Governance*. Stanford: Stanford University Press.

Held, D. 2003. *Cosmopolitanism: A Defence*. Cambridge: Polity Press.

Holton, R. 2009. *Cosmopolitanisms: New Thinking and New Directions*. Basingstoke: Palgrave.

Jansen, S. 2009. Cosmopolitan Openings and Closures in Post-Yugoslav Antinationalism, in *Cosmopolitanism in Practice*, edited by M. Nowicka and M. Rovisco. Aldershot: Ashgate, 73–92.

Jones, P. 2007. Cosmopolitanism and Europe: Describing Elites or Challenging Inequalities? in *Cosmopolitanism and Europe*, edited by C. Rumford. Liverpool: Liverpool University Press, 72–86.

Kendall, G., Skrbiš, Z. and Woodward, I. 2009. *The Sociology of Cosmopolitanism: Globalization, Identity, Culture and Government*. Basingstoke: Palgrave.

Kleingeld, P. 2007. Kant's Second Thoughts on Race. *The Philosophical Quarterly*, 57, 573–92.

Kleingeld, P. 2009. Kant's Changing Cosmopolitanism, in *Kant's Idea for a Universal History with a Cosmopolitan Aim: A Critical Guide*, edited by A. Rorty and J. Schmidt. Cambridge: Cambridge University Press, 171–86.

Kögler, H. 2005. Constructing a Cosmopolitan Public Sphere – Hermeneutic Capabilities and Universal Values. *European Journal of Social Theory*, 8(3), 297–320.

Krossa, A.S. 2009. Conceptualising European Society on Non-Normative Grounds: Logic of Sociation, Glocalisation, and Conflict. *European Journal of Social Theory*, 12(2), 249–64.

Kurasawa, F. 2004. A Cosmopolitanism from Below: Alternative Globalization and the Creation of a Solidarity without Bounds. *European Journal of Sociology/ Archives Européennes de Sociologie*, 45(2), 233–55.

Kurasawa, F. 2007. *The Work of Global Justice. Human Rights as Practices*. Cambridge: Cambridge University Press.

Lamont, M. and Aksartova, S. 2002. Ordinary Cosmopolitanisms: Strategies for Bridging Racial Boundaries among Working-Class Men. *Theory, Culture & Society*, 19(4), 1–25.

Mignolo, W. 2000. The Many Faces of Cosmo-polis: Border Thinking and Critical Cosmopolitanism. *Public Culture*, 12(3), 721–48.

Muthu, S. 2003. *Enlightenment Against Empire*. Princeton: Princeton University Press.

Nash, K. 2006. Political Culture, Ethical Cosmopolitanism and Cosmopolitan Democracy. *Cultural Politics*, 2(2), 193–212.

Nava, M. 2002. Cosmopolitan Modernity: Everyday Imaginaries and the Register of Difference. *Theory, Culture & Society*, 19(1–2), 81–99.

Nava, M. 2007. *Visceral Cosmopolitanism. Gender, Culture and the Normalisation of Difference*. Oxford and New York: Berg.

Nowicka, M. and Kaweh, R. 2009. Looking at the Practice of UN Professionals: Strategies for Managing Differences and the Emergence of a Cosmopolitan Identity, in *Cosmopolitanism in Practice*, edited by M. Nowicka and M. Rovisco. Aldershot: Ashgate, 51–71.

Nowicka, M. and Rovisco, M. 2009. *Cosmopolitanism in Practice*. Aldershot: Ashgate.

Pollock, S. 2000. Cosmopolitan and Vernacular in History. *Public Culture*, 12(3), 591–625.

Pollock, S., Bhabha, H.K., Breckenridge, C.A. and Chakrabarty, D. 2000. Cosmopolitanisms. *Public Culture*, 12(3), 577–89.

Robertson, A. 2010. *Mediated Cosmopolitanism: The World of Television News*. Cambridge: Polity.

Robins, K. 2006. *The Challenges of Transcultural Diversities: Transversal Study on the Theme of Cultural Policy and Cultural Diversity*. Strasbourg: Council of Europe Publishing.

Rovisco, M. 2010. Reframing Europe and the Global: Conceptualising the Border in Cultural Encounters. *Environment and Planning D: Society and Space*, 28, 1015–30.

Santos, B. S. and Rodriguez-Garavito, C. (eds). 2005. *Law and Globalization from Below: Towards a Cosmopolitan Legality*. Cambridge: Cambridge University Press.

Skrbiš, Z. and Woodward, I. 2007. The Ambivalence of Ordinary Cosmopolitanism: Investigating the Limits of Cosmopolitan Openness. *The Sociological Review*, 55(4), 730–47.

Skrbiš, Z., Kendall, G. and Woodward, I. 2004. Locating Cosmopolitanism: Between Humanist Ideal and Grounded Social Category. *Theory, Culture & Society*, 21(6), 115–36.

Tarrow, S. 2005. *The New Transnational Activism*. Cambridge: Cambridge University Press.
Werbner, P. 1999. Global Pathways: Working Class Cosmopolitans and the Creation of Transnational Ethnic Worlds. *Social Anthropology*, (7)1, 17–35.
Vandenberghe, F. (forthcoming). Towards a Cosmopolitan Theory of Recognition between States, in *Justice and Recognition: A Symposium with Axel Honneth*, edited by Sobotka, M. et al. Prague: Prague University Press.
Vertovec, S. and Cohen. R. (eds). 2002. *Conceiving Cosmopolitanism – Theory, Context, and Practice*. Oxford and New York: Oxford University Press.

PART I
Cultural Cosmopolitanism

Cosmopolitan Sociology: Outline of a Paradigm Shift

Ulrich Beck

Cosmopolitanism has undergone a renaissance in recent years, however the sociological significance of this renaissance is easily missed. As I hope to show, the point is that cosmopolitanism has ceased to be merely a controversial idea and ideal; in however distorted a form, it has left the realm of philosophical castles in the air and has entered reality. Indeed, it has become the defining feature of a new era, the era of reflexive modernity, in which the national gaze operating with an unproblematized assumption of neat correspondence between nation, territory, society, politics and culture is missing reality. Thus the word 'cosmopolitan' becomes indispensable for describing a situation in which 'humanity' and 'world' are not merely thinkable but unavoidable social, political and moral categories for the human condition. This is why a world that has become cosmopolitan urgently demands a new standpoint, the cosmopolitan outlook, from which we can grasp the social and political realities in which we live and act. The cosmopolitan outlook is both the presupposition and the result of a conceptual reconfiguration of our modes of perception.

In order to conceptualize this in social scientific terms there is a need to turn the often misunderstood concept of cosmopolitanism from its philosophical head onto its social scientific feet (see also Beck and Grande 2010).

First, I will call into question one of the most powerful convictions about society and politics, one which binds both social actors and social scientists: methodological nationalism. Methodological nationalism equates modern society with society organized in territorially limited nation-states.

Second, I propose to draw an essential distinction between cosmopolitanism in a normative philosophical sense and cosmopolitization as a social scientific research programme.

Third, I am going to illustrate this paradigm shift by re-mapping transnational social inequality and, fourth, global risk. Fifth, and finally, I will pick up the question: what does 'methodological cosmopolitanism' mean?

Critique of Methodological Nationalism

Methodological nationalism assumes that the nation, state and society are the 'natural' social and political forms of the modern world. It assumes that humanity is naturally divided into a limited number of nations, which on the inside, organize themselves as nation-states, and on the outside, set boundaries to distinguish themselves from other nation-states. It goes even further: this outer delimitation, as well as the competition between nation-states, presents the most fundamental category of political organization. Indeed, the social science stance is rooted in the concept of the nation-state. It is a nation-state outlook on society and politics, law, justice and history, that governs the sociological imagination. And it is exactly this methodological nationalism that prevents the social science from getting at the heart of the dynamics of modernization and globalization, both past and present: the *unintended* result of the radicalization of modernity is a disempowerment of Western states, in sharp contrast to their empowerment before and during the nineteenth-century wave of globalization (Beck 2007).

Where social actors subscribe to this belief I talk of a 'national outlook'; where it determines the perspective of the social scientific observer, I talk of 'methodological nationalism'. The distinction between the perspective of the social actor and that of the social scientist is crucial, because there is only a historical connection between the two, not a logical one. This historical connection – between social actors and social scientists – alone gives rise to the axiomatics of methodological nationalism. And methodological nationalism is not a superficial problem or minor error. It involves both the routines of data collection and production and basic concepts of modern sociology and political science like society, social inequality, state, democracy, imagined communities.

It is evident that, in the nineteenth century, European sociology was formulated within a nationalist paradigm and that any cosmopolitan sentiments were snuffed out by the horrors of the Great Wars. In the methodological nationalism of Emile Durkheim, fraternity became solidarity and national integration. He, of course, has in mind the integration of the national society (France) without even mentioning, naming or thinking about it (but it is also true that at the same time Durkheim referred to cosmopolitanism as a possibility). In fact, not using the adjective 'national' as a universal language does not falsify but might sometimes even prove methodological nationalism. Max Weber's sociology involved a comparative study of economic ethics of world religions, but the political inspiration for his (political) sociology was nationalistic. In North America, the same national paradigm is evident. Of course, Talcott Parsons adopted a comparative sociological approach and was a student of European social thought, but his sociological interest and approach was American. Most classical sociology today is the study of the 'national society' under the umbrella of 'society'. We should not forget that classical sociology was the product of national struggles, the Franco-German War of 1870 and the First World War at the beginning of the twentieth century (Beck 2007, Beck and Grande 2010).

The critique of methodological nationalism should not be confused with the thesis that the end of the nation-state has arrived. One does not criticize methodological individualism by proclaiming the end of the individual. Nation-states (as all the research shows – see also the different contributions in this volume) will continue to thrive or will be transformed into transnational states (for example, the European Union). The decisive point is that national organization as a structuring principle of societal and political action can no longer serve as the orienting reference point for the social scientific observer. One cannot even understand the re-nationalization or re-ethnification trend in Western or Eastern Europe and other parts of the world without a cosmopolitan perspective. In this sense, the social sciences can only respond adequately to the challenge of globalization if they manage to overcome methodological nationalism and to raise empirically and theoretically fundamental questions within specialized fields of research, and thereby elaborate the foundations of a newly formulated cosmopolitan social science (Beck and Grande 2010, Beck and Sznaider 2006, Weiß 2010).

The Crucial Distinction between Normative Cosmopolitanism and Empirical-Analytical Cosmopolitization

We can distinguish three phases in the way the word 'globalization' has been used in the social sciences: first, denial; second, conceptual refinement and empirical research; third, 'cosmopolitization'. The initial denial is over because the theoretical and empirical refinement revealed a new social landscape in the making (for example, among many others, Bauman 1998, Beck 2000, Beisheim et al. 1999, Held et al. 1999, Randeria 2001, Sassen 2003). Its dominant features include *interconnectedness*, which means dependency and interdependency of people across the globe. Virtually the entire span of human experiences and practices is in one way or another influenced by the overwhelming interconnectivity of the world. (This is not be confused with world system and dependency theories.)

The third phase uncovers the core unseen, unwanted consequence of this global interconnectivity: the end of the 'global other'. The global other is here in our midst. Of course, one of the outstanding examples is the cartoon controversy (Kunelius et al. 2007). The cartoons epitomize the intersection of the global and local when it comes to communication and conflict in the digital age and to politics too. The global other is and stays in our midst, cannot be excluded any longer. Or to put it this way: even if the Danish government would decide to exclude all Danish or non-Danish Muslims it would not solve the conflict, in fact, the opposite clearly would happen: a global outrage and explosion of conflicts. And exactly this is my point: asking to clearly distinguish between philosophical cosmopolitanism and social scientific cosmopolitization. Cosmopolitanism in Immanuel Kant's philosophical sense means something active, a task, a conscious and voluntary choice, clearly the affair of an elite, a top-down issue (Kant 1983, 1996). But today in reality a 'banal', 'coercive' and 'impure' cosmopolitization unfolds unwanted, unseen, very powerful and confrontational beneath the surface or behind the façade of persisting national spaces, jurisdictions and labels; from the top of the society down to everyday life in families, work situations and individual biographies – even as national flags continue to be raised and even if national attitudes, identities and consciousness are strongly being reaffirmed. So the new volcanic landscapes of 'societies' have to be re-mapped on the macro level as well as on the micro level, and horizontally through the main fields of communication, interaction and social and political practices.[1]

Like climate change, most of the main impetuses for social and economic transformations in the new century do not differentially or exclusively apply to certain limited groups of nations. Consider the following: global free trade and financialization, corporate deterritorialization and transnationalized production, globalized labour use, competition and class conflicts, globalized policy consulting and formulation (coerced by the IMF, etc.), Internet communication and cyberspace, globally orchestrated bioscientific manipulation of life forms (gradually including human bodies), global risks of all kinds (financial crisis, terrorism, AIDS, swine flu, etc.), transnational demographic realignments (migration of labour, spouses, children), cosmopolitanized arts and entertainments and, last but not least, globally financed and managed regional wars. There are no permanent systematic hierarchies, sequences or selectivities by which different groups of nations – whether at different levels of development, in different regions or of different ethnicities and religions – are exposed to these new civilizational forces in mutually exclusive ways. Wanted or not, they are every nation's and every person's concern because they are structurally enmeshed with the new civilization process which I call '(reflexive) cosmopolitization'; and the civilizational condition thereby shared across the globe is '(reflexive or) Second Modernity' (Beck 2006, Beck et al. 1994, Beck and Grande 2010, Chang 2010).

The recent world history seems to dictate that surviving, let alone benefiting from, these new civilizational forces require every nation to actively internalize them and one another. The sociological implication is: the other is in our midst!

Isolationist efforts – whether spoken in terms of trade protectionism, religious fundamentalism, national fundamentalism, media and Internet control or otherwise – are readily subjected to international moral condemnations (and, to some extent, ineffective). In fact, accepting or refusing these forces remains beyond wilful political or social choices because they are globally reflexive (like the cartoon conflict demonstrates) – that is, compulsively occurring through the cosmopolitan imperative: cooperate or fail!

Cosmopolitization can be studied in many fields: in relation to migration, class, family, science, state, the individual, the region, the religions, the international relationships, but is also very evident when it comes to social inequality and global risks.

---

1   For the discussion on the distinction between – 'pure' – cosmopolitanism and – 'impure' – cosmoplitization see also Beck and Grande (2010), Calhoun (2010), Chang (2010), Gilroy (2010), Levy (2010), Maharaj (2010), Sznaider (2010) and Zhang (2010).

Re-Mapping Social Inequality in the Age of Climate Change

The national outlook on social inequality is inward orientated. It stops at the borders of the nation-state. Social inequalities may blossom and flourish on the other side of the national garden fence, that is, at best, cause for moral outrage, but politically irrelevant. A clear distinction must be made, therefore, between the reality of social inequality and the political problem of social inequality (cf. Beck 2010). National boundaries draw a sharp distinction between politically relevant and irrelevant inequality. Inequalities within national societies are enormously magnified in perception; at the same time inequalities between national societies are faded out. The 'legitimation' of global inequalities is based on an institutionalized 'looking the other way'. The national gaze is 'freed' from looking at the misery of the world. It operates by way of a double exclusion: it excludes the excluded. And the social science of inequality, which equates inequality with nation-state inequality, is unreflectively party to that. It is indeed astonishing how firmly global inequalities are 'legitimated' on the basis of tacit agreement between nation-state government and nation-state sociology – a sociology programmed to work on a nation-state basis and claiming to be value-free.

My point is: the performance principle legitimates national inequality, the nation-state principle legitimates global inequality (in another form). How? The inequalities between countries, regions and states are accounted politically incomparable. In a perspective bounded by nation-state, politically relevant comparisons can only be played out within the nation-state, never between states. Such comparisons, which make inequality politically explosive, assume national norms of equality. That is why even massive differences in income between persons with the same qualifications but different nationality only then have a political force if they can be related to a horizon of perception of common equality. Such a common frame only emerges when the persons belong to the same nation or the European Union or are employed in the same company, even if in different national subsidiaries.

Yet that is precisely what the national gaze fades out: the more norms of equality spread worldwide, the more global inequality is stripped of the legitimation basis of institutionalized looking away. The wealthy democracies carry the banner of human rights to the furthest corners of the earth, without noticing that the national border defences, with which they want to repel the streams of migrants, thereby lose their legitimation. Many migrants take seriously the proclaimed human right of equality of mobility and encounter countries and states which – not least under the impact of increasing internal inequalities – want the norm of equality to stop short at their fortified borders. Put in other words that means: the conception of social inequality, based on principles of nationality and statehood, misleads analysis. Most theorists of class, including Pierre Bourdieu, who thought so extensively about globalization in his final years, identify class society with the nation-state. The same is true of Immanuel Wallerstein (1974, 1980, 1989), John H. Goldthorpe (2002), in fact also of almost all non-class theory sociologists of inequality (and incidentally also of my individualization thesis [Beck 1992]).

Without the concept of locational social vulnerability it is impossible to understand the implications of climate change for the cosmopolitan re-mapping of inequalities. In recent years, however, social vulnerability has become a key dimension in the sociological analysis of inequalities in world risk society: the globalization of industrial capitalism produces a radical unequal exposure to hardly definable risks, and the resulting inequalities must largely be seen as expression and product of power relations in the national and global context. Social vulnerability is a sum concept, encompassing means and possibilities, which individuals, communities or whole populations have at their disposal, in order to cope – or not – with the threats of climate change (or financial crises).

A understanding of vulnerability certainly has a crucial relationship to the future, but also has historical depth. The 'cultural wounds' which, for example, result from the colonial past, constitute an important part of the background to understanding border-transcending climate conflicts (Kasperson and Kasperson 2005). The significance of this could be deserved at the Copenhagen Climate Summit in December of 2009. The developing countries – like Brazil, South Africa and India (in US wishful thinking, all partners in the formation of a global alliance of democracies to push back against authoritarian powers) – decided that their status as post-colonial nations was more important than their status as democracies. Like the Chinese they argued that it is fundamentally unjust to cap the greenhouse gas emissions of poor countries at a lower level than the emissions of the United States or the European Union; all the more so since the industrialized West is responsible for the foreign-induced climate risks from which they suffer. Revealingly, both Brazilian and Chinese leaders have made the same pointed joke – likening the United States to a rich man who, after afflicting others by gorging himself at a banquet, then invites the neighbours in for coffee and asks them to split the bill! Thus, because of the question of (in)justice incorporated in the cosmopolitics of climate change there is no Global Green New Deal so far and the United States is losing the free world.

The cosmopolitan re-mapping of inequality has to take account of three parameters:

1. The globalization of social inequality can no longer detach itself from the globalization of social equality.
2. The social science of social inequality can no longer rely on the premise of the distinction between national and international. The equation of social and national inequality which methodological nationalism adopts has become a source of error par excellence.
3. The founding premise of social science, the distinction between social and natural inequality, has become untenable.

Anyone who thinks these three components together encounters a paradox: the more norms of equality are acknowledged globally, the more insoluble the climate problem becomes and the more devastating the social-ecological inequalities. Not a cheerful prospect! But it is precisely this incorruptible realism, open to the world that is designated by the concept of the 'cosmopolitan outlook' (actor perspective) and methodological cosmopolitanism (observer perspective). It's not a matter of any official rhetoric of world fraternity, but of sharpening perceptions in everyday life, in politics and scholarship for the unbounded explosive force of social inequality in the age of climate change and globalization. This cosmopolitan realism certainly encompasses the possibility that nation-state governments will assert themselves militarily or even run amok because of the loss of autonomy they have experienced.

To summarize: methodological nationalism is based on a double assumption of congruence: on the one hand the congruence of territorial, political, economic, social and cultural boundaries; on the other, the congruence of actor perspective and social scientific observer perspective. The premise of the normative-political nationalism of actors becomes unreflectedly the premise of the social scientific observer perspective. These congruence assumptions are mutually reinforcing. The historical trend, however, is running in the opposite direction: territorial, state, economic, social boundaries continue to exist, but they are no longer coterminous! The necessary paradigm shift can build on three insights:

- social classes are only one of the historical forms of inequality;
- the nation-state is only one of the historical frames of interpretation;
- 'the end of the national class society' does not mean 'the end of social inequality', on the contrary: inequality both in the national and the transnational sphere is exacerbated.

Today we are seeing a kind of repetition of the process Max Weber (1988) was observing when he analysed the origins of modern capitalism. Except that now this process is taking place on a global scale. Weber said we have to look at the separation of family household and capitalist enterprise – that is: the emancipation of economic interests. At present we are witnessing the emancipation of economic interests from national ties and control bodies. That means the *separation of power and politics*. The emergent nation-state developed institutions of politics and power which were able to limit the injuries of modern industrial capitalism. This took place within the territorial borders of the nation-state and was a kind of marriage between power and politics, one that is now ending in divorce. Accordingly power is becoming more diffuse, partly transferred into cyberspace, to financial markets and mobile capital, partly shifted onto individuals who now have to cope with the attendant risks alone. And at present there is no equivalent of the sovereign nation-state in sight.

Risk Society's Cosmopolitan Moment

The theory of world risk society maintains: modern societies are shaped by new kinds of risks and manufactured uncertainties, their foundations are shaken by the global anticipation of global catastrophes. Such perceptions of global risk are characterized by three features (cf. Beck 2009):

1. *De-localization*: its causes and consequences are not limited to one geographical location or space, they are in principle omnipresent.
2. *Incalculableness*: its consequences are in principle incalculable; at bottom it is a matter of 'hypothetical' risks, which, not least, are based on science, induced not-knowing and normative dissent.
3. *Non-compensability*: the security dream of First Modernity was based on the mastery of the unsafe consequences and dangers of decisions; accidents could occur, as long as and because they were considered compensable. Once the global finance system has collapsed, once the climate has changed irrevocably; once terrorist groups possess weapons of mass destruction – then it's too late. Given this new quality of 'threats to humanity' – argues François Ewald (2002) – the logic of compensation breaks down and is replaced by the principle of precaution by prevention. Not only is prevention taking precedence over compensation, we are also trying to anticipate and prevent risks whose existence has not been proven.

So what is meant by risk society's 'cosmopolitan moment'? Climate change exacerbates inequalities between the poor and the rich, between centre and periphery – but simultaneously dissolves them. The greater the planetary threat, the less the possibility that even the wealthiest and most powerful will avoid it. Climate change is both hierarchical and democratic. Climate change is pure ambivalence: it also releases the cosmopolitan imperative: cooperate or fail.

The current, seductive naïve catastrophic realism is mistaken. Climate risks are not identical with climate catastrophes (Beck 2009). Climate risks are the anticipation of future catastrophes in the present. This 'present future' of climate risks is real, the 'future future' of climate catastrophes, on the other hand, is (still) unreal. Yet even the anticipation of climate change sets a fundamental transformation in motion in the here and now. Ever since it has ceased to be disputed that the ongoing climate change is man-made and has catastrophic consequences for nature and society, the cards in society and politics have been dealt anew – worldwide. That's why climate change by no means leads directly and inevitably to apocalypse; it also affords the opportunity of overcoming the national narrowness of politics and of developing a cosmopolitan realpolitik in the national interest.

To the extent that a world public becomes aware of the fact that the nation-state system is undermined by global risks (climate change, global economic crises) which bind underdeveloped and developed nations to one another, then something historically new can emerge, namely a cosmopolitan vision in which people see themselves both as part of an endangered world and as part of their local histories and survival situations.

Accordingly climate change – like ancient cosmopolitanism (Stoicism), the *ius cosmopolitica* of the Enlightenment (Kant) or crimes against humanity (Hannah Arendt, Karl Jaspers) – releases a 'cosmopolitan moment and momentum'. Global risks entail being confronted with the global other. They tear down national borders and mix the local with the foreign, not as a consequence of migration, but rather as a consequence of 'interconnectedness' and risks. Everyday life becomes cosmopolitan: people have to conduct and understand their lives in an exchange with others and no longer exclusively in an interaction with their own kind.

In order to understand and conceptualize this we have to give up the assumption that community-building is only possible on the basis of positive integration through shared values and norms, and need to get accustomed to the idea that community-building can also result from conflicts through negative values (crises, risks, threat of annihilation). Therefore we have to distinguish between self-induced and foreign-induced risks. In the case of 'self-endangerment' those who decide upon risks and those who are affected by these risks belong to one social or cultural group; this holds true for the European and US-American path of modernization. Whereas in the case of 'foreign endangerment' decision makers and people affected belong to different countries, cultures, world regions; this corresponds to the post-colonial path of modernization.

Thereby the issue of inequality and rule is placed in the 'logics' of global risks itself. The risk requires a decision, hence a decision maker, and generates radical asymmetry between those who take, define and profit from a risk and those who have to accept the risk and bear the 'unseen side-effects' of the decisions taken by others, maybe even by paying with their lives, not having had the chance to participate in the decision-making process. It is indeed of great cosmopolitical relevance to distinguish self-induced endangerment and foreign-induced endangerment, since the relationship amongst entire world regions is portrayed as power relations characterized by the externalization of self-produced threats to others. The rich and powerful produce and profit from the risks of climate change, while the poor and powerless suffer and struggle for their existence due to the side-effects of our decisions.

Methodological Cosmopolitanism: The Problem of the Unit of Research

A key question thrown up by the cosmopolitan turn in the social sciences is this: what research unit forms the (appropriate) basis of social theory and research? Or more precisely: how can research units *beyond* methodological nationalism be found and defined which allow us to understand processes of cosmopolitization and to make comparative analyses of variations in cosmopolitan modernity? What are the reference points of social scientific analysis if, on the one hand, one wants to free it from the 'container' of the nation-state but, on the other, not take refuge in abstract concepts of 'world society'? Empirical research in such diverse disciplines as anthropology, geography or political science has in recent years developed a large number of concepts, all with the aim of breaking down the supposedly 'natural' equation of 'society/nation/state'. Paul Gilroy's conceptualization of the *Black Atlantic* (1993), Saskia Sassen's identification of the *Global City* (1991), Arjun Appadurai's notion of 'scapes' (1996), Martin Albrow's concept of the *Global Age* (1996) and our own analysis of *Cosmopolitan Europe* (Beck and Grande 2007) are examples of this kind of research.

This variety of concepts and approaches can be usefully systematized with the help of two distinctions. On the one hand, new units of research may be distinguished according to whether they refer to processes of transnationalization or to transnational structures. An example of the former would be transnational migration processes, an example of the latter would be 'diaspora communities' in which migrants create new forms of transnational (co-)existence. A second distinction relates to the range and the location of cosmopolitization. Range involves the question of the role that the unit of research of the national, that is the nation-state, nation cultures, etc., (still) plays in the age of cosmopolitization. Location involves the question of the level at which emphasis of cosmopolitization is laid – above the national: world regions, world religions; below the level of the national: the local, the family, the individual, the enterprise, work, etc. One possibility, of course, is that the nation-state and the national continue to exist, but lose their epistemological monopoly position, for example, because they become integrated in new forms of political organization and societal order. The methodological consequence would be that new units of research have to be found, which contain the national, but no longer coincide with the national. We would describe this as 'embedding the national'.

A more far-reaching possibility is that the research object of the national is replaced by other foci; which does not necessarily mean that the national becomes obsolete or irrelevant ('replacing the national').

Table 1.1 Units of analysis in methodological cosmopolitanism

	Processes	Structures
Embedding the national	'Compressed modernization' (Chang 1999, 2010); cosmopolitan Europeanization (Beck and Grande 2007); 'recursive cosmopolitization' (Levy 2010)	Transnational policy regimes (Grande 2004); global assemblages (Sassen 2006); world regions (Katzenstein 2005)
Replacing the national	'Ships in motion' (Gilroy 1993); supply chain capitalism (Tsing 2009); 'cosmopolitan innovations' (Tyfield and Urry 2009)	World religions; transnational migrant networks (Glick Schiller 2009); border zones; global city; the local; the family; the individual

It is frequently assumed and/or argued that the unchanged or newly growing importance of the state legitimates methodological nationalism. But that is based on a false equation of actor and observer perspective. Even if the nation-state gains functionally in importance, it can lose its epistemological monopoly position as the unit of research, because the investigation of the cosmopolitization process can only succeed if other foci are moved centre stage. This way you can construct a table to sum up the conceptual tool box of methodological cosmopolitanism (see Table 1.1).

Ships in motion: replacing the national with transcontinental processes

One of the first and most radical alternatives to methodological nationalism (though it wasn't described in this way) was introduced by Paul Gilroy. In his seminal study he did not take the national 'container' but a transcontinental space, the *Black Atlantic* (1993), as the field for his theorizing and empirical research. Gilroy convincingly argued that the ideas of nation, nationality and national belongings do have epistemological consequences: they affirm a research programme and practice of 'cultural insiderism', based on essentializing ethnic difference. Gilroy's starting point is not a fixed entity, instead the *image of ships in motion* between Europe, America, Africa and the Caribbean is the central symbolic principle of organizing his research.

A similar approach, replacing the national as basic unit of research by new transnational processes, was taken by Anna Tsing (2009) in her research on forms of transnational supply chain capitalism. In contrast to theories of growing capitalist convergence and homogeneity, her analysis points to the fundamental role of difference in mobilizing capital, labour and other resources. The focus and unit of analysis in her research is again not a fixed entity but a process: labour mobilization in supply chains, as it depends on the performance of gender, ethnicity, nationality, religion and citizen status. Her analysis reveals that diversity is of central importance to global capitalism and not merely decorative.

Transnational networks and border zones: replacing the national with new transnational structures

In the last decade there has been a substantial amount of research in the field of transnational studies (Khagram and Levitt 2008, Pries 2008, Vertovec 2009). Irrespective of different research objects and academic disciplines they have in common that they replace the national as unit of analysis with new structures which can be observed at a multiplicity of levels. Most innovative here is research on transnational migration by Nina Glick Schiller (2009) and others (cf. Vertovec 2009). They privilege a constructivist view of territorial spaces, in which transnational social formations – such as transnational networks, kinship groups, migrant organizations and diaspora communities – cross and overlap the territories of nation-states without necessarily having a global reach.

In historical studies a similar approach has been introduced recently as transnational historiography. This questions the nation-state centred concentration on the history of states, border zones and inter-regional transfer flows. Instead attention is paid to the configuration and political functions of border zones. This allows an analytical distinction between processes of nation-formation and territorialization. In contrast to the nation-state centred perspective it suggests analysing nation-state borders not as clear limits, but as fluid and inclusive border areas (Hopkins 2002, Thelen 1999, Tyrrell 1999). Of course in historical studies there has been since the nineteenth century a tension between the national focus and the thematic study of for example feudalism, the Enlightenment, Industrial Revolution, Fascism; the study of the fluidity of border regions is also quite old, a good example is Claudio Magris's *Danube* (1999) – of course essayistic and literature-oriented rather than social scientific – and not least there's the ground-breaking work of Karl Schlögel (2003). Put another way transnational historiography sounds good but it's really an answer to an American question – that is, of overcoming a specific US American provincialism.

Embedding the national in new transnational structures and processes

An initial example is '*transnational policy regimes*' (Grande 2004, Grande and Pauly 2005, Grande et al. 2007). This refers to new forms of transnational institution building which have established themselves in a number of global regulation spheres such as climate protection, Internet regulation or the taxation of transnational enterprises. These institutions represent interaction relationships which are not defined by a national area of operation, but by practical regulation problems; they include very different and extremely variable participating groups and extend to diverse territorial levels. Consequently these policy regimes are the relevant research units for an empirical analysis of transnational politics. Crucial here, admittedly, is that these new institutions do not replace nation-states, but instead integrate them. The nation-states are embedded in new transnational systems of regulation and it is one of the most important tasks of empirical analysis to investigate the specific importance of nation-states in these institutions. Where the nation-state continues to dominate, as we can at present observe in the case of climate policies, there the transnational threatens to become the 'showcase of the national'.

Another example of why it may be necessary to continue to choose the nation-state as research unit and nevertheless overcome the narrowness of methodological nationalism is to be found in the work of Daniel Levy (2010), Natan Sznaider (2010), Levy and Sznaider (2010) and Saskia Sassen (2006). They show that globalization processes derive from transformations within nation-states and gain their dynamic there, whether it's a case of the rise of the global capital market or of networks of committed human rights activists (Kurasawa 2007). In short: the national space becomes a highly complex 'showcase of the global'. Precisely because of the interconnectedness of the world many things begin locally, even if on occasion in unlocalized closeness. Thus it is neither national nor global, but cosmopolitan.

Outlook: The Paradigm Shift in the Social Sciences

It is evident that the taken-for-granted nation-state frame of reference – 'methodological nationalism' – prevents the social sciences from understanding and analysing the dynamics, ambivalences and opportunities of the cosmopolitan human condition in the twenty-first century. A methodological nationalist as well as a national politician, who attempts to deal with global risks in isolation resembles a drunken man, who on a dark night is trying to find his lost wallet in the cone of light of a street lamp. To the question 'Did you actually lose your wallet here?', he replies, 'No, but in the light of the street lamp I can at least look for it'.

But sociology and political science are not the only disciplines under pressure, economics is too. There is a situation vacant: a theorist is sought to succeed Mr Keynes, transnationally. The need is now for a clever reflexive regulation (philosophy) on a global scale, including new actors like transnational corporations, the World Bank, IMF, Attac, Greenpeace, etc. In the EU, there is an equal need for much stronger political institutions – a European Minister for Economic Affairs – to complement the central bank. But the greatest need of all is a new theory of the mixed economy, framed for the global marketplace of today, as the now defunct Keynesian system was framed for the national post-war economies.

We are under the spell of a sociology, whose foundations were conceived and developed in the past hundred years. The first century of sociology is over. On the way into the second, which has now begun, the space of sociological imagination and research has to be opened up and determined anew, that is opened up to the cosmopolitan constellation. Learning about others is not simply an act of cosmopolitan open-mindedness but an integral part of learning about and understanding the reality of ourselves or even viewing ourselves as other. A cosmopolitan sociology means a sociology which reflects on the ontologized premises and dualisms of a nation-state sociology – such as national and international, us and them, internal and external – in their significance for the grammar of the political and the social, as for the determination of the sociological field of investigation, and in this way gains a new sociological frame of reference to all kind of subjects. A cosmopolitan sociology clearly distinguishes itself from a universalist one, because it doesn't start out from something abstract (usually derived from a European historical experience and context, for instance 'society' or 'world society' or 'world system' or the 'autonomous individual', etc.). Instead key concepts like dependence, interdependence, interconnectedness take centre stage along with the methodological questions posed by them: how do we research the interdependent world? Cosmopolitan sociology, therefore, opens up indispensable new perspectives on seemingly isolated, familiar, local and national contexts. But we are just beginning there are more problems than solutions, more questions than answers. But we sociologists are not the first. With this new 'cosmopolitan vision' we follow the empirical and methodological paths which other disciplines – such as contemporary anthropology, geography, ethnology, historiography – have already taken with enthusiasm.

Bibliography

Albrow, M. 1996. *The Global Age: State and Society Beyond Modernity*. Cambridge, UK/Stanford, CA: Polity Press/Stanford University Press.

Appadurai, A. 1996. *Modernity at Large: Cultural Dimensions of Globalization*. Minneapolis: University of Minnesota Press.

Bauman, Z. 1998. *Globalization: The Human Consequences*. New York: Columbia University Press.

Beck, U. 1992. *Risk Society: Towards a New Modernity*. London/Newbury Park/New Delhi: Sage Publications.

Beck, U. 2000. *What Is Globalization?* Cambridge, UK/Malden, MA: Polity Press.

Beck, U. 2006. *The Cosmopolitan Vision*. Cambridge, UK/Malden, MA: Polity Press.

Beck, U. 2007. The cosmopolitan condition: why methodological nationalism fails. *Theory, Culture & Society*, 24(7–8): 286–90.

Beck, U. 2009. *World at Risk*. Cambridge, UK/Malden, MA: Polity Press.

Beck, U. 2010. Remapping social inequalities in an age of climate change: for a cosmopolitan renewal of sociology. *Global Networks*, 10(2): 165–81.

Beck, U. and Grande, E. 2007. *Cosmopolitan Europe*. Cambridge, UK/Malden MA: Polity Press.

Beck, U. and Grande, E. 2010. Varieties of second modernity: the 'cosmopolitan turn' in social and political theory and research. *British Journal of Sociology*, 61(3): 409–43.

Beck, U. and Sznaider, N. 2006. Unpacking cosmopolitanism for the social sciences: a research agenda. *British Journal of Sociology*, 57(1): 1–23.

Beck, U., Giddens, A. and Lash, S. 1994. *Reflexive Modernization: Politics, Tradition and Aesthetics in the Modern Social Order*. Cambridge: Polity Press.

Beisheim, M., Dreher, S., Walter, G., Zangl, B. and Zürn, M. 1999. *Im Zeitalter der Globalisierung? Thesen und Debatten zur gesellschaftlichen und politischen Denationalisierung*. Baden-Baden: Nomos Verlagsgesellschaft.

Calhoun, C. 2010. Beck, Asia and second modernity. *British Journal of Sociology*, 61(3): 597–619.

Chang, K.-S. 1999. Compressed modernity and its discontents: South Korean society in transition. *Economy and Society*, 28(1): 30–55.

Chang, K.-S. 2010. The second modern condition? Compressed modernity as internalized reflexive cosmopolitanism. *British Journal of Sociology*, 61(3): 444–64.

Ewald, F. 2002. The return of Descartes' malicious demon: an outline of a philosophy of precaution, in *Embracing Risk: The Changing Culture of Insurance and Responsibility*, edited by T. Baker and J. Simon. Chicago/London: University of Chicago Press, 273–301.

Gilroy, P. 1993. *Black Atlantic: Modernity and Double Consciousness*. Cambridge, MA: Harvard University Press.

Gilroy, P. 2010. Planetarity and cosmopolitics. *British Journal of Sociology*, 61(3): 620–6.

Glick Schiller, N. 2009. A global perspective on migration and development. *Social Analysis*, 53(3): 14–37.

Goldthorpe, J.H. 2002. Globalisation and social class. *West European Politics*, 25(3): 1–28.

Grande, E. 2004. Vom Nationalstaat zum transnationalen Politikregime – Staatliche Steuerungsfähigkeit im Zeitalter der Globalisierung, in *Entgrenzung und Entscheidung. Was ist neu an der Theorie reflexiver Modernisierung?* edited by U. Beck and C. Lau. Frankfurt am Main: Suhrkamp, 384–401.

Grande, E. and Pauly, L.W. (eds). 2005. *Complex Sovereignty: Reconstituting Political Authority in the Twenty-first Century*. Toronto/Buffalo/London: University of Toronto Press.

Grande, E., König, M., Pfister, P. and Sterzel, P. 2007. Globalization, political transnationalization, and the future of the nation-state – a comparison of transnational policy regimes, in *Globalization: State of the Art and Perspectives*, edited by S.A. Schirm. London/New York: Routledge, 98–121.

Held, D., McGrew, A., Goldblatt, D. and Perraton, J. 1999. *Global Transformations: Politics, Economics and Culture*. Cambridge, UK/Stanford, CA: Polity Press/Stanford University Press.

Hopkins, A.G. (ed.). 2002. *Globalization in World History*. New York: W.W. Norton.

Kant, I. 1983. Idea for a universal history with a cosmopolitan purpose, in *Perpetual Peace and Other Essays on Politics, History and Morals*, by I. Kant. Indianapolis: Hackett, 29–39.

Kant, I. 1996. Toward perpetual peace: a philosophical project, in *Practical Philosophy*, by I. Kant. Cambridge: Cambridge University Press, 311–51.

Kasperson, J.X. and Kasperson, R.F. 2005. *The Social Contours of Risk*, 2 volumes. London/Sterling, VA: Earthscan.

Katzenstein, P.J. 2005. *A World of Regions: Asia and Europe in the American Imperium*. Ithaca: Cornell University Press.

Khagram, S. and Levitt, P. (eds). 2008. *The Transnational Studies Reader: Intersections and Innovations*. London/New York: Routledge.

Kunelius, R., Eide, E., Hahn, O. and Schroeder, R. (eds). 2007. *Reading the Mohammed Cartoons Controversy: An International Analysis of Press Discourses on Free Speech and Political Spin*. Bochum/Freiburg: Projektverlag.

Kurasawa, F. 2007. *The Work of Global Justice: Human Rights as Practices*. Cambridge: Cambridge University Press.

Levy, D. 2010. Recursive cosmopolitization: Argentina and the global human rights regime. *British Journal of Sociology*, 61(3): 579–96.

Levy, D. and Sznaider, N. 2010. *Human Rights and Memory*. University Park: Penn State University Press.

Magris, C. 1999. *Danube: A Sentimental Journey from the Source to the Black Sea*. London: Harvill Press.

Maharaj, S. 2010. Small change of the universal: beyond modernity? *British Journal of Sociology*, 61(3): 565–78.

Pries, L. (ed.). 2008. *Rethinking Transnationalism: The Meso-Link of Organizations*. Abingdon/New York: Routledge.

Randeria, S. 2001. *Local Refractions of Global Governance: Legal Plurality, International Institutions, the Post-Colonial State and NGOs in India*. Habilitation. Free University Berlin.

Sassen, S. 1991. *The Global City: New York, London, Tokyo*. Princeton: Princeton University Press.

Sassen, S. 2003. Globalization or denationalization? *Review of International Political Economy*, 10(1): 1–22.

Sassen, S. 2006. *Territory, Authority, Rights: From Medieval to Global Assemblages*. Princeton: Princeton University Press.

Schlögel, K. 2003. *Im Raume lesen wir die Zeit: Über Zivilisationsgeschichte und Geopolitik*. München: Carl Hanser Verlag.

Sznaider, N. 2010. Rewriting the Persian letters. *British Journal of Sociology*, 61(3): 627–33.

Thelen, D. 1999. The nation and beyond: transnational perspectives on United States history. *Journal of American History*, 86(3): 965–75.

Tsing, A. 2009. Supply chains and the human condition. *Rethinking Marxism*, 21(2): 148–76.

Tyfield, D. and Urry, J. 2009. Cosmopolitan China? Lessons from international collaboration in low-carbon innovation. *British Journal of Sociology*, 60(4): 793–812.

Tyrrell, I. 1999. Making nations/making states: American historians in the context of empire. *Journal of American History*, 86(3): 1015–44.

Vertovec, S. 2009. *Transnationalism*. London: Routledge.

Wallerstein, I. 1974. *The Modern World-System, Vol. I: Capitalist Agriculture and the Origins of the European World-Economy in the Sixteenth Century*. New York/London: Academic Press.

Wallerstein, I. 1980. *The Modern World-System, Vol. II: Mercantilism and the Consolidation of the European World-Economy, 1600–1750*. New York: Academic Press.

Wallerstein, I. 1989. *The Modern World-System, Vol. III: The Second Great Expansion of the Capitalist World-Economy, 1730–1840s*. San Diego: Academic Press.

Weber, M. 1988. Die protestantische Ethik und der Geist des Kapitalismus, in *Gesammelte Aufsätze zur Religionssoziologie*, by M. Weber, Vol. 1. Tübingen: J.C.B. Mohr.

Weiß, A. 2010. Vergleiche jenseits des Nationalstaats. Methodologischer Kosmopolitismus in der soziologischen Forschung über hochqualifizierte Migration. *Soziale Welt*, 61(3–4): 295–311.

Zhang, J.Y. 2010. The cosmopolitization of science: experience from Chinese stem cell scientists. *Soziale Welt*, 61(3–4): 257–76.

Cosmopolitanism and Consumption

Jennie Germann Molz

Introduction

Attempts to define "cosmopolitanism" often tend to distinguish between the political and cultural connotations of the term. On the one hand, cosmopolitanism, as a form of global citizenship, has specific political and institutional implications related to global governance, world democracy and moral debates regarding human rights. On the other hand, many scholars argue that cosmopolitanism also refers to the cultural realm of citizenship and is therefore bound up in questions of identity, community and belonging in a globalized world. In other words, as Ulf Hannerz puts it, "cosmopolitanism has two faces ... one is more cultural, the other more political" (2006: 9). Hannerz (2006: 5) captures the "two faces" of cosmopolitanism in his list of the various things "cosmopolitan" can stand for:

> [S]omeone with many varied stamps in his or her passport; or a city or a neighborhood with a mixed population; or, with a capital C, a women's magazine, at least at one time seen as a bit daring in its attitudes; or an individual of uncertain patriotic reliability, quite possibly a Jew; or someone who likes weird, exotic cuisines; or an advocate of world government; or, again with a capital C, a mixed drink combining vodka, cranberry juice, and other ingredients.

Contrasting the political dimensions of cosmopolitanism ("uncertain patriotic reliability" and advocacy of "world government") against its cultural dimensions (travel, urban culture, exotic cuisine, and fashion and lifestyle magazines), this particular combination of examples highlights two important points. First, these examples suggest that cosmopolitanism is not just an abstract theoretical or political project, but that it is also "actually existing," emerging in material, everyday practices and "habits of thought and feeling" (Robbins 1998: 2). Second, these references to travel, tourism, fashion, food and drink strongly associate cosmopolitanism with consumption. If cosmopolitanism is indeed a "form of consumption" (Binnie and

Skeggs 2004: 41), then understanding cosmopolitanism entails an examination of the habits of thought, feeling and practice related to consumption.

Intensified academic interest in cosmopolitanism as a cultural form and as a form of consumption is perhaps not surprising when understood in the broader context of social change over the past few decades. Since the 1980s, social life, especially in the west, has been largely shaped by globalization and by what many scholars have identified as a general shift from a producer to a consumer society (Lash and Urry 1994, Bauman 1998). As western societies have moved from production-centered capitalism, with its focus on work and the conditions of labor, to consumer capitalism, with its focus on leisure, taste and style, consumption has played an increasingly vital role in the patterning of social life, as a means of civic participation, and as a site of individual and collective identity construction (Bourdieu 1984). Similarly, many theories of globalization place culture and consumption front and center alongside politics and economy. In his influential article "Disjuncture and difference in the global cultural economy," Appadurai (1990) characterizes globalization as a framework of overlapping "scapes" that encompasses economic, political *and* cultural global flows that characterize "international capital as deeply as they do international clothing styles" (297). Appearing in the same volume on "Global Culture," Hannerz's (1990) article "Cosmopolitans and locals in world culture" sets the tone for thinking of cosmopolitanism as a cultural orientation toward globalization. Indeed, Hannerz acknowledges that his line of thinking in that piece, which will be discussed in more detail in the next section, emerged out of his interest in the cultural aspects of globalization. Highly influential in their own right, these pieces by Appadurai and Hannerz reflect a wider consensus among scholars that globalization has brought increased attention to the role of culture and consumption in the organization of everyday life.

The purpose of this chapter, therefore, is to consider how cosmopolitanism has become associated with the cultural dimensions of consumption. The chapter begins by outlining in further detail several cultural approaches to cosmopolitanism and consumption and then discusses three related debates—briefly summarized as homogeneity versus heterogeneity; inclusion versus exclusion; and "superficial" versus "authentic" cosmopolitanism—that shape this field of study. The chapter concludes that these debates pivot not on the separation of culture and politics, but rather on a convergence of the two. In this sense, consumption becomes a contested "cosmopolitical" terrain upon which the tendency for consumer-based capitalism to reproduce trenchant social inequalities is countered by the political potential for consumption to serve as a more ethical form of engagement between people.

Cosmopolitanism as Cultural Orientation

The connections between cosmopolitanism, culture and consumption are often traced back to Ulf Hannerz's (1990) discussion of "cosmopolitans and locals" and John Urry's (1995) concept of "aesthetic cosmopolitanism." Both of these works identify cosmopolitanism as a cultural orientation that emerges in response to a culturally complex world. Hannerz defines cosmopolitanism as "a state of mind" and a cultural skill, conveying an "orientation, a willingness to engage with the Other ... a state of readiness, a personal ability to make one's way into other cultures, through listening, looking, intuiting and reflecting" (Hannerz 1990: 239). According to Hannerz, whether cosmopolitans travel the world or stay home and consume the exotic array of food, fashion and other cultural products that globalization makes available in their own neighborhoods, they are characterized primarily by their openness to other cultures. Not only do cosmopolitans demonstrate a kind of cultural competence "in maneuvering more or less expertly" within a variety of cultural systems, they actively "search for contrasts rather than uniformity" and express a "delight in difference" (Hannerz 1990: 239). Cosmopolitanism thus refers to an intellectual skill, an aesthetic *savoir faire*, and an affective pleasure in experiencing and navigating through cultural difference.

Urry elaborates on Hannerz's description of the cosmopolitan in his model of "aesthetic cosmopolitanism," which portrays the cosmopolitan as a highly mobile, curious and reflexive subject who delights in and desires to consume difference. Urry describes "aesthetic cosmopolitanism" as a cultural disposition that has developed alongside the growth of popular tourism and the penchant for "consuming" foreign places. Similar to Hannerz's definition of cosmopolitanism, Urry describes a cultural disposition that involves "a stance of openness towards divergent experiences from different national cultures" and "a search for and delight in contrasts between societies rather than a longing for uniformity or superiority" (Urry 1995: 167). According to Urry, the key features of "aesthetic cosmopolitanism" include extensive mobility; curiosity about and appreciation of other places and cultures; a willingness to risk moving beyond the "tourist bubble"; a reflexive ability to locate one's own society and culture in a broader historical and geographical context; and a "semiotic skill" (Urry 1995: 167). In these accounts, cosmopolitanism does not refer to global citizenship merely as a political or institutional status in terms of global governance, but as a cultural disposition embodying sentiments, affiliations and interpretive skills that transcend local and national boundaries.

Urry's "aesthetic cosmopolitanism" is distinctive in that it is "firmly anchored in the practices of popular *consumer culture*" (Tomlinson 1999: 201, emphasis in original). The skills and attitudes expressed in "aesthetic cosmopolitanism" are cultural symptoms of the emergence of a novel form of "consumer citizenship" that defines the modern experience: "A modern person is one who is able to exercise those rights and who conceives of him or herself as a consumer of other cultures and places" (Urry 1995: 165). Indeed, cosmopolitanism, as expressed through travel and consumption, has become an ordinary feature of daily modern life in western societies, a point Urry makes by referring to Hebdige's concept of "mundane cosmopolitanism." Hebdige explains that people are world travelers, either directly or via their televisions: "It is part of being 'taken for a ride' in and through late-twentieth century consumer culture. In the 1990s everybody [at least in the 'west'] is more or less cosmopolitan" (Hebdige, in Urry 1995: 167). This kind of everyday cosmopolitanism constitutes a more recent line of theorization that also firmly links cosmopolitanism to culture and consumption.

Everyday articulations of cosmopolitanism are perhaps best characterized in Beck's (2003, 2004, 2006) concept of "banal cosmopolitanism." Drawing on Billig's (1995) formulation of "banal nationalism," which describes how political consciousness is molded through daily routines, Beck argues that participating in unremarkable daily routines, like shopping, eating or listening to music, produces new cosmopolitan identities. Reflecting on the example of food, Beck (2003: 37) explains:

> *If we are what we eat, none of us is national anymore ... We are now all used to finding foodstuffs that used to be separated by continents and cultures freely available side-by-side as mass market commodities. This selection ... is the basic ingredient of a culinary cosmopolitanism. ... World society is in some ways baking in the oven and broiling in the pan.*

Beck's culinary illustration of "banal cosmopolitanism" reveals it to be intimately tied to practices of consumption. Indeed, he identifies "banal cosmopolitanism" explicitly as a form of cultural consumption, not only of food, but also of music, fashion and lifestyles, that makes us all "more cosmopolitan than we think" (Beck 2003: 38). In this sense, consumption engenders a particular cosmopolitan consciousness in relation to cultural difference.

In her studies of metropolitan London in the early 1900s, Nava (2002, 2007) explores in detail the everyday expressions of an emerging cosmopolitan consciousness in early twentieth-century consumer culture. Concerned with vernacular practices of "the global modern everyday," Nava (2002: 89) pays attention to the articulation of a cosmopolitan imagination in the mundane practices of shopping. In her analysis of the opening of Selfridge's department store in London in 1909, Nava illustrates the way designs, fashions and cultural products from abroad helped to cultivate among middle-class women a "cosmopolitan structure of feeling." This feeling captured "the fluidity and excitement of modern urban life, physical mobility and encounters with strangers ... and, above all, the advent of a new modern consciousness: a psychic, social and visceral readiness to engage with the new, with difference" (Nava 2002: 82). While this consciousness was novel at the beginning of the last century, by now, Nava concludes, difference has become a familiar and unremarkable feature of vernacular cosmopolitanism in urban culture today.

Along with Hannerz and Urry, Nava understands cosmopolitanism as a cultural orientation toward difference, however her analysis specifically highlights the affective and desirous elements of this orientation. In this sense, her analysis helps to illustrate the way cosmopolitanism is embedded in everyday "habits of thought and feeling" (Robbins 1998: 2). These conceptualizations of cosmopolitanism as a structure of feelings and fantasies, as a set of cultural skills and competences, and as part of the "banal" makeup of every day life, signify an important shift from thinking about the cosmopolitan as an abstract political figure to thinking about the cosmopolitan as a lifestyle consumer. In other words, global citizenship revolves not just around political engagement or civic participation, but also around cosmopolitan tastes, styles and patterns of consumption.

Nava's work also emphasizes the way the cosmopolitan imagination and related forms of cosmopolitan consumption were, and continue to be, shaped by gender, race and class. In this sense, her analysis provides an important corrective to the models of cosmopolitanism outlined by Hannerz and Urry, both of which have been critiqued by feminist and postcolonial scholars for failing to acknowledge the particularly Euro-American, white, male and privileged perspective the cosmopolitan figure assumes. Like Nava, many of these critics have sought to account for the way gender, race, class, ethnicity and sexuality shape cosmopolitan patterns of consumption and position cosmopolitan subjects unequally in what Massey (1993) has called the power-geometry of time–space compression. For example, in a critical reading of Hannerz's distinction between cosmopolitans and locals, Jones and Leshkowich (2003) question Hannerz's categorization of Nigerian women as "local." They take issue with his explanation that the women's cross-border smuggling of frozen fish sticks, dehydrated milk and baby clothes did not "go beyond the horizons of urban Nigerian culture" and therefore did not count as cosmopolitan (Hannerz 1990: 238). To Jones and Leshkowich, in contrast, these goods strongly hint at cosmopolitan aspirations and the desire to acquire "the material goods literally to fashion themselves (and, in this case, their children) as cosmopolitans conversant with global heterogeneity" (Jones and Leshkowich 2003: 16). This implicit gendering of the "local" as feminine and the "cosmopolitan" as masculine reflects "a widespread 'masculinist' tendency in studies of globalization" that tends to erase "how gender and other factors unequally shape access to processes of cultural production and material accumulation" (Jones and Leshkowich 2003: 16, and see Nava 2002: 88, Freeman 2001). This and similar analyses draw attention to the complex articulation of difference in the realm of cosmopolitan consumption, especially as cosmopolitan desires are negotiated alongside the commodification of difference. They reveal the way commodity objects, everyday consumer activities such as eating, shopping, dressing and traveling, and imaginative and mediated terrains of consumption are infused with power and politics. The sections that follow provide an overview of these tensions and the paradoxes that frame critical debates around cosmopolitanism and consumption.

Commodifying Difference: Homogeneity versus Heterogeneity

Appadurai asserts that the central problem of globalization is the "tension between cultural homogenization and cultural heterogenization" (1990: 295). He points out that increased global flows of media, technology, people and capital have led to a sense of standardization in some realms, such as the appearance of McDonald's golden arches around the world; at the same time, he notes, cultural forms rarely travel intact and tend to be appropriated or altered in different cultural contexts.

For many theorists, however, what is at stake in cultural globalization is not a simple distinction between homogeneity and heterogeneity. Some suggest that cultural forms and practices are more likely to be implicated in "global structures of common difference" than to fall neatly into binary categories of global hegemony or local appropriation (Wilk 1995: 117), while others argue that cultural globalization results in a more contingent, indeterminate and hybrid form of culture (Bhabha 1994, Pieterse 1995, 2004).

In either case, the tensions between homogenization and heterogenization have shaped much of the scholarship in the field of cultural globalization over the past two decades and continue to pose a particularly significant paradox in the relationship between cosmopolitanism and consumption. On the one hand, the forms of aesthetic or banal cosmopolitanism described earlier entail a desire to consume cultural difference. On the other hand, the very act of consuming difference results in, at best, a hollowing-out or watering-down of that difference, and at worst, a form of appropriation and symbolic oppression of the Other. This paradox is reflected in hooks' chilling observation that "the commodification of difference promotes paradigms of consumption wherein whatever difference the Other inhabits is eradicated, via exchange, by a consumer cannibalism that not only displaces the Other but denies the significance of that Other's history through a process of decontextualization" (hooks 1992: 431). If consumption eradicates difference, then *cosmopolitan* consumption seems to be an impossible proposition.

One way this paradox manifests itself is in spaces of cosmopolitan consumption, such as shopping malls, global cities and tourist destinations, where the homogenizing effects of globalized architectural styles and transnational industry standards are held in tension with the diversity of local products and cultures on offer in those places (Ritzer 2005, Urry 1995, Sheller and Urry 2004, Zukin 1996). Aware that they are competing on a global stage for capital investment and tourists, cities brand themselves as cosmopolitan by offering world-class accommodations, transportation and entertainment, while at the same time accentuating unique environmental or cultural features that make visiting that particular place worthwhile. According to Harvey (1990: 271), what becomes important in this global milieu is "the building and signaling of [each place's] unique qualities in an increasingly homogeneous but fragmented world." According to some theorists, cosmopolitanization also constitutes a new form of urban renewal through which cities capitalize on cultural diversity to transform themselves into globalized spaces of consumption (Binnie and Skeggs 2004, Binnie et al. 2006, Bodaar 2006).

In this and other ways, cosmopolitanism has proved useful to capitalism's imperative to move into new markets. As Marx and Engels (1952 [1848]: 46–7) explain, capitalism is, in its very nature, cosmopolitan:

> *The need for a constantly changing market chases the bourgeoisie over the whole surface of the globe. It must settle everywhere, establish connexions everywhere ... the bourgeoisie has through its exploitation of the world market given a cosmopolitan character to production and consumption in every country.* [Emphasis added]

According to Binnie and Skeggs (2004), the notion that cosmopolitanism is itself part of the cultural logic of global capitalism has significant implications not only for the production and consumption of cultural difference, but also for the ethical purchase of cosmopolitanism as a mode of cross-cultural understanding. To make this point, Binnie and Skeggs contrast the position taken by Beck (2000) and Cheah (1998) with a more cynical perspective expressed by Žižek (1997) and Brennan (1997). Whereas Beck and Cheah see cosmopolitanism as creating new forms of engagement with others, both Žižek and Brennan argue that cosmopolitanism is merely a guise under which the logic of late capitalism exploits and markets difference. For example, Binnie and Skeggs (2004) argue that branding gay urban spaces as "cosmopolitan" is less about creating a space for genuine encounters across lines of sexuality or class and more about marketing sexuality as cultural difference. Instead of creating authentic connections between strangers, cosmopolitan differences are valued, quite literally, for their marketability. Engagement with others becomes a question of knowing their value: "Is their culture worth knowing, experimenting with?" (Skeggs 2004: 159).

Within the consumer logic of late capitalism, then, cultural difference underpins a cosmopolitan style, but not necessarily a cosmopolitan ethic. Beck (2006: 150–1) argues that this logic extends to cosmopolitanism itself: "Cosmopolitanism has itself become a commodity: the glitter of cultural difference fetches a good price. Images of an in-between world, of the black body, exotic beauty, exotic music, exotic food and so on, are globally cannibalized, re-staged and consumed as products for mass markets." The result is a "safe form of multiculturalism" (Binnie et al. 2006: 250) that allows the privileged cosmopolitan consumer to get close to the Other, but not too close or too involved (see Ahmed 2000). According to Kalra et al. (2005), even the transgressive potential of hybridity falls prey to the commodifying logic of capitalism, relegated to a kind of "benign multiculturalism" that allows the cosmopolitan to consume cultural products from the diaspora—such as music, film and literature—and yet remain ignorant of the "places that are being bombed and crippled by the actions of imperialism resurfaced" (48).

What is significant here is the way the capitalist process of commodification is seen to deplete or contain cultural difference, resulting instead in what Jones and Leshkowich (2003) describe as "homogenized heterogeneity." Homogenized heterogeneity refers to the way cultural differences are identified and appreciated, but then appropriated in ways that diminish those differences or marginalize them in relation to global modernity. When this happens, "difference is transformed. Its edges are smoothed and its contours are flattened so that it fits more neatly into its assigned pigeonhole in the global display of culture" (Jones and Leshkowich 2003: 14, and see Wilk 1995). In this sense, commodification reduces the concepts of hybridity, diversity and cultural difference to the "occasional experience of exotic commodities which can be repackaged to sustain the insatiable trade in new forms of cultural identity" (Papastergiadis 2000, cited in Kalra et al. 2005: 101).

Cosmopolitanism often entails fantasies of transcending cultural differences, but as the analyses described above suggest, consumerist ideology tends to reproduce the very social divisions cosmopolitanism claims to dissolve. Given the tendency for commodification to incorporate and exploit cultural differences, can cosmopolitan aspirations toward universality ever be realized through practices of consumption? In her study of the Hmong diaspora, Schein (1998) describes the transnational commodity relations through which comparatively well-off Hmong residing in the United States obtain traditional costumes and cultural goods produced by their Miao "brethren" in China, with whom they purportedly share cultural ties. Schein argues that these commodity relations reveal a key contradiction: "In one sense, their messages are of horizontal fraternity ... But in another sense, they have been constructed on a bedrock of inexorable disparity" (Schein 1998: 167). This contradiction between "horizontal fraternity" and "inexorable disparity" points toward another paradox in cosmopolitan consumption that pits ideals of cosmopolitan inclusiveness against uses of cosmopolitanism as a marker of distinction.

Cosmopolitanism as Distinction: Inclusion versus Exclusion

By consuming a cosmopolitan array of media images, travel experiences, food and fashion, consumers around the world are promised membership in the global community via the marketplace. At the same time, cosmopolitan consumption requires a level of knowledge, competence and sophistication that distinguishes the discerning consumer from the parochial hoi polloi. In this sense, cosmopolitan consumption connotes universality at the same time that its logic of distinction reproduces material and symbolic inequalities based on hierarchies of race, class, gender, ethnicity and sexuality. This paradox shapes a second set of debates over the inclusive potential versus the exclusive effects of cosmopolitan consumption.

According to many scholars, the global flows of media images help foster a cosmopolitan consciousness by enabling viewers to imagine the lives of other people living in other places around the world and to locate their own lives in this global context (Appadurai 1990, Urry 2000, Szerszynski and Urry 2002, 2006, Schein 1999, Beck 2006) These "mediascapes," which are consumed primarily in people's living rooms, are seen as a form of "banal cosmopolitanism" (Beck 2006) and as a vital underpinning to the cosmopolitan disposition toward cultural difference described by Hannerz (1990) and Urry (1995). The extent to which these images bring viewers to a more sophisticated understanding of the world beyond their doorstep or merely reproduce culturally-based hierarchies and generally-held assumptions about the world is certainly a point of debate (see Lutz and Collins 1993, Parks 2003). Nevertheless, several studies suggest that this mundane consumption of global media has an inclusive effect, helping people to feel part of a wider global community.

In their UK-based media study, Szerszynski and Urry (2002, 2006) argue that exposure to increasingly large volumes of visual flows depicting foreign cultures and global imagery helps to generate a cosmopolitan disposition amongst viewers. According to their findings, global imagery transmitted through television and advertising constitutes "a 'publicly screened' cosmopolitan culture" that brings the world into people's homes and extends their awareness of the world beyond the domestic realm (Szerszynski and Urry 2002: 461). Experiencing "the simultaneity of events and the knowledge of this simultaneity all over the world," according to Beck (2006: 42), results in an "inner cosmopolitanization" or a "globalization of emotions and empathy." In other words, the global media not only enables people to imagine the world beyond their own locality, but to *feel* a kind of cosmopolitan connection to the world community.

Whereas Szerszynski and Urry develop their argument from the perspective of British viewers, Schein's (1999) research on media consumption in post-socialist China reveals a particularly Chinese form of cosmopolitanism. Schein observes that even though Chinese consumers in post-Mao China could not afford to travel or purchase foreign goods, they fulfilled their desire to "acquire worldliness" by consuming a panorama of transnational programming depicting "the world's goods and lifestyles" (1999: 360). For Schein, this global commodity desire, effected through the consumption of satellite broadcasts and media imagery rather than the purchase of actual commodities, constituted a kind of "imagined cosmopolitanism" that provided at least the illusion of spatial, class, gender and race mobility, and an escape from the constraints of economic, geohistorical and political exclusions. Central to this desire to participate, even in symbolic ways, in global consumer culture, Schein argues, was a longing for inclusion, "horizontal comradeship," and the eradication of "the differentials of power and wealth that otherwise amount to exclusions" (1999: 360). At the other end of the class spectrum, Ong (1999) describes how affluent Hong Kong residents used consumption as a means to detach themselves from local economic, political and social constraints in advance of the island's return to Chinese rule. Opting instead for a free-floating, "flexible citizenship," these wealthy Chinese consumers purchased real estate, made business investments, or enrolled their children in private schools abroad as a means of establishing residency in multiple places. In this case, their purchasing power enabled them to perform a material kind of cosmopolitan citizenship that their poorer counterparts could only imagine.

Schein's and Ong's findings align with Ferguson's assertion that consumption of "cosmopolitan" goods and lifestyles constitutes a claim to membership in global society. In his review of anthropological research in postcolonial Africa, Ferguson notes that many researchers interpreted Africans' acquisition of the material goods and social manners of their European colonizers either as a form of mimicry, or as a process of indigenization. In contrast, Ferguson sees postcolonial Africans' consumption of European fashions, goods, cosmetics and lifestyles as an expression of their desire "to be full and equal citizens of a modern urban society" (Ferguson 2002: 555). By adopting European dress and manners, Ferguson argues, African consumers were not imitating their white colonizers or appropriating these goods into indigenous meaning structures. Instead, they were asserting their "political and social rights to full membership in a wider society" (555). Here, cosmopolitanism is held to its ideals of universality and inclusion, and consumption of international or "western" goods, images and lifestyles constitutes a claim to membership in the modern world society.

This longing for equal membership in the global community is evident, as well, in the consumption practices of other non-western groups. For example, in his description of a second-hand marketplace in Tonga, Besnier (2004) describes how Tongans use consumption practices to articulate a modern and cosmopolitan self. In the act of buying and selling objects sent by their diasporic relatives, Tongans demonstrate membership in global modernity through their access to western commodities, knowledge of western culture, fluency in English, and above all, participation in the cornerstone of modernity: consumer culture. Fadzillah (2005) tells a similar story about rural teenage girls in northern Thailand who sell beauty products for multinational corporations like Amway and Avon. She notes that by involving themselves with the commodity world of the global beauty industry, these girls move literally and symbolically beyond their rural backgrounds and align themselves instead with the "cosmopolitan" world of travel, money and international beauty. In India, the influx of international brands has made global lifestyles available to urban middle-class women who negotiate ideals of Indian femininity within a context of global media and flows and international measure of beauty. According to Munshi (2001), these "Globo–Indians" consume cosmetics and beauty products in order to perform a "modern" global version of womanhood.

These studies identify the intense and ambivalent desires embedded in practices of cosmopolitan consumption at the "subaltern" end of the power-geometry of globalization, where fantasies of cosmopolitan inclusion rub up against social, economic and political exclusions based on gender, race and class. Schein's and Ong's analyses show how access to the material artifacts of cosmopolitanism is regulated by class, while Fadzillah's and Munshi's accounts make it clear that cosmopolitanism at this end of the power spectrum is highly feminized. As Schein acknowledges, such desires to transcend spatial or social differences do not "presume any actual diminishment of difference among media consumers around the world, but rather *its disavowal* as an effect of the consumption of global media" (1999: 360–1). According to these analyses, consumption—of media images as well as of material goods—enables postcolonial "subaltern" classes to participate in global modernity and to legitimize their membership in the global community. At the same time, however, these strategies of propelling oneself into a putatively inclusive cosmopolitan world community often rely on practices of distinction and exclusion based on familiar hierarchies of race, class and gender. Besnier acknowledges that in Tonga, cosmopolitanism is "an important prestige-manipulation tool" that allows high-ranking and wealthy Tongans to "assert their superiority over commoners, the poor, and the poorly connected" (2004: 11). Cosmopolitan consumption is as much a marker of exclusion, then, as it is a means of transcending hierarchies of difference.

Despite the aspirations toward cosmopolitan inclusion described above, a more familiar critical reading of cosmopolitanism depicts it as an exclusive class position reserved for a mobile, bourgeois elite with expensive tastes and jet-set lifestyles (Featherstone 2002, Vertovec and Cohen 2002, Calhoun 2002). These "cosmocrats" are known primarily by their global connoisseurship, their affinity for international travel and consuming foreign places, and an "acquired taste for artifacts from around the world" (Vertovec and Cohen 2002: 7). In this sense, tastes, preferences and cultural competencies involved in cosmopolitan consumption operate as markers of distinction rather than inclusion (Bourdieu 1984). This is especially evident in cosmopolitan orientations toward food and fashion.

In one sense, the global mobility of culinary styles and the increased availability of ingredients from around the world signals a kind of democratic "cosmopolitan omnivorousness" (Woodward et al. 2008: 214). In another sense, however, the knowledgeable consumption of exotic foods constitutes a strategy of exclusion that distinguishes the cosmopolitan elite from the parochial masses. In his study of "ethnic" restaurants in Sydney, Hage (1997) demonstrates how eating ethnic foods serves as a classificatory practice. In one Sydney suburb with a thriving ethnic restaurant culture, Hage finds that residents distinguish themselves as daring, sophisticated and worldly in contrast to the unsophisticated population of another area of Sydney lacking in "authentic" ethnic restaurants. Hage also observes that the white diners in this Sydney suburb consume not just foreign foods, but the cultural diversity that food represents. As Hage puts it, these "cosmo-multicultural" consumers do not just eat the spicy curry, but "eat" the *difference* between the curry and the pesto (Hage 1997: 129).

Consuming difference in this way, Hage (1997: 129) suggests, requires a "certain distance from the materiality of the food" that allows for consumption, not of the food itself, but of the difference between foods. These instances of "tasting" cultural difference are less about embodied encounters with the immigrants who prepare and serve the food than they are about marketing diversity as a tourist attraction (Hage, 1997: 121, see also hooks 1992, Heldke 2003, Germann Molz 2007). In this case, knowing how to navigate and consume the global flows of food and cuisines becomes a marker of distinction that reinscribes difference in three ways: first through the consumption of cultural diversity signified by the various cuisines; second through the separation between self and Other required to "sample" this cultural diversity; and then again as wealthy suburbanites distinguish themselves from their working-class counterparts in another neighborhood.

The global flows of fashion are another arena where some people's claims to cosmopolitan knowledge and competence are upheld while other claims are marginalized or excluded. As Jones and Leshkowich (2003: 9) point out, "style [is] an important terrain for negotiations over power." This is evident in Nava's (1996, 2002) study of early twentieth-century shopping culture in London, which reveals that women's forays into cosmopolitanism via fashion and shopping were, at the same time, undermined by anxious discourses that characterized female desires for consumer goods as insatiable, irrational and even pathological. Female consumption, in other words, was seen as an inferior form of participation in an emerging global modernity. If the consumption practices of these white, middle-class, urban women were deemed insufficient markers of membership in global society, then where does that leave the claims to cosmopolitanism asserted by the Chinese, Tongan, Thai, Indian or African consumers described earlier? How is their participation in global consumer culture kept in its place, so to speak? Jones and Leshkowich's analysis of the recent emergence of Asian styles on the global fashion scene is instructive in this sense. Jones and Leshkowich (2003: 5) acknowledge that, in one sense, "the global interest in Asian dress might seem to open new democratic forms of cross-cultural exchange," however, "no matter what form these fashions may take and no matter how praised they may be by fashion elites located in the centers of power, they get defined as somehow lesser than, somehow Other to, and somehow more feminized than their perennial Western foil." In this way, "Other" claims to cosmopolitan legitimacy serve as the constitutive limit for western, elite assertions of cosmopolitan authority. As these studies reveal, cosmopolitan consumption tends to reproduce social divisions rather than providing equal membership in a global community. This engenders a deep skepticism about the limited potential of consumption as a strategy for practicing global citizenship.

Consumer-Citizenship: "Superficial" versus "Authentic" Cosmopolitanism

A third key debate revolves around the links between cosmopolitan consumption and political claims of global citizenship. Within this debate, we can discern two distinct but related modes of cosmopolitanism: a "superficial" cosmopolitanism that entails dabbling in cultural difference; and a more "authentic" cosmopolitanism that translates into deeper forms of cross-cultural engagement (Kendall et al. 2009). On the one hand, critics identify certain forms of cosmopolitan consumption as little more than an aesthetic appreciation or recognition of cultural difference that remains on the surface, so to speak (Beck 2006, Chaney 2002, Regev 2007). In this case, cosmopolitanism entails a primarily stylistic engagement with cultural difference, concerned more with what looks, tastes or feels interesting than with the political or economic conditions of production and consumption. In contrast to this kind of "depthless" cosmopolitanism, some scholars have argued that cosmopolitan consumption may also involve an ethico-political orientation concerned with humanity, the "oneness of the world," and the possibility of a more just world order (Szerszynski and Urry 2002). Consumers see their actions in the marketplace as deeply intertwined with democratic ideals, with the material and political welfare of others across the world, and with the well-being of the global environment. This "authentic" form of cosmopolitanism, which sees consumption as a potentially civic act, emphasizes the political as opposed to aesthetic dimension of global citizenship.

According to Urry (1999), globalization has extended the rights, responsibilities and risks that constitute citizenship beyond the confines of the nation-state, implicating individuals in universal and de-territorialized modes of membership. He notes that the rights, responsibilities and risks that constitute this liberal model of global citizenship involve both aesthetic elements (such as the rights to travel internationally, to consume other places, and to access global media; or the responsibility to respond to images that address people as differentiated citizens of the globe), but also ethical and political elements (such as a responsibility to be informed about the state of the globe or to act on behalf of the globe as a whole rather than in terms of shared identity interests; or the right to form social movements with citizens of other states to protest state or corporate powers). The tension between the aesthetic and ethico-political dimensions of global citizenship inflects the debate between "superficial" and "authentic" cosmopolitan consumption as well. The question is: can cosmopolitan consumption be both? Scholars wonder whether "exposure to other cultures—from buying bits of them to learning to partake in their beliefs and practrices—[will] lead to a fundamental change in attitudes?" (Vertovec and Cohen 2002: 9). Put simply, are "global shoppers" likely to "endorse human rights issues or feel generous toward migrants and refugees?" (Woodward et al. 2008: 13)

Critics doubt that consumption practices and commodified forms of cosmopolitanism can lead to "genuine" forms of cosmopolitan engagement, often citing the inherent paradoxes surrounding commodification, difference, inclusion and exclusion discussed earlier (Vertovec and Cohen 2002, Calhoun 2002, Binnie and Skeggs 2004, Jubas 2007). For these critics, cosmopolitan commodities and lifestyles skim the surface of cultural difference, providing few channels for political agency or incentives for fostering genuine cross-cultural encounters. Heldke (2003: 22) argues that the cosmopolitan pleasure in consuming difference and novelty through cultural commodities like "ethnic" food, for instance, relies on, and indeed preserves, the consumer's ignorance about that other culture. Cosmopolitan consumption serves up, as Hage (1997: 118) puts it, "multiculturalism without the migrants" and "foreign-ness without the foreigners." Sociopolitical issues like human rights, migration, ethnic cleansing or global wealth inequalities are apparently not on the menu for the cosmopolitan consumer.

Calhoun agrees that consumption practices have limited purchase in the realm of global citizenship. The global mobility of Chinese food or McDonald's, he says, "tells us little about whether to expect democracy on a global scale, successful accommodation of immigrants at home or respect for human rights across the board" (Calhoun 2002: 105). Calhoun refers to cultural consumables, such as tourism, food, music and fashion, as the "easy faces of cosmopolitanism." Consuming these commodities may be culturally broadening, he argues, "but they are not hard tests for the relationship between local solidarity and international civil society" (Calhoun 2002: 105). Furthermore, the deeper cosmopolitanism burrows into capitalism, the more likely it is to reproduce rather than transcend deep and systemic inequalities. Calhoun sees little, if any, transgressive potential in what he calls "consumerist cosmopolitanism": "If there is to be a major redistribution of wealth, or a challenge to the way the means of production are controlled in global capitalism, it is not likely to be guided by cosmopolitanism as such" (Calhoun 2002: 106).

This attenuation of the political potential of consumption may stem from the fact that consumers often purchase clothing or electronic goods with no sense of where they were manufactured. They are unwittingly implicated in global trade circuits that link them to the wider world (Beck 2004, 2006, Timmerman 2008). Indeed, because the capitalist logic through which cultural difference is commodified relies on a material and emotional distancing, consumers are able to ignore or disavow unpalatable differences when they make their purchases. In this case, Beck explains, cosmopolitanism can emerge as the "latent" or "unconscious" side effect of world trade or transnational interdependencies. The question Beck poses is whether such "latent" forms of cosmopolitanism can underpin any kind of substantive political agency, or whether they are doomed to be "'trivial,' negligible or even dubious" (Beck 2004: 134).

Appadurai's discussion of "fetishism" is useful in synthesizing these perspectives. Drawing on Marx's notion of commodity fetishism, Appadurai (1990) introduces two new forms of fetishism that underpin cultural globalization: "production fetishism" and "fetishism of the consumer." Production fetishism refers to efforts to brand as "local" commodities and services that are actually produced through globally distributed circuits of management, material resources and labor. For example, production fetishism makes it possible to market Volkswagens as "national" products, even though they are assembled from parts sourced from all over the world (Beck 2006: 40–1). In this case, Appadurai (1990: 307) argues, the locality "becomes a fetish which disguises the globally dispersed forces that actually drive the production process." The counterpart to this is the "fetishism of the consumer," by which the consumer is transformed into a sign that stands in for real agency. Here, Appadurai argues, mediated images and ideas of consumer agency replace actual agency, and they do so in such subtle ways that "the consumer is consistently helped to believe that he or she is an actor, where in fact he or she is at best a chooser" (1990: 307). In this formulation, there seems to be little hope for achieving global political agency through consumption.

Other scholars are far more optimistic about the potential relationship between culture, consumption and citizenship. For one thing, argues Beck (2006: 41–2), even "banal" cosmopolitanism equips individuals with the skills necessary for navigating in an increasingly global world:

> What seems … to be 'eclecticism' or 'inauthenticity' … can be understood in terms of a new reflexivity. Here elements from many different countries and cultures are continually compared, rejected, combined and remixed. Thought through to its conclusion, there arises a whole network of everyday practices and skills to deal with a high degree of interdependence and globality.

For another, a cosmopolitan consciousness or "structure of feeling," even one cultivated through consumption, is seen as the foundation for an emerging cosmopolitan civil society (Stevenson 1997, Meijer 1998, Urry 2000, Kendall et al. 2009). According to Urry, participating in cosmopolitan consumer culture through international travel or exposure to global media images is far more connected to citizenship and citizen rights than skeptics acknowledge. He argues that the rights to travel and to consume other cultures and places are, themselves, markers of citizenship. What is emerging, Urry (2000) suggests, is a "consumer citizenship" that challenges previous distinctions between private and public spheres and makes possible new forms of civic participation and political resistance.

Stevenson (2002) similarly argues that consumption is precisely a political site where cosmopolitan citizenship might be enacted. For Stevenson, because shopping requires consumers to make daily ethical choices about the products they buy and the way they inhabit private and public space, consumption constitutes an ethical, moral and political domain that is central to citizenship, despite a "masculine logic that sees it as a peripheral activity" (Stevenson 2002: 310). Fully invigorating "consumer-citizenship" as a substantive civic subjectivity relies, Stevenson argues, not just on the development of formal cosmopolitan institutions, but also on a cosmopolitan sensibility structured around respect for ecological and cultural diversity, concern for social inequities, moral acceptance of human rights (2002: 314). In this sense, consumer society has the potential to become an arena for political action and cosmopolitan solidarity.

An example of these new forms of consumption-based political participation are the various campaigns and forms of "ethical," "sustainable" or "compassionate" consumption that seek to promote global causes via the marketplace. Boycotts of fashion brands that employ sweatshop labor abroad, advocacy of "fair trade" or "green" commodities, and issues-based marketing campaigns like Product (RED) and Make Poverty History, have all framed global civic participation in the context of consumption (Sáiz 2005, Seyfang 2005, Jubas 2007, Nash 2008). These emerging consumption trends blur the distinction between "authentic" and "superficial" forms of cosmopolitan consumption, posing the real possibility that consumption can bring about sociopolitical change but also raising serious critiques about the way these campaigns mobilize well-worn stereotypes that perpetuate social hierarchies and related material inequalities. Are these consumer campaigns examples of global political action, or do they further illustrate Appadurai's notion of "consumer fetishism"?

This debate has coalesced to a significant degree around the Product (RED) brand campaign (see Himmelmani and Mupotsa 2008). Launched in 2006 by U2's lead singer, Bono, and the company's CEO, Bobby Shriver, Product (RED) partners with iconic global brands to sell (RED) branded consumer goods in order to raise awareness and money in the fight against AIDS in Africa. Sarna-Wojcicki (2008: 14) identifies Product (RED) as a form of "causumerism," which she defines as "a particular mode of political activism through consumer choice" that empowers shoppers to "make a statement with their purchases." By channeling consumers' cosmopolitan consciousness via purchasing power, Product (RED) has raised more than $100 million and garnered extensive publicity for the Global Fund, an organization that fights AIDS, tuberculosis and malaria worldwide. On the one hand, commentators applaud this material success and acknowledge Product (RED)'s ability to mobilize celebrities, corporations and consumers to its cause. At the same time, however, critics ask whether this kind of "compassionate consumerism" (Kuehn 2008) is genuinely transformative, especially in light of the reductive effects wrought by the campaign.

According to these critics, the marketing discourse surrounding Product (RED) reinforces a series of social hierarchies that pivot on implicit distinctions between "us" and "them," "first world consumers" and "African AIDS patients," saviors and victims (Sarna-Wojcicki 2008: 14, Jungar and Salo 2008). In this discourse, Sarna-Wojcicki explains, "the empowerment promised by (RED) is limited to the shopping mall of the 'first world consumers,' excluding African voices from the 'cause.' … (RED), like other cause based initiatives, is claiming to raise 'awareness,' yet the topic of AIDS and Africa is rendered in monolithic images and reductive descriptions" (2008: 28). Cosmopolitan shoppers can thus buy into a cause without disrupting their own values and daily habits, without questioning their deeply held assumptions about the relationship between Africa and the west, and without committing to riskier forms of political activism.

Moves toward ethical or compassionate consumption underscore the fact that consumption is always political, but as the critiques described above suggest, they provide no easy answers about how a cosmopolitan consciousness should be mobilized into just, sustainable and ethical modes of engagement with other people. Cosmopolitan consumption may promote certain structures of feeling about "humanity" or the "world as a whole," and indeed people may be deeply transformed personally by the cross-cultural encounters made possible by their consumption practices, but the extent to which *feeling* cosmopolitan translates into action, or even concern, on behalf of human rights or struggles for a better world and issues of global justice remains unclear. Is there transformative potential within cause-based consumption, or are "ethical" and "compassionate" consumption merely marketing trends designed to preserve the status quo? Can a viable cosmopolitical agenda for global social justice be attained through consumption? Or must cosmopolitical aims necessarily be pursued outside of the regime of consumption? These questions will remain central as scholars continue to grapple with the inherent paradoxes of cosmopolitan consumption.

Conclusion: Towards a Cosmopolitics of Consumption

One of the ways to make sense of the debates discussed in this chapter is to return to Hannerz's (2006) distinction between the "two faces of cosmopolitanism, culture and politics." It is clear that consumption, as a set of practices and as a logic, refuses to stay put on the "culture" side of this coin. Instead, the critical analyses outlined above bring our attention to the political dimensions of cosmopolitan consumption. In these accounts, consumption is revealed to be implicated not only in the political economy of capitalism, the reiteration of social inequalities, and the simultaneous appropriation *and* disavowal of difference, but also in claims to membership in global society and in forms of collective action and civic participation. In other words, the scholarship reviewed here suggests that the two faces of cosmopolitanism are joined, albeit uneasily, in a "cosmopolitics of consumption."

A key question at stake in this cosmopolitics of consumption is whether consumption will be a friend or an enemy of cosmopolitan society (Beck 2000). Despite several optimistic gestures toward the political potential of cosmopolitan consumption, most of the scholarly critiques reviewed in this chapter seek to convince us that the more deeply cosmopolitanism becomes implicated in the commodifying logic of late capitalism, the more it will resemble what Beck (2006: 20) refers to as "deformed cosmopolitanism." For Beck, "deformed cosmopolitanism" is not the result of the active pursuit of cosmopolitan political ideals, but rather is the unintended cultural effect of globalization, a fate that "merely befalls us" (2006: 20). In contrast, Beck suggests that a "non-deformed cosmopolitanism" emerges from "the sense of partaking in the great human experiment in civilization ... and hence of making a contribution to world culture" (2006: 21). The task for a "cosmopolitics of consumption" is to better understand how consumption might be practiced as a way of participating in, contributing to and "re-forming" a cosmopolitan world culture.

Bibliography

Ahmed, S. 2000. *Strange Encounters*. London: Routledge.
Appadurai, A. 1990. Disjuncture and difference in the global cultural economy. *Theory, Culture and Society*, 7(2–3), 295–310.
Bauman, Z. 1998. *Globalization: The Human Consequences*. Cambridge: Polity.
Beck, U. 2000. The cosmopolitan perspective: sociology of the second age of modernity. *British Journal of Sociology*, 51, 79–105.
Beck, U. 2003. *Conversations with Ulrich Beck, with J. Willms*. Cambridge: Polity.
Beck, U. 2004. Cosmopolitical realism: on the distinction between cosmopolitanism in philosophy and the social sciences. *Global Networks*, 4(2), 131–56.
Beck, U. 2006. *Cosmopolitan Vision*. Cambridge: Polity.
Besnier, N. 2004. Consumption and cosmopolitanism: practicing modernity at the second hand marketplace in Nuku'alofa, Tonga. *Anthropological Quarterly*, 77(1), 7–45.
Bhabha, H. 1994. *The Location of Culture*. London: Routledge.
Billig, M. 1995. *Banal Nationalism*. London: Sage.
Binnie, J. and Skeggs, B. 2004. Cosmopolitan knowledge and the production and consumption of sexualized space: Manchester's gay village. *The Sociological Review*, 52(1), 39–61.
Binnie, J., Holloway, J., Millington, S. and Young, C. 2006. Grounding cosmopolitan urbanism: approaches, practices and policies, in *Cosmopolitan Urbanism*, edited by J. Binnie, J. Holloway, S. Millington and C. Young. London: Routledge, 1–34.
Bodaar, A. 2006. Multicultural urban space and the cosmopolitan "other": the contested revitalization of Amsterdam's Bijlmermeer, in *Cosmopolitan Urbanism*, edited by J. Binnie, J. Holloway, S. Millington and C. Young. London: Routledge, 171–86.

Bourdieu, P. 1984. *Distinction*. London: Routledge and Kegan Paul.
Brennan, T. 1997. *At Home in the World: Cosmopolitanism Now*. Cambridge, MA: Harvard University Press.
Calhoun, C. 2002. The class consciousness of frequent travellers: towards a critique of actually existing cosmopolitanism, in *Conceiving Cosmopolitanism*, edited by S. Vertovec and R. Cohen. Oxford: Oxford University Press, 86–109.
Chaney, D. 2002. Cosmopolitan art and cultural citizenship. *Theory, Culture and Society*, 19(1–2), 157–74.
Cheah, P. 1998. Introduction part II: the cosmopolitical – today, in *Cosmopolitics*, edited by B. Robbins and P. Cheah. Minneapolis: University of Minnesota Press, 20–41.
Fadzillah, I. 2005. The Amway connection: how transnational ideas of beauty and money affect northern Thai girls' perceptions of their future options, in *Youthscapes*, edited by S. Maira and E. Soep. Philadelphia: University of Pennsylvania Press.
Featherstone, M. 2002. Cosmopolis: an introduction. *Theory, Culture and Society*, 19(1–2), 1–16.
Ferguson, J.G. 2002. Of mimicry and membership: Africans and the "new world society." *Cultural Anthropology*, 17(4), 551–69.
Freeman, C. 2001. Is local: global as feminine: masculine? Rethinking the gender of globalization. *Signs: Journal of Women, Culture and Society*, 26(4), 1007–37.
Germann Molz, J. 2007. Eating difference: the cosmopolitan mobilities of culinary tourism. *Space and Culture*, 10(1), 77–93.
Hage, G. 1997. At home in the entrails of the west, in *Home/World: Space, Community and Marginality in Sydney's West*, edited by H. Grace, G. Hage, L. Johnson, J. Langsworth and M. Symonds. Annandale: Pluto, 99–153.
Hannerz, U. 1990. Cosmopolitans and locals in world culture. *Theory, Culture and Society*, 7(2–3), 237–51.
Hannerz, U. 2006. Two Faces of Cosmopolitanism: Culture and Politics. Barcelona: Fundació CIDOB.
Harvey, D. 1990. *The Condition of Postmodernity*. Cambridge, MA: Blackwell.
Heldke, L. 2003. *Exotic Appetites*. London: Routledge.
Himmelmani, N. and Mupotsa, D. 2008. (Product)Red: (re)branding Africa? *The Journal of Pan African Studies*, 2(6), 1–12.
hooks, b. 1992. *Black Looks: Race and Representation*. London: Turnaround.
Jones, C. and Leshkowich, A.M. 2003. The globalization of Asian dress: re-orienting fashion or re-orientalizing Asia? in *Re-Orienting Fashion: The Globalization of Asian Dress*, edited by S.A. Niessen, A.M. Leshkowich and C. Jones. Oxford: Berg, 1–48.
Jubas, K. 2007. Conceptual confusion in democratic societies: understandings and limitations of consumer-citizenship. *Journal of Consumer Culture*, 7, 231–54.
Jungar, K. and Salo, E. 2008. "Shop and do good?" *The Journal of Pan African Studies*, 2(6), 92–102.
Kalra, V., Kaur, R. and Hutnyk, J. 2005. *Diaspora and Hybridity*. Sage: London.

Kendall, G., Woodward, I. and Skrbiš, Z. 2009. *Sociology of Cosmopolitanism: Globalization, Identity, Culture and Government*. London: Palgrave Macmillan.

Kuehn, K. 2008. *Compassionate Consumerism: Healing Africa Through Gap's Product (RED) Campaign*. Paper presented at the International Communication Association, Montreal, Quebec, Canada, May 21, 2008, available at www.allacademic.com/meta/p234360_index.html. Accessed November 20, 2009.

Lash, S. and Urry, J. 1994. *Economies of Signs and Space*. London: Sage.

Lutz, C. and Collins, J. 1993. *Reading National Geographic*. Chicago: University of Chicago Press.

Massey, D. 1993. Power-geometry and a progressive sense of place, in *Mapping the Futures*, edited by J. Bird, B. Curtis, T. Putnam, G. Robertson and L. Tickner. London: Routledge, 59–69.

Marx and Engels 1952 [1848]. *Manifesto of the Communist Party*, trans. S. Moore. Moscow: Progress Press.

Meijer, I. 1998. Advertising citizenship: an essay on the performative power of consumer culture. *Media, Culture and Society*, 20, 235–49.

Munshi, S. 2001. "Marvellous me": the beauty industry and the construction of the "modern" Indian woman, in *Images of the "Modern Woman" in Asia*, edited by S. Munshi. Richmond: Curzon, 78–93.

Nash, K. 2008. Global citizenship as show business: the cultural politics of Make Poverty History. *Media Culture and Society*, 30(2), 167–81.

Nava, M. 1996. Modernity's disavowal: women, the city and the department store, in *Modern Times: Reflections on a Century of English Modernity*, edited by M. Nava and A. O'Shea. London: Routledge, 38–76.

Nava, M. 2002. Cosmopolitan modernity: everyday imaginaries and the register of difference. *Theory Culture Society*, 19(1–2), 81–99.

Nava, M. 2007. *Visceral Cosmopolitanism*. Oxford: Berg.

Ong, A. 1999. *Flexible Citizenship: The Cultural Logics of Transnationality*. Durham, NC: Duke University Press.

Parks, L. 2003. Our world, satellite televisuality, and the fantasy of global presence, in *Planet TV*, edited by L. Parks and S. Kumar. New York: New York University Press, 74–93.

Pieterse, J. 1995. Globalization as hybridization, in *Global Modernities*, edited by M. Featherstone, S. Lash and R. Robertson. London: Sage, 45–68.

Pieterse, J. 2004. *Globalization and Culture: Global Mélange*. Oxford: Rowman and Littlefield.

Regev, M. 2007. Cultural uniqueness and aesthetic cosmopolitanism. *European Journal of Social Theory*, 10(1), 123–38.

Ritzer, G. 2005. *Enchanting a Disenchanted World*. 2nd Edition. Thousand Oaks: Pine Forge Press.

Robbins, B. 1998. Actually existing cosmopolitanism, in *Cosmopolitics*, edited by P. Cheah and B. Robbins. Minneapolis: University of Minnesota Press, 1–19.

Sáiz, A.V. 2005. Globalization, cosmopolitanism and ecological citizenship, in *Citizenship, Environment, Economy*, edited by A. Dobson and A.V. Sáiz. London: Routledge, 7–22.

Sarna-Wojcicki, M. 2008. Refigu(red): talking Africa and Aids in "causumer" culture. *The Journal of Pan African Studies*, 2(6), 14–31.

Schein, L. 1998. Importing Miao brethren to Hmong America: a not-so-stateless transnationalism, in *Cosmopolitics*, edited by P. Cheah and B. Robbins. Minneapolis: University of Minnesota Press, 163–91.

Schein, L. 1999. Of cargo and satellites: imagined cosmopolitanism. *Postcolonial Studies*, 2(3), 345–75.

Seyfang, G. 2005. Shopping for sustainability: can sustainable consumption promote ecological citizenship, in *Citizenship, Environment, Economy*, edited by A. Dobson and A.V. Sáiz. London: Routledge, 137–54.

Sheller, M. and Urry, J. 2004. Places to play, places in play, in *Tourism Mobilities*, edited by M. Sheller and J. Urry. London: Routledge, 1–10.

Skeggs, B. 2004. *Class, Self, Culture*. London: Routledge.

Stevenson, N. 1997. Globalization, national cultures and cultural citizenship. *The Sociological Quarterly*, 38(1), 41–66.

Stevenson, N. 2002. Consumer culture, ecology and the possibility of cosmopolitan citizenship. *Consumption, Markets and Culture*, 5(4), 305–19.

Szerszynski, B. and Urry, J. 2002. Cultures of cosmopolitanism. *Sociological Review*, 50(4), 461–81.

Szerszynski, B. and Urry, J. 2006. Visuality, mobility and the cosmopolitan: inhabiting the world from afar. *British Journal of Sociology*, 57(1), 113–31.

Timmerman, K. 2008. *Where Am I Wearing? A Global Tour to the Countries, Factories and People that Make Our Clothes*. New York: Wiley.

Tomlinson, J. 1999. *Globalization and Culture*. Cambridge: Polity.

Urry, J. 1995. *Consuming Places*. London: Routledge.

Urry, J. 1999. Globalization and citizenship. *Journal of World–Systems Research*, 5(2), 311–24.

Urry, J. 2000. The global media and cosmopolitanism. Paper to the Transnational America Conference, Bavarian American Academy, Munich, June 2000. Available at www.lancs.ac.uk/fass/sociology/papers/urry–global–media.pdf. Accessed November, 20 2009.

Vertovec, S. and Cohen, R. 2002. Conceiving cosmopolitanism, in *Conceiving Cosmopolitanism: Theory, Context, Practice*, edited by S. Vertovec and R. Cohen. Oxford: Oxford University Press, 1–22.

Wilk, R. 1995. Learning to be local in Belize: global systems of common difference, in *Worlds Apart: Modernity through the Prism of the Local*, edited by D. Miller. London: Routledge, 110–33.

Woodward, I., Skrbiš, Z. and Bean, C. 2008. Attitudes toward globalization and cosmopolitanism: cultural diversity, personal consumption and the national economy. *British Journal of Sociology*, 59(2), 207–26.

Žižek, S. 1997. Multiculturalism, or, the cultural logic of multinational capitalism. *New Left Review*, 225, 28–52.

Zukin, S. 1996. Space and symbols in an age of decline, in *Re-presenting the City*, edited by A. King. New York: New York University Press, 43–59.

3

Cosmopolitan Openness

Zlatko Skrbiš and Ian Woodward

Introduction

The word cosmopolitanism is increasingly commonly used although it continues to escape an easy definition. Philosophers and sociologists find it difficult to define the term and they are at pains in agreeing just who befits the label 'cosmopolitan'. In this sense they are no different from ordinary citizens who – often just because they like the hipness of the fad word 'cosmopolitan' – use it to describe their lives, experiences and tastes. There are different ways of being cosmopolitan but what most cosmopolitans share is a disposition of openness to the world around them. This may sound nebulous and trite but openness is probably one characteristic that most theorists of cosmopolitan agree on and it is also one common theme connecting a vast majority of conceptions of cosmopolitanism through its history: from Diogenes to Kant (1983), Nussbaum (1996) to Derrida (2000).

Yet, while cosmopolitanism and openness are in a symbiotic relationship, the relationship is not a mechanical one. As we argued elsewhere (Skrbiš and Woodward 2007: 734), we should not think of the relationship between the two as being one of the continuum where more perceived openness towards difference and the other somehow corresponds with a more intensely cosmopolitan identity. Looking another way, the idea of openness serves as a kind of an epistemological principle of cosmopolitanism: it limits and fixates the definitional horizon by reminding us that beyond openness lies a sphere of all things un-cosmopolitan. As we will show in the first part of this chapter, drawing on key examples from the history of the cosmopolitan idea, there exist a strong and historically enduring association between cosmopolitanism and the idea of openness.

Most would agree that openness and cosmopolitanism both engender something positive and enabling, evoking acceptance and engagement rather than distance and rejection. This positive impulse is not only central to the idea of cosmopolitanism; it is its driving force. Yet, the place of openness in discussions of cosmopolitanism is somewhat obscured: it is implicitly rather than explicitly spoken about; it refers to something abstract rather than concrete and articulated; it captures the 'spirit' of an idea of cosmopolitanism rather than its manifestations. This is both the strength and weakness of the concept of openness.

In terms of the genesis of the idea of cosmopolitan openness, we find it centrally embedded in the works of thinkers from radically different eras. It is a core idea behind Diogenes' (born 412 BC) lapidary statement 'I am a citizen of the world'. This statement includes two key points. On the one hand, it professes a degree of detachment from the local and an inherently critical distance to immediacy. On the other, it decrees a sense of openness that allows an individual to embrace the world community which is quite different and apart from the world that one is embedded in. The idea is also critical to Immanuel Kant's (1724–1804) understanding of cosmopolitanism, particularly his conceptions of peace and hospitality. Yet, his openness is quite different from Diogenes': whereby Diogenes presupposes some degree of unrestricted universalism, Kant's openness is a more regulated one, limited through his recognition of the role that the states play in regulating both peace and hospitality. More recently, the idea of openness is central to Martha Nussbaum's (1996) intervention about cosmopolitan education. In her view, education – and by implication one's worldview – must be inherently international and cosmopolitan in orientation. Students, she argues, must be encouraged to open up and learn not only about their immediate environment but also about other places and cultures. Leaving aside the debate that followed (Cohen 1996), there is no doubt that the productive legacy of Nussbaum's intervention rests critically and centrally on the idea of openness, postulating universalism and humanity as a reference point for moral judgements and practical action.

In short, what this short historical excurse demonstrates is that the history of cosmopolitan thought is a history of use of the idea of openness although largely in terms of abstract ideals, such as openness towards humanity, valuing of universalism and embracing of diversity that comes as an inevitable consequence of moving beyond local and particular. There is no need to put openness on a pedestal and proclaim it the newfound God of the cosmopolitan ideal. What it offers, however, is a noteworthy intersection between concepts that have had an enduring relationship. Building on our previous arguments about the agenda for cosmopolitanism research, this chapter will extend our earlier efforts to make cosmopolitanism a sharper conceptual and analytical tool through an exploration of openness. Initially we set the call for this agenda (Skrbiš et al. 2004) as a simple reaction to those who render cosmopolitanism a simple figure of speech and an excuse to hyperventilate on free-spirited and non-constrained cosmopolitan fantasies. We categorically opposed those conceptions of cosmopolitanism which treat it as 'something of a fantasy – a comforting illusion, but one that may not be at all analytically useful' (Skrbiš et al. 2004: 119). Later, we endeavoured to show how cosmopolitan openness is understood through the everyday experiences of ordinary citizens who have no understanding of cosmopolitanism as a philosophical or social theoretical concept but who operate with basic and popular notions of the idea. Instead of asking them about their 'cosmopolitanism', by following in Lamont and Aksartova's (2002: 2) footsteps, we wanted to ground people's dispositions in everyday experiences such as travel, shopping or thinking about 'other' cultures (see also Skrbiš and Woodward 2007; Calcutt et al. 2009). We acknowledge the apparently paradoxical ambition to invest into an abstract and blunt concept of openness in order to make another blunt and abstract concept (cosmopolitanism) sharper and more useful. But the history of interweaving between cosmopolitanism and openness, the embeddedness of the cosmopolitan idea in the idea of openness, provides a strong justification for such an undertaking.

In what follows we explore contemporary expressions of openness by firstly outlining the structural and systemic conditions which make it such a relevant contemporary concept. The first part of this discussion focuses on the enabling dimensions of contemporary openness, associated with various types of mobility and an ever-expanding global fluidity. The second part of this story relates to the social structural uptake of these raw materials. This dynamic creates a critical tension for the concept of openness which we explicate. In the second part of this chapter we analyse the dimensions of openness as they are observable in outlooks, practices and values of individuals. At no point do we suggest to be prescriptive, even less reductive, concerning how openness could be measured. Our goal is, however, to show that openness is not a decorative and hip accoutrement for the contemporary cosmopolitanism scholar but a useful analytical tool. Finally, we interrogate the cultural and political implications of openness as we recognize that openness is far from universal and neutral but rather a contested point of view based on position and privilege.

The Socio-Cultural Contexts of Contemporary Openness

Two significant socio-cultural trends – historically unprecedented in terms of intensity and scope – contextualize and provide a structural, systemic basis for the current relevance of openness as a way of conceptualizing cosmopolitanization processes. The first of these trends emerges from a familiar story regarding the volume and velocity of global flows. The second, which potentially mitigates the effects and consequences of the first or at least complicates it, concerns the reception, uptake and consequences of such flows. In the section below we deal with each process in some detail.

The first is that the contemporary era is one of increased mobility, exchange and fluidity. Research into mobility asserts a set of facts describing key facets and characteristics of the contemporary social world associated with globalization, technological changes, fluidities and speed. These dimensions of global capitalism provide some of the raw materials and the scene-setting for the current cosmopolitan agenda. Though cosmopolitanism does not directly spring from these mobilities *per se*, in many cases the various types of mobility are an important pathway to and wellspring of the cosmopolitan way of seeing. Mobility theory asserts that the world is characterized by unprecedented levels of movement and fluidity: capital, people, information and objects move about the globe more frequently, in greater volume and with greater speed. As recently asserted (*The Economist* 2009: 85) 'For the first time in history, across much of the world, to be foreign is a perfectly normal condition'. Increasingly, the global reach of economic and cultural interactions intensify, and though their movement is surveilled, monitored and sometimes prevented by nation states – some notably more than others – it is a truism that these intentions recognize fewer boundaries than ever before. This in itself provides an important cosmopolitan context. Moreover, even if one's body or material belongings cannot be mobile, imaginative and virtual forms of mobility are increasingly afforded and encouraged by traditional media, but more so by the global connectivity of computers and the Internet. Though it has most recently coalesced into a consolidated field of inquiry, this facet of contemporary globalization processes has been acknowledged in social theory since the 1980s, pointing to the annihilation of spatial barriers and the development of communities of interest and empathy both beyond and within national borders (Harvey 1989; Tomlinson 1999; Lash and Urry 1987).

Though this largely materially-driven openness has reached a recent intensity that is unrivalled, it is an historically situated process. Marx, of course, famously understood that the world was becoming more cosmopolitan, if only in the name of capitalism's voracious and exploitative expansion. As recent scholarship has pointed out (for instance Latour 1993), there are a variety of material bits which activate and construct these emergent exchange networks: technologies like shipping, navigation, storage and maps, for example. At its basis this is often commercial capitalist activity, moving commodities and production technologies about and across boundaries in response to consumer demand enervated by new status desires of various capitalized social classes. Reflecting on the historical development of such an arrangement, Braudel (1992) illustrates that the everyday fact of the emerging global economy of the sixteenth to nineteenth centuries was its constitution as a system for exchanging ideas and cultural difference. Though Braudel discusses many examples of this, in assigning fashion a special place as a motor of economic growth and trade based in the carriage of aesthetic and decorative forms, he picks up on an important point. As it circulates ever more widely, fashion objects carry innovation, novelty and difference as their trademarks, but they also speak to changing desires for difference, newness or innovation within fractions of the consumer population – people's taste for something culturally novel, often experienced as the *joie de vivre* and energy of a culture (see also Campbell 1987). When lack of contentedness with one's current material life was provoked through an increasing awareness of the different, exotic, plain better or more interesting, one was forced to confront and overcome the 'ceiling of the possible' determined by one's local environment (Braudel 1992: 435). In the case of fashion, when the phantasms of aspirant social classes were stimulated, consumer demand and entrepreneurship kicked the economy into action, drawing in non-local, exotic colours, designs, materials and scents. Braudel quotes seventeenth-century dramatist Thomas Dekker, who highlights how fashion is underpinned by a process of aestheticized cultural exchange:

> *His codpiece is with Denmark, the collar, his Duble and the belly in France, the wing and narrow sleeve in Italy: the short waste hangs over a Dutch*

Botchenstall in Ultrich: his huge slopes speak Spanish: Polonia give him the Bootes. (Braudel 1992: 321)

Nava's (1998) historical account is somewhat in sympathy with Braudel, but incorporates the visceral and sensual directly, by illustrating how cosmopolitan discourses were incorporated into commercial promotions by Selfridges department store, London, in the early twentieth century. While Selfridges was 'founded at the height of British Imperialism' it promoted a 'cosmopolitanism which was modern, urban and cultured' (Nava 1998: 166) by its demonstration of intellectual and aesthetic openness through advertising, store facilities and layout and promotions which privileged cultural difference as a desirable status distinction. While this was a deployment of cosmopolitanism that was related to the growth of modern consumer cultures, representations of luxury and display, and the imbrication of conspicuous signifiers of identity and social status, Nava argues that this does not necessarily diminish its potential critical or transformative efficacy as a cultural text. Indeed, she suggests that the selling of these 'mundane' or 'domesticated' (Nava 2002: 94) forms of cosmopolitan styles goes hand-in-hand with more fundamental and progressive social structural changes. They may, in fact, be the harbingers of wider social changes.

This is an important historical observation about the material-aesthetic basis of openness, and a very productive expansion of the discourse of cosmopolitan openness which fuses aesthetics, everyday commerce and the allure of visual difference within commercial public spaces (Nava 2007). This observation illustrates that there is a historically contextualized and ongoing expansion of intensified exchanges in late modern or second-modern culture; enabled and stimulated through economic, institutional and social ties, but of course ineradicably permeated by cultural baggage. This increased mobility of people and things is a fact of globally integrated social relations which is obvious through careful historical study, but also now more than ever is it a social fact (Beck 2006). The availability of 'things of difference' constitutes significant raw material for the development of openness as a reflexive response to cultural and social difference.

It is here we come to our second major assertion concerning the structural conditions of openness: this process creates greater opportunities for a cosmopolitan openness to be fostered, but does not necessarily guarantee it. The key reason for this is outlined in the following aspect of our argument which relates to the socially and culturally structured uptake and subsequent 'possession' of these forms of aestheticized difference. Our analysis points to the need for considering the impact of actual practices of consumption and appropriation in relation to these forms; that is, their mode of uptake, reception and use. Though it is an attractive idea to suggest sheer availability and display of cultural difference in such areas as food, dress, customs and habits and styles of leisure can lead to genuine and lasting processes of democratization by elevating the non-local within the realm of a state or empire, this remains something of an open question empirically. In contemporary literatures on consumption, omnivorousness and cultural difference, we can see some important pointers regarding the differential reception and use of these images and objects.

Chaney (2002) has described how shifting aesthetic and cultural economies, coupled with the rising importance of cultural citizenship, have generated the possibility of deploying cosmopolitan symbols as signs of distinction, at least for select groups within a population. He defines the cosmopolitan cultural citizen as having heterogeneous tastes, and the ability to transcend native culture by adopting a learned indifference to local goods (Chaney 2002: 158). Cosmopolitans are geographically and culturally mobile, and must have the capacity to interpret things as cosmopolitan, and especially distinguish it from the comfort and familiarity of the local. As Hall (2002: 26) has put it, cosmopolitanism requires the ability to draw upon and enact vocabularies and discourses from a variety of cultural repertoires. The cosmopolitan has the technical and intellectual resources or 'capital' to gain employment across national boundaries, and typically has an ability to traverse, consume, appreciate and empathize with cultural symbols and practices that originate outside their home country. This is where forms of cultural capital come most strongly into play regarding forms of cosmopolitanization, comprising both a threat and an opportunity in regard their full expression.

The best empirical explorations of this issue comes from sociological studies of cultural consumption. Such literatures begin in substantial form with Bourdieu, but importantly, moving towards what might be understood as a 'cosmopolitanization of Bourdieu' through new ideas of plurality, performativity and flexibility – indeed aspects of 'openness' – in consumption practices. In literatures on cultural consumption in the wake of Pierre Bourdieu's (1984) rather monolithic account of the cultural empire of French national tastes, this idea of pluralization has reached its strongest empirical expression in the work of Peterson and colleagues (Peterson and Kern 1996). Their research shows that possessing tastes for things across and beyond one's location in the social spectrum becomes incorporated into structures of social difference, infusing cultural difference objects with interpretable markers of social status and honour within particular cultural scenes and circuits. For example, Peterson (1990) asserts that the World Music genre, defined as incorporating music of non-Western origin, is likely to be the preferred music of the affluent baby-boomers, and predicts that it may replace classical music as the music of the intellectual classes into the twenty-first century. Van Eijck (2000: 216) has speculated that one attraction of these forms of music 'lies in the musical experiment and the juxtaposition of diverse musical elements'. But more than this, we want to suggest that such cosmopolitan omnivorousness becomes a symbol of social status and of one's moral worth. It is a particular type of cultural capital that demonstrates one is able to appreciate the cultural products and practices of others, suggesting openness and flexibility, which are 'important resources in a society that requires social and geographical mobility, "employability", and "social networking"' (Van Eijck 2000: 221). Such a credential is an important emergent form of capital which is a necessary outlook one must possess to be perceived as civilized and educated, argue Peterson and Kern (1996: 906).

Ironically, while this makes insularity and cultural narrowness an outdated set of habits, it also elevates the love of, and desire for, cultural difference to the realm of fashion and exclusivity. Though variety and curiosity – the hallmarks of the omnivorous disposition – may in one sense seem to negate snobbery and lead to a flattening of cultural difference, such traits can also be associated with connoisseurship, cultural possession, mastery and a desire for the exceptional and rare which are the basis of subtle processes of cultural differentiation and exclusion. Part of Peterson and Kern's (1996) conclusion is that standards of 'good taste' now involve knowledge and consideration of cultural goods produced outside one's own national culture. Indeed, in some circles, cultural difference and its 'mastery' becomes a highly valued status marker. As Peterson (1997: 87) puts it: being high status now does not require snobbishness, but means having 'omnivorous' tastes. Being attuned to the cultural outputs of others requires a sense of inclusivity and the appreciation of cultural difference which are the hallmarks of cosmopolitan openness, yet it also requires frames of interpretation, cultural experiences and learning which are available on the basis of possessing various types of social capital. These culturally acquired, social possessions, of course, are unevenly distributed.

Following our discussion of these two socio-cultural contexts of cosmopolitan openness, we now turn attention to identifying some key dimensions of such openness. We do this in an effort to delineate the common elements normally associated with the idea of cosmopolitan openness.

Four Central Dimensions of Cosmopolitan Openness

We see cosmopolitanism as something that happens in people's lives but we also acknowledge that the concept of cosmopolitanism suffers because in addition to being a social category, it is also understood as a social ideal (Hollinger 1995). It is important to acknowledge that this messiness is nothing extraordinary in social sciences where conceptual bifurcation is not an exception but a rule. Even the most basic of social science concepts such as class are contaminated with a multitude of assumptions about what they do, or should, represent. Indeed, class may be a good example to use because the only way to understand class is to painstakingly assemble the many characteristics, locations and experiences which allow us to identify one's class position. The same principles apply when it comes to the concept of cosmopolitanism and cosmopolitan openness. We refuse to believe those who argue that the cosmopolitan cannot (and even should not!) be practically interrogated (cf. Skrbiš et al. 2004).

How do we move on from perceptions that the concept of cosmopolitan openness is vague, abstract, aspirational and thus analytically weak? We propose defining some minimal common ground in the domains of disposition and practice which will help us delineate the key parameters of cosmopolitan openness. To move away from an abstract principle of cosmopolitan openness that lacks an Archimedean point of reference, we are making a case for a more empirically defined domains – a minimal vocabulary as it were – which will help us define, express (and possibly measure) what we mean by cosmopolitan openness. These four foci are:

1. the question of attachment and belonging;
2. mobilities;
3. cosmopolitan ethics and reflexivity; and
4. consumption and flows.

Attachment and belonging

This point is about the very core principle driving the cosmopolitanism debate. It can be traced back to the lapidary statement by Diogenes about 'being a citizen of the world'. This is perhaps the most important theme in any discussion of openness not only because it directly addresses the thought that gave rise to the philosophical idea, but because it invites an individual as reflexive subject to reflect upon and define their position in the world. The idea of 'being a citizen of the world' is unquestionably a litmus test of cosmopolitan belonging. Not only does this question allow us to understand and measure people's sense of cosmopolitan belonging. There is a range of ways in which this question can be pursued, depending on the mode of investigation. This question is not only philosophically embedded in the cosmopolitan principle itself but is also empirically assessable. In terms of qualitative research it can be interestingly articulated in conversational contexts (Calcutt et al. 2009; Savage et al. 2005; Pichler 2008; Skrbiš and Woodward 2007). It is also well captured by using survey techniques which allow us, just as in conversational contexts, to measure the gradations of belonging from family, local community, region, state, to global community (Phillips 2002; Woodward et al. 2008). The probing into people's sense of attachment and belonging must acknowledge that any expression of sentiments of attachment and belonging are inherently reflexive and changeable.

Mobility

The contemporary world is characterized by unprecedented mobility, both corporeal (travel of people) and virtual and its significance has been captured in contemporary social thought (Urry 2000). Indeed, it is global media outlets which allow people to derive potential benefits from virtual mobility (see Hebdige 1990; Szerszynski and Urry 2006). Although these benefits are generally considered to be predominantly positive given they bring people 'closer together', they are equally capable of alerting people to new dangers and vulnerabilities, linking these dangers with specific groups which give rise to fears and anxieties (Poole 2002; Skrbiš and Woodward 2007). This tension between benefits and dangers, allure and detesting of cultural difference as a result of experience of mobility is as fascinating as it is unpredictable (Skrbiš and Woodward 2007). The individual's attitudes towards (and experiences of) mobility can importantly influence one's cosmopolitan openness and the effect on how a person perceives and deal with cultural difference.

Cosmopolitan ethics and a reflexive style of cosmopolitan engagement

The question of cosmopolitan openness is inherently about human ethics, which is why we see it one of the four critical foci. Perhaps the critical defining feature of the cosmopolitan ethic is the acceptance and institution of self-problematizing relationships with cultural difference. The movement from a restricted to an elaborated set of codes of cultural engagement (Bernstein 1972; Emmison 2003) rests on a deepening relationship with the raw material of globality. This deepening relationship has been referred to as a 'reflexive' style of cosmopolitan engagement (Kendall et al. 2009). In this style of cosmopolitanism, the individual can become a type of cultural aficionado and expert, familiar with culturally strange styles, sometimes to establish status within particular social reference groups or networks, but also for the pleasure gained by cultivating aspects of the self as a way of being in the world. But – crucially – along with this possibly voracious desire for cultural novelty, this style of engagement reflects a deeper and more culturally skilled engagement with otherness. It shows some desire and willingness to be challenged and learn from different cultural experiences, and perhaps most importantly it shows some implicit value preference for the explicit de-hierarchization of culture on political or ethical grounds. In seeking out new, marginal and geographically dispersed forms of culture, it necessarily eschews the idea that local is best, that the limits of one's cultural consumption rest within the nation or region, and that 'culture' is something most frequently produced by educated middle-classes in the urban regions of advanced, Western nations. On a broader canvas, it acknowledges the potential of cultural immersion and exchange to enhance self. The reflexive cosmopolitan shows a genuine commitment to living and thinking beyond the local or nation and is more likely to act in cosmopolitan ways that are ethically directed. If consumption or leisure forms the basis of the cosmopolitan action for this type, it is combined with an ethical or political ethos which renders such consumption meaningful in terms of valuing cultural difference. For example, what might have been interpreted by someone else as a repulsive, disgusting or difficult travel experience could be recast in this reflexive frame as revelatory, stimulating, challenging and even life-changing. Ideally, the reflexive cosmopolitan feels little or no political commitment to local and national contexts and in fact is likely to show an irony, almost bordering on suspicion, towards their own national myths and discourses. This demonstrates a broad willingness to step outside stable, privileged and established power categories of selfhood.

Consumption and cultural flows

The most common form of openness – a response to the ubiquity of global flows of objects and people – is unproblematically experienced and indeed often positively embraced by citizens of many nationalities in particular circumstances and settings, especially where matters of choice, variety, freedom and positive experimentation are emphasized. Underpinned by powerful discourses of variety and abundance, self-cultivation and individual empowerment, this form of openness is the one most citizens of Westernized nations routinely experience in their daily lives and indeed frequently profess to positively enjoying. It springs from cosmopolitanization processes, in the sense that cosmopolitanism infuses commodities and becomes a type of commodity in its own right (Beck and Sznaider 2006: 41), but because at its heart it is individualized, it cannot be said to constitute a robust or mature form of cosmopolitanism. Elsewhere, and on the basis of our empirical inquiries, we have called this a 'sampling' type of cosmopolitan action because it involves positive engagement with stylistic, sensual and aesthetic differences in the name of entertainment, expanding personal tastes and the pursuit of elaborated repertoires for experiencing pleasure (Skrbiš and Woodward 2007; Kendall et al. 2009).

Importantly, we wish to emphasize that this sampling type of cosmopolitan action is not the only possible response to the ubiquity of global flows and is not necessarily implicitly unreflexive in practice, though we do suggest that it does not always constitute or lead to more complex forms of cosmopolitan orientation. Often, in such an orientation towards cultural openness, what is evident are reflex-like responses to the mere fact of the globalizing world which are rapid, apparently rational and self-interest maximizing in the context of greater individual choice or freedoms. But, crucially, these are quite fragile expressions, easily challenged or countered along lines of worry about national culture and economic security (Woodward et al. 2008). In this case, its positive consequences for the development of a critical, self-problematizing cosmopolitanism will be meagre, making people apparently 'indifferent' to difference in their daily lives (Ollivier 2008), accepting it as a mere fact of their existence. For others, such experiences may be a response to globality which offers the chance of cultivating and expanding personal repertoires of cultural action. This type of openness is textured by cosmopolitanization as a social fact, but constitutes only an immediate response to the surfaces of this fact. These forms of openness typically lack any apparent critical engagement or self-problematizing possibilities, they are almost purely self-enhancing and presumably result in little change or even substantial challenge to core aspects of selfhood. What is more, as we note, these forms of openness have a very brittle foundation which is vulnerable to threats to one's self-interest, or the perceived interests of a national collective. Yet, they do demonstrate a willingness to act outside the boundaries of the nation and to seek novel cultural experiences. In this sense, they are nascent forms of cosmopolitanism: a type of sampling that is perhaps a pathway to, or building block of, deeper cosmopolitan attitudes.

The Cultural and Political Consequences of Openness in Consumptive Contexts

Our attempts to introduce a lexicon for understanding of cosmopolitan openness notwithstanding, we acknowledge some important political and cultural consequences of efforts to ground cosmopolitan openness. We cannot uncritically accept that concepts like openness and its cosmopolitan partners such as 'inclusivity' and 'appreciating difference' are unproblematic. Such attitudes may be based on relationships of 'ownership and entitlement' (Skeggs 2004) whereby certain groups, by virtue of their capacity to define the meaning of cultural objects, places and peoples, are able to value and propertize cultural difference in an ultimately exclusive and exclusionary way, even in the name of cosmopolitan acceptance of difference. It may be that openness is in fact merely a cultural outlook that constitutes a form of cultural appropriation. Skeggs (2004: 158–9) points out that to command such cultural resources and draw them into oneself for the purposes of building or enhancing self is a form of 'embodied entitled subjectivity'. Skeggs' (2004) emphasis on the mediative and transformative powers of the cosmopolitan outlook as a type of *enablement* is valuable, for it captures the power relationship inherent in consumptive relationships in the name of cosmopolitanism. Like the sense of the cosmopolitan as an enhanced, 'ideal symbolic specialist' (Kendall et al. 2009), Skeggs understands that to be cosmopolitan is a way of seeing (Hannerz 1990), and then a way of appropriating cultural difference in ways which suits one's purposes, which does of course constitute a type of cultural power one group of people have at the expense of others. At once, such practices purport to suggest that otherness is valued, but at the same time they tend to value only certain forms of otherness, frequently for the purpose of enhancing self, and through categories established via legitimated means of cultural authority. In this sense, they are an appropriation based upon certain moral attributions: one knows what is to be valued, one knows what is culturally useful and one knows to what potential uses such resources could be put. This is not a wholehearted and holistic acceptance of cultural difference, but necessarily partial and contextual.

The entitled practice of consumers being able to 'pick and choose' products from around the world according to their own preferences and desires, comes with particular types of risks in regard to cosmopolitan openness. While this may evoke a sense of participatory 'cosmo-multiculturalism' (Hage 1998), complete with the indulgence of fantasies of authenticity, the open cosmopolitan culture fosters an individual's accumulation of transnational symbols, and his or her surface-oriented experience of another culture, such as food, and superficial ways of life. An important consideration here is that such consumption is also a form of symbolic accumulation that accrues consumer capital differentially. While the empirical links between consumption practices and forms of ethical cosmopolitanism are unmapped, the theoretical territory for its interpretation is powerfully clear. According to Hage (1998), working broadly within and extending the critical power of Bourdieu's framework, such practices always involve operating from a position of symbolic power and dominance. Hage sees this ability to 'pick and choose' as a form of appropriation by a dominant culture through means of symbolic manipulation. In this way, such forms of cross-cultural engagement are politically charged and result in contradictory tendencies. On the one hand they are about experiencing and consuming difference and potentially positive in helping to construct everyday forms of ethical cosmopolitanism, and on the other they are a form of appropriation whereby cultural difference is consumed, subsumed and ultimately dominated within robustly established cultural frameworks.

On all these matters, the particular application of Bourdieu's methodological-conceptual framework applied by both Skeggs and Hage is extremely valuable, although we suggest that their understanding of cosmopolitanness as principally a type of middle-class subjectivity that goes hand-in-hand with the resources offered by an identity-obsessed consumer culture may be restrictive in some cases, and underspecified in others. For example, what about working-class cosmopolitanisms, and the possibility for an ethic of valuing otherness which works independently of the market and propertized accumulative processes? Moreover, is it possible that consumption-based engagements with otherness actually have the capacity to initiate deeper cosmopolitan sentiments and act as pathways to a more critical form of cosmopolitanism? In our view, this last question remains one of the most puzzling, yet unaddressed and indeed critical questions in the field, given that most people who come into contact with cosmopolitan otherness will do so in the context of consumptive, commodified settings and experiences, such as tourist travel, markets and festivals, travel journalism, global media spectacles, music and food. A way of advancing this issue, we argue, is to conceptualize and look for openness as a performative and strategic practice, pointing to the fact that there are numerous ways of being open, rather than a single, universal type of openness. As each is a way of being open, with its own sets of assumptions and ways of seeing difference, it thus has different consequences for an individual, and for their relations with otherness. We also urge researchers to pay attention to both the pathways to openness and the threshold points which mark the pathways to becoming open. A person is not necessarily always open to cultural difference, but through various learning processes or aspects of biography and personal experience, one may become more open, or indeed more prejudiced. Social psychological research in the field of contact theory suggests some important considerations for this research agenda. Though it emerges from experimental and individual research procedures which sociologists are likely to find limiting, in rigorously attending to the antecedents and interrelations of familiarity, liking and prejudice it can assist in directing sociological investigation. For example, in a meta-analysis of contact studies, Pettigrew and Tropp (2006) suggest that while familiarity and contact with different groups may generally reduce prejudice and increase the likelihood of liking culturally different groups, such situations are not guaranteed. For example, enjoying one experience of intercultural contact, such as eating at an Indian restaurant, may be limited to such contexts and not extended beyond them. People may feel that they like the individuals involved within these limited interactions and contexts, for example, but this may not extend to the group as a whole. Likewise, people may be more positively disposed to some aspects of difference, such as food, but remain anxious about other aspects of culture such as specific cultural practices or values. All up, context, circumstance, a range of individual factors, scope and scale remain important determinants of the outcomes of intercultural contact, and suggest that there should be no assumed relationship between consumptive experiences and the development of cosmopolitan outlooks. Given the ubiquity and variety of mundane consumptive experiences that form the basis of everyday cosmopolitanism, we suggest specifying and interrogating the relationships between consumptive practices and cosmopolitan outlooks and values should be central to empirical investigations into the nature of contemporary cosmopolitanism.

Conclusion: Making Openness a Useful Concept in Cosmopolitan Studies

Openness as a cultural outlook and practice is context and object dependent. This feature is perhaps its best chance of survival in the conceptual battles that must continue to take place if explorations of cosmopolitanism are to yield valuable empirical research. The implication of this context dependency is that openness has a performative dimension, it must be brought into social frames by actors who mobilize particular ways of seeing, which elevate openness as a relevant and operational schema or discourse. Thus, openness it neither a universal concept, nor necessarily more or less ubiquitous. It is more of a strategy, resource or frame for managing meaning. Openness is not the same thing for every person, nor is it the same for each person across particular settings. It may rest on similar conceptual dimensions, such as curiosity for example, though its objects can be diverse, as can its users. This means that researchers must look not to absolute expressions of openness, but to its performance, effervescence and manifestation across a diversity of settings by a diversity of people. While there is good reason to think that types of openness based upon the educated contemplation of people, music or objects is associated more with particular privileged classes, then again qualities of openness can be displayed within working classes, migrant and marginal communities. The emerging literatures that continue to complicate in useful ways the rather restrictive idea of the omnivore demonstrate this feature aptly (Ollivier 2008; Warde et al. 2007).

While openness is thus a relatively fuzzy and sometimes even decidedly blunt social science concept, if we incorporate it into a performative frame of inquiry it begins to yield more utility. In terms of our own empirical research into cosmopolitanism (Skrbiš and Woodward 2007; Woodward et al. 2008; Calcutt et al. 2009) we found that people adopted what could be seen as an ambivalent and largely self-centred relationship to cosmopolitan experience that rested upon an individualist embracing of cosmopolitan openness in some realms and a fear or rejection of cosmopolitan ideals of openness within others. We see this ambivalence as a structural feature of the discourse of ordinary cosmopolitanism whereby individuals are making reflexive and deliberative judgements in relation to local and global domains. In this sense, cosmopolitanism is not an ideal type but a negotiated, performed frame of reference for dealing with openness to everyday cultural difference. People become not simply more or less open and cosmopolitan, but they reservedly deploy their cosmopolitan openness, thus allowing us to reconcile the frequently occurring gaps between people's philosophical commitment to cosmopolitan openness and often parochial practices. If anything, our research shows that most people are likely to be ambivalent cosmopolitans, seeing the resources of cosmopolitanism as a tool for negotiation of life chances in an increasingly interconnected and open world.

Bibliography

Beck, U. 2006. *The Cosmopolitan Vision*. Cambridge: Polity.
Beck, U. and Sznaider, N. 2006. Unpacking cosmopolitanism for the social sciences: a research agenda. *British Journal of Sociology*, 57(1), 1–23.
Bernstein, B. 1972. *Class, Codes and Control*. London: Paladin.
Bourdieu, P. 1984. *Distinction: A Social Critique of the Judgement of Taste*. London: Routledge.
Braudel, F. 1992. *Civilisation and Capitalism, 15th – 18th Century*. Berkeley: University of California Press.
Calcutt, L., Woodward, I. and Skrbiš, Z. 2009. Conceptualizing otherness: an exploration of the cosmopolitan schema. *Journal of Sociology*, 45(2), 169–85.
Campbell, C. 1987. *The Romantic Ethic and the Spirit of Modern Consumerism*. New York: Blackwell.
Chaney, D. 2002. Cosmopolitan art and cultural citizenship. *Theory, Culture and Society*, 19(1–2), 157–74.
Cohen, J. (ed.). 1996. *For Love of Country*. Boston: Beacon Press.
Derrida, J. 2000. *On Hospitality*. Stanford: Stanford University Press.
The Economist 2009. The others. 19 December, 85–7.
Emmison, M. 2003. Social class and cultural mobility: reconfiguring the cultural omnivore thesis. *Journal of Sociology*, 39(3), 211–30.
Hage, G. 1998. *White Nation. Fantasies of White Supremacy in a Multicultural Society*. Annandale: Pluto Press.
Hall, S. 2002. Political belonging in a world of multiple identities, in *Conceiving Cosmopolitanism: Theory, Context, Practice*, edited by S. Vertovec and R. Cohen. Oxford: Oxford University Press, 25–31.
Hannerz, U. 1990. Cosmopolitans and locals in world culture. *Theory, Culture & Society*, 7, 237–51.
Harvey, D. 1989. *The Condition of Postmodernity*. Oxford: Blackwell.
Hebdige, D. 1990. Fax to the future. *Marxism Today*, January, 1118–23.

Hollinger, D.A. 1995. *Postethnic America: Beyond Multiculturalism*. New York: Basic Books.

Kant, I. 1983. To perpetual peace: a philosophical sketch, in *Perpetual Peace and Other Essays on Politics, Heritage and Morals*, translated by Ted Humphrey. Indianapolis: Hackett Pub. Co., 107–39.

Kendall, G., Woodward, I. and Skrbiš, Z. 2009. *The Sociology of Cosmopolitanism*. London: Palgrave Macmillan.

Lamont, M. and Aksartova, S. 2002. Ordinary cosmopolitanisms: strategies for bridging racial boundaries among working class men. *Theory, Culture and Society*, 19(4), 1–25.

Lash, S. and Urry, J. 1987. *The End of Organised Capitalism*. UK: Polity Press.

Latour, B. 1993. *We Have Never Been Modern*. Hemel Hempstead: Harvester Wheatsheaf.

Nava, M. 1998. The cosmopolitanism of commerce and the allure of difference: Selfridges, the Russian ballet and the tango 1911–1914. *International Journal of Cultural Studies*, 1(2), 163–96.

Nava, M. 2002. Cosmopolitan modernity: everyday imaginaries and the register of difference. *Theory, Culture and Society*, 19(1–2), 81–99.

Nava, M. 2007. *Visceral Cosmopolitanism: Gender, Culture and the Normalisation of Difference*. Oxford: Berg.

Nussbaum, M.C. 1996. Patriotism and cosmopolitanism, in *For Love of Country*, edited by J. Cohen. Boston: Beacon Press.

Ollivier, M. 2008. Models of openness to cultural diversity: humanist, populist, practical and indifferent omnivores. *Poetics*, 36(2–3), 120–47.

Peterson, R.A. 1990. Audience and industry origins of the crisis in classical music programming: towards world music, in *The Future of the Arts*, edited by D.B. Pankratz and V.B. Morris. New York: Praeger.

Peterson, R.A. 1997. The rise and fall of highbrow snobbery as a status marker. *Poetics*, 25, 75–92.

Peterson, R.A. and Kern, R.M. 1996. Changing highbrow taste: from snob to omnivore. *American Sociological Review*, 61, 900–7.

Pettigrew, T.F. and Tropp, L.R. 2006. A meta–analytic test of intergroup contact theory. *Journal of Personality and Social Psychology*, 90(5), 751–83.

Phillips, T. 2002. Imagined communities and self-identity: an exploratory quantitative analysis. *Sociology*, 36(3), 597–617.

Pichler, F. 2008. How real is cosmopolitanism in Europe? *Sociology*, 42, 1107–26.

Poole, E. 2002. *Reporting Islam: Media Representations and British Muslims*. London: I.B. Tauris.

Savage, M., Bagnall, G. and Longhurst, B. 2005. *Globalization and Belonging*. London: Sage.

Skeggs, B. 2004. *Class, Self, Culture*. London: Routledge.

Skrbiš, Z. and Woodward, I. 2007. The ambivalence of ordinary cosmopolitanism: investigating the limits of cosmopolitan openness. *Sociological Review*, 55(4), 730–47.

Skrbiš, Z., Kendall, G. and Woodward, I. 2004. Locating cosmopolitanism: between humanist ideal and grounded social category. *Theory, Culture and Society*, 21(6), 115–36.

Szerszynski, B. and Urry, J. 2006. Visuality, mobility and the cosmopolitan: inhabiting the world from afar. *The British Journal of Sociology*, 57(1), 113–31.

Tomlinson, J. 1999. *Globalization and Culture*. Cambridge: Polity.

Urry, J. 2000. *Sociology Beyond Societies: Mobilities for the Twenty–First Century*. London: Routledge.

Van Eijck, K. 2000. Richard A. Peterson and the culture of consumption. *Poetics*, 28 (2/3), 207–24.

Warde, A., Wright, D. and Gayo-Cal, M. 2007. Understanding cultural omnivorousness: or, the myth of the cultural omnivore. *Cultural Sociology*, 1(2), 143–64.

Woodward, I., Skrbiš, Z. and Bean, C. 2008. Attitudes toward globalization and cosmopolitanism: cultural diversity, personal consumption and the national economy. *The British Journal of Sociology*, 59(1), 207–26.

4

Mega-Events and Cosmopolitanism: Observations on Expos and European Culture in Modernity

Maurice Roche

This chapter explores the changing relationships between 'mega-events' – (or international public cultural event genres like World's Fairs (hereafter 'expos') and Olympic Games (see Roche 2000) – and forms of cosmopolitanism. It takes a long-term socio-historical perspective on the development of both mega-events and modern society, considering mega-events both as modernizing factors and also as illuminating some of the possibilities and limitations of modern societies as cosmopolitan social orders. Mega-events can be subjected a variety of interpretations. These range from the overly optimistic, which acquiesce in their claimed contributions to modern civilization, to the overly pessimistic, which critically reduce them to only their capitalistic and hegemonic aspects. The view taken in this chapter aims to avoid these polarities, and to be more nuanced and realistic. Taken overall the socio-historical analysis and account of expos the chapter suggests that mega-events and the socio-cultural processes associated with them can be provisionally assessed to have contributed positively to the development of European-level culture and civil society in the modern period (also see Roche 2000: ch. 8 and 2011).

The chapter is divided into two main sections. In the first section the concept of cosmopolitanism is discussed and two aspects of its meaning, namely analytic and normative are indicated. A 'negative' or 'minimal' conception of its normative meaning is briefly outlined. These concepts are used in assessing mega-events in the rest of the chapter. In this section also the main mega-event genres are introduced. In the second section some key forms of 'actually existing' cosmopolitanism are outlined, and these are discussed as aspects of the social character and impacts of mega-events, particularly expos. The chapter considers the cosmopolitan character of mega-events primarily with reference to European culture over the course of the modernization process. In this context it also makes passing reference to the related but contrastive experience of the United States. It draws on my work in the sociological analysis of mega-events, of European society and of European cosmopolitanism (respectively in Roche 2000, 2010, 2007).[1]

Cosmopolitanism, Europe and Expos: Perspectives and Principles

Cosmopolitanism as a perspective, or better a problematic, in social theory and sociology, both in general and in its application to understanding European society and culture, has two aspects which need to be clearly distinguished. On the one hand there is an analytical aspect, oriented to the understanding of social realities and what 'is'. On the other hand there is a normative aspect, oriented to envisaging a better social world which 'ought' to be made real (Roche 2007). An *analytic* socio-historical issue for the chapter is to consider how Europe's mega-events and their related socio-cultural processes could be said to have contributed to the maintenance and renewal of cosmopolitan traditions. Besides this analytic issue there is also the *normative* aspect of cosmopolitanism. Since at least the eighteenth-century European Enlightenment this strand in modernity's self-reflection has, among other things, involved the envisaging of ideal moral and political worlds in universalistic (and transnational) terms through such concepts as 'world citizenship' and of the nature and equality of human beings in terms of their potential for rationality and autonomy.

Granting the intellectual significance of the analytic–normative conceptual distinction, then, this chapter attempts to keep linkages and potential feedback relationship between analytic and normative perspectives in view. So, in terms of the analytic aspect it will be suggested that expos in Europe, as elsewhere, provide a cultural space and platform for the simultaneous display of conflicting and contrapuntal themes, both non- or anti-cosmopolitan themes connected with nationalism and also forms of 'actually existing' cosmopolitanism. The latter can be recognized in, among other things, the expos' promotion of universalistic ideologies such as those involved in science (understood as a transnational phenomenon) and the innovations it involves in knowledge and technology, their display of culturally diverse product designs, architectures and so on, and in their mixing of national hosts and international visitors. In addition in terms of the normative aspect, it will be suggested that a minimal or negative conception of cosmopolitanism is the

---

[1] Other work on the sociology of mega-events relevant to the theme of cosmopolitanism includes that on their national and global citizenship aspects (Roche 2001a, 2002), their nationalistic and globalization aspects (2001b, 2006a, 2006b), and their lifeworld and lived time aspects (2003). For an additional discussion of cosmopolitanism in relation to expos see Roche 2011.

most appropriate version of the concept of cosmopolitanism to apply to mega-events like expos, and to understanding and critically assessing their conflicting themes and characteristics, and also arguably more broadly in the interpretation of European culture.

From an analytic perspective and in general terms European history evidently provides an enigmatic context in terms of which to reflect on cosmopolitanism. Over the course of early and later phases of modernity the European social formation became organized into discrete nation-states. European peoples became organized into distinct and competitive forms of 'nations' and 'nationalities', and in some significant cases into the hyper-national forms of modern 'empires' (Roche 2010: chs 3–5). Europe's histories of nationalism and xenophobia, of war and imperialism, represent un- and anti-cosmopolitan tendencies within the modernization process (Roche 2010: chs 3–5, also Mazower 1998).

However these tendencies have developed in parallel with more complex and communicative histories of trade, cultural exchange and international cooperation, of which the international and supra-national organization of the European Union is the pre-eminent example in the contemporary period. European nations, in spite of their frequent ideological and mythological claims to being ethnic nations and mono-cultures, actually emerged historically from processes of cultural mixing and as de facto multi-cultures. In addition Europeans' recurrent interests (for whatever reason, whether positive or negative) in intra-continental travel and migration have added to the cultural mixtures which make up European nations. Finally Europe's deep historical exchanges with and/or openness to influence by ideas and values, people and goods from the Middle East, Central Asia and the Far East continues into the contemporary period to add to the processes of cultural mixing which have always characterized European society and culture. In each of these respects Europe has always also retained contrapuntal forms of collective memory, cultural tradition and self-understanding, which we can refer to, in analytical terms, as being 'cosmopolitan' traditions and indeed 'heritages'. To set the scene for the discussion of mega-events and their relation to such contrapuntal forms of cosmopolitanism in this chapter we can now outline cosmopolitanism's normative and analytic aspects a little further.

Normative cosmopolitanism

The normative idea that Europe *ought* to be a cosmopolitan society, and indeed that Europeans ought to see themselves as cosmopolitans, characterizes much of the contemporary sociology and social theory of Europe and the EU.[2] Normative cosmopolitanism, among other things, refers to perspectives which give a priority to moral and political universals over what by comparison appear as the moral and political particularities associated with perspectives such as communitarianism

---

2   On cosmopolitan themes in the sociology of Europe see for instance Beck and Grande 2007, and Delanty and Rumford 2005; also Roche 2010: ch. 9.

and nationalism. During the Enlightenment it was formulated in terms of such concepts as 'world citizenship' and humanistic rationalism, and expressed in terms of interests in humanitarian internationalism both in ideology and political practice.[3] In our period, in addition, it can be formulated in terms of the concept of human rights and expressed in terms of interests in the theory and practice of global governance (see Held 1995, 2004).[4]

'Negative utilitarianism' advocates the universal moral imperative to promote the minimization of the greatest pain of the greatest number rather than the more familiar 'positive' (and arguably utopic) imperative to maximize the greatest happiness of the greatest number.[5] In my view, comparable with this we can conceive of a 'negative or minimalistic cosmopolitanism'.[6] This is particularly relevant to understanding European society given Europe's deep traditions and potential for 'incivility' (Roche 2010: chs 3–5, and 9). From this minimalistic cosmopolitan perspective priority, both in theoretical and practical terms, needs to be assigned to the attempt to understand, address and ameliorate the causes and conditions of the denials of otherness, difference and peaceful coexistence involved in many kinds and levels of physically violent and abusive behaviour between people. This includes violence of the inter-state kind (war), of the inter- and intra-community kind (particularly that associated with xenophobia and 'racism') and of the domestic kind (particularly that inflicted by males on women and children). The EU has aspired to play a role at each of these levels, and thus could be interpreted as developing and being guided by a particular version of negative or minimalistic normative cosmopolitanism.[7]

---

3   On the idea of 'world citizenship' see Immanuel Kant's classic discussion (Kant 1963 (originals 1784–95)), also principles in the social theory of Marx and nineteenth-century socialism (for references see Roche 2007).
4   See Held 1995 and 2004; also Delanty and Rumford 2005, and Rumford 2007 (Introduction).
5   A negative utilitarian approach to ethics and politics has attracted support from various quarters, notably including that from the critical rationalist perspective of the philosopher of science Karl Popper, see for instance Popper 1962: vol. 1, ch. 5.
6   For directly relevant discussions see for instance Fine 2006 and 2007, also Kaldor 2002; for a more generally relevant social theoretical discussion of cosmopolitanism see Delanty 2010.
7   On the EU's role in international peace-keeping and more broadly in the promotion of peaceful coexistence and cooperation between nations and world regions see for instance McCormick 2007 and Telo 2007. On the EU's role in monitoring and attempting to counter xenophobia and 'racism' see for instance the European Agency 2007. (On these latter problems see Modood and Werbner 1997 and Wrench and Solomos 1993. On the EU's role in recognizing and countering domestic violence see for instance Euronet 2005 and EC 2005.)

Analytic cosmopolitanism

From the socio-historical approach taken in this chapter cosmopolitanism is best seen as an analytic perspective with normative implications rather than as an exclusively normative perspective. Consistent with this it is worth observing that writers on cosmopolitanism refer as often to analytic conceptions, such as 'banal' and 'actually existing' forms of cosmopolitan, as they do to normative conceptions (see Beck and Grande 2007, Calhoun 2002). By the former they refer to empirical and existential realities of cultural diversity and hybridity and to processes of the change and adaptation of local factors to global forces. In addition, as will be considered further later, there is the presence in Europe's history and identity of various less than ideal but once definitely 'actually existing' forms of cosmopolitanism, in the morally highly problematic histories and heritages of European empires.[8] Arguably to attempt to understand Europe sociologically is, among other things, to be willing to get to know and to engage with the 'actually existing' cosmopolitan realities of such culturally mixed and hybrid cross-continental social phenomena as empires and their heritages, trading cities and their networks, religious pluralism, high cultures (for instance institutionalized science) and popular cultures (for instance consumer culture).

Analytic cosmopolitanism guides sociological and social theoretical analysis in very different directions than the well-trodden paths mapped out in European academia under the pervasive influence of official and popular ideologies of nationalistic modernization and its associated mythologization of unmixed ('pure') ethnicities and mono-cultures.[9] Rather it guides sociology towards the study of Europe's pervasive social realities of mixture and hybridity, sometime known about and intended, most often barely known about and/or unintended. These social realities and their ethical implications no doubt vary according to time and place, but they are extensive and comparable enough for us to be able to refer to them as constituting a 'condition' in European society.[10] Europe's analysable 'cosmopolitan condition(s)' can be seen as a set of situations of mixed but shared fate which underpin and motivate normative and ideological reflection and expression, conflict and debate (Roche 2007) and in particular motivate an interest in the minimal or negative version of cosmopolitanism sketched above.

Cosmopolitanism and mega-events

'Mega-events' refer to international public and popular cultural events, particularly the two main genres of international exhibitions or World's Fairs

---

8 On this see Roche 2007, also Stevenson 2007 and Van der Veer 2002.
9 For instance see Beck and Grande 2007 on 'methodological nationalism', also Delanty 2010: ch. 2.
10 For comparable types of use of the notion of 'condition' in social analysis see Harvey 1989 and van Steenbergen 1994.

(or expos) and international sport events of which the first and still the biggest is the Olympic Games (Roche 2000). They were always hosted by a nation-state and thus prominently displayed the particularistic nationalistic symbols and values of their hosts. However simultaneously and contrapuntally, through the multi-national character of their organization, they also carried and disseminated more internationally and universalistically-oriented values. Thus they presented themselves as having cosmopolitan aspects both analytically and normatively.

Each of the main genres of mega-event developed traditions of normative discourse connected with universalistic notions, such Enlightenment-derived ideas and ideals as 'human progress' and 'international peace', 'civilization' and 'education', 'human communication' and 'human cooperation'.[11] These were codified into formal aspirations, ideologies and institutional charters by key event-organizing agencies such as the IOC (International Olympic Committee) and BIE (Bureau of International Expositions), together with their associated socio-cultural 'movements'. These discourses and ideologies typically evolved to contain strong cosmopolitan themes. These include reference to such universalistic (and transnational) concepts as human rights (see Lechner and Boli 2005: chs 1, 4 and *passim*, Roche 2002) and also the equal and rational character of human individuals particularly as expressed in the value of 'education' for human development. As regards the latter, the expo movement and event genre can be claimed to have addressed (and to continue to address) the cosmopolitan value of education directly in the cognitive terms of promoting access to and openness to the scientific worldview together with the technological innovation this worldview makes possible. Comparably the Olympic movement and event genre (in its ideology of 'Olympism') have addressed this value in the more indirect somatic terms of the promotion of the various (health, moral and educational) benefits for people which can be claimed for sport competition and training. Besides its reference to human individuals the value of education has also been connected with collective, but again transnational and effectively cosmopolitan, notions of human development in the form of 'human progress' and 'civilization'. Particular and local versions of these values have also often been claimed as aspirations and potential benefits of particular expos and mega-events.

Mega-events' versions of normative cosmopolitanism, as in these claimed educational and progressive aspects, can be conceived as being positive, maximalist and even utopic. By contrast the discussion in this chapter suggests that it would be more useful to interpret mega-events' normative cosmopolitanism in more minimalist or negativist terms. That is to say, typically masses of culturally diverse people gather at mega-events to share in elements of common experience. Host organizers and their publics typically attempt to set aside whatever xenophobic strands have been woven into their national traditions. They set out to 'welcome the world', to extend hospitality to international visitors and express varying degrees of openness to and interest in participating nations, their displays and their visiting

---

11 Enlightenment origins of some of these conceptions can be traced in Kant's enduringly influential thinking (Kant 1963).

publics. Most visitors perform versions of the minimalistic cosmopolitan values of 'peaceful coexistence' and basic coordination among strangers. This takes the form of basic socio-temporal rituals of synchronization and socio-spatial rituals of interactional choreography which are characteristic of situations of mass co-presence at major events. In addition the common or sharable collective emotions created in these situations, together with the sharable memories they generate (Roche 2003), represent elements of the preconditions for transnational communication among people who are strangers and in other ways culturally diverse. This additional proto-communicative potential raises the possible normative cosmopolitanism of mega-events somewhat beyond the minimalistic conception which is otherwise my focus here.

We are now in a position to consider in more detail the at times contested and convoluted socio-genesis of some of these normative cosmopolitan aspects of expos in the socio-history of some of the 'actually existing' forms of cosmopolitanism commonly associated with them in the modern period. These latter forms include the conflicted form associated with European empires, but they particularly include what can be referred to as 'modernist' and 'touristic' forms of cosmopolitanism.

Mega-Events and Cosmopolitanism: Cultural Forms and Historical Developments

Mega-event cultural event genres were 'invented' in the mid-nineteenth century (expos) and late nineteenth century (Olympic Games). Although these genres were ideologically flexible and institutionally relatively frail they were enduring and were only briefly abandoned during the periods of world war in the twentieth century. Otherwise they have retained their presence in international and global culture over the course of the major period of modernization and through to the contemporary period. The modern mega-event genres were launched in the mid and late nineteenth century and established themselves as key new elements in the international cultural calendar relatively rapidly through processes of cross-national competition and emulation. The first international expo was staged by the British in London in 1851 and prompted the Americans and French to follow suit in staging expos in 1853 and 1855 respectively. Expos were staged on a relatively frequent but irregular calendar from that time on. A generation or so later the French-inspired Olympic Movement staged the first of the modern Olympic Games in Athens in 1896. The Movement established a regular four-year calendar for the occurrence of the Games, and apart from the uncertainties of the early Olympics which were staged as parts of expos (1900 Paris, 1904 St Louis and 1908 London) and the intervention of the world wars, this has operated through to the contemporary period.

Mega-events were (and remain) self-consciously 'modern' international events of a scale which (at least in the west) was historically unprecedented in terms of visitor attendance. Expos typically run for six or so months and have reliably proven capable of attracting crowds which accumulate into the tens of millions over this period. While most visitors would be citizens of the host nation their international and 'actually existing' cosmopolitan character would be evidenced in the fact that a certain proportion of participants would also be from other countries, both people associated with the visiting national exhibitions and also international tourists. Events of these kinds have occurred according to a more or less formalized calendar since the late nineteenth century in most of the leading modernizing societies, particularly Britain, France and the United States, but also including many other nations.[12]

Expos typically contained a conflicting mix of political and cultural vectors and these were connected with the slow development of international and ultimately global levels of culture and cosmopolitanism in complex and variable ways. Vectors which provided some, albeit transitory, socio-cultural basis for normative cosmopolitan values include those connected with the promotion of the culture of 'modernity' and, arguably, the linkage between touristic and consumer aspects of modern popular culture. We come to these more supportive 'actually existing' forms of cosmopolitanism associated with expos in a moment. First it is worth noting a vector which particularly characterized European expos and which had a more ambiguous and conflictual relationship with normative cosmopolitanism, namely that involving the production of 'imperial expos'.

The European nations which staged expos for a century from the mid-nineteenth century to the mid-twentieth century, particularly Britain and France, organized and thought of themselves not only as capitalist economies but also as colonial and imperial powers. The producers of expos reflected and refracted this in the various imperially-angled versions of internationalism and cosmopolitanism they promoted. These versions could range from a relatively benign but still explicitly hierarchic, patronizing and oppressive representations of submerged nations and colonized ethnicities (as in the case of Canada and Australia in British Empire expos) to explicitly and ideologically racist conceptions of 'others' (for instance African tribes) subjected to European 'civilizing missions'. The imperial theme had been part of national expos in France in the 1840s and was an important part of the first international expo in London in 1851. Britain was the world's leading industrial and imperial power in this period and used the 1851 expo to display its industrial achievements and its imperial possessions. Britain and France later developed explicitly imperial aims and rationales for many of their expos. The United States' expos in this period also presented its own, albeit more ideologically disguised, version of imperialism (Rydell 1984, 1993).[13]

---

12 On the socio-history of expos in particular see Greenhalgh 1988, Roche 1998, 2000, Rydell 1984, 1993, Rydell and Gwinn 1994, Rydell and Kroes 2005, and Schroeder-Gudehus and Rasmussen 1992.
13 The profoundly anti-cosmopolitan ideological and practical vector of racism was, until the Second World War, often associated particularly with the imperial dimension of expos, and also to varying degrees with the other two dimensions discussed here. This

In addition to and in contradiction with the imperial vector other political and cultural vectors were manifest in mega-events in the late nineteenth century and pre-First World War periods. These forms of 'actually existing' cosmopolitanism were more supportive of versions of normative cosmopolitanism. These vectors have in various ways reasserted themselves in the post-Second World War period through to the present. To oversimplify the situation for the purposes of exposition we can focus the discussion on two historically important forms of analytic or 'actually existing' cosmopolitanism connected with expos. Firstly there is a form that we can refer to as 'modernist' cosmopolitanism. This refers, among other things, to the way in which expos exposed mass publics to the recurrently transformative power and flow of modern technologies from around the world to create what could be experienced as the possibility of 'progress' in all spheres of life, from work to leisure, from the domestic to the public, from the informational and communicational to the sensory and the hedonistic. Secondly there is a form of cosmopolitanism that we can refer to as 'touristic cosmopolitanism' and which is associated with the consumer culture promoted by expos. Each of these types of cosmopolitanism remains significant in contemporary culture, and we can now consider each of them in a little more detail.

Modernist cosmopolitanism

The national and international networks of elites and professionals who designed and produced expos in the late nineteenth century, as much as the masses and publics who attended, felt themselves to be participants in a new visibly dynamic and transformative civilization. Expos appeared to mark and chart a new civilization committed to 'progress'. This civilization was perceived as being a distinctively 'modern' as well as being a 'world' civilization, and expos provided recurrent public 'theatres' in which to stage and experience developments in it. This is the sense in which we can say that expos, through the international structures of their organization, the universalistic values they proclaimed and the technological contents sourced from around the world that they presented, provided (and still provide) contexts for the promotion and development of 'modernist' forms of cosmopolitanism. Expos originally offered a new mass form of 'rational recreation', and the genre has continued to offer this through to the present. The attraction of expos for the mass publics which typically attended them was always what we can call the 'info-tainment' character of the core and distinctive form of experience they offered.

In terms of the 'information' aspect of this experience – visitors would get to see and celebrate impressive exhibitions of the promise of 'modernity', namely power and 'progress', and to some extent or another would experience the drama of being

---

racist and xenophobic vector within the culture of expos counter-balanced and indeed conflicted with their otherwise more normatively positive cosmopolitan tendencies, and it is explored at greater length in Roche 2000: ch. 3.

made to feel as if they were 'witnesses to history'. On the one hand they would experience new developments in the progress of human technological 'mastery of nature' and the taming of natural forces. On the other hand they would experience new technological applications which were perceived as being likely, sooner or later, to change and presumably 'improve' the material life conditions of the mass of the people, people 'like them', middle and working class people, 'citizens' even, visiting the expo. Key examples here in the nineteenth century are those of electric light and electrification in general, and engineering-based architecture (for instance the Crystal Palace and the Eiffel Tower at the London 1851 and Paris 1889 expos respectively) and in the twentieth century the peaceful uses of nuclear power (Brussels 1958). In the field of communication technologies examples are successive new developments from the telephone, to film, to radio, to television.

In terms of the entertainment aspect of expo visits – this kind of informative and educational experience would be presented to and received by visitors as if it were intrinsically 'fun', a dramatic, festive and celebratory experience in its own terms, and one comparable to the other more explicitly entertaining and consumerist elements of expos, such as the great fairs and architectural spectacles they also contained.

Touristic cosmopolitanism

There is a final version of analytic 'actually existing' cosmopolitanism which we now need to consider. That is, mega-events, particularly expos, can be interpreted as promoting 'touristic cosmopolitanism'. This is the version of inter-cultural co-presence and exchange connected with the development of modern societies' and individuals' commitments to 'consumer culture', and particularly to the influential mobile version of this culture, namely that of tourism. It need hardly be noted in passing that this mobile version of consumerism continues to be highly relevant to understanding the nature and dynamics of societies and their culture in the contemporary period. Indeed arguably this cultural institution and cultural industry, together with its associated forms of cosmopolitan attitudes, is becoming increasingly powerful and influential in the early twenty-first century as both a carrier and driver of the processes of globalization which characterize our times (see Roche 2010: ch. 8). The connection of expos with 'touristic consumerism' can be analysed in three main aspects.

The first and most obvious aspect is that most visitors attending the expos had to become tourists in order to get to them. The relative minority of international visitors had to engage in the newly developing mass transport systems and technologies of steamship travel or long-distance railway travel, and a large proportion of domestic visitors had to become 'excursionists' and use the new railway systems. The birth of the cultural industry of tourism, which became so dominant nationally and globally, both as an industry and as a form of cultural experience in the late twentieth century, and which in many ways is virtually consonant with the concept of 'post-modern' times[14] occurred in parallel with, and in close connection with, the development of international expos. The expos themselves provided powerful 'new age', if temporary, tourist attractions in the mid and late nineteenth century. Pre-eminently in the case of Paris, but also in other cities, they left an accumulation of 'event heritage' architecture which contributed to the permanent tourist attraction of major cities (Roche 2000: ch. 5). Also they were occasionally used to promote tourism and even to attract and recruit migrants to major continental regions or imperial colonies, as in the 1915 and 1939 San Francisco expos in relation to California and the US West coast and the 1924/5 London (Wembley) expo in relation to India, Canada and Australia.

To briefly indicate the importance of expos for the development of the tourist industry both nationally and internationally in the mid/late nineteenth century it is sufficient to point to the growth in Britain of the prototypical tourist company, Thomas Cook. It is true that the tourist industry, as led and illustrated by the growth of Thomas Cook's operation selling 'railway excursions' in the 1840s, grew on the back of the growth of steam-powered transport systems in the mid-nineteenth century, in particular the massively important growth of railways. Nevertheless people needed motives as well as locomotives to travel, and the great expos helped to provide these motives and popularize these demands, beginning with Cook's tourism operation (Buzard 1993).

A second aspect of the expo-touristic consumerism link is that usually what was most impressive to the new mass public visiting late nineteenth century expos about the products on display, apart from their unprecedented quantity and quality, was the fact that most of them had been brought to the expo from all over the world. The actual or fantasy consumption of these unfamiliar 'foreign' and 'exotic' goods and/or of the images associated with them provided an early version of the kind of vicarious experience of touristic sensations through consumption that we are now very familiar with in contemporary culture, and which contribute to a mundane aspect of 'the cosmopolitan imagination' embedded in the everyday consumption of goods and images in contemporary capitalist society.[15]

Finally, in a number of different ways the mass public of the expo host nation typically encountered an unprecedented range of foreigners and people from very different cultures. In his account of this aspect of expos Greenhalgh suggests that there were a variety of ways in which 'others' were encountered at these events. These included as diplomats, as servants in exotic leisure and entertainment zones,

---

14 On the sociology of tourism in modernity see the classic analyses by MacCannell 1989 and Urry 1990, also Apostolopoulos et al. 1996, Rojek and Urry 1997 and Wang 1999.

15 On late nineteenth century expos as precursors of contemporary consumerism see, for instance, Featherstone 1991, Richards 1990, Pred 1991, de Cauter 1993, and Gunning 1994; also Williams 1982 on the influence of the French expos on the development of consumer culture. For a searching discussion of 'the cosmopolitan imagination' see Delanty 2010.

and as 'educational'/'scientific' objects in racist 'human displays' of 'primitive cultures' (Greenhalgh 1988: 82). We can suggest that this amounted to a kind of vicarious and virtual tourism, tourism-without-the-travel, in which the Others and their tourist sights and ways of life 'come to you' rather than 'you going to them'. Mass publics became very familiar with more benign versions of this process in the early twentieth century through the impact of film on popular culture (Gunning 1994) and again in the late twentieth century through the pervasive influence of the mass communication medium of television in particular.

Connected with the propagation of popular attitudes and experiences of 'touristic consumerism' oriented to the national and international spheres is the notion that this also had implications for how people living in big modern urban environments began to view their own cities. The latter were key socio-material locations of and foci for the process of 'modernization' and for various types of attempt to make the 'progress' modernity offered into a lived reality. The quasi-touristic encounter, at least with the sophisticated versions of 'foreigners' discussed above, contributed to a popular taste for participation in a cosmopolitan dimension of the public culture of the times.

Expos and their associated influx of foreign tourists and travellers, lent a periodic focus to the emerging 'actually existing' cosmopolitanism of modern cities. The cosmopolitanism of the international expo event site was an exaggerated microcosm of the kind of cosmopolitanism characteristic of nineteenth-century and twentieth-century urbanism, particularly the cultural mixtures present in most capital cities, but also in other large cities, especially those acting as trading and migrant centres. The expos themselves were designed by leading architects and urban planners and experienced by visitors, as 'cities-in-miniature' and as 'ideal cities'. Hence the name for Chicago's 1893 site 'the White City'[16] which was also later used as the name for one of London's main sites for the series of virtually annual imperial expos held there in the 1908–14 period.

The de facto urban cosmopolitanism of expos as transient 'ideal cities-in-miniature' propagated the normatively cosmopolitan-friendly public attitudes and practices. Outside of expos nineteenth-century city-dwellers interacted with an emerging set of popular cultural urban forms, institutions and 'industries' – namely 'public' museums and art galleries and also department stores, large scale fairs and theme parks, and each of these forms was stimulated by expo events.[17] Obviously museums, art galleries and fairs predate nineteenth-century expos and have a long institutional history in Western Europe in particular (Bennett 1995). However even

---

16   On the 1893 Chicago expo in this context see Findling 1994 and Rydell 1984. For a relevant discussion of the 1904 St Louis expo in terms of touristic consumer culture see Gunning 1994.

17   On various linkages between expos and the institutions of the modern urban museum see Rydell 1993, Macdonald and Fyfe 1996, and Bennett 1995. On equivalent linkages between expos and the institution of the modern department store see Williams 1982. On the linkage between expos and the touristic consumer culture institutionalized in the modern theme park see Roche 2000: ch. 5, also Kasson 1978.

these were qualitatively transformed by the international expo movement and the stimulus they gave to cultural modernization. This resulted, in the case of museums and art galleries, in a new level of popular recognition of and access to institutions and their particular mixtures of national, international and transnational cultural contents, which were previously class-exclusive and elite-oriented. In the other cases, notably department stores and theme parks, these quintessential consumerist and touristic forms and institutions were either effectively created as concepts by the international expo movement, or their development was rapidly accelerated and widely diffused by them. Versions of these kinds of institutions and industries were pioneered in expos and provided substantial settings and experiences within the experience of these events. National and international publics visiting expos interacted with these settings, understanding themselves in terms of the de facto cosmopolitan cultural frameworks expos promoted involving info-tainment, touristic consumerism and 'modern'/'modernizing' urbanism.

Conclusion: Cosmopolitanism, Mega-Events and Europe

This chapter has addressed the main mega-event genres, particularly expos, as key cases of the development of cosmopolitan culture in western modernity in general and European modernity in particular through a brief socio-historical review of the expo genre. There were two main stages in the discussion, firstly a social theoretical inquiry into analytic and normative understandings of cosmopolitanism in relation to Europe. From an analytical perspective we have noted that mega-events embodied not only nationalistic and anti-cosmopolitan histories, attitudes and practices but also proto-cosmopolitan ones. So the second and main section of the chapter presented a socio-historical analysis of the main forms of analytic 'actually existing' cosmopolitanism associated with expos, namely the ambiguous and contradictory imperial form and, more importantly the modernist and touristic forms.

In addition, from a normative perspective we asked in the introduction what the significance of mega-events might be particularly for minimalistic interpretations of cosmopolitanism in a European context. Mega-events and their associated socio-cultural processes may or may not have achieved the maximalist cosmopolitan goals to which their organizers have often claimed to aspire, whether in Europe or other parts of the world. But the suggestion from the review undertaken in this chapter is that, given Europe's histories of war, oppression and genocide, it would be normatively better and more relevant to investigate and interpret the social roles and influences of such events and processes in minimal or negative cosmopolitan terms. These terms focus on the principle of peaceful coexistence. This requires moral agents to tolerate the actual or potential embodied co-presence of non-threatening others and their participation in a sharable world. In addition it is also connected with principles which value hospitality in terms of enabling the access of others to conditions of peaceful co-presence. Viewed in historical perspective, if they achieved nothing more, most European expos in the modern and contemporary periods can be reasonably viewed as having embodied these sorts of principles to a greater or lesser extent.

The European social formation can be conceived of as involving the development of a European-level 'civil society' and 'civil space' (Roche 2010: ch. 9). In both in their analytic and normative interpretation such notions offer ways of understanding the potential normative roles of mega-events and their festive culture in the sociohistorical contexts and the contemporary contexts of European society. Such events, and the network of national and sub-national festive events which they overarch, can be interpreted as having helped to produce and reproduce European civil space in at least the minimally cosmopolitan sense of providing valuable instances and models of peaceful coexistence and co-presence.[18] While such events may not necessarily have been highly interactional and communicative, nonetheless they can be interpreted as typically having had normatively positive and celebratory characteristics for the varied publics who visited and participated in them. Such event histories, memories and models provide encouragement for cultural politics and cultural policy-making in contemporary Europe, both at national and EU levels, to pursue the production of major cultural events. Expos and other megaevents might in the future, as they often have in the past, offer Europeans visions and experiences of what they deeply need to know, namely that a non-threatening 'minimally cosmopolitan' European society and culture could be more than an idle wish, that, however transient, it could be a practical and lived reality.

Acknowledgement

I would like to thank the editors, particularly Maria Rovisco, for their suggestions about the chapter's treatment of topics and its general shape.

Bibliography

Apostolopolous, Y., Leivadi, S. and Yiannakis, A. (eds). 1996. *The Sociology of Tourism: Theoretical and Empirical Investigations*. London: Routledge.
Beck, U. and Grande, E. 2007. *Cosmopolitan Europe*. Cambridge: Polity.
Bennett, T. 1995. 'The exhibitionary complex', in *The Birth of the Museum: History, Theory and Politics*, edited by T. Bennett. London: Routledge, ch. 2.
Buzard, J. 1993. *The Beaten Track: European Tourism, Literature and Culture 1800–1918*. Oxford: Oxford University Press.

---

18   On the cosmopolitan aspects of touristic culture and events see for instance Roche 2000: ch. 5, 2009, 2011; Picard and Robinson 2006.

Calhoun, C. 2002. 'The class consciousness of frequent travelers: towards a critique of actually existing cosmopolitanism', in *Conceiving Cosmopolitanism: Theory, Context, Practice*, edited by S. Vertovec and R. Cohen. Oxford: Oxford University Press, ch. 6.

De Cauter, L. 1993 'The panoramic ecstasy: on world exhibitions and the disintegration of experience'. *Theory, Culture and Society*, 10, 1–23.

Delanty, G. 2010. *The Cosmopolitan Imagination*. Cambridge: Cambridge University Press.

Delanty, G. and Rumford, C. 2005. *Rethinking Europe: Social Theory and the Implications of Europeanization*. London: Routledge.

EC 2005. *The Daphne Experience 1997–2003: Europe Against Violence Towards Children and Women*. Brussels: European Commission (DG Justice, Freedom and Security).

Euronet 2005. *What about us? Children's Rights in the European Union: Next Steps*. Ruxton report. Brussels: European Children's Network.

European Agency 2007. *Report on Racism and Xenophobia in the Member States of the EU*. Vienna: European Agency for Fundamental Rights.

Featherstone, M. 1991. *Consumer Culture and Postmodernism*. London: Sage.

Findling, J. 1994. *Chicago's Great World's Fairs*. Manchester: Manchester University Press.

Fine, R. 2006. 'Cosmopolitanism and violence: difficulties of judgement'. *British Journal of Sociology*, 57 (1), 49–67.

Fine, R. 2007. *Cosmopolitanism*. London: Routledge.

Greenhalgh, P. 1988. *Ephemeral Vistas: The Expositions Universelles, Great Exhibitions and World's Fairs*. Manchester: Manchester University Press.

Greenhalgh, P. (ed.). 2000. *Art Nouveau 1890–1914*. London: V&A Publications.

Gunning, T. 1994. 'The world as object lesson: cinema audiences, visual culture and the St. Louis World's Fair 1904'. *Film History*, 6, 422–44.

Harvey, D. 1989. *The Condition of Postmodernity*. Oxford: Blackwell.

Held, D. 1995. *Democracy and the Global Order: From the Modern State to Cosmopolitan Governance*. Cambridge: Polity Press.

Held, D. 2004. *Global Covenant: The Social Democratic Alternative to the Washington Consensus*. Cambridge: Polity Press.

Kaldor, M. 2002. 'Cosmopolitanism and organized violence', in *Conceiving Cosmopolitanism: Theory, Context, Practice*, edited by S. Vertovec and R. Cohen. Oxford: Oxford University Press, ch. 17.

Kant, I. 1963. *On History* (original documents 1784 to 1795), edited by L. Beck. New York: Bobbs-Merrill Co. Ltd.

Kasson, J. 1978. *Amusing the Million: Coney Island at the Turn of the Century*. New York: Hill & Wang.

Lechner, F. and Boli, J. 2005. *World Culture: Origins and Consequences*. Oxford: Blackwell Publishing.

MacCannell, D. 1989. *The Tourist*. 2nd edn. London: Macmillan.

McCormick, P. 2007. *The European Superpower*. London: Palgrave.

Macdonald, S. and Fyfe, G. (eds). 1996. *Theorizing Museums*. Oxford: Blackwell.

Mazower, M. 1998. *Dark Continent: Europe's Twentieth Century*. London: Penguin.

Modood, T. and Werbner, P. (eds). 1997. *The Politics of Multiculturalism in the New Europe*. London: Zed Books.

Picard, D. and Robinson, M. (eds). 2006. *Festivals, Tourism and Social Change*. Clevedon: Channel View Publications.

Popper, K. 1962. *The Open Society and its Enemies*. Vols 1 and 2, 4th edn. London: Routledge.

Pred, A. 1991. 'Spectacular articulations of modernity: the Stockholm exhibition of 1897'. *Geografiska Annalerm*, 73 B 1, 45–84.

Richards, T. 1990. *The Commodity Culture of Victorian England: Advertising and Spectacle 1851–1914*. Stanford: Stanford University Press.

Roche, M. 1998. 'Mega-events, culture and modernity: expos and the origins of public culture'. *International Journal of Cultural Policy*, 5 (1), 1–31.

Roche, M. 2000. *Mega-Events and Modernity: Olympics and Expos in the Growth of Global Culture*. London: Routledge.

Roche, M. 2001a. 'Citizenship, popular culture and Europe', in *Culture and Citizenship*, edited by N. Stevenson. London: Sage, 74–98.

Roche, M. 2001b. 'Modernity, cultural events and the construction of charisma: mass cultural events in the USSR in the interwar period', *Cultural Policy*, 7 (3), 493–520.

Roche, M. 2002. 'The Olympics and "global citizenship"'. *Citizenship Studies*, 6 (2), 165–81.

Roche, M. 2003. 'Mega-events, time and modernity'. *Time and Society*, 12 (1), 99–126.

Roche, M. 2006a. 'Nationalism, mega-events and international culture', in *Handbook of Nations and Nationalism*, edited by G. Delanty and K. Kumar. London: Sage, ch. 22.

Roche, M. 2006b. 'Mega-events and modernity revisited: globalisation and the case of the Olympics', in *Sports Mega-Events: Social Scientific Analyses of a Global Phenomenon*, edited by J. Horne and W. Manzenreiter. Oxford: Blackwell, ch. 2.

Roche, M. 2007. 'Cultural Europeanisation and the "cosmopolitan condition": EU regulation and European sport', in *Europe and Cosmopolitanism*, edited by C. Rumford. Liverpool: Liverpool University Press, ch. 8.

Roche, M. 2009. 'Mega-events and micro-modernization: on the sociology of the new urban tourism', in *Event Tourism*, edited by S. Page and J. Connell. London: Routledge.

Roche, M. 2010. *Exploring the Sociology of Europe: An Analysis of the European Social Complex*. London: Sage.

Roche, M. 2011. 'Festivalisation, cosmopolitanism and European culture: on the socio-cultural significance of mega-events', in *Festivals and the Cultural Public Sphere*, edited by G. Delanty, L. Giorgi and M. Sassatelli. London: Routledge, ch. 8.

Rojek, C. and Urry, J. (eds). 1997. *Touring Cultures: Transformations of Travel and Theory*. London: Routledge.

Rumford, C. (ed.). 2007. *Europe and Cosmopolitanism*. Liverpool: Liverpool University Press.

Rydell, R. 1984. *All the World's a Fair: Visions of Empire at American International Expositions 1876–1916*. Chicago: Chicago University Press.

Rydell, R. 1993. *World of Fairs: The Century-of-Progress Expositions*. Chicago: Chicago University Press.

Rydell, R. and Gwinn, N. (eds). 1994. *Fair Representations: Worlds Fairs and the Modern World*. Amsterdam: VU University Press.

Rydell, R. and Kroes, R. 2005. *Buffalo Bill in Bologna: The Americanisation of the World, 1869–1922*. Chicago: Chicago University Press.

Schroeder-Gudehus, B. and Rasmussen, A. 1992. *Les Fastes du Progrès: Le guide des Expositions Universelles 1851–1992*. Paris: Flammarion.

Stevenson, N. 2007. 'Cosmopolitan Europe, post-colonialism and the politics of imperialism', in *Europe and Cosmopolitanism*, edited by C. Rumford. Liverpool: Liverpool University Press, ch. 4.

Telo, M. 2007. *Europe: A Civilian Power? – European Union, Global Governance and World Order*. London: Palgrave.

Urry, J. 1990. *The Tourist Gaze*. London: Sage.

Van der Veer, P. 2002. 'Colonial cosmopolitanism', in *Conceiving Cosmopolitanism: Theory, Context, Practice*, edited by S. Vertovec and R. Cohen. Oxford: Oxford University Press, ch. 10.

Van Steenbergen, B. 1994. *The Condition of Citizenship*. London: Sage.

Wang, N. 1999. *Tourism and Modernity: A Sociological Analysis*. Oxford: Elsevier Science.

Williams, R.H. 1982. *Dream Worlds: Mass Consumption in Late Nineteenth Century France*. Oxford: University of California Press.

Wrench, J. and Solomos, J. (eds). 1993. *Racism and Migration in Western Europe*. Oxford: Berg.

The Cosmopolitan City

Christina Horvath

The inhabitants of the contemporary world's largest cities share the experience of diversity and otherness in their everyday life. In an increasingly global context, great metropolises are often seen as metonyms for the world reunited in one city where racial, ethnic, religious, cultural and sexual differences can be encountered and practiced daily. While certain commentators celebrate this diversity as the very factor that makes twenty-first century cities successful, vibrant places, others assess it with concern, associating growing immigrant communities with the rise of criminality. Cities themselves generally value representations of their own cultural diversity as a staple upon which their branding strategies can be based yet in some cases they may avoid references to their multicultural neighborhoods, considering these too difficult to integrate into their marketable images. In either case, metropolises of global reach are hubs of transnational networks where diasporic people can negotiate their identities and affiliations by perpetually revisiting "old ideas of home, nation and homeland" (Ball 2004: 25). For this reason, migrants cannot see transnational metropolises such as London or Paris as simply local or national cities. These former imperial centers have always been linked to worlds of difference since their "local" places have been interfused with a "global" network of relations and regions extending far beyond them. Focusing on the idea of the city as a space of encounter between cultures, this chapter proposes to examine competing notions of the cosmopolitan, transnational, multicultural and postcolonial city in order to explore various forms of difference which are valued in or, on the contrary, excluded from contemporary urban discourses. A series of key issues linked to cosmopolitan cities such as the questions of cultural capitals, multiethnic neighborhoods, gentrification, city branding and commemorative practices will be discussed in a case study exploring various ways in which contemporary Paris is represented in scholarly and political discourses as well as literary and cinematographic narratives.

Cosmopolitan Paris

Well-known for being a cultural capital since the eighteenth century, Paris is most often referred to as a cosmopolitan metropolis. Despite the indubitably multicultural character of the city and the massive presence of postcolonial migrants, the adjective "cosmopolitan" is generally preferred to "multicultural" which is used with a certain reluctance in French political discourses. The terms "cosmopolitan" and "multicultural" are competing notions: they both describe the particularities of contemporary world cities. However, multiculturalism refers mostly to the presence of ethnic, religious or sexual difference in cities or to claims for the recognition of cultural otherness (Joppke and Lukes 1999: 1) while cosmopolitanism evokes the idea of world citizenship and promotes identities which are not territorially based (Breckenridge et al. 2002: 2). Kosnick notes that both cosmopolitanism and multiculturalism exhibit "a certain openness, eagerness, and ability to engage with different cultural traditions and orientations that are strange in their origin" (Hemelryk Donald et al. 2009: 36) and reject exclusively parochial cultural attachments with the aim to reconcile the principle of equality with the recognition of positively valued difference. Since multiculturalism is concerned with territorially limited spaces such as nations, cities or single neighborhoods, multicultural metropolises are communally defined as territories that need to integrate minority populations regardless of their transnational affiliations and mobilities. Multiculturalist urban policies are therefore expected to look at the city as a local space where minority claims can be accepted within the limits determined by the rules of liberal democratic political models. Official multiculturalism was first instituted in the 1970s in postcolonial societies such as Canada and Australia "that lacked nation-founding myths and clear breaks with their colonial past" (Joppke and Lukes 1999: 3) and defined themselves as "multiple cultures existing under the roof of a neutral state." Although this multicultural model is today predominant in North America, its popularity remains rather limited in France where natives are regarded as universal individual-citizens directly linked to the nation-state, and national-political membership requires the acceptance of French cultural values. The Republican model leaves little room for multicultural claims arising from minority groups, as it is well illustrated by the long-lasting debate about the right of Muslim girls to wear the Islamic veil in French public schools.

As a model for society, multiculturalism proposes two concurrent urban models. On the one hand, it celebrates hybridity, intermingling and mongrelization and sees the city as a fusion of cultures; on the other hand it considers the metropolis as a mosaic of distinct cultural and ethnic backgrounds that coexist within a community encouraging and welcoming difference. We will see that neither of these images plays a considerable role in French city branding strategies. While Hatziprokopiou notes that most British cities including London are promoted as multicultural sites of "branded difference" (Hemelryk Donald et al. 2009: 14), dominant images of Paris remain essentially French and evoke mainly connotations with French cultural references such as French history, fashion, art or cuisine.

The more universally oriented notion of cosmopolitanism conceptualizes cities as nodes in a global cultural network and considers them as the endpoints of migratory movements that produce cultural mosaics. Originating in ancient Greek thought and Kantian philosophy, cosmopolitanism reflects a universalistic conception of human belonging. Paris can be seen as a cosmopolitan metropolis since it is inscribed in transnational population flows which transcend the boundaries of the nation-state. Like London, New York and other world cities, Paris constitutes also a nod in cultural flows which are partly ordered by center–periphery relationships. As Hannerz (1996: 128) suggests, cosmopolitan world cities are centers to which "people from different parts of the world look, even from considerable distance and often from one continent to another, as fairly durable sources of new culture." These places are sites from which a wide variety of ideas and cultural forms might spread during a certain period of time. Although they might undergo shifting fortunes in this respect and become less significant with the time, many of these cities continue to play an important role as centers of new cultures. Most of the time, they are characterized by the presence of four social categories which have in common to develop strong ties to some other place in the world: highly skilled, mobile individuals belonging to the managerial classes, Third World populations, people specializing in expressive activities including art, design, fashion, or cuisine and tourists (Hannerz 1996: 129–31). Although cities like New York, London or Tokyo exemplify better global cities understood as the control center of global economy (Sassen 1991), Paris continues to attract a large amount of transnational people belonging to all four categories and can be considered as something more and qualitatively different than a manifestation of French national culture.

On the other hand, the cosmopolitan city is predominantly associated with transnational elites able to navigate between and within different cultures thanks to their education, confidence, cultural capital and money. Friedmann and Wolff (1982: 322) note that "transnational elites are the dominant class in the world city, and the city is arranged to cater to their life styles and occupational necessities." For Binnie et al. (2006: 7), cosmopolitanism is founded on "an openness to, desire for and appreciation of, social and cultural difference" which is associated with gentrification and urban formations of the "new middle class" and bound up with notions of knowledge, cultural capital and education. Hannerz (1996: 103) describes the cosmopolitan mindset as "an orientation, a willingness to engage with the Other" which entails an intellectual and esthetic openness toward divergent cultural experiences and requires a "state of readiness, a personal ability to make one's way into other cultures, through listening, looking, intuiting, and reflecting."

Unlike multiculturalism which, based on the anthropological concept of culture as a specific form of life, inherited a comprehensive and anti-elitist notion of cultures in the plural, the cosmopolitan ideal implies less an absence of belonging to a nation-state than "the possibility of belonging to more than one ethnic and social localism simultaneously" (Werbner 2008: 34). As Hannerz (1996: 204) points out, the cosmopolitan may embrace an alien culture, but he does not become committed to it. Mobility that may constitute a key aspect of the cosmopolitan stance doesn't suffice to turn one into a cosmopolitan. Labor migrants, tourists who tend to be more spectators than participants or exiles who wish to preserve a threatened, uprooted sense of self are less likely to develop a cosmopolitan attitude than expatriates who have chosen to live abroad for some period and who know that they can go home when it suits them. Associated to the city, cosmopolitanism is understood as a series of practices linked with the production deployment of cultural capital, mainly by the new middle and gentrifying classes who consider themselves as "globally oriented, particularly through artistic and intellectual pursuits which draw them into international cultural circuits" (Binnie et al. 2006: 15). As Binnie et al. (2006: 15) argue, cosmopolitan urban identities find physical expression in gentrified urban settings through local territory and encounters commodified through ethnic restaurants, import stores, international media and architectural forms: "Thus the socialization of cosmopolitan global identities and the generation of encounters with difference and diversity find their locus in particular 'consumptionscapes' in the city." In a similar way, Cohen (1997: 167) sees global cities as international and cosmopolitan, partly because they are more integrated to other global cities than to their original national context, but also because prevalent "tastes, consumption patterns and forms of entertainment are drawn more from an emerging global culture than from the national culture."

The term cosmopolitanism is frequently used in tandem with two other notions: transnationalism and postcolonialism, both referring to massive population displacement which had occurred in the context of globalization since the era of decolonization. In his study of postcolonial London, John Clement Ball (2004) uses interchangeably both terms that appear simultaneously in the title of his book *Imagining London: Postcolonial Fiction and the Transnational Metropolis*. Focusing on the experience of colonial or postcolonial migrants who have come to live in London, Ball (2004: 31) describes everyday life in the British metropolis as one that involves "a dynamic inhabitation and negotiation of a spatial spectrum that extends from the most local inhabited space, the body, outwards through the home, the neighborhood, the community, the city, the nation, and beyond the most global inhabited space, the world." Building on Michael Peter Smith's theory of transnational urbanism, the author argues that inhabitants of transnational cities develop interstitial identities which go beyond such binary oppositions as local and global insofar as their everyday local experience is informed by phenomena and networks that "defy easy boundary-setting" (Smith 2001: 117). In *Postcolonial London: Rewriting the Metropolis*, John McLeod (2004) pursues a similar goal to the one set by Ball. He studies London's postcolonial re-writing in narratives by African, Asian and Caribbean writers and explores different attitudes to the metropolis' diasporic transformation resulting from migration and emerging hybrid communities and the heterogeneous, diverse and transnational character of the city's society and culture. The adjective "transnational" which appears regularly in critical work dealing with the multiethnic population of cosmopolitan London, also refers to a recent shift in migration which since the 1980s has become less a directed movement with a point of departure and a point of arrival than an ongoing flow between several locations. In this sense, transnational cities can be equated to postcolonial metropolises which cannot be seen as simply local or national entities because of their past and present overseas linkages.

While London's role in postcolonial imagery is widely studied in the Anglophone world, postcolonial re-writings of Paris trigger little interest in France. Even if the transition from Paris as a French metropolis and Western intellectual capital to a globalized and transcultural world city is as frequently represented in film and novels as London's transnational change, until recently critics in the Hexagon have devoted little attention to postcolonial Paris. This denial of the city's historical, cultural and ethnic diversity started to change in the 1990s with the publication of a series of work concerned with North- and Sub-Saharan African cultural and literary production in France, published mostly by scholars working at American universities such as Michel Laronde, Benetta Jules-Rosette, Odile Cazenave, Mireille Rosello, Alec Hargreaves or Dominic Thomas. In their introduction to the volume *Francophone Postcolonial Studies*, Charles Forsdick and David Murphy (2003) argue that, although Paris' status as a postcolonial city is striking, the predominantly nation-centered concept of Frenchness and the only fleeting recognition of the role played by colonial expansion in the formation of national and Republican identity led not only to an active suppression of colonial memory but also to a strong reluctance in the French academia to engage with postcolonial theory. As a result of this legacy, majority cultural gatekeepers in France tend to consider multiculturalism and postcolonial theory as Anglo-Saxon inventions alien to France's Universalist traditions and often refuse recognition to artists of immigrant origin who produce diasporic or multicultural representations of Paris that contradict dominant narratives of the French capital. As Hargreaves argues, the literature, films and other art forms produced by France's postcolonial minority's have been studied and valorized far more extensively outside France – especially in the English-speaking world – than within the country in which their creators live (Forsdick and Murphy 2003, Hargreaves 2007).

Dominant French discourses which tend to ignore Paris' colonial legacy and multicultural diversity generally favor images of the city as the world's unique cultural capital. In *The World Republic of Letters* Pascale Casanova (2004: 24) attempts to demonstrate that just in the same way as the eighteenth-century London became the center of the world economy, nineteenth-century Paris imposed its cultural hegemony as the undisputed capital of Western painting and literature and maintained its unique position as "the city endowed with the greatest literary prestige on earth" until the recent emergence of a polycentric globalized space. In the international literary space which was formed in the sixteenth century as the result of long-lasting rivalries between emerging national states and their languages, France's central position was based on the greatness of its national literary past, its historical and literary legitimacy, and the universal recognition of its greatest authors. The exceptional status of Paris as the world's leading literary capital, argues Casanova, was due to the city's "non-national" and "ahistorical" character corresponding both to the timeless nature of works of art recognized as "classics" and to the universal, cosmopolitan values associated with literary legitimacy. The emergence of Paris as a literary and cultural capital was made manifest on the one hand by the city's countless descriptions in novels and poems and, on the other hand, by its universally acknowledged power of conferring literary recognition to writers of immigrant origins such as Octavio Paz, Samuel Beckett, Danilo Kiš or Cioran. For Casanova, Paris' uniqueness as a literary capital lies precisely in the cosmopolitan stance of its literary population and the city's relatively strong emancipation from national politics:

> *Because France was the least national of literary nations, it was able to manufacture a universal literature while consecrating works produced by outlying territories – impressing the stamp of littérarité upon texts that came from farflung lands, thereby denationalizing and departicularizing them, declaring them to be acceptable as legal tender in all the law of universality in the world of letters against the ordinary political laws of nations, France became an alternative model for writers from every part of the literary world who aspired to autonomy. (Casanova 2004: 87)*

Casanova (2004: 29) sees the only shortcoming of the universality which made Paris "the homeland of [all] those free spirits who have not found a homeland" in the ongoing domination of Francophone writers who have been the only authors unable to look to Paris for consecration and liberation. Unlike London, another literary center that successfully rallied under the British banner a wide range of postcolonial Commonwealth authors from various countries, Paris "never took an interest in writers from its colonial territories; or more precisely, it long despised and mistreated them as a species of extreme provincials, too similar to be celebrated as exotic foreigners but too remote to be considered worthy of interest" (Casanova 2004: 122).

Celebrating Paris as a global capital of culture and literature, Casanova asserts that cosmopolitan attitudes played a central role in the recognition of literary work produced by transnational avant-gardes. Intellectual elites concentrated in the French capital tended to favor universal values against territorial ones, thereby contributing to the emergence of a universal literary modernity. However, they remained curiously indifferent toward the expressions of cultural otherness within the Francophone literary space and the emergence of new, alternative images of Paris, produced by postcolonial migrants. Today, in an era described as "a transitional phase, passing from a world dominated by Paris to polycentric and plural world" (Casanova 2004: 164) these attitudes are evolving, due as much to interurban rivalry to seize literary and cultural power, as to the increasing globalization and commercialization of the publishing industry.

Diasporic Communities and Multicultural Neighborhoods

With a territory of 8,700 hectares, Paris is a relatively small capital city compared to other European metropolises such as London (32,100 ha) or Madrid (60,700 ha).

Another notable difference that distinguishes Paris from most European capitals is an unusually sharp divide separating the densely populated inner city from the surrounding suburbs that feature looser settlements (Pinçon and Pinçon-Charlot 2004: 8). The city's boundaries are composed by social housing estates, sport establishments and the Boulevard Périphérique composed of two concentric carriageways: an inner and an outer ring. Constructed in 1958 on the former site of the last remaining city walls, this orbital motorway separates a relatively homogeneous inner city containing only a limited number of ethnic enclaves and multiethnic neighborhoods and demographically diverse suburbs known as "banlieues." Most peripheral areas are marked by concentrations of large-scale, predominantly high-rise social housing projects and problems usually associated with inner-city areas in the UK and North America. Suburban neighborhoods in France evoke the negative connotations of social exclusion and geographic segregation. As the etymologic origin of the term suggests, "banlieues" are places of banishment and exclusion, located on the outskirts of the city and separated from the center by rigid boundaries that emphasize their non-belonging to the system.

French urban policies are radically different from the British or American ones insofar as their main object is not community but space. As Mustafa Dikeç (2007: 4) observes, "this is almost necessary so since the French Republican tradition emphasizes a common culture and identity, and any reference to communities is deliberately avoided because they imply separatism, which is unacceptable under the principle of the 'one and indivisible' republic." Although in French media and political discourses "banlieues" are usually considered as a threat to security and largely associated with ethnic minority population by the amalgamation of urban immigration and delinquency, inner city neighborhoods are evolving under the principle of "mixité sociale." This means that since the renovation program commissioned by Napoleon III and led by Haussmann between 1852 and 1870, social classes considered as "dangerous" have been continuously rejected on the city's periphery, while the inner city continued to evolve as a space of encounter, exchange and cohabitation between various social, professional or demographic categories. In their sociological analysis of Paris, Michel Pinçon and Monique Pinçon-Charlot (2004) note the existence of various axes dividing the urban space into economically privileged quarters in the West and predominantly working-class neighborhoods situated in the East or quarters marked by a higher density of cultural institutions and intellectual life on the left bank of the city of the Seine and to commerce on the right bank. Despite their attempt to list major divides, the authors of this major monograph only evoke a few diasporic or multiethnic neighborhoods such as the "Goutte d'Or," the Tamil quarter and the neighbourhood known as "les Abbesses." Located near the underground station Barbès-Rochechouard, the "Goutte d'Or" is described as a quarter shaped by several successive waves of immigration starting in the 1860s with the rural exodus depicted in Emile Zola's novel *The Dram-Shop* (1877), followed by the arrival of workers from Eastern Europe, Spain, Italy, North and Sub-Saharan Africa and most recently from Asia. Resulting from the intermingling of populations coming from a multitude of geographic locations, the neighborhood is described as a colorful mix of ethnic groups whose peaceful cohabitation is illustrated by the undisturbed coexistence of their shops and restaurants in the same neighborhood. As opposed to the Goutte d'Or's ethnic hotchpotch, the Tamil quarter is depicted as an apparently homogeneous ethnic neighbourhood located between the railway stations Gare du Nord and Gare de l'Est, in the 10th district of Paris. Yet the Tamils who arrived in France in the 1970s to escape civil war in Sri Lanka live in the suburbs and not in this neighborhood where their shops, restaurants and two temples are located, therefore their presence doesn't change considerably the social composition of the district which remains predominantly French. Finally, the description of the quarter known as "les Abesses" is mainly based on Jean-Pierre Jeunet's film, *Amélie* (2001) that is set in the village-like neighborhood located around the eponymous underground station and depicted in a strongly idealized way as an example of the intermingling of various demographic and ethnic categories. For Michel and Monique Pinçon, "les Abesses" represents at the same time demographic change, the survival of traditional forms of sociability and solidarity threatened by rising property prices and gentrification as well as an emerging new myth of Paris triggered by the success of the movie worldwide.

In this sociological study, the above-mentioned Parisian quarters appear as the perfect embodiments of the harmonious cohabitation of different ethnic and social groups in the French capital. This idea of social and demographic mix has been a constant preoccupation of urban planners and administrators in Paris since the end of the nineteenth century. The term "mixité" was used for the first time in 1973 by the Minister of Public Works Olivier Guichard to designate the aim of making different social classes cohabit in the same communes, neighborhoods or even buildings in order to prevent spatial segregation. As a result of ongoing processes of gentrification and demographic change, Paris' population is today younger than the national average (36 percent aged between 20 and 39 in Paris against only 28 percent in France) and more strongly marked by the presence of people of immigrant origins. As the percentage of immigrants is generally slightly higher in working-class neighborhoods, the intermingling of social and ethnic categories is strongly interlinked. Pinçon notes that in 1994, 9.4 percent of France's immigrants lived in Paris, although Parisians only represented 3.6 percent of the country's population. Foreigners represented 14.5 percent of the city's inhabitants and they were not evenly distributed: their concentration was higher in the North-Eastern and Eastern districts (18th, 19th and 20th; 2nd, 3rd, 10th and 11th) as well as in the wealthy 8th and 16th districts. However, these differences remained relatively insignificant, ranging from 10 percent to 22 percent, which illustrates the relative success of urban policies aiming to avoid the emergence of predominantly diasporic enclaves.

Cosmopolitan City Branding in Paris and Elsewhere

On July 6, 2005, Paris lost the bidding race for holding the 2012 Summer Olympic Games against London after a 54–50 vote of the International Olympic Committee. By deploying the slogan "the world in one city," London put forward its cosmopolitanism as a captivating diversity to attract the major sporting event while Paris relied on its typical French qualities and placed a great emphasis on France's passion for sport and the city's rich cultural heritage with regard to Olympism. This strategic difference exemplifies as much the popular adoption of cosmopolitanism as place branding cultural disposition in Britain as the French reluctance to hold out new urban differences and alternative cultural forms to attract investment or tourism. Doreen Massey (2007: 4) assesses the British Olympic bid as a claiming of a place identity based on the city's cultural and ethnic diversity a "mixity of lived practices," the "criss-crossing of multiple allegiances," a "convivial demotic cosmpopolitanism" rather than a multiculturalism consisting in the mere "juxtaposition of, and negotiated relations between, mutually boxed-in communities."

In an article published in 2009, Kira Kosnick observes the important role that urban cultural diversity has come to play in the branding efforts of metropolitan centers across the globe: "The 'rich mix' that many cities can offer figures prominently in contemporary place marketing, most important against the background of growing interurban competition for tourism, creative talent, and investment. In many locations, ethnocultural diversity has come to be accepted as a key asset and requirement for urban development by city officials, business executives and planners alike" (Hemelryk Donald et al. 2009: 28). As Richard Florida and other influential urban studies theorists have argued, economic growth depends today on the cities' ability to share in the flow of the creative classes (Florida 2002) and urban diversity is a key component for the creation of a climate of tolerance and openness in which innovation can flourish. The cosmopolitan qualities of world-openness, creativity and diversity play a strategic role in marketing experts' efforts to reposition cities successfully in the global arena. London's multicultural neighborhoods such as Chinatown or Brick Lane have been not only powerful elements in the successful Olympic bid but also examples of the general trend of transforming ethnic quarters into "sites of branded difference," "places of leisure and consumption" and signifiers of "acceptable" and "packaged" difference (Hemelryk Donald et al. 2009: 14). Neoliberal and entrepreneurial forms of urban governance creating deep inequalities are often criticized for displaying visible loci of ethnic diversity as celebratory emblems of London's diversity while the unofficial counterparts of these branded, ideal places remain largely unnoticed and unvalued. On the other hand, the emergent multicultural Paris has little or no role to play in official branding efforts in contemporary France. Ethnic enclaves such as the Turkish quarter at Strasbourg-Saint-Denis or the Asian quarter near the underground station Porte d'Ivry do not feature at a central place either in official city guides or in the failed Olympic bid that favored Parisian landmarks representing traditional ideas of Frenchness such as the Eiffel Tower, Champ de

Mars and the Palace of Versailles. Marked by a strong attachment to the Republican tradition, the contemporary restructuring of the French state goes hand-in-hand with a strong emphasis on a common culture and identity, the fragmentation of which would be seen as a threat to the social and political integrity of France.

Rosemary Sales describes London's Chinatown as a branded urban place where "Chinese culture can be consumed as part of a 'global ethnic supermarket'" (Hemelryk Donald et al. 2009: 45). This central-London neighborhood, which was once a ghetto for underprivileged migrants, has become institutionalized by the city's authorities. Although it remains important to Chinese migrants whom it provides with material resources such as food and information, it features prominently on London's tourist maps and welcomes visitors who constitute henceforth the majority of the New Year celebrations' audience. In a study published in 2009, Michel Pinçon and Monique Pinçon-Charlot describe the Parisian "Chinatown" of Porte d'Ivry as the successful fusion of a former working-class neighborhood with a high percentage of Jewish, Algerian, Portuguese, Uruguayan and Chilean migrant population and a very heterogeneous population arriving in the mid-1970s from South-East Asia. Less central than London's Chinatown, the Parisian Asian quarter is dominated by a series of tower blocks constructed in the 1960s as part of an urban regeneration project which aimed to attract a middle-class population, thereby promoting social cohesion. Despite the failure of this plan, the neighborhood is far from being an Asian ghetto: it is inhabited not only by Chinese, Vietnamese, Cambodian and Laotian people but also by important African and Caribbean populations. Unlike London's Chinatown, the neighborhood's ethnic shops, restaurants and temples are mainly frequented by the Asian community but the New Year celebrations attract also Parisians. In 2004, in the framework of the Year of Chinese Culture in France, the parade was exceptionally staged in central Paris, on the Avenue of Champs-Elysées. The event, featuring more than 7,000 costumed performers, drew a crowd of 200,000 spectators and was assessed by the media as the first non-French cultural event to be held at a key Parisian landmark location, with municipal authorities covering more than one-third of the costs. We can see in this unprecedented event a sign that the Republic is slowly coming to terms with an emerging mongrel Paris which encapsulates otherness, fragmentation and heterogeneity; as well as a new place granted to cosmopolitan features in Paris's urban branding strategies.

Images of an Emerging Mongrel Paris

In parallel with the gradual recognition of ethnic minority artists who have been "making inroads to the cultural mainstream" (Forsdick and Murphy 2003: 146), images of a multicultural and mongrel Paris have emerged in documentary cinema as well as in cinematographic and literary narratives. We can see a recent example of this trend in *La Goutte d'Or: vivre ensemble* (*The Goutte d'Or: Living Together*, 2010), a documentary movie directed by Bruno Lemesle. The film is an attempt to put forward ideas of solidarity and diversity in one of Paris' most significant multicultural neighbourhoods. Located in the 18th district, between the underground stations Barbès-Rochechouart and Château-Rouge, La Goutte d'Or encompasses the biggest African food market of the capital as well as numerous North and Sub-Saharan African ethnic shops, restaurants and various places of worship such as the mosque Polonceau and the Church Saint-Bernard. The latter is an important Parisian landmark associated with the struggle of "Sans-Papier" since the eviction in 1996 by police of 300 undocumented immigrants who had taken sanctuary in the church for several months. Lemesle's aim is to rehabilitate the image of the quarter, better known by the Parisians for its drug dealers, illegal street market and African prostitutes than for its numerous cultural associations and unique multiethnic community who miraculously survived the 1983 restructuration as well as the actual urban regeneration plan. The film shows problems linked to poverty, insalubrious housing conditions and illegal immigration through the prism of various inhabitants ranging from Maghrebi immigrant workers to a young female academic of Algerian descent specialized in the history of immigration, and from African housewives raising several children in unhygienic conditions to social activists who fight for the creation of appropriate social housing in the neighborhood.

Unlike Lemesle's modest documentary, scarcely sponsored by the SCAM, a French association supporting multimedia creation, *9/3, Mémoire d'un territoire* (*9/3, Memories of a Territory*, 2008) was produced for the French television channel Canal+ which broadcasted it on September 29, 2008. Directed by renowned French Algerian filmmaker Yamina Benguigui, the film benefitted from exceptional media coverage and triggered vehement reactions from historians who accused Benguigui of distorting the history of Seine-Saint-Denis. Recalling three periods of the administrative region located in the North-East of Paris, the documentary investigates the industrial fabric, the housing considerations and the successive waves of immigration from 1860 to today, with a special focus on the Spanish, Italian, Algerian and Caribbean communities. Although the region is often associated with urban violence and the riots that occurred in 2005, these don't constitute a central element in the film. Benguigui is more interested in denouncing two centuries of segregation which started with the relocation of dangerous industries to the North-East of Paris. Due to the pollution, the lack of hygiene and successive epidemics, workers were rapidly decimated and replaced by migrants, coming first from the French countryside and European countries and later from the former colonies. The industrial pollution of this period created waste including lead, arsenic, or hydrocarbon which has polluted the ground waters and soils to the present day. By revealing the shortcomings of large-scale housing projects constructed on industrial grounds at the lowest possible cost, the documentary accuses urban planners and authorities of having planned or accepted the predictable emergence of today's ghettos. The elegiac musical background associated with a series of interviews with disenchanted inhabitants of the stigmatized region contributed to a melodramatic effect that has been seriously criticized as manipulative by historians who reproach the filmmaker that she censored their contribution by cutting elements that contradicted the intended message of the film.

While the documentary shows the region known as 9-3 as a multicultural area where immigrants from various origins live together, in her more recent TV film *Aïcha* (2009) located in the same area, Benguigui proposes to focus exclusively on the daily life of the Algerian community. The Boumazza family lives in the Eastern part of Bobigny, in a high-rise housing project, separated from Paris only by the orbital motorway. The film's main character, the family's 23-year-old daughter, suffers from the stifling cultural traditions and yearns for independence. This young Parisian of Algerian descent who is reluctant to break away from her family, balances between two cultures and two worlds. The film evokes most of the ethnic stereotypes associated with Muslim communities in France: it conveys images of Islamists recruiting followers in the tower blocks, shows bright law school graduates who struggle to find work because of their ethnic origins and young girls who undergo virginity tests or accept arranged marriages as their only way to escape parental control. Yet, despite its sometimes reductive portraiture of the French-Algerian characters, this ethnic comedy honored at the La Rochelle film festival is the first French telefilm dedicated to multicultural neighborhood in the greater Paris area to be broadcasted on a French TV channel prime time.

Unlike *Aïcha* that features little interaction between the native French and the Algerian ethnic minority populations apart from the protagonist's timid flirt with a young French architect in charge of the regeneration of the neighborhood, Cédric Klapish's *When the Cat's Away* (*Chacun cherche son chat*, 1996) exemplifies the much valued French principle of "mixité sociale." Set in the Bastille neighborhood, a recently gentrified former working-class area in Eastern Paris, the film shows massive solidarity between inhabitants belonging to various age groups, social classes, occupational and gender categories and ethnic groups. The main character is a young make-up artist, Chloe, who shares an apartment with her homosexual friend, Michel. When she goes on holiday for one week, she leaves her cat Gris-gris with an old neighbor who lets the animal escape. On Chloe's return, the whole neighborhood is mobilized to find the missing cat, including the African workers of the neighboring cabinet-making workshop, the mentally retarded Maghrebi youth Djamel, the painter Belcanto, the regular costumers of the nearby bistro and a network of old ladies who find their unique entertainment in this hilarious quest. Searching the neighborhood for the cat becomes a pretext for the exploration of a Parisian quarter which has an exceptionally rich history of immigration, mongrelization and working-class solidarity. Marked by the high concentration of craft industry, the quarter formerly known as "Faubourg Saint-Antoine" had attracted workers from the French provinces and overseas since the seventeenth century until it became in the 1960s a quarter valued by artists and bohemians who converted the former industrial workshops into painters' studios. The subsequent gentrification of the quarter is well illustrated by Klapish's movie which shows the Bastille area's vibrant nightlife attracting young people from all over the capital, the urban regeneration signified by numerous construction sites omnipresent in the film and the departure of elderly inhabitants and artists who cannot afford the rising rents and property prices. Chloe, who initially likes to hang out in the trendy "Pause Café" with a young drummer living in the neighborhood, gradually develops a preference for the old-fashioned working-class bistro and the painter Belcanto. Klapish uses this metaphor to show that in this truly cosmopolitan Parisian neighborhood the solidarity between inhabitants prevails over boundaries of age, gender or ethnicity. Although racial difference is less central in this movie than in Benguigui's film, Djamel's figure is conceived to demonstrate the inhabitants' ability to accept ethnic otherness, in the same way as Michel's character illustrates their tolerant attitudes toward sexual difference.

In a more recent film, *Paris* (2008), Cédric Klapish offers another cosmopolitan vision of the French capital, depicted this time in its entirety as a complex network of human relations and a node in global population flows. This idea is mainly illustrated by two immigrant characters, Khadija, a student of North-African background, and Benoit, the Cameroonian clandestine who risks his life by attempting the dangerous crossing of the Straits of Gibraltar to enter France illegally. Born and bred in France, Khadija is a Parisian, yet she encounters prejudices because of her ethnic otherness when she tries to find employment in a bakery. Eventually hired for the job, she proves exceptionally hard-working, thereby earning the respect of her racist employer. Benoit is the only character in the movie whose story is partly set in another location than Paris. We encounter him for the first time at a holiday resort in Cameroon where he works as a swimming instructor. Despite not having legal paperwork to immigrate, he decides to make his way to Paris to join his brother who works there as a cleaner, but also to respond to the invitation of Marjolaine, a Parisian model with whom he made acquaintance at the resort hotel. The destinies of these immigrant characters inscribe Paris in the global network of population displacement and depict the postcolonial metropolis as a much-coveted destination which both attracts and resists immigrants from the former colonies.

With the gradual recognition of artists belonging to various Diasporas, alternative images of Paris depicted as a postcolonial metropolis have increasingly managed to secure a place at the high table of the city's literary representations. We can see an example of this diversification of Parisian imagery in the work of Alain Mabanckou, one of the most successful contemporary African writers published in France, who offers two contradictory variants of diasporic Paris in two novels published in the space of a decade: *Bleu-Blanc-Rouge* (*Blue-White-Red*, 1998) and *Black Bazar* (2009). A common characteristic of both novels is to show Paris exclusively through the prism of West-African immigrants. In the first text, a main character called Massala Massala arrives as an illegal immigrant to Paris. The first part of the novel is set in Africa, Paris appears only in the conversations and phantasms of the characters as an idealized city where luxury items, high-brow cultural products and Parisian landmarks associated with emblematic notions of French identity are easily available for everyone. This portraiture of city contrasts singularly with the images of marginalization and spatial and social exclusion encountered in the second part set in Paris which ends with the eviction of the protagonist by the French authorities. Images of Paris are exploited in the novel to show the capital as a lure that attracts migrants but remains beyond their reach, with the noticeable exception of a few segregated places such as an overpopulated squat in the 14th district, the African market in the 18th district and a series of underground stations where the protagonist engages in an illegal commerce of monthly public transport passes purchased with stolen cheques under false identity.

The narrator of *Black Bazar* has a fundamentally different experience of Paris. Unlike Massala Massala, he is neither naive not disenchanted in his ways of considering the metropolis in which he seems to be perfectly in his element. His main difference with the immigrant character in the previous novel lies not in his more regular contact with the French ethnic majority population or his greater access to symbolic places of Frenchness but in his thorough knowledge of a parallel, diasporic Paris which constitutes the scene of his daily social life and professional activities. He chooses his friends and romantic partners exclusively from the African Diaspora and has only superficial contacts with members of other ethnic groups such as the Arab who runs the local shop or a racist Afro-Caribbean neighbor. Yet he belongs not only to the West-African community whose diversity is put on display at the Jip's bar, but also to a subculture of high fashion called "sape" which is practiced widely by members of the Diaspora. Purchasing expensive designer clothes in Italy and selling them in Paris to the members of the community is a lucrative activity which requires the practice of diasporic places such as the Château-Rouge area and its market, les Halles, where the protagonist regularly encounters other African migrants of diverse national and ethnic backgrounds in his favorite bar and the suburbs where members of the Diaspora come together for major social events. The protagonist of *Black Bazar* doesn't seem to be excluded from emblematic Parisian places such as the avenue of Champs-Elysées or the Eiffel Tower but these symbolic landmarks have little appeal to him. Nonetheless, the narrator of Mabanckou's novel is subject to a positive evolution: living initially in a self-sufficient ethnic enclave, he progressively develops a more cosmopolitan attitude after he discovers his vocation as a writer and shows an increasing interest in cultural difference after his encounter with a white Belgian woman.

The Postcolonial Paris and its Recent Commemorative Landmarks

Charles Forsdick and David Murphy (2003: 1) observe that the landmarks of French national memory described in the collection of essays *Lieux de mémoire* published by Pierre Nora are restricted to the geographic area of the Hexagon. According to the authors, the non-recognition of the role played by the former colonies in the shaping of national identity is symptomatic of the general amnesia concerning the immigrants' contribution to French culture. Whereas France and Great Britain are experiencing similar processes of "reverse colonization," Parisian reactions to the transformation of the former imperial center into a postcolonial metropolis are very different from the ones observed in London. Policies celebrating the multicultural city led in London to the implementation of several commemorative places such as the Museum of London, holding collections on the impacts that immigrants have had on the city. In 2007 the exhibit "Belonging: Voices of London's Refugees" looked at the contribution which refugees have made to London. Another exhibit displayed in the Museum in Docklands entitled "Journey to the New World," presented the facts and fables behind the first European voyages to America. In 2004, a hub of four museums, the Museum of London, London's Transport Museum, Croydon Museum and Heritage Service and the Jewish Museum launched an integrated website amalgamating voice recordings and images with the aim of showcasing London's history, culture and religions. This online resource entitled "Exploring 20th Century London" dedicates an important place to the history of immigration, communities, local identities and shared experiences. Introducing the visitor to "a myriad of overlapping communities, each bound together by a sense of people having something in common and a distinct identity" (www.20thcenturylondon.org.uk), the website presents the development of bohemian neighborhoods such as Chelsea or Hampstead; ethnic quarters including the Italian, German, Chinese, Russian, East European, Jewish and French communities located in Clerkenwell, Charlotte Street, Limehouse, Whitechapel or Aldgate; and places associated with the emerging gay community such as Soho. The website extensively deals with the settlement of Caribbean workers in the areas of Notting Hill Gate and Brixton and the development of multicultural communities such as Stepney featuring Maltese, West Indian, Pakistani, Greek and Italian establishments or Whitechapel where the Bangladeshi community replaced the Jewish one.

Although until recently commemorative places of colonial and postcolonial history were extremely rare in Paris, the last few years witnessed a decisive change in the French attitude with regard to the creation of sites dedicated to the history, the arts and the cultures of the former colonies or to postcolonial immigration. The "Cité Nationale de l'Histoire de l'Immigration" opened in October 2007 with a mission to contribute to the recognition of the integration of immigrants into French society and advance the views and attitudes on immigration in France. The collection occupies the Palais de la Porte Dorée, formerly the home of the Musée National des Arts d'Afrique et d'Océanie, designed by Albert Laprade for the Colonial Exhibition of 1931. It displays a permanent installation, "Benchmarks," which showcases the history and culture of immigration in France from the early nineteenth century to the present and contains interactive exhibits presenting immigrant stories in multimedia form.

Another museum displaying collections of indigenous art, cultures and civilizations from Africa, Asia, Oceania and the Americas was opened in June 2006. Located close to the Eiffel Tower, the Quai Branly Museum is a new emblematic Parisian landmark which contains the exhibits of the now closed Musée National des Arts d'Afrique et d'Océanie and the ethnographic department of the Musée de l'Homme. The launch of this new center displaying artifacts many of which were acquired in the former colonies marks a turning point in French cultural identity and dominant attitudes toward difference. The museum not only displays exhibits dedicated to "primitive art" but also offers series of conferences and workshops. It hosts a so-called "université populaire" which proposes discussions and debates on the notions of difference, memory, colonial history, decolonization and otherness.

Another cultural milestone in the French Republic's progressive coming to terms with ethnic and cultural diversity was the admission of tribal and aboriginal art in the prestigious Louvre which opened in 2000 a wing devoted to masterpieces from Africa, Asia, Oceania and the Americas. This event of symbolic importance was supported by President Jacques Chirac, a fervent admirer of primitive art. In November 2006 the museum hosted a series of events entitled "The Foreigner's Home," a multidisciplinary program focused on displacement, immigration and exile. Nobel Prize winner African-American writer Toni Morrison, who was invited to host a "conversation" between the arts around a theme of her choice, selected the topic of foreigners enriching countries where they settle. Featuring an installation by the American choreographer William Forsythe and the German sculptor and video artist Peter Welz, a live concert by the Malian musician Toumani Diabaté, a retrospective of movies by the African-American director Charles Burnett, debates with transnational writers Edwige Danticat, Michael Ondaatje, Fatou Diome and Boubacar Boris Diop and a poetry slam with popular rappers in front of Géricault's "Medusa," the project demonstrated the creative energy of displaced populations.

Finally, two recent exhibits at the Parisian Hôtel de Ville demonstrated the City of Light's new willingness to acknowledge diversity as well as postcolonial or transcultural memory. Inaugurated in April 2009, a series of photographs, documents and personal belongings related to the nearly 70,000 immigrants from the French West Indies in the 1960s–1980s were exhibited under the title "Mémoires d'outremer." Commemorating for the first time colonial history and slavery on an emblematic site in central Paris, a massive wall was displayed as part of the exhibit, featuring the names of slaves liberated from French colonies in 1848. In February 2010, another exhibit entitled "Paris: 150 years of immigration" was displayed outside the Hôtel de Ville, celebrating the French capital's multicultural roots and ethnically and culturally mixed population. Despite vehement public debates surrounding the creation of new commemorative sites and the sometimes controversial reception of exhibits presenting new approaches to the themes of multicultural society and colonial or postcolonial history, the launch of these new Parisian landmarks demonstrates clearly the emergence of a new cosmopolitan stance acknowledging diversity and multiculturalism as part of the contemporary French culture and Parisian identity.

Conclusion

Today's global metropolises are cosmopolitan cities where racial, ethnic, religious, cultural and sexual differences make part of the inhabitants' daily experience and practice. This feature can be assessed in different ways in urban discourses of self-representation and city branding. While certain cities such as London value representations of their own cultural diversity and use it as the main selling proposal in their branding strategies, other metropolises like Paris conceive their multicultural aspects as contradictory with their marketable images. In the case of Paris, branding strategies predominantly emphasize traditional images of Frenchness and seek to promote a culturally homogeneous identity which correspond less and less to the city's population. These opposed marketing strategies go hand-in-hand with different ways of using the notions of "cultural capitals" versus "cosmopolitan," "transnational," "multicultural" and "postcolonial" cities in urban discourses. It is striking that French discourses describing Paris traditionally favor the first two adjectives, while the latter three more regularly feature in contemporary depictions of London.

These differences in the cities' self-representation do not result from significant differences in the metropolises' history or organic structures. Paris has performed the same role as London as a major gateway city for overseas migrants. Because of their size and the structure of their labor markets and the career opportunities and cultural assets they offer, both capitals are key migrant destinations. They also share similar patterns in post-war immigration which in both cities consisted of three main waves: the labor immigration of the 1950s attracting workers mainly from the former colonies, the family reunification of the 1970s and 1980s and today's post-industrial migration comprising a mixture of asylum seekers and highly skilled international migrants. Currently, Paris and London are both experiencing the same processes of gentrification and growing internationalization, play a comparable role as cultural capitals and constitute similar nodes in global cultural flows.

Differences in both metropolises' predominant narratives of self-representation are rather due to the importance of Republican ideology in France which advocates integration through assimilation while contemporary neoliberal Britain is more tolerant toward communities displaying their cultural difference and less uncomfortable with its colonial legacy. These fundamental differences are particularly well demonstrated by both countries' respective commemorative practices and by the reluctance in French academia to study in literature, films and other art forms diasporic or multicultural representations of Paris that contradict dominant narratives of the French capital. However, in recent years, both artists and academics seem to have been taking a growing interest in Paris' colonial legacy and multicultural diversity. A similar shift can be observed in urban policies and educative and commemorative practices which are exemplified by recent exhibits dedicated to immigrant contribution to Parisian history and French national identity.

Bibliography

Ball, J.C. 2004. *Imagining London: Postcolonial Fiction and the Transnational Metropolis.* Toronto, Buffalo and London: University of Toronto Press.

Blanchard, P., Bancel, N. and Lemaire, S. 2005. *La Fracture coloniale: La société française au prisme de l'héritage colonial.* Paris : La Découverte.

Binnie, J., Holloway, J., Millington, S. and Young, C. 2006. *Cosmopolitan Urbanism*. London: Routledge.
Breckenridge, C.A., Pollock, S., Bhabha, H. and Chakrabarty, D. 2002. *Cosmopolitanism*. Durham, NC: Duke University Press.
Casanova, P. 2004. *The World Republic of Letters*. Cambridge, MA: Harvard University Press.
Cohen, R. 1997. *Global Diasporas. An Introduction*. London: UCL Press.
Dikeç, M. 2007. *Badlands of the Republic: Space, Politics and Urban Policy*. Oxford: Blackwell.
Florida, R. 2002. *The Rise of the Creative Class: And How it's Transforming Work, Leisure, Community and Everyday Life*. New York: Perseus Book Group.
Forsdick, C. and Murphy, D. 2003. *Francophone Postcolonial Studies: A Critical Introduction*. Oxford: Oxford University Press.
Fourcaut, A., Bellanger, E. and Flonneau, M. 2007. *Paris/Banlieues: Conflits et solidarités*. Grane: Creaphis.
Friedmann, J. and Wolff, K. 1982. World city formation: an agenda of social action. *International Journal of Urban and Regional Research*, 6, 309–44.
Gilroy, P. 1992. *There Ain't No Black in the Union Jack. The Cultural Politics of State and Nation*. London: Routledge.
Hamnett, C. 2003. *Unequal City. London in the Global Arena*. London: Routledge.
Hannerz, U. 1996. *Transnational Connections*. London: Routledge.
Hargreaves, A. 2007. *Multi-Ethnic France: Immigration, Politics, Culture and Society*. London: Routledge.
Hemelryk Donald, S., Kofman, E. and Kevin, C. 2009. *Branding Cities. Cosmopolitanism, Parochialism and Social Change*. London: Routledge.
Joppke, C. and Lukes, S. 1999. *Multicultural Questions*. Oxford: Oxford University Press.
Les Immigrés en France, INSEE-Références, édition 2005.
Mabanckou, A. 1998. *Bleu-Blanc-Rouge*. Paris: Présence Africaine.
Mabanckou, A. 2009. *Black Bazar*. Paris: Seuil.
McLeod, J. 2004. *Postcolonial London: Rewriting the Metropolis*. London: Routledge.
Massey, D. 2007. *World City*. Cambridge: Polity Press.
Pinçon, M. and Pinçon-Charlot, M. 2004. *Sociologie de Paris*. Paris: La Découverte.
Sassen, S. 1991. *The Global City*. Princeton: Princeton University Press.
Smith, M.P. 2001. *Transnational Urbanism: Locating Globalization*. Oxford: Blackwell.
Stébé, J.-M. 1999. *La Crise des banlieues*. Paris: Presses Universitaires de France.
Stora, B. 2007. *La Guerre des mémoires. La France face a son passé colonial*. Paris: éditions de l'Aube.
Werbner, P. 2008. *Anthropology and the New Cosmopolitanism. Rotted, Feminist and Vernacular Perspectives*. Oxford: Berg.

Films

Benguigui, Y. (2008) *9/3, Memories of a Territory*.

Benguigui, Y. (2009) *Aïcha*.
Jeunet, J.-P. (2001) *Amélie*.
Klapish, C. (1996) *When the Cat's Away*.
Klapish, C. (2008) *Paris*.
Lemesle, B. (2010) *The Goutte d'Or: Living Together*.

Websites retrieved on October 20, 2010

www.mediapart.fr/club/edition/les-invites-de-mediapart/article/241008/le-9-3-de-yamina-benguigui-un-usage-falsifie-de

www.lagendagolfe.com/ViewArticle.asp?Page_Id=36

www.china.org.cn/english/2004/Jan/85464.htm

www.nytimes.com/2006/11/15/world/europe/15iht-entracte.3550088.html?_r=1

www.eurocheapo.com/blog/paris-free-cultural-exhibits-at-the-hotel-de-ville.html

www.nytimes.com/2006/11/15/world/europe/15iht-entracte.3550088.html?pagewanted=2&_r=1

www.louvre.fr/media/repository/ressources/sources/pdf/DPToniMorrisonlightENGLISH_v2_m56577569831144595

www.history.ac.uk/ihr/Focus/Migration/resources.html

www.20thcenturylondon.org.uk/

6

Paradoxes of Postcolonial Vernacular Cosmopolitanism in South Asia and the Diaspora

Pnina Werbner

Introduction

It is now more than 20 years since the fatwa calling for the death of Salman Rushdie, transmitted globally from Tehran, was pronounced by the Ayatollah Khomeini. *The Satanic Verses*, the book that evoked the wrath of the Ayatollah, was written by an Indian-born Pakistani postcolonial novelist; a Cambridge graduate living in London and writing in English. The book was an open and explicit attack on all 'fundamentalist' pretences to purity, whether Islamic, Hindu or neoliberal, and it responded to the threat posed by the Iranian Islamic revolution, President Zia's Islamizing military dictatorship in Pakistan, the rise of the Hindu nationalist Right in India and the emergence of Thatcherite Britain with its doctrinaire neoliberal philosophy. Against all those 'pure' fundamentalisms, the book extolled an 'impure' culture and religion imbued with popular and global aesthetics: of poetry, music, cinema, art. It portrayed an alternative society – a multicultural Britain, a tolerant peaceful India, an open, universal Sufi Islam. Its very language was hybrid – English mixed with Urdu words and expressions – and one of its anti-heroes, Gabriel, was a famous Indian cinema actor in religious 'mythologicals'. In the novel, the Prophet Muhammad was depicted as a poet in spite of himself. But, as many scholars recognize (e.g. Fischer and Abedi 1990, see Werbner 2002), to understand the book's message a reader would have to be familiar with the central paradigmatic myths and intellectual writings of a wide range of intellectual traditions: the Koran, the Hindu *Mahabarata*, Gramsci, Fanon, Blake, Shakespeare, Persian satirical poetry. Whatever the novelist's intentions, this very diversity of mythological and epic sources makes it inaccessible to Muslims and non-Muslims alike. The world-embracing fusion of Indian, Islamic and English literary epic traditions allegorized in *The Satanic Verses* is lost, in other words, on most readers. Diaspora South Asian Muslims – and indeed Muslims worldwide – could not be blamed thus for thinking that *The Satanic Verses* was a deliberate, iconoclastic, offensive, even blasphemous vilification of the Prophet of Islam, the 'Perfect Man' of Sufi tradition.

Rushdie's project of fusing different traditions and representing the enormous diversity of India's vernacular cultures had begun even earlier, in *Midnight's Children*, the novel that told the story of India's birth as a nation. As he explained in a preface to the 2006 paperback edition, his aim in the novel was to create 'a literary idiolect that allowed the rhythms and thought patterns of Indian languages to blend with the idiosyncrasies of "Hinglish" and "Bambaiyya", the polyglot street slang of Bombay' (2006: xiv). The central plot of this novel relates to the hero's telepathic capacity to hear and comprehend the 'inner monologues of all the so-called teeming millions, of masses and classes alike' that 'babbled in everything from Malayalam to Naga dialects, from the purity of Lucknow Urdu to the Southern slurrings of Tamil' (ibid.: 232).

Like *Midnight's Children*, the present chapter considers the Indian subcontinent and its global diaspora(s) as a vernacular cosmopolis, divided by religion, nation and language, and yet nevertheless united by mutually comprehensible popular aesthetics. The task posed here is, in the first instance, to disentangle the ambiguities inherent in the very notion of vernacular cosmopolitanism before going on to analyse, first, Sufi pilgrimage cults in South Asia and the diaspora and second, Indian film, popularly known as 'Bollywood' and now having a global reach, as vernacular cosmopolis. Within South Asia, I will argue, Bollywood transcends the spaces of the region's cultural and religious diversity, despite its deep divisions. This encompassing capacity is one rooted in Indian popular cinema's sensual aesthetics, which has arguably created a Bollywood 'sensorium'.[1] Unlike Rushdie's intentional and sometimes deliberately provocative literary and vernacular hybridities, Bollywood's sensorium, much like its American counterpart, Hollywood, appears to have grown organically out of the contributions and appropriations of a multitude of artists, writers and performers, drawing on diverse traditions, many of whom originate from India's diverse minorities, alongside the majority Hindu and Hindi-speaking population.

Before pursuing this argument further, the need is first to disentangle what we mean by vernacular cosmopolitanism.

Vernacular Cosmopolitanism

The notion of vernacular cosmopolitanism has been used to refer to alternative, particularly non-Western, forms of cosmopolitanism, the latter defined broadly as an openness to difference, whether to other ethnic groups, cultures, religions or nations.[2] As a concept that joins contradictory notions of local specificity and universal enlightenment, vernacular cosmopolitanism can be located at the crux

---

1   I owe this insight to Marie Gillespie.
2   For a range of examples, see the contributions to Werbner (2008).

of current debates on cosmopolitanism. These pose the question whether the local, parochial, rooted, culturally specific and demotic may coexist with the translocal, transnational, transcendent, elitist, enlightened, universalist and modernist – whether boundary-crossing demotic cultures and migrations may be compared to the sophisticated cultures of globetrotting travellers or the moral worldview of deracinated intellectuals. Indeed, the question is often reversed to ask whether there can even be an enlightened normative cosmopolitanism which is not rooted, in the final analysis, in patriotic and culturally committed loyalties and understandings. Kwame Anthony Appiah (1998), for example, evokes the notion of cosmopolitan 'patriotism', a 'rooted' cosmopolitanism, and proposes that cosmopolitans begin from membership in morally and emotionally significant communities (families, ethnic groups) while espousing notions of toleration and openness to the world, the transcendence of ethnic difference and the moral responsibility for and incorporation of the other. As he recognizes, postcolonial migrants elites may and do feel sentimentally attached to several homes in several different countries.

Seen theoretically, then, vernacular cosmopolitanism belongs to a family of concepts all of which combine in similar fashion apparently contradictory opposites: cosmopolitan patriotism, rooted cosmopolitanism, cosmopolitan ethnicity, working class cosmopolitanism, discrepant cosmopolitanism.[3] Such conjunctions attempt to come to terms with the conjunctural elements of postcolonial and precolonial intercultural and political encounters, while probing the conceptual boundaries of cosmopolitanism and its usefulness as an analytic concept.

The parameters of vernacular cosmopolitanism remain, however, ambiguous: are we talking about demotic forms of travel and trade across borders in the postcolonial world, as in the case of the Senegalese Mourides described by Diouf (2000), or of the tolerant worldviews of Sufi labour migrants working in the Gulf, whom I describe elsewhere as 'working class cosmopolitans' (Werbner 1999)? Or are we talking of non-European but nevertheless high cultures produced and consumed by non-Western elites, such as those of the Sanskritic, Urdu, Persian, Arabic or Ottoman worlds? The Sanskritic cosmopolis in precolonial Asia, Pollock tells us (2000), spanned an area extending from Afghanistan to Java and from Sri Lanka to Nepal in the first millennium, a non-Western but nevertheless cosmopolitan literary world that he contrasts with the vernacular traditions that succeeded it. Are we to define, by analogy, contemporary Hindi/Urdu, Cantonese or Southeast Asian mass-consumer and mediatized cultural worlds as cosmopolitan, or as vernacular, or both?[4]

In disentangling these conceptual ambiguities we are confronted with a paradox: since all vernacular languages or cultures are naturally, organically, hybrid and hybridizing, in the way argued by Bakhtin (1981), while at the same time they retain their distinctive local, even parochial identity, then the conjunction of the vernacular with the cosmopolitan appears to be an internal contradiction, an

---

3   On cosmopolitan ethnicity see Richard Werbner (2002).
4   On the latter see contributions to Robinson (2007).

oxymoron. But this view implies a closing of space, an extremely restricted local localness. Hence Briggs argues that

> [O]ne of the cornerstones of projects of modernity has been to construct a moral opposition between vernacularism and cosmopolitanism that denigrates the former and valorises the latter ... [in order to maintain] elite control over vernacular subjects. (Briggs 2005: 77)[5]

My argument here is that, by contrast, the South Asian vernacular cosmopolis, represented and embodied most saliently in Indian popular cinema, is a hybrid mixture of a wide range of traditions and languages within the space of South Asia. Its eclectic origins and heteroglossic, carnevalesque assemblages have led commentators to note its transcendent, extra-national self-contained cultural 'autonomy' (Gopal and Moorti 2008: 15), articulating an 'alternative cosmopolitanism' and offering a counterpoint to 'neotraditionalist discourses' of nation (ibid.: 32). This enables it to reach out across the whole region, to Muslims, Hindus and Sikhs, to Pakistanis and Indians. Since the 1980s, this distinctively South Asian cosmopolis has sometimes been threatened by a Hindi takeover, but in a more recent countermovement, the undermining of the polyglot, heteroglossic, carnevalesque assemblage that Bollywood represents appears to have failed as the genre increasingly moves into a new phase – that of diasporizing and opening up globally. Indeed, the continuous dialectic in Indian film between local and cosmopolitan vernaculars, between the pure and the impure, the fundamentalist and syncretic, represents, perhaps, the wider story of South Asia and its diasporas, a proposition that I hope will become clearer in the course of this chapter.

Popular versus Elite Forms of Vernacular Cosmopolitanism

Can the novels of colonial and postcolonial intellectuals written in the language of the imperial colonist, be regarded as exemplars of vernacular cosmopolitanism? Against this claim, Timothy Brennan has argued that third world novels in English by diasporic writers such as Salman Rushdie, while admittedly promoting genuine aesthetic novelty or 'hybridity' within the English novel, are celebrated because they fit a Western liberal aesthetics and novelty-dominated consumer market. By contrast, politically committed third world novelists like the Egyptian Naguib Mahfouz, who write from within richly layered indigenous aesthetic traditions and address Arab audiences beyond the English-speaking metropolis, are marginalized (Brennan 1997: 37–43). In similar vein Aijaz Ahmad, reflecting on the new Urdu writers' realist literary movement in South Asia in the 1930s, critiques Frederic

---

5   Briggs' argument, against that view, that both Boas and Du Bois advocated a kind of vernacular cosmopolitanism. The weakness in his argument is that he often tends to equate cosmopolitanism with globalization.

Paradoxes of Postcolonial Vernacular Cosmopolitanism

Jameson's essentialist proposition that all 'Third' world literature is ultimately to be read as 'nationalist allegory' – a response to the 'experience of colonialism and imperialism'. The lumping together of all 'Third World' novels as the Other of the West, Ahmad proposes, effaces the autonomous bases of non-Western literatures and effectively constitutes them as an 'absence', a negative mirroring (Ahmad 1992: 100 and *passim*). Yet not only, he says, is most literature outside the West not even written in English; even more crucially, far from being exclusively preoccupied with the confrontation of their nations with imperialism and colonialism, the agendas of the Urdu realist writers were often highly complex and internally focused, demanding that

> *a critique of others (anti-colonialism) be conducted in the perspective of an even more comprehensive, multifaceted critique of ourselves: our class structures, our familial ideologies, our management of bodies and sexualities, our idealisms, our silences. (Ahmad 1992: 118)*

In other words, there can be no separation of the agonism of internal moral debates from broader ethical questions surrounding ethnic or national differences.

The dichotomy identified by Brennan or Ahmad appears to set a limit to high-cultural vernacular cosmopolitanism: they are novels inspired by a cosmopolitan world consciousness but written in the vernacular and thus accessible only in translation to Western readers. Against that, it may be argued that colonial and postcolonial novels that incorporate the vernacular into an imperial world language, much as Rushdie does, occupy a unique border zone defining the limits of vernacular cosmopolitanism. A fascinating example from the Philippines is that of José Rizal's anti-colonial masterpiece, *Noli me Tangere*, published in Berlin in 1887 and written in Spanish, the language of the colonial master, understood at the time by only 5 per cent of the Philippines' population. The novel, a satirical critique of race, class and cruel clerical mendacity, is cosmopolitan in its intellectual allusions to world literature and languages[6] while being embedded in the vernacular: in words, places, persons and scenes intimately familiar to Filipinos. As Benedict Anderson comments poetically,

> *Rizal's Spanish text is bejewelled with Tagalog words and expressions. Sometimes they are deployed for sheer comic effect, sometimes to deepen the reader's sense of the conflicts between peninsular Spaniards, creoles, mestizos and Indios. But most often they simply reflect, as did the Anglo-Indian that developed in Victorian times, the casual penetration of the imperial vernacular by local languages. (1998: 241)*

---

6 Hence Benedict Anderson makes the point that almost a fifth of the 64 chapters of *Noli* begin with epigraphs 'taken from poets, dramatists, philosophers, the Bible ... and come in Spanish, Italian, Latin, and even Hebrew' (2005: 51). We find references in the novel to a 'Filipino Rothschild' (p. 255), to Aristotle's categories (p. 464), all in the spirit of a new world in which 'the old gods are gone' (p. 465).

So too, *Noli* is

> *replete with references to, and descriptions of, streets, churches, neighbourhoods, cafés, esplanades, theatres, and so forth. ... The density of these places and placenames are among the elements that give the reader the most vivid sense of being drawn deep inside the novel. (1998: 243)*

This localizing and vernacularizing movement in the novel, along with its emancipatory cosmopolitan message, enable its readers to 'imagine' a nation on the edge of being born out of its multifarious ethnic groups and dialects (Anderson 1983: 26–7, 30).

As in the Philippines, so too in postcolonial Nigeria, the dilemma posed by the highly restrictive domestic readership for original novels for Anglophone Nigerian writers is how to develop 'expressive forms which acknowledge the history of local symbolic and cultural practices and which strive for a direct didactic or political impact' (Smith 2005: 280); they resist the view that one 'can become a member of the cosmopolitan literary ecumene *only* by taking the bend in the road which leads away from home' (*ibid.*: 281, italics in the original), but the reliance on an international readership compels novelists to adopt a 'cosmopolitan tenor' (*ibid.*: 10) while not abandoning the specifically Nigerian vernacular 'cadences, resonances and nuances of the language' (*ibid.*: 285).

If hybridized Anglophone or Latino colonial and postcolonial novels occupy the border zone between third world vernacular writings and Western aesthetic works, much of the scholarly interest in vernacular cosmopolitanism has focused on indigenous, demotic or popular forms of intercultural life worlds. In particular, the notion that there are many, different, cosmopolitan practices with their own historicities and distinctive worldviews, all coexisting in late modernity, has led to an exploration of marginal cosmopolitanisms. Homi Bhabha, who possibly coined the term vernacular cosmopolitanism, is uneasy with Martha Nussbaum's image of the self as at the centre of a series of concentric circles, with universal liberal values privileged above family, ethnic group or nation (Nussbaum 1994). The notion of a borderless cosmopolitan community seems inadequate, he says, in relation to the millions of refugees and migrants fleeing violence and poverty. Drawing on Appiah's vision, Bhabha proposes a 'cosmopolitan community envisaged in *marginality*', a border zone which he terms vernacular cosmopolitanism (1996: 195–6).

The challenge to the idea that cosmopolitans are necessarily members of the elite was first posed by James Clifford who reflects on the status of companion servants, guides and migrant labourers, and the grounds of equivalence between privileged and unprivileged travellers (1992: 106–7). Critiquing Hannerz's (1992) original depiction of cosmopolitan subjectivity as elitist, Clifford (1992: 107) proposes that 'the project of comparing and translating different travelling cultures need not be class- or ethno-centric'. The differential, often violent, displacements that impel locals to travel create, he says, 'discrepant' cosmopolitanisms (Clifford 1992: 108).

Paradoxes of Postcolonial Vernacular Cosmopolitanism

Despite the fact that Hannerz (2004: 77) has revised his position, acknowledging that more people beyond the elite may now be identified as cosmopolitan, he nevertheless notes that 'bottom-up' cosmopolitans are unlikely to be recognized as such in their own environment. This raises the critical question of cosmopolitan consciousness: in what sense does cosmopolitanism need to be grounded in an open, experimental, inclusive, normative consciousness of the cultural other? Such a consciousness would need to include elements of self-doubt and reflexive self-distantiation, an awareness of the existence and equal validity of other cultures, other values, and other mores. Is travel without such an inclusive consciousness cosmopolitan? Does travel inevitably lead to such openness and reflexivity? Despite their global commercial acumen, Senegalese Mouride traders are said to engage in 'rites of social exclusiveness' so that 'Mouride diasporic culture is homogenised in a way that excludes foreign values' (Diouf 2000: 694, 695). Similarly, members of the jet-setting wealthy Chinese overseas trading diaspora studied by Aihwa Ong, with their multiple passports and multiple homes in different countries, appear to lack the kind of cultural openness and sensitivity normally associated with cosmopolitanism. Diasporas, by definition, are heterogeneous, and not all their members are equally cosmopolitan. Sometimes it is factory workers rather than wealthy merchants who display more openness to their non-diasporic compatriots (Werbner 1999). Diasporic intellectuals may be alienated from working class compatriots despite their celebration of cultural hybridity as Friedman (1997) has suggested. But not all diasporic elites are so alienated. Similarly, not all Senegalese in Italy are inward looking, even if Mourides regard Italy as a 'polluting' environment. Riccio reports that Senegalese in Italy are a multi-ethnic and multi-religious community who seek, as one migrant told him, not 'only to look for jobs. To emigrate is to know new things, to broaden one's horizons in such a way that one can bring back home what one discovered and learned'.

It has been argued that cosmopolitanism is always 'situated' (Robbins 1998, Werbner 2008) and this is all the more so in the case of vernacular cosmopolitanism. Indeed, much depends on context. Some environments are more cosmopolitan than others. Zubaida (1999) invokes the 'legendary cosmopolitan enclaves of Cairo, but especially Alexandria, the paradigm case of Middle Eastern cosmopolitanism' – a hub of ideas, religions, goods and people from East and West, protected by an imperial context. Thessalonica was, according to Kenneth Brown (2006), 'a great Balkan cosmopolitan city for centuries, a veritable Babel of languages, religions, cultures and local traditions'. Ashis Nandy describes the cosmopolitanism of contemporary Cochin on the Malabar coast – 'the ultimate symbol of cultural diversity and religious and ethnic tolerance' (Nandy 2002: 158 *passim*). If we take vernacular cosmopolitanism to refer to a multi-centred world, beyond the West, in the sense proposed by Arjun Appadurai (1990), it is perhaps among the elites of such cosmopolitan cities in South Asia and elsewhere that distinctive vernacular cosmopolitanisms are created.

Complex Diasporas[7]

Given this potential for an inclusive vernacular cosmopolitanism in South Asia, what happens when economic migrants from the whole subcontinent, divided by nationality, religion and language but united by a shared popular culture, cuisine, music and custom, settle permanently in a Western country like Britain or the United States? What kind of diasporas does such a heterogeneous and yet in many ways homogeneous group form?

One result is the emergence of two alternative visible diasporic public spheres in Britain created by South Asian settlers,[8] the one, 'pure' nationalist or religious, the other resistant and yet complicit, produced through the entertainment industry – commercial film, novels and other media – that tells a story of cultural hybridity and cosmopolitanism, of inter-generational conflict, inter-ethnic or inter-racial marriage, family politics and excesses of consumption; a cultural arena produced by British South Asians intellectuals, that makes its distinctive contribution to British and South Asian popular culture by satirizing the parochialism and conservatism of the South Asian immigrant generation.

The fact that, as in South Asia, similar vernacular cultural tastes, cuisines, music, sport, poetry, fashion and film are widely enjoyed across vast geographical regions points to a key feature of late modern diasporas (and indeed of some earlier ones) which has remained so far untheorized in the scholarly literature. The Jewish model of diaspora, often taken as archetypal, is in a critical sense misleading, because Jewish religion, culture and national political orientation (to Zion, to the memory of the Holocaust) coincide, despite geographical dispersion and despite internal religious or political disagreements. This is true also of the Armenian and Greek diasporas, each of which shares a place of origin, unique history and specific Christian liturgical tradition. But where vast cultural regions of consumption do *not* simply coincide with either religion or national homelands, as is true for South Asians, Middle Eastern Arabs, Latin Americans, Afro-Caribbeans and possibly even Chinese, we may talk of '*complex*' or '*segmented*' diasporas; segmented, because members of such diasporas may unite together in some contexts and oppose each other in other contexts. Their members' identities, in other words, are not fixed but situationally determined. In such complex, segmented diasporas the fact that people from a particular region share a rich material culture of consumption, both high cultural and popular, and sometimes a dominant religion (e.g. Islam, Catholicism) across a large number of nation-states, creates public arenas and economic channels for cooperation and communal enjoyment, *which cut across the national origins or religious beliefs of performers and participants.*

The South Asian regional diaspora of vernacular cultural consumption in no way determines either political loyalties and commitments or more focused exilic yearnings for a lost homeland. It is quite possible for people from a single cultural region to be locked in bitter national or religious conflicts. In the diaspora, however,

---

7   This section is extracted from Werbner (2004).
8   On different cultural arenas in the diasporic public sphere see Werbner (2002).

the sharing of a regional culture can create cross-cutting ties and the potential for transcendent coalitions and alliances which mitigate such conflicts.

Regional and inter-regional cultural sharing, a vernacular cosmopolitanism, is rooted in many respects in shared traditions of ritual and celebration. Among these I want to single out here one in particular: Sufi pilgrimage regional cults.

Pilgrimage and Sufi Regional Cults

Pilgrimage centres, whether Mecca, Rome, or the basilica of Our Lady in Guadalupe in Mexico, attract millions of devotees annually. They come from many different countries, and many have travelled long distances. Such shrines seem to epitomize the utopian vision of the Prophet Isaiah when he prophesized that at the end of the days 'all nations will flow' to the mountain of God in peace. Victor Turner labelled the harmony at great pilgrimage centres as 'communitas', the erasure of structure and hierarchy. Against that, much anthropological research has shown that shrines can be sites of conflicts and misunderstanding, often between co-religionists regarding the significance of the sacred centre, and different visions of Christianity or Islam. In contemporary South Asia, however, where communal violence between Hindus and Muslims has made religion intensely politicized, pilgrimage shrines to Sufi saints are widely held to be havens of amity between Muslims and Hindus; of a genuinely vernacular cosmopolitanism.

This utopian vision of Sufism and Sufi pilgrimage has, however, had its critics. They argue against the view among Indian postcolonial scholars (e.g. Nandy 1990) who extol syncretic folk religions, such as that practised at saints' shrines, as the answer to India's religious 'fundamentalisms' and their associated communal conflicts. Peter van der Veer, for example, argues that although Muslim shrines attract both Muslim and Hindu worshippers, they do so for different reasons: whereas for Muslim followers, a spiritual relationship to the saint, or *pir*, is of central importance, Hindus see the *dargah* mainly as a healing domain specializing in the cure of demonic illnesses. Consequently, Muslims and Hindus are clearly divided by different degrees of participation and non-participation in rituals defined as Islamic, such as prayers in the mosque (1994a: 207, 1994b). Sufi shrines, in other words, do not provide the context for intercultural communication. Other scholars, however, such as Helena Basu (1998) or Saheb (1998), have shown that there are indeed Muslim shrines that create islands of Hindu and Muslim communal harmony.

Those on the negative side of the debate like van der Veer maintain that the mere presence of Hindus at Muslim shrines cannot be taken as a sign of a commonly shared, syncretic folk-religion. Rather, the different meanings and values associated with pilgrimages and visitations to Muslim shrines must be carefully delineated. Against that, on the positive side others argue that while the interpretation of the meaning of pilgrimage rituals or of the saint may vary, Hindus and Muslims worship *in amity* (see also Werbner 2010). This inclusive aspect of local Islam is stressed by Saheb (1998), for example, as being the 'universalist' dimension of the cult of Nagor-e-Sharif in Tamil Nadu. At that shrine, established since the sixteenth century, various communities of Hindus and Muslims come from as far away as Sri Lanka and Singapore, and participate as equals in the processions to the shrine centre, but Hindus construct the saint as a deity, whereas for the Muslims he was/is an extraordinary man. Clearly, the charismatic power embodied by a Sufi shrine is dependent on the cosmological ideas actors bring to bear on his image.

Despite this divergence of interpretation, Muslims do not perceive of the presence of Hindus at shrines as indicative of non-Islamic practices. On the contrary, the symbolic repertoires of regional saints' cults in South Asia reinforce beliefs in the universalism of Islam. The Sufi fable of saintly world renunciation and closeness to God is widely shared throughout the region. Even though each specific cult is deeply embedded in and shapes a local environment, all address similar ontological themes related to death, place and embodiment through which sanctity and sainthood are constructed (see Werbner 2003). To argue that these practices are marginal to the 'true' Islam represented by the mosque and the *ulema* is to misrecognize the centrality of eschatological ideas about redemption and salvation to Islam more generally.

In the perception of followers and devotees, saints' shrines create a haven of blessed tranquillity and peace, *sukun*, within an alternative universe of ethical meanings. Rather than being merely a magical source of healing, for devotees saintly charisma embodies an emotional and moral space and is at the hub of a sacred topography. In different ethnographic contexts in South Asia, the sacred aura of a saint, his *baraka*, *karamat* or *faiz*, is revealed as an embodied quality of exemplary persons. These outstanding individuals create for followers and supplicants spaces of potential freedom which extend geographically across administrative and even national boundaries. They bring into dialectical conjunction a series of apparent opposites – between universalism and particularism, inclusiveness and exclusiveness, hierarchy and equality. They deny the importance of difference. All followers are united in their devotion and love of the saint, alive or dead. The vitality of Sufism thus derives not only from the ritual devotional practices around saints' shrines, but from the way ritual is embedded in Sufi mystical philosophy, emotional proximity and a utopian imaginary of an alternative social order.

The intercultural atmosphere of tolerance evident at Sufi annual festivals in South Asia can be found elsewhere in the Muslim world too. Schielke (2008) describes the carnivalesque atmosphere at annual *mulid* festivals in Egypt, marked by an ethos of joyful inclusiveness. Differences between Islamic religious tendencies, gender or class are erased so that a 'famous actress can eat next to a beggar, and there is no difference between them'. Attempts by Islamic reformists in the Egyptian administration to control what they regard as the disorderly dimensions of these festivals, with their crowds, music, trangressive alcohol drinking, gambling and spontaneous mingling between the sexes in intercultural amity, seem to be, in the long run, doomed to failure, however.

The annual celebration at a saint's lodge or shrine in South Asia gathers together individual supplicants and pilgrims alongside organized groups of devotees and disciples who visit the festival annually and cultivate a special relation to the saint and the Sufi tariqa or order he founded. These groups often travel great distances to attend the annual ritual. They frequently come from different linguistic, ethnic and even religious groups. Although the celebration marks the high point of the year, it cannot be understood apart from the more enduring links that constitute the organization of the order.

Inclusivity, a form of vernacular cosmopolitanism, is thus a key feature of South Asian Sufi cults. Saiyed echoes other scholars when he contends that it is through Sufi shrines that 'the subcontinent saw the best part of Hindu-Muslim integration', and that it was 'the personal and spiritual influence of various saints that ... allowed for the peaceful coexistence of the two communities for several centuries on the Indian subcontinent' (Saiyed 1989: 242). The experience of communitas at pilgrimage centres, the true sense of love and camaraderie, comes from membership in a specific but deterritorialized organization. Jurgen Frembgen describes the pilgrimage to the shrine of Lal Shabaz Qalandar in Sehwan in Sind, a thirteenth-century shrine of a saint who preached peace between Hindus and Muslims, which nevertheless has sustained a regional cult organization (Frembgen 2011). Its disciples are *qalandar* dervishes who often grow their hair wild and are mendicants or faqirs. At the shrine during the *'urs* they dance a devotional dance known as 'dhammal', a frenzied and ecstatic swirl of the head and body performed to the rhythmic beat of the *dhole* (a big barrel-shaped drum). Bells, gongs, cymbals and horns make a thunderous din, while the dervishes, clad in long robes, beads, bracelets and coloured head-bands, whirl faster and faster in a hypnotic trance, until with a final deafening scream they run wildly through the doors of the shrine to the courtyard beyond. The devotees come from all over Pakistan. They make their way to the shrine in organized groups known as *jamaats* to arrive in time for the annual festival. They meet regularly with one another at the places where they usually live.

Sufi orders create global pathways along which labour migrants travel. In a case study told to me by a migrant at the lodge centre in Pakistan, he recounted how he overcame his trials and tribulations with the aid of his Sufi *shaykh* (for details see Werbner 1999). For Hajji Suleiman, during his transnational peregrinations 'home' was condensed in the image of his Sufi saint whom he mustered before his inner eye whenever he needed courage to confront superiors and foreigners. That image was always with him. His experience of overseas travel was thus not one of alienation but of triumphant mastery, rooted in his localized faith in his *shaykh* – which was, simultaneously, very much also a faith in Islam as a world religion. Hence, one of the most exhilarating aspects of his migration experience for him was the sense of Islam as a boundary-crossing global faith. His voluntary labour at the tomb of Abdul Qadr Gilani in pious service to God while working on a building site confirmed his identity in his own eyes as a cosmopolitan who is at home everywhere just as God is everywhere. So too, the pilgrimage to Mecca, which he performed several times during his stay in the Middle East, provided him with an experience of membership in a global community. He was determined to have that experience, even at the risk of losing a valuable job.

Although a simple man from a poor background and with little formal education, Hajji Suleiman clearly felt that the experience of labour migration has transformed him. He was competent now in the traditions of others. He understood the Japanese, his employers, intimately, having observed their minutest customs. By the same token, he had also observed the customs, habits and idiosyncrasies of Hindus, Bangladeshis, Arabs and Iraqis. He appeared to have had close cross-cultural friendships. His confidence was such that learning another language was regarded by him as a small matter. But when he considered moving to Europe, it was nevertheless from the vantage point of his most valued identity as a Sufi. If he moved to Holland, it would be with the mission to found a branch of his order there. He would utilize the Arabic picked up in the Gulf to create a cross-national Sufi community of Pakistanis, Turks and Arabs. He was certain he could do that, since he had lived with Muslims from other countries already. The world was mapped by him in terms of his Sufi order. Holland is an empty place, a void, since there is no branch of the order there. His perspective as a Sufi member of his *shaykh*'s transnational regional cult shapes his cosmopolitanism and provides it with a sense of order.

The Dialectics of Vernacular Cosmopolitanism: Bollywood

The relations between Sufi followers, venerators of saints' shrines, with their more inclusive and tolerant worldviews, and the iconoclastic, puritanical Islamists, have been antagonistic and highly politicized for hundreds of years in South Asia, and the battles have carried over into Britain, though in a attenuated form. The same puritans have also condemned Pakistani wedding ritual celebrations, with their overt sensuality, fun, dance, song and music. These too contain many themes that are widely prevalent across the whole of South Asia and its diasporas, from the use of turmeric and henna to ritual clowning and bawdy singing (see Werbner 2002/1990). Music and songs travel across the boundaries of religious communities. Not surprisingly, then, romance, love and weddings figure prominently in the shared vernacular cosmopolis of Bollywood.

Not only Muslims but the Hindu Right have objected to Bollywood as a site of 'vice' and loose morals. For Muslim hardliners, Bollywood is the epitome of all that is Hindu and beyond the pale. But the emergence of Bollywood, like the emergence of Hollywood, tells quite a different story. Foreigners, minorities and Muslims were there from the start. As Tabish Khair, an Indian scholar based at Aarhus University in Denmark, explains,[9] 'Bollywood' was only briefly, if ever, 'Hindi' cinema. To the extent that the term stands for 'mainstream Bombay cinema', until the 1980s Bollywood was dominated by Urdu, with its historical Muslim, high-cultural associations. All the major writers of Bombay cinema in the 1940s, 1950s and 1960s wrote in Urdu. Some were famous Urdu writers. A conscious use of

---

9   In a collaborative research project proposal I am currently preparing alongside others.

Hindi began creeping into Bollywood only in the 1980s. Although both Hindi and Urdu developed from a common trunk, nevertheless there are differences between the two languages today, and the two have been written and spoken (and heard) as different languages, at the very least by the middle classes, from early in the twentieth century onwards, if not earlier. Until the 1970s, no Bollywood actor could 'get away' with a 'Hindi' accent (s instead of sh, k instead of q in some words, etc.); they had to have an Urdu accent. The language was also Urdu, or Hindustani (Hindi + Urdu= the common trunk) leaning heavily towards Urdu. Parsis and especially Anglo-Indians, who were significant in the early silent films, largely disappeared in the talkies because they mostly did not have a chaste Urdu diction. Bombay cinema only became equated with Hindi post-1970s, when it came to be caught up in quasi-nationalist discourse.

This has obscured many aspects of Bombay cinema, and particularly the large-scale involvement of Muslims and other minorities in the industry. The most recent change in Bollywood as a linguistic and national film genre has been the adoption of a kind of semi-anglicized Hindustani accent by some of the younger stars today. This would have had audiences laughing themselves to death even two decades ago, but the new creolized linguistic turn once again has the capacity to reach out across the religious, national and ethnic divisions in the subcontinent – between Hindi and Urdu, India, Pakistan and Bangladesh, Hindus, Muslims, Bengalis and Sikhs.

Like Bollywood, the term 'diaspora' too cannot be used unproblematically when it comes to the Bombay cinema. One has to bear in mind two types of 'diaspora': South Asian communities outside India and different linguistic and cultural communities within colonial India and its emergent postcolonial nations. Right from the beginning, Bombay cinema attracted people from all over India. During Partition this meant that some people, like Raj Kapoor or Dilip Kumar, who were actually from Pakistan, ended up staying on in India, and some, like Saadat Hasan Manto, ended up leaving for Pakistan. There were also Parsis, Indian Jews and Anglo-Indians in the industry. Ashok Kumar, the first real star, was a Bengali. The appeal of Bombay cinema in the context of the global South Asian diaspora can only be understood if it is put in the context of its development and continuation as part of and inflected by its internal subcontinental 'diasporas'. It has always been an aesthetic and cultural melting pot, and hence its appeal was broader – and felt not only in India but in the rest of Asia, Africa and Eastern Europe, even before it came to the attention of Western viewers.

Diasporic South Asian audiences in the West appropriate and perform Bollywood songs and dances, irrespective of origin: Jewish Indians in Israel, Muslim Indians in East and South Africa, Sikhs in Britain, all draw from the Bollywood sensorium selectively, to perform and celebrate their own cultural events during weddings, in nightclubs, even in Hindu temples. This includes minority sexual communities such as gay South Asians (Dudrah 2006). Diasporics figure in Bollywood movies, now shown in mainline cinemas in the UK, just as these movies now include songs, dances and travel beyond the borders of India. The imagination of the vernacular cosmopolis which is South Asia has expanded beyond the boundaries of the subcontinent, along with its diasporas.

Bollywood clearly does not belong to a single, pure culture. It has created its own imaginary country, as Javed Akhtar playfully argues:

> There is one more state in this country and this is Hindi cinema ... Hindi cinema's culture is quite different from Indian culture, but it is not alien to us, we understand it. Hindi cinema is our closest neighbour. It has its own world, its own tradition, its own symbols, its own expressions, its own language and those who are familiar with it understand it. (Kabir 1999: 35, see also Gopal and Moorti 2008: 15)

It is this capacity to share popular culture across communal divisions which has allowed the different South Asian diasporas in the UK and elsewhere to coexist harmoniously, despite conflicts on the subcontinent. Bollywood is now playing a part of what has been called 'celluloid diplomacy' between India and Pakistan, allowing imports of Indian movies and other cultural products between the two countries. The threat to this fragile peace currently being negotiated, and with it a loss of a shared world of aesthetic pleasure, understandings and openness to hybridity, caricature, playfulness, fun, music and song, comes from the hardliner puritans, whether Muslims or Hindus.

Acknowledgements

A version of this chapter was first presented at the Graduate School Fall Colloquium on 'Reconvening Asia: Embodiment, Transformation, Space', School of Asian Languages and Cultures, University of Michigan, Ann Arbor, 23 October 2009, and drew on an ESRC research proposal to study 'Bollywood from the Margins'. I am grateful to the participants in the colloquium and especially to Tabish Khair, Gabriele Shenar, Rachel Dwyer, Raminder Kaur, Marie Gillespie and Rosie Thomas for their salient contributions to my understanding of Bollywood.

Bibliography

Ahmad, A. 1992. *In Theory: Classes, Nations, Literatures*. London: Verso.
Anderson, B. 1983. *Imagined Communities*. London: Verso.
Anderson, B. 1998. *The Spectre of Comparisons*. London: Verso.
Anderson, B. 2005. *Under Three Flags: Anarchism and the Anti-Colonial Imagination*. London: Verso.
Appadurai, A. 1990. Disjuncture and Difference in the Global Cultural Economy. *Theory, Culture and Society*, 7, 295–310.

Appiah, K.A. 1998. Cosmopolitan Patriots, in *Cosmopolitics: Thinking and Feeling Beyond the Nation*, edited by P. Cheah and B. Robbins. Minneapolis: University of Minnesota Press, 91–116.

Bakhtin, M. 1981. *The Dialogic Imagination*, trans. Caryl Emerson and Michael Holsquist. Austin: University of Texas Press.

Basu, H. 1998. Hierarchy and Emotion: Love, Joy and Sorrow in a Cult of Black Saints in Gujarat, India, in *Embodying Charisma: Modernity, Locality and the Performance of Emotion in Sufi Cults*, edited by P. Werbner and H. Basu. London: Routledge, 117–39.

Bhabha, H. 1996. Unsatisfied: Notes on Vernacular Cosmopolitanism, in *Text and Nation*, edited by L. Garcia-Morena and P.C. Pfeifer. London: Camden House, 191–207.

Brennan, T. 1997. *At Home in the World: The Cosmopolitan Now*. Cambridge, MA: Harvard University Press.

Briggs, C.S. 2005. Genealogies of Race and Culture and the Failure of Vernacular Cosmopolitanisms: Rereading Franz Boas and W.E.B. Du Bois. *Public Culture*, 17(1), 75–100.

Brown, K. 2006. Some Aspects of Cosmopolitanism. Paper presented at the Association of Anthropologists conference, Keele University, April 2006.

Clifford, J. 1992. Traveling Cultures, in *Cultural Studies*, edited by L. Grossberg, C. Nelson and P.A. Treichler. London: Routledge, 96–116.

Diouf, M. 2000. The Senegalese Murid Trade Diaspora and the Making of a Vernacular Cosmopolitanism. *Public Culture*, 12(3), 679–702.

Dudrah, R.K. 2006. *Bollywood: Sociology Goes to the Movies*. New Delhi: Sage Publications.

Fischer, M. and Abedi, M. 1990. *Debating Muslims: Cultural Dialogues in Postmodernity and Tradition*. Madison: University of Wisconsin Press.

Frembgen, J.W. 2011. *At the Shrine of the Red Sufi: Five Days and Nights on Pilgrimage in Pakistan*, translated from German by Jane Ripken. Karachi: Oxford University Press.

Friedman, J. 1997. Global Crises, the Struggle for Cultural Identity and Intellectual Porkbarrelling: Cosmopolitans Versus Locals, Ethnics and Nationals in an Era of De-Hegemonization, in *Debating Cultural Hybridity: Multi-Cultural Identities and the Politics of Anti-Racism*, edited by P. Werbner and T. Modood. London: Zed Books, 70–89.

Gopal, S. and Moorti, S. 2008. Introduction: Travels of Hindi Song and Dance, in *Global Bollywood: Travels of Hindi Song and Dance*, edited by S. Gopal and S. Moorti. Minneapolis: University of Minnesota Press, 1–60.

Hannerz, U. 1992. *Cultural Complexity: Studies in the Social Organisation of Meaning*. New York: Columbia University Press.

Hannerz, U. 2004. Cosmopolitanism, in *A Companion to the Anthropology of Politics*, edited by D. Nugent and J. Vincent. Oxford: Blackwell, 69–85.

Kabir, M.N. 1999. *Talking Films (Conversations on Hindi Cinema with Javed Akhtar)*. New Delhi: Oxford India.

Nandy, A. 1990. The Politics of Secularism and the Recovery of Religious Tolerance, in *Mirrors of Violence*, edited by V. Das. Delhi: Oxford University Press, 64–93.
Nandy, A. 2002. *Time Warps*. London: Hurst.
Nussbaum, M. 1994. Patriotism and Cosmopolitanism. *The Boston Review*, XIX(5).
Pollock, S. 2000. Cosmopolitan and Vernacular in History. *Public Culture*, 12(3), 591–625.
Riccio, B. 2004. Transnational Mouridism and the Afro-Muslim Critique of Italy. *Journal of Ethnic and Migration Studies*, 30(5), 929–44.
Rizal, J. 1887 [1996]. *Noli me Tangere*, trans. Ma. Soledad Lcason-Locsin. Makati: Bookmark.
Robbins, B. 1998 Comparative Cosmopolitanisms, in *Cosmopolitics: Thinking and Feeling Beyond the Nation*, edited by P. Cheah and B. Robbins. Minneapolis: University of Minnesota Press, 246–64.
Robinson, K. (ed.). 2007. *Southeast Asian and Pacific Cosmopolitans: Self and Subject in Motion*. London: Palgrave.
Rushdie, S. 1981/2006. *Midnight's Children*. London: Vintage Books.
Rushdie, S. 1988. *The Satanic Verses*. London: Virago.
Saheb, S.A.A. 1998. A 'Festival of Flags': Hindu-Muslim Devotion and the Sacralising of Localism at the Shrine of Nagore-e-Sharif, in *Embodying Charisma: Modernity, Locality and the Performance of Emotion in Sufi Cults*, edited by P. Werbner and H. Basu. London: Routledge, 55–76.
Saiyed, A.R. 1989. Saints and Dargahs in the Indian Subcontinent: A Review, in *Muslim Shrines in India: Their Character, History and Significance*, edited by C.W. Troll. Delhi: Oxford University Press, 240–56.
Schielke, S. 2008. Policing Ambiguity: Muslim Saints-Day Festivals and the Moral Geography of Public Space in Egypt. *American Ethnologist*, 35(4), 539–52.
Smith, A. 2005. Distance Between You and Your Home: The Estrangement of Postcolonial Writing. *Sociological Review*, 53(2), 275–93.
Van der Veer, P. 1994a. *Religious Nationalism: Hindus and Muslims in India*. Berkeley: University of California Press.
Van der Veer, P. 1994b. Syncretism, Multiculturalism and the Discourse of 'Tolerance', in *Syncretism/Anti-Syncretism*, edited by C. Stewart and R. Shaw. London: Routledge, 196–211.
Werbner, P. 1999. Global Pathways: Working Class Cosmopolitans and the Creation of Transnational Ethnic Worlds. *Social Anthropology*, 7(1), 17–35.
Werbner, P. 2002/1990. *The Migration Process: Capital, Gifts and Offerings among British Pakistanis*. Oxford: Berg, paperback POD edition with a new introductory preface.
Werbner, P. 2002. *Imagined Diasporas among Manchester Muslims: The Public Performance of Pakistani Transnational Identity Politics*. Oxford: James Currey Publishers, and Santa Fe: New School of American Research.
Werbner, P. 2003. *Pilgrims of Love: The Anthropology of a Global Sufi Cult*. London: Hurst Publishers, and Bloomington: Indiana University Press.

Werbner, P. 2004. Theorising Complex Diasporas: Purity and Hybridity in the South Asian Public Sphere in Britain. *Journal of Ethnic and Migration Studies*, 30(5), 895–911.

Werbner, P. (ed.). 2008. *Anthropology and the New Cosmopolitanism: Rooted, Feminist and Vernacular Perspectives*. ASA Monograph No. 45. Oxford: Berg.

Werbner, P. 2010. Beyond Division: Women, Pilgrimage and Nation Building in South Asian Sufism, in special issue on 'Gender, Religious Change and Sustainability,' edited by G. Samuels and S. Rosario. *Women's Studies International Forum*, 33(3).

Werbner, R. 2002. Cosmopolitan Ethnicity, Entrepreneurship and the Nation: Minority Elites in Botswana. *Journal of Southern African Studies*, 28(4), 731–53.

Zubaida, S. 1999. Cosmopolitanism and the Middle East, in *Cosmopolitanism, Identity and Authenticity in the Middle East*, edited by R. Meijer. London: Curzon, 15–34.

Diaspora and Cosmopolitanism

Vinay Dharwadker

During the last two decades of the twentieth century, postcolonial writers, and theorists as well as scholars of the African diaspora, working primarily in the humanities, established broad connections between migration and diaspora, on the one hand, and the hybridization of languages, identities, aesthetic forms, and cultural practices, on the other. In the opening decade of the new millennium, commentators on cosmopolitanism and globalization extended these arguments to project a more general equivalence between diaspora and cosmopolitanism. Over the same 30 years or so, however, scholars in the emerging field of diaspora studies, working chiefly in the social sciences and on a range of diasporas, suggested that certain core features render diasporic formations anticosmopolitan. This contradiction between diaspora as inherently cosmopolitan—a proposition based primarily on theoretical speculation—and diaspora as intrinsically anticosmopolitan—a proposition grounded mainly in empirical studies—has become the central paradox that we need to resolve at the intersection of the phenomena called "diaspora" and "cosmopolitanism."

But the contradictory claims of postcolonial theory and black British cultural studies, in one direction, and diaspora studies, in the other, cannot be explained as merely a divergence of opinion, a contest of interpretations, or even a consequence of disciplinary differences. Rather, the polarization of cosmopolitanism and anticosmopolitanism that ruptures diasporic formations seems to arise from instabilities that lie deeper within the phenomena themselves. In my opening sections, I shall therefore chart the trajectories of the most influential arguments on both sides, looking especially at how migration and diaspora are related to each other and to hybridity, creolization, syncretism, and cosmopolitanism. In the middle sections, I shall examine the convergences and disjunctions among different approaches to diaspora and the tensions they generate, using the Jewish Diaspora and the Indian labor diaspora as contrasting but representative paradigms. In the final sections, I shall then resolve some of the dilemmas posed by the cosmopolitan and anticosmopolitan alignments of diasporic consciousness and experience in theory as well as practice.

Migration and Hybridity

Historically, the association of diaspora and cosmopolitanism in postcolonial and cultural studies derives from a series of links between migration and hybridity and diaspora and creolization. An early stage of this development appears in Salman Rushdie's arguments about migration and hybridity in and around his controversial novel, *The Satanic Verses* (1988). Defining an imaginative schema (in the Kantian sense) in an anticipatory essay published in 1986, Rushdie observes that "the migrant is, perhaps, the central or defining figure of the twentieth century," and that migration "offers us one of the richest metaphors of our age" (*ibid.*: x). Moreover,

> *The very word metaphor, with its roots in the Greek words for bearing across, describes a sort of migration, the migration of ideas into images. Migrants—borne-across humans—are metaphorical beings in their very essence; and migration, seen as a metaphor, is everywhere around us. We all cross frontiers; in that sense, we are all migrant peoples. (Ibid.: xii)*

This amalgam of ideas becomes the organizing principle of the novel, which explores every aspect of emigration, immigration, and migrancy from "a migrant's-eye view of the world." As Rushdie says about the book roughly one year after Ayatollah Khomeini's fatwa against it:

> *The Satanic Verses ... is written from the very experience of uprooting, disjuncture and metamorphosis (slow or rapid, painful or pleasurable) that is the migrant condition, and from which, I believe, can be derived a metaphor for all humanity. ... Standing at the centre of the novel is a group of characters most of whom are British Muslims ... struggling with just the sort of great problems that have arisen to surround the book, problems of hybridization and ghettoization, of reconciling the old and the new. ... The Satanic Verses celebrates hybridity, impurity, intermingling, the transformation that comes of new and unexpected combinations of human beings, cultures, ideas, politics, movies, songs. It rejoices in mongrelization and fears the absolutism of the Pure. Mélange, hotchpotch, a bit of this and a bit of that is how newness enters the world. It is the great possibility that mass migration gives the world ... The Satanic Verses is for change-by-fusion, change-by-conjoining. It is a love-song to our mongrel selves. (1991: 394)*

As this passage shows clearly, Rushdie makes migration the primary ground for the intermingling of cultures and identities, and equates the migrant condition with the condition of hybridity in general.

Writing in England around the same time, Homi K. Bhabha uses a philosophical, psychoanalytical, and political framework, rather than a literary schema, to argue that hybridity "is never simply a question of the admixture of pre-given identities or essences," but instead is "the perplexity of living as it interrupts the representation of the fullness of life" (1990: 314). Here the "fullness of life" obliquely designates the homogenous community that the sovereign Euro-American nation-state ideologically attributes to itself; whereas the "perplexity of living" points to the "exiles and émigrés and refugees" and "the gathering of people in the diaspora: indentured, migrant, interned," who have left "other worlds" and are, literally and figuratively, knocking at their host nation's gates (1994: 139). Their liminality places them in *"neither the One ... nor the Other ... but something else besides,* which contests the terms and territories of both"—that is, it situates them neither in the hostland (the métropole, the Occident) nor in the homeland (the colony, the Orient), but in a situation (the diaspora) that differs from both, and constitutes the "Third Space" of their hybridity (1994: 28).

Drawing as much on the account of linguistic hybridization—the double-voicing of all utterances—in Mikhail Bakhtin (1981: 358–62, 429), as on the divergent accounts of enunciation in Michel Foucault (1972) and Jacques Derrida (1986), Bhabha treats this figurative space also as the universal "Third Space of enunciation," in which all human communication is fashioned. It therefore "represents both the general conditions of language and the specific implication of the utterance" (that is, both *langue* and *parole*), serving as "the precondition for the articulation of cultural difference," in which we "emerge as the others of ourselves" (1994: 36–9). As an "interstitial" site, the Third Space stands between those who represent and those who are represented, or between dominant host and subordinate guest, rendering "the structure of meaning and reference an ambivalent process," and thereby opening "the way to ... an *inter*national culture, based not on the exoticism of multiculturalism or the *diversity* of culture, but on the inscription and articulation of culture's *hybridity*" (1994: 38). It is in this "in-between" space that diasporic populations appropriate the language of their hosts, and use it to reshape both homeland and hostland ways of life, and hence to create "their own distinctive cultures" or hybrid identities (Ashcroft et al. 1998: 118).

Rushdie's dynamic mapping of migration, in part, sets the stage for the principle that the world is not merely a configuration of fixed objects, codes, "structures, organizations, and other stable social forms," but, in Arjun Appadurai's words, is also "a world of flows" that is "fundamentally characterized by objects in motion," including "ideas and ideologies, people and goods, images and messages, technologies and techniques" (2001: 5). In coining migration as the master-trope of a world in motion, however, Rushdie—and Bhabha, following him—does not distinguish clearly between migration and diaspora, ignoring the elementary fact that every diaspora involves migration, but every migration does not involve or result in a diaspora. As James Clifford remarks, "Diasporic populations do not come from elsewhere in the same way that 'immigrants' do" (1994: 307); and, as Kim D. Butler observes, a diaspora is constitutively a large, collective formation (whereas a migration is typically centered around individuals and families); and its population is dispersed to at least two different destinations, develops a self-consciousness about its group identity, and "dwells-in-displacement" for at least two generations. Diasporas thus "combine individual migration ... with the collective history of group dispersal," and also involve the "regenesis of communities abroad" (2001:

191–2)—a process that neither Rushdie nor Bhabha explores in any detail when equating migration or diaspora with hybridity.

Diaspora and Creolization

For black British cultural theorists around the close of the twentieth century, the intermingling that is characteristic of the African diaspora is not quite Bhabha's abstract hybridity. Rather, under colonialism, it is the literal "mongrelization" of the European and African races that Rushdie invokes and, more or less concurrently, a "mélange" of black and white cultures. According to Stuart Hall (1990), "what is uniquely ... Caribbean" about the African diaspora in Britain is "precisely the mixes of color, pigmentation, physiognomic type; the 'blends' of tastes that are Caribbean cuisine; the aesthetics of the 'cross-overs', of 'cut-and-mix' ... which is the heart and soul of black music." In Hall's perspective, the hybridity of this phenomenon is defined by the semantic root of the term, as a condition produced "by combining two different elements" or by "a mixture," so that

> *diaspora does not refer ... [merely] to those scattered tribes whose identity can only be secured in relation to some sacred homeland to which they must at all costs return. ... The diaspora experience ... is defined, not by essence or purity, but by the recognition of a necessary heterogeneity and diversity; by a conception of 'identity' which lives with and through, not despite, difference; by hybridity. Diaspora identities are ... constantly producing and reproducing themselves anew, through transformation and difference. (244)*

While Hall, a sociologist, draws on the social sciences, Kobena Mercer (1988), a commentator on Afro-Caribbean aesthetic practices, adopts a more humanistic perspective:

> *Across a whole range of [black diasporic] cultural forms there is a powerfully syncretic dynamism which critically appropriates elements from the master-codes of the dominant culture and creolizes them, disarticulating the given signs and rearticulating their symbolic meaning otherwise. The subversive force of this hybridizing tendency is most apparent at the level of language itself where creoles, patois, and Black English decenter, destabilize, and carnivalize the linguistic domination of 'English'. (255)*

Mercer thus equates hybridity not only with biological grafting, but also with creolization (literally, a linguistic process) and with syncretism (an ideational process), and then expands the equation to include "practices of interculturation," which involve the most general process of combining elements from two cultures to produce a third, unprecedented one.

In the late 1980s and early 1990s, Paul Gilroy brings together this range of concepts to analyze the African diaspora and its cultures under slavery, colonization, and postcolonial (re)dispersion on an intercontinental scale. In *"There Ain't No Black in the Union Jack"* (1987), for instance, he takes the position that

> The assimilation of blacks [into European society] is not a process of acculturation but of cultural syncretism. ... In the context of modern Britain this has produced a diaspora dimension ... [in which] non-European traditional elements, mediated by the histories of Afro-America and the Caribbean, have contributed to the formation of new and distinct black cultures amidst the decadent peculiarities of the Welsh, Irish, Scots and English. (155–6)

In *The Black Atlantic* (1993), he goes on to argue that "The contemporary black English [people] ... stand between (at least) two great cultural assemblages. ... locked symbiotically in an antagonistic relationship marked out by the symbolism of [the] colors ... black and white." In such a situation, one choice is to fall back "on the idea of cultural nationalism," which would exclude a diasporic community from the "natural" nation of their hostland:

> Against this choice stands another, more difficult option: the theorisation of creolisation, metissage, mestizaje, and hybridity. From the viewpoint of ethnic absolutism [which valorizes the hostland's majority as the singular norm of citizenship], this would be a litany of pollution and impurity. (2)

Further analysis shows that, apart from Rushdie, who uses the word "cosmopolitan" for some of the phenomena he explores (such as the metropolis and the postcolonial city), the cultural theorists of the 1980s and 1990s, such as Bhabha, Hall, Mercer, and Gilroy, do not explicitly attribute cosmopolitanism to diaspora. As both Ania Loomba (1998) and Leela Gandhi (1999) point out in their influential critiques of postcolonialism, the primary association in the field remains that between diaspora and hybridity, whether the latter is taken in Bhabha's sense or not. Even the (re-)emergence of cosmopolitanism as a major interdisciplinary field around the millennial moment does not change the situation: most scholars simply reinterpret hybridity as cosmopolitanism, assuming that both equally represent a condition that combines elements from two or more disparate sources. Summing up this trend in the context of cosmopolitanism and globalization, for example, Nicholas Van Hear (1998) remarks that

> For many such commentators ... migrants and transnationals are cosmopolitans, while those who stay behind are parochials. ... Transnational populations are ... thrusting, energetic entrepreneurs or cultural innovators, breathing life into the societies that accommodate them. A stimulating heterogeneity is ... produced by migration and mixing. Transnationalism is redolent of multiplicity, pluralism and fertile hybridity. (253)

In the first decade of the twenty-first century, theorists essentially add cosmopolitanism to the existing inventory of terms associated with diaspora, so that James Clifford's representative list from 1994—"border, travel, creolization, transculturation, hybridity, and diaspora" (303)—is modified in Falu Bakrania's version of 2008 as "creolization, syncretism, bricolage, borderland, fusion, and cosmopolitanism," with each element now correlated to "migration, diaspora, transnationalism, and globalization" (536).

Diaspora Studies and its Paradigms

Definition of diaspora

Diaspora studies draws primarily on the disciplines of history, political science, sociology, and anthropology, and on fields such as social theory, ethnography, and women's studies. As a consequence, it often approaches its object of investigation with assumptions, methods, concepts, analytical frameworks, and archives that differ significantly from those of postcolonial theory and black cultural studies. The divergence is clearest in the definitions and paradigms that diaspora studies employs.

The definition of diaspora most widely invoked in the field is by William Safran (1991), from the inaugural issue of the journal *Diaspora*. The "concept of diaspora," he says, should be "applied to expatriate minority communities whose members share several of the following characteristics":

> 1) they, or their ancestors, have been dispersed from a specific original 'center' to two or more 'peripheral,' or foreign, regions; 2) they retain a collective memory, vision, or myth about their original homeland—its physical location, history, and achievements; 3) they believe that they are not—and perhaps cannot be—fully accepted by their host society and therefore feel partly alienated and insulated from it; 4) they regard their ancestral homeland as their true, ideal home and as the place to which they or their descendants would (or should) eventually return—when conditions are appropriate; 5) they believe that they should, collectively, be committed to the maintenance or restoration of their original homeland and to its safety and prosperity; and 6) they continue to relate, personally or vicariously, to that homeland in one way or another, and their ethnocommunal consciousness and solidarity are importantly defined by the existence of such a relationship. (83–4)

This seeks to be a comprehensive and culturally open definition, making room for as many variations as possible, but it falls short on several fronts. As Clifford points out, in general, "no society can be expected to qualify on all counts, throughout its history"; and "the discourse of diaspora will necessarily be modified as it is translated and adopted" under changing circumstances (1994: 306). Moreover, the definition can fail in particular cases: it cannot accommodate some principal features of the African diaspora, for example; and, as Safran admits, it cannot account for the Gypsies, who are "a truly dispersed and homeless people" and constitute "a classic diaspora," but whose homelessness derives from "their nomadic culture," due to which "they have no precise notion of their place of origin, no clear geographical focus, and no history of national sovereignty," and hence "have no myth of return" (1991: 87). Part of the difficulty is that Safran models his conception on the Jewish Diaspora; and, even though he does not promote it explicitly as the norm, he acknowledges that none of the other major instances—the African, the Armenian, the Greek, the Chinese, and the Indian diasporas—"fully conforms" to its "ideal type." But the applicability of Safran's list even to his Jewish model is uncertain: Clifford points out incisively that "large segments of Jewish historical experience do not meet the test of ... the last three criteria"; "there is little room ... for the principled ambivalence about physical return and attachment to land ... [in] Jewish diasporic consciousness, from biblical times on;" and it also excludes "Jewish anti-Zionist critiques of teleologies of return" (1994: 305).

Influential as it has been in diaspora studies, Safran's definition raises other issues that are significant in the context of cosmopolitanism. Much of the definition is cast in terms of a diaspora's consciousness about its own condition, and hence is intensely subject-centered. In anchoring diaspora to its members' experiences, memories, perceptions, choices, and actions, the definition naively replicates the philosophical, political, and methodological difficulties that handicapped the Subaltern Studies project in its early stages, for instance, when it attempted to (re-)construct Indian history in terms of subaltern consciousness (Spivak 1988). Moreover, Safran overtly views diasporas from the position of host nation-states, classifying them, to begin with, as "expatriate minority communities," and hence as potentially troublesome constituencies to be tolerated (rather than welcomed) and contained (within the category of minorities). Furthermore, Safran's long definition does not foresee the political, ethical, and moral complications created by a diaspora's "double consciousness" of belonging both *here* and *there*—by the division of its loyalties between hostland and homeland. As I shall show later, locating the characteristics of diaspora in the subjectivity of its members, in the divided political loyalties of its double consciousness, or in an ideology of the (host) nation-state jeopardizes not only the potential connection between diaspora and cosmopolitanism, but the very existence of diaspora itself.

Normativity of the Jewish diaspora

For many scholars, a central intellectual issue in this context concerns the general role of the Jewish paradigm in the field of diaspora studies. Should the dispersion of the Jews, viewed in the light of its magnitude and historical priority and as a continuous phenomenon over 2,500 years or so, constitute the norm by which we determine whether the dispersions of other people count as diasporas? The analysis of Clifford, together with that of Daniel and Jonathan Boyarin (1993), strongly suggests that Jewish diasporic experience and consciousness vary so much over time, space, documented circumstance, and self-understanding, that it may be impossible to reduce them to a single, coherent paradigm. Even if a uniform pattern could be constructed, its use as the standard to judge all other diasporas would immediately pose innumerable theoretical, interpretive, methodological, and political problems.

The complexity of the situation becomes evident when we examine some of the arguments for the Jewish Diaspora as a norm. Irma McClaurin (2008) points out that Steven Vertovec, for instance, observes that "the current over-use and under-theorization of the notion of 'diaspora' among academics, transnational intellectuals and 'community leaders' alike—which sees the term become a loose reference conflating categories such as immigrants, guest-workers, ethnic and 'racial' minorities, refugees, expatriates and travelers—threatens the term's descriptive usefulness" (357). His collaborator, Robin Cohen, an equally prominent figure in the rapid interdisciplinary expansion of diaspora studies since about 1990, distances himself from the inclusiveness more forcefully by responding that "Natural scholarly caution would invite rejection of this profligacy" (2001: 3643). Cohen's phrasing signifies that, for him, neither analogy nor "apparent theoretical and experiential coherence" are legitimate grounds for the field's "new pluralism." He is troubled even by the fact that, starting around the mid-twentieth century, "other groups saw themselves as victims of forcible dispersion in a manner similar to the ancient Jews and used the expression 'diaspora' as a self-description of their fate." Referring edgily to the Armenian diaspora (following the Ottoman and Turkish genocides of 1894–6 and 1915–16), the African diaspora (under the Atlantic slave trade after 1492), and the Irish diaspora (after the potato famine of the 1840s), he asserts that "A number of conventional historians would wish to go no further with the idea of diaspora." But, to his dismay, beginning in the 1980s, "Many ethnic groups … defined themselves as 'diasporas,' or were so recognized by scholars or journalists;" and, in the course of the 1990s, the academic journal *Diaspora*, with its "manifesto … for openness," identified as many as "34 ethnic groups as diasporas," with numerous other groups also "casually referred to" in the same way (2001: 3642–3).

McClaurin does not mention Cohen, but she does identify Donald Akenson as an outspoken proponent of the normativity of the Jewish Diaspora, noting that, for him, the "most pristine application" of the term "diaspora" is to the Jewish phenomenon alone. "That is why," says Akenson, "were we to be master of our vocabulary, 'diaspora' would be a term limited only to the ancient Hebrews and their descendents, the modern Jews. To use the word 'diaspora' even as a metaphor for other groups is to replace a precise connotation with a fuzzy one" (McClaurin 2008: 357). It is not at all clear that, in Akenson's perspective, the Indian diaspora (now over 20 million people) and the Chinese diaspora (now 50 million), for example, would qualify as legitimate diasporas (Dufoix 2008: 41–50; Cohen 2001: 3643).

Akenson's provocative stance invites at least three counterpositions. The first reminds us that the term universalized by the "new pluralism" of diaspora studies is the ancient Greek *diaspora*, and not, say, the Hebrew *galut*. The term for diaspora has spread, not from the Hebrew Torah, but from the Greek rendering of that text as the Old Testament of the Christian Bible, which is not a canonical text of Judaism. Hence, by definition—if not also by the very process of textual dissemination, as theorized by Jacques Derrida—the translated term "diaspora" cannot be controlled by a desire "to be master of our vocabulary": it is a part, not of "our" vocabulary, but of someone else's vocabulary.

Another counterposition, arising from the third criterion on Safran's list, points out that the Jewish Diaspora explicitly resists biological creolization and, contrary to appearances, even cultural hybridity, which is why Jewish identity remains historically distinct and genealogically definable after two-and-a-half millenniums of dispersions and re-dispersions across much of the earth (see Ohliger and Munz 2003: 3–4). But the Jewish Diaspora's resistance to creolization is trammeled in a profound historical irony; for it is precisely the Jewish people who, in early and middle modernity, are identified by their European Others as paradigmatic cosmopolitans—fellow-subjects of European states who are reviled, attacked, and then almost exterminated over the *longue durée* for, among other reasons, being "rootless cosmopolitans" (see Dharwadker 2001: 89–91). This tragic irony, in which resistance to creolization somehow equals cosmopolitanism, prises apart the fusion creolization, hybridity, and cosmopolitanism in postcolonial and black cultural studies; and it does so by demonstrating that a figurative extension of the biological conceptions embedded inside creolization and hybridization does not necessarily yield a valid conception of cosmopolitanism.

Not least, the third counterposition underscores the fact that Akenson's desire to police the application of diaspora "only to the ancient Hebrews and their descendants, the modern Jews," goes against the grain of the linguistic hybridity of the word itself, and to the weight of cosmopolitanism that has coalesced associatively around it. Diaspora is neither merely an ancient Hebrew signifier, nor merely an ancient Greek one, nor merely a modern English or French one, even though its significations slide in and out of all these and other languages historically as well as transhistorically. Most importantly, this lexical and semantic hybridity— an instance of Bakhtin's determinate linguistic property of double-voicing in an utterance—is not of Jewish or Hebrew origin, and thereby undermines Akenson's proprietorial angst. The canonical Greek translation of the Book of Deuteronomy, prepared in the second century, picked *diaspora* to correspond to *galut* because the Greek term had been used as early as Thucydides' *History of the Peloponnesian War* (circa 400 BC) to describe the "scattering" of the Aeginetan people across Hellas, after the Athenian army forcibly expelled them from their native island of Aegina for "inveterate" enmity toward the Athenian city-state, and for instigating that war (II, 27; 1994: 394). For the translators who produced the Old Testament, a dispersion of a people from their homeland—especially a forced scattering after a catastrophic public event—was not exclusively a Jewish experience, which is why it was translatable in the first place. In short, the ancient Greek term, *diaspora*, was a cosmopolitan, inclusive, and universalizing rendering of *galut*; whereas Akenson's desire to claim that diaspora as such—the signifier as well as its significations—is exclusively Jewish or Hebrew stems from a particularistic and anticosmopolitan view of the phenomenon.

Since Safran's relatively pluralistic definition of diaspora allows many formations to be identified as diasporas, at least loosely, it is cosmopolitan in and of itself, and also makes room (under its third criterion) for diasporic cosmopolitanism as syncretism, creolization, or hybridity. But reductions of Safran's paradigm that try to elevate the Jewish Diaspora to the status of a singular norm are rooted in exclusionary anticosmopolitanism, and hence attenuate the possibilities of connecting the diasporic and the cosmopolitan.

Counter-example of the Indian labor diaspora

The interplay of cosmopolitan and anticosmopolitan elements that becomes visible when we evaluate the normativity of the Jewish Diaspora in diaspora studies is transfigured when we juxtapose it against the dynamics of the Indian indentured-labor diaspora. A core feature of the Indo-Caribbean diaspora, which emerged between the mid-nineteenth and the early twentieth centuries, is that its members were "late arrivers" at their destination. At the time of their arrival, their so-called host society already had a prior, twofold diasporic structure containing dispersed European colonizers and transplanted African groups—without a surviving aboriginal community to serve as an indigenous host. Since the 1840s, the cumulative Indian diaspora experience in the Caribbean has consequently been one of marginalization by the dominant European colonial minority as well as competing Afro-Caribbean labor, and hence of a double "marginality in their adopted homes." Within the Indo-Caribbean diaspora, as Victor Ramraj (1992) observes, there is an "inevitable division between assimilationists and traditionalists," namely, those who advocate integration with the "host" society, and those who promote resistance by maintaining homeland traditions. In Caribbean idiom, this is the division between those who are for and those who are against creolization (77–8). But even when individuals or groups of subcontinental origin are willing to assimilate, the twin-layered social structure around them prevents full integration; the divisions between the European and Afro-Caribbean populations force the Indians to choose between the two "hosts," creating new inequities of power and further alienating them from the community with which they choose not to align themselves. Indo-Caribbeans who Anglicize themselves (and hence emerge as an elite comprador group serving the Europeans) are at odds with Afro-Caribbeans (a subaltern group), as well as with members of their own community who creolize with the latter.

Ramraj aptly remarks that, within the Indian diaspora in the Caribbean, the conflicts between assimilationists and traditionalists often disrupt family and community life, usually with traumatic consequences for individuals (1992: 78). Against this backdrop, at least so far as representations in Indo-Caribbean literature are concerned, a "creolized" individual of Indian origin is usually identified as a "cosmopolitan," but the latter is someone who is Europeanized or Anglicized, rather than someone who has adopted the culture of Afro-Caribbean blacks. Moreover, in contrast to many of their counterparts of African origin, members of this Indian diaspora by and large do not seek to return to their homeland; and, in spite of the traditionalists among them, do not engage significantly with a nativism seeking to reinstitute supposedly authentic homeland identities (81–2, 84). In other words, the belated Indian labor diaspora in the Caribbean disturbs the characteristic structure of diasporic double consciousness that black cultural theorists, among others, take for granted—splitting it further, as it were, into a triple consciousness. At the same time, the triangulated situation of the Indo-Caribbean diaspora reminds us that, at the grassroots level, the circumstances of biological creolization and cultural syncretism impart to these phenomena more layers than the two-way transactions (between Afro-Caribbeans and Europeans) on which black cultural theorists concentrate.

Indentured-labor diasporas, however, are not uniform in time and space, and Vijay Mishra's extraordinary 1992 account of the Indian diaspora in Fiji compels an even deeper questioning of the ideas prevalent in postcolonial and diaspora studies. Mishra focuses on "*girmit* ideology," in which *girmit* is a Hindi-English creolization of "agreement," the contract for indenture that individuals signed before they were transported by ship, usually from Calcutta (Kolkata) or Madras (Chennai), to the Pacific islands, in the last quarter of the nineteenth century. "*Girmit* ideology" refers to a "false consciousness" (and a false self-consciousness), in the classic Marxist sense, that arises in the diaspora and prevents it from facing up to "historical realities" (3).

Mishra argues that when indentured laborers were displaced from north India to the Fiji Islands, starting in 1879, the horrors of the journey, long-term disillusionments after arrival, and betrayals about a return at the end of the contract period resulted in a "nostalgic transmission" of the homeland's culture to the diaspora. In submitting to this nostalgia, however, "the diaspora itself became a fossilized fragment of the original nation" that it had relinquished (1–2). In theory, a fragment of any nation can "duplicate in itself the dynamics of the totality" from which it has been broken off; a diaspora tries imaginatively to construct a "new world" for itself in its hostland, using elements from its homeland culture; but, since it is a fragment, it cannot fully actualize the "inherent principle of dynamic growth" that drives the totality it has left behind. The diaspora's potential for innovation and revolutionary change at the border of disparate cultures is therefore "overtaken by the triumph of the 'fossil'" and its own "structural inadequacies" and failures then lead it to "the construction of ghostly enemies"—"phantoms" that include the European colonizer in Fiji (indistinguishable from the colonizer left behind at home), as well as indigenous Fijian society (as mediated by European colonialism) (2).

Mishra therefore finds that the Indian diaspora in Fiji reconstitutes a "Mother India" that cannot interact with its hostland; and that indigenous Fijian society, trapped in European colonial conceptions of itself, cannot acknowledge the historical reality of the Indian diaspora in its midst (3). In this situation, stretching over more than a century, the "fossilized fragment" of subcontinental origin is caught between a homeland "whose dynamism it [cannot] ... duplicate" and a hostland "whose social formations it cannot totally adopt," even as it "cannot return to the [homeland] for either emotional sustenance or cultural capital." *Girmit* ideology thus produces a "false consciousness" among diasporic Indians in Fiji that "blinds" them to the realities of Fiji life and politics; that gives them an "inferiority complex" and a paranoia induced by "phantom enemies;" and that prevents them for relating successfully to Indians in other diasporas and to Indians at home (7–8). Mishra therefore underscores the impossibility of assimilation, even as he stresses the impossibility of a return, at least in the circumstances that circumscribe indentured labor; and he implies that, if assimilation is impossible, then cosmopolitanism, as the co-existence of disparate cultures, is impossible. Moreover, his account entails that, if diaspora consciousness can carry a "double consciousness" (as in the African diaspora), which becomes a source of creative cultural creolization or syncretism, then it can also carry a "false consciousness" (as in the case of the *girmit* ideology in Fiji), which renders both hybridity and cosmopolitanism untenable.

Initially establishing this interpretation of the Indo-Fijian situation more than a decade before Safran proposed his definition of diaspora—and several years before Rushdie, Bhabha, Gilroy and others constructed their pictures of hybrid diasporas—Mishra pre-emptively undercuts the idea that some measure of cultural mixing is inevitable under migration and dispersion; and that maintaining contact with other branches of the diaspora, sustaining the homeland at a distance, and nurturing the dream of a return are indispensable features of this condition. *Girmit* ideology retains only the first two of Safran's criteria (the fact of dispersion and the memory or vision of the homeland); but even with those, its impact as a false consciousness (which, by definition, cannot grasp its own falsity) is at best that of distortion. It is possible, then, that diasporic consciousness as such is consumed by a pervasive false consciousness; and if it collapses under its own weight, then it dissolves Safran's entire consciousness-centered conception of diaspora. Given such a possibility, the tragedy of diaspora, as Mishra envisions it, is its utter obliteration of home, memory, consciousness, future, assimilation, belonging, transformation, and dispersion itself.

Cosmopolitan and Anticosmopolitan Diasporas

Cosmopolitanism under globalization

Once we have encountered characterizations of the diasporic condition such as Mishra's and Safran's, we can no longer assume that migration and diaspora, hybridity and creolization, and cosmopolitanism and anticosmopolitanism, are interconnected in a straightforward way. But a direct equation between diaspora and cosmopolitanism (re-)emerges on either side of the millennial moment, when scholars begin to investigate the "new diasporas" under globalization, which mostly prove to be dispersions of professionals and corporate personnel of the kind that Robin Cohen has identified in his typology of diasporas (see 2001: 3643).

According to Van Hear (1998), one of the "social dimensions of globalization" is "the emergence of a world middle class or elite which shares tastes and values … and which is sharply distinct in terms of wealth, resources and culture from the lower classes of the society in which it is located." While some of its members may be part of various diasporas around the globe, the class as a whole is not diasporic; but it is "assertively cosmopolitan and is characterized by widely spreading transnational connections" (252–3). In Van Hear's assessment, some scholars in the social sciences conclude that this is a new variety of cosmopolitanism connected to contemporary globalization, and that "Diasporas are … the bearers of this cosmopolitanism." In the context of "globally dispersed ethnic groups," he highlights the position of Joel Kotkin around 1992, for whom "These global tribes are today's quintessential cosmopolitans. … [and] it is likely that such dispersed people—and their worldwide business and cultural networks—will increasingly shape the economic destiny of mankind" (253).

Uncritical celebration, however, is not the only response to dispersion and cosmopolitanism under globalization; Christopher Lasch, for instance, offers a more negative early evaluation, based on the class characteristics and lifestyles of the emergent cosmopolitans. "The new elites," he observes in 1995, "which include not only corporate managers, but all those professions that produce and manipulate information—the lifeblood of the global market—are far more cosmopolitan, or at least more restless and migratory, than their predecessors." Personal and professional "advancement" and "upward mobility" seem to be their only goals, and

> 'Multiculturalism' … suits them to perfection, conjuring up the agreeable image of a global bazaar in which exotic cuisines, exotic styles of dress, exotic music, exotic tribal customs can be savored indiscriminately, with no questions asked and no commitments required. The new elites are at home only in transit … theirs is essentially a tourist's view of the world. (Lasch 1996: 254)

On an economic and cultural canvas of vast proportions, however, "the cosmopolitanism of the favored few, because it is uninformed by the practice of citizenship, turns out to be a higher form of parochialism … [in which] their acknowledgement of civic obligations does not extend beyond their own immediate neighborhoods" (254). Van Hear, Kotkin, and Lasch thus give us divergent assessments of diaspora and cosmopolitanism under contemporary globalization, but they uniformly posit a direct connection between the two phenomena, and link both to socioeconomic class.

Diaspora and anticosmopolitanism

Despite recent trends in relation to globalization, however, several features of diaspora still stand out as anticosmopolitan. The first is the aporia of assimilation: the ideology of the nation-state as the host of immigrants and diasporas (with the United States serving as a paradigmatic "melting pot") projects full assimilation as an attainable ideal, but diasporic experience in the long duration and on a global scale repeatedly unmasks the impossibility of assimilation—not just in practice, but in its very conception. If assimilation is fundamentally impossible, then diaspora as long-term settlement in a foreign land can never result in "intermingling" (in Rushdie's phrase), in creolization, hybridization, or cultural cross-fertilization (in Gilroy's terms), or in a cosmopolitanization of guest and host populations.

A second anticosmopolitan factor appears when the state-apparatus in a host nation, representing what Safran (2003) identifies as "the Jacobin ideology ... of the socioculturally and politically homogenous *état–nation*" (439)—which is still overt in France, but is often covert in other Western countries now—seeks to contain the immigrant and diaspora populations in its midst using the category of minorities. Even when this happens within a state-policy framework of ameliorative multiculturalism, the principal effect of the host's minoritization of guest communities is always negative: it pre-empts precisely the kind of social and cultural integration that might render both hostland and diaspora transparently cosmopolitan (Ramraj 1992: 77, 83).

A third anticosmopolitan dimension, which Gabriel Sheffer (1995) as well as Cohen (1997) and others explore in detail, emerges around the definition of a diaspora from the point of view of a host nation, not only as a minority but also as an ethnic formation. While minority-status imposes the "numbers game" of democracy and political representation on a diaspora community, the attribute of ethnicity brings into play its racial, linguistic, religious, national, and cultural differences from other groups in the host society, especially from the dominant numerical majority. An ethnic classification thus conceptually segregates a diasporic minority as (merely) a particular group, in contrast to a majority whose ethnic particularity is suppressed, and whose cultural identity is elevated to a self-evidently normative universal. A hostland's identification of a social group as an ethnic minority, however, is often ambivalent in practice, because many minorities also adopt it as an empowering instrument of self-identification; in such a context, a diaspora community may use this double-edged identification as the framework for its ethno-nationalism—its explicit political as well as racial, linguistic, religious, and cultural commitment, not to its host nation *here*, but to its original homeland *there* (to use Bhabha's phrase again). When a host society labels ethnic minorities explicitly, it enlarges the gap that groups of foreign origin have to bridge in order to assimilate into its so-called mainstream, and thus forestalls cosmopolitan integration; when a diaspora adopts an ethnic label as a signifier of its displaced nationalism, it consciously rejects the possibility of a cosmopolitan identity for itself. The anticosmopolitanism is even more marked when a diaspora defines itself, and is defined by others, as a religious diaspora (such as a Muslim, Sikh, or Coptic diaspora) within an ethnic-minority framework: religion and cosmopolitanism are antagonistic because the former most often aligns itself with an unqualified universalism, whereas the latter aligns itself with secularism and cultural relativism (or, in Anthony Appiah's formula, with "universalism plus difference") (see Dharwadker 2001: 202).

A fourth anticosmopolitan element appears as an outcome of the double consciousness that theories of the African diaspora especially emphasize. The concept draws on W.E.B. Du Bois's observation in his classic, *The Souls of Black Folk* (1903), that "It is a peculiar sensation, this double-consciousness, this sense of always looking at one's self through the eyes of others. ... One ever feels his twoness,—an American, a Negro; two souls, two thoughts, two unreconciled strivings; two warring ideals in one dark body" (45) In general, diasporic consciousness is double consciousness, the constant consciousness of belonging here as well as there, to hostland as well as homeland, without relinquishing either. But, politically, this double consciousness can give birth to a divided allegiance in a diaspora, driving it to intervene in the affairs of its homeland, often covertly and sometimes even in betrayal of its hostland. As Robin Cohen (2005) puts it, in the "more complex, pluralist world" we inhabit, "diasporas can be a force for stability ('peace–makers') as well as a force that amplifies and even creates conflict ('peace-wreckers')," playing "significant and varied roles in the whole range of activities in the conflict cycle" far from where they are currently located (179, 180). A divided loyalty of this type is often committed to a "purist," "separatist," or "restorative" vision of the homeland, and hence may be aggressively anticosmopolitan in its interventions.

Cosmopolitanism as Cultural Ambidexterity

The multiple manifestations of diasporic anticosmopolitanism remind us that any effort to equate hybridity (or creolization) with cosmopolitanism poses two conceptual obstacles. One appears in Gayatri Spivak's extrapolation from Bhabha's position, that "all identities are irreducibly hybrid" (which she calls an "'obvious' fact"), and in her concomitant assertion of "the irreducible hybridity of all language" (1999: 155, 164). But if all individual and group identities are hybrid, then all national, subnational, and transnational communities are *homogenous in their very hybridity*, and we are again left with the task of differentiating one identity, group, or community from another—exactly the task that hybridity was supposed to perform in the first place. In other words, the theory of hybridity, originally designed to articulate and explain difference, paradoxically ends up becoming an instrument of homogeneity, with everything in the world uniformly construed as hybrid. To reinstate difference, we then need a theory of meta-hybridity to explain how and why one hybrid is different from another—which constitutes, at best, a *reductio ad absurdum*.

The other obstacle appears in the tacit simplification that hybridity must be the same as cosmopolitanism because both somehow involve a mixing of elements from two or more sources. But while the linguistic origin of hybridity, like that of creolization, lies in a notion of intermingling, does cosmopolitanism really mean an admixture of cultures? A cosmopolitan is a citizen of the world because she has the capacity to be at home in *different* societies; but to be so does not necessarily mean that she mixes different cultures. Rather, it means that she is able to switch back and forth between places and cultures, so that when she is at one location she follows the codes appropriate to it, and when she is at another location, she changes over to the codes required there. This entails that a cosmopolitan *differentiate* among her cultural locations; and that she practice what linguists and anthropologists call code-switching (which occurs in bilingualism or multilingualism) rather than code-mixing (which occurs in linguistic creolization). W.E.B. Du Bois got the distinction exactly right in 1903, when he noted that the "double-consciousness" of "the American Negro" is such that "He would not Africanize America" and, at the same time, "He would not bleach his Negro soul in a flood of white Americanism. ... He simply wishes to make it possible for a man *to be both a Negro and an American*" (45; emphasis added). The double consciousness of the African diasporic subject that Hall and Gilroy, among others, invoke must therefore remain distinct from his biological or cultural creolization: the former is the embodiment of his cosmopolitanism, whereas the latter is the embodiment of his hybridity (understood, despite Bhabha's animadversions, simply as "intermingling"). As I have suggested elsewhere, the cosmopolitan subject

> *does not linger liminally between two cultures but stands quite firmly in both of them. He is likely to be ambivalent about each of the cultures he inhabits, but his ambivalence is subsumed by his cultural ambidexterity, an equal or commensurate facility in two or more cultural systems concurrently. ... [T]he ambidextrous subject tries to maintain a critical distance toward two cultures so that he can act in both without sacrificing either.* (Dharwadker 1997: 123–4)

We can therefore say that the cosmopolitan subject is culturally ambidextrous, and switches codes between the distinct, co-existing cultures in which she is at home to commensurate degrees; her cosmopolitanism is analogous to multilingualism, and hence represents a culture of translation. In contrast, the hybrid or Creole subject inhabits a single culture of her own, which emerges in the intermingling of two prior cultures; she mixes (and mixes up) their codes, and is no longer fully at home in either in its unmixed form; her condition is therefore analogous to an admixture of languages (as in a pidgin or Creole), and hence represents a culture of creolization. That is, hybridity or creolization does not necessarily result in the cultural ambidexterity that defines cosmopolitanism. This distinction between cosmopolitanism and creolization enables us to explain the anticosmopolitanism of diasporas: whenever a diaspora is unable to inhabit its homeland and its hostland with commensurate facility, even its hybridization or creolization of those cultures cannot prevent it from becoming anticosmopolitan. When a diaspora is denied an opportunity, or is unable to achieve cultural ambidexterity—the condition of actively inhabiting two distinct cultures, and translating them into each other without reducing them to an undifferentiated amalgam—it ceases to be cosmopolitan.

Conclusion

The foregoing discussion stresses the fact that the terms "diaspora" and "cosmopolitanism" are both multilayered and ambiguous; their significations can be simplified, but the concepts they represent are manifold, changing over time and in context. It is virtually impossible to determine the relation between diaspora and cosmopolitanism without clearly distinguishing between migration and diaspora; the two phenomena are asymmetrical, because every diaspora involves migration, but every migration is not part of a diaspora. A view popularized by postcolonial theory and black British cultural studies, clustered around the humanities, suggests that diasporas are inherently cosmopolitan; but diaspora studies, which often uses ideas and methods developed in the social sciences, suggest that some diasporas, or some features of all diasporas, may be intrinsically anticosmopolitan. If it is possible for the members of a diaspora to assimilate into a host society, then it is possible for them to be creolized or to become hybrid or cosmopolitan; if, however, assimilation is impossible, then cosmopolitanism is also an impossibility. In many diasporas, the impossibility of a return to a homeland may also alter the relation of diaspora to cosmopolitanism.

In order to better understand what diasporas are, it is necessary to complicate our present understanding of creolization, which contributes to diasporic cosmopolitanism in vital ways. In the Caribbean, for example, multiple diasporas co-exist and relate to each other differently, with no one diaspora unambiguously constituting a host society; in such circumstances, creolization is a fractured process interlinking different diasporas in disparate ways, and hence creating divergent forms of cosmopolitanism. It is equally necessary to modify our understanding of what diaspora consciousness may be; how the double consciousness (sometimes splitting into multiple levels of consciousness) of immigrants, ethnic groups, and minorities in a host society shapes or reshapes it; and how, especially, diasporic consciousness may actually collapse into a self-canceling false consciousness. We also need to engage in a comprehensive economic analysis of diaspora, and especially to comprehend the role of socioeconomic class in the formation of diasporas and diaspora consciousness; as part of this, we need to define and understand subaltern diasporas and elite diasporas, and the respective roles they play in modern diasporic movements. The relation of diaspora to cosmopolitanism frequently depends on how diasporas creolize in particular circumstances, what kinds of diaspora consciousness and double consciousness they develop, and especially what their economic and class dimensions are. Most importantly, however, it is necessary to reconceptualize what hybridity is, what its relation is to creolization (whether taken literally or figuratively), and whether it can be identified with cosmopolitanism. Current theoretical accounts of hybridity lead to contradictions, especially with regard to cultural difference—the very phenomenon hybridity is supposed to embody and explain; and, in some respects, hybridity, creolization, and cosmopolitanism prove to be quite incommensurate with each other. Given the complexity of diaspora as a phenomenon characterized by long duration and global reach, it may be especially productive to redefine cosmopolitanism as cultural ambidexterity, which cannot merely be equated with either hybridity or creolization.

Bibliography

Appadurai, A. 2001. Grassroots globalization and the research imagination, in *Globalization*, edited by A. Appadurai. Durham, NC: Duke University Press, 1–21.
Ashcroft, B., G. Griffiths, and H. Tiffin. 1998. *Key Concepts in Post-Colonial Studies*. London: Routledge.
Bakhtin, M.M. 1981. *The Dialogic Imagination: Four Essays*. Edited by M. Holquist, translated by C. Emerson and M. Holquist. Austin: University of Texas Press.
Bakrania, F. 2008. Hybridity, in *International Encyclopedia of the Social Sciences*, edited by W.A. Darity, Jr. 2nd edition. Detroit: Macmillan Reference USA, 3, 535–7.
Bhabha, H.K. 1990. DissemiNation: time, narrative, and the margins of the nation, in *Nation and Narration*, edited by H.K. Bhabha. London: Routledge, 291–322.
Bhabha, H.K. 1994. *The Location of Culture*. London: Routledge.
Boyarin, D. and J. Boyarin. 1993. Diaspora: generation and the ground of Jewish identity, in *Theorizing Diaspora: A Reader*, edited by J.E. Braziel and A. Mannur (2003). Malden: Blackwell, 85–118.
Butler, K.D. 2001. Defining diaspora, refining a discourse. *Diaspora*, 10(2), 189–219.
Clifford, J. 1994. Diasporas. *Cultural Anthropology*, 9(3), 302–38.
Cohen, R. 1997. *Global Diasporas: An Introduction*. Seattle: University of Washington Press.
Cohen, R. 2001. Diaspora, in *International Encyclopedia of the Social and Behavioral Sciences*, edited by N.J. Smelser and P.B. Baltes. Amsterdam: Elsevier, 6, 3642–5.
Cohen, R. 2005. New roles for diasporas in international relations. *Diaspora*, 14(1), 179–83.
Derrida, J. 1986. *Margins of Philosophy*. Translated by A. Bass. Chicago: University of Chicago Press.
Dharwadker, V. 1997. Print culture and literary markets in colonial India, in *Language Machines: Technologies of Literary and Cultural Production*, edited by J. Masten, P. Stallybrass, and N. Vickers. New York: Routledge.
Dharwadker, V. (ed.). 2001. *Cosmopolitan Geographies: New Locations in Literature and Culture*. New York: Routledge.
Du Bois, W.E.B. 1903. *The Souls of Black Folk*. Signet Classic edition, with new introduction by Randall Kenan, 1995. New York: Penguin.

Dufoix, S. 2008. *Diasporas*. Translated by W. Rodarmor. American edition, with a foreword by R. Waldinger. Berkeley: University of California Press.

Foucault, M. 1972. *The Archaeology of Knowledge and The Discourse on Language*. Translated by A.M. Sheridan Smith. New York: Pantheon.

Gandhi, L. 1999. *Postcolonial Theory: A Critical Introduction*. New Delhi: Oxford University Press.

Gilroy, P. 1987. *"There Ain't No Black in the Union Jack": The Cultural Politics of Race and Nation*. American edition, with new foreword by Houston A. Baker, Jr., 1991. Chicago: University of Chicago Press.

Gilroy, P. 1993. *The Black Atlantic: Modernity and Double Consciousness*. Cambridge, MA: Harvard University Press.

Hall, S. 1990. Cultural identity and diaspora, in *Theorizing Diaspora: A Reader*, edited by J.E. Braziel and A. Mannur (2003). Malden: Blackwell, 233–46.

Lasch, C. 1996. *The Revolt of the Elites and the Betrayal of Democracy*. New York: Norton.

Loomba, A. 1998. *Colonialism/Postcolonialism*. New York: Routledge.

McClaurin, I. 2008. Diaspora, in *International Encyclopedia of the Social Sciences*, edited by W.A. Darity, Jr. 2nd edition. Detroit: Macmillan Reference USA, 2, 356–8.

Mercer, K. 1988. Dialogic culture and the dialogic imagination: the aesthetics of black independent film in Britain, in *Theorizing Diaspora: A Reader*, edited by J.E. Braziel and A. Mannur (2003). Malden: Blackwell, 247–60.

Mishra, V. 1992. The girmit ideology revisited: Fiji Indian literature, in *Reworlding: The Literature of the Indian Diaspora*, 1–12, edited by E.S. Nelson. New York: Greenwood Press.

Ohliger, R. and R. Munz. 2003. Diasporas and ethnic migrants in twentieth-century Europe: a comparative perspective, in *Diasporas and Ethnic Migrants: Germany, Israel and Post-Soviet Successor States in Comparative Perspective*, edited by R. Munz and R. Ohliger. London: Frank Cass, 3–17.

Ramraj, V. 1992. Still arriving: the assimilationist Indo–Caribbean experience of marginality, in *Reworlding: The Literature of the Indian Diaspora*, 1–12, edited by E.S. Nelson. New York: Greenwood Press, 77–85.

Rushdie, S. 1986. Introduction, in *On Writing and Politics: 1967–1983*, by G. Grass, translated by R. Manheim. New York: Harcourt, ix–xv.

Rushdie, S. 1988. *The Satanic Verses*. New York: Viking.

Rushdie, S. 1991. *Imaginary Homelands: Essays and Criticism 1981–1991*. London: Granta and Viking.

Safran, W. 1991. Diasporas in modern societies: myths of homeland and return. *Diaspora*, 1(1), 83–99.

Safran, W. 2003. Recent French conceptualizations of diaspora. *Diaspora*, 12(3), 437–41.

Sheffer, G. 1995. The emergence of new ethno-national diasporas, in *Sociology of Diaspora: A Reader*, edited by A.K. Sahoo and B. Maharaj. Jaipur: Rawat, 1, 43–62.

Spivak, G.C. 1988. Subaltern studies: deconstructing historiography, in *Selected Subaltern Studies*, edited by R. Guha and G.C. Spivak. New York: Oxford University Press, 3–32.

Spivak, G.C. 1999. *A Critique of Postcolonial Reason: Toward a History of the Vanishing Present*. Cambridge, MA: Harvard University Press.

Thucydides. 1994. The history of the Peloponnesian War. Translated by R. Crawley, revised by R. Feetham. In *Great Books of the Western World*, volume 5: Herodotus, Thucydides. M.J. Adler, series editor. Chicago: Encyclopaedia Britannica, 343–616.

Van Hear, N. 1998. *New Diasporas: The Mass Exodus, Dispersal and Regrouping of Migrant Communities*. Seattle: University of Washington Press.

PART II
Political Cosmopolitanism

8

Cosmopolitanism and Natural Law: Rethinking Kant

Robert Fine

Kant's Cosmopolitanism and Natural Law

For the contemporary student of cosmopolitanism, Kant's vision of a cosmopolitan condition-to-come provides a rich and ever re-readable resource. Kant's political writings have become 'classic' texts of contemporary cosmopolitanism.[1] The critically minded cosmopolitan understands we cannot simply repeat Kant's eighteenth-century vision – that it is necessary to iron out inconsistencies in his thinking, radicalize it where its break from the old order of nation states is incomplete, draw out latent connections between peace and social justice, and modernize in terms of differences in historical context and conceptual framework – but a core cosmopolitan intuition is that Kant's cosmopolitanism remains as relevant to our times as it was to his own (Bohman and Lutz-Bachman 1997). To my mind, the return to Kant is fully justified by the richness of what we find in the texts but I do wish question the narrative within which the return to Kant is typically framed. In this narrative we are reminded of the strong cosmopolitan currents running through eighteenth-century enlightenment thought; then we are warned that in the long nineteenth century these cosmopolitan currents succumbed to nationalism, imperialism, racism, anti-Semitism and technology; finally we are reassured we are now in a position to remember the dead and recover enlightenment's cosmopolitan insight (Schlereth 1997). This narrative offers a consoling story of birth, death and rebirth. The widely held view that eighteenth-century cosmopolitanism left little

---

[1] The student of Kant's cosmopolitanism can find his ideas on this subject developed in his political writings published between 1784 and 1798, most systematically formulated in *The Metaphysics of Morals* (published 1797) and especially in the part entitled the 'Metaphysical Elements of the Theory of Justice' (or for short *Metaphysics of Justice*). Kant's political essays include 'Idea for a universal history with a cosmopolitan purpose' (1784); 'An answer to the question: "what is enlightenment?"' (1784); 'On the common saying: "This may be true in theory but it does not apply in practice"' (1793); 'Perpetual peace: a philosophical sketch' (1795); and 'The contest of faculties' (1798). They are collected in Kant (1991).

or no legacy for the long century that followed may be represented by Theodor Adorno's remark in *Negative Dialectics* that Hegel's alleged deification of the nation state was reactionary in comparison with Kant's cosmopolitan point of view (Adorno 1990) or by Jürgen Habermas' remark in *The Inclusion of the Other* that what Kant understood is that the idea of right is best suited to the identity of *world citizens*, not to that of citizens of a particular nation state, but that this insight was lost when the universalistic elements of right were swamped by the particularistic self-assertion of one nation against another (Habermas 1998). Sankar Muthu concludes his fine book on *Enlightenment against Empire* with a statement (outside the area of his expertise) that the cosmopolitanism characteristic of the enlightenment was unable to endure into the nineteenth century because of a sea change that occurred in philosophical assumptions, argument and temperaments (Muthu 2003: 259).[2]

To be sure, today cosmopolitans are reluctant to accept the conceptual framework in which Kant articulated his cosmopolitanism. Jürgen Habermas, for example, designates as 'metaphysical' the idea he finds in Kant that the cosmopolitan perspective can be accounted for primarily as an a priori demand of reason. He wishes to abandon this 'metaphysical' baggage on the 'post-metaphysical' ground that human beings are the authors of the laws to which they are subject. While Kant declared over the noise of battle that Providence, the Laws of Nature and the Cunning of Reason were inexorably taking human society forward to a universal cosmopolitan end, today Habermas looks for a space in which the political urgency of cosmopolitan solidarity may be given its due. He shies away from transcendental deductions in the conviction that cosmopolitanism represents the rational will of self-conscious and freely deliberating citizens and not the a priori deductions from the postulates of practical reason. He conceives cosmopolitanism as a shared project citizens can join and fashion in their own image, not as a rationally ordained blueprint projected onto reality (Habermas 1998). The dropping of natural law in the name of post-metaphysical principles has, however, not been a painless move. On the one hand, by turning his back on natural law, Habermas deprives himself of a powerful tool he might otherwise use to explain precisely why our response to new and difficult social conditions should take a cosmopolitan form. On the other

---

[2] The social theorists and philosophers of the long nineteenth century – Hegel, Marx, Nietzsche, Weber, Durkheim – were disciples of Kant's cosmopolitanism to a greater extent than is usually recognized. The sphere of their investigations was the fate of humanity in the modern bourgeois world and their benchmark remained that of humanity as a whole (Chernilo 2007). However, we cannot simply by-pass their critiques of Kant. They understood that the idea of right is a social form of subjectivity rooted in modern ethical life; a contradictory social form that arises late in human history and can suffer all manner of reversals (not least the right to the product of one's own labour transmutes into the right of the capitalist to expropriate the product of one's labour); a transitory social form that can transmute into a terrifying administrative power over society. If we try simply to jump over nineteenth-century social theory, the risk is that we end up repeating the illusions of eighteenth-century natural law in a less critical mode.

hand, Habermas allows natural law to return through a back door by depicting cosmopolitanism as a rational necessity that simply '*must* be institutionalised' (Habermas 1998: 179). To the extent that the rational necessity of cosmopolitanism is not up for discussion but derived from the universal principles of right, it might appear that the common sense of even the most post-metaphysical cosmopolitans remains more indebted to Kant's metaphysical approach than they might acknowledge. We tend to see ourselves as surpassing those philosophies of history, such as Kant's, which represent cosmopolitanism as the *telos* of social evolution but this does not stop our own time-consciousness following a teleological logic (Fine and Smith 2003, Smith and Fine 2004).

My argument is that Kant's cosmopolitanism should be situated in the framework of modern natural law. The key objection to this claim is that Kant's cosmopolitanism represented a move away from the natural law concept of *ius gentium* – that natural law was precisely the tradition from which Kant departed. Indeed, Kant was famously critical of many of the most celebrated natural law theorists – Grotius, Pufendorf, Vattel and the rest – as 'sorry comforters' whose justifications of the supremacy of state sovereignty were unable to provide for a lawful and peaceful community of nations based on universal law (Brown 2005, Hoffe 2006). It is true that Kant was critical of the natural law tradition but I maintain that his critique of traditional natural law was executed in the service of modern natural law. Kant did not break from natural law, he modernized it.

Let us clarify our terms. Modern natural law theory put the idea of right at the centre of its world. It was in the name of right that it attacked the old order of servitude, inequality and superstition; diagnosed the 'corruptions', 'inconveniences' and 'pathologies' characteristic of the new bourgeois order; and analysed the legal, moral and political requirements of this ascendant society. Modern natural law provided the epistemological framework in which philosophers of right analysed new forms of social inequality, political misrule and cultural isolation that accompanied the growth of bourgeois society and prescribed remedies through projects of educational reform, social intervention and political transformation. Its premise was the right of private property which made possible not only the liberty and equality of property owners but also the wealth of nations. Its concern was over the new forms of injustice brought into being by the rise of modern civil society. Its solution was the development of new moral, legal and political forms in which the injustices of civil society could be remedied (Fine 2002). In the final stage of its journey modern natural law presented international law as the form of inter-state relations in which the principle of sovereignty could be upheld.

The natural law tradition long preceded the Enlightenment. In early modernity it provided a language for the legitimation of hierarchies of inequality. Stephen Toulmin recounts that the Greek composite, 'cosmopolis', was in fact central to the natural law tradition. It expressed the unity of the *cosmos* (the order of nature) and the *polis* (the order of human society) – an idea of harmony in which the structure of nature would reinforce a just social order. It meant that what God is to nature, so too the king is to the state, the husband to his wife and the father to his family (Toulmin 1992). Traditional natural law presupposed two different kinds of law, natural and positive: natural laws emanating from nature, positive laws posited by human beings (Colletti 1972). Traditional natural law was not just a theory of natural law but a theory that privileged natural law over positive laws. It limited the field of human legislation so that even the highest power *on earth* was subject to its rule. Otto Gierke summarized this way of thinking thus: 'whatever statute or act of government contradicted the eternal and immutable principles of natural law was utterly void and would bind no one' (Gierke 1958).

By putting forward the idea of 'right' at the core of its thinking modern natural law showed its superiority to the natural law tradition. It broke from traditional natural law by basing itself on the idea of equal right but drew from the tradition the universalistic insight that natural law applies to all times, all places, all societies, all people (Chernilo 2010). It revealed so-called 'old rights' to be no more than entrenched privileges of the Church, state and nobility but it could only put the idea of right at the centre of its thinking by rationalizing its existence (Fine 2002). It overcame natural law in its traditional form only to reconstruct it in a modern form by naturalizing the institutions of capitalist society. It declared with Hobbes that 'obedience to the civil law is the law of nature' (Hobbes 1996). It dissolved the traditional myth of a morally infused state of nature but reconstituted its own form of abstraction in the idea of a multiplicity of atomized individuals in a chaotic state of nature. In empirical versions of modern natural law this abstraction was disguised as an empirical observation; in formal versions, especially that of Kant, this disguise was stripped away and the speculative character of this abstraction admitted. This did not stop Kant from turning relations of bourgeois society into the a priori condition of social organization – or more specifically into the a priori condition of the asocial form of sociality that results from a multitude of conflicting interests. As Gillian Rose put it, Kant could only conceive of uniting individuals 'externally' since he presupposed from the start the existence of a multitude of isolated and competing individuals (Rose 1981). Bourgeois society was the hidden premise of Kant's philosophy of right.

Kant's Cosmopolitanism and the System of Right

Near the start of the *Metaphysics of Justice* Kant writes that 'the student of natural right ... has to supply the immutable principles on which all positive legislation must rest' (Kant 1991: 132). For Kant, the immutable principles of 'right' cannot be based on what the law happens to say in any particular place or time; it can only be drawn from the realm of natural laws defined as laws to which 'an obligation can be recognised *a priori* by reason without external legislation' (Kant 1996: 26). This was crucial to the *critical* content of Kant's philosophy of right. For if universal laws were based simply on what the law is empirically, in the manner of positivist jurisprudence, they might offer no more than an endorsement of the status quo. There could be no clearer statement of Kant's self-positioning within the natural law tradition. The return to Kant's cosmopolitanism is at once a return to natural law, indeed to what was arguably the high point of the natural law tradition.

The great strength of Kant's reconstruction of natural law theory lay in the systematic character of his methodology as he moved from the simplest and most abstract elements of the system of right to increasingly more complex and concrete forms (Cavallar 1999). Kant argued that the idea of natural right is realized in practice through a progression of laws and institutions beginning with private law, moving on to public law, thence to international law and finally to cosmopolitan law. He begins with the idea of right in general as 'the sum of those conditions within which the will of one person can be reconciled with the will of another in accordance with a universal law of freedom' (Intro §B). Kant maintains that freedom is only possible under law because individuals can only be free in relation to others. In his 'Theory and Practice' essay he elaborates this relational concept of right:

> *The whole of concept of external right is derived from the concept of freedom in the mutual external relationships of human beings ... Right is the restriction of each individual's freedom so that it harmonizes with the freedom of everyone else in so far as this is possible within the terms of a general law. And public law is the distinctive quality of the external laws which make this constant harmony possible. Since every restriction of freedom through the arbitrary will of another party is termed coercion, it follows that a civil constitution is a relationship among free men who are subject to coercive laws, while they retain their freedom within the general union with their fellows.* (Kant 1991: 73)

As Richard Beardsworth observes, 'one form of freedom and coercion (the force-field of arbitrary wills) is replaced by another form of coercion and freedom: the force of public law' (Beardsworth 2011). Kant acknowledges that public law is necessarily coercive and can become despotic but he argues that the risk has to be taken because a universal system of public law is the only form yet discovered in which my right of subjective freedom can be reconciled with yours. Kant argues that the right to subjective freedom is the natural right of every human being but that it requires legal and political supports if it is to have peremptory and not merely provisional validity (Flikschuh 2000).

From this beginning Kant addresses the elements of private law: for example, the idea of a subject (*persona*) as a possessor of rights whose 'moral personality is nothing but the freedom of a rational being under moral laws'; the idea of a 'thing' (*res*) as 'an object of free will that itself lacks freedom'; the separation of property from mere physical possession; the idea that there is nothing in the world, not even one's honour, that cannot be turned into alienable property. Kant then takes the reader from the sphere of private law to that of public law where he deduces from the 'Idea of the state as it ought to be' the institutional forms of a republican constitution: a representative legislature to establish universal norms, an executive to subsume particular cases under these universal norms, a judiciary to determine what is right in cases of conflict, and the constitutional separation of powers to keep these spheres of activity distinct in accordance with the 'moments of its concept' (Kant 1996: §45). Kant's ideal state grounded in reason – or as he put it, a perfect *societas civilis* – was to be a republic resting on the rule of law, representative government and the separation of powers.

Gillian Rose has noted that the juridical categories Kant deduced as rational forms of an ideal political community are for the most part categories of Roman law (Rose 1981: 84). One of the limitations of this approach has been observed in a seminal essay by Manfred Riedel: it concerns Kant's inability to distinguish between civil society and the state (Riedel 1984). Kant inherited the old European tradition that goes back to Aristotle's κοιωυια πολιτικη (political community) whose classic formula was the fusion of state and civil society. It was not possible within this framework to understand civil society in its modern form; that is, as a de-traditionalized society separated on one side from the family and on the other from the state (Hegel 1991: §182). In this respect Kant fell short of the empirical wing of natural law, notably Adam Ferguson and Adam Smith, as well as Hegel, since Scottish political economy played a massive part in dissecting the anatomy of bourgeois civil society and Hegel's *Philosophy of Right* played an equally massive part in conceptualizing civil society as a distinctive sphere of social life (Fine 2001, Fine and Vazquez 2006). Kant's conceptual inability to distinguish civil society and the state was bound to have ramifications for his theory of cosmopolitanism.

The next stage of Kant's journey from the spheres of private and public law took him to the spheres of international and then cosmopolitan law. Following the same 'deductive' method Kant sought to derive the forms and practices of an ideal international order from the juridical postulates of practical reason. His project was to extend the philosophy of right beyond its national limitations and address the idea of right in what we might call extra-societal relations. This involved him a two step strategy: the first to do with the chasm separating the theory of international law from its actual practical existence in the world; the second to do with the conceptualization of cosmopolitan law as well as its actualization. Kant distinguished between international law which roughly speaking refers to relations between one state and another, and cosmopolitan law which refers to relations between individuals of one state and individuals of another *and* between individuals of one state and another state as a whole. Whilst states alone are subjects of international law, individuals are *also* subjects of cosmopolitan law.

Kant attacked the 'depravity' of the existing international order because he saw it as lacking any effective legal relations and as perpetually prone to wars between states. He recognized that the *theory* of international law (*ius gentium*) was well established but insisted it was more semblance than substance because it lacked the abstract coercive force required of any genuine law. In the eyes of Kant, the natural law tradition merely painted a legal gloss on a system in which rulers granted themselves the licence to go to war as they pleased, used any means of warfare necessary, exploited newly discovered colonies as if they were lands without people, and treated foreigners within their own lands as aliens without rights (Kant 1991: 103–5). Kant was not the first to claim that existing international relations functioned more like a Hobbesian war of all states against all than a properly functioning legal order but what was most innovative in his approach was his attempt to understand and remedy this situation. He argued that 'the greatest evils which oppress civilised nations are the result of war' not least because wars were becoming a graveyard of human rights for nations as a whole and not just for their armed forces. Kant's dictum was that politics could no longer justify wars in terms of sovereign prerogative or glory. Henceforth 'all politics', as he put it, 'must bend the knee before right' (Kant 1991: 174 and 231).

Kant emphasized the need to develop international legal norms to limit the damage caused by wars. The 'old right' of sovereigns to declare war without consulting their subjects must be annulled; citizens must have the right to give their consent to any declaration of war; wars must be conducted in accordance with principles which leave states with the possibility of entering a 'state of right' after the war; barbaric acts of warfare must be criminalized (Kant 1991: 166). More radically, Kant sought to unpack the institutional conditions that would make it possible for all wars to be superseded and standing armies abolished. Here the main problem was that, in the absence of any external legal authority, international laws were interpreted and applied by the warring states themselves. Kant argued that an international authority over that of states had to be established that would be in some ways akin to the national authority of the Leviathan over individuals, *except* – and this was a major proviso – that this domestic analogy must not be over-stretched. Kant reiterated that the rational deduction from the idea of universal right could *not* be a world state but this has not stopped some commentators from attributing to Kant the belief that a society of world citizens would supersede political states (Bull 1977). Kant explained that he was opposed to the creation of a world state because there was nothing to stop it turning into a 'universal despotism', a despotism writ large. Kant looked rather to the establishment of a Federation or League of Nations based on mutual cooperation and voluntary consent among a plurality of independent states. He envisaged that such a Federation could start with an alliance of republics but would eventually encompass 'all the nations of the earth' (Kant 1991: 105–14). This conclusion was deeply rooted in the systematic character of Kant's metaphysics. The Federation of Nations would not supersede the independence of states but would challenge the turning of state independence into the absolute (Brown 2005). On the one hand, the rights of states would be relativized downward in relation to citizens (the task of republicanism); on the other, they would be relativized upward in relation to international law (the task of the Federation). What we find in Kant's cosmopolitanism is not a critique of the state as such but a critique of the deification of the state in doctrines of absolute state sovereignty. His point was that every sphere of right – private and public right in the domestic field and international and cosmopolitan right in the international field – was to have its due in the system of right as a whole.

The other markedly innovative aspect of Kant's political writings was to develop the concept of cosmopolitan right, that is, rights ordinary people should have in relation to foreigners and foreign states when they engage in international commerce, migration, travel or flight. Kant restricted cosmopolitan right to the right to hospitality individuals should possess as citizens of the world – the right to visit all regions of the world, initiate communication with other peoples, try to engage in commerce with them and appeal to them for help. Kant is often criticized for restricting the extent of this right – 'the other can turn him away if this can be done without destroying him' (Kant 1991: 105–8) – but it is important to see the context in which he made such statements (Benhabib 2004). Kant was seeking to avoid abuses committed in the name of the 'right of hospitality', notably those unleashed on non-European people by European states and trading companies. Kant referred to the 'Jesuitism' of colonial interpretations of 'universal hospitality' designed to justify the subjugation of non-European peoples on the pretext that they mistreated European travellers – 'travellers' who were actually armed invaders. He attacked the 'inhospitable conduct' of so-called civilized states which spoke of 'visiting' foreign countries but actually were engaged in conquering them. He defended the right of non-European peoples to their own ways of life even if they did not share European commercial values. Towards the end of the section on 'cosmopolitan right' in the *Metaphysics of Justice* Kant repudiated justifications of European colonialism in terms of 'bringing culture to uncivilised peoples' and purging the home country of 'depraved characters'. This improbable combination, Kant argued, simply glossed over the extermination, enslavement and abuse of colonized peoples (Kant 1996: §62).

Sankar Muthu has done us a great service in demonstrating how radically opposed Kant was to European imperial practices (Muthu 2000 and 2003). He pointed out that Kant was not a standard bearer of cosmopolitan morality as it is normally conceived. Kant believed everyone should be a 'friend of human beings as such' but noted:

> *The benevolence present in love for all human beings is indeed the greatest in its extent, but the smallest in its degree; and when I say that I take an interest in this human being's well-being only out of my love for all human beings, the interest I take is as slight as an interest can be. (Cited in Muthu 2000: 23–4)*

Kant argued that 'love for a particular group' and 'general love for the entire human race' are each fraught with dangers: the former because it breeds indifference to 'the class of men with whom <one> stands in no connection'; the latter because 'the friend of humanity ... cannot fail to dissipate his inclination through its excessive generality and quite loses any adherence to individual persons' (*ibid.*). Faced with this difficulty, Kant (in a manner to be followed by Durkheim) looked to the formation of a patriotism in which the citizen could both express 'fealty to his country' and promote the 'well-being of the entire world'. He envisioned a world of multiple interconnections – one that required that we come to terms with the global dynamics of modern society.

Natural Law and History

Kant recognized that the cosmopolitan ideals that once lit up the dawn of the French revolution quickly succumbed to wars of conquest both in Europe and in the non-European world which were marred by horrifying instances of injustice. His obstinacy, however, lay in attempting to reconcile the principle on which the world revolution was turning, the rise of national self-determination, with universal principles of right. The form of this reconciliation was not predetermined and in the non-European world he defended the right of national self-determination in the face of colonial conquest. From a moral point of view Kant maintained that the duty to act in accordance with the principles of right was incumbent both upon rulers however great the sacrifice they had to make, upon ordinary people whether or not public opinion recognized it, and upon European nations engaged in imperial expansion. From a historical point of view he argued that longer-term historical tendencies were conducive to cosmopolitan ideas and practices. He pointed to the economic utility of cosmopolitanism in a commercial age in which peaceful exchange is more profitable than war and plunder; the political utility of cosmopolitanism for states faced with the escalating costs and risks of modern warfare; the plausibility of cosmopolitanism in an age in which citizens have the opportunity both to reach a higher level of political maturity and to have a greater voice in political decision making; and above all the salience of cosmopolitanism to a world marked by the growing interconnectedness of peoples: 'the peoples of the earth have entered in varying degrees into a universal community, so that a violation of rights in one part of the world is felt everywhere' (Kant 1991: 107–8).

Kant acknowledged countervailing tendencies, for example, that republican citizens may be civilized 'only in respect of outward courtesies and proprieties'. He argued, however, that the germ of enlightenment necessarily evolves towards a universal end, 'the perfect civil union of humankind' and that this universal purpose was 'guaranteed by no less an authority than the great artist *Nature* herself' (Kant 1991: 50 and 114). In Kant's teleology 'the means nature employs to bring about the development of innate capacities is that of antagonism with society'. The 'unsocial sociability of men', as he famously put it, pushes humanity forward (Kant 1991: 44). Nature may offer us a salutary education but it is 'harsh and stern' in its pedagogy. It does so by way of great hardships even to the extent of nearly destroying the whole human race. In this teleology there is no rosy optimism, no resignation in the face of violence, and no justification of violence today in the name of perfection tomorrow. What we find is something altogether more interesting: a struggle in dark times to retain faith in the possibility of human progress and to translate this faith into practice.

Kant's cosmopolitanism may be read as part a collective effort to radicalize the distinctive accomplishment of eighteenth-century revolutions: the declarations of the rights of man and citizen. If the idea of the rights of man signified that every 'man' should be conceived as a bearer of rights, it contrasted with traditional societies in which personality was a privileged status distinct from the majority of the population. Roman law distinguished between the status of persons who had the right to have rights and slaves who did not. By contrast, the declarations of the rights of man and citizen universalized the status of personality so that every man could in principle be deemed a bearer of rights. The more radical wing of eighteenth-century republicanism recognized the multiple exclusions present in practice in the declarations of the rights of man and citizen, but argued that they provided the framework in which struggles for the rights of women, slaves, colonial subjects, Jews, workers, criminals, lunatics and other excluded groups could be attached to the original republican conception (Hunt 2007). From the Black Jacobins of Saint Domingue to the petitions of Olympe de Gouges the excluded had most to gain from the universality of rights. The specific contribution of Kant was to address the contradiction between the universality of the idea of the rights of man and its particular national existence. It seemed that the rights of man stopped at the gates of the city: no citizen, no rights.

Kant's search for a solution led him down three connected paths: the expansion of republican forms of government, the enhancement of international law and the establishment of international legal authority. It was a prescient vision of reform but, as his successors could see more clearly, one that could also reproduce the very problems it set out to solve. The affinity between cosmopolitanism and republicanism could be contradicted by the inversion of the rights of man into a duty of unconditional obedience to the state which grants these rights and into a feeling of unthinking patriotism among citizens who identify with the state. The extension of republicanism could be contradicted by the means by which it was achieved: war, colonial conquest, human suffering. The formation of a voluntary League of Nations might well not provide the alchemy for turning perpetual war into perpetual peace and could be contradicted by its own principles of voluntarism and self-determination. Insofar as Kant shared the dream of modern natural law, a dream transformed into a political method by the French Revolution, that the rational way of dealing with problems is to 'sweep away the inherited clutter from traditions, clean the slate and start again from scratch' (Toulmin 1992: 175), he could not know how heavily the burden of history weighs upon the present.

Kant's relation to the natural law tradition was more like a dialogue than a rupture. The natural law jurists he lumped together as 'sorry comforters' were closer to him than he acknowledged: they were the first to give the world a regular system of natural jurisprudence, the first to conceive of the unity of the human race in spite of its division into nations, the first to argue that universal human unity was a natural law even if it went unacknowledged by those who held that the duties of humanity ought to be conferred on compatriots alone. *Ius gentium* stood for legal principles that were binding despite the absence of higher authority: treaties had to be respected, states had to recognize one another reciprocally as sovereign, the conduct of war had to preserve the possibility of a future peace (Hegel 1991: §333). States were not considered merely as private persons but as members of a society in which every state was entitled to be recognized as an independent power in the eyes of other states. As Hegel observed, when Napoleon declared that 'the French Republic is no more in need of recognition than the sun is' this illusion of self-sufficiency was his undoing. Grotius and Pufendorf defended the sovereignty of states but also treated states as moral personalities with civil obligations to one another. Christian Wolff looked to Europe as a forerunner of a time when 'the voice of nature will reach the civilised peoples of the world and they will realise that all men are brothers'. Vattel subordinated the interests of a particular society to 'the ties of the universal society which nature has established among men' and looked to commerce and communication as media through which this *civitas maxima* could be established. Kant overstated his own break from the tradition of natural law and in so doing also overstated the break represented by the rise of republicanism (Tuck 2001).

Hegel observed in *The Philosophy of Right* that republican states may require the consent of the people to go to war or at least to finance war, but responsibility for making war and peace and for the command of armed forces does not generally lie with the people but with the rulers. In any event the people may be more prone to martial enthusiasm than their rulers. The very rationality of republican institutions can be a source of popular identification with them and the trust people have in the state may encourage them to identify their interests with the interests of the state (Hegel 1991: §268). In times of war, when the independence of the state is at risk, popular identification with it is likely to be intensified and lead to a situation in which the rights of individuals become a matter of indifference compared with the survival of the state (§145A). Citizens may be required to sacrifice themselves to the interest of the state, however much their self-sacrifice is represented as an act of individual valour (Hegel 1991: §328R). Wars can be as useful for republican as for other states as a means of averting internal unrest and consolidating the power of the state within. They can appear ethical because they elevate the interest of the community as a whole over the private interest of the individual, patriotism over private enrichment. And there is plenty of scope for republican states to go to war if they feel they have suffered an injury from another state or the security of its people is at risk. A League of Nations, though designed to put an end to war, is quite capable of constructing its own enemies and starting new wars (Hegel 1991: §324A).

In the tradition of natural law thinking Kant imposed his own *Sollen* – his own prescriptions of what political community ought to be – on society. It was not always a particularly liberal prescription in the customary sense of the term. He wrote in the *Metaphysics of Justice* that the formation of a republican state is a rational necessity everyone must recognize and that people must be forced into state formation if they fail to do so of their own accord. In another passage he wrote that the unilateral will of property owners *must* give way to a 'collective, universal and powerful Will' and that people must obey the law once they have entered into a 'civil condition' (§8). In another passage he wrote that the duty of the citizen is to 'endure even the most intolerable abuse of supreme authority' and that the 'well-being of the state' must not be confused with 'the welfare or happiness of the citizens of the state' (§86). In another he insists that the state legislature can do 'absolutely no injustice to anyone' and that 'the people's duty <is> to endure even the most intolerable abuse of supreme authority' (§86). Whilst Kant affirmed the right and duty of citizens to think for themselves, he restricted this right and duty to 'the use which anyone may make of it as a man of learning addressing the entire reading public' (Kant 1991: 55); otherwise, as in the case of an officer receiving a command from his superiors or a clergyman receiving an order from the church, they must obey since the freedom of citizens does not lie in their capacity to choose for or against the law but only in their 'internal legislation of reason' (§28).

These normative prescriptions doubtless mirror something of the nature of modern political community but a certain state-consciousness still haunts the antechambers of Kant's discussion. He gives a roughly accurate empirical account of the organization of power in modern republican states (albeit without fully recognizing the social character of civil society) and then converts these empirical facts into juridical postulates of practical reason. To paraphrase Marx, he rediscovers the idea of 'right' in every sphere of law he depicts. Once we explore the dark side of the modern state – the social inequalities and class conflicts of civil society, the overweening power of the executive, the narrow limits of representation, the military machines it constructs, its interest in war and conquest, its tendency to present itself as an 'Earthly God' – the prospect of ratcheting cosmopolitanism onto these materials is bound to appear less promising.

Perhaps the least appealing aspect of Kant's cosmopolitanism has to do with his anthropological writings, which are sometimes indicted for their racist resonances (McCarthy 2009: 42–68). Kant has been accused of serving as a philosophical source of race-thinking *avant la lettre* and at face value his representation of Native Americans as too weak for hard work, Africans as adapted to the culture of slaves, Asians as civilized but static and Europeans as capable of progress towards perfection do seem to reinforce these charges. They appear either to reveal the susceptibility of even the most enlightened philosophers to the prejudices of their day or to reveal the imperialistic character of cosmopolitanism itself. My own inclination is to go down neither of these roads. The more difficult and interesting path, to my mind, would be to revisit the anthropology in the light of Kant's natural law theory. For all its manifold limitations, Kant's theorization of 'race' was opposed to polygenetic views of the origins of the human species, that is, to the view that the different races had no common origin and no possibility of a common end. If Kant's anthropology was an attempt to explain differences between the races in terms of geographical, climactic and economic conditions (between hunting, pastoral, agricultural and commercial modes of production), then we might read his monogenetic argument as an attempt to demonstrate that so-called racial differences do not challenge the biological unity of the human race and that even the unequal differentiation of human types finds its teleological purpose in nature's plan that all natural capacities are destined to be developed throughout the human species and that the universality of the human condition is becoming a legal, political and moral norm. I do not wish to nail my flag to this mast but a definite advantage of this reading is to rescue the unity of Kant's own philosophical, political and anthropological writings.

Conclusion: Cosmopolitanism Beyond Natural Law?

Hegel recognized that the greatness of Kant's cosmopolitan vision lay in the fact that he had 'some inkling of the nature of spirit ... to assume a higher shape than that in which its being originally consisted' and that in this respect he was superior to those for whom spirit remained an 'empty word' (Hegel 1991: §343R). Kant understood that it is a matter of 'infinite importance' that 'a human being counts as such because he is a human being, not because he is a Jew, Catholic, Protestant, German, Italian, etc.' (Hegel 1991: §209R). Hegel, however, adds his own notes of realism. For example, in his *Philosophy of History* he comments that among European states there naturally arises a common interest in preserving their own power and independence but also that the balance of power between them is continually being threatened and can lead to conditions of mutual mistrust. Thus when the Thirty Years' War resulted in the utter desolation of all parties, the Peace of Westphalia brought to a close this period of perpetual war by establishing a legal framework which ratified the coexistence of religious parties and established a system of rights based on human will rather than divine command. The Treaty of Westphalia (1648) was a major step forward in the liberation of political life from the control of the Church. It marked the replacement of blind obedience to divine law by the principle of obedience to the laws of one's own making. Executive powers previously the property of dynastic families were transferred into functions of the state. Privileges of the feudal nobility were curtailed and transformed into official state positions. The dependence of the people on noble masters was broken and dependence on the state came in its stead. Feudal retinues were replaced by standing armies. These developments in turn created new powers and new imbalances of power which disrupted the formation of a common interest among states. The story does not of course end in Hegel's own times.

Kant's philosophy of right was a critical philosophy. His natural law theory was critical in that it sought to change the world. It did not stop at what was empirically given whether this was supported by the authority of the state, the agreement of human beings or the inner moral feelings of individuals. It did not trust in any publicly recognized truth. When it encountered difficulties in distinguishing what is right among a variety of opinions, it based its judgement on genuine concern for the concept itself. His cosmopolitanism was at its most radical when it pushed at the boundaries of natural law theory and advanced it not as a blueprint for an ideal legal and political order-to-come but as a reminder of what human freedom makes possible. Kant puts this sense of possibility very well when he writes:

> *Humanity is by its very nature capable of constant progress and improvement without forfeiting its strength ... no one can or ought to decide what the highest degree may be at which mankind may have to stop progressing, and hence how wide a gap may still of necessity remain between the idea and its execution. For this will depend on freedom, which can transcend any limit we care to impose.* (Kant 1991: 189–91)

Kant's critical idealism was based on the idea of 'cancelling' the empirical world in favour of the a priori and beneath its formal criteria definite social institutions were, as Hegel put it, 'smuggled in'. His insistence on the importance of the idea of right became inadequate when he took something conditioned by specific social relations and transformed it into the absolute. When we refuse to consider the subjective dispositions of individuals, there is always the temptation to impose a utopian blueprint on them.

Perhaps this is another way of saying that the seeds of transforming Kant's critical idealism into something more conventional were already present in the natural law approach. The deduction of the institutional forms of right from postulates of practical reason can have conservative as well as critical appropriations. At the time of Kant's writing, international law operated largely in terms of treaties and other agreements between sovereign states; the idea of republican statehood was restricted to Europe and America; the rest of the world was either under their imperial control or outside world society altogether; there was no United Nations and no concept of human rights as such. Today, writing in the wake of the century of catastrophe, it might appear that the elements of the cosmopolitan condition have finally come into place. The risk is that an unmediated appropriation of Kant's cosmopolitan thinking can turn his critical idealism into something more akin to an uncritical positivism. The other legacy we might draw from Kant is to try once again to separate the rational kernel of Kantian natural law theory from its mystical shell in our own efforts to come to terms with the dynamics of global society and confront the barbarism within.

Acknowledgements

I should like to thank Richard Beardsworth, Gurminder Bhambra, Glynis Cousin and Lydia Morris for their suggestions.

Bibliography

Adorno, T. 1990. *Negative Dialectics*. London: Routledge.
Arendt, H. 1992. *Lectures on Kant's Political Philosophy*. Edited with an interpretive essay by Ronald Beiner. Chicago: Chicago University Press.
Beardsworth, Richard. 2011. *Cosmopolitanism and International Relations Theory*. Cambridge: Polity Press.
Benhabib, S. 2004. *The Right of Others: Aliens, Residents, and Citizens*. Cambridge: Cambridge University Press.
Bohman, J. and Lutz-Bachmann, M. (eds). 1997. *Perpetual Peace. Essays on Kant's Cosmopolitan Ideal*. Cambridge, MA: MIT Press.

Brown, C. 2006. Kantian cosmopolitan law and the idea of a cosmopolitan constitution. *History of Political Thought*, 27(4), 661–84.
Brown, G. 2005. State sovereignty, federation and Kantian cosmopolitanism. *European Journal of International Relations*, 11(4), 495–522.
Bull, H. 1977. *The Anarchical Society: A Study of Order in World Politics*. London: Macmillan.
Cavallar, G. 1999. *Kant and the Theory and Practice of International Right*. Cardiff: University of Wales Press.
Chernilo, D. 2007. A quest for universalism: re-assessing the nature of classical social theory's cosmopolitanism. *European Journal of Social Theory*, 10(1), 17–35.
Chernilo, D. 2010. On the relationship between social theory and natural law: lessons from Karl Löwith and Leo Strauss. *History of the Human Sciences*, 23(5), 91–112.
Colletti, L. 1972. Rousseau as critic of civil society, in *From Rousseau to Lenin*, trans. John Merrington and Judith White. London: New Left Books.
Fine, R. 2001. *Political Investigations*. London: Routledge.
Fine, R. 2002. *Democracy and the Rule of Law: Marx's Critique of the Legal Form*. Caldwell: The Blackburn Press (new edition of Pluto Press 1984).
Fine, R. 2003. Kant's theory of cosmopolitanism and Hegel's critique. *Philosophy and Social Criticism*, 29(6), 609–30.
Fine, R. 2007. *Cosmopolitanism*. London: Routledge.
Fine, R. and Smith, W. 2003. Jürgen Habermas' theory of cosmopolitanism. *Constellations*, 10(4), 469–87.
Fine, R. and Vazquez, R. 2006. Freedom and right in modern society: reading Hegel's *Philosophy of Right*. *Law and Sociology, Current Legal Issues*, 8, 241–53.
Flikschuh, K. 2000. *Kant and Modern Political Philosophy*. Cambridge: Cambridge University Press.
Gierke, Otto Friedrich von. *Natural Law and the Theory of Society, 1500 to 1800*. Cambridge.
Habermas, J. 1998. Kant's idea of perpetual peace: at two hundred years' historical remove, in *The Inclusion of the Other: Studies in Political Theory*. Cambridge, MA: The MIT Press.
Hegel, G. 1991. *Philosophy of Right*. Edited by A.W. Wood and translated by H.B. Nisbet, Cambridge: Cambridge University Press.
Hobbes, T. 1996. *Leviathan*. Cambridge: Cambridge University Press.
Hoffe, O. 2006. *Kant's Cosmopolitan Theory of Law and Peace*. Cambridge: Cambridge University Press.
Hunt, L. 2007. *Inventing Human Rights: A History*. New York: W.W. Norton.
Kant, I. 1987. *Critique of Judgment*. Translated by Werner S. Pluhar. Cambridge: Hackett Publishing Company.
Kant, I. 1991. *Kant: Political Writings*. Edited by H. Reiss. Cambridge: Cambridge University Press.
Kant, I. 1996. *The Metaphysics of Morals*. Translated and edited by Mary Gregor, introduction by Roger Sullivan. Cambridge: Cambridge University Press.

McCarthy, G.T. 2009. *Race, Empire, and the Idea of Human Development*. Cambridge: Cambridge University Press.

Muthu, S. 2000. Justice and foreigners: Kant's cosmopolitan right. *Constellations*, 7(1), 23–44.

Muthu, S. 2003. *Enlightenment against Empire*. Princeton: Princeton University Press.

Riedel, M. 1984. *Between Tradition and Revolution: The Hegelian Transformation of Political Philosophy*. Cambridge: Cambridge University Press.

Rose, G. 1981. *Hegel Contra Sociology*. London: Athlone.

Schlereth, T. 1997. *The Cosmopolitan Ideal in Enlightenment Thought: Its Form and Function in the Ideas of Franklin, Hume and Voltaire*. Notre Dame: University of Notre Dame Press.

Smith, W. and Fine, R. 2004. Kantian cosmopolitanism today: John Rawls and Jürgen Habermas on Immanuel Kant's *Foedus Pacificum*. *Kings College Law Journal*, 15(1), 5–22.

Toulmin, S. 1992. *Cosmopolis: The Hidden Agenda of Modernity*. Chicago: University of Chicago Press.

Tuck, R. 2001. *The Rights of War and Peace: Political Thought and the International Order from Grotius to Kant*. Oxford: Oxford University Press.

Cosmopolitanism, Democracy and the Global Order

David Held

Cosmopolitanism is concerned to disclose the ethical, cultural and legal basis of political order in a world where political communities and states matter, but not only and exclusively. In circumstances where the trajectories of each and every country are tightly entwined, the partiality of 'reasons of state' needs to be recognized. While states are hugely important vehicles to aid the delivery of effective public recognition, equal liberty and social justice, they should not be thought of as ontologically privileged. They can be judged by how far they deliver these public goods and how far they fail; for the history of states is marked, of course, not just by phases of bad leadership and corruption but also by the most brutal episodes. A cosmopolitanism relevant to our global age must take this as a starting point, and build an ethically sound and politically robust conception of the proper basis of political community, and of the relations among communities.

This chapter examines why cosmopolitanism remains a compelling political philosophy and approach to global challenges. The first section sets out the context of cosmopolitanism; that is, an explanation of why cosmopolitanism is relevant to global political and social problems. It focuses on cosmopolitan values rooted in leading international regimes and organizations. The section that follows explores the structure and meaning of cosmopolitanism in more detail, and sets out how I understand this important concept. The third section discusses the relation between cosmopolitan values and principles and the idea of a cosmopolitan legal community. The final two sections examine the significance of these notions in meeting many of today's global challenges. The argument is that the multilateral order is inadequate, and the principles that underpin it are inappropriate, to the global issues faced in the twenty-first century. Cosmopolitanism, it is contended, discloses a more suitable and productive approach. Accordingly, the chapter offers an account of the relevance of cosmopolitanism to global challenges, rather than a defence of cosmopolitanism against leading criticisms (see Held 1995, 2004, Archibugi 2009).

The Context of Cosmopolitanism

Thinking about the future of humankind on the basis of the early years of the twenty-first century does not give grounds for optimism. From 9/11 to the 2006 war in the Middle East, terrorism, conflict, territorial struggle and the clash of identities appear to define the moment. The wars in Afghanistan, Iraq, Israel/Lebanon, Israel/Gaza and elsewhere suggest that political violence is an irreducible feature of our age. Perversely, globalization seems to have dramatized the significance of differences between peoples; far from the globalization of communications easing understanding and the translation of ideas, it seems to have highlighted what it is that people do not have in common and find dislikeable about each other (Bull 1977: 127). Moreover, the contemporary drivers of political nationalism – self-determination, secure borders, geo-political and geo-economic advantage – place an emphasis on the pursuit of the national interest above concerns with what it is that humans might have in common.

Yet, it is easy to overstate the moment and exaggerate from one set of historical experiences. While each of the elements mentioned poses a challenge to a rule-based global order, it is a profound mistake to forget that the twentieth century established a series of cosmopolitan steps towards the delimitation of the nature and form of political community, sovereignty and 'reasons of state'. These steps were laid down after the First and Second World Wars which brought humanity to the edge of the abyss – not once but twice. At a time as difficult as the start of the twenty-first century, it is important to recall why these steps were taken and remind oneself of their significance.

From the foundation of the UN system to the EU, from changes to the laws of war to the entrenchment of human rights, from the emergence of international environmental regimes to the establishment of the International Criminal Court, people have sought to reframe human activity and embed it in law, rights and responsibilities. Many of these developments were initiated against the background of formidable threats to humankind – above all, Nazism, fascism and Stalinism. Those involved in them affirmed the importance of universal principles, human rights and the rule of law in the face of strong temptations to simply put up the shutters and defend the position of only some countries and nations. They rejected the view of national and moral particularists that belonging to a given community limits and determines the moral worth of individuals and the nature of their freedom, and they defended the irreducible moral status of each and every person. At the centre of such thinking is the cosmopolitan view that human well-being is not defined by geographical or cultural locations, that national or ethnic or gendered boundaries should not determine the limits of rights or responsibilities for the satisfaction of basic human needs, and that all human beings require equal moral respect and concern. The principles of equal respect, equal concern, and the priority of the vital needs of all human beings are not principles for some remote utopia; for they are at the centre of significant post-Second World War legal and political developments.

Cosmopolitanism, Democracy and the Global Order

What does 'cosmopolitan' mean in this context? (see Held 2002). In the first instance, cosmopolitanism refers to those basic values which set down standards or boundaries which no agent, whether a representative of a global body, state or civil association, should be able to violate. Focused on the claims of each person as an individual, these values espouse the idea that human beings are in a fundamental sense equal, and that they deserve equal political treatment; that is, treatment based upon the equal care and consideration of their agency, irrespective of the community in which they were born or brought up. After over 200 years of nationalism, sustained nation-state formation and seemingly endless conflicts over territory and resources, such values could be thought of as out of place. But such values are already enshrined in the law of war, human rights law, the statute of the ICC, among many other international rules and legal arrangements.

Second, cosmopolitanism can be taken to refer to those forms of political regulation and law-making which create powers, rights and constraints which go beyond the claims of nation-states and which have far-reaching consequences, in principle, for the nature and form of political power. These regulatory forms can be found in the domain between national and international law and regulation – the space between domestic law which regulates the relations between a state and its citizens, and traditional international law which applies primarily to states and interstate relations. This space is already filled by a host of legal regulation, from the legal instruments of the EU and the international human rights regime as a global framework for promoting rights, to the diverse agreements of the arms control system and environmental regimes. Within Europe the European Convention for the Protection of Human Rights and Fundamental Freedoms and the EU create new institutions and layers of law and governance which have divided political authority; any assumption that sovereignty is an indivisible, illimitable, exclusive and perpetual form of public power – entrenched within an individual state – is now defunct (Held 1995: 107–13). Within the wider international community, rules governing war, weapons systems, war crimes, human rights and the environment, among other areas, have transformed and delimited the order of states, embedding national polities in new forms and layers of accountability and governance. Accordingly, the boundaries between states, nations and societies can no longer claim the deep legal and moral significance they once had in the era of classic sovereignty. Cosmopolitanism is not made up of political ideals for another age, but embedded in rule systems and institutions which have already altered state sovereignty in distinct ways, and have been endorsed by societies of diverse faiths.

The Structure of Cosmopolitanism

However, the precise sense in which these developments constitute a form of 'cosmopolitanism' remains to be clarified, especially given that the ideas of cosmopolitanism have a long and complex history. For my purposes here, cosmopolitanism can be taken as the moral and political outlook which builds upon the strengths of the post-1945 multilateral order, particularly its commitment to universal standards, human rights and democratic values, and which seeks to specify general principles upon which all could act. These are principles which can be widely shared, and form the basis for the protection and nurturing of each person's equal interest in the determination of the forces and institutions which govern their lives.

Cosmopolitan values can be expressed formally, and in the interests of brevity, in terms of a set of principles (Held 2002). Eight principles are paramount. They are the principles of:

1. equal worth and dignity;
2. active agency;
3. personal responsibility and accountability;
4. consent;
5. collective decision-making about public issues through voting procedures;
6. inclusiveness and subsidiarity;
7. avoidance of serious harm; and
8. sustainability.

While eight principles may seem like a daunting number, they are interrelated and together form the basis of a compelling ethical and political orientation – an orientation which helps illuminate what it is that humankind can have in common.

The first principle is that humankind belongs to a single moral realm in which each person is regarded as equally worthy of respect and consideration (Beitz 1994, Pogge 1994). To think of people as having equal moral value is to make a general claim about the basic units of the world comprising persons as free and equal beings (Kuper 2000). To uphold this principle is not to deny the significance of cultural diversity and difference but to affirm that there are limits to the moral validity of particular communities (Nussbaum 1997: 42–3). In the post-Holocaust world, these limits have been recognized in the United Nations Charter and in the human rights regime, among many other legal instruments (Held 2004: part 3).

The second principle recognizes that, if principle 1 is to be universally recognized and accepted, then human agency must be conceived as the ability to shape human community in the context of the choices of others. Active agency bestows opportunities to act (or not as the case may be), and duties to ensure that independent action does not curtail and infringe upon the life choices and opportunities of others (unless sanctioned by negotiation or consent: see below). Active agency is a capacity both to make and pursue claims and to have such claims made and pursued in relation to oneself.

The first two principles cannot be grasped fully unless supplemented by principle 3. At its most basic, this principle can be understood to mean that it is inevitable that people will choose different cultural, social and economic projects and that such differences should be welcomed and accepted (Barry 1998: 147–9). Actors have to be aware of, and accountable for, the consequences of actions, direct or indirect, intended or unintended, which may radically restrict or delimit the choices of others.

The fourth principle, consent, recognizes that a commitment to equal worth and equal moral value, along with active agency and personal responsibility, requires a non-coercive political process in and through which people can negotiate and pursue their public interconnections, interdependencies and life chances.

Principles 4 and 5 must be interpreted together. For principle 5 acknowledges that while a legitimate public decision is one that results from consent, this needs to be linked with voting at the decisive stage of collective decision-making and with the procedures and mechanisms of majority rule. The consent of all is too strong a requirement of collective public responses to key issues (Held 2002: 26–7). Principle 5 recognizes the importance of inclusiveness in the process of granting consent, while interpreting this to mean that an inclusive process of participation and debate can coalesce with a decision-making procedure which allows outcomes accruing from majority support (Dahl 1989).

The sixth principle, the principle of inclusiveness and subsidiarity, connotes that those significantly affected by public decisions, issues or processes, should, *ceteris paribus*, have an equal opportunity, directly or indirectly through elected representatives, to influence and shape them. According to this principle, collective decision-making is best located when it is closest to and involves those whose life expectancy and life chances are determined by significant social processes and forces. On the other hand, this principle also recognizes that if the decisions and issues are translocal then political associations need to have a wider than local scope and framework of operations.

The seventh principle is for allocating priority to the most vital cases of need and, where possible, trumping other, less urgent public priorities until such a time as all human beings, de facto and de jure, are covered by the first six principles; that is to say, until they enjoy the status of equal moral value and active agency, and have the means to participate in their respective political communities and in the overlapping communities of fate which shape their needs and welfare. Accordingly, if the requirements specified by the principle of avoidance of serious harm are to be met, public policy ought to be focused, in the first instance, on the prevention of conditions of most pressing vulnerability marked by immediate, life-and-death consequences.

The eighth principle, sustainability, specifies that all economic and social development must be consistent with the stewardship of the world's core resources which are irreplaceable and non-substitutable. Sustainable development is best understood as a guiding principle to assure equal worth and active agency of future generations.

The eight principles can best be thought of as falling into three clusters. The first cluster (principles 1–3) sets down the fundamental organizational features of the cosmopolitan moral universe. Its crux is that each person is subject of equal moral concern; that each person is capable of acting autonomously with respect to the range of choices before them; and that, in deciding how to act or which institutions to create, the claims of each person affected should be taken equally into account. The second cluster (principles 4–6) forms the basis of translating individually initiated activity, or privately determined activities more broadly, into collectively agreed or collectively sanctioned frameworks of action or regulatory regimes. Public power can be conceived as legitimate to the degree to which principles 4, 5 and 6 are upheld. The final principles (7 and 8) lay down a framework for prioritizing urgent need and resource conservation. By distinguishing vital from non-vital needs, principle 7 creates an unambiguous starting point and guiding orientation for public decisions. While this 'prioritizing commitment' does not, of course, create a decision procedure to resolve all clashes of priority in politics, it clearly creates a moral framework for focusing public policy on those who are most vulnerable, and who would be unable to act autonomously without certain material capacities. By contrast, principle 8 seeks to set down a prudential orientation to help ensure that public policy is consistent with global ecological balances and that it does not destroy irreplaceable and non-substitutable resources.

It could be objected at this point that, given the plurality of interpretive positions in the contemporary world (social, cultural, religious and so on), it is unwise to construct a political standpoint which depends upon overarching principles. For it is doubtful, the objection could continue, that a bridge can be built between 'the many particular wills' and 'the general will' (see McCarthy 1991: 181–99). In a world marked by a diversity of value orientations, on what grounds, if any, can we suppose that all groups or parties could be argumentatively convinced about fundamental ethical and political principles? Yet I would argue that the principles of cosmopolitanism are the conditions of taking cultural diversity seriously, and of building a democratic culture to mediate clashes of the cultural good. They are, in short, about the conditions of just difference and democratic dialogue. The aim of modern cosmopolitanism is the conceptualization and generation of the necessary background conditions for a 'common' or 'basic' structure in which individual and social activity can take place (cf. Rawls 1985: 254ff.).

Thus, while a modern cosmopolitanism acknowledges a plurality of values and a diversity of moral conceptions of the good (how would it be otherwise?), it entails, as one commentator aptly put it, 'a particular type of political arrangement, one which, for one, allows the pursuit of different conceptions of good' (Tan 1998: 283). Only polities that acknowledge the equal status of all persons, that seek neutrality or impartiality with respect to a wide range of personal ends, hopes and aspirations, and that pursue the public justification of social, economic and political arrangements can ensure a basic or common structure of political action which allows individuals to pursue their projects – both individual and collective – as free and equal agents. Hence, cosmopolitan principles are the principles of democratic public life, stripped of one crucial assumption – never fully justified in any case in liberal democratic thought, classic or contemporary – that these principles can only be enacted effectively within a single circumscribed, territorially based political community.

A distinction can be made between 'thick' and 'thin' cosmopolitanism (see Held 2005, for a discussion). There are those for whom membership of humanity at large means that special relationships (including particular moral responsibilities) to family, kin, nation or religious grouping can never be justified because the people involved have some intrinsic quality which suffices alone to compel special moral attention, or because they are allegedly worth more than other people, or because such affiliations provide sufficient reason for pursuing particular commitments or actions. Against this, there are those who recognize that while each person stands in 'an ethically significant relation' to all other people, this is only one important 'source of reasons and responsibilities among others' (Scheffler 1999: 260). Cosmopolitan principles are, in this context, quite compatible with the recognition of different 'spheres' or 'layers' of moral reasoning (Walzer 1983). As I understand cosmopolitanism, it should be thought of as closer to the second position than the first; cosmopolitanism lays down regulative principles that delimit and govern the range of diversity and difference that ought to be found in public life. It discloses the proper framework for the pursuit of argument, discussion and negotiation about particular spheres of value. Cosmopolitanism thus sets down a set of procedural principles for political life. Of course, the principles of autonomy, dialogue and tolerance are open to objection; they have been contested throughout the modern period. But if they are rejected, it is important to be clear that what is being cast aside is the willingness to test the generalizability of political claims and interests, to pursue the deliberative justification of these, and to ensure the accountability of power in all its forms.

Global Challenges and Cosmopolitan Law

The idea of cosmopolitan law invokes the notion of a domain of law different in kind from the law of states and the law made between one state and another for the mutual enhancement of their geo-political interests. Kant, the leading interpreter of the idea of such a law, saw it as the basis for articulating the equal moral status of persons in the 'universal community' (1970: 108). For him, cosmopolitan law is neither a fantastic nor a utopian way of conceiving law, but a 'necessary complement' to the codes of national and international law, and a means to transform them into a public law of humanity (see Held 1995: ch. 10). While Kant limited the form and scope of cosmopolitan law to the conditions of universal hospitality – the right to present oneself and be heard within and across communities – it is understood here more broadly as the appropriate mode of representing the equal moral standing of all human beings, their entitlement to equal liberty and to forms of governance founded on deliberation and consent. In other words, cosmopolitan law should be thought of as the form of law which best articulates and entrenches the eight principles of cosmopolitan order. If these principles were to be systematically entrenched as the foundation of law, the conditions of the cosmopolitan regulation of public life could initially be set down.

At the heart of a cosmopolitan conception of global order is the idea that citizenship can be based not on an exclusive membership of a territorial community but on general rules and principles which can be entrenched and drawn upon in different settings. The meaning of citizenship thus shifts from membership in a community which bestows, for those who qualify, particular rights and duties to an alternative principle of world order in which all persons have equivalent rights and duties in the cross-cutting spheres of decision-making which can affect their vital needs and interests. As Habermas has written, 'only a democratic citizenship that does not close itself off in a particularistic fashion can pave the way for a *world citizenship* ... State citizenship and world citizenship form a continuum whose contours, at least, are already being becoming visible' (1996: 514–15). There is only a historically contingent connection between the principles underpinning citizenship and the national community; as this connection weakens in a world of overlapping communities and fate, the principles of citizenship must be rearticulated and re-entrenched. Moreover, in light of this development, the connection between patriotism and nationalism becomes easier to call into question, and a case built to bind patriotism to the defence of core civic and political principles – not to the nation or country for their own sake (Heater 2002). Only national identities open to diverse solidarities, and shaped by respect for general rules and principles, can accommodate themselves successfully to the challenges of the global age. Ultimately, diversity and difference, accountability and political capacity, can flourish only in a cosmopolitan legal community (see Brunkhorst 2005, Held 2002). The global challenges we face are better met in a cosmopolitan legal framework.

The key reasons for this should be highlighted for clarity. First, cosmopolitan values have played, as previously noted, a constitutive role in the development of important aspects of the international and global political realm, and these continue to be of great relevance in the framing of core general civic and political principles. Second, the world of 'overlapping communities of fate', of interlocking and interdependent relations across borders and sectors of society, generated by globalization, binds the fortunes of people together across countries in dense networks and processes. Third, if the complex and demanding political issues that this gives rise to are to be resolved, not by markets or geo-political might, but by mechanisms of deliberation, accountability and democracy, then a cosmopolitan legal order can be seen to set down a fair and inclusive political framework to address them, internationally and globally.

Global challenges today can be thought of as divided into three types – those concerned with sharing our planet (global warming, biodiversity and ecosystem losses, water deficits), those concerned with sustaining our life chances (poverty, conflict prevention, global infectious diseases) and those concerned with managing our rulebooks (nuclear proliferation, toxic waste disposal, intellectual property rights, genetic research rules, trade rules, finance and tax rules) (cf. Rischard 2002). In our increasingly interconnected world, these global problems cannot be solved by any one nation-state acting alone. They call for collective and collaborative action – something that the nations of the world have not been good at, and which they need to be better at if these pressing issues are to be adequately tackled.

While complex global processes, from the financial to the ecological, connect the fate of communities to each other across the world, global governance capacity is under pressure. Problem-solving capacities at the global and regional level are weak because of a number of structural difficulties, which compound the problems of generating and implementing urgent policy with respect to global public goods and bads. These difficulties are rooted in the post-war settlement and the subsequent development of the multilateral order itself.

The problems faced by international agencies and organizations stem from many sources, including the tension between universal values and state sovereignty built into them from their beginning. For many global political and legal developments since 1945 do not just curtail sovereignty, but support it in distinctive ways. From the UN Charter to the Kyoto Protocol, international agreements often serve to entrench the international power structure. The division of the globe into powerful nation-states, with distinctive sets of geo-political interests, was embedded in the articles and statutes of leading IGOs (see Held 1995: chs 5 and 6). Thus, the sovereign rights of states are frequently affirmed alongside more universal principles. Moreover, while the case can be made that universal principles are part of 'the working creed' of officials in some UN agencies such as the United Nations Children's Fund (UNICEF), UNESCO and the World Health Organization (WHO) and NGOs such as Amnesty International, Save the Children and Oxfam, they can scarcely be said to be constitutive of the conceptual world and working practices of many politicians, national or international (Barry 1999: 34–5).

In addition, the reach of contemporary regional and international law rarely comes with a commitment to establish institutions with the resources and clout to make declared universal rules, values and objectives effective. The susceptibility of the UN to the agendas of the most powerful states, the partiality of many of its enforcement operations (or lack of them altogether), the underfunding of its organizations, the continued dependency of its programmes on financial support from a few major states, the weaknesses of the policing of many environmental regimes (regional and global) are all indicative of the disjuncture between universal principles (and aspirations) and their partial and one-sided application. Four deep-rooted problems need highlighting (see Held 2004: ch. 6).

A first set of problems emerges as a result of the development of globalization itself, which generates public policy problems which span the 'domestic' and the 'foreign', and the interstate order with its clear political boundaries and lines of responsibility. These problems are often insufficiently understood or acted upon. There is a fundamental lack of ownership of many of them at the global level. A second set of difficulties relates to the inertia found in the system of international agencies, or the inability of these agencies to mount collective problem-solving solutions faced with uncertainty about lines of responsibility and frequent disagreement over objectives, means and costs. This often leads to the situation where the cost of inaction is greater than the cost of taking action. A third set of problems arises because there is no clear division of labour among the myriad of international governmental agencies; functions often overlap, mandates frequently conflict, and aims and objectives too often get blurred. A fourth set of difficulties relates to an accountability deficit, itself linked to two interrelated problems: the power imbalances among states and those between state and non-state actors in the shaping and making of global public policy. Multilateral bodies need to be fully representative of the states involved in them, and they rarely are.

Underlying these four difficulties is the breakdown of symmetry and congruence between decision-makers and decision-takers. The point has been well articulated recently by Kaul and her associates in their work on global public goods. They speak about the forgotten equivalence principle; that is, the span of a good's benefits and costs should be matched with the span of the jurisdiction in which decisions are taken about that good (see Kaul et al. 2003). At its root, such a principle suggests that those who are significantly affected by a global public good or bad should have a say in its provision or regulation. Such a principle of equivalence could be circumscribed by a concept of the right to protection from grievous harm. In this way, 'all-inclusiveness' would entail deliberation and engagement in policies that seriously affect life expectations and life chances (Held 2004: ch. 6, cf. Buchanan and Keohane 2004).

Yet, all too often, there is a breakdown of 'equivalence' between decision-makers and decision-takers, between decision-makers and stakeholders and between the inputs and outputs of the decision-making process. Pressing examples include climate change, the impact of trade subsidies, AIDS management and the question of intellectual property rights. Thus, the challenge is to find ways to align the circles of those to be involved in decision-making with the spillover range of the good under negotiation, that is to address the issue of accountability gaps; to create new organizational mechanisms for policy innovation across borders; and to find new ways of financing urgent global public goods. Legitimate political authority at the global level cannot be entrenched adequately without addressing the representative, organizational and financial gaps in governance arrangements. Cosmopolitan principles point the way forward.

To restore symmetry and congruence between decision-makers and decision-takers requires a reframing of global governance and a resolve to address those challenges generated by cross-border processes and forces. This project must take as its starting point, in other words, a world of overlapping communities of fate. Recognizing the complex processes of an interconnected world, it ought to view certain issues – such as industrial and commercial strategy, housing and education – as appropriate for spatially delimited political spheres (the city, region or state), while seeing others – such as the environment, pandemics and global financial regulation – as requiring new, more extensive institutions to address them. Deliberative and decision-making centres beyond national territories are appropriately situated when the principle of all-inclusiveness can only be properly upheld in a transnational context; when those whose life expectancy and life chances are significantly affected by public matter constitute a transnational grouping; and when 'lower' level decision-making cannot manage satisfactorily transnational or global policy questions. Of course, the boundaries demarcating different levels of governance will always be contested, as they are, for instance, in many local, sub-national regional and national polities. Disputes about the appropriate jurisdiction for handling particular public issues will be complex and intensive; but better complex and intensive in a clear cosmopolitan framework (in which cosmopolitan law frames political power) than abandoned simply to powerful geo-political interests (dominant states) or market based organizations to resolve them alone (see Held 2004: ch. 6).

Accordingly, states are hugely important vehicles to aid the delivery of effective public regulation, equal liberty and social justice, but they should not be thought of as ontologically privileged. They can be judged by how far they deliver these public goods and how far they fail. The same can be said about political agents operating beyond the level of the nation-state. They are by no means necessarily noble or wise, and their wisdom and nobility depend on recognizing necessary limits on their action, limits which mark out legitimate spaces for others to pursue their vital needs and interests. IGOs and INGOs, like states, need to be bound by a rule based order which articulates and entrenches cosmopolitan principles. Only such an order can underwrite a political system which upholds the equal moral standing of all human beings, and their entitlement to equal liberty and to forms of governance founded on deliberation and consent. Here are the grounds to build a politically robust and ethically sound conception of the proper basis of political community, and of the relations among communities in a global age. We need to build on the cosmopolitan steps of the twentieth century and deepen the institutional hold of this agenda.

Political Openings: Towards a Cosmopolitan Global Order

Surprisingly perhaps, it is an opportune moment to rethink the nature and form of contemporary global governance and the dominant policies of the last decade or so. The policy packages that have largely set the global agenda – in economics and security – are failing. The Washington Consensus and Washington security doctrines – or market fundamentalism and unilateralism – have dug their own graves. The most successful developing countries in the world (China, India, Vietnam, Uganda, among them) are successful because they have not followed the Washington Consensus agenda, and the conflicts that have most successfully been diffused (the Balkans, Sierra Leone, Liberia, among others) are ones that have benefited from concentrated multilateral support and a human security agenda. Here are clues as to how to proceed in the future. We need to learn to follow these clues and learn from the mistakes of the past if the rule of law, accountability and the effectiveness of the multilateral order are to be advanced.

In addition, the political tectonic plates appear to be shifting. With the faltering of unilateralism in US foreign policy, uncertainty over the role of the EU in global affairs, the crisis of global trade talks, the growing confidence of leading emerging countries in the world economy (China, India, Brazil), and the unsettled relations between elements of Islam and the West, means business as usual seems unlikely at the global level in the decades ahead. It is highly improbable that the multilateral order can survive for very much longer in its current form, and a new political space is being opened up.

Of course, cosmopolitanism has its enemies that may exploit this space (see Archibugi 2009). But I argue that cosmopolitanism constitutes the political basis and political philosophy of living in a global age. In a world of overlapping communities of fate, individuals need to be not just citizens of their immediate political communities, but of the wider regional and global networks which impact upon their lives. Under such conditions, people would come, in principle, to enjoy multiple citizenships – political membership, that is, in the diverse communities which significantly affect them. This overlapping cosmopolitan polity would be one that in form and substance reflected and embraced the diverse forms of power and authority that operate within and across borders. A cosmopolitan polity can only be satisfactorily entrenched if a division of powers and competencies is recognized at different levels of political action and interconnectedness – levels which correspond to the degrees to which public issues stretch across borders and significantly affect diverse populations. Such a polity must embrace diverse and distinct domains of authority, linked both vertically and horizontally, if it is to be a successful servant of cosmopolitan principles and practices. The possibility of a cosmopolitan polity must be linked to an expanding framework of states and agencies bound by cosmopolitan principles and rules. How should this be understood from an institutional point of view? Initially, the possibility of cosmopolitan politics would be enhanced if the UN system actually lived up to its Charter. Among other things, this would mean pursuing measures to implement key elements of the rights Conventions, and enforcing the prohibition on the discretionary right to use force (see Falk 1995). However, while each move in this direction would be helpful, it would still represent, at best, a move towards a very incomplete form of accountability and justice in global politics. Thus, a cosmopolitan polity would need to establish an overarching network of public fora, covering cities, nation-states, regions and the wider global order. It is possible to conceive of different types of political engagement on a continuum from the local to the global, with the local marked by direct and participatory processes while larger domains with significant populations are progressively mediated by representative mechanisms. The aim would be to establish a deliberative process whose structure grounds 'an expectation of rationally acceptable results' (see Habermas 1996). Such a process can be conceived of in terms of diverse public spheres in which collective views and decisions are arrived at through deliberation, deliberation which is guided by the test of impartiality, as opposed to that of simple self-interest, in the formation of political will and judgment. Accordingly, a cosmopolitan polity would seek the creation of an effective and accountable administrative, legislative and executive capacity at global and regional levels to *complement* those at national and local levels. Political cosmopolitanism involves the development of administrative capacity and independent political resources at regional and global levels as a necessary complement to those in local and national polities. At issue is the strengthening of the administrative capacity and accountability of regional institutions like the EU along with developing the administrative capacity and forms of accountability at the level of the UN system itself. A cosmopolitan polity does not call for a diminution per se of state power and capacity across the globe. Rather, it seeks to entrench and develop political institutions at regional and global levels as a necessary complement to those at the level of the state. This conception of politics is based on the recognition of the continuing significance of nation-states, while arguing for layers of governance to address broader and more global questions. The aim is to forge an accountable and responsive politics at local and national levels alongside the establishment of representative and deliberative assemblies in the wider global order; that is, a political order of transparent and democratic cities and nations as well as of regions and global networks. The institutional requirements of political cosmopolitanism include:

- Multilayered governance and diffused authority.
- A network of democratic fora from the local to the global.
- Enhancing the transparency, accountability and effectiveness of leading functional IGOs; and building new bodies of this type where there is demonstrable need for greater public coordination and administrative capacity.
- Use of diverse forms of mechanisms to access public preferences, test their coherence and inform public will formation.
- Establishment of an effective, accountable, international police/military force for the last-resort use of coercive power in defence of cosmopolitan law.

Is a cosmopolitan global order utopian? There are many reasons for pessimism: globalization has not just integrated peoples and nations, but created new forms of antagonism. The globalization of communications does not just make it easier to establish mutual understanding, but often highlights what it is that people do not have in common and how and why differences matter. Ethnic self-centredness, right-wing nationalism and unilateralist politics are once again on the rise, and not just in the West. Yet, the circumstances and nature of politics have changed. Like national culture and traditions, cosmopolitanism is a cultural and political project, but with one difference: it is better adapted and suited to our regional and global age. However, the arguments in support of this have yet to be articulated in the public sphere in many parts of the world; and we fail here at our peril.

Against the background of 9/11, the current unilateralist stance of the United States, the desperate cycle of violence in the Middle East and elsewhere, the advocacy of cosmopolitanism may appear like an attempt to defy gravity or walk on water! And, indeed, if it was a case of having to adopt cosmopolitan principles and institutions all at once, or not at all, this would be true. But it is no more the case than was the pursuit of the modern state – as a system of circumscribed authority, separate from ruler and ruled – at the time of Hobbes. Over the last several decades the growth of multilateralism and the development of international law has created cosmopolitan anchors to the world. These are the basis for the further consolidation of the hold of cosmopolitan principles and institutions. Moreover, a coalition of political groupings could emerge to push these achievements further, comprising European countries with strong liberal and social democratic traditions; liberal groups in the US polity which support multilateralism and the rule of law in international affairs; developing countries struggling for freer and fairer trade rules in the world economic order; non-governmental organizations, from Amnesty International to Oxfam, campaigning for a more just, democratic and equitable world order; transnational social movements contesting the nature and form of contemporary globalization; and those economic forces that desire a more stable and managed global economic order.

Bibliography

Archibugi, D. 2009. *The Global Commonwealth of Citizens*. Princeton: Princeton University Press.
Barry, B. 1998. International society from a cosmopolitan perspective, in *International Society: Diverse Ethical Perspectives*, edited by D. Mapel and T. Nardin. Princeton: Princeton University Press, 144–63.
Barry, B. 1999. Statism and nationalism: a cosmopolitan critique, in *Global Justice*, edited by I. Shapiro and L. Brilmayer. New York: Nomos XLI, 12–66.
Beitz, C. 1994. Cosmopolitan liberalism and the states system, in *Political Restructuring in Europe: Ethical Perspectives*, edited by C. Brown. London: Routledge, 123–7.
Brunkhorst, H. 2005. *Solidarity*. Cambridge, MA: MIT Press.
Buchanan, A. and Keohane, R. 2004. The preventive use of force: a proposal. *Ethics and International Affairs*, 18(1), 1–22.
Bull, H. 1977. *The Anarchical Society*. London: Macmillan.
Dahl, R.A. 1989. *Democracy and its Critics*. New Haven: Yale University Press.
Falk, R. 1995. *On Humane Governance*. Cambridge: Polity Press.
Habermas, J. 1996. *Between Facts and Norms: Contributions to a Discourse Theory of Law and Democracy*. Cambridge: Polity Press.
Heater, D. 2002. *World Citizenship*. London: Continuum.
Held, D. 1995. *Democracy and the Global Order: From the Modern State to Cosmopolitan Governance*. Cambridge: Polity.
Held, D. 2002. Law of states, law of peoples. *Legal Theory*, 8(1), 1–44.
Held, D. 2004. *Global Covenant*. Cambridge: Polity
Held, D. 2005. Principles of cosmopolitan order, in *The Political Philosophy of Cosmopolitanism*, edited by G. Brock and H. Brighouse. Cambridge: Cambridge University Press, 10–27.
Kant, I. 1970. *Kant's Political Writings*. Edited and introduced by H. Reiss. Cambridge: Cambridge University Press.
Kaul, I., Conceição, P., Goulven, K. and Mendoza R. (eds). 2003. *Providing Global Public Goods*. Oxford: Oxford University Press.
Kuper, A. 2000. Rawlsian global justice: beyond the law of people to a cosmopolitan law of persons. *Political Theory*, 28, 640–74.
McCarthy, T. 1991. *Ideals and Illusions*. Cambridge, MA: MIT Press.
Nussbaum, M. 1997. Kant and cosmopolitanism, in *Perpetual Peace: Essays on Kant's Cosmopolitan Ideal*, edited by J. Bohmann and M. Lutz-Bachmann. Cambridge, MA: MIT Press.

Pogge, T. 1994. Cosmopolitanism and sovereignty, in *Political Restructuring in Europe: Ethical Perspectives*, edited by C. Brown. London: Routledge.
Rawls, J. 1985. Justice as fairness: political not metaphysical. *Philosophy of Public Affairs*, 14(3), 223–51.
Rischard, J.-F. 2002. *High Noon*. New York: Basic Books.
Scheffler, S. 1999. Conceptions of cosmopolitanism. *Utilitas*, 11, 255–76.
Tan, K. 1998. Liberal toleration in the law of peoples. *Ethics*, 108, 276–95.
Walzer, M. 1983. *Spheres of Justice*. Oxford: Martin Robertson.

10

ASHGATE RESEARCH COMPANION

Cosmopolitanism and the Struggle for Global Justice

Gillian Brock

Introduction

According to a widely used account of what cosmopolitanism is, the key idea is that every person has global stature as the ultimate unit of moral concern and is therefore entitled to equal respect and consideration no matter what her citizenship status, or other affiliations happen to be (Pogge 1992). Cosmopolitanism would seem to prohibit discrimination, exploitation and aggression towards others, and is, therefore, at least potentially a significant force in the struggle to secure justice on a global scale. In this chapter I discuss the ways in which cosmopolitanism has been both helpful and (mistakenly) feared in the struggle for global justice, with particular attention to debates in political philosophy. I first clarify the ways in which cosmopolitanism may be neutrally defined, before discussing its relationship to globalization and global justice. I then briefly discuss a couple of widely used distinctions in discourse on cosmopolitanism before beginning a more lengthy discussion of different cosmopolitan accounts of global justice which are to be found in the literature, paying particular attention to prominent debates. I also address the issue of whether cosmopolitanism is in tension with other affiliations and commitments, such as attachment to family, local communities or nations, before briefly considering a very current debate concerning whether the state matters to egalitarian conceptions of distributive justice. Finally, I briefly consider the importance of human rights in securing global justice and the ways in which we might further promote the instantiation of cosmopolitanism in the world.

Two Aspects of being a "Citizen of the World"

Some of the earliest proponents of cosmopolitanism (such as Diogenes and Cicero) rejected the idea that one should be importantly defined by one's city of origin, as was typical of Greek males of the time.[1] Rather, they insisted that they were "citizens of the world." The Stoics' idea of being a citizen of the world neatly captures the two main aspects of cosmopolitanism, especially as it is frequently understood today. These are: a thesis about identity and one about responsibility. As a thesis about identity, being a cosmopolitan indicates that one is a person who is influenced by various cultures. Cosmopolitanism as a thesis about responsibility generates much discussion, as we see below.[2] Roughly, the idea is that as a cosmopolitan, one should appreciate that one is a member of a global community of human beings. As such, one has responsibilities to other members of the global community. As Martha Nussbaum elaborates, one owes allegiance "to the worldwide community of human beings" and this affiliation should constitute a primary allegiance (Nussbaum 1996: 4). As a thesis about responsibility, cosmopolitanism guides the individual outward from local obligations, and prohibits those obligations from crowding out responsibilities to distant others. Cosmopolitanism highlights the responsibilities we have to those whom we do not know, but whose lives should be of concern to us. The borders of states, and other boundaries considered to restrict the *scope* of justice, are irrelevant roadblocks in appreciating our responsibilities to all in the global community. On this account, cosmopolitanism is clearly useful in the struggle for global justice. But not all have perceived this to be the case, given some widespread misconceptions about what this entails which are discussed next.

Misconceptions about cosmopolitanism in discussion of globalization and global justice

Talk about cosmopolitanism is often closely associated with discourse about globalization and global justice. Though these are, in general, different topics, they often have strong points of intersection, as we see.

What is the field of global justice concerned with or what should it be about? If we examine actual Global Justice Movements in the world, such as those represented by (say) the World Social Forum,[3] we notice that there are a number of quite different groups that can be identified as concerned with issues of global justice.[4] These

---

[1] For an excellent history of cosmopolitanism, see Pauline Kleingeld (2006).

[2] For some of this debate see Brock and Brighouse (2005) and Brock and Moellendorf (2005).

[3] More information about this organization can be found at their official home page: www.forumsocialmundial.org.br.

[4] The Global Justice Movement is a movement of movements and includes a variety of groups dedicated to promoting aspects of global justice such as fair trade. Prominent examples of key movements would be "Via Campesina," which coordinates peasant organizations, agricultural workers, rural women,and indigenous communities, in efforts to promote small-scale sustainable agriculture; "Jubilee 2000," which is a Christian organization aiming to relieve indebtedness of developing countries; and "Peoples' Global Action" which coordinates grassroots campaigns aimed at resistance to capitalism. (All of these have websites and can easily be located on the web.)

include: trade unionists, farmers, indigenous peoples, environmentalists, and so forth. These groups often have common grievances, such as opposition to the way globalization is unfolding in the world today, the dominance of multinational corporations or economic interests throughout the globe with a feared withering away of local cultures, devastation for local economies, intensified destruction of the environment, deepening exploitation, the apparent unconcern with the most vulnerable and marginalized, and so forth. Though members of the so-called Global Justice Movement have common points of struggle, they often resist congealing into an overarching political program, despite occasional victories (such as those achieved at, or represented by, the World Social Forum). A central claim made by some of these marginalized groups is that they want less interference especially from global actors. Perhaps despairing of ever getting any meaningful chance to be given a real voice and input in decisions that crucially affect them, perhaps also skeptical given bad histories of interference, domination or oppression, given their current and expected future marginalization, they (apparently) frequently ask now simply to be left alone to live their lives as they see fit. Others, perhaps more hopeful about what their activism can accomplish, demand changes to our global governance arrangements, such as changes to the rules governing the World Trade Organization. Chief among these would be changes that take more seriously fairness for the world's worst off and most vulnerable, by distributing the costs and benefits of globalization more evenly.

Academic philosophical theorizing about global justice has, in some important ways, been more narrowly focused, though it does incorporate the concerns of such activists. Theorizing about global justice has been dominated by issues of global distributive justice over the last two decades, though this is not to say that other issues have been entirely neglected. Various theorists advocate different models of global justice which might consist of several components such as advocating: a more equal distribution of resources globally (Beitz 1979, Pogge 1989, Moellendorf 2002, Tan 2004); that every person be well positioned to enjoy the prospects for a decent life (Nussbaum 2006, Miller 2007, Brock 2009); more global equality of opportunity (Caney 2005, Moellendorf 2002); universal respect for and promotion of human rights (Shue 1980, Beitz 2009, Miller 2007, van Hooft 2009); promotion of the autonomy of peoples who stand in relations of equality with one another (Rawls 1999, Miller 2007); or criteria governing intervention, especially military intervention, in the affairs of states (Moellendorf 2002, Tan 2000, Buchanan and Keohane 2005). There is also much debate about how best to realize the desired elements, what principles should govern our interactions at the global level, and how to improve the management of our global affairs, including how best to govern globalization (Held 1995, Cabrera 2004, Weinstock 2005). Also prominent is a debate about the role of national self-determination in accounts of global justice and space for local affiliation and partiality (Miller 2007, Tamir 1993). Contemporary theorizing on global justice has also been enormously influenced by John Rawls' work, especially his *The Law of Peoples* (1999), which is discussed below.

The question of what cosmopolitan justice entails is very much a current topic of debate, with people defending a full spectrum of views. Indeed, the critical mass of scholars actively working on the topic today endorse forms of egalitarianism which would be quite antithetical to the neo-liberal agenda, as I discuss. For the anti-globalization movement, cosmopolitanism is sometimes feared because it is construed as another way to justify the relentless spread of capitalism throughout the globe and the liberal discourse associated with cosmopolitan values is nothing more than global capitalism's useful handmaiden.[5] This view involves a misconception about the diversity of positions that are rightly construed as cosmopolitan. One could see oneself as a member of a global community of human persons for all sorts of reasons, such as religious commitments – Christianity is often thought of in this connection – and there is also a strong Marxist justification for holding this position as well. There is no need to suspect at the outset that talk of cosmopolitanism necessarily entails commitment to neo-liberal, capitalist views about economic justice.

There are economic forms of cosmopolitanism, some proponents of which advocate free trade (these include Adam Smith and Milton Friedman). However, there are also as many communist and socialist versions of economic cosmopolitanism as well (as advocated by, say, Marx, Engels and Lenin), which encourage proletarians of the world to unite and to recognize their common interests in promoting a global economic order more aligned with workers' interests rather than those of capital. What is cosmopolitan about both of these familiar economic views is simply the idea that the preferred economic model transcends the boundaries of a nation-state. Current debates about what cosmopolitan justice consists of typically bypass the debate about modes of production.

Two Distinctions Concerning Cosmopolitanism

Two distinctions are widely used in the literature. I review these next.

1. Moral and institutional cosmopolitanism

The crux of the idea of moral cosmopolitanism is that every person has global stature as the ultimate unit of moral concern and is therefore entitled to equal consideration no matter what her citizenship or nationality status. Thomas Pogge gives a widely cited synopsis of what are thought to be the key ideas:

---

[5] The "anti-globalization movement" refers to those various groups who oppose globalization. Because they may do so for various reasons, it is hard to define the movement concisely, but some of the more prominent grounds include opposition based on fear concerning the global spread of capital, or the perceived threat to self-determination and/or political autonomy, or threats to environmental conservation, and so forth.

> *Three elements are shared by all cosmopolitan positions. First, individualism: the ultimate units of concern are human beings, or persons – rather than, say, family lines, tribes, ethnic, cultural, or religious communities, nations, or states. The latter may be units of concern only indirectly, in virtue of their individual members or citizens. Second, universality: the status of ultimate unit of concern attaches to every living human being equally – not merely to some sub-set, such as men, aristocrats, Aryans, whites, or Muslims. Third, generality: this special status has global force. Persons are ultimate units of concern for everyone – not only for their compatriots, fellow religionists, or such like. (Pogge 1992: 48–9)*

Cosmopolitanism's force is best appreciated by considering what it rules out. For instance, it rules out positions that attach no moral value to some people, or weights the moral value some people have differentially according to their race, ethnicity or nationality. Furthermore, assigning ultimate rather than derivative value to collective entities such as nations or states is prohibited. If such groups matter, they matter because of their importance to individual human persons rather than because they have some independent, ultimate (say, ontological) value.

A common misconception is that cosmopolitanism requires a world state or government. A distinction is sometimes drawn in the literature between moral and institutional cosmopolitanism (also referred to in the literature variously as "legal" or "political" cosmopolitanism). Institutional cosmopolitans maintain that fairly deep institutional changes are needed to the global system in order to realize the cosmopolitan vision adequately (Cabrera 2004, Held 1995). Moral cosmopolitans need not endorse that view, in fact many are against radical institutional transformations (Nussbaum 2006). Cosmopolitan justice requires that our global obligations (such as protecting everyone's basic human rights or ensuring everyone's capabilities are met to the required threshold) are effectively discharged. However, a number of suitable arrangements might do this effectively. There are various possibilities for global governance that would not amount to a world state. These include mixtures of delegating responsibilities for particular domains to various institutions, with multiple agencies able to hold each other accountable, and other ways of reconfiguring the structure of governance bodies at the global level (such as the United Nations) so they are brought into line better with cosmopolitan goals (Held 1995, Weinstock 2005, Grant and Keohane 2005).

2. Weak versus strong cosmopolitanism

The way in which this distinction is typically drawn (for example Miller 2000: 174) is that weak cosmopolitanism underwrites, as requirements of justice, only the conditions that are universally necessary for human beings to lead minimally decent lives, whereas strong cosmopolitans are committed to a more demanding form of global distributive equality that will aim to eliminate inequalities between persons beyond some account of what is sufficient to live a minimally decent life. So, what is weak or strong on this account is the extent of one's commitments to redistribution.[6]

Cosmopolitan Justice, Rawls' *Law of Peoples*, and Some of His Prominent Cosmopolitan Critics

Cosmopolitan justice can be argued for from a number of theoretical perspectives. After all, there are different conceptions of how to treat people equally especially with respect to issues of distributive justice, and this is often reflected in these different accounts. Cosmopolitan justice could be argued for along various lines, including: utilitarian (prominently, Singer 1972); rights-based accounts (Shue 1980, Jones 1999, Pogge 2002); along Kantian lines (O'Neill 2000); Aristotelian or capabilities-based (Nussbaum 2000, 2006); and contractarian (Beitz 1979, Pogge 1989, Moellendorf 2002, Brock 2009). In recent years, one popular way of arguing for cosmopolitan justice has taken contractarian forms, following a very prominent debate between John Rawls and his critics. Because of its enormous dominance in current debates on cosmopolitan justice in political philosophy, I discuss this next.

In *A Theory of Justice* (1971), John Rawls sets out to derive the principles of justice that should govern liberal societies. Because one's position in society can distort one's judgments about justice in profound and yet unrealized ways, Rawls sets out to shield us from this source of bias in constructing a powerful and ingenious normative thought experiment. The idea is that you are to imagine yourself in a hypothetical choosing situation (the "original position") in which you are to select the principles of justice which will govern your society. In this choosing situation you are behind a "veil of ignorance" in which you are deprived of all knowledge of who you are in society. The veil of ignorance, coupled with the facts that you are going to have to choose the basic principles to govern the society (a weighty matter) and you will have to live with these choices (you will be bound by the "strains of commitment"), are powerful constraints on what sorts of principles would not be chosen. You would not, for instance, choose principles that support a slave society, he argues, as you may end up being in the position of a slave or someone else who is badly off. Rather, you would seek to ensure that the worst off position is as good as possible, given the knowledge that you may end up having to occupy it. More positively, he famously argues for two principles; namely, one protecting equal basic liberties and a second permitting social and economic inequalities when (and only when) they are both to the greatest benefit of the least advantaged (the

---

6   A worry I have with the way this distinction is drawn is that it seems to exclude almost no one with defensible views on global justice. Even Rawls ends up as a weak cosmopolitan on this account (a label he himself explicitly rejected). Perhaps this distinction needs to be replaced with more nuanced ones to play some continuing, useful role in the literature.

Difference Principle) and attached to positions that are open to all under conditions of fair equality of opportunity (the Fair Equality of Opportunity Principle). In *A Theory of Justice*, Rawls' focus is on the principles that should govern closed communities—paradigmatically, nation-states. Cosmopolitans such as Charles Beitz (1979) and then Thomas Pogge (1989) argued that these two principles should apply globally. After all, if the point of the veil of ignorance is to exclude us from knowledge of factors which are distorting, yet arbitrary, from a moral point of view, surely where one happens to have been born (or citizenship) qualifies as one of those quintessentially arbitrary factors from a moral perspective?

Cosmopolitans were then understandably disappointed when Rawls later explicitly argued against the global extension. He argued that, though the two principles should apply within liberal societies, they should not apply across them. Rather, in the international arena, Rawls thinks different principles would be chosen (in a second original position occupied by representatives of different, well-ordered peoples) and these would include principles acknowledging peoples' independence, their equality, that they have a right to self-defense, that they have duties of non-intervention, to observe treaties, to honor a limited set of rights, to conduct themselves appropriately in war, and to assist other peoples living in unfavorable conditions. A crucial factor for this apparently quite different position is the fact that in the global context it is *peoples* rather than *individual persons* that must make decisions about justice. Our membership in a "people" makes for a very different justice context for Rawls. In the space provided, I cannot do justice to all the complexities of Rawls' sophisticated account, but for good exposition of the views and critical discussion of these see Martin and Reidy (2006), Moellendorf (2002) and Tan (2004). Here I focus on just a few commonly identified points of tension between Rawls and some of his prominent cosmopolitan critics. Later in the chapter we further discuss the relevance (if any) that membership in groups such as peoples or nations might have to accounts of global justice.

In *The Law of Peoples* (1999), Rawls engages directly with central claims made by some cosmopolitans, namely those who argue the Difference Principle should apply globally. He takes up Beitz's claim that, since a global system of cooperation already exists between states, a Global Difference Principle should apply across states as well. Rawls argues against this, for a couple of reasons, but notably, because he believes that wealth owes its origin and maintenance to the political culture of the society rather than (say) to its stock of resources. Furthermore, any global principle of distributive justice we endorse must have a target and a cut-off point. Rawls believes we have a duty "to assist burdened societies to become full members of the Society of Peoples and to be able to determine the path of their own future for themselves" (1999: 118). Unlike his understanding of cosmopolitan commitments to a Global Difference Principle, Rawls believes his principles have a target, which is to ensure the essentials of political autonomy and self-determination.

Rawls' *Law of Peoples* has generated much criticism. One of the most frequently raised objections is that the background picture Rawls invokes incorporates outmoded views of relations between states, peoples and individuals of the world. Rawls presupposes that states are (sufficiently) independent of one another, so that each society can be held largely responsible for the well-being of its citizens, at least in the case of well-ordered peoples (that is, those reasonable liberal and decent peoples not suffering unfavorable conditions). Furthermore, according to Rawls, differences in levels of wealth and prosperity are largely attributable to differences in political culture and the virtuous nature of its citizens. Critics point out, however, that Rawls ignores both the extent to which unfavorable conditions may result from factors external to the society and that there are all sorts of morally relevant connections between states, notably that they are situated in a global economic order that perpetuates the interests of wealthy developed states with little regard for the interests of poor, developing ones. We who live in the affluent, developed world cannot thus defensibly insulate ourselves from the misery of the worst off in the world, because we are complicit in keeping them in a state of poverty.

Thomas Pogge has done much to show the nature and extent of these incriminating connections (1994, 2001, 2002, *inter alia*). According to Pogge, two international institutions are particularly worrisome: the international borrowing privilege and the international resource privilege. Any group that exercises effective power in a state is recognized internationally as the legitimate government of that territory, and the international community is not much concerned with how the group came to power or what it does with that power. Oppressive governments may borrow freely on behalf of the country (the international borrowing privilege) or dispose of its natural resources (the international resource privilege) and these actions are legally recognized internationally. These two privileges have enormous implications for the prosperity of poor countries (for instance) because these privileges provide incentives for coup attempts, they often influence what sorts of people are motivated to seek power, they facilitate oppressive governments being able to stay in power, and, should more democratic governments get to be in power, they are saddled with the debts incurred by their oppressive predecessors, thus significantly draining the country of resources needed to firm up fledgling democracies. All of this is disastrous for many poor countries. Because foreigners benefit so greatly from the international resource privilege, they have an incentive to refrain from challenging the situation (or worse, to support or finance oppressive governments). For these sorts of reasons, the current world order largely reflects the interests of wealthy and powerful states. Local governments have little incentive to attend to the needs of the poor, since their being able to continue in power depends more on the local elite, foreign governments and corporations. We (in affluent developed countries) have a responsibility to stop imposing this unjust global order and to mitigate the harms we have already inflicted on the world's most vulnerable people. As an initial proposal for us to begin to make some progress in the right direction, Pogge suggests that we impose a Global Resources Tax of roughly 1 percent to fund improvements to the lives of the worst off in developing societies (Pogge 1994).

So, critics point out that Rawls ignores the extent to which societies suffering unfavorable conditions frequently result from factors external to that society, and that national policies are often shaped, or even decided by, international factors. They also argue that the boundedness and separateness of political communities is difficult to sustain in our world today, due to phenomena such as globalization and integration (Hurrell 2001). Rawls assumes we can talk coherently of bounded political communities that can constitute self-sufficient schemes of political cooperation. However, critics argue this is an untenable assumption. Some authors concentrate on showing that we actually have a system of global cooperation between societies and how this would give rise to obligations to the worst off (Hinsch 2001). Others believe that it is insulting to characterize the relations between states of the world as cooperative, since in reality the relationship is rather one of domination and coercion (Forst 2001).

Several critics, then, argue that the basic global structure is a scheme of coercive institutions that importantly affects individuals' life prospects. It should be transformed so that it becomes a fair scheme of cooperation among all citizens of the world. For many of these critics, this is best modeled by considering a global original position in which decision-makers have no knowledge of any morally arbitrary features, including country of citizenship. Using this kind of strategy, popular claims are that we should endorse a Global Difference Principle (permitting economic inequalities just in case they work to improve the situation of the worst off in the world) or Global Equality of Opportunity (Moellendorf 2002, Caney 2005, Tan 2004), though other options, such as arguing for what is needed for a decent life (a "sufficientarian" account of global distributive justice) are also attractive (Brock 2009, Miller 2007, Nussbaum 2006).

Several other kinds of criticisms are also voiced including that the notion of a people is not sufficiently clear or important to do the work Rawls thinks it can do (Pogge 1994, Kuper 2000). Furthermore, since Rawls often takes the boundaries of states to mark off distinct peoples, his view runs into difficulties. If we take a people to be constituted by commonalities such as shared language, culture, history or ethnicity, then the official state borders and peoples do not coincide well. National territories are not typically comprised of a single people, nor is it clear that individuals belong to one and only one people (Pogge 1994).

Another common observation is that Rawls' arguments for his abridged list of human rights is defective. For one thing, critics charge that Rawls' failure to include democratic rights is quite mistaken. Amartya Sen, for instance, provides extensive evidence to support the claim that non-democratic regimes have severely adverse consequences for the well-being and human rights of those over whom they rule (1999: 147–8, 154–5). Sen also argues that respect for human rights and ideas of democracy are not simply Western values, but rather that substantial elements of these ideas can be found in all major cultures, religions and traditions.

Rawls argues for a respectful relationship between states (as representatives of peoples). Indeed, he argues that liberal democratic regimes have an obligation to deal with illiberal decent hierarchical regimes as equals, and not to endeavor to impose their values on them. Some might think that Rawls' views appropriately acknowledge the importance of our cultural or national affiliations. Andrew Kuper (2000) argues that Rawls may take cultural pluralism seriously but he does this at the expense of taking seriously the reasonable pluralism of *individual persons*. Well-ordered hierarchical societies may well contain individuals who hold liberal ideas.

Rawls' account incorporates the wrong kind of toleration for such societies at the expense of liberal values. Rawls' view is not sufficiently sensitive to the individuals within states. Indeed, it would seem that Rawls, in defending non-liberal states as he has, would be forced to defend the rights of states to impose inegalitarian policies on its citizens, even if a majority of the citizens were vigorously against such policies (Blake 2005: 23).

Rawls aims at a realistic utopia, but critics charge that the result is neither sufficiently realistic nor utopian (for example Kuper 2000). It is not sufficiently realistic because, critics claim, he has not taken account of all the relevant realities; for instance, of interdependence or domination in the global arena. To the extent that he has not captured all the salient realities, his Law of Peoples is not as "workable" and likely to sustain ongoing cooperative political arrangements and relations between peoples. Furthermore, critics contend that the view is not very utopian in that the political (moral) ideals used are too tame to constitute much of an advance over the status quo. In his bow to realism, Rawls has tried to ensure that the Law of Peoples results in stability, yet the Law of Peoples he endorses is potentially very unstable because, arguably, stability is only really achieved when just arrangements are in place and Rawls has offered us nothing more than a modus vivendi with oppressor states. Defenders of Rawls' views, such as Samuel Freeman (2006) and David Reidy (2006) continue to defend Rawls' views against these charges.[7]

The debate between Rawls and his Cosmopolitan critics continues. Its prominence is not hard to understand since it highlights key issues that must be taken seriously in cosmopolitan normative theorizing, such as:

1. Just how do we blend what is "realistic" with normative consideration?
2. How should groups such as "peoples" matter in our theorizing about cosmopolitan justice?
3. What are the limits of what we should tolerate in the interests of a peaceful world order?
4. How (if at all) can we reconcile tolerating illiberal regimes with the equal respect all individuals in the world deserve?
5. Should peace or justice be our goal in the global realm?

What Role is there for Partiality in Accounts of Global Justice, according to Cosmopolitans? Reconciling Cosmopolitanism with Other Commitments

Do cosmopolitans make room in their theorizing for the special attachments and commitments that fill most ordinary human beings' lives with value and meaning? Do these affiliations conflict with our commitments to global justice?

---

7   For more discussion on this debate see Martin and Reidy (2006) and Brock (2009: ch. 2).

A common misconception about cosmopolitanism concerns how a cosmopolitan must view her relations to those in local or particular communities, namely, that she must eschew such attachments in favour of some notion of impartial justice that the individual must apply directly to all, no matter where they are situated on the globe. But this is by no means entailed by several of the sophisticated accounts of cosmopolitanism on offer today (see, for instance, Brock and Brighouse 2005). Indeed, most contemporary cosmopolitans recognize that for many people, some of their most meaningful attachments in life derive from their allegiances to particular communities, be they national, ethnic, religious or cultural. Their accounts often seek to define the legitimate scope for such partiality, by situating these in a context which clarifies our obligations to one another. Cosmopolitan justice provides the basic framework or structure and thereby the constraints within which legitimate patriotism may operate (see, for instance, Tan 2004, 2005). Cosmopolitan principles should govern the global institutions, such that these treat people as equals in terms of their entitlements (regardless of nationality and power, say). However, once the background global institutional structure is just, persons may defensibly favor the interests of their compatriots (or co-nationals, or members of other more particular groups), so long as such partiality does not conflict with their other obligations, for instance, to support global institutions. So cosmopolitan principles should govern the global institutions, but need not directly regulate what choices people may make within the rules of the institutions. One of the strengths of Tan's view is that even though cosmopolitan justice provides the justification for the limits of partiality towards group members, the value of those attachments is not reduced to cosmopolitan considerations, which is arguably a flaw with other attempts (for example Nussbaum 1996).

A simple way to show how there is a gap between the cosmopolitan's position and what anti-cosmopolitans fear is this. Cosmopolitanism is essentially committed to these two central ideas: first, the equal moral worth of all individuals, no matter where they happen to be situated on the planet and what borders separate them from one another. Second, there are some obligations that are binding on all of us, no matter where we are situated. But acknowledging these two ideas still leaves plenty of room to endorse additional obligations, which derive from more particular commitments, and the preference some may have to spend discretionary resources and time on particular communities or attachments important to one's life plans and projects. In order to know just what constitutes our discretionary resources, and what our basic obligations to one another are, we need the input of cosmopolitan justice. So long as we act in ways consistent with those commitments, there are no residual ethical concerns. Whether or not there is still room for conflict depends on how much is packed into cosmopolitan justice. Very strong forms of egalitarian duties might leave little room; weaker ones might leave more. And yet we can appreciate that conceptually, at least, there is no tension here as feared.[8]

---

8   Recall that this sort of solution to the issue of how our global responsibilities can be reconciled with our local ones applies primarily to the issue of global *distributive* justice. Other principles may certainly be overlaid on these to deal with rectifying

The Circumstances of Egalitarian Justice: A Current Debate Concerning How and Whether the State Makes a Difference to Our Commitments to Equality

A current debate rages between cosmopolitan egalitarians and "statist" egalitarians. This debate is between those egalitarians who believe that full egalitarian justice applies within the state but not outside it ("statists"), and those who believe the state does not, and cannot, make this kind of difference to one's commitment to egalitarian distributive justice (cosmopolitans).

There are several forms of the argument. One kind emphasizes the fact that states are legally able to coerce whereas the lack of a global legal coercive authority rules out the need for global equality (Blake 2002, Miller 1998). The idea here is that legal coercion must be justifiable to those who will find their autonomy restricted. This coercion would be justifiable if no arbitrary inequalities are permissible in the society, hence we get a strong commitment to traditional egalitarian conceptions of distributive justice. This form of argument has been criticized from several directions. One line of attack is to dispute the idea that coercion is necessary for a concern with egalitarian distributive justice. There may be other reasons to care about equality in the absence of coercion. Another way to criticize this argument is to emphasize that even if we agree that coercion triggers egalitarian duties of justice, coercion in the global sphere being rampant, the necessary ingredients for egalitarian duties of justice are present at the global level.

A second version of the "equality among compatriots but not among non-compatriots" position argues that when we make laws within a state, we become "joint-authors" of the laws of our society (Nagel 2005). This shared involvement triggers egalitarian duties. But there is no relevant analog in the global context: there is no global law making process, and so no global legislation of which all persons are similarly joint-authors. This argument has been challenged in several ways, including questioning whether joint authorship of legislation is necessary for the requisite concern (Caney 2008) and also arguing that even if it is, similar processes can be found in the global context (Cohen and Sabel 2006).

Debate continues on numerous fronts about whether and how equality matters at the global level. Current questions that are still hotly debated include these:

1. What are the circumstances for triggering egalitarian duties of justice?
2. What is the scope of egalitarian justice? In particular, can a case be made that these should apply globally?

Debate also continues about several other issues which have a long history in political philosophy as applied to the state, namely:

---

past injustices. For more discussion on how to reconcile particular and cosmopolitan commitments see, for instance, Brock (2002).

3. What should we be trying to equalize? Capabilities (Nussbaum 2006), access to primary goods (Tan 2004), opportunities (Moellendorf 2002, Caney 2001), positive freedom (Gould 2004) and the value of resources (Steiner 1999) are just some of the candidates that have been presented with many sophisticated accounts also being developed, such as that we should promote standing in relations of equality with one another (relational egalitarianism).[9]
4. Why and how does equality matter? Here a debate rages between, for instance, luck egalitarians (Tan 2004, 2009) and relational egalitarians (Anderson 1999).

The field is rich with new possibilities here. In particular, the idea that what we should be trying to achieve in the global sphere is a certain kind of equality in our relations with one another is gaining increasing attention.

Cosmopolitanism and Global Justice in the World: Concluding Remarks

In many ways the widespread and growing commitment to the importance of human rights in regulating our international affairs is something of a cosmopolitan achievement in the struggle for global justice. The fact that we have a document that clearly specifies the entitlements that all human beings have is quite remarkable, given the diversity of worldviews and perspectives represented among the world's people. Furthermore, we have an international legal order that has certain commitments to uphold these entitlements. All those states that are members of the United Nations are (technically, at least) committed to respecting human rights. And there is wide proliferation of treaties and agreements based on these commitments to human rights. The cosmopolitan idea that each person has equal moral worth and deserves some fundamental protections and entitlements is not just a theoretical position but has made some significant inroads in international law and global policy-making, though this is not to deny that we still have far to go before the cosmopolitan vision is adequately instantiated in the world. Moves to promote global solidarity and community are often helpful in the struggle to ensure each person really is accorded the dignity and equal moral worth to which they are entitled. To that end, Nussbaum's suggestion (1996) that we educate for world citizenship is very important. School curricula should be revised to promote more understanding of our global problems, and more opportunity to understand and create empathy with others no matter where they are situated.

---

9   For more on this alternative see Brock (2009: ch. 12).

Bibliography

Anderson, E. 1999. What is the Point of Equality? *Ethics*, 109, 287–337.
Beitz, C. 1979. *Political Theory and International Relations*. Princeton: Princeton University Press.
Beitz, C. 2009. *The Idea of Human Rights*. Oxford: Oxford University Press.
Blake, M. 2002. Distributive Justice, State Coercion, and Autonomy. *Philosophy and Public Affairs*, 30, 257–96.
Blake, M. 2005. International Justice. *Stanford Encyclopedia of Philosophy*, http://plato.stanford.edu/entries/international-justice.
Brock, G. 2002. Liberal Nationalism versus Cosmopolitanism: Locating the Disputes. *Public Affairs Quarterly*, 16, 307–27.
Brock, G. 2005. Egalitarianism, Ideals, and Cosmopolitan Justice. *Philosophical Forum*, 36, 1–30.
Brock, G. 2009. *Global Justice: A Cosmopolitan Account*. Oxford: Oxford University Press.
Brock, G. and Brighouse, H. 2005. *The Political Philosophy of Cosmopolitanism*. Cambridge: Cambridge University Press.
Brock, G. and Moellendorf, D. 2005. *Current Debates in Global Justice*. Dordrecht: Springer.
Buchanan, A. and Keohane, R. 2005. The Preventive Use of Force: A Cosmopolitan Institutional Proposal, in *Global Institutions and Responsibilities: Achieving Global Justice*, edited by C. Barry and T. Pogge. Malden: Blackwell, 253–79.
Cabrera, L. 2004. *Political Theory of Global Justice: A Cosmopolitan Case for the World State*. London: Routledge.
Caney, S. 2001. Cosmopolitan Justice and Equalizing Opportunities. *Metaphilosophy*, 32, 113–34.
Caney, S. 2005. *Justice Beyond Borders: A Global Political Theory*. Oxford: Oxford University Press.
Caney, S. 2008. Global Distributive Justice and the State. *Political Studies*, 57, 487–518.
Cohen, J. and Sabel, C. 2006. Extra Republicam Nulla Justitia? *Philosophy and Public Affairs*, 34, 147–75.
Forst, R. 2001. Towards a Critical Theory of Transnational Justice. *Metaphilosophy*, 32, 160–79.
Freeman, S. 2006. The Law of Peoples, Social Cooperation, Human Rights, and Distributive Justice. *Social Philosophy and Policy*, 23, 29–68.
Gould, C. 2004. *Globalizing Democracy and Human Rights*. Cambridge: Cambridge University Press.
Grant, R. and Keohane, R. 2005. Accountability and Abuses of Power in World Politics. *American Political Science Review*, 99(1), 29–43.
Held, D. 1995. *Democracy and the Global Order: From the Modern State to Cosmopolitan Governance*. Stanford: Stanford University Press.
Hinsch, W. 2001. Global Distributive Justice. *Metaphilosophy*, 32, 58–78.

Hurrell, A. 2001. Global Inequality and International Institutions. *Metaphilosophy*, 32, 34–57.
Jones, C. 1999. *Global Justice*. Oxford: Oxford University Press.
Kleingeld, P. 2006. Cosmopolitanism. *Stanford Encyclopedia of Philosophy*, http://plato.stanford.edu/entries/international-justice.
Kuper, A. 2000. Rawlsian Global Justice: Beyond the *Law of Peoples* to a Cosmopolitan Law of Persons. *Political Theory*, 28, 640–74.
Kymlicka, W. 1995. *Multicultural Citizenship: A Liberal Theory of Minority Rights*. Oxford: Oxford University Press.
Martin, R. and Reidy, D. 2006. *Rawls's Law of Peoples: A Realistic Utopia?* Malden: Blackwell.
Miller, D. 2000. *Citizenship and National Identity*. Cambridge: Polity Press.
Miller, D. 2007. *National Responsibility and Global Justice*. Oxford: Oxford University Press.
Miller, R. 1998. Cosmopolitan Respect and Patriotic Concern. *Philosophy and Public Affairs*, 27(3), 202–24.
Moellendorf, D. 2002. *Cosmopolitan Justice*. Boulder: Westview Press.
Nagel, T. 2005. The Problem of Global Justice. *Philosophy and Public Affairs*, 33, 113–47.
Nielsen, K. 1988. World Government, Security, and Global Justice, in *Problems of International Justice*, edited by S. Luper-Foy. Boulder: Westview Press.
Nussbaum, M. 1996. Patriotism and Cosmopolitanism, in *For Love of Country: Debating The Limits of Patriotism*, edited by J. Cohen. Boston: Beacon Press.
Nussbaum, M. 2000. *Women and Human Development*. Cambridge: Cambridge University Press.
Nussbaum, M. 2006. *Frontiers of Justice: Disability, Nationality, Species Membership*. Cambridge, MA: Belknap Press.
O'Neill, O. 2000. *Bounds of Justice*. Cambridge: Cambridge University Press.
Pogge, T. 1989. *Realizing Rawls*. Ithaca: Cornell University Press.
Pogge, T. 1992. Cosmopolitanism and Sovereignty. *Ethics*, 103, 48–75.
Pogge, T. 1994. An Egalitarian Law of Peoples. *Philosophy and Public Affairs*, 23(3), 195–224.
Pogge, T. 2001. Priorities of Global Justice. *Metaphilosophy*, 32, 6–24.
Pogge, T. 2002. *World Poverty and Human Rights*. Cambridge: Polity Press.
Rawls, J. 1971. *A Theory of Justice*. Cambridge, MA: Harvard University Press.
Rawls, J. 1999. *The Law of Peoples*. Cambridge, MA: Harvard University Press.
Reidy, D. 2004. Rawls on International Justice: A Defense. *Political Theory*, 32, 291–319.
Reidy, D. 2006. Political Authority and Human Rights, in *Rawls's Law of People: A Realistic Utopia?*, edited by Rex Martin and David Reidy. Malden: Blackwell, 169–88.
Scheffler, S. 1999. Conceptions of Cosmopolitanism. *Utilitas*, 11, 255–76.
Scheffler, S. 2001. *Boundaries and Allegiances*. New York: Oxford University Press.
Sen, A. 1999. *Development as Freedom*. Oxford: Oxford University Press.

Shue, H. 1980. *Basic Rights: Subsistence, Affluence, and U.S. Foreign Policy*. Princeton: Princeton University Press.

Singer, P. 1972. Famine Affluence, and Morality. *Philosophy and Public Affairs*, 1(3), 229–43.

Steiner, H. 1999. Just Taxation and International Redistribution. *Nomos*, 41.

Sypnowich, C. 2005. Cosmopolitans, Cosmopolitanisms, and Human Flourishing, in *The Political Philosophy of Cosmopolitanism*, edited by G. Brock and H. Brighouse. Cambridge: Cambridge University Press, 55–74.

Tamir, Y. 1993. *Liberal Nationalism*. Princeton: Princeton University Press.

Tan, K.-C. 2000. *Tolerance, Diversity, and Global Justice*. University Park: Pennsylvania State University Press.

Tan, K.-C. 2004. *Justice Without Borders: Cosmopolitanism, Nationalism, and Patriotism*. Cambridge: Cambridge University Press.

Tan, K.-C. 2005. The Demands of Justice and National Allegiance, in *The Political Philosophy of Cosmopolitanism*, edited by G. Brock and H. Brighouse. Cambridge: Cambridge University Press, 164–79.

Tan, K.-C. 2008. A Defense of Luck Egalitarianism. *The Journal of Philosophy*, 105(1), 665–690.

Van Hooft, S. 2009. *Cosmopolitanism: A Philosophy for Global Ethics*. Stocksfield: Acumen.

Weinstock, D. 2005. The Real World of (Global) Democracy. *Journal of Social Philosophy*, 37(1), 6–20.

Cosmopolitan Memory and Human Rights

Daniel Levy and Natan Sznaider

Cosmopolitanism has long been the prerogative of certain elites frequently associated with urban environments. Indeed it is commonplace to perceive of cosmopolitans as rootless universalists who situate themselves outside the national community. However, recent advances in the literature direct our attention to extensive cosmopolitan imaginations permeating diverse geographies, strata of society and the political, cultural and legal domains of many countries (Delanty 2009, Levy and Sznaider 2010). In this chapter we argue that global changes have ushered in new forms of memory cultures transforming the national premises that hitherto dominated collective identifications, breaking down the dichotomy between local and cosmopolitan solidarities. More specifically, we deploy collective memory as analytic lens to focus on how public negotiations over past human rights abuses shape the balance of universal prescriptions and particular forms of solidarity. The emergence of a Human Rights Regime, we suggest, reflects the political-cultural and institutional embodiment of a new cosmopolitanism through which global concerns and local experiences become enmeshed.

We begin this chapter by elaborating on the significance of collective memory as an analytical tool and its centrality for meaning making. Next, we revise the conventional approach to memory which confines it to national boundaries. Instead, we highlight the factors that have contributed to the cosmopolitanization of memory cultures. The second section provides a historical overview addressing the implications these changes have for the transformation of legitimate sovereignty. Here we study the role of Holocaust memory for the subsequent emergence of a global Human Rights Regime. We then shift our attention to the theoretical surcharge cosmopolitan memories carry for human rights politics and the concomitant transformation of sovereignty. Finally we examine the role global media images have for the diffusion of cosmopolitan human rights ideals and emerging forms of solidarity. Concluding the chapter is a discussion of how fragile cosmopolitan sovereignty is when confronted with terrorism and other forms of political violence that threaten to undo the nascent manifestations of cosmopolitan statehood.

Collective memory has become a ubiquitous term dominating the public and scholarly imagination during the last two decades. True to its multidisciplinary character there has been little agreement on a concise definition (Olick and Robbins 1998). Yet much of the literature draws on the works of Maurice Halbwachs, for whom memories are not merely mediated but constituted in social frameworks. 'It is in society that people normally acquire their memories. It is also in society that they recall, recognize, and localize their memories' (Halbwachs 1992: 38). Studying and theorizing memory is thus not a matter of reflecting philosophically on inherent properties of the subjective mind or its neurological functions but of identifying shifting social frames where memories are embedded. Memory is situated in *social* frameworks (for example family, national and personal experiences anchored by symbolic markers), externalized in *cultural* signs (for example archival repositories such as memorials and museums), and shaped by *political* circumstances (for example wars, catastrophes and debates generating lasting meanings of these events). The forms and contents of memories thus vary according to social organization, historical circumstances and the groups to which individuals belong. Analysing group memories allows us to understand what categories people employ to make sense of their lives, their social, cultural and political attachments. That is, the political, cultural and social imageries which command normative attention.

The literature on memory, however, remains widely wedded to a nation-state model. Ironically, the territorial conception of national culture – the idea of culture as 'rooted' – was itself a reaction to the enormous changes during the *fin de siècle*. It was a conscious attempt to provide a solution to the 'uprooting' of local cultures that the formation of nation-states necessarily involved. Sociology understood the new symbols and common values, transmitted primarily through the consolidation of cultural memories by establishing links to foundational pasts, as means of integration into a new unity. The triumph of this perspective can be seen in the way the nation-state has ceased to appear as a project, and has instead become widely regarded as something natural. Accordingly, the nation-state reflects a

> *spatial understanding of the possibility of political community, an understanding that necessarily gives priority to the fixing of processes of historical change in space. Not only does the principle of state sovereignty reflect a historically specific resolution of questions about the universality and particularity of political community, but it also fixes that resolution within categories that have absorbed a metaphysical claim to timelessness. ... Time and change are perceived as dangers to be contained. (Walker 1990: 172–3)*

But during the last two decades we have witnessed a cultural (and by extension temporal) turn in the social sciences and humanities, of which the emerging cosmopolitan research agenda is a part.

At the beginning of the twenty-first century, globalization is posing a challenge to the idea that binding history and borders tightly together is the only possible means of social and symbolic integration. This crisis of territoriality has significant theoretical implications as the spatially rooted understanding of culture is being challenged by the disentanglement of nation and state. Contrary to conventional approaches which associate memory with national identifications, we propose a cosmopolitan conception of memory focusing on the simultaneity of universal and particular outlooks. We do not treat universalism and particularism as moral choices, but rather look at them as co-extensive modes of existence which can change over time. We historicize these notions, thereby de-moralizing them, while retaining them as valuable sociological tools. This has consequences, which we have addressed as the cosmopolitanization of memories (Levy and Sznaider 2002, 2005). Rather than presuppose the congruity of nation, territory and polity, cosmopolitan memories are based on and contribute to nation-transforming idioms, spanning territorial and linguistic borders. The formation of cosmopolitan memories does not eliminate the national perspective, but renders nationhood into one of several options of collective identification. The cosmopolitan turn suggests that particular orientations towards the past need to be re-evaluated against the background of global memory scapes. This is not to say that memory is no longer articulated within the nation-state, but that we witness a pluralization of memories, both in empirical terms but also considering its normative validation, which has given way to a fragmentation of memory, no longer beholden exclusively to the idea of the nation-state. A cosmopolitan perspective does not entail a denial of the persistent reality of the nation for social actors. It suggests, rather, that the contemporary nation-state itself and new forms of nationalism are best understood if the social-scientific observer adopts a cosmopolitan perspective. As Beck writes, 'the experience of an actual removal of boundaries, which may in turn trigger a reflex of neo-national closure, requires a cosmopolitan approach for its analysis' (Beck 2004: 133). In this light, a cosmopolitan methodological shift derives its analytical force from elucidating the relationship between processes of actual cosmopolitanization and the persistence or resurgence of political self-descriptions that are tied to a nationalist normativity.

The Cosmopolitanization of Sovereignty: Memory and Human Rights

One key interpretive issue is the transition from heroic nation-states to a form of statehood that establishes internal and external legitimacy through its support for sceptical narratives challenging the kind of foundational quasi-mythical pasts, which previously served as generation-transcending fixed points. These post-heroic symptoms of statehood are based on a critical engagement with past injustices and the incorporation of human rights rhetoric and practices. This is manifested, among other things, in the large number of historical commissions, official apologies and the active role of human rights organizations in public debates about usable pasts. Through the analytic prism of memories of rights abuses we provide an explanation for the salience of human rights norms as a globally available repertoire of legitimate claim-making. Public negotiations about memories of failures to address past human rights abuses (for example legislative measures, historical revisionism, educational measures and commemorative practices), we argue, shape the balance of particular identifications and universal mandates. Hence we consider the recent proliferation of human rights ideals as a new form of cosmopolitanism, exemplifying a dynamic through which global concerns become part of local experiences. Whereas universalism frequently implies the dissolution of the particular, the cosmopolitan gaze provides an analytic lens that shows how particular national and ethnic memories are not erased but transformed.

Nowhere is the cosmopolitan tension between particular attachments and universal aspirations more apparent than in the ways in which memories of human rights abuses have informed emerging conceptions of state sovereignty. Human rights discourse has become an omnipresent feature of international politics. Images of human rights abuses and the attendant political rhetoric seeking to assuage mass atrocities suffuse the global media. While many obstacles remain towards the fulfilment of human rights ideals, human rights declarations, formulated as a set of rules, regulations and norms, do constitute a challenge to one of the central tenets of sovereignty, namely the principle of non-interference in so-called 'internal affairs'. When it comes to certain types of abuses, human rights are about humans and not about members of specific states. The end of the Cold War in 1989 and the emergence of global interdependencies have highlighted the tensions between the imperatives of a Human Rights Regime,[1] the unbounded universal 'we' and the prerogatives of sovereignty, the political community, the bounded 'we'.

This dichotomous view certainly has relevance, but it is our contention that the consolidation of the Human Rights Regime has not so much led to the erosion of state sovereignty but rather to its transformation. More specifically, human rights themselves have become a principle of political legitimacy, inaugurating a new kind of politics (Levy and Sznaider 2006b, 2010). Although the rights revolution of the last two decades has not always deterred human rights abuses, it has created strong normative and institutional foundations able to penetrate the shield of sovereign impunity. Increasingly, compliance with a set of human rights norms – such as dignity and rights for all – is circumscribing the legitimacy of unacceptable state actions. Adherence to a minimal set of human rights ideals has become a significant, albeit uneven, factor in global politics and a prerequisite to preserving legitimate sovereignty.

We examine the link between human rights and sovereignty through the analytic prism of historical memories. Historical memories refer to shared understandings of and responsibilities for the significance the past has for the present concerns of a community. Through memory, a political community validates, challenges and reproduces itself. More specifically, we argue that historical memories of past

---

[1] The notion of a 'Human Rights Regime' refers to a system that is 'defined as principles, norms, rules and decision-making procedures around which actor expectations converge in a given issue-area' (Krasner 1982: 185).

failures to prevent human rights abuses have become a primary mechanism through which the institutionalization of human rights idioms and their legal inscription during the last two decades have transformed sovereignty. The global proliferation of human rights norms is driven by the public and frequent, ritualistic attention to memories of their persistent violations. The emergence of this global 'memory imperative' finds its expression in a set of political and normative expectations to engage with past injustices.

One factor that has contributed to a rapprochement between particular (national) identifications and universal (human rights) orientations in many countries is the aforementioned decoupling of nationhood and state. The state is increasingly considered a neutral institution which regulates the affairs of its citizens without necessarily providing an exclusionary sense of belonging. Clearly states have retained most of their sovereign functions, but the basis for their legitimacy is no longer primarily conditioned by a contract with a bounded nation. It is also determined by a state's adherence to a set of nation-transcending human rights ideals. Thus legitimacy is mediated by the extent to which states engage with (or commit to) an emerging Human Rights Regime, blurring the boundaries of internal and external affairs.

This cosmopolitanization of sovereignty is the result of particular historical conjunctures (the end of the Cold War, the Balkan wars of the 1990s, as well as repeated failures of this new Human Rights Regime to prevent acts of ethnic cleansing and genocide). Historically, it is a European phenomenon that emerged against the backdrop of memories of the Second World War and the Holocaust (Levy and Sznaider 2005). On the basis of these memories the nascent United Nations formulated various human rights conventions thereby establishing a global context. War atrocities themselves had not previously led to the triumph of human rights. They were not part of international relations prior to the Second World War: the Covenant of the League of Nations did not even contain explicit references to human rights. In contrast, human rights have a central place in the preamble and Article 1 of the UN Charter. The link between the Holocaust and the emergence of a moral consensus about human rights is particularly evident in the genesis and the consolidation of the Universal Declaration of Human Rights that was adopted by the General Assembly of the newly formed United Nations on 10 December 1948. The Declaration, as well as the UN charter itself, must be understood as direct responses to the shared moral revulsion of the delegates to the Holocaust – a sentiment that was also reflected in the direct connection between the Declaration and some of the legal principles established in the Nuremberg war crime trials. This link was also manifested in the close working relationship between the United Nations War Crimes Commission and the Human Rights Division of the nascent United Nations (Morsink 1999). In both cases, concerns about the illegality of retroactive jurisprudence were overcome by replacing conventional (that is, national) legal principles with the broader notion of international law and its implicit appeal to a civilized consciousness, now viewed as a safeguard against the barbarous potential of national sovereignty.

Together they were decisive in shaping the way contemporary human rights norms limit state sovereignty by providing international standards for how states can treat their own citizens. Human rights are therefore less a matter of philosophical or religious worldviews, but based on historical experiences and concomitant memories of catastrophes. Memories of the Holocaust have evolved into a universal code that is now synonymous with an imperative to address past injustices (both legally as well as in commemorative terms). It is against this background of particular national narratives and the normative universal imperative of reconciliation as response to human rights violations, that the dualism between victim and perpetrator memories is organized and ultimately fades. The vanishing of concrete personal memories is accelerated through the Americanization, that is universalization, of Holocaust representations. As a result, the dichotomy of perpetrators and victims is displaced and a third epistemological vantage point surfaces: that of the passive bystander and an attendant witness perspective. We shall return to this in our discussion of global media representations below.

Although the 'memory imperative' originated with the centrality of Holocaust memories during the 1990s, it has become a code for human rights abuses as such. By now the Holocaust had been reconfigured as a de-contextualized event. Memories of the Holocaust shape the articulation of a new rights culture. Once this new rights culture is in place, it no longer needs to rely on its original articulation (in this case the memory of the Holocaust) but it assumes strong normative powers. The Holocaust is now a concept that has been dislocated from space and time precisely because it can be used to dramatize any act of injustice, racism or crime perpetrated anywhere on the planet (Levy and Sznaider 2010). Most opposition to injustice is now articulated through the categorical denial and remedial efforts of rights violations. The victims of the present can no longer find salvation in the future but must be redeemed by connecting their experience to an iconographic past of human rights violations. Nation-states engage (or are expected to) with their own history in a cosmopolitan fashion which entails the recognition of the Other in forms of acknowledging past injustices and associated narratives. This dynamic explains both the importance of human rights norms as a globally available repertoire of legitimate claim-making and the particular appropriation of this universal script.

Rather than presupposing an abstract notion of political interests (grounded, for instance, in power or capital), we probe how, once institutionalized, human rights idioms themselves constitute political interests shaping power balances and by extension the contours of cosmopolitan sovereignty. Memory politics of human rights have become a new form of political rationality and a normative requirement for state legitimacy. Sovereign rhetoric is increasingly evaluated by the extent to which it is related to the legal recognition of human rights. To be sure, memory clashes abound, providing ample evidence that the prominence of human rights does not imply the end of the national and at times even raises the spectre of re-nationalization or re-tribalization. However, the prevalence of human rights, the mediated proliferation of memories of human rights abuses and their association with particularistic politics does signify the diminishing normative return of nationalism in international politics.

The choice of cosmopolitanism as a new moral and political idiom in this connection is not arbitrary. It relates to political and intellectual forms predating the era of the nation-state. Crucially, it has resurfaced at a time when the basic premises of the nation-state have been challenged and the shape of its sovereignty is being transformed. Cosmopolitanized memories capture the social modalities dealing with difference, such as universalism, relativism, ethnicity, nationalism and multiculturalism. Universalist versions of cosmopolitanism (for example Nussbaum 2002) oblige us to respect others as equals as a matter of principle, yet for that very reason it does not involve any requirement that would arouse curiosity or respect for what makes others different. Even more, the particularity of others is sacrificed to a postulate of universal equality which denies its own context of emergence and interests. In contrast, cosmopolitan memories presuppose a 'universalistic minimum' involving a number of substantive norms that must be upheld at all costs. These substantive norms include the sanctity of the body (Turner 2006) and the avoidance of unnecessary cruelty (Sznaider 2001). We use the term 'cosmopolitan common sense' when we have good reasons to assume that most individuals would be willing to defend this minimum (Beck and Sznaider 2006: 19).

Fragmentation and de-contexualization of memory cultures

In the following we highlight two dimensions of cosmopolitanized memory politics that are particularly important for theorizing the prominence of human rights and the transformation of sovereignty: the fragmentation of memories reflective of and contributing to the decoupling of nation and state; and the de-contextualization of memories, compelling the abstraction of concrete historical suffering thereby facilitating nation-transcending identifications with others. The fact that memories are no longer exclusively beholden to the idea of the nation-state is of central importance. Today there is a pervasive trend towards national and global introspection that has prompted numerous countries around the world to 'come to terms with their past' (Levy and Sznaider 2005). 'Inventions of Nationhood' during the nineteenth century were based on heroic conceptions and formative myths that were transmitted by 'traditional' and 'exemplary' forms of narrativity. In contrast, the history of Western European nation-states during the last quarter of the twentieth century was characterized by a self-critical narrative of their national pasts. While traditional and exemplary narratives deploy historical events to promote foundational myth, sceptical narratives also incorporate events that focus on past injustices committed by one's own nation. Cosmopolitanized memories thus evolve in the context of remembered continuities that view the past of the nation through its willingness to come to terms with injustices committed in its name.

This focus on memories of past injustices is accompanied by another tendency; namely, the transition from *history politics* which is characterized by a state-centric dynamic (through official commemorations, textbooks and so on) to *memory history*, which corresponds to the fragmentation of memories and their privatization (Diner 2003). This transformation manifests itself in the changing relationship of memory and history. The difference between memory history and conventional historical narratives is instructive. History is a particularized idea of temporal sequences articulating some form of (national) development. Memory, on the other hand, represents a co-existence of simultaneous phenomena and a multitude of pasts. (National) history politics corresponds to the *telos* of modernity (as a kind of civic religion). Memory can dissolve this sequence, which is a constitutive part of history. Memory history is a particular mnemonic mode which moves away from state supported (and state supporting) national history.

The previous (attempted) monopoly by the state to shape collective pasts has given way to a fragmentation of memories borne by private, individual, scientific, ethnic, religious and other mnemonic agents. Although the state continues to exercise an important role in how we remember its history, it now shares the field of meaning production with a host of other players. Modes of collective memory are being cosmopolitanized and also exist on supra- and sub-national levels. As the state loses its privileged command over the production of collective values (for example nationalism), human rights memories become politically and culturally more consequential.

In both the national and global case, the success of identification with distant others is found on the ability to produce shared memories that at once generate concrete references (to heroic deeds of the nation or particular human rights atrocities) and the possibility to draw abstract identifications from them (the need to forget the misdeeds of the nation as Ernest Renan put it, and remember selectively as the uneven pursuit of human rights appears to indicate). It is a delicate balance, which has come under increased pressure with the aforementioned proliferation and fragmentation of memories. The claim that the nation-state is an unproblematic container for solidarity is profoundly a-historical. Ironically, when national cultures were invented, they were open to the same criticisms as those directed at global culture today. They were dismissed as superficial and inauthentic substitutes for local cultures that were once rich in tradition. The nation was taken to task for being too large and alienating, an unlikely source of identification (Weber 1976).

In his seminal 1983 treatise on the origins of nationalism, Benedict Anderson quips about the limits of solidarity when he poses the rhetorical question 'Who would be willing to die for the European Community?'. This comes as somewhat of a surprise, given Anderson's constructivist approach which stipulates that all communities, and especially nations, are entities that are fundamentally imagined. The very belief that there is something fundamental at their root is the result of a conscious myth-building process. To come into existence, the nation-state at the *fin de siècle* depended on a process by which existing societies used representations to turn themselves into new wholes that would act immediately on people's feelings and on which they could base their identities; in short, making them into groups with which individuals could identify. The essential point of Anderson's thesis, which is often overlooked, is that a new system of values requiring self-sacrifice and willingness to live together is necessary in the transition to nationhood. In the pre-modern era, solidarity was based primarily on direct contact with those close (ethical boundaries corresponded to village boundaries); with the 'nationalization of the masses', it became necessary to identify with many other people via an 'imagined community'. We do not know each other, and yet we feel united as citizens of the same country.

This distant quality also permeates the salience of universal (human) or particular (national) rights as they are mediated, among other things, by the extent to which memories of past human rights abuses are transmitted in concrete or abstract forms. The latter are proliferating with the cosmopolitanization of memories. Human rights matter only to the extent that their universality is recognized. This recognition, in turn, is engendered through a process of de-contextualization by which memories of concrete (particular) atrocities are transformed into abstract (universal) violations of humanity. Without this de-contextualization it is difficult to re-contextualize memories of human rights as abstract categories and thus ensure their recognition as universal lessons for humanity. This process of abstraction is also necessary in order to re-inscribe memories of past atrocities into particular experiences. At the same time, this process of abstraction does little to change the fact that communities transmit different memories of the past, based largely on the extent to which memories of past abuses are a concrete part of shared experiences or whether they lack the kind of proximity (or distance) that allow them to become abstract principles. Accordingly, the strength of human rights principles in a given national context is the product of the tenuous balance of particular (concrete) and universal (de-contextualized) memories. The latter are in essence a form of forgetting. The relationship between memory and forgetting has received significant attention in the literature (Ricoeur 1999). However, contrary to most views, we do not treat memory as an antidote to forgetting. Instead we suggest that institutionalized memories of human rights abuses imply forgetting. The institutionalization of such memories and thus their ability to mobilize legitimate political claims is largely based on the process of de-contextualization, which in turn requires a shift from concrete memories to abstract remembrance. There is a move away from the concrete (that is particular) experience towards a more abstract (that is universal) message in order to reappropriate and recast one's own memories of past abuses in the contours of a globalized human rights discourse. As a result, we are frequently witnessing the institutionalization of the remembrance of barbarous acts at the expense of memories of the barbarity of these acts.

The distinction between memory and remembrance is not incidental. Nor can it be reduced to the so-called instrumentalization of memories. Memory vacillating between the concrete and the abstract, and its implied de-contextualization, can be related to three dimensions. It inheres in the course of action that gives memories their ritualistic strength. Ritualization depends on mediation, which by definition requires a certain form of abstraction. Considering the various channels through which memories of past human abuses are communicated, we consider this as a process of mediated forgetting. Failure to remember is also implied insofar as proximity to that which is remembered can shape the relative political-cultural significance it has for a community. Put differently, the universality of human rights necessitates a certain distance from the actual events that are being remembered. Lastly, the immanence of this dynamic is not just the product of historical and geographic proximity, but is also the result of temporal distance from the events that are being remembered.

One way of looking at this phenomenon empirically is to focus on the de-contextualization of memories of human rights abuses, which function as a precondition for the spread of human rights as a universally recognized idiom. The de-contextualization of particular memories of human rights abuses and their universal re-appropriation can be addressed by distinguishing between who is remembering and what is remembered. Moreover, cosmopolitan memories of human rights abuses are circumscribed by the historical occurrence of a forgiveness narrative that has further contributed to the shift from memory to remembrance and a corresponding transition from concrete individual to more abstract collective dimensions (Levy and Sznaider 2006a). Memories of human rights violations have become a subject of public negotiations and been subjected to the imperatives of forgiveness and reconciliation (Olick 2007).

By historicizing human rights, we thus propose a political sociology of human rights that is not based on some universalized metaphysical appeal but primarily transmitted through the proliferation of globally produced memories of failures to address human rights abuses. These mnemonic practices are firmly embodied in historical references (for example Holocaust, Balkan wars, Rwanda) and institutional manifestations (for example International War Crime Tribunals). The main difference between the universalistic origins of human rights and their recent cosmopolitan manifestations is that the latter unfold on the background of a globalized imagination. This does not imply convergence or homogenization. But rather the emergence of a locally situated recognition that sees humanity as a meaningful category of membership, in a culturally, politically and legally consequential fashion which is in line with de-nationalized conceptions of membership. Exclusion from the nation is no longer synonymous with exclusion from the protection of the state. The continuous transposition of cosmopolitan memories about failures to prevent human rights abuses has changed the conditions of membership. The surplus of legitimacy which human rights conceptions currently enjoy is neither an irreversible nor an evenly distributed process. Memories of human rights abuses, as well as failures to address them in time, are thus facets of a conflictual conception of collective memory. Memory is diverse and plural. It tells more than one story. Often these stories are contradictory and do not recount one single narrative. And they do not need to. Witnesses in trials make this point quite clearly. This is particularly relevant to contemporary debates in liberal democracies where national cultures and their homogeneous conceptions of the collectivity are challenged by the multicultural compositions of their societies.

The cosmopolitan turn and the proliferation of human rights and recognition are closely related to the aforementioned changes in moral sentiments since 1945. Memories of the great wars have transformed human rights sensibilities, at least in Western liberal democracies. Can there be a cosmopolitan reaction to the ever-present spectacle of human rights violations? Are 'we' responsible for the suffering of remote others? How should people respond when confronted with pictures of the beaten, tortured and murdered? With compassion? What does compassion mean in the context of a globalized human rights politics? Compassion involves an active moral impetus to address others' suffering.

There is a strong relationship between human rights consciousness and the emergence of a globalized cosmopolitan and liberal society, with its distinctive features of an expanded global awareness of the presence of others and the equal worth of human beings driven by memories of past human rights violations. Through these memories and their institutionalization in international conventions, the nature and sentiments of compassion have changed. Cruelty is now understood as the infliction of unwarranted suffering, and compassion is an organized, public response to this evil, as in human rights politics. With the lessening of profoundly categorical and corporate social distinctions triggered by the memories of barbarism, compassion can become more extensive and set a politics of human rights into motion. The capacity to identify with others, and in particular with others' pain, is promoted by the profound belief that others are similar to us. This identification is based on ontological equality.

Cosmopolitan media images

However, both the 'memory imperative' and the cosmopolitan recognition of the other require recurrent forms of mediation in order to sustain the Human Rights Regime. Here the globalization of media images plays a crucial role (Tester 2001). Developments in the field of communications go hand-in-hand with new forms of memory (Silverstone 2007). According to Patrick Hutton (1993), oral cultures rely on memories of lived experiences. In cultures of literacy, however, we 'read' to retrieve forgotten wisdom from the past. The invention of the printing press to produce books and newspapers was crucial in this process of reconstructing the past. How do the new global media transform memory cultures? The technological revolution that introduced the printing press textualized culture. The printed text led to an externalization of knowledge and laid the foundation for references to shared knowledge. The global media have led to yet another revolution in the reception of knowledge, values and memories by promoting a visual culture. We now remember things with the aid of images, which helps to explain why exhibitions, films, memorials and other media are becoming so important.

Compassion enters into current debates on the universal and contextual foundations of ethics as depicted in the global media. Globalization transforms cultures and their meaning making vocabularies. This transformation becomes evident when the particularities that make up a culture are divorced from their original spatial (that is, local and national) contexts. Culture can no longer be understood as a closed national space, because it now competes constantly with other spaces. Transnational media and mass culture such as film and music loosen the national framework without abandoning it entirely. The globalization of communication technologies challenges national identities by confronting the viewer with the presence of others. In the process, conceptions and ideas about the world come into conflict with exclusivist notions of national self-understanding. Even television viewers who never leave their hometown must integrate global value systems that are produced elsewhere into their local frame of reference. The rise of rapid, electronically based communication has led to an interlocked system diminishing the political-cultural salience of national borders. The immediate speed and imagery of the new global communications facilitate a shared consciousness and cosmopolitan memories that span territorial and linguistic borders.

Many of these global developments are possible only because of technological breakthroughs in electronic media. One particularly important feature for the globalization of the human rights discourse is the rise of media events, where a live and concentrated local action can be shared by the world (Dayan and Katz 1992). This is how the world is transported into the local. Distant others can be part of, and engender, emotions of everyday life. Human rights politics is put into action when the sight of suffering leads to political action intended to lessen the suffering of others. This is only possible when a language is shared which makes the suffering of others understandable. For the current suffering of others to be made comprehensible it must be integrated into a cognitive structure that is connected to the memory of other people's suffering. In this way, earlier catastrophes become relevant in the present and can determine a future that is articulated outside the parameters of the nation-state. However, there are communal boundaries to this globalized compassion.

A Cosmopolitan Leviathan?

As much as the end of the Cold War constituted an important juncture for the consolidation of the Human Rights Regime, the terrorist attacks of 11 September 2001 and their geopolitical aftermath have added a new urgency to debates about the political status of human rights, sovereign prerogatives and the potential for cosmopolitan memory cultures. Terrorism challenges the political salience of human rights principles and frequently causes the state to revert to one of its founding imperatives: the provision of security for its citizens (Sznaider 2006). When people feel insecure they will appreciate the security the state can provide. If they fear nothing more than violent death they will accept the state as ultimate protector. Anti-terrorist measures and expanding executive powers frequently infringe upon civic and human rights and have led some to demand that sovereignty be less conditional (Ignatieff 2004). Terrorism shifts attention away from state abuse and redirects national memories to failures of the state to protect its citizens.

However, despite these challenges, or perhaps precisely because of them, even the national interest rhetoric through which anti-terrorist measures are justified continues to be articulated in the global context of a human rights discourse. The recurrence of strong executive powers and national interest politics weaken international legitimacy and require extensive justifications vis-à-vis human rights standards. Current suspensions of human rights are not taking place in the middle of political crises but rather in the context of ongoing political reconfigurations. International terrorism is occurring at a historical moment when the classic nation-state is being transformed, a state which monopolized the means of violence and whose task it was to neutralize the fear of violent death into civilized channels. As soon as the state is recognized as the only source of legitimate violence, people internalize the state's authority as the 'mortal god', to employ Hobbes's metaphor of the Leviathan. This means that the state needs to be worshipped as the new legitimate god, introducing a modern sovereignty in which God's sovereignty was transferred to the state.

Since the terror attacks on 11 September, international politics have left the realm of calculability and the rules of warfare must be renegotiated. The Westphalian Order, grounded on the notion that a stable and peaceful political order can only be maintained by mutually supportive vows of non-intervention between political entities, no longer holds. The modern Human Rights Regime is premised on the notion that the prevention of human suffering takes precedence over the principle of sovereignty. This is the opposite of Hobbes and runs counter to the state's claim to provide security. The perceived suffering of strangers and the impulse to alleviate that suffering is one of the unintended consequences of the global process. The strength of human rights consists not only in their institutionalization but also in the realization, perpetuated by continuous reminders of past failures, of their fragility. Every time gross human rights violations are committed, they are not perceived as evil but as a (our) political failure, carrying the seeds, at least potentially, of real action. Memories of past abuses which by definition remind us of a breakdown of the regime, have been driving human rights remedies and have further raised the political costs of committing such abuses.

From a cosmopolitan perspective, however, universal human rights and particular national interests no longer exist as two extremes. Studying cosmopolitanized memories provides a diagnostic prism that allows us to historicize the balance of particular attachments and universal aspirations rather than stipulate their mutual exclusiveness or a universal trajectory. These developments are not merely epiphenomenal but are integral to how memories of human rights operate. Much of the debate on cosmopolitanism revolves around implicit or contested understandings of belonging. This is doubtless compounded by the vagueness of the concept of identity itself (Brubaker and Cooper 2000). For most social scientists, strong forms of belonging are constructed through a naturalized image of the nation, with manifestations such as communitarianism and ethno-nationalism, to name two possibilities. Cosmopolitanism, by contrast, is often characterized (both in its normative version and by its nationalist opposition) as the breakdown of boundaries, referring to humans rather than embedded people. Underlying this dualistic perception is the assumption that belonging operates primarily (or sometimes even exclusively) in the context of communal allegiance expressive of thick solidarities. Conversely, Craig Calhoun reminds us that we need not succumb to the opposite fallacy, which presents cosmopolitan identity 'as freedom from social belonging rather than a special form of belonging, a view from nowhere or everywhere, rather than from particular social spaces' (Calhoun 2003: 532). We thus employ a notion of cosmopolitanism that not only demands a universalistic minimum but also presupposes a particularistic one that recognizes the existence of communal fate and attachment. The respective balance of particularism and universal modes, we suggest, can be identified in changing forms of memories and sovereignty.

In both national and cosmopolitan cases, the success of identification with distant others is ultimately relying on a balanced notion of thick attachments with concrete others (for example, kin, local) and thinner versions of solidarity (for example, the nation, the global). The point is not that we dispense with thick forms of belonging, but rather that we explore identities as the coexistence of thick attachments and thin orientations. This view is premised on the notion that meaningful identities are predicated on particular attachments, which are always embedded in the story of the communities from which we construct our identities. Particularism becomes a prerequisite for a cosmopolitan orientation. Rather than treat cosmopolitanism as negating nationalism, we see cosmopolitanized memories as potential mediators between the particular and global horizons against which identifications unfold.

Bibliography

Anderson, B. 1983. *Imagined Communities. Reflections on the Origins and Spread of Nationalism*. London: Verso.

Beck, U. 2004. Cosmopolitan realism: on the distinction between cosmopolitanism in philosophy and the social sciences. *Global Networks*, 4(2), 131–56.

Beck, U. and Sznaider N. 2006. Unpacking cosmopolitanism for the social sciences: a research agenda. *British Journal of Sociology*, 57(1), 1–23.

Brubaker, R. and Cooper, F. 2000. Beyond 'identity'. *Theory and Society*, 29, 1–47.

Calhoun, C. 2003. 'Belonging' in the cosmopolitan imaginary. *Ethnicities*, 3, 531–53.

Dayan, D. and Katz, E. 1992. *Media Events: The Live Broadcasting of History*. Cambridge, MA: Harvard University Press.

Delanty, G. 2009. *The Cosmopolitan Imagination: The Renewal of Critical Social Theory*. Cambridge: Cambridge University Press.

Diner, D. 2003. *Gedächtniszeiten. Über Jüdische und andere Geschichten*. Munich: C.H. Beck.

Halbwachs, M. 1992. *On Collective Memory*. Edited by Lewis A. Coser. Chicago: University of Chicago Press.

Hutton, P. 1993. *History as an Art of Memory*. Hanover: University Press of New England.

Ignatieff, M. 2004. *Lesser Evil: Political Ethics in an Age of Terror*. Princeton: Princeton University Press.

Krasner, S. 1982. Structural causes and regime consequences: regimes as intervening variables. *International Organization*, 36, 185–205.

Levy, D. and Sznaider, N. 2002. Memory unbound: the Holocaust and the formation of cosmopolitan memory. *European Journal of Social Theory*, 5(1), 87–106.

Levy, D. and Sznaider, N. 2005. *Memory and the Holocaust in the Global Age*. Philadelphia: Temple University Press.

Levy, D. and Sznaider, N. 2006a. Forgive and not forget: reconciliation between forgiveness and resentment, in *Taking Wrongs Seriously: Apologies and Reconciliation*, edited by E. Barkan and A. Karn. Palo Alto: Stanford University Press, 83–100.

Levy, D. and Sznaider, N. 2006b. Sovereignty transformed: a sociology of human rights. *British Journal of Sociology*, 57(4), 657–76.

Levy, D. and Sznaider, N. 2010. *Human Rights and Memory*. Pennsylvania: Penn State University Press.

Morsink, J. 1999. *The Universal Declaration of Human Rights Origins, Drafting, and Intent*. Philadelphia: University of Pennsylvania Press.

Nussbaum, M. 2002. *For Love of Country?* Boston: Beacon Press.

Olick, J.K. 2007. *The Politics of Regret. On Collective Memory and Historical Responsibility*. London: Routledge.

Olick, J.K. and Robbins, J. 1998. Social memory studies: from 'collective memory' to the historical sociology of mnemonic practices. *Annual Review of Sociology*, 24(1), 105–40.

Ricoeur, P. 1999. Memory and forgetting, in *Questioning Ethics*, edited by R. Kearney and M. Dooley. London: Routledge, 5–12.

Silverstone, R. 2007. *Media and Morality: On the Rise of the Mediapolis*. London: Polity Press.

Sznaider, N. 2001. *The Compassionate Temperament: Care and Cruelty in Modern Society*. Boulder: Rowman & Littlefield.

Sznaider, N. 2006. Terrorism and the social contract. *Irish Journal of Sociology*, 15(1), 7–23.

Tester, K. 2001. *Compassion, Morality and the Media*. Buckingham: Open University Press.

Turner, B.S. 2006. *Vulnerability and Human Rights*. University Park: Penn State University Press.

Walker, R.B.J. 1990. State sovereignty, global civilization, and the rearticulation of political space. World Order Studies Program, Occasional Paper no. 18, Princeton University.

Weber, E. 1976. *Peasants into Frenchmen: The Modernization of Rural France, 1870–1914*. Palo Alto: Stanford University Press.

The Cosmopolitical[1]

Pheng Cheah

What I am calling "the cosmopolitical" is the concrete force field or domain in which moral politics or political morality becomes articulated beyond the state form such that "the political" becomes, by ethical necessity, "cosmopolitical," in a conjuncture in which we cannot say definitively that there are actually existing mass-based cosmopolitanisms that have displaced the national imagining of political community or that a global government has rendered obsolete the organization of human existence by the territorial state form. The gradual emergence of the cosmopolitical accompanies the development of cosmopolitanism from an intellectual ethos to a vision of a global political consciousness that is generated and sustained by institutional structures. The central problem that has troubled modern cosmopolitanism from its moment of inception in eighteenth-century European philosophy to the globalized present is whether we live in a world that is interconnected enough to generate, on the one hand, institutions that have a global reach in their regulatory function, and on the other hand, a global form of political consciousness or solidarity, a feeling that we belong to a world, that can take root within and be sustained by these institutions and influence their functioning in turn. Any theory of cosmopolitanism must therefore address two related questions, first, an empirical question concerning the cosmopolitan extensiveness of a regulatory power embedded in institutions, and second, a question about the normativity of these institutions, whether they can be in a relation of mutual feedback with a global political consciousness that voices the universal interests of humanity and tries to maximize human freedom. If both these questions cannot be answered satisfactorily, cosmopolitanism remains an intellectual ethos of a select clerisy, a form of consciousness without a mass base. The cosmopolitical refers to a material global condition that, in the current conjuncture, has not yet generated a mass-based cosmopolitan consciousness.

---

1   Portions of this chapter are adapted and reprinted by permission of SAGE Publications Ltd., London, Los Angeles, New Delhi, Singapore and Washington DC, from Pheng Cheah "Cosmopolitanism," *Theory, Culture and Society*, SAGE © 2006; also by permission of the publisher from *Inhuman Conditions: On Cosmopolitanism and Human Rights* by Pheng Cheah, Cambridge, MA: Harvard University Press © 2006 by the President and Fellows of Harvard College.

Cosmopolitanism in Modern European Philosophy

D'Alembert's entry in the *Encyclopédie* notes that "cosmopolitan" derives from the Greek words for "world" (cosmos) and "city" (polis) and that it refers to "un homme qui n'a point de demeure fixe, ou bien un homme qui n'est étranger nulle part [a man without a fixed abode, or better, a man who is nowhere a stranger]" (Diderot and d'Alembert 1751–1765: 4, 297). The term's philosophical usage to indicate a "citizen of the universe," however, emphasizes that this intellectual ethos or spirit is not one of rootlessness. Instead, what is imagined is a universal circle of belonging that involves the transcendence of the particularistic and blindly given ties of kinship and country. The cosmopolitan therefore embodies the universality of philosophical reason itself, namely its power of transcending the particular and contingent. Hence, the popular view of cosmopolitanism as an elite form of rootlessness and a state of detachment and nomadic non-belonging is mistaken. The cosmopolitan's universal circle of belonging embraces the whole of humanity. When cosmopolitanism is criticized for being a form of elitist detachment, the real point of dissatisfaction is that it is merely an intellectual ethos or perspective espoused by a select clerisy because the philosophers of the French Enlightenment could not envision feasible political structures for the regular and widespread institutionalization of mass-based cosmopolitan feeling. The bonds of humanity, whether they are predicated in terms of reason or moral sentiment, may be the strongest possible ties. But for various reasons, not many people are able to feel their pull. Rousseau lamented that in relations between different societies, the Law of Nature, or natural pity, the original root of social virtues such as clemency and humanity, has lost

> *almost all the force it had in the relations between one man and another, [and] lives on only in the few great Cosmopolitan Souls [grandes ames cosmopolites] who cross the imaginary boundaries that separate Peoples and, following the example of the sovereign being that created them, embrace the whole of Mankind in their benevolence.* (1766: 174)

The true inaugurator of modern cosmopolitanism is Immanuel Kant. Kant retained the idea of membership to humanity as a whole by insisting on the importance of "knowledge of man as a citizen of the world [*des Menschen als Weltbürgers*]" in his writings on pragmatic anthropology and universal history (1968a: 400). However, Kant was primarily concerned with man as a practical being and actor in history, someone who not only knows the world as a spectator of a play but knows his way about the world as a participant (1968a: 400). A world-citizen acts from the pluralistic standpoint of humanity as a collective actor as opposed to that of an egoistic individual (Kant 1968a: 411). Accordingly, Kant articulated at least four different modalities of cosmopolitanism that would become the main topoi of contemporary discussions of the concept in normative international relations theory (including accounts of global civil society and the international public sphere), liberal political economy and theories of globalization. These different modalities, which are part of a systemic whole, are: a world federation as the legal and political institutional basis for cosmopolitanism as a form of right; the historical basis of cosmopolitanism in world trade; the idea of a global public sphere; and the importance of cosmopolitan culture in instilling a sense of belonging to humanity.

What Kant calls "a universal *cosmopolitan existence*" is nothing less than the *regulative idea* of "a perfect civil union of mankind" (1968b: 47). It is a constitutional global federation of all existing states that is "based on *cosmopolitan right* [*Weltbürgerrecht*], in so far as individuals and states, coexisting in an external relationship of mutual influences, may be regarded as citizens of a universal state of mankind [*allgemeinen Menschenstaats*] (*ius cosmopoliticum*)" (Kant 1968e: 203n). Although it would not possess the coercive means of enforcement available to a world-state, it would nevertheless be a legitimately institutionalized world community, able to make rightful claims on its constituent states regarding their treatment of individuals and other states. Individual states would retain their sovereignty, but would be held accountable by a universal citizenry — humanity — with regard to issues such as disarmament and imperialist expansion. Kant's world federation would therefore fall somewhere between the political community of the state in its lawful relations with other states and a world-state.

Kant regarded state sovereignty as inviolable because the state was formed through an original contract by rational consensual individual wills. He also believed that the state had a fundamental role in the moral-cultural education of its citizens. Hence, his idea of cosmopolitan right remained restricted. The cosmopolitan community is a federation of states and not of world citizens, and the ultimate purpose of "a cosmopolitan system of public political security [*weltbürgerlichen Zustand der öffentlichen Staatssicherheit*]" is to bring about lasting peace so that states can devote their time and efforts to the cultural education of their citizens and increase their aptitude for morality instead of wasting their resources on expansionist war efforts (Kant 1968b: 44–7). Consequently, the scope of cosmopolitan right is limited to the provision of hospitality. It is "the right of a stranger not to be treated with hostility when he arrives on someone else's territory," a mere right of resort and not a right of a guest to expect to be entertained (Kant 1968e: 213–16). The protection of individual rights that we call "human rights" does not fall under cosmopolitan right but is left to the civil constitution of each state (Kant 1968e: 204–6). Matters concerning relations between states such as the principle that a state has no right to use its citizens for war against other states are also not governed by cosmopolitan right, but fall under the right of peoples (*Völkerrecht*) (Kant 1968d: 467–9).

In Kant's view, world trade provided the historical basis of cosmopolitan unity. As the spirit of commerce spreads throughout the world, states find that it is in their self-interest to enter into a world federation to prevent war and violence because these deplete their financial power (*Geldmacht*) (1968e: 226). Moreover, the unity brought about by trade and other forms of encounter between countries creates something like a global public sphere that will safeguard cosmopolitan right by protesting any violations of it in the same manner that a critical national public sphere safeguards the rights of citizens vis-à-vis the territorial state:

> *the peoples of the earth have thus entered in varying degrees into a global community, and it has developed to the point where a violation of rights in one part of the world is felt everywhere. The idea of a cosmopolitan right is therefore not fantastic or overstrained; it is a necessary complement to the unwritten code of political and international right, transforming it into a public right of humanity [öffentlichen Menschenrechte]. (Kant 1968e: 216–17)*

In addition, forms of culture also instill a deeper subjective sense of cosmopolitan solidarity or the feeling of belonging to humanity by encouraging universal social communication and sympathy. The fine arts and the sciences play a crucial role in developing our humanity (*Menschheit*) because they involve "a universally communicable [*allgemein mitteilen*] pleasure" (Kant 1968c: §83, 321). The humanities (*humaniora*) cultivate our mental powers by instilling in us "the universal feeling of sympathy, and the ability to engage universally in very intimate communication. When these two qualities are combined, they constitute the sociability [*Geselligkeit*] that befits humanity and distinguishes it from the limitation of animals" (Kant 1968c: §60, 300).

It is important to emphasize that although the different modalities of cosmopolitanism exhibit universalistic tendencies, unlike the philosophers of the French Enlightenment, Kant did not conflate the normativity of cosmopolitanism with that of moral reason and universal freedom. True freedom or autonomy could only be found in a kingdom (*Reich*) of ends, a systematic union of all rational beings through the moral law that each member is to treat himself and all others never merely as means but always at the same time as ends in themselves. Such a community could never be realized in the finite, sensible world because all sensible existence, including the actions of human beings, is determined by circumstances and principles that are not wholly rational, for instance, sensuous impulses and inclinations in the case of human action. The best we can hope for is that cultivation will curb our sensuous inclinations so that our resistance to acting out of obedience to the moral law can be minimized. What cultural education within the external institutional framework of a cosmopolitan federation attempts to create is "humanity," the unity of the species as an empirical consciousness in general. But this can only be a simulacrum that asymptotically approximates the realm of ends.

Marx's Proletarian Cosmopolitanism and the Mistaken Antinomy between Cosmopolitanism and Nationalism

The distinction between the normativity of morality and that of cosmopolitan right indicates that cosmopolitanism is not identical to moral freedom but is merely an institutional vehicle for its actualization. Consequently, cosmopolitanism is not necessarily opposed to nationalism in the way that universalism is opposed to particularism. Both forms of solidarity are alternative vehicles for the actualization of moral freedom. It is also erroneous to regard cosmopolitanism as the transcendence of the particularistic and parochial limits of the nation-form because cosmopolitanism may in fact precede the popular nation-state in history and nationalism in the history of ideas. Significantly, Kant does not have an understanding of the nation (*Volk*) as a self-conscious and strong form of popular solidarity that constitutes the basis for political solidarity. Like many of his contemporaries in the eighteenth and early nineteenth century, Kant spoke of the character of nations as a set of distinctive acquired or artificially cultivated traits that have developed from an innate character. However, national character is not considered a basis of solidarity. Solidarity only comes about in a civil condition (a society with distributive justice) and this is instituted by an original contract that constitutes the people as an articulated whole (*Volk, populus*) and the state (which has rights over the people) in one and the same moment (Kant 1968a: 174, Kant 1968d: §41, §43). Hence, for Kant, the people is defined by the state. "It is absurd," he suggests, "to speak of the majesty of a people [*Volksmajestät*]," as a cause of war. It is the majesty of a state that leads a ruler "to order thousands of people to immolate themselves for a cause that does not truly concern them" (Kant 1968e: 209).

This means that Kant's cosmopolitanism is not opposed to nationalism but to absolutist statism. His vision is formulated prior to the spread of popular nationalism in Europe, the period between 1825 and 1831 where nationality, in search of statehood, emerges for the first time as the primary basis of revolution. This period saw the rise of Greek, Belgian, and Polish nationalist movements, first aroused by the Napoleonic invasion, and now rebelling against their Ottoman, Dutch, and Russian governments for the primary reason that these were foreign regimes. Formulated too early to take into account the role of nationalism in the transition between the age of absolutism and the age of liberalism, Kant's cosmopolitanism is more a philosophical republicanism and federalism designed to reform the absolutist dynastic state than a theory opposing the modern theory of nationality. Indeed, because Kant writes at a time when the phenomenon and concept of "the nation" is still at an embryonic stage, he points out that the Right of Peoples or Nations (*Völkerrecht*) is a misnomer since it actually refers to the lawful relation of states to one another, *ius publicum civitatum* (Kant 1968d: §53, 466).

Kant could not predict that global capitalism was also the material condition of possibility of a different type of collective glue with similar humanizing aims. Like cosmopolitanism, nationalism in the initial moment of its historical emergence is a popular movement distinct from the state that also sought to provide rightful regulation for the behavior of absolutist states toward their subjects (Anderson 1991). Before the tightening of the hyphen between nation and state through official nationalism, the ideals of cosmopolitanism and European nationalism in its early stirrings are almost indistinguishable (Meinecke 1917). Prestatized nationalism had an unbounded and cosmopolitan extensiveness and patriotism was viewed as a concrete actualization of ideals and ends that would merely be abstract under cosmopolitanism. One could describe Giuseppe Mazzini's argument that the nation is the only historically effective threshold to humanity as well as the nationalism of

Johann Gottlieb Fichte (1808) as types of cosmo-nationalism (Mazzini 1961, Fichte 1978). Cosmo-nationalist themes are revived in the republican nationalism of Sun Yat-sen, the father of modern China, the idea of the proletarian nation in early Chinese socialism, and the decolonizing nationalisms of Frantz Fanon and Amilcar Cabral (Meisner 1967: 47–8, Fanon 1963, Cabral 1979).

In the history of ideas, the notorious tensions between nationalism and cosmopolitanism become more apparent from Marx onwards. For Marx, proletarian cosmopolitanism is no longer just a normative horizon of world history or a matter of right growing out of international commerce. It is a necessary and existing form of solidarity grounded in the global exploitation that has resulted from the global development of forces of production. In stark contrast to Kant's vision of cosmopolitanism, Marx's characterization of the nation and its appendages—national economy, industry, and culture—in naturalistic and primordial terms in the *Manifesto of the Communist Party* (1848) indicates that a significant sense of national belonging had already developed (Marx and Engels 1932b). But the nation is a false natural community, an ideological construction that masks the class interests of less developed bourgeois states such as the various German states and obscures the truly cosmopolitan essence of economic activity and civil society. Because economic activity transcends territorial borders, modern civil society is inherently cosmopolitan. "It embraces the whole commercial and industrial life of a given stage and, insofar, transcends the state and the nation, though, on the other hand again, it must assert itself in its external relations as nationality and internally must organise [*gliedern*] itself as a state" (Marx and Engels 1932a: 25–6). The proletarian revolution must be directed against the national state because it contradicts the unbounded nature of civil society qua medium and form of economic activity. Because universal exploitation creates a universal class in advanced countries that has been dispossessed and freed of any illusions by utter immiseration, the bourgeois ideology of "humanity" will be demystified and bourgeois cosmopolitanism will be sublated (*aufgehoben*) and replaced by the cosmopolitan solidarity of the proletariat.

Marx's proletarian cosmopolitanism is thus different from Kant's pre-nationalist cosmopolitanism. Kant missed the potential of popular nationalism as an emancipatory force against statism because he could not predict that the material interconnectedness brought about by capitalism would engender the bounded political community of the nation. Marx's socialist cosmopolitanism is an anti- and post-nationalism that reduces the nation to an ideological instrument of the state. He dismissed nationalism although he witnessed its rise. Identifying the nation too hastily with the bourgeois state, Marx reduced the nation to an ideological instrument of the state and saw nationalism as a tendentious invocation of anachronistic quasi-feudal forms of belonging in modernity. However, this antagonistic relation between socialist cosmopolitanism and nationalism has almost never been maintained from a historical-practical standpoint. The uneven character of capitalism as an actually existing global system implies an irreducible disparity between the working-class in different parts of the world. This has repeatedly posed obstacles for the formation of a global proletarian consciousness or world community based on labor. The national question was most notably raised in response to anti-colonialist struggles in Asia and Africa. In the historical scene of decolonization, it is not only the material economic wealth that workers have produced that needs to be reappropriated. The nation's spiritual or cultural personality has been taken away by territorial imperialism and continues to be expropriated by neocolonial forces. In Amilcar Cabral's exemplary reformulation, national liberation is "the phenomenon in which a socio-economic whole rejects the denial of its historical process … [T]he national liberation of a people is the regaining of the historical personality of that people, it is their return to history through the destruction of the imperialist domination" (Cabral 1979: 130). Imperialism determines that the primary shape of struggle for the (neo)colonized peoples who make up the mass of the world's population is nationalist. To remove the *nation* from the global circuit of property and commodification so that its people can have access to the products of their labor, the people must first achieve or regain their rightful cultural *personality*, which imperialism has violently usurped.

The same challenges to the formation of cosmopolitan solidarity continue to be raised today by popular nationalist responses to neocolonialism and uneven development. Two central issues stand out here. First, in a world where the nation-state is the primary form of political organization, can socialist cosmopolitanism have an adequate institutional basis if it does not work through a form of popular nationalism that seeks to shape state actions in accordance with the interests of humanity? Second, does a post-nationalist form of cosmopolitan solidarity leave peoples in the postcolonial South vulnerable to the unequal and predatory imperatives of capitalist globalization under its current neoliberal dispensation?

The Challenges of Contemporary Globalization: New Cosmopolitanisms or the Cosmopolitical?

Although visions of cosmopolitanism have mutated from an intellectual ethos to an institutionally grounded global political consciousness, this institutional grounding has been called into question by the uneven character of global capitalism. There is an inadequation or lack of fit between the material interconnectedness brought about by global capitalism and the degree of formation of global solidarities. In other words, we cannot automatically assume that experiences of a globalizing world where people, things, and events have become more and more connected necessarily leads to and forms the substrate for a cosmopolitan form of politics that displaces that of the nation-state form. In the past decade, various processes of contemporary globalization such as transcultural encounters, mass migration and population transfers between East and West, First and Third Worlds, North and South, the rise of global cities as central sites for the management of global financial and business networks, the formation of transnational advocacy networks, and the proliferation of transnational human rights instruments has led to greater hopes that this inadequation can be overcome and that feasible global forms of political consciousness have in fact arisen. It is suggested that whatever its shortcomings, contemporary transnationalism furnishes the material conditions for new radical cosmopolitanisms from below that can regulate the excesses of capitalist globalization. In comparison with older philosophical approaches, some of the proponents of new cosmopolitanism attempt to dissociate it from universal reason, arguing that cosmopolitanism is now a variety of actually existing practical stances that are provisional and can lead to strategic alliances and networks that cross territorial and political borders. However, these new cosmopolitanisms still contain a normative dimension. It is claimed that they are normatively superior to more parochial forms of solidarity such as nationalism and that they represent, however provisionally, the interests of humanity because they exhibit a degree of autonomy from the imperatives of economic globalization.

Theories of new cosmopolitanism are essentially syntheses of three different arguments, which can be found in different combinations. First, it is suggested that cultural and political solidarity and political agency can no longer be restricted to the sovereign nation-state as a unified spatio-temporal container because globalization has undermined many of the key functions from which the nation-state derives its legitimacy. Second, the various material networks of globalization are said to have formed a world that is interconnected enough to generate political institutions and non-governmental organizations that have a global reach in their regulatory functions as well as global forms of mass-based political consciousness or popular feelings of belonging to a shared world. Third, this new cosmopolitan consciousness is characterized as a more expansive form of solidarity that is attuned to democratic principles and human interests without the restriction of territorial borders. In some cases, it is also suggested that the new cosmopolitan consciousness is in a relation of mutual feedback with emerging global institutions, taking root and finding sustenance from these institutions and influencing their functioning in turn.

The thesis of the spatial-geographical destriation of the world economy is most clearly expressed in Saskia Sassen's work on global cities. Whereas the globalization of industrial production under post-Fordism created a hierarchical new international division of labor between center and periphery, Sassen argues that the outstripping of industrial capital by much more profitable non-industrial forms of capital such as international finance and the production of high-value specialized producer services crucial for the managing of global production networks (such as legal, accounting, and business management services) has led to the rise of new geographical formations, global networks of interlinked cities, that no longer respect the center–periphery distinction. New York, London, and Tokyo, the paradigmatic global cities, have become dislocated from their respective nation-states, and function instead as "a surplus-extracting mechanism vis-à-vis a 'transnational hinterland'," "as a transterritorial marketplace" in which each plays a different complementary role (Sassen 1991: 127, 327). These networks are a complex border-zone that facilitates the penetration of the nation-state by global forces.

However, for "the partial unbundling" of the nation through global economic processes to have any normative significance, it has to be aligned with the rise of new supranational political formations that can replace the normative deficit caused by the nation's weakening. Otherwise, the denationalization of the state merely serves the predatory rights of global capital. Here, the focus inevitably shifts to the concomitant proliferation of global political institutions radiating from the UN system and organizations and discourses centered on human rights and the rise of a new cosmopolitan culture through transnational migration and global cultural and media flows (Sassen 1998: 21–2). A combination of these two phenomena is seen as constituting globalization's normative payoff, namely a cosmopolitan political culture that exceeds the imperatives of merely economic globalization.

The progressive implications of a cosmopolitanism arising from the social experience of global cities—a cosmopolitan corporate work culture, the sophisticated consumption patterns of this high-income bracket, and the global culture of its growing immigrant population from the Third World—who are needed to support the lifestyle of the former group—is, however, dubious. The cosmopolitanism of corporate workers is essentially the cosmopolitanism of a new technocratic professional class whose primary aims in life are profit-making and conspicuous consumption. The only feelings of solidarity manifest here are to the global firm as a terrain for professional self-interest and advancement. This type of attachment is gradually disseminated throughout the world through the global outsourcing of white-collar jobs, which in turn establishes more bridges for higher-end South–North migration.

Similar questions should be raised about the cosmopolitanism of transnational underclass migrant communities in the North. Contemporary studies of global culture that focus on postcoloniality often connect this kind of cosmopolitanism to the political culture of human rights activism as evidence of the post-national spatialization of politics. For example, Arjun Appadurai has grouped transnational NGOs and philanthropic movements, diasporic communities, refugees, and religious movements under the rubric of actually existing "postnational social formations," arguing that these organizational forms are "both instances and incubators of a postnational global order" because they challenge the nation-state and provide non-violent institutional grounding for larger-scale political loyalties, allegiances, and group-identities (1993: 421). It is claimed that these global social and political movements emanate from the grassroots level and exhibit autonomy from dominant global economic and political forces ("grassroots globalization" or "globalization from below") and that they can be the sustaining basis for transcending or overcoming the constraining discourse of nationalism/statism (Appadurai 2000).

The connection between transnational migrant experiences of global cultural diversity and institutionalized forms of cosmopolitan solidarity, however, remains largely unelaborated. The world is undoubtedly interconnected and transnational mobility is clearly on the rise. But this does not inevitably generate meaningful cosmopolitanisms in the robust sense of pluralized world political communities. One should cast a more discriminating eye at the various emergent forms of cosmopolitanism and distinguish them in terms of how they are connected to the operations of neoliberal capital. For instance, over and above interventions on behalf of underprivileged migrant minority groups on an ad hoc basis, to what extent can activist cosmopolitanisms take root in the latter in a consistent manner to generate a genuinely pluralized mass-based global political community within the Northern constitutional nation-state as distinguished from the defensive identity politics of ethnic, religious, or hybrid minority constituencies? Can these cosmopolitanisms be embedded in a global community in the South forged from transnational media networks?

It is doubtful whether transnational migrant communities can be characterized as examples of cosmopolitanism in the robust normative sense. It is unclear how many of these migrants feel that they belong to a world. Nor has it been ascertained whether this purported feeling of belonging to a world is analytically distinguishable from long-distance, absentee national feeling. It is moreover uncertain that cultural minorities who have achieved multicultural recognition in Northern constitutional democracies are naturally sensitive to the plight of their former compatriots in the peripheries. They are more likely to be driven by the desire for upward class mobility and to become the new bearers of the imperatives of national/regional economic competition. The example of Asian-American entrepreneurship shows that Americans of South Asian, Chinese, or Vietnamese heritage often lead the vanguard of outsourcing initiatives in their countries of origin, justifying super-exploitation in the name of transnational ethnic solidarity. The NRI (Non-Resident Indian) businessman or multinational executive professes diasporic patriotism as he sets up call centers in India, just as the diasporic Chinese investor who exploits cheap female labor in Southern Chinese factories wishes to benefit people in his ancestral village. The argument that transnational print and media networks extend a world community beyond transnational migrancy to include peoples dwelling in the South has to reckon with the banal fact that many in the South are illiterate and/or do not have access to a television or hardware capable of receiving CNN and Rupert Murdoch's Asia-based Star TV.

What is sorely missing from celebrations of new cosmopolitanism in the softer social sciences and cultural studies is a thorough discussion of the normative implications of globalization, or more precisely the relationship between universality or weaker normative forms of wide inclusivity and the global extensiveness of economic, political, and cultural processes. There are, however, more recent arguments from philosophy that suggest that contemporary post-Cold War human rights regimes, other emergent transnational legal and political institutions, and the so-called international civil society of NGOs constitute a contemporary revival and updated affirmation of Kant's vision of cosmopolitanism. Among these arguments, that of the German philosopher, Jürgen Habermas, is the most sophisticated. For Habermas, the curse of globalization turns out to be a blessing in disguise. In his view, globalization is not reducible to global capitalism, but has relatively autonomous cultural and political aspects that create the conditions for an *Aufhebung* (transcendence/sublation) whereby the earlier national shell that imprisoned democratic republicanism will be destroyed and its kernel or truth-content, preserved in the form of deliberative democratic procedures, will rise up phoenix-like to a higher supranational state of existence.

First, the homogeneous national-cultural base of civil-political solidarity, which is already undermined by the global dissemination of mass culture, is further eroded by economically-driven South to North and East to West migration, which changes the ethnic, religious, and cultural composition of European nations. Habermas regards such cultural pluralization/multiculturalization of society as a boon. Xenophobic conflicts and the tyranny of the hegemonic cultural majority can only be controlled by the construction of a multicultural civil society that respects the differences of minority cultures. Hence, transnational migration, Habermas argues, actually accelerates the decoupling of political culture from the pre-political identity of the majority cultural group so that it can be completely co-extensive with the public-discursive democratic process (Habermas 2001: 71–6). Second, following Ulrich Beck's thesis of the rise of a world risk society, Habermas suggests that political solidarity is also decoupled from its national base by the creation of globally shared risks such as ecological and environmental damage, international organized crime such as the traffic in arms, drugs, and women. Because the political interests of the people affected by such global issues will no longer be co-extensive with the territorially-based decisions of nation-states, these actions will suffer from a legitimation deficit (Habermas 2001: 68–71). Third, the growing number of regulatory political institutions and forms of cooperation at various levels beyond the nation-state that attempt to compensate for its declining competencies suggest the blurring of the distinction between foreign and domestic policy, thereby indicating the irreversible development of a genuinely global politics (Habermas 2001: 70–1). These bodies range from the United Nations and its agencies to international regimes, some more tightly organized than others, such as NAFTA, ASEAN, and the European Union, as well as informal networks of NGOs. Finally, the increasing proliferation of human rights instruments indicates the emergence of a weak form of cosmopolitan solidarity, that of a quasi-legal community of world citizens.

Habermas's cosmopolitan vision consists of a dynamic complex of interconnected public spheres at both the national and transnational level rather than a world organization. He emphasizes the importance of global *Öffentlichkeit* for democratizing the processes of international negotiation that lead to agreements between states (Habermas 2001: 110). Insofar as such processes connect internal nation-state politics to policies of world organization, global *Öffentlichkeit* exploits existing structures for the formation of solidarity in national public spheres to further develop cosmopolitan solidarity in individual citizens and foster a world domestic policy on the part of state actors. This is a significant update on Kant's idea of a global public sphere, which Habermas argues, is now more securely actualized through global communications. Examples of its emergence and development stretch from the polarized global public debates over the Vietnam War and the Gulf War (and we may now add the US invasion of Iraq) to the series of UN-organized conferences over important global issues such as poverty, population growth, and the status of women. Although the global public attention and world opinion elicited by these global summits is channeled through national public sphere structures and is issue-specific and temporary, the ability of the international civil society of transnational NGOs to create and mobilize transnational public spheres through press and media coverage indicate the beginnings of more permanent communicative structures for genuine global debate. Such NGO participation gives greater legitimacy to the deliberations of international negotiating systems by making them transparent for national public spheres and reconnecting them to grassroots decision-making.

Although it offers a thorough elaboration of the normative implications of globalization for the formation of a new cosmopolitanism for the contemporary world, Habermas's project is unfeasible for three reasons. First, because the key features of Habermas's cosmopolitan vision are projected from the Euro-American-centric prototype of the Northern constitutional welfare state, it relies on a utopian over-idealization of the cosmopolitan virtues of Northern states, something that must increasingly be doubted after the US invasion of Iraq. Second, the criteria that make the First World welfare state the ideal model depend on a high degree of economic development that cannot be attained in the postcolonial South because its capacities have been actively deformed by the structures of the global economy. Postcolonial states forced to undergo structural adjustment, especially those in Africa and Latin America, are too impoverished to provide social welfare to their citizens. Worse still, states adopting the neoliberal path of export-oriented industrial development actively sacrifice the welfare of their people to provide conditions to attract transnational capital flows. This scenario is not exactly friendly to any of the three aspects of democratic will-formation (political participation, the expression of political will, or the public use of reason) Habermas desires and celebrates. Finally, while a degree of mass-based cosmopolitan solidarity has arisen in the domestic domains of Northern countries in response to exceptionally violent events such as the Vietnam War, the Rwandan genocide, or the war in Iraq, it is unlikely that this solidarity will be directed in a concerted manner toward ending economic inequality between countries because Northern civil societies derive their prodigious strength from this inequality. Indeed, we can even say that global economic inequality is simultaneously the material condition of possibility of democratic legitimation in the North Atlantic and that which hampers its achievement in the postcolonial South.

The impasses of Habermas's cosmopolitan project raise several broader questions: is the international division of labor the unacknowledged condition and therefore also the non-transcendable limit of all new cosmopolitanisms? If national forms of solidarity remain important, especially for economically weak countries bearing the brunt of capitalist exploitation, does uneven development constitute a crippling impediment to the formation of cosmopolitan solidarity? Does it place such constraints on cosmopolitanism's efficacy that we may regard it as a constitutive condition of contemporary arguments for the transcendence of nationalism, the limit beyond which theories of cosmopolitanism lose their coherence and become unworkable? In this regard, it is important to note that although transnational advocacy networks at the grassroots level may be animated by principles that are global in scope, although they are unconnected to traditional political parties within the national system of electoral democracy or national unions, and are able to voice their interests at global fora such as the World Social Forum, members of these movements and the participants in such fora may not have transcended feelings of national solidarity or the desire to make their respective nation-states take better care of its people. For instance, the central concept of food sovereignty—the idea that "every people, no matter how small, has the right to produce their own food"—articulated by the Sem Terra Movement, a movement of landless agrarian workers based in Brazil, indicates that although the movement's goals are global in scope, it begins from the principle of a people's national integrity (Stedile 2004: 43). Moreover, the activities of these social movements have to connect with the nation-state at some point because it is the primary site for the effective implementation of equitable objectives for redistribution at a large scale.

The feasibility of institutionalizing a mass-based cosmopolitan political consciousness therefore very much remains an open question today. It is not enough to fold the pluralistic ethos of older cosmopolitanisms into the institutionalized tolerance of diversity in multicultural societies. This kind of cosmopolitanism is only efficacious within the necessarily limited frame of the (now multiculturalized) democratic state in the North Atlantic that is sustained by global exploitation of the South. This type of limited cosmopolitanism has a more insidious counterpart in the state-sponsored cosmopolitanism of developed countries in Asia. Here, cosmopolitanism degenerates into a set of strategies for the biopolitical improvement of human capital. It becomes an ideology used by a state to attract high-end expatriate workers in the high-tech, finance, and other high-end service sectors as well as to justify its exploitation of its own citizens and the lower-end migrant workers who bear the burden of the country's successful adaptation to flexible accumulation. Cosmopolitanism is here merely a symbolic marker of a country's success at climbing the competitive hierarchy of the international division of labor and maintaining its position there. At the same time, however, capitalist globalization has made the urgency of a cosmopolitical frame of analysis unquestionable. But the force field of the cosmopolitical that is thereby generated is uneven. It does not clearly lead to the formation of cosmopolitanisms that are necessarily progressive or emancipatory. Hence, new cosmopolitanisms (and theories about them) as well as nationalisms need to be repeatedly inscribed within or re-embedded in this uneven force field that is their substrate and the material conditions of their genesis so that their consequences can be adequately evaluated and assessed at every turn.

Bibliography

Anderson, B. 1991. *Imagined Communities: Reflections on the Origin and Spread of Nationalism*. 2nd edition. London: Verso.

Appadurai, A. 1993. Patriotism and its futures. *Public Culture*, 5(3), 411–29.

Appadurai, A. 2000. Grassroots globalization and the research imagination. *Public Culture*, 12(1), 1–19.
Cabral, A. 1979. *Unity and Struggle: Speeches and Writings*, translated by Michael Wolfers. New York: Monthly Review.
Diderot, D. and d'Alembert, J.L.R. 1751–1765. *Encyclopédie ou Dictionnaire raisonné des Sciences, des Arts, et des Métiers*. Paris: Briasson, David, Le Breton, Durand.
Fanon, F. 1963. *The Wretched of the Earth*, translated by Constance Farrington. New York: Grove Weidenfeld.
Fichte, J.G. 1978. *Reden an die Deutsche Nation*. Hamburg: Felix Meiner.
Habermas, J. 2001. *The Postnational Constellation: Political Essays*, translated and edited by M. Pensky. Cambridge, MA: MIT Press.
Kant, I. 1968a. Anthropologie in pragmatischer Hinsicht, in *Werkausgabe XII*, edited by W. Weischedel. Frankfurt am Main: Suhrkamp, 397–690.
Kant, I. 1968b. Idee zu einer allgemeinen Geschichte in weltbürgerliche Absicht, in *Werkausgabe XI*, edited by W. Weischedel. Frankfurt am Main: Suhrkamp, 31–50.
Kant, I. 1968c. Kritik der Urteilskraft, in *Werkausgabe X*, edited by W. Weischedel. Frankfurt am Main: Suhrkamp.
Kant, I. 1968d. Die Metaphysik der Sitten, in *Werkausgabe VIII*, edited by W. Weischedel. Frankfurt am Main: Suhrkamp.
Kant, I. 1968e. Zum ewigen Frieden. Ein philosophischer Entwurf, in *Werkausgabe XI*, edited by W. Weischedel. Frankfurt am Main: Suhrkamp, 191–251.
Marx, K. and Engels, F. 1932a. Die Deutsch Ideologie, in *Marx/Engels Gesamtausgabe Vol. 1:5*, edited by V. Adoratskij. Berlin: Marx–Engels Verlag.
Marx, K. and Engels, F. 1932b. Manifest der kommunistischen Partei, in *Marx/Engels Gesamtausgabe Vol. 1:6*, edited by V. Adoratskij. Berlin: Marx–Engels Verlag, 523–57.
Mazzini, G. 1961. *The Duties of Man and Other Essays*, translated by T. Jones. London: J.M. Dent.
Meinecke, F. 1917. *Weltbürgertum und Nationalstaat: Studien zur Genesis des deutschen Nationalstaates*. Munich: R. Oldenbourg.
Meisner, M. 1967. *Li Ta-chao and the Origins of Chinese Marxism*. Cambridge, MA: Harvard University Press.
Rousseau, J.-J. 1766. Discourse on the origin and the foundations of inequality among men, in *The Discourses and Other Political Writings*, edited and translated by V. Gourevitch (1997). Cambridge: Cambridge University Press, 111–246.
Sassen, S. 1991. *The Global City. New York, London, Tokyo*. New Jersey: Princeton University Press.
Sassen, S. 1998. *Globalization and its Discontents*. New York: New Press.
Stedile, J.P. 2004. Brazil's landless battalions: the sem terra movement, in *A Movement of Movements: Is Another World Really Possible?*, edited by T. Mertes. New York and London: Verso, 17–48.

Hermeneutic Cosmopolitanism, or: Toward a Cosmopolitan Public Sphere

Hans-Herbert Kögler

Introduction:
On the Very Idea of a Cosmopolitan Public Sphere

The idea of a cosmopolitan public sphere may seem both self-evident and paradoxical, depending which layers of the concept are tapped into first. Self-evident if we are taken by the implicit normative potential of a public sphere, understood as the dialogical space in which "the forceless force of the better argument" (Habermas) alone is to hold sway. If an idealized conception of rational discourse is made the core of our understanding of public social communication, the boundaries must indeed seem endless. Given that here all are engaged in a counterfactually presupposed power-free enterprise—one destined toward finding the best solution to an issue, or the best articulation of relevant needs and interests—everyone capable of meaningful participation seems legitimately entitled to be heard and taken into account. Given, furthermore, that we find ourselves within an ongoing state of globalization which affects about every essential sphere of social life, a normatively acceptable public sphere must indeed appear to be cosmopolitan. It seems to imply a world public (*Weltöffentlichkeit*) or global citizenship that articulates its self-understanding by means of an all-inclusive transnational dialogue.

Yet if we are first led to the public sphere as a socially emergent dimension of the modern nation-state, its feasibility in the global context may look quite different. At best, it may shine as the desirable utopian vision of a transnational academic elite that transports its post-Marxist hopes of a transnational classless world citizenship into a procedural model of how "all people united" collectively define their common interest. At worst, it may look as the toothless paper tiger of free-floating intellectuals who project and superimpose their own supra-national and intercultural habitus onto a fragmented and deeply divided global world—

one which in reality is far from approaching a communicative sphere of mutual understanding, debate, and interest-articulation. The talk about "cosmopolizing" the state-based public sphere would thus be a sidetrack. It would miscalculate the possibility (and perhaps also the desirability) of a transnational sphere of communication that, in spite of being more inclusive and open, would lack the state-based grounding of rights based on shared national citizenship, together with the required means of implementing them.

Against this conflicting backdrop of the idea of a cosmopolitan public sphere (how can any truly communicative, that is rational, public sphere *not* be truly inclusive, that is, cosmopolitan? And: what could a public sphere *beyond* the grounding in a national-state possibly mean, that is practically amount to?), I set out to clarify the *socially existing and normatively acceptable* grounds of public global dialogue. At stake is the possibility of cultural-political communication that realizes itself in a state beyond the state—that is transnational and yet culturally and socially grounded ("rooted," if you wish). The envisioned transnational communicative sphere would unleash its normative and progressive force less by direct political influence, and rather by establishing, as it were, in the minds of the cultural agents, a new scope or framework, a new dimension of assessing what, who, and how something is going to be taken into account concerning the issues at stake. Here, agents are engaged in serious public dialogue outside the boundary of the state, without the legal and institutional guarantees, without even the nation-state induced "thick conceptions" of its shared histories, value-perspectives, and legal-institutional frames. A cosmopolitan consciousness, exemplified in the critical and reflexive orientation of each of its representatives, would both unleash contextual resources for new, shared ideas and values, as much as it would enhance the cognitive distance between agents and their taken-for-granted cultures and backgrounds.

However, participants would nonetheless remain thoroughly grounded in specific cultural, national, and historical contexts. And yet, while the cultural backgrounds remain indispensable resources of understanding as well as concrete contexts of application and realization, they similarly become repositioned and reconfigured in light of a context-transcending perspective. Hermeneutic cosmopolitanism involves a stronger detachment and distanciation from thick backgrounds than the complementarity of local rootedness and universal moral ideals that Anthony Appiah's "rooted cosmopolitanism," for example, seems to suggest.[1] Rather, agents come to situate their self-understanding *sub specie*

---

[1] For Appiah, the cultural background constitutes a rooted context of ethical obligations, while moral obligations provide an agent with a universal perspective (Appiah 2005; see also 2006). It seems that Appiah has cleaved too far apart cultural rootedness and cosmopolitan consciousness, missing (1) how concrete contexts become as such challenged and transformed via encounters with other perspectives and norms, and (2) how universal moral ideals are always understood through concrete cultural perspectives and backgrounds. I thus try to show how situated agents can critically transform their culturally rooted self-understanding via continuously enlarged moral *and* cultural self-conceptions. Thanks to Ben Hoffman for discussion of this point.

universalis—and yet such a universal viewpoint emerges only from an ongoing elaboration of cognitive input by concrete contexts. It thus follows that this "cosmopolitan perspective"—to answer in advance the challenge that this sounds still "liberal" and "context-free"—is an ongoing but situated reinterpretation of issues in light of a widened framework, without suggesting or presupposing a defined set of pre-fixed or pre-set universal values or standards. And this in turn means that the conception of a global public sphere involves a strong emphasis on the mutuality and interchangeability of perspectives as part of the process of engaging in the exchange of viewpoints and information.

Accordingly, the hermeneutic idea of a cosmopolitan public sphere is primarily based on dialogical understanding and exchange, in the sense of a communicative process in which the back-and-forth of intentionally relevant beliefs and assumptions are constantly tested and confirmed. Importantly, this rules out models of the public (*Öffentlichkeit*) or public knowledge as merely requiring equal access to information, or full transparency of all information with regard to all participants. While as such worthwhile ideals, they leave out the necessary mutuality and perspective-taking that alone can satisfy high normative standards of a truly intersubjective public sphere.

Furthermore, the intersubjective public dialogue will be considered the *ultima ratio* of reality with regard to the beliefs, values, and assumptions that are brought up, articulated, in its realm. The meanings are real inasmuch as they can be generated and understood within the mutual exchange of perspectives, such that public dialogue is here granted an autopoietic force. The communicative articulation of perspectives stemming from diverse backgrounds makes shared as well as diverging assumptions explicit and known, thus acquiring existence as public knowledge. This satisfies the highest criteria of true mutual intersubjectivity, because now values and value-perspectives cannot be introduced as pre-established, as "already-known-to-be-true-or-right"—they will have to be confirmed by the process. The process has to be constantly (re-)confirmed by those who express their commitments to this form of serious public dialogue.

Finally, the value-orientation that inheres in this public sphere is not solely oriented at mutual understanding in the substantive strong sense of consensus-building; rather, the immense intensification of cultural difference and contextual particularity involves that reflexive self-distanciation, cognitive appreciation of diverse cultural values and practices, and insights into multiple forms of political, cultural, and symbolic expressions of social power become central aspects of dialogical understanding. Because the commitment to dialogical exchange involves both a willingness to explain, defend, and unfold one's own claims and premises, as much as it requires a cognitive openness to new, divergent, and challenging views, substantive background assumptions concerning the self, the symbolic order, or the right political organization cannot be made the ground of mutual understanding. Cosmopolitan dialogue must be flexible enough to incorporate the wide range of accessible beliefs and practices, without thereby foregoing its own meta-normative orientation toward mutual understanding.

We saw that this hermeneutic process will have to take place "en dehors d'état," outside or without the state, as global dialogue is not backed by state decree, by a shared history, army or constitution. But it must still find its resources in the concrete social practices agents are currently engaged in. Those practices must be capable of generating the respective dialogical reality we are looking for. The question thus becomes: on which bases, on the grounds of what evidence, capacities, or cultural-political resources, could we envision the establishment of the desired dialogical attitude such that the reality of a transnational public sphere will be more than an intellectual chimera? What are the resources that human agency entails such that concrete social agents may become capable of orienting themselves within a cosmopolitan mode of self-understanding? How can subjects, given that their existing self-identities are thoroughly shaped by concrete cultural, social, and political arrangements, ascend to a cosmopolitan point of view? How can subjects that are defined by concrete value-laden role expectations, bound and grounded within functioning social fields, transcend those symbolic and practical affiliations to assume the role of the world citizen?

This chapter will be concerned with answering these questions. The approach will be hermeneutic—yet not solely understood as a method, but rather as a social-ontological approach to human agency whose intentionality, cultural and social embeddedness, and linguistically mediated normative orientation toward issues and objects is emphasized as defining human identity. This provides a general framework for the multiple substantive conceptions of cultural backgrounds that emerge within a dialogical exchange. It thus allows us to address the issue of values and value-orientations without building on a liberal model of agency and values, as well as assessing values after the acceleration of the process of globalization. Values should be conceived as generated *within* social practices, which suggests (1) that any value-orientation has to emerge from and remain (to a certain extent) grounded in concrete cultural contexts and practices; and (2) that those practices are themselves generated in terms of dialogical relations—which thus entails the potential to unleash a more radical, context-transcending mode of dialogical orientation.

Situated agents, understood according to a model of self-constitution via dialogical perspective-taking, can be seen as capable of taking a cosmopolitan perspective vis-à-vis themselves and others, which allows us to profile several important capabilities for a cosmopolitan public sphere. The trick is to show that these hermeneutic capabilities entail practically achievable normative goals for public dialogue beyond and above the boundaries of states, and to show how their specific implementation does justice to the high normative goals that we set out as required for a cosmopolitan public sphere.

Values, Human Agency, and Dialogical Relations

In philosophical discourse, the concept of value has long been met with suspicion. Neo-Kantian in origin, it seemed to presuppose a disembedded, solitary subject capable of orienting itself toward a self-contained realm of meaning entities—pure values, as it were. Those values were to provide meaning and justification to an otherwise contingent, arbitrary, and ultimately unjustified way of life. With the hermeneutic, pragmatic, and poststructuralist critique of the founding subject, the reference to values as a grounding source withered away. Now it is the embedded and symbolically mediated beliefs and practices that in turn provide the resources for value-assumptions. Now subjects, by articulating and justifying the normative aspirations and implications of their actions, seem to rely on a groundless ground, on the ever-shifting cultural landscapes of their particular backgrounds (Lash 1998, Beck et al. 1994).

As such, it may thus appear that the very practice of value-articulation, of providing a reflexive justification for one's intentional actions and goals, becomes vain, as it abstracts and generalizes contextual beliefs and assumptions that must lose their relevance and significance once de-contextualized. Worse, those validity claims or value-orientations may well turn into sources of symbolic power and hegemonic impositions once applied outside of their home-contexts, once they are extrapolated to settings and practices other than their originating ones. Is not every explicit validity or truth claim just another veiled attempt to subdue the other, to impose our value-regime on the other's being, to subject the subjects yet once more to a regime alien to their own agency and potential self-realization?

And yet, the reference to some kind of value-orientation seems indispensable, as our hint to agency and self-realization highlights. In addition, the challenge and critique of existing beliefs and practices requires the readiness to explicate the grounds on which the critic assumes her right to question an existing practice, and thus refers back to the need of some kind of justificatory source. Even if criticism were to proceed "immanently," as often invoked, any critical practice as such transcends the status quo and must do so in light of a projected, however implicitly envisioned, state, if only one beyond what there is. The question thus arises *what form the unavoidable value-orientation of our critical beliefs and practices can or should possibly take*. This question assumes enhanced relevance in the context of *globalization*, as the complexity and differences of local beliefs and practices is increasingly networked and interrelated, enhancing the predicament of both finding a common ground of shared values *and* of becoming aware of the immense diversity of contexts and cultures (Sullivan and Kymlicka 2007). If it is true that we cannot avoid being normative, if value-orientations are built into our being as human-cultural beings, and if it is also true that those value-orientations are inextricably linked with concrete contexts, than a *mediation between values and contexts* must be found. Such a mediation, however, cannot be ordained *ex officio* by the privileged intellectual, but has to be reached *by the very agents* whose values are at stake.

I suggest that the basic capacity to engage in productive dialogue, that is the common orientation toward a shared subject matter that is approached through mutual perspective-taking and critically assessed in terms of symbolic and practical background assumptions, points to an answer. We must avoid reducing subjects to unreflectively situated effects of contexts, as little as we can suggest a universal value-scheme that decides what all must share and honor as such. The path left open is thus the processual dialogical achievement of shared values, reflectively articulated in a mutual give-and-take. Yet we must first show how the *culturally embedded value-orientations are capable of serving as a source for a dialogical, reflexive, and critical reconstitution of values in a globally expanded value-horizon*. And to do so we need a basic model of how value-orientations are anchored in human agency.

Now, the hermeneutic-pragmatic turn in social theory brought to the fore the constitutive role of *embedded agency* (Kögler 2006). Agents are now understood to be situated in symbolically and practically structured *life worlds* which provide constitutive and inescapable horizons for all they do, feel, intend, and experience (Schütz 1967, Giddens 1984). Subjects are intentionally oriented, that is their thoughts are about something, they perceive something, and they intend to do something. To get this approach into place as our backdrop for the possibility of a cosmopolitan public sphere, I want to remind us of three of its essential insights.

1. Every intentional speech act is in its meaning dependent on a holistic and in its entirety inexplicable background. Most simple statements like "the cat is on the mat" or "the grass is green" assume a shared horizon, as altering background assumptions (such as a dead cat glued to the mat or fake grass) show (Searle 1989, Dreyfus 1980, 1993). Explicating such assumptions draws on further assumptions, and so on. Since intentional agency depends in its meaningfulness largely on language, it remains inescapably bound to a holistic and symbolically mediated background, which is always culturally specific. This background, however, exists literally in terms of speech acts that are maintained through the dialogical practices of socially situated agents, and thus forms (1) a necessary recourse for meaning, and (2) allows for reflexive and critical analysis vis-à-vis explicitly thematized aspects. (McCarthy and Hoy 1994)
2. While intentional agency is symbolically mediated (and thereby always dialogically constituted), the holistic background is internally differentiated — that is it does not consist in language or symbolic means alone. The different layers which consist of material practices and emotional-affective dimensions as well must be seen as co-constituting the backdrop for one's intentional acts. On the one hand, the linguistic terms are not self-sufficient meaningful entities, but make sense in the context of embodied interactions, thus social practices form an essential layer (Wittgenstein 1953, Bourdieu 1990). This dimension forms a "traditional" layer exercised as routine acts and rules, grounded in acquired dispositions typical of the respective social contexts. On the other hand, those intentions and rules are always embodied in particular agents, which means that there is also the unique, individual, emotionally colored dimension of an always slightly different perspective on the issues and practices at stake. Thus the attunement (Heidegger 1962) of an agent to a context and its "values," integrated into the overall scheme, plays a constitutive role. The practical dimension and the subjective dimension coalesce with the strictly speaking symbolic dimension, in which a conceptual scheme shapes whatever reality or the world are supposed to be like.

3. Finally, it is crucial to see that the interactive symbolic and practical relations are prior to the differentiated poles of an agent (who intentionally or even reflexively targets something as something) and the other (that is objects, other agents, or abstracted values) (Cassirer 1953, Lee 1997). The correlative roles of "I" and "it" (or "you"), of subject and object/co-subject, of intentional disclosure and intentional meaning, are emergent abstractions, are always tied back to their relational origin. Agency is thus an emergent relational phenomenon, derived from early empathetic encounters in which interactive settings allow the continuous and subtle abstractions of features, in part by introducing propositional symbolic systems, which in turn constitute reflexive agency (Kögler and Stueber 2000). The conscious self-identity of an agent thus remains in some way tied to its cultural background. But this also means—important for avoiding substantive conceptions of self-identity and human personhood in a global context—that the formal presupposition of dialogical encounters, which is provided by the capacity to differentiate into a self-related and an other-related pole, allows for a wide variety of substantive conceptions of self-identity.

Beyond the State: World-citizenship as Cultural Agency

If we now employ the hermeneutic-pragmatic conception of agency for our vision of cosmopolitanism, the task is to see how the inevitable intertwinement and interconnectedness of agents and cultures after globalization is to lead to an *adequate self-understanding of this process*. The objective structures that define social relations on a global order are to be reconstructed such that socially situated agents can understand themselves as active participants in the process, as subjects that understand, and can react to, what is happening. It is therefore that I evoke the concept of a cosmopolitan public sphere, namely to suggest a field in which agents reflexively and in an engaged manner participate in interpreting and defining their own as well as the common good.

Yet saying this immediately brings to mind the fact that the classic modern concept of the (bourgeois?) public sphere was inextricably tied to the emerging modern state (Habermas 1989, Eder 2006). The contested process of shaping and integrating subjects into the state order provided a context in which solidarity could be based on shared citizenship, on the assumption that one belongs to the same national-political order and thus assumes the status of a valuable, rightful subject. Precisely this context is missing at the global level. How, then, could the concept of a cosmopolitan public sphere be justified, or even conceptualized? How are processes of mutual understanding, deliberation, and collective action to be understood without the framework of an emerging (world-)state (for which United Nations and other global organizations do not provide an equivalent)?

The question arises whether a global public sphere can be grounded in dialogical social practices, which express and sustain the dialogical capacities of agents, without the backdrop of the state—including the backdrop of a world state. There may be *historical signs* for this: the emerging awareness of economic, political, social, and military interconnectedness, expressed by global social movements concerning climate change, nuclear arms control, and so on; an increasing empathetic concern for remote others, expressed in the outpouring of solidarity and support for victims of drastic natural disasters, such as the 2004 Tsunami or the earthquake in Haiti, but also regarding the genocidal situation in Darfur; and the vast expansion of the close co-existence with previously remote others, which transformed previously "homogenous" societies into ones that understand themselves as multi-ethnic and thus globally defined. Given that these phenomena may be taken as symbolic indicators for the possibility of a post-national public sphere, we set out to explore how cognitive resources entailed in human agency may allow us to envision a public dialogue on a global scale.

From its inception the public sphere has been understood as a third space between state and society: "It is neither a political institution nor a social institution, but an instance from which these institutions are observed and their meaning (especially their legitimacy) is communicated in either an affirmative or critical way" (Eder 2006: 333). It thus constitutes a somewhat free-floating symbolic space in which speech acts prevail and the formation and exchange of opinions persists. And while the beliefs and assumptions trace back to social and cultural backgrounds, and while the will-formation becomes relevant for a particular national government, this definition entails a certain freedom from the actual social and political contexts and fields within a particular culture. And yet, especially in its early classical formulations, the concept remains, as we saw, focused on the nation-state. The public sphere is seen as a realm in which free and equal citizens both exchange and form their opinions about relevant matters, as they pertain to their own lives within the emerging European nation-states (Habermas 1989). While this conception still locates the public sphere as a communicative space between state and society, it does so, however distanced and oppositional, within the larger confines of the nation-state. Therefore, if our task is to explore the viability of a public sphere on the cosmopolitan level, we may first have to address the very idea that the nation-state and the public sphere constitute a suggestive, if not necessary, constellation. At stake is whether the orientation of public opinion and belief formation is necessarily be oriented toward a national context. Instead I suggest that the relation between nation-state and public sphere is a highly contingent one when looked at in light of the practices and capabilities necessary to sustain a critical public dialogue.

1. Often and in many socially formalized contexts, institutionalized state-orders (*Staatsordnungen, Ordnungen des Rechtsstaats*) do not contribute toward realizing, but rather tend to undermine the recognition and development of dialogical values and agent-based capacities in social practices and fields. The conception of citizens united in a shared politico-cultural order tends to smooth over the vast discrepancies that exist among citizens, who exist in very different modes of access and resource-availability with regard to

contexts and institutions that allow meaningful critical participation in public debates (Bourdieu 1999). Under the umbrella of shared citizenship, this perspective covers up vast interest- and resource inequalities even among those "inside" the citizen-conception, as much as it builds a bedrock identity against foreigners, delinquents, immigrants, and otherwise socially "different" subjects who are both symbolically and institutionally excluded from participation (Benhabib 2006, Bohman 1998). This exclusion operates not merely by means of a general ideological scheme, but via adopted first- and second-person attitudes in members of nation-states who refuse to recognize the thereby identified and classified others as entitled dialogue-partners in matters of public concern.

2. Often and in many concrete institutional contexts, the state "hosts" instrumentalist social practices that turn agents into "human capital," into a material to be utilized in functional social sub-systems. By assuming the existence of an overarching state, whose citizens are deemed publicly organized, the actual systems that organize the social world are allowed to operate within a Foucauldian-like scenario enacting micro-practices that actively undermine the development of dialogical capacities by producing adjusted, manipulable subjects (Foucault 1979, 1994). Within the economic sub-system, for instance, a whole host of new practices is constantly tested, installed, revoked, and reinvented whose sole focus is higher efficiency via flexible work time, capital flow, investments strategies, and so on. Within education, practices that aim at better measurement, assessment, and streamlined production of results, are implemented against the holistic understanding of more adequate critical learning strategies. And within mass culture, the entertainment complex captures more and more "shares" of the mass media so that even domains formerly restricted to reflective and critical practices become scarce or themselves dominated by criteria of cheap entertainment and mass approval (Adorno and Horkheimer 2002).

3. Yet besides those normalizing practices, social venues and cultural practices do exist which actively foster dialogical modes of self-understanding and critical reflexivity. The point here is that these reflexive practices are not constitutively dependent on the state, nor are they best understood as emergent cultural products from within a unified national heritage. A view that sees the state as crucial tends to either ignore or misinterpret those venues that in fact transcend the limits of a specific nation-state scenario. Often, national treasures or traditions are recounted and narrated in a form that either fully excludes or at least minimizes the extent to which intercultural influences shaped the respective national culture. Impressionism without Japanese Ukiyoe, the US constitution without the Iroquois (or the French Enlightenment), nineteenth-century philosophy without Buddhism, are but a few examples of such symbolic exclusions, denying the insight that the "fusion of horizons" (Gadamer 1989) often extents into the original core of a tradition. In turn, context-bridging interpretive practices emerge from particular niches within a "national horizon." The export or mutual discovery

of human rights or environmental concerns can serve as examples, but also, for instance, the recent adaptation of US-American hip hop by Western Europe's disadvantaged immigrant youth, which creatively produced their own inspired forms of cultural expression and production. Fueled by an omnipresent worldwide web and facile traveling to follow up in person and connect on the ground, the boundary of the nation-state has become just one among many "limits," and concrete experiential sources, rather than national boundaries, become the real "ties that bind"(Urry 2000).

4. Perhaps most fundamentally, however, defining the public sphere mainly in the context of the state misconstrues how values are situated and embedded within social practices, by assuming that the state provides the constitutive foundation for such values in the first place. The point here is not to deny that a legal-constitutional framework plays an essential role in guaranteeing rights. But it is to assert, as Hegel already saw, that the actualization of those rights depends as well on intersubjective socio-cultural networks, including family and civil society, in which substantive value-orientations represent social relations which sustain agent-based resources for realizing normative orientations and aspirations. Those background cultures must, to a certain degree, support and reflect higher-order value-orientations if those are to have any impact (Pippin 2008, Honneth 1996, Buchwalter 2001).

Accordingly, the state itself relies on the formation of certain cultural capabilities that are (1) crucial for the development of a public sphere, but (2) not intrinsically connected to the existence of separate nation-states. We must now turn to analyze those features of cultural agency that can ground our intuitive idea of global citizens encountering one another in the medium of public dialogue.

Cultural Capabilities for Cosmopolitan Dialogue

What is crucial is thus to turn to the formative context for self-identity (Sugarman and Sokol 2010). This move will reveal the boundaries of self-identity to be a highly flexible, never fully fixed limit of self-understanding. The relevant cognitive capabilities have no intrinsic constitutive relation to the national context and are not restricted by any particular cultural or national context. It is because of this that we can approach an idea of citizenship as world-citizenship, that is as cultural agency such that the national context or horizon will appear as merely one symbolic-cultural boundary, below which lie many different layers of cognitive perspectives, belief-systems, and value-orientations.

I thus claim that we can (1) identify certain capabilities that have to underlie the rationally acceptable notion of a responsible and reflective citizen, and (2) that the capabilities which make cultural agents worthwhile actors within a state always already entail the resources to go beyond the state (Kögler 2005). The most basic capacities required for meaningful participation in an intersubjective public sphere include dialogical perspective-taking, mutual respect, and critical reflexivity. They are acquired in concrete cultural settings based on direct intersubjective encounters. Those capacities coalesce with the emergence of an agent's self-identity, but provide general features that can be constantly re-applied and expanded. In other words, the capabilities of (1) empathetically understanding another concretely situated human agent, of (2) respecting another human agent as entitled and worthy of the same rights and resources as oneself, and of (3) being able to critically question and challenge generally accepted notions and beliefs—all these have their ultimate source in the agent's socially emergent self-identity. These agent-based hermeneutic capabilities are socio-ontologically basic and thus prior to any higher-order social organization, be this the state or any other social constellation or field.

An agent will become an agent only insofar as he or she becomes an active participant in concrete modes of role-taking, which as *play* is emergent with one's linguistic and socially cognitive (intersubjective) abilities (Mead 1934, 1982, Bruner 1990, Sugarman and Sokol 2010, Kögler 2010). These modes of role-playing, where one *concretely takes on the perspective of another*, are but a (necessary and retained) stage of cultural agency. Emergent from the back-and-forth movement of imaging oneself in concrete roles is an understanding of one's own and the other's role as role-takers as such. Roles become conscious as roles that can be occupied by anyone—the idea of the human agent per se is born (Habermas 1983/1987). Within the new framework, the idea of equality, and the same rules and resources granted to everyone, becomes possible. It is again tied to a new mode of linguistic understanding, namely the mode of addressing another as a (potentially infinite) reason-giver, as an equal subject capable of understanding an issue as such-and-such, finally, as someone who can teach me as much as he or she may learn from me. The abstraction from concrete roles, perspectives, and modes of life has here the function to enable a *universally shared idea of human agency* (one which is often immediately invoked to ground universal human rights or cross-cultural values).

But the processual abstraction from the empathetic mode of role-taking toward the position of the "Generalized Other" (Mead 1934) will also enable, beyond the universalized second-person point of view, an objectifying, third-person approach toward oneself and one's context and peers. It thus entails the resources for *critical reflexivity*, thereby enabling a third mode of discourse that challenges widely shared and established ideas, conceptual assumptions, and institutional arrangements. The capacity for critical discourse, besides those for empathetic and normative discourse, complements what are essential elements of a democratic public sphere. If all three capabilities are globally applied—if they come to define basic background assumptions and capacities within the dialogical orientation of situated agents vis-à-vis one another at a global level—we can speak of the emergence of a cosmopolitan public sphere (Kögler 2005, see also Delanty 2010).

Yet what we now need to know is how these capabilities can be concretely realized within the confines of public transnational communication, which represents an extremely heightened dimension of mediated dialogue. Employing the model of dialogue at this level safeguards the intentional understanding of agents vis-à-vis other agents as socially situated, culturally embedded and rational co-subjects. The point is to maintain this stance in light of and by means of *the media* that are necessary to gain access to subjects situated in foreign contexts and cultures. A hermeneutically informed cosmopolitanism would thus approach the relevant media and respective information in a manner such that the crucial experiential-normative aspects are allowed to emerge, such that (1) agents are seen as requiring the necessary capabilities to make sense of the relevant information, and (2) the media themselves are thematized and analyzed vis-à-vis their capacity to convey the necessary meaning.[2]

The general framework within which all exchange and understanding of meaning operates is the intentional orientation toward something, which is linguistically mediated, based on substantive background assumptions and practices, and co-disclosed with other agents in social settings. The understanding of another will thus always proceed via an understanding of the other's perspective on something, which is mediated by my own background beliefs and yet allows access to another's views and values (Gadamer 1989). Now this process happens in early developmental scenarios face-to-face, and dialogue is usually understood as the actual exchange of beliefs and assumptions with another. Yet the very formation of identity, as we saw, proceeds via the imaginary assumptions of roles, it entails the generalizing abstraction of roles toward a universal role or standpoint, and it includes the representation of objective affairs, thus an objectifying capacity. In other words, *concrete dialogue* itself entails the imaginary, abstractive, and objectifying features that define the *mediated dialogue* with others who are absent, accessible only through the symbolic medium. What is now crucial is that the interpretive access to the other via that medium will be one which preserves *the subjective relation with the other*. And here the three aforementioned capabilities come into play as a constitutive hermeneutic force to create a *dialogical medium of understanding*.

First, the other can and needs to be approached as a concretely situated, that is both culturally and emotionally defined, individual. The narrative reconstruction of the biographical context of another, or of especially important events, in a light that makes the other accessible as an experiencing agent, marks one feature of preserving the other's agency. The empathetic potential that builds our selves as unique selves via a dialogical-experiential relation to others can be employed to distant others such that they become "real," become tangible as subjects

---

2 Empirical research supports the assumption that global media like the Internet and globalized TV can foster the building of transnational spheres of deliberation, consciousness-formation, and political self-understanding. By asking the "simple empirical question: with the development of global processes especially the global media, is cosmopolitanism becoming more widespread?" John Urry finds "a widespread cosmopolitanism: There was a strong awareness of the global flows of money commodities, and pollution; of extended relations connecting them to other peoples, places, and environments; of the blurring boundaries of nation, culture and religion; and of a diverse range of possible local, national, and global experiences" (Urry 2000: 2, 9). Thanks to Murray Skees for discussion of this point. See also Ionescu 2008, Thompson 1995, Poster 1995, and Cohen 1996.

experiencing pain, defeat, hope, humiliation, triumph. The empathetic discourse enables an emotional-affective bonding, creating an affective solidarity with others. Yet two cautionary remarks are in order: first, this empathetic perspective-taking will be adequate and successful in preserving true intersubjectivity only if it is itself reflexively mediated by an understanding of contextual, cultural and value-orientational differences, so as to avoid an ethnocentric projection of one's own culturally mediated affective states onto others (Makreel 2000, Kögler 2000). Second, the other cannot be made into an "object" of pity or sympathy, depleting the other's agency by overly defining the other's situation in terms of the affective factors. The point is rather to approach the other as a concrete individual in terms of a unique, narratively accessible biography or life-situation, and to thus develop a level of encounter that includes the first-person perspective of the real and concrete other (Nussbaum 2002, Godrej 2009).

Furthermore, the other is understood as reflexive agent, for whom the expansion of concrete roles eventually leads to a generalized understanding of roles as rules—and therefore as a rational subject per se. The hermeneutic perspective thus does not rule out a universal perspective; it is rather keen on insisting that such a perspective is based on a process of concrete abstraction, which allows for the reconstruction of beliefs and assumptions that are considered valid based on the concrete processes of communication. The cosmopolitan dialogue presupposes the assumption that the other is a rational co-subject, in the sense that he or she is capable of reflexively assessing the reasons and evidence for a view or position vis-à-vis a shared subject matter. But this assumption does not mean that the consensus about the subject matter at stake is guaranteed, nor that the failure to reach such consensus is identical with a failure in "understanding." The hermeneutic horizon thus includes the acknowledgment that not every experience or phenomenon is fully conveyable within the confines of the linguistically mediated process, such that the full force of the phenomenon can be shared as such for the other. But it insists on mutual respect vis-à-vis the other within a dialogical relation, such that the possible input and attempt for any possible experience is kept open. And it also insists and is aware of the fact that the consensus reached on certain universal ideas or norms, such as human rights, receives its support differently in different contexts, and is compatible with different sources of justification. Cosmopolitan dialogue is geared toward developing a sensibility regarding how universal human rights are differently understood according to the respective contexts without curtailing their normative force (Healy 2000, 2006).

Therefore, it is thirdly important to combine the hermeneutic recognition of equality with a self-objectifying perspective, the result of which would be an accompanying representation of the relations of power and domination inherent in certain contexts. The rejection of an abstract and detached universalism which would disregard the self-understanding of cultural contexts is prone to throw out the normative baby with the context-insensitive bathwater. Instead, the normative recognition of the other as a situated rational agent cannot come at the cost of disregarding, both cognitively and then politically, the effects of power and oppression on agents. Cultural difference is not allowed to be a cover-up for culturally oppressive norms, for the subordination of groups and classes to existing hierarchies of power, to the denunciation and humiliation of politically, culturally, or socially dissident agents. Mediated dialogue is very well capable of reporting, representing, and denouncing political and cultural orders of symbolic violence, as it is capable to inform and reveal modes of oppression and violence as they pertain to hitherto unreachable spheres. By integrating the empathetic concern with concrete life-trajectories, the respect for the self-determining powers of situated agents per se, and the actual constraints and challenges that agents face in their respective political and power-defined context, cosmopolitan dialogue can be realized by new media such as the Internet and critical reportages that become available on a global TV and information market. From Tiananmen Square to the revolt against the generals in Burma, from the mass demonstration against the Iranian regime to the red shirts in Thailand, the struggles against power become ever more accessible on a global scale. What is required is both an attitude of empathetic, normative, and critical openness with regard to their meaning, and a system of mass media that develops the social resources to put those hermeneutic capabilities into play.

The Cosmopolitan Consciousness—Dialogically Conceived

We are now in a position to see that the formation of self-identity, which is a process of continuously expanding perspective-taking without a natural boundary at any level, including cultural, national, or geographical limits, entails the potential to demarcate essential capabilities for a reflexive global consciousness. The objective tendencies entailed in the developmental emergence of agency can potentially be enacted so that agents themselves become capable of actively engaging and participating in the process, and to do so in a justifiable, normatively desirable manner. In other words, I suggest that we take the empirical potential entailed in human agency and put it, as it were, before the agents' intentional orientations, thus turning it into value-orientations that agents can, if they choose to do so, reflectively endorse.

We saw that intentional agency is value-oriented, aiming at some object or goal, and that those orientations are always embedded in a holistic cultural background. In the global scenario, the reflexive awareness of the embeddedness of (formerly authoritative) validity and truth claims reaches a new level. To develop a reflexive sense of one's own tradition within the context of the plural perspectives represented in a cosmopolitan public sphere is a major challenge, but it also entails the opportunity to transform the commitment toward one's values into a *fallibilistic consciousness* of validity—with validity here understood as the outcome of a dialogical process and construction. This process thus abandons the transcendental or metaphysical hope of absolute knowledge, yet without abandoning agents to the particularism of their respective contexts. It rather aims at a *reflexive openness* toward the mediation of value-commitments with concrete backgrounds and experiences from which they continue to draw their strength and content.

The fact that the global public sphere lacks an immediate political addressee such as a national government, combined with the dramatic increase of cultural, religious, political, and historical differences in its background positions, heightens the awareness of the hermeneutic challenge embedded in any intersubjective understanding. It brings to the fore the (always present, albeit oft ignored) need to make, to whatever extent necessary, explicit and articulate those background beliefs, assumptions, and dispositions that shape the explicit intentional orientation at something as something. The global challenge faces this human-scientific conundrum in a morally dramatized form, because here the other is not texts or cultural beliefs or practices as objects of understanding. Rather, the other is one whose concerns are those of real subjects, as co-citizens of the global space of one's co-existence. This said, the fact that the cosmopolitan dialogue exists itself in a space beyond or above the nationalized political frames, rather than directly intended at (national-)political will formation, foregrounds its nature as a *Verständigungsdiskurs*—that is as a dialogue emphatically aimed at *understanding* the other.

Agents thus encounter and approach one another with an understanding of themselves as sharing some value-orientation, some symbolically mediated perspectives, as well as social practices and institutions; they also commit themselves to be subject to the *rule of reciprocity* which does not per se privilege any perspective over another one, as it requires everyone to take into account the perspective of the other. This means, for instance, that the debate over whether local or universal standards of morality apply at a global level is reconceived here such that the values that may deserve to be counted as universal do so only if emerging from the interchange (Sullivan and Kymlicka 2007). What becomes universal is instead the intersubjective orientation toward open and reflexive dialogue, in which subjects define themselves as engaged with the most distant other, as bound by a shared global fate and experience, by the need to reconstruct one's own belief, perspective, and interest in light of how it relates to anyone affected, based on the shared capabilities that enable culturally situated global citizens to engage with one another in this context.

Cosmopolitan dialogue thus enacts the basic hermeneutic potential to move in-between and among contexts, without aiming to reach as such a detached level of abstraction. It makes use of the always concretely mediated, and yet general capacity of *imaginative-narrative perspective-taking*. This basic feature of human agents as language users can be unleashed to open up concrete life worlds of others. Foregrounding this feature makes sure that the empathetic concern for the situated other, to understand the motivation, background meaning, and force of the other's perspective, remains a central concern within the context of global dialogue. Yet since intentional agency is drawing on holistic background assumptions, embedded in social practices, the need for a self-objectifying perspective of power and structural domination emerges as well. Social practices involve hierarchical relations of power and domination, and they exercise their efficiency by a variety of means, including the macro-structural formation of conditions that pervasively structure, discipline, and thus constitute the self-understanding of situated agents. A reflexive self-construction of a global public sphere has to (1) thematize the objective processes of power that define its background context, and (2) to utilize the self-distanciating potential that intercultural dialogue provides to unearth the old and new forms of power that inhere in the involved cultural and national contexts.

Far from guaranteeing the establishment of a global public sphere, the basic hermeneutic capabilities represent but resources for its possible normative horizon. Recognizing situated validity-claims, engaging in empathetic perspective-taking, and critically analyzing power will have to be moments of a global dialogue in which agents would be able to fully recognize themselves as reconstructing and constructing shared as well as diverging values after globalization.[3]

Bibliography

Adorno, T.W. and Horkheimer, M. 2002. *Dialectic of Enlightenment*. Stanford: Stanford University Press.
Appiah, A.K. 2005. *The Ethics of Identity*. Princeton: Princeton University Press.
Appiah, A.K. 2006. *Cosmopolitanism: Ethics in a World of Strangers*. New York: W.W. Norton.
Beck, U. Giddens, A. and Lash, S. 1994. *Reflexive Modernization*. Stanford: Stanford University Press.
Benhabib, S. 2006. *Another Cosmopolitanism*. Oxford: Oxford University Press.
Bohman, J. 1998. The globalization of the public sphere: cosmopolitan publicity and the problem of cultural pluralism. *Philosophy and Social Criticism*, 24(2/3), 199–216.
Bourdieu, P. 1990. *The Logic of Practice*. Stanford: Stanford University Press.
Bourdieu, P. 1999. *The Weight of the World*. Stanford: Stanford University Press.
Bruner, J. 1990. *Acts of Meaning*. Cambridge, MA: Harvard University Press.
Buchwalter, A. 2001. Law, culture, and constitutionalism: remarks on Hegel and Habermas, in *Beyond Liberalism and Communitarianism*, edited by R. Williams. Albany: SUNY Press, 207–27.
Cassirer, E. 1953. *The Philosophy of Symbolic Forms, Vol. 1, Language*. New Haven: Yale University Press.
Cohen, J. 1996. The public sphere, the media, and civil society, in *Rights of Access to the Media*, edited by A. Sajó and M. Price. The Hague: Kluwer Law International, 19–50.

---

3   I want to thank Cosimo Zene, John McCumber, Alphonso Lingis, Andrew Buchwalter, Mitchell Haney, Farah Godrej, Murray Skees, Ben Hoffman, and Rosa de Jorio for helpful comments and discussion.

Delanty, G. (ed.). 2006. *Handbook of Contemporary European Social Theory*. London and New York: Routledge.
Delanty, G. 2010. *The Cosmopolitan Imagination: The Renewal of Critical Theory*. Cambridge: Cambridge University Press.
Dreyfus, H. 1980. Holism and hermeneutics. *Review of Metaphysics*, 34(1), 3–24.
Dreyfus, H. 1993. *Being-in-the-World: A Commentary on Heidegger's Being and Time*. Cambridge, MA: The MIT Press.
Eder, K. 2006. Making sense of the public sphere, in *Handbook of Contemporary European Social Theory*, edited by G. Delanty. London and New York: Routledge, 333–46.
Foucault, M. [1975] 1979. *Discipline and Punish*. New York: Pantheon Books.
Foucault, M. [1976] 1994. *History of Sexuality: An Introduction*. New York: Vintage Books.
Gadamer, H.-G. [1960] 1989. *Truth and Method*. New York: Crossroads.
Giddens, A. 1984. *The Constitution of Society*. Berkeley and Los Angeles: University of California Press.
Godrej, F. 2009. Towards a cosmopolitan political thought: the hermeneutics of interpreting the other. *Polity*, 41, 135–65.
Habermas, J. [1981] 1983/7. *Theory of Communicative Action, Vol. 1 and 2*. Boston: Beacon Press.
Habermas, J. 1989. *The Structural Transformation of the Public Sphere*. Cambridge, MA: The MIT Press.
Healy, P. 2000. Self–other relations and the rationality of cultures. *Philosophy and Social Criticism*, 26(6), 61–83.
Healy, P. 2006. Human rights and intercultural relations: a hermeneutico-dialogical approach. *Philosophy and Social Criticism*, 32(4), 513–41.
Heidegger, M. [1927] 1962. *Being and Time*. New York: Harper & Row.
Honneth, A. 1996. *The Struggle for Recognition: The Moral Grammar of Social Conflicts*. Cambridge, MA: The MIT Press.
Ionescu, L. 2008. European public sphere and information management. *Cinematographic Art and Documentation*, 3, 4–12.
Kögler, H.-H. 1999. *The Power of Dialogue: Critical Hermeneutics after Gadamer and Foucault*. Cambridge, MA: The MIT Press.
Kögler, H.-H. 2000. Empathy, dialogical self, and reflexive interpretation: the symbolic source of simulation, in *Empathy and Agency: The Problem of Understanding in the Human Sciences*, edited by H.-H. Kögler and K. Stueber. Boulder: Westview Press, 194–221.
Kögler, H.-H. 2005. Constructing a cosmopolitan public sphere: hermeneutic capabilities and universal values. *European Journal of Social Theory*, 8(3), 297–320.
Kögler, H.-H. 2006. Hermeneutics, phenomenology, and philosophical anthropology, in *Handbook of Contemporary European Social Theory*, edited by G. Delanty. London and New York: Routledge, 203–26.
Kögler, H.-H. 2010. "Agency and the Other: on the intersubjective roots of self-identity," in Sugarman, J. and Sokol, B. *Human agency and development*. Special Issue of New Ideas in Psychology.

Kögler, H.-H. and Stueber, K. (eds). 2000. *Empathy and Agency: The Problem of Understanding in the Human Sciences*. Boulder: Westview Press.

Lash, S. 1998. *Another Modernity, a Different Rationality*. London: Blackwell Publishers.

Lee, B. 1997. *Language, Metalanguage, and the Semiotics of Subjectivity*. Durham, NC and London: Duke University Press.

McCarthy, T. and Hoy, D. 1994. *Critical Theory*. Oxford: Blackwell.

Makreel, R. 2000. From simulation to structural transposition: a Diltheyan critique of empathy and defense of *Verstehen*, in *Empathy and Agency: The Problem of Understanding in the Human Sciences*, edited by H.-H. Kögler and K. Stueber. Boulder: Westview Press, 181–93.

Mead, G.H. 1934. *Mind, Self, and Society*. Chicago: University of Chicago Press.

Mead, G.H. 1982. *The Individual and the Social Self*. Chicago: University of Chicago Press.

Nussbaum, M. 2002. *Women and Human Development: The Capabilities Approach*. Oxford: Oxford University Press.

Pippin, R. 2008. *Hegel's Practical Philosophy: Rational Agency as Ethical Life*. Cambridge: Cambridge University Press.

Poster, M. 1995. *CyberDemocracy: Internet and the Public Sphere*. Online, available at: www.hnet.uci.edu/mposter/writings/democ.html (accessed: May 13, 2010).

Schütz, A. 1967. *The Phenomenology of the Social World*. Evanston: Northwestern University Press.

Searle, J. 1989. *Intentionality*. Cambridge: Cambridge University Press.

Sugarman, J. and Sokol, B. 2010. Human agency and development. *New Ideas in Psychology*, special issue.

Sullivan, W. and Kymlicka, W. 2007. *The Globalization of Ethics*. Cambridge: Cambridge University Press.

Thompson, J. 1995. *The Media and Modernity*. Cambridge: Polity Press.

Urry, J. 2000. *The Global Media and Cosmopolitanism*. Online, available at: www.comp.lancs.ac.uk/sociology/056ju.html (accessed: May 13, 2010).

Wittgenstein, L. 1953. *Philosophical Investigations*. Cambridge: Cambridge University Press.

Cosmopolitan Citizenship

Nick Stevenson

If the history of twentieth-century Europe could be written as a struggle between capitalism and socialism then with the coming down of the Berlin Wall in 1989 few were in any doubt as to who had won. The socialist dream of an egalitarian and work based society had, it seemed, floundered upon the rocks of authoritarian, state-managed societies. However the triumphalist liberalism that greeted the end of Eastern European socialism with ideas of "the end of history" has since had to be revised. If the idea of a peaceful planetary nation-state oriented liberal democracy always seemed an impossible dream given the ecological damage, inequality, and general human misery that it requires then some have recently been proposing more cosmopolitan versions of this vision. Here there is a recognized need for global solutions to global problems. Issues of environmental degradation, global poverty, refugee crises, and other features can only be faced in the context of post-national versions of citizenship. Proponents of a new cosmopolitan age argue that citizens need to break with the hegemony of the nation-state so that democracy can find new levels of expression in our global era. A genuinely cosmopolitan citizenship would come about when citizens had the possibility of participating within a polity that was not exclusively tied to national borders. For such a sense of citizenship to become meaningful it would need to offer a sense of rights, duties, and democratic accountability beyond the nation.

However if this view has its roots in the last decade of the twentieth century, after 9/11 and the war in Iraq such ideas already seem to be wearing thin. The war on terror responsible for Abu Ghraib, Guantánamo Bay, extraordinary rendition, "regime change," the disastrous wars in Afghanistan and Iraq and of course the promotion of neoliberalism. In this respect, I would argue that cosmopolitan ideas need to be rethought in terms of trying address the practical problems of the present. In this setting proposals for world government seem not only utopian but increasingly wide of the mark.

Here I want to investigate the idea of cosmopolitanism in the European setting. This is not because ideas of cosmopolitanism or global citizenship can only be European. More likely there will be many attempts to reinvent citizenship in a transnational age. However, as we shall see, I am keen to avoid the view of cosmopolitanism as if it comes from "nowhere." If cosmopolitan citizenship currently has a foothold in the world then it is in the European setting. The European Union (somewhat imperfectly) represents attempts by nation-states to pool sovereignty in order to help resolve or at least face a number of shared collective problems. However unlike many other cosmopolitan authors I see no reason to suppose that this model is transportable outside of Europe and severely doubt it provides a model of a future world state. However the European Union not only partially disconnects the idea of citizenship from the nation (granting rights to mobility and representation) but can also be connected to a rich vein of European thought and reflection.

The idea of the cosmopolitan joins together a notion of global citizenship as well as the capacity to live with the "Other." Cosmopolitan critique is suspicious of dogmatism and should be as alive to the fundamentalism of neoliberalism as to the promotion of pure or separatist identities. However there exist many different tendencies within cosmopolitan thinking. Here I shall explore the ways in which the idea of cosmopolitanism can be traced through different traditions within European thought and practice. This is not to argue that cosmopolitanism is specifically European, however this discussion aims to outline what cosmopolitanism might mean in the European setting. In this respect, I aim to explore the ways in which this rich vein of thinking might be reinvented and applied to some of the current problems of the present. As we shall see, the cosmopolitan projects of the past have been most effective when they have sought to offer alternative possible worlds, rather than building unrealistic utopias in the sky. There is a need for cosmopolitan arguments and imaginations to come down to earth and more concretely connect with the democratic possibilities of the present. Here my argument is that whatever the rightness of cosmopolitan political sensibilities they are unlikely to get very far without a substantial revival in the fortunes of democratic citizenship. However in doing this I want to draw inspiration from European intellectual traditions that have pointed out that the democratic settlement in the European context has a dark side. For example, much of the debate on cosmopolitanism takes place without explicit reference to the work of either Jean-Paul Sartre (2006) or Franz Fanon (1965). Both Sartre and Fanon are important for pointing to how universal ideas of human rights and democracy did little to disrupt colonial ideas of a racial hierarchy that arguably continue to haunt Europe today. Here they remind us that we can both uphold notions of human rights without it necessarily disrupting culturally ingrained ideas of superiority and inferiority and the practices of domination. Questions of cosmopolitanism therefore cannot operate outside of a concern for questions of culture and respect and how these issues are tied to notions of race as well as class, gender, and sexuality. Missing from much liberal commentary on cosmopolitanism is a sense that cultures of disrespect can indeed continue to operate within political cultures that respect democratic procedures and human rights. A human right to an education does not guarantee the right to an education that is not structured through relations of dominance and exclusion. This is why a European cosmopolitanism needs to be the meeting point between universalism and questions of cultural difference and Otherness.

European Cosmopolitan Worlds

Historically the idea of cosmopolitanism can be traced back to the Stoics (third century BC) but has since then found expression in the writing of both Immanuel Kant and Hannah Arendt. According to the philosopher Kwame Anthony Appiah (2006) cosmopolitanism in its various guises involves the idea that we have obligations to distant others and that to value human lives means to take an interest in activities and values that make them meaningful. There may of course be times when attempts to be both citizens of the world while valuing difference come into conflict, but we become cosmopolitan through the attempt to deal with this challenge. Notably however the ways in which intellectuals and thinkers have sought to realize these political goals varies greatly depending upon the social, historical, and cultural context.

For Kant the idea of a cosmopolitan order was built upon the need to construct a confederation of states that had renounced violence while being governed by the rule of law. The root of the problem of war lay with states coming into conflict with one another, and with their capacity to mobilize standing armies. The overriding cosmopolitan principle being that "no state shall forcibly interfere in the constitution and government of another state" (Kant 1970: 96). For its own security each state should seek to establish a federation whereby separate states are "welded together as a unit" (Kant 1970: 102). Whereas "savages" seek to protect their right to wage wars, Kant clearly believed that the granting of rights to citizens would both enhance the prospects of peace and bring to an end the hitherto lawlessness of nation-states. Indeed many have argued that the formation of the European Union on the principles of human rights and democracy is the realization of Kant's dream of peaceful co-existence. In this argument, the European Union (despite some of the claims of the Euro-skeptics) is not a state, but rather serves to "preserve and secure the freedom of each state in itself" (Kant 1970: 104).

The republican view following Kant is that democratic rule requires an international order of democratic states. The development of genuinely civil societies not only requires internal pacification, but also the rule of law governing the actions of states. This would change the foundation of citizenship that has existed in the majority of democratic states. In exchange for civil and political rights, citizens accept that they may become combatants during wars. However after the total wars of twentieth-century Europe many have become aware that ideas of civil society need to find a more global expression (Kaldor 2003). The limitation of the idea of genuinely pacified civil societies "internal" to Western democratic states allowed colonial powers to participate in a politics of violent conquest. A genuinely international "civil" society requires an international system that is subject to the rule of law. If Europe is our current best expression of this ideal many can be perhaps forgiven for thinking that the current polarizing rhetoric in respect of the "war on terror" makes its expansion seem unlikely.

David Harvey (2001) has argued that it is easy to detect a different Kant to that which is so loved by liberal cosmopolitanism. This is a Kant who is caught within the contradictions and evasions of Enlightenment thinking. As the cultural historian George L. Mosse (1978) has argued, racism is not an aberration of Enlightenment thinking but actually integral to its foundation. Many will undoubtedly find such a view uncomfortable, however, it is hard to comprehend the entirely shameful history of European scientific racism without coming to a similar conclusion. The Enlightenment passion for the categorization of "man" in relation to "nature" seemingly paved the way for numerous reflections on the racial hierarchy of peoples and cultures. Much of the work of eighteenth-century anthropologists sought to classify the white race in such a way that stressed its correspondence with middle-class values of orderliness and being law-abiding. Even the most "rational" of Enlightenment thinkers like Kant did not escape these formulations given he argued that there were four main races: White, Negro, Mongol, and Hindu. These races provided the basis for appearance, intelligence, and potential human development. Notably these mutable ideas were followed by later generations of racial biologists and scientists who linked questions of race to ideas of civilization and ultimately to notions of degeneration. Indeed if for Kant the peoples of hot lands were timid, lazy, and superstitious we might ask to what extent universal principles actually operate as a form of discrimination rather than as a shared good? (Harvey 2001: 275). Does the Euro-centrism of Kant tell us less about a possible future civilized world and more about the need of European intellectuals to feel superior?

This is indeed what the post-colonial critic Gayatri Spivak (1999) has argued in relation to Kant. Spivak argues that for Kant civility is a learnt through culture that inevitably has limited conditions of entry for non-European peoples. Indeed it is the desire upon the part of Europeans to be global legislators that reproduces the binary opposition between master and the native. Kant unknowingly reproduces "the axiomatics of imperialism" (Spivak 1999: 37). Yet we might remind ourselves that Kant is by no means exceptional within the history of European philosophy in his attachment to the belief in the superiority of Western civilization. Indeed Bhikhu Parekh (1995) has similarly discovered that Western liberal writers such as Locke and Mill viewed non-Europeans with contempt. This is the point, he reasons, where liberalism can itself become illiberal. Such a view simply assumes that a European way of life is best and that there is nothing of value to be learnt from an intercultural dialogue with other traditions of thinking. Inevitably the division between the "civilized" and the "primitive" reproduces a racialized logic that seeks to uphold Western forms of superiority.

Hannah Arendt's cosmopolitan vision was both inspired by that of Kant but was formulated in the context of the nationalism, racism, and totalitarianism of the twentieth century. Arendt (1986: xi) writes:

> *Antisemitism (not merely the hatred of the Jews), imperialism (not merely conquest), totalitarianism (not merely dictatorship) – one after the other, one more brutally than the other, have demonstrated that human dignity needs a new guarantee which can be found only in a new political principle, in a new law on earth.*

Arendt's cosmopolitanism is formulated in the context of the beginnings of international law and in the Nuremberg charter. This introduced the idea of "crimes against humanity" that despite the criticism it has received Arendt endorsed. Such a notion is built upon the idea that individuals can be held accountable for their actions irrespective of the laws of their own state. Arendt (1977) explores these features in her famous book on the trail of Adolf Eichmann, a former Nazi who had claimed in his defense that he was merely following orders from superiors. The cosmopolitan principle at work here is that each of us is responsible for the other, and that this responsibility cannot be contained within the walls of the nation-state. The prospect of being a global citizen or cosmopolitan then depended upon both the development of international law, respect for human diversity, and the capacity of individuals to be responsible. For the cosmopolitan the crimes of "the final solution" were not simply an affront to the Jews but an attack upon humanity. More specifically Arendt was particularly concerned to stress that cosmopolitan responsibilities should not be reliant upon human goodness, but were better placed in the hands of institutions that granted their citizens equal rights. The ability to act in the public then should not depend upon questions of personal morality, but alternatively would rest upon the public conscience of citizens. Part of Arendt's reasoning comes from her recognition that Eichmann was an ordinary man who did not lack a sense of morality or duty. The only sure way to guard against crimes against humanity was to integrate the masses into republics based upon rights and the rule of law where people were motivated by the need to uphold a public morality (Cannovan 1992). However Arendt (2000) was not an uncritical supporter of human rights. If the idea of the "rights" of humans have been with us since the end of the eighteenth century, then so has the limitation that the enforcement of human rights treaties and agreements depends upon your attachment to a nation-state. If on the one level Arendt wisely cautioned that even if world government were possible it may not look like some of the more idealistic accounts available within political theory then on the other it is those who lose their national citizenship who are among the world's most vulnerable citizens. As Zygmunt Bauman (2004a) reminds us, refugees and immigrants are the perfect scapegoat during our current turbulent times. If they, like the global power elite, are constantly crossing the borders of national societies they are also a vivid representation of the precarious state of humanity.

Refugees remind us that we too may become redundant and surplus to requirements. However I would also argue that refugees and stateless peoples also remind us of the importance of national communities in securing the rights of the majority. Indeed the sense of being under "threat" by those who are crossing over borders can breed a sense of national victimhood. Rather than those fleeing war, genocide, and oppression being the object of our concern it is "we," the host members of the national community, who become the "real" victims. Omer Bartov (2000) has carefully demonstrated how a sense of national victimization within the European context has been mobilized to obscure the poor treatment of minority communities in the past. It is then we "the majority" who are suffering from the standards of political correctness, lack of welfare provision, education, and "alien" invasion that obscures our inhumanity. Perhaps here we need to remind ourselves of one of the many lessons we might take from the Holocaust. Tzvetan Todorov (1999) distinguishes between so-called "vital values" where my exclusive concern is with my own life and well-being and what we might call "moral values" that suggest that there are indeed principles or at very least human standards that go beyond the need to simply pursue my own limited interests. There is then no cosmopolitan citizenship without a cosmopolitan morality or ethical sensibility.

However ideals of a universal cosmopolitanism were quickly displaced by the beginning of the Cold War. Such ideas were unlikely to take root in a world that was divided between the logics of two destructive superpowers. It is mistaken to think that the cosmopolitan ideal only re-emerges after the end of the Cold War. Elsewhere I have argued that European peace movements like CND (Campaign for Nuclear Disarmament) and END (European Nuclear Disarmament) struggled to dismantle the bloc system through the promotion of intellectual and cultural exchange (Stevenson 1999). Here the fear was that the Cold War promoted an atmosphere of paranoia and hostility with democracy being the main casualty. The aim of European peace movements was quite literally to unfreeze the Cold War from below through the promotion of dialogue. The historian and public intellectual E.P. Thompson (1982) memorably captured the logic of superpower nuclear escalation through what he called exterminism. The polarization of East and West into two antagonistic blocs not only reinforced the dominance of NATO and the Warsaw Pact but potentially pushed the possibility of Europe being the site of a nuclear war. The peace movement was urged to build alliances across the blocs in order to promote cultural understanding and intellectual exchange. Mary Kaldor (2003) similarly recognizes the importance of European peace initiatives in helping question the development of militarism and dismantle the oppositions between East and West in favor of a more cosmopolitan emphasis upon human interconnectedness. While many have argued that the revolutions of 1989 failed to produce a new political ideology, Kaldor (2003: 75) argues that "East Europeans invented a new form of politics." The collapse of the distinction between the West and the non-Western in a world of global interconnection ushers in the possibility of genuinely cosmopolitan concerns and passions. Through the spread of global media has come an increasing sense of shared humanity to which we all belong. Cosmopolitan or global citizenship it seems has a long association with the changing fortunes of the European continent and its intellectual traditions.

If many of these arguments have a direct bearing upon the idea of cosmopolitan thought today they also need to be extended. With the end of the Cold War many have argued that the time is now right to reinvent cosmopolitanism for our own times. Due to the intensification of economic, political, and cultural globalization today the world after the Cold War is more easily understood through a web of global interdependence. According to Zygmunt Bauman (2006) interconnected global societies have rapidly expanded our moral responsibilities. This has meant that in our time the distinction between direct responsibility for killing and killing through neglect becomes increasingly questionable. If Arendt focused upon the responsibilities we all share in respect of our actions, then current indifference to the globe's fragile ecological balance and human misery as the result of poverty would equally seem to be a matter for cosmopolitan concern. The United Nations reports that there has been an increase in 25 million chronically undernourished people since 1996, leaving a total of 850 million people globally without enough to eat. These features are also evident in questions related to global warming whereby the ecological footprint of wealthy societies is likely to have a hazardous impact upon their own as well as poorer nations. Cosmopolitanism in our own time would need to continually remind global humanity of the ways in which we are historically, culturally, and of course morally interconnected with one another, while also seeking to struggle for a form of politics that seeks to accommodate the difference of strangers.

Ulrich Beck (2006) has recently sought to ambitiously rethink the very basis of the social sciences along these lines. The aim here has been an attempt to address what a genuinely critical theory might come to mean in the twenty-first century. Beck argues if the theoretical tangles of postmodernism have now run their course, then cosmopolitanism aims to return the social sciences to more "real world" concerns. In this the cosmopolitan viewpoint holds that the social sciences needs to dispense with the limitations of methodological nationalism by adopting more complex and genuinely global perspectives. Rejecting the idea that globalization can be understood within the dimensions of economic globalization, cosmopolitanism aims to help us appreciate the multidimensional nature of current social transformations. The idea of interconnected global societies is not something that happens outside the walls of the nation-state but literally happens in more local contexts. From the intensification of cultural intermixing to the development of global social movements and from the emergence of the global ecological crisis to the movement of refugees we have seemingly surpassed the world of exclusive national societies.

According to Beck and Sznaider (2006) cosmopolitanism "should be chiefly conceived of as globalization from within, as internalized cosmopolitanism." What is genuinely "new" in this situation is not necessarily cultural intermixing and global interdependence but an enhanced awareness of these features through the formation of something like a global public sphere. In other words, cosmopolitanism requires a politics of translation through the domain of culture to help us appreciate the global interdependency of questions related to our shared ecological, economic, and moral worlds. If methodological nationalism still seeks to discover what is distinctive about each nation, cosmopolitanism helps us appreciate ways in which the globe is experiencing new levels of interconnection and intercultural dialogue. If there is indeed a growing awareness that we exist in a network of responsibilities then equally it would seem we need to move our horizons from the nation to a greater appreciation of more global uncertainties. As Beck defines it resistance to these initiatives may come from an unwillingness to abandon "the nation" as the domain of our thinking for the admittedly less certain project of trying to understand an increasingly uncertain global world.

For Beck and Sznaider (2006: 19) the dimensions of fact and value can become bridged through the development of what they call "cosmopolitan common sense."

This is the assumption that much of humanity would be ready to uphold a minimal set of universal norms. Notably they mention freedom from torture, enslavement, and religious intolerance as being relatively self-evident, widely shared norms. Here the central question becomes which cosmopolitan institutions? What is often pointed to in this setting is the development of permanent human rights courts, the strengthening of the United Nations and more international treaties and agreements (Held 2004). This would of course mean that global institutions would themselves need to become more powerful than the world's most powerful states. However such a noble idea in the context of the present seems like a lost cause. As Chantal Mouffe (2005) argues, the consequence of attempting to integrate the world into a unified model of liberal democracy would be widely understood as an attempt to increase the power of the West. A reconstructed cosmopolitan approach to modernity would need to accept that there are indeed plural modernities that do not discount universal human rights, but argue that they cannot simply be seen as a universal good. Mouffe here is indicating that the meaning of "human rights" cannot be decided outside of the contours of hegemonic struggle and political forms of antagonism. Instead of a reformed United Nations seeking to impose a universal order better to argue for an appreciation of an increasingly multipolar world. This view would argue that there are indeed multiple globalizations that cannot be contained within ideas of the West and the rest. Such a world is likely to be made up of large regional units (Latin America, Africa, Europe, China, the United States) that will articulate different political rationalities and citizenships. This cancels the idea that the European project articulates the basis for a future global cosmopolitan polity. Further it also opens the possibility of there being multiple cosmopolitan or global citizenships that may be in agreement with each other but equally will find themselves in competition.

Following Chantal Mouffe (2005) cosmopolitans should give up the idea that the aim is to impose a single liberal model upon the rest of the world. Demands for a cosmopolitan peace are probably better served through a global balance of powers than United Nations reform. As Tzvetan Todorov (2005) comments it is unlikely the United Nations could ever ensure justice given that the armed might belongs to individual states. We still live in a world where the dominant military powers are nation-states. Hence my argument is less for a construction of a global cosmopolitan order, but more for European citizens to defend their social and political values in a multipolar world. Such a view seeks to build upon what I take to be Arendt's cosmopolitan realism where rather than overly investing in the possibility of a new utopian world order emerging at some point in history ordered by the values of global justice and human rights we would do well attend to more complex and often messy realities. We might equally add here that while the idea of Europe could indeed act as a counterweight to some of the imperial ambitions of the United States it is unlikely to ever replace it as a global power. European citizens are unlikely to wish to carry the financial cost of building themselves as a military power of equal standing. However as Zygmunt Bauman (2006: 240) has wisely counseled, Europe's mission perhaps remains the attempt to promote values other than military might. To achieve these we would need to discuss the possibility of a European humility that has emerged after colonialism. If the cosmopolitan mission is likely to take plural paths here I wish to explore what Europeans may learn from both their own history and attempt to develop a cosmopolitan polity. Indeed Raewyn Connell (2007) has argued that much globalization theory takes the European experience as central and as a consequence marginalizes other modernities. My argument similarly contends that cosmopolitanism is less about a global vision from nowhere but has actually grown out of a European modernity seeking to address European issues and concerns. There is no easy escape from a Euro-centric ethnocentrism for the version of cosmopolitanism I am seeking to defend albeit one that welcomes the view of the Other. This does not of course mean that Europe does not have a global role or indeed might not be able to offer "universals," but it does mean that questions of cosmopolitan citizenship should more adequately seek to address the intellectual and historical context within which much of its central concerns were founded. However if the idea of European cosmopolitanism has come out of a historical experience of colonialism, slavery, human rights abuse, extreme nationalism, and the Holocaust then today it is threatened by neoliberalism.

Neoliberalism and Cosmopolitanism

Cosmopolitan critique then has thus far failed to adequately account for the development of neoliberal forms of globalization. Since the 1980s the growing impact of neoliberal policies has meant enhanced processes of deregulation, privatization, and an ideology of the lean state. The growing impact of neoliberalism is currently underestimated within much cosmopolitan thinking given the stress on the need to think beyond the nation. In particular, given the emphasis that cosmopolitanism places upon the pluralization of the cultural domain, I want to argue that it displaces the extent to which the market can be said to have colonized cultural and political life. Such features arguably replay earlier debates within the globalization literature between homogenization and cultural difference. Notably commodification strategies can lead to either the spread of cultural difference or homogenization, but the key point here is more the ways in which public forms of culture become increasingly subject to the discipline of the market.

In David Harvey's (2006) terms neoliberalism can be seen as an attempt to restore the power of the capitalist ruling-classes after the breakdown of social democracy. Neoliberalism has resulted in increased social inequality, the development of an entrepreneurial culture, and a blaming of the lower classes for lacking the necessary competitive strength in a cut-throat market. Neoliberalism's "success" is measured by its defenders through its ability to undermine the solidarity of oppositional organizations like trade unions, the privatization of public resources, the reduction of taxes, and the fostering of a climate favorable for business. Andre Gorz (1999), in this setting, argues that "new style" European social democracy has had to increasingly adapt itself to the "reality" of global markets. This has led to social democracy adopting the rhetoric of international competitiveness. These developments have resulted in the distribution of wealth upwards into the board rooms and away from the shop floor. Indeed despite recent talk of a European "third way" between social democracy and capitalism, the commodification of the public is unlikely to be held in check without a reinvestment in the idea of the social state (Bauman 2004b, Giddens 1998).

The development of monetarism, privatization, and the reduction of government spending was developed in the United States and then transported globally through institutions such as the IMF and the World Bank. Indeed if the period of European imperialism has now passed the United States has over the course of the twentieth century fostered a new kind of imperial rule. America became the hegemonic power in a world determined by national struggles for independence and the Cold War. For David Harvey (2003), if racism was the ruling ideology of European imperialism the United States has historically sought to conceal its global ambitions in abstract universalism. The United States presents itself as the global defender of freedom by defending free markets and private property. The internal image promoted by the United States and the face it presents to the rest of the world relies upon it being identified as a promoter of civilized values. There were of course evident contradictions during this period of hegemony such as the suppression of democratic and populist attempts to promote social democracy in Latin America. However the global strategy of the United States during the Cold War was over-determined by the need to combat the real or imagined influence of the Soviet Union. The American empire was able to do this by supporting the revival of its potential economic competitors through the development of favorable trade relations, financial assistance, and multilateral institutions. As Leo Panitch and Sam Gindin (2005: 112) comment, "this was the first empire fully oriented to the making of global capitalism."

Under neoliberal hegemony New York has become the financial center of the global economy and is increasingly driven by processes of progressive economic privatization (or "accumulation by dispossession") (Harvey 2003). While the intellectual roots of neoliberalism can be traced back to the 1930s and 1940s, Harvey (2003) argues that these ideas were used to reform capitalist practice after the oil crisis in 1973. Similarly to European imperialism at the end of the nineteenth century, neoliberalism can be seen as a response to the internal problems of capitalist accumulation. Accumulation by dispossession works through the forcing open and privatization of markets, usually through the IMF and WTO. If the over-accumulation of capital leads to a surplus of capital that cannot be profitably invested then privatization enables capital to be put to use. Notably in this analysis the end of the Cold War and the opening up of China has drawn the globe into a genuinely world market. However the sociologist Michael Mann (2003) has argued that American power remains more limited than many currently like to believe. Mann points to both the unwillingness of the United States (despite Iraq) to occupy foreign nations in the ways exemplified by the Europeans and the fact that despite their economic dominance they cannot directly force neoliberalism on sovereign states, opening the possibility of national forms of resistance. As Immanuel

Wallerstein (2006) has argued the position of the United States as a world power has been substantially weakened by the Iraq War. The neo-conservative attempt to reaffirm American power, honor and hegemony is in ruins. We are then on the cusp of increasing multilateral divisions in world power with no one center maintaining overwhelming superiority.

The arrival of a more multipolar world led Hardt and Negri (2000) to argue that our current era cannot be described as imperialist with any intellectual precision. If imperialism in the past meant the expansion of the state due to crisis tendencies within capitalism then the current era is better characterized as being governed by global capital and the declining power of nation-states. Instead of a politics of imperialism, Hardt and Negri propose the dominance of a postmodern Empire. The global economy has been postmodernized through processes of heterogeneity, deterritorialization, and differentiation in such a way that has deconstructed any clear contrast between the First and Third World. This effectively means that imperial politics is mostly finished, with no nation-state ever likely to be as powerful as European nations at the end of the nineteenth century. The rule of Empire then is not the direct rule of a single power but actually constitutes a power shift to a boundless order that exists within a universal space. Yet if David Harvey's account does not differentiate the power of global capitalism then Hardt and Negri neglect to recognize the pivotal role of the United States as the one remaining superpower. Indeed as Chantel Mouffe (2005) comments, their analysis of Empire offers little beyond a kind of ultra-Leftism which opposes "the people" to global capitalism. Gone is any idea of state, nation, or indeed world-region in terms of organizing political identities and potentially alternative political projects. Any lasting significance that the memory of European-style social democracy might have in seeking to curb the worst excesses of a market economy is too quickly banished from the analysis (Moschonas 2002). However what is missing from the analysis thus far is the question as to what extent the idea of Europe might provide an alternative or at least break on the American model of capitalism? Here many cosmopolitan thinkers have argued that if it is to do so in the future then a new European project needs to be imagined in the future.

European Cosmopolitan Publics

The idea of the public depends upon a politics of contestation and languages and practices that aim to educate and engage modern citizens. Along with the decline of social democracy and the triumph of neoliberalism has come the erosion of the Left/Right divide. The displacement of the language of progressive development that accompanied the rise of European social democracy has led many to abandon the idea of "culture" as being an educative project (Hoggart 1957). If the language of the market still prefers to reduce education to the language of strategic advantage and market opportunity and to treat ideas of the public as the place of choice then more critical notions of the public sphere should insist upon their role as places of potential learning and self-criticism. Notions of the public hold out the possibility of us becoming critical citizens and of building a more informed and educated curiosity about the shared worlds within which we move.

In this context Habermas' (2001) notion of constitutional patriotism has been seen by many as holding out the possibility of building upon Europe's democratic rather than colonial heritage. Here collective loyalty is consolidated within a commitment to the language of citizen's rights and responsibilities rather than the ethnos of national identities. Similarly Craig Calhoun (2001) argues that rather than engaging in the languages of "civilization" such a model aims to build a shared sense of European solidarity through public forms of communication. European identity then is constituted through overlapping and multiple forms of dialogue and identification. Habermas (2001, 2003) aims to give the European project a sense of utopia and unfulfilled destiny after the decline of communism. If the Marxist dream for Europe was of a world built upon the educated and emancipated labor of workers then a cosmopolitan Europe will be built through the constraint of nationalism and capitalism so that we are able to build public spaces built on the principles of pluralism, democracy, and social solidarity beyond the nation-state. Here Habermas seeks to imagine a European society that has moved beyond nationalist hatred and the downward pressure exerted by global competition on welfare systems. For Habermas without the careful construction of a federal European state the idea of Europe is likely to be dominated by a neoliberal race to the bottom, racist border controls, and nationalist forms of regression. In this respect, the European Union's ability to secure an institutional basis for human rights and democracy announces the beginning of Europe's progressive project and not its end point.

The European Union itself has sought to institute a transnational public sphere in order to foster a sense of shared identification amongst its citizens. These efforts have included educational projects, cultural, and artistic events (including the European city of culture) and communications policy in addition to other initiatives. The main problem here is that despite the impact of globalization and the fragmentation of identity much public conversation remains organized through specifically national cultures. Despite these drawbacks, both Habermas and the European Union have consistently argued for a composite sense of identity that does not necessarily compete with national identity, but recognizes the possibility of having local, national, and global identities. The aim here being to both integrate national identities into an inclusive framework and thereby potentially domesticating nationalist hostility. As Habermas (2001: 77) argues a European-wide civic solidarity can only come into being in the European setting if it *pays* to be a citizen. As nation-states lose their power to order economic life it is only through a renewal of solidarity through the European Union that would save politics from neoliberalism.

Pierre Bourdieu (2001, 2003) has similarly called for a European social movement to defend civilized values (the rights to an education, health, culture, and work) against the power of the market. More specifically Bourdieu (2003: 29) argues that neoliberalism has introduced:

A mode of production that entails a mode of domination based on the institution of insecurity, domination through precariousness: a deregulated financial market fosters a deregulated labor market and thereby the casualisation of labor that cows workers into submission.

In this respect, modern capitalism has progressively undermined the practice of democratic citizenship. In our economic lives the market has instituted a dual labor market of overworked and stressed professionals and low status and unskilled jobs with few career prospects. While they are both subject to neoliberal pressures of downsizing, increasing insecurity, and market uncertainty, this division institutes a cultural divide between global citizens who are international, polyglot, and polycultural and the locals who are more likely to take refuge in nationalism and parochialism.

The aim of a European social movement would be to "restore politics" (Bourdieu 2003: 38). Such a social movement would need to build upon many of the concrete objectives of a multitude of social movements in areas such as housing, employment, health, and the environment. For Bourdieu, central to these movements are a shared sense of civic activism and a rejection of the regressive politics of neoliberalism. The reason that Europe becomes central to these arguments is twofold. Firstly the existence of a European polity at a transnational level converts cosmopolitanism into a possibility. The explicit focus of a European social movement would be to argue that Europe must be more than a central bank, bureaucracy, and single currency. The democratic aim would be to replace the European Commission with a genuine executive responsible to an elected parliament. Secondly the dominance of European trade amongst fellow Europeans helps destroy some of the myths of the global economy. As Bourdieu (2001: 36) reports, "70 per cent of the trade of European countries is with other European countries."

Bourdieu's argument is that meaningful citizenship, stable employment, and welfare all depend upon the invention of a European civil society. Etienne Balibar (2002, 2004) has similarly argued for a European citizenship that includes all the communities that are historically present on European territory. In particular he seeks to connect the expansion of the market and uncertainty into the cultures of everyday life and the intensification of populist racism. There is no European country that can claim to have been immune to popular ideas that have consistently linked the arrival of "foreigners," increased competition over jobs and the decline of shared living standards. However in ultra-nationalist rhetoric it is notable that this is not just a rejection of the non-European but also the rejection of other Europeans. While it is the Arab, the black, and the Muslim who are the consistent focus of popular racism, such features are also increasingly accompanied by an intensification of anti-European sentiment. This is particularly evident in the context of the enlargement of the European Union promoting the mobility of labor from the former Eastern Europe. Similarly with Bourdieu, Balibar calls for the development of a new European social movement that works across national boundaries that would need to mutually address the right to difference as well as measures that sought to correct the global economy.

Similarly we might point to Ulrich Beck's (2006) idea of cosmopolitan Europe that becomes constructed through a struggle to confront the traditions that stem from aggressive nationalism, genocide, and colonialism. Yet for Beck the reflexive project of a Europe of self-criticism is threatened by the continuation of nationalism. This is the idea that democracy could (if it not were for the EU) become recentered within the nation-state at some later point. Here Beck agrees with Habermas that such a project is wholly unrealistic in a world being reconstituted through the global flows of money, knowledge, and people. If Beck and Habermas perceive a future Europe emerging through both the recognition of Europe's internal cosmopolitan complexity and need to combat neoliberalism then Bourdieu and Balibar prefer to emphasis the role of social movements and the active citizen. If they all agree that the idea of Europe is central to combating the regressive politics of neoliberalism they disagree whether this process is essentially bottom-up or top-down. These visions are not necessarily contradictory as a different Europe would inevitably depend upon the capacity of citizens to challenge the current trajectory of Europe and thereby usher in a more concrete form of cosmopolitanism.

However the rise of Right-wing anti-immigration political parties across a resurgent nationalist Europe should be reason enough to halt a European self-congratulatory language that prefers to perceive some realities rather than others. For a genuinely grassroots cosmopolitan Europe to emerge it will require a number of critical cultural initiatives that cut across civil society, popular culture, education and national borders. Such features would also need to include an understanding of how a neoliberal Europe through the promotion of economic inequality and uncertainty can itself be connected to a politics of fear and concerns about the alienness of the Other. We might be equally skeptical, following Balibar and Bourdieu, that we are on the cusp of a popular citizen's Europe that is about to emerge from below. The current state of the European Left seems ill-prepared to take on such a role despite the desirability of such a project. Notably Susan George (2008) articulates a passionate case for a people's Europe built upon the 2005 French and Dutch "No" votes to the European constitution. However despite her argument that the Lisbon Treaty is a neoliberal treaty with little to offer the citizens of Europe there is little evidence to suggest that Europeans are about to encounter a resurgence in citizen's activity of this type. Much critical thought in this respect is mainly concerned to defend the achievements of the past in respect of maintaining the emancipatory effect the building of common systems of welfare had on the lives of many ordinary citizens.

Conclusion

The European cosmopolitan project perhaps needs to be reconceived as a social experiment in search of a convincing narrative to keep it alive. For previous generations this was provided by the memory of the slaughter of the European wars of the twentieth century. However a new narrative is now required in face of the threat of neoliberalism, the erosion of social citizenship, and widespread racism. By this I do not mean that there could be a single European morality, but more that cosmopolitanism needs to find a way to appeal to the vast majority of ordinary people and not just politicians and political theorists. Anthony Giddens (2007) recognizes to this extent that the diverse European social model needs to be defended against neoliberal deregulation. Rather than nationalist regression a politics of hope needs to defend and extend not only free mobility for European citizens, but also common access to a welfare system. If a world government is too utopian then the cosmopolitan project needs to come down to earth and be seen to deliver benefits for non-elites.

Further I would add that Europeans might also wish to remember that Europe was the place of the Enlightenment project. Tzvetan Todorov's (2009) recent defense of the principles of critical freedom, tolerance, and humanitarian concern are all based upon the recognition that they have their roots in an Enlightenment culture. Yet as should be clear by now (and for some of the reasons I have mentioned) we now have to recognize the Enlightenment as a profound if not unambiguous event. If the European Enlightenment was the source of humanism and ideas around progress it both promoted civilized values as well as racism and nihilism. As John Gray (1995) argues, the project for the autonomous use of reason failed to recognize both its groundlessness and that the appeals to morality are more often appeals to tradition. Instead my argument would be that the European project needs to recognize its historically constructed nature, and that it has emerged as much out of the need to uphold principles such as human rights and democracy as it has to respond to suffering (Beck 2006). In this respect, there needs to be greater recognition that the European Union is both necessary in a global age but that it has emerged out of the concerns of philosophers and thinkers who sought to provide practical solutions to the present. A renewed emphasis upon European cosmopolitanism would require the meeting ground between philosophical concerns that sought to learn the lessons of the past, but did so in such a way that attempted to meet the needs of the future. If citizens of the future are to engage with genuinely global problems they cannot do this solely from the point of view of the nation-state. There is in this respect no going back to the European Enlightenment, but we need to remember a time when critical thinkers felt it possible to fashion a more emancipated world and improve the common lot of a shared humanity. If the first European Enlightenment mainly sought to create a space for critical reason in the face of tradition today we face different problems. As I have argued throughout, cosmopolitan citizenship is more about how to construct a sense of solidarity with our fellow citizens across borders without producing a sense of the Other. How this might be achieved while also recognizing national cultural and other distinctions is a project which will preoccupy many critical thinkers for some time to come.

Bibliography

Appiah, K.A. 2006. *Cosmopolitanism: Ethics in a World of Strangers.* London: Penguin.
Arendt, H. 1977. *Eichmann in Jerusalem: A Report on the Banality of Evil.* London: Penguin.
Arendt, H. 1986. *The Origins of Totalitarianism.* London: Andre Deutsch.
Arendt, H. 2000. The perplexities of the rights of man, in *The Portable Hannah Arendt*, edited by P. Baehr. London: Penguin Classics.
Balibar, E. 2002. *Politics and the Other Scene.* London: Verso.
Balibar, E. 2004. *We, The People of Europe? Reflections on Transnational Citizenship.* Princeton: Princeton University Press.
Bartov, O. 2000. *Mirrors of Destruction: War, Genocide, and Modern Identity.* Oxford: Oxford University Press.
Bauman, Z. 2004a. *Wasted Lives: Modernity and its Outcasts.* Cambridge: Polity Press.
Bauman, Z. 2004b. *Europe: An Unfinished Adventure.* Cambridge: Polity Press.
Bauman, Z. 2006. *Liquid Fear.* Cambridge: Polity Press.
Beck, U. 2006. *Cosmopolitan Vision.* Cambridge: Polity Press.
Beck, U. and Sznaider, N. 2006. Unpacking cosmopolitanism for the social sciences: a research agenda. *The British Journal of Sociology*, 57(1), 1–23.
Bourdieu, P. 2001. *Acts of Resistance: Against the New Myths of our Time.* Cambridge: Polity Press.
Bourdieu, P. 2003. *Firing Back: Against the Tyranny of the Market.* Cambridge: Polity Press.
Calhoun, C. 2001. The virtues of inconsistency: identity and plurality in the conceptualisation of Europe, in *Constructing Europe's Identity*, edited by C.E. Cederman. London: Lynne Reiner Publishers.
Cannovan, M. 1992. *Hannah Arendt: A Reinterpretation of Her Political Thought.* Cambridge: Cambridge University Press.
Connell, R. 2007. *Southern Theory.* Cambridge: Polity Press.
Fanon, F. 1965. *The Wretched of the Earth.* London: Penguin.
George, S. 2008. *We the Peoples of Europe.* London: Pluto Press.
Giddens, A. 1998. *The Third Way: The Renewal of Social Democracy.* Cambridge: Polity Press.
Giddens, A. 2007. *Europe in the Global Age.* Cambridge: Polity Press.
Gorz, A. 1999. *Reclaiming Work.* Cambridge: Polity Press.
Gray, J. 1995. *Enlightenment's Wake.* London: Routledge.
Habermas, J. 2001. *The Postnational Constellation.* Cambridge: Polity Press.
Habermas, J. 2003. Toward a cosmopolitan Europe. *Journal of Democracy*, 14(4), 86–100.
Hardt, M. and Negri, A. 2000. *Empire.* Cambridge, MA: Harvard University Press.
Harvey, D. 2001. Cosmopolitanism and the banality of geographical evils, in *Millennial Capitalism and the Culture of Neoliberalism*, edited by J. Comfort and J.L. Carmaroff. Durham, NC: Duke University Press, 529–64.
Harvey, D. 2003. *The New Imperialism.* Oxford: Oxford University Press.

Harvey, D. 2006. *Spaces of Global Capitalism: Towards a Theory of Uneven Geographical Development*. London: Verso.
Held, D. 2004. *Global Covenant: The Social Democratic Alternative to the Washington Consensus*. Cambridge: Polity Press.
Hoggart, R. 1957. *The Uses of Literacy*. London: Chatto and Windus.
Kaldor, M. 2003. *Global Civil Society: An Answer to War*. Cambridge: Polity Press.
Kant, I. 1970. Perpetual peace: a philosophical sketch (1795), in *Kant: Political Writings* (1st Edition), edited by H.S. Reiss. Cambridge: Cambridge University Press, 43–130.
Mann, M. 2003. *Incoherent Empire*. London: Verso.
Moschonas, G. 2002. *In the Name of Social Democracy: The Great Transformation: 1945 to the Present*. London: Verso.
Mosse, G.L. 1978. *Towards the Final Solution: A History of European Racism*. London: J.M. Dent and Sons Ltd.
Mouffe, C. 2005. *On the Political*. London: Routledge.
Panitch, L. and Gindin, S. 2005. Superintending global capital. *New Left Review*, 35, 112.
Parekh, B. 1995. Liberalism and colonialism: a critique of Locke and Mill, in *The Decolonisation of Imagination*, edited by J.N. Pieterse and B. Parekh. London: Zed Books, 81–98.
Sartre, J.P. 2006. *Colonialism and Neocolonialism*. London: Routledge.
Spivak, G. 1999. *A Critique of Postcolonial Reason: Toward a History of a Vanishing Present*. Cambridge, MA: Harvard University Press.
Stevenson, N. 1999. *The Transformation of the Media*. London: Longman.
Thompson, E.P. 1982. *Zero Option*. London: Merlin Press.
Todorov, T. 1999. *Facing the Extreme: Moral Life in the Concentration Camps*. London: Weidenfeld and Nicholson.
Todorov, T. 2005. *The New World Disorder: Reflections of a European*. Cambridge: Polity Press.
Todorov, T. 2009. *In Defence of the Enlightenment*. London: Atlantic Books.
Wallerstein, I. 2006. The curve of American power. *New Left Review*, 40, 77–94.

Cosmopolitan Borders: Bordering as Connectivity

Anthony Cooper and Chris Rumford

Introduction

It is often said that a cosmopolitan is someone who is at home anywhere in the world, or, expressed in slightly more formal terms, a citizen of the world; and it is such ideas that have led to cosmopolitanism being considered utopian. The problem is actually not that cosmopolitan ideas are utopian per se, but rather that they assume that the world is much more open and accessible than it really is, even a world defined by the logics of globalization ('borderless world' being a very misleading term in this regard). What is needed in order to properly understand the relationship between the individual and the world, it might be argued, is a clearer sense of how the would-be cosmopolitan can become connected to the world in a concrete and meaningful, rather than aspirational or abstract, sense.

In its more optimistic iterations cosmopolitanism may promise the earth, but it is more useful – and more down to earth – when it causes us to rethink the place of individuals in the world and their relationship with Others, on the one hand, and the communities to which they may belong (or distance themselves from, or are distanced from), on the other. Rather than to simply see cosmopolitanism as heralding a world of footloose individuals – 'tourists and vagabonds' in Bauman's (1998) terms – it is more productive to view it as being centrally concerned with the changing relationships which are occurring between individuals, their communities and the world (Rumford 2008a). Cosmopolitan thinkers often criticize the tendency amongst non-cosmopolitans to assume the primacy of national belonging in the modern world. But by the same token, it is naive to assume that the cosmopolitan automatically belongs in or to the world. Such belonging does not occur easily; it is the outcome of a political project and/or the availability of cosmopolitan opportunities. As such, understanding ways in which people can and do belong to the world is centrally important. As Beck (2007: 162) says, '[t]o belong or not to belong – that is the cosmopolitan question'. What is needed, it is argued in this chapter, in order to understand the nature and possibility of this belonging is a sense of the means by which would-be cosmopolitans can connect to and access the world, through what Delanty (2006: 27) terms 'moments of world openness'.

This chapter advances the case that the border is a prime site for connecting individuals to the world, bringing them into contact with Others and causing them to reassess their relations with the (multiple) communities to which they may or may not belong. In Beck's (2000: 51–2) terms, borders should be conceived of as 'mobile patterns that facilitate overlapping loyalties'. As outlined in this chapter the border is best thought of as a 'quilting point' (or 'anchoring point' – *point de capiton* in Žižek's Lacanian term) which makes the cosmopolitan experience a real possibility; making connectedness possible, encouraging contact with others and negotiations of difference.

One legacy of globalization is a world of proliferating borders – rather than a 'borderless world' – and it is these borders which facilitate the mobility upon which many commentators believe that cosmopolitans thrive; as we will see later borders can be 'engines of connectivity' at the same time as fulfilling more traditional duties as markers of division and difference. However, we would caution against equating cosmopolitanism with mobility in a straightforward way (*pace* Urry): the unfettered mobility enjoyed by the privileged elites is no indicator of the permeability or otherwise of borders, as conventionally understood. Mobility, or rather the facilitation of certain kinds of mobility, is a product of (certain kinds of) borders, not a consequence of their absence. The borders responsible are those which are increasingly designed to speed up flows for 'goods' while filtering out the 'bads', such as the 'smart' borders which have arisen in the period since 11 September 2001. Over the past decade or so understandings of social and political transformations have been strongly influenced by the 'mobilities turn' (Cresswell 2006, Urry 2007, Adey 2009). This literature tends to see borders as secondary to the mobilities that undermine them (but see Salter 2008). This priority needs to be rethought: borders can generate new kinds of mobility rather than simply being transformed or eroded by mobility.

This chapter is organized in the following way. The section that follows outlines the changing nature of borders and how these changes have been apprehended by social scientists. It also outlines the case for why borders can be thought of as cosmopolitan, an idea which at first blush appears rather counterintuitive. We then turn our attention to the 'vernacularization of borders' and outline the case for borders being 'quilting points' bringing the cosmopolitan experience within the grasp of ordinary people, not just the elites. The chapter then proceeds to explore in some detail the networking connectivity of borders and offers two short case studies – Melton Mowbray and Calais – of borders-as-connectivity and more specifically of the ways in which citizens can construct borders or utilize bordering opportunities in order to connect to the world. It is argued that citizen bordering, or 'borderwork', as it is termed here, demonstrates the vernacularization of cosmopolitanism, and, as such, this particular aspect of contemporary borders can tell us much about the nature of 'practical cosmopolitanism'.

Towards Cosmopolitan Borders

When we consider borders, cosmopolitan or otherwise, we must dispense with the idea that borders always correspond to the edges of a nation-state. The idea that borders can now be diffused throughout society (Balibar 2002) has become widely recognized throughout the social sciences (if not wholeheartedly accepted). This shift in understanding has been supplemented by a whole range of important changes in the ways we comprehend borders, driven by the need to understand the variety of borders and bordering processes that exist in a changing and unpredictable world. In the contemporary literature the following have emerged as key changes in the nature of borders.

The first change is the idea that 'borders are everywhere', mentioned above. This registers the multiple sites of bordering that now exist; at airports, Eurostar terminals and maritime ports, but also in other locations, many of which would not be thought of as borders in the conventional sense: in travel agencies and other offices where travel documents are issued and databases checked, along motorways where trucks are scanned and car number plates monitored, and shopping on the Internet where credit card usage leads to the 'transaction mining' of information for security purposes. The second change is the recognition that borders mean different things to different people and act differently on different groups. This is Balibar's (2002) idea of polysemy, an idea which suggests that borders are becoming 'asymmetrical membranes' (Hedetoft 2003) or acting like 'firewalls' (Walters 2006). These metaphors point to borders being designed so as to allow the passage of 'desirables' while keeping out 'undesirables'. The UK has developed polysemic borders in its attempt to create 'security in a global hub' (Cabinet Office 2007) through e-borders designed to be 'open to business but closed to terrorists and traffickers'.

The third change is the acknowledgement that borders can be remote and distant from the territory they are designed to protect. The UK now is now developing 'offshore borders all over the world' (Home Office 2007) in order to prevent undesirables from starting their journey to the UK. The Eurostar train link has introduced 'juxtaposed' borders so that UK passport control takes place at Gare du Nord and French passport control at St Pancras. In Lahav and Guiraudon's (2000) terms 'borders are not always at the border'. The fourth change follows from the first three: borders are mechanisms to 'control mobility rather than territory' (Durrschmidt and Taylor 2007: 56). The traditional idea that borders lock-down territory or form a security perimeter for the sovereign nation-state has given way to the idea of the border as a conduit, speeding up transit where necessary, blocking passage when required. Finally, the fifth change in understanding is that borders are conceptualized less as things (lines on a map) but as processes. The diffusion and dispersal of borders, their polysemic qualities and their remoteness means that borders are not what or where they used to be. It is for these reasons that it makes more sense to talk about processes of bordering rather than fixed or territorial borders, although of course walls are still employed at many border locations (Turner 2007).

So far we have outlined the changing nature of borders but have not yet looked in detail at the argument for borders becoming more cosmopolitan. For many people, the idea of 'cosmopolitan borders' is an oxymoron. So in what sense can we think of borders as cosmopolitan borders? In the second half of this section we will outline three key ways in which processes of bordering are becoming cosmopolitanized. The importance of taking the idea of cosmopolitan borders seriously, we believe, is to be found not in the fact that borders are changing in novel ways, although this important enough to warrant attention, but because the changing nature of borders can tell us much about cosmopolitanism.

First, the idea that bordering is not only the business of the nation-state is core to the cosmopolitan borders thesis. In Europe, the EU has emerged as a major actor in the business of creating, relocating and dismissing borders. The EU shifts the borders of Europe every time it enlarges, it turns national borders into European borders, it regulates and harmonizes European borders through Frontex, its borders agency, and it has the power to decide where the important borders in Europe are to be found (Rumford 2007). More important in the context of this chapter is the activity of ordinary people in contributing to processes of bordering. This activity, people making, shifting or dismantling borders, is here termed 'borderwork' (Rumford 2008a, 2008b). This dimension of bordering is largely absent from the border studies literature in which it is understood that people can utilize borders for their own advantage, as smugglers, tourists and market traders frequently do, and that people are active in marking the (state) border through shows of nationalist fervour or grassroots protest, for example. It is rarely given consideration that citizens (and non-citizens) may be active in constructing or dismantling borders as a form of political opportunism or self-empowerment. This borderwork may or may not take place at the edge of a polity, but is in fact more likely to take the form of bordering dispersed throughout society, as Balibar has theorized (Rumford 2006). One argument advanced here is that borderwork represents a vernacularization of cosmopolitanism, now no longer entirely an elite pursuit if borderwork is everyday practice which takes place at a plurality of sites throughout society. If borders are increasingly dispersed and diffused throughout society, and borders are central to our understanding of cosmopolitanism, as is argued here, then ordinary people, through their daily encounter with, and negotiation of, borders can be said to have cosmopolitan experiences on a routine basis.

Second, borders as connective tissue. Borders are conventionally thought to divide one polity from another but they are also able to connect, not just proximate entities, but, it is argued here, globally. This builds upon van Schendel's (2005) notion that borderlanders are able to 'jump' scales (local, national, regional, global) through their everyday practices and their 'mental maps', and therefore do not experience the national border only as a limit: what forms a barrier to some can present itself as a gateway to others. People can 'invoke' the scale of the border themselves; as a 'local' phenomenon, a nation-state 'edge', or as a transnational staging post, thereby allowing them to access the border as conduit. Borders can work to provide transnational or global connectivity by allowing people to project themselves beyond their locality by constructing new networking opportunities.

This connectivity also further reinforces the vernacularization of cosmopolitanism, opening up political opportunities and avenues of empowerment to ordinary people. The connectivity potential of borders will be expanded upon in the latter part of this chapter.

Third, the possibility of seeing from the border and the alternative perspective that this offers. There is a precedent for identifying the border as a key cosmopolitan site. Walter Mignolo has argued that 'border thinking' is a core component of critical cosmopolitanism. For Mignolo, critical cosmopolitanism comes from the 'exterior of modernity', in other words coloniality (Mignolo 2000: 724). Border thinking – 'the transformation of the hegemonic imaginary' from the perspective of the excluded – is a tool of critical cosmopolitanism (Mignolo 2000: 736–7). As an adjunct to this we can propose that 'seeing from the border' is a key dimension of cosmopolitan borders. This involves more than a recognition that it is possible to view a border from both sides. Rather than simply 'looking both ways' across a border we need to aspire to look from the border. Placing border perspectives – thinking and seeing from the border – as central components of critical cosmopolitanism has several important consequences, not least of which is the centrality of borders to understanding the world: borders are increasingly important in the study of political and social transformations. It also means that borders can change the way we think of cosmopolitanism.

The (national) border has traditionally been associated with territory, its delimitation and security, and the dominant image of the border is the fortified line, the security wall, or the site of a military face-off between antagonistic forces. For these reasons, the existence of the border has tended to 'distort' territory, turning the land in proximity to the border into an intensified terrain of surveillance and suspicion, and the border itself into an exceptional space where time and distance do not conform to standard measurement. This is particularly true in respect of our experience of crossing the border; an inordinate amount of time spent travelling a very small distance (the distance between two check-points or from one side of passport control to the other), the few steps it takes to cross the border requiring an unusual amount of effort (to satisfy bureaucratic requirements) and the short walk across the borderline being injected with ritual importance, nationalist coding and perhaps unaccountable feelings of guilt (Lofgren 2002). Although passing across a border normally involves only a small physical distance it is a movement from one watershed to another; in terms of culture, of political regime, of language and so on. This conventional view of borders as 'magnifiers of difference' needs to be updated in many respects (for example, in the sense that the intensity of borders is diminished by being located in so many places throughout society) but in other respects is still of great relevance. Nowadays the features of the border that come to the fore are not necessarily the intensity of transit or the symbolic significance of the small step into the unknown, but the ways in which the border can act as a portal offering access to the national, transnational and the global. It is to these dimensions of borders that we now turn in order to develop the core argument of the chapter on the connective potential of borders.

The Bordering of Networks and the Networking of Borders

Boer (2006: 9) suggests that there is too much emphasis on what a border is and where it is to be found, rather than viewing bordering as a process, and thus addressing the who, how and importantly why of border construction (see also van Houtum 2005). In this part of the chapter we want to move this idea forward by examining the associated questions of why and how particular bordering practices are enacted, as well as showing why this 'grassroots' or 'bottom-up' bordering is visible to some but not to others. We want offer a bottom-up, grassroots, reading of bordering that explains how ordinary people can use borders to create networks of connectivity rather than simply remaining passive recipients of borders imposed as mechanisms of division or thresholds to be crossed. In other words, we wish to show how ordinary people can construct, negate and/or redefine borders in order to network their identities. Thinking about borders from this perspective goes some way to addressing questions that are central to the study of cosmopolitanism, in particular: 'how are ordinary individuals and groups making sense of their identities and social encounters in ways that can be said to be cosmopolitan?' (Nowicka and Rovisco 2009: 1), as well as offering new insights and direction to debates within border studies.

Therefore we will now proceed to examine the ways in which borders can be networked, inasmuch as borders are not necessarily opposed to mobilities and flows and at the same time problematize the idea that bordering is by definition mainly divisionary. We will then consider how individuals use networks to their own ends, before contrasting two preliminary case studies – the English town of Melton Mowbray and the French port of Calais – to show how borderwork is performed on the ground by ordinary people, as well as illustrating our central premise: that borders can connect as well as divide.

The idea that borders can be networked – and ultimately that borders can represent tissues of connectivity – is on the surface problematic considering how such a conceptualization of the border runs counter to the dominant binaries of networks/places, inside/outside and so on. Conventional readings of borders posit them as divisionary, connected to territory, and state-centred, while, in contrast, 'postmodern spaces of flows, de-territorialized connections and de-localized identities' (Axford 2006: 4) are seen by many to be the antithesis of bordered space inasmuch as, by definition, they render borders ineffectual. Indeed many idealist descriptions of cosmopolitanism stand opposed to a world in which, to quote Deleuze and Guattari (1986: 42), 'the modern state defines itself in principle as the rational and reasonable organisation of a community'. However, as should now be apparent, this is not the cosmopolitanism or border theory on offer here. Rather, in order to better understand how people inhabit, make sense of and engage with the contemporary world it is crucial to formulate a version of cosmopolitanism in which borders – and processes of bordering – are explicitly included.

What is important is to understand borders, and processes of bordering, spatially rather than as fixed or ridged 'thin' lines. Stuart Elden (2009: xxvii) makes the point that 'boundaries only become possible in their modern sense through a notion of space, rather than the other way around', adding 'a properly critical political theory of territory needs to investigate the quantification of space and the role of calculative mechanisms in the commanding of territory, and the establishment of borders'. In other words the modern territorial border is constructed through the imposition of a Cartesian idea of space which is external, material, absolute and objective, rather than belonging to a cognitive and subjective category internal to the subject as argued by Aristotle and later by Kant. For Elden it is space (or a particular and dominant definition of it) that defines the border and not the border that defines space in terms of its compartmentalization. This is useful when theorizing borders as being spatial in their own right, as being borderlands (Donnan and Wilson 1999), spaces of negotiation (Boer 2006), or even as whole regions or countries (Balibar 2004a), where the border extends well beyond the location of any physical or visible 'dividing line'.

Another way to theorize borders in spatial terms, that is, in ways that do not simply connect borders to a particular definition of compartmentalized space, is the idea of mobile, mobility-dependent and networked borders. Here, as we have already discussed, borders are increasingly understood as being less about keeping people and things out inasmuch as they are increasingly required to filter and manage mobilities both within and outside of state territory. 'The concept of the social will in the future', as sociologist John Urry (2000: 1) tells us, 'be one particularly deployed by especially national forces seeking to moderate, control and regulate these variously powerful networks and flows criss-crossing their porous borders'. Placing primacy on networks and mobilities in this way conforms to Urry's (2000: 210) notion that mobilities rather than societies should be the main focus of sociology, as well as Manuel Castells' (2000: 1) assertion that in a post-industrial era, a space of flows has come to dominate a space of places.

The idea of network borders asserts a particular network/border relationship. Networks do not by definition simply cross borders with ease, in the same way that borders, by definition, cannot be simply theorized as being employed to stop them. Rather, borders and networks share 'a mutually constitutive dynamic' (Axford 2006: 6), in the sense that localities are connected to 'larger' geographical spaces and scales in such a way that 'we have', as Dicken et al. (2001: 97) sum up, 'a mutually constitutive process: while networks are embedded within territories, territories are, at the same time, embedded into networks'. Crucial, however, is the need to go beyond privileged levels of analysis, that is, to go beyond theorizing borders at the level of state territoriality (Axford 2006: 3).

Moving beyond the distinct network/border dialectic in this way has important implications for borders and bordering processes. Acknowledging the intrinsic and reciprocal relationship between mobility, territory and borders can help to understand borders as being networked themselves and allow borders to take on strange new properties. One of the ways in which borders and networks 'hold hands' is the idea that borders are increasingly designed to embrace mobility not only in ways that render borders mobile in themselves, but also to the extent that some borders actually require mobility to be recognized as borders. Three common examples of networked borders within the literature will highlight this.

First, often called 'remote control' (Lahav and Guiraudon 2000), truck drivers that frequent major transport routes across Europe, usually destined for the UK, are being encouraged to repeatedly check their cargo for illegal immigrants using increasingly sophisticated methods commonly found at traditional border sites (Walters 2006: 194), long before reaching and crossing the line demarcating UK territory. It is in this sense that border can be seen to be networked along the major transport routes of Europe.

The second example is Nick Vaughan-Williams' notion of the 'citizen-detective'. Here citizens themselves can be said to be undertaking bordering practices, such as downloading pictures of wanted suspects onto mobile phones, or being provided with phone numbers to ring if a suspected or suspicious person is identified. Vaughan-Williams (2008: 63) argues that the use of the citizen-detective, through such schemes as the as the 'Life Savers' anti-terrorist hotline in London (basically a phone number that can be stored on mobile devices and dialled if the user deems someone acting suspiciously), redefines the position of the border as well as explaining its proliferation and diffusivity. In this way, connected to surveillance practices, the border remains 'a site where a control takes place on the movement of subjects' (Vaughan-Williams 2008: 63).

Finally, for the third example of borders being networked and spatial we return to the concept of juxtaposed borders touched upon earlier. To reiterate, the UK border control is now present in Brussels and Paris, and in reciprocal fashion, the French border control is present at St Pancras Eurostar terminal in London. Such border rationale is particularly endorsed because it is seen as both a securitization strategy as well as a means of stemming the perceived wave of 'illegal' immigrants heading for the UK. The idea of juxtaposed border will be further touched upon in our second case study in which we look at the French Channel port of Calais.

These examples help to highlight the way in which borders are becoming mobile, spatial and diffuse, and designed to monitor and filter the mobility of individuals. In these cases it is important to emphasize that without the literal physicality of movement either by the border itself, or people and things across the border, they stop being borders. Traditional, fixed, static, borders – usually located at the periphery of states – tend to be purposefully visible (and exuding an air of permanence), performing as they do functions associated with state territoriality and sovereign power: the traditional border is 'a site, par excellence, for the staging of such performances' (de Lint 2008: 167). They do not need people or goods to be crossing them in order to be seen to be borders. The UK's juxtaposed borders located in Brussels and Paris on the other hand would not be immediately recognizable as borders if mobility across them was not regular. In the absence of mobility it would also be difficult to recognize borders enacted by 'remote control' or performed by the citizen detective because of the absence of any distinct crossing point or particular location. These bordering processes are mobile to the point of complete diffusion. The type of bordering processes described in these three examples are in many ways dispensable, disposable borders, in the sense that they are deployed where and when needed in order to satisfy a specific and singular demand. They are, as Balibar (2004b: 1) has stated, 'dispersed a little everywhere, wherever the movement of information, people and things is happening and is controlled'. And, when required, these dispensable borders can, relatively simply, be disbanded or shifted elsewhere.

On the other hand, it should also be apparent that the three examples above illustrate how borders and processes of bordering have become more securitized of late, reflecting the concerns of an increasingly busy sub-field of the border studies literature which sees the mobility and diffusion of borders as a product of the heightened perception of security threats (see for example, Walters 2006, and Vaughan-Williams 2010 amongst others). These examples are indicative of the way the state is still considered to be the primary borderer, regardless of how diffused or networked the border in question may be. In other words, while the securitization of borders, highlighted in the contemporary literature, has undoubtedly fuelled the transformation of borders, that is, theorized them to be more mobile, networked and mobility dependent, they are still reliant on divisionary processes enacted by the state in top-down fashion.

Re-Orienting Borders

Many border descriptions tend to revolve around notions of crossing, maintaining, managing, stopping or performing. Certain studies have shown that those crossing borders tend to develop more 'cosmopolitan' attitudes than those who do not, that is, 'border crossers' tend to be more open to foreigners and outside influences because of their border-crossing experiences (see Mau et al. 2008). In this vein much has been written about the positive experience of border crossing. 'When as a child I went on vacation', Boer (2006: 3) writes, 'one of the attractions was the crossing of the boundary between countries' (see also Donnan and Wilson 1999). Other directions of study have highlighted possible 'reciprocities' between border, borderer and bordered, in terms of how the act of crossing, experiencing and contesting borders can change the border itself. Inge E. Boer (2006) argues that borders or boundaries offer subjective, temporary and changeable spaces of negotiation, the outcome of which changes the boundary dynamic. Papadopoulos et al. (2008: 163) argue that the post-national diffusion and transformation of borders, touched upon above, should not be understood in terms of states simply trying exert their power, rather border transformation can be explained as a result of complex struggles between types of mobility control and more fluid, nomadic forces of resistance. However it is also crucial that we think of borders as something more than things to be simply crossed, or things that are put in place to prevent, facilitate or hinder crossing. In other words, can borders be networked in such a way that empowers non-state actors? Further, can borders be re-orientated, or even constructed anew, in order to facilitate connectivity?

Ulrich Beck (2002: 19) talks about a pluralization of international borders, a 'globalization from within' causing disagreements over the drawing of borderlines, and what he views as the 'axiom of the incongruity of borders'. In other words bordering hierarchies are levelled in the sense that state borders no longer become the all-defining catch-all borders that define other (potential) borders. Beck is alluding to notions of identity formation and affirmation, that is the loosening of cultural boundaries, in which the national border no longer fixes or imposes dominant meta-narratives under which other borders operate. In doing so Beck points to border 'change' and the possibility of drawing new borders while at the same time questioning old ones. He argues 'borders are no longer predeterminate, they can be chosen [and interpreted], but simultaneously also have to be redrawn and legitimated anew' (Beck 2002: 19). In addition Delanty (2007: 10) has argued that, in relation to EU borders, 'the border is becoming a site of cosmopolitan reorientations in previously divided identities'. For Delanty (2007: 10), therefore, 'the border is not just a conflict zone where a primordial clash of civilizations is played out. The border takes many different forms and includes sites of negotiation'.

While conventional understandings of the border have tended to prevent or manage connectivity, we argue that the same borders can facilitate connections. Larsen et al. (2006: 11) hold that networks 'should be viewed as an accomplishment, involving and made possible through various network tools such as cars, buses, trains, planes, laptops, networked computers, personal organisers, mobile phones, text messages and so on'. We would suggest that borders may be also be 'tools of networking', and in the remaining part of the chapter we will introduce two case studies to illustrate this point.

Melton Mowbray

The town of Melton Mowbray in the UK is famous for its food products, particularly pork pies and Stilton cheese, and in 2008 the European Union (EU) granted Protected Geographical Indication (PGI) status for its famous pies after a long, arduous and hard-won battle. For Melton the implication of PGI status means that only pies produced within a certain designated (bordered) area, located around the town, can be branded as being Melton Mowbray pies. This case study is important when theorizing the possibility of cosmopolitan borders for the following reasons. First, Melton provides an example of borderwork in the sense that it highlights 'bottom-up', 'grassroots' border construction. As we have argued this ability of citizens, non-citizens and non-state actors to take a lead role in border construction and border maintenance creates sites of cosmopolitan encounters and experiences that are not restricted to the periphery of state territory. Moreover these sites of cosmopolitan encounters are in themselves experienced by people other than those whose passports allow easy (rite of) passage (see Salter 2007).

In the case of Melton Mowbray, the PGI border amounts to a European border in the midst of the UK making it theoretically possible to describe Melton as being located on a European border. More pertinently the way in which such tangible but non-state borders can be implemented by an array of non-state actors highlights ways in which cosmopolitanism can be enacted that does not solely amount to notions of crossing (or being allowed to cross). Although legitimated by the EU, the PGI border was proposed, constructed and contested by ordinary people living in and around Melton, as well as those elsewhere who had an (economic) interest in the Melton brand name. Not surprisingly those producers who were being effectively 'bordered out' stringently contested the border, delaying its implementation, but eventually losing the legal ability to brand their pies as well as, of course, large sums of money. Therefore the of idea 'doing' bordering implicit in this example, we would argue, is intrinsic to ideas of enacting cosmopolitanism, that is, looking at the ways in which cosmopolitanism manifests in real terms – a question put forward and discussed earlier in this chapter. Consequently the Melton example shows how cosmopolitanism, manifest through bordering, is experienced differently (the idea of getting your border in first empowers some at the expense of others) and at different places (localities) far removed from traditional sites of bordering and traditional perceptions of cosmopolitanism.

Second, and overlapping with the first point, Melton also provides an example of how the (non-state) PGI border connects Melton to the world beyond its immediate locality. As touched upon above, the 'pork pie' border is a European border, connecting Melton to other food- and drink-producing towns and regions (such as Champagne and Parma). In another sense, it allows Melton to market itself as a 'food capital' to project itself on the global food map. In other words, the border empowers Melton to define and project its own distinct identity in ways that are not only local or national but also transnational and global. The border, in this case, serves to orient localities towards 'global socio-cultural landscapes, and not towards immediate neighbours' (Durrschmidt and Taylor 2007: 54, see also van Schendel 2005), and it is in this sense that the border becomes a networked border and a tool of networking.

Third, this example highlights the visibility/invisibility aspect of cosmopolitan borders. Like the mobility-dependent borders described earlier, there may be a difficulty in recognizing these new borders as being borders in the sense that they are visible to some but not to others. Cosmopolitan borders may not be recognized as borders in the traditional sense in terms of their locality or function. In the case of Melton, the border is invisible to all but local producers, competing manufacturers and gastronomes. Still, when the border came into force it cost some producers millions of pounds to relocate factories, while other producers lost the right to brand their products as 'Melton Mowbray' pies. If we view the new border around Melton in terms of connectivity, the border becomes visible through its function, in the same way that for Georg Simmel (1994: 6) the bridge 'accomplishes the connection between what is separated not only in reality and in order to fulfil practical goals, but also making it directly visible'. In other words, the connectivity aspects of borders can make visible dynamic and cosmopolitan border functions that were previously unseen. Seeing the connectivity function of borders in this way informs us of how to see like a border as discussed at the beginning of this chapter.

Calais

The next case study is markedly different from the previous example – the border of interest is a traditional state territorial border – but nevertheless serves to highlight the rich variety of bordering practices that can be said to be cosmopolitan. The northern French port of Calais overlooks what is approximately the narrowest point of the English Channel, and is situated close to major transport roots and hubs such as the ferry port, Eurostar and Eurotunnel terminals and Channel Tunnel entrance. To this end Calais has featured prominently in the media over the last 10 years for its association with (illegal) immigration, particularly in relation to the now closed Red Cross Centre at nearby Sangatte and the formation of various refugee camps in waste areas across the town. Calais is also the location of one of the UK's juxtaposed borders, located there not surprisingly because of perceived threats associated with immigration.

In terms of cosmopolitan borders and connectivity, Calais is interesting for the following reasons. First, the border is being transformed and redefined by a multitude of non-state actors, including the migrants themselves, in ways that are not always deemed desirable by the national governments of France and the UK. Such activity has transformed Calais from what could once be described as a minor border to a major border zone. Whereas in Melton it was a 'new' border that was the focus of endorsement and contestation involving an array of different actors, in Calais the focus is on a traditional state territorial border championed and contested by many different borderworkers including the state, resulting in transforming bordering processes and agendas. In many ways the border is being transformed in the way that Papadopoulos et al. (2008) describe; the border is changing in response to those who contest or experience it, while at the same time those doing the contesting are changing in response to the border and being empowered in the process. This resistance to (imposed) state apparatus highlights the way in which borders must be considered central to cosmopolitan formulations, while at the same time, of course, inserting cosmopolitanism into bordering practices. Rather than state borders being conceptualized as objects of prevention or facilitation – the latter determining who is cosmopolitan and the former determining who is not – focusing on bordering processes and thus interactions at the border uncovers meaningful ways in which borders can be involved in our active experiences of the world. It is an active experience because borders do not have to by definition imposed by states, but rather they can be manipulated and changed in response to, and when in contact with, non-state borderworkers. The empowerment of non-state actors, and their ability to actively impact upon bordering processes, as is the case in Calais, can offer valuable insights concerning how cosmopolitanism is, and can be, practised and performed by different people and organizations, as well as the ways in which cosmopolitanism impacts within but also upon the world.

Second, and in terms of the connectivity, the border zone, as a result of the borderwork mentioned above, is bringing together many different groups (under logics of equivalence and difference in Laclau's (2007) terms) to the point where the border acts as a node connecting Calais to a diverse range of extensive networks (of policing, securitization, humanitarianism, social movements, criminal activity). The border becomes what Inge E. Boer (2006) has described as a space of negotiation in which different individuals and groups, including the governments of France and the UK, converge on the Calais border in order to contest its meaning. This can happen at the border site, for example a month-long gathering bringing together many different interest groups from many countries organized by the campaign group No Borders. It can also happen elsewhere, for example protests and meetings highlighting events at Calais and held in Bristol, Cambridge and other locations in the UK by NGOs and campaign groups.

Conclusion

Borders are central to cosmopolitanism, but not because crossing borders is traditionally thought to be part of the cosmopolitan experience. The border is central because it connects individuals to the world, and, at the same time, it allows them to negotiate their membership (in or out) of communities and to join with or break away from the nation-state. In other words, the border as 'quilting point' makes possible the autonomization of individuals (and also the autonomization of communities) (Rumford 2000). In this chapter we have sought to acknowledge and add meaning to the idea that borders are transforming – that they are dispersed throughout society, mean different things to different people, and that they can be distant from the territory that initiated them. At the core of the idea of cosmopolitan borders is the idea of borderwork: the ability of non-state actors to take part in bordering activity. Moreover, this borderwork allows for novel forms of connectivity: non-state actors can connect by utilizing bordering opportunities centred on construction, negation, narration and negotiation. Borders should not be taken for granted, either in their location or as state constructs located in solely divisionary practices, but rather be seen as potential mechanisms of everyday empowerment, that while uncertain, can nevertheless provide new possibilities, experiences and potentialities for people in their everyday lives. As Boer (2006: 13) alludes, 'if we accept [borders] but take them as uncertain, not lines, but spaces, not ridged but open to negotiation. The resulting uncertain territories are the ground we all stand on together'.

Bibliography

Adey, P. 2009. *Mobility*. London: Routledge.
Axford, B. 2006. The dialectic of borders and networks in Europe: reviewing 'topological presuppositions'. *Comparative European Politics*, 4(2/3), 160–82.
Balibar, E. 2002. *Politics and the Other Scene*. London: Verso.

Balibar, E. 2004a. *Europe as Borderland*. The Alexander von Humboldt Lecture in Human Geography, 24 November 2004, Institute for Human Geography, Universiteit Nijmegen, the Netherlands.

Balibar, E. 2004b. *We, the People of Europe? Reflections on Transnational Citizenship*. Princeton: Princeton University Press.

Bauman, Z. 1998. *Globalization: The Human Consequences*. Cambridge: Polity Press.

Beck, U. 2000. *What is Globalization?* Cambridge: Polity Press.

Beck, U. 2002. The cosmopolitan society and its enemies. *Theory, Culture and Society*, 19, 17–44.

Beck, U. 2007. Cosmopolitanism: a critical theory for the twenty-first century, in *The Blackwell Companion to Globalization*, edited by G. Ritzer. Oxford: Blackwell, 162–76.

Boer, I.E. 2006. *Uncertain Territories: Boundaries in Cultural Analysis*. Amsterdam: Rodopi.

Cabinet Office. 2007. *Security in a Global Hub: Establishing the UK's New Border Arrangements* Online, available at: www.cabinetoffice.gov.uk/media/cabinetoffice/corp/assets/publications/reports/border_review.pdf (accessed: 15 September 2010).

Castells, M. 2000. *The End of the Millennium*. Oxford: Blackwell.

Cresswell, T. 2006. *On the Move: Mobility in the Modern Western World*. London: Routledge.

Delanty, G. 2006. The cosmopolitan imagination: critical cosmopolitanism and social theory. *British Journal of Sociology*, 57(1), 25–47.

Delanty, G. 2007. Peripheries and borders in Western Europe. *Eurozine*. Online, available at: www.eurozine.com/articles/2007-08-29-delanty-en.html (accessed: 15 September 2010).

Delanty, G. 2009. *The Cosmopolitan Imagination*. Cambridge: Cambridge University Press.

Deleuze, G. and Guattari, F. 1986. *Nomadology: The War Machine*. New York: Columbia University Press.

de Lint, W. 2008. The security double take: the political, simulation and the border. *Surveillance & Society*, 5(2), 166–87.

Dicken, P., Kelly, P. and Yeung, H. 2001. Chains and networks, territories and scales: towards a relational framework for analysing the global economy. *Global Networks*, 1, 89–112.

Donnan, H. and Wilson, T. 1999. *Borders: Frontiers of Identity, Nation and State*. Oxford: Berg.

Durrschmidt, J. and Taylor, G. 2007. *Globalization, Modernity and Social Change*. Houndmills: Palgrave.

Elden, S. 2009. *Terror and Territory: The Spatial Extent of Sovereignty*. London: Minnesota University Press.

Hedetoft, U. 2003. *The Global Turn: National Encounters with the World*. Aalborg: Aalborg University Press.

Home Office. 2007. *Securing the UK Border: Our Vision and Strategy for the Future*. Online, available at: www.homeoffice.gov.uk/documents/securing-the-border (accessed: 15 September 2010).

Laclau, E. 2007. *On Populist Reason*. Verso: New York.

Lahav, G. and Guiraudon, V. 2000. Comparative perspectives on border control: away from the border and outside the state, in *The Wall Around the West: State Borders and Immigration Controls in North America and Europe*, edited by P. Andreas and T. Snyder. London and Lanham: Rowman and Littlefield, 55–80.

Larsen, J., Urry, J. and Axhausen, K. 2006. *Mobilities, Networks, Geographies*. Aldershot: Ashgate.

Lofgren, O. 2002. The nationalization of anxiety: a history of border crossings, in *The Postnational Self: Belonging and Identity*, edited by U. Hedetoft and M. Hjort. Minneapolis: Minnesota University Press, 250–74.

Mau, S., Mews, J. and Zimmerman, A. 2008. Cosmopolitan attitudes through transnational social practices? *Global Networks*, 8(1), 1–24.

Mignolo, W.D. 2000. The many faces of cosmo-polis: border thinking and critical cosmopolitanism. *Public Culture*, 12(3), 721–48.

Nowicka, M. and Rovisco, M. (eds). 2009. *Cosmopolitan in Practice*. Aldershot: Ashgate.

Papadopoulos, D., Stephenson, N. and Tsianos, V. 2008. *Escape Routes*. London: Pluto Press.

Rumford, C. 2000. European cohesion? Globalization, autonomization, and the dynamics of EU integration. *Innovation: the European Journal of Social Science Research*, 13(2), 183–97.

Rumford, C. 2006. Theorising borders. *European Journal of Social Theory*, 9(2), 155–69.

Rumford, C. 2007. Does Europe have cosmopolitan borders? *Globalizations*, 4(3), 327–39.

Rumford, C. 2008a. *Cosmopolitan Spaces: Europe, Globalization, Theory*. London: Routledge.

Rumford, C. 2008b. Introduction: citizens and borderwork in Europe. *Space and Polity*, 12(1), 1–12.

Salter, M. 2007. Govermentalities of an airport: heterotopia and confession. *International Political Sociology*, 1, 49–66.

Salter, M. (ed.). 2008. *Politics at the Airport*. Minnesota: Minnesota University Press.

Simmel, G. 1994. Bridge and door. *Theory Culture Society*, 11, 5–10.

Turner, B. 2007. The enclave society: towards a sociology of immobility. *European Journal of Social Theory*, 10(2), 287–304.

Urry, J. 2000. *Sociology Beyond Societies: Mobilities for the Twenty First Century*, New York: Routledge.

Urry, J. 2007. *Mobilities*. Cambridge: Polity Press.

van Houtum, H. 2005. The geopolitics of borders and boundaries. *Geopolitics*, 10, 672–9.

van Schendel, W. 2005. Spaces of engagement: how borderlands, illicit flows, and territorial states interlock, in *Illicit Flows and Criminal Things: States, Borders, and the Other Side of Globalization*, edited by W. van Schendel and I. Abraham. Bloomington: Indiana University Press, 38–68.

Vaughan-Williams, N. 2008. Borderwork beyond inside/outside? Frontex, the citizen-detective and the war on terror. *Space and Polity*, 12(1), 63–80.

Vaughan-Williams, N. 2010. The UK border security continuum: virtual biopolitics and the simulation of the sovereign ban. *Environment & Planning D: Society & Space*, 28(6), 1071–83.

Walters, W. 2006. Border/control. *Europe Journal of Social Theory*, 9(2), 187–203.

PART III
Debates

Critical Cosmopolitanism

Fuyuki Kurasawa

Introduction

At this particular historical and theoretical juncture, discourses of cosmopolitanism in the human sciences are multiplying to the extent that the term itself risks dissolving into an empty signifier. Hence, before considering the implications of adding the qualifier 'critical' to the idea of cosmopolitanism, we need to define the latter more precisely. For our purposes, the literature on cosmopolitanism advances and draws upon three principals meanings. At the most general level, cosmopolitanism designates a worldview according to which subjects understand themselves as citizens of the world or belonging to humankind as a whole, whether in opposition to or superimposed upon their membership of territorially- or socio-culturally-delimited communities (city-states, nations, civilizations, religious or ethnic groups, etc.).[1] In a second, complementary sense, cosmopolitanism refers to an ethos of worldliness, of seeking to engage with the world as one's dwelling-place or home; frequently, this dimension is referred to as an openness to difference and commitment to cultural pluralism (Hannerz 1990), which thus imply a refutation of parochial or nativist tendencies. To be cosmopolitan, then, signifies a capacity for multiperspectivism, that is to say, to move between and be able to decode a wide array of divergent socio-cultural practices and belief-systems, as well as to be familiar with the self-understandings of various groups across the world. Third, cosmopolitanism identifies a belief in human unity and a consequent attachment to humankind *in toto* (Tagore 1997). Often supported by a humanist universalism that advocates recognition of the worth of all civilizations' and societies' contributions to social life, such a cosmopolitan outlook seeks to translate seemingly incommensurable cultural frameworks to make them mutually intelligible. Accordingly, it questions the 'self-evidentness' of categorical dichotomies commonly employed to hierarchically divide parts of humankind from

---

[1] The word itself originated with the ancient Greek Cynics (Diogenes: 'I am a citizen of the world' [*kosmou polites*]) and the Greco-Roman Stoics (e.g. Seneca) (Nussbaum 2002a), although the principle of identifying with humankind is found in several Western and non-Western intellectual traditions.

each other (savage/civilized, 'East'/'West', etc.), as well as exclusionary discourses grounded in essentialized group characteristics (racism, ethno-racial nationalism, 'cultural separatism' and religious fundamentalism, amongst others) (Sen 2005).

If, at first glance, these definitional elements seem to be relatively innocuous, their reframing in the terms of critical theory—to produce an explicitly *critical* cosmopolitanism—enables us to underscore their more radical implications by exposing the considerable gap between the normative aspirations contained in the three significations detailed above and their actualization in the current world order. Hence, the articulation of normativity and socio-historically informed analysis characterizing critical cosmopolitanism pushes beyond formal advocacy and recognition of cosmopolitan ideals—world citizenship, wordliness and human unity—in two ways: through a negative critique of the structural obstacles and relations of domination preventing such ideals from being presently achieved, and through a reconstructive critique of alternative perspectives and practices by which cosmopolitan principles can be grounded in the material world. In particular, from the vantage-point of critical theory, the key question is one of shifting the conception of cosmopolitanism from being strictly a set of subjective or attitudinal dispositions towards other human beings (that is to say, a product of a person's will, volition or moral sentiments) towards a more substantive and systemic project of universal emancipation tackling structurally-produced sources of inequality and global injustices blocking the exercise of individual and collective capabilities and the flourishing of human potential. To sum up, then, critical cosmopolitanism is defined by its pluralist egalitarianism and emancipatory universalism, as well as its materialist substantivism.

Referring back to the first of the three aforementioned meanings from such a perspective, world citizenship becomes less a matter of voluntary self-identification with humankind than one of gauging the unequally distributed capacity to exercise the rights entailed by being a citizen of the globe. Extending the paradox which Arendt identified regarding the stateless in postwar Europe (Arendt 1968), one might argue that regardless of the fact that all human beings may formally claim that the world is their polis (and thus that they are the bearers of universal rights), only those who are already recognized as citizens of rich and relatively powerful nation-states can actually have such rights substantiated via their institutional protection, advancement and enforcement. In other words, occupying a dominant position within Westphalian, nation-state-centric regimes of citizenship is currently a necessary precondition for the meaningful exercise of the cosmopolitan ideal of viewing oneself as a citizen of the world. Furthermore, critical cosmopolitanism puts into question the exclusionary design of these national frames of citizenship, which restrict participation in deliberation and decision-making as well as material entitlements to membership of a specific territorially-bounded political community, while leaving those constituted as territorially or legally outside of such communities (citizens of other nation-states or undocumented migrants, respectively) with few if any civil-political or socio-economic rights. From a critically cosmopolitan stance, then, such rights and the capacities to exercise them should be decoupled from legally-sanctioned belonging to particular territories, thereby being equally accessible to all human beings wherever they are located and whenever they choose or need to enact them (Balibar 2004); only then will the notion of being a citizen of the world become substantive in practice.

Likewise, two dimensions of critique specified above can guide a reinterpretation of the cosmopolitan ethos of worldliness and intercultural openness. On the one hand, critical cosmopolitanism insists on the fact that treating the world as one's home is akin to feeling that 'the world is one's oyster', namely, a stance that can only be adopted by members of dominant groups, whose considerable symbolic and material power provides them with a degree of agency allowing them to view the globe as an unfettered space within which they can realize their expectations and execute their projects of self-cultivation or transformation of external reality. In addition, being worldly can all too easily become a strategy of distinction (Bourdieu 1984), according to which members of groups with high levels of economic and cultural capital are able to establish their superiority vis-à-vis dominated groups. Hierarchical differentiation in various fields is thereby generated by the ability to be or become worldly, which can be equated with the 'class consciousness of frequent travellers' (Calhoun 2003). In this sense, worldliness becomes reduced to the ability to travel to distant lands, to be at the cutting edge of global trends, and to consume non-local, 'exotic' goods and services—activities that are misrecognized by those partaking in them as choices available to all participants in a field and as indicators of cultural sophistication rather than socio-economic dominance. Based on such a logic, the vast majority of the world's population is condemned to a perpetual non-cosmopolitan status, here again misrecognized as a matter of voluntarily unsophisticated decision-making instead of an effect of the severe restriction in the range of options available to those suffering from socio-economic deprivation. When expressed in these terms, cosmopolitan worldliness can also be a kind of thin multiculturalism, limited to facile or domesticated, consumerist modes of interaction with unfamiliar socio-cultural expressions (food, music, etc.) and never extending beyond a liberal concern for tolerance; it is this sort of multicultural capitalist ideology that is taught in the world's leading business schools and global management programmes, where thin cosmopolitanism is seen as a social facilitator of transnational trade and investment relations.

By contrast, critical cosmopolitanism underscores the existence of a worldly sensibility from below, grounded in ordinary ways of thinking and acting. For many human beings, whose structural positions in the world economy exclude them from the elitist brand of cosmopolitanism denoted above, worldliness is an everyday reality fuelled by several globalizing processes: interculturally expansive social imaginaries shaped by transnational flows of persons, ideas and images (Appadurai 1996), which are facilitated by the Internet and mobile technologies; the mundane processes of cultural translation and interpretation required to make sense of ubiquitous globalized manifestations of popular culture (e.g. Bollywood films or Brazilian *telenovelas* overseas); and the social interactions conducted in a variety of languages between inhabitants of global cities with others of different socio-cultural backgrounds and persuasions. At the same time, critical cosmopolitanism is not content with the liberal model of multicultural diversity, seeking a thicker and more normatively demanding mode of intercultural engagement composed, for heuristic purposes, of three analytical components: an outward turn, characterized by a willingness to encounter different ways of doing and thinking that prompt a radical decentring of familiar or proximate cultural and ethical horizons; a moment of in-betweenness, whereby one negotiates and attempts to make different socio-cultural worldviews intelligible to oneself; and an outward turn, marked by an expanded viewpoint through which to denaturalize and radically put into question the *doxa* of one's own socio-cultural worldviews and practices (Kögler 2005, Kurasawa 2004). Particularly notable in demarcating a critical cosmopolitanism from its liberal multicultural counterpart is this third step, for the capacity for self-critique of habitual discourses, rituals and belief-systems via intercultural perspectivism demands a kind and degree of hermeneutical depth and relativizing interrogation that are beyond the purview of the tolerance for diversity.

Finally, for critical cosmopolitanism, what undergirds the principle of human unity is not simply a notion of living in a global village—that is to say, the creation of transnational bonds of interdependence bonds attributable to globalizing forces—but the normative commitment to the moral equality of all human beings (Nussbaum 2002a, Benhabib 2006). Aside from opposing modes of social domination at every scale, this implies a rejection of essentializing forms of thought hierarchically dividing the globe into discrete and inherently incommensurable cultural or civilizational zones, which are often accompanied by xenophobic or racialized constructs of otherness (the foreigner, the non-believer, etc.). Similarly, the ethical orientation to humankind as a whole requires pursuing arduous processes of intercultural dialogue across apparently intractable global divides, in order to generate a contingent yet egalitarian discourse of universal emancipation informed by a plurality of understandings of the good and the just.

Theoretical Frames

Critical cosmopolitanism's normative and analytical components are refracted through three principal theoretical paradigms, each of which foregrounds a different dimension of the overarching framework of thought. The first approach is a neo-Kantian one, since it formulates universal norms of moral equality while drawing inspiration from Kant's prescient vision of a pacified domain of international relations secured through a world federation of states and peoples. Neo-Kantians advocate for the institutionalization of such universal norms through an enforceable, legally binding regime of global governance, thus putting forth proposals for the juridification of cosmopolitan principles via international law and constitutional mechanisms (Held 1995, Bohman and Lutz-Bachmann 1997, Habermas 1998a). Because it would regulate all actors in global politics, cosmopolitan legality erodes the idea of states' absolute and undisputed sovereignty over administrative territories and their populations. A specifically Habermasian variant of neo-Kantian cosmopolitanism hones in on intersubjective procedures of public deliberation and the practice of discourse ethics to formulate cosmopolitan principles and institutional configurations. As such, this variant interrogates structural arrangements and procedures that constitute membership of specific political communities in exclusionary terms (e.g. the aforementioned regimes of national citizenship), thus preventing certain persons from fully participating in decision-making processes and being able to make claims as rights-bearing subjects (Benhabib 2006, Fraser 2008).

The second theoretical paradigm through which to formulate critical cosmopolitanism is Levinasian in character, being mainly preoccupied with the notion of openness to difference and an ethical stance towards alterity. For Levinas, ethics signifies the ontological primacy of being-for-the-other, as an infinite and unconditional cosmopolitan responsibility without spatial or socio-cultural restrictions; human rights mean nothing less than being responsible for the rights of the other human (Levinas 1999, Douzinas 2007), for the stranger whose radical difference cannot be assimilated or domesticated into sameness. At one level, this leads theorists of difference to continuously remain vigilant about the implicit bounds of humanity in Euro-American discourses of cosmopolitanism, and to question whom these discourses constitute as human and whom is considered outside of humankind's limits (abject others towards whom we may feel no responsibility) (Butler 2004). At another level, Levinasians reformulate cosmopolitanism by radicalizing the Kantian concept of hospitality, which is converted into an a priori and unrestricted duty to welcome, and be with and for, the other in her or his alterity (Derrida 2001). What binds us together as humans is this responsibility to others, as well as recognition of common experiences of loss and mourning that expose our shared state of interdependence and vulnerability vis-à-vis others (Butler 2004).

With its emphasis on egalitarianism and emancipatory political struggles, neo-Marxism represents the third of critical cosmopolitanism's theoretical approaches. Although sympathetic to some of the aspirations of liberal cosmopolitans, neo-Marxists assert that, when deprived of a materialist basis, such aspirations either deliberately or inadvertently correspond to ideological expressions of the latest, highly globalized neoliberal phase of capitalism. If stripped of the sorts of political demands specified above, the ideals of being citizens of the world and feeling at home in the latter can become paeans to affluent consumerism (world music, fusion restaurants, etc.) and socio-economic deregulation to open up transnational markets (by facilitating 'free trade' of goods and services and the unregulated circulation of capital flows between countries) (Calhoun 2003, Hardt and Negri 2000, Harvey 2009). Moreover, this neoliberal logic is selective about the principle of 'freedom of movement' across national borders, applying it to economic and cultural elites (as investors, businesspeople, or tourists) while ignoring the plight of the vast majority of the world's population in the global South, which is subject to re-regulation through ever more restrictive Northern immigration and citizenship regimes (Balibar 2004). By contrast, neo-Marxism concentrates on how public discourse and agonistic political struggle can create socially thick bonds of solidarity between social movements and forces resisting neoliberal capitalism, by forming progressive networks within global civil society that aim to enact the egalitarian principles of critical cosmopolitanism through a restructuring of the global socio-economic order (Tarrow 2005). In other words, for human beings to have the substantive capacities to treat the entire world as their polis, to experience it as their home and to participate in a unified human community, cosmopolitan thinking and practice cannot but address systemic sources of inequality and domination in the world economy, including discourses of neoliberalism and its institutional infrastructure (the World Bank, the International Monetary Fund, the World Trade Organization, etc.).

Critical Cosmopolitanism's Three Facets

For explanatory purposes, the political, economic and cultural aspects of critical cosmopolitanism can distinguished from one another. The cosmopolitical approach and the theme of cosmopolitan democracy represent the most ambitious and detailed programmes of organizational reform of the current system of global governance (Archibugi 2008, Archibugi et al. 1998). Among the key proposals have been a bolstering of international law to formally entrench cosmopolitan norms and thus bring interstate relations and non-statist transnational actors under the aegis of enforceable juridical mechanisms, as well as the transformation of existing multilateral international organizations in order to curb national sovereignty and hold all actors on the global stage accountable to such mechanisms or organizations (e.g. via an expansion of the mandate and powers of the International Criminal Court to prosecute all perpetrators of mass human rights violations). Concretely, this means that such violations are to be halted, either through the use of sanctions against those committing them or, as a last resort and under specific conditions, through multilateral military intervention. If all human beings are to have equal standing in practice, instances of situational and structural violence targeting them cannot unfold with impunity—regardless of where they take place or whom they affect; from a critical cosmopolitan perspective, genocide and famine cannot be met with indifference or a solely geopolitical calculus. Cosmopolitical theorists are also concerned with the further democratization of processes of transnational political governance, chiefly by increasing the participation of global civil society in deliberation within international forums and institutions through the creation of a parliamentary structure within the infrastructure of the United Nations. To undermine the dependence of human rights upon national citizenship, critical cosmopolitanism can also support the development of a multiscaled architecture of rights, which are to apply unconditionally to all human beings and be democratically negotiated through subnational and transnational processes.

Not to be neglected in the elaboration of the political aspects of critical cosmopolitanism are analysts of global civil society, who draw attention to the roles of transnational activist networks, social movements and non-governmental organizations in the creation of informal cosmopolitan practices and worldviews (Kumar et al. 2009, Tarrow 2005). Such transnational networks may employ a 'boomerang pattern' (Keck and Sikkink 1998) of spatially nested political activism, bypassing hostile or unresponsive domestic governments to mobilize external resources and allies within global civil society, which, in turn, can exercise 'rebound' pressure on these governments. This cosmopolitanism from below is being stimulated by the proliferation and growing integration of supranational political coalitions, who pursue campaigns tackling borderless problems: environmental damage, war, women's and indigenous rights, crimes against humanity, neoliberal capitalism and its institutions of governance, and so on (Keck and Sikkink 1998, Kurasawa 2007).

The starting point of critical cosmopolitanism's economic dimension is a refusal to accept the structural violence and abject living conditions wrought upon large segments of the world's population, both via the operations of global capitalism and the growing North–South divide. Thus, in the first instance, cosmopolitan discourse aims to elaborate a moral grammar of justification for the urgent task of global redistribution of material resources, as a means to alleviate severe poverty and elevate the living standards of marginalized groups (notably women and the poor in the global South). Given that most citizens accept the legitimacy of redistributive obligations to the fellow members of their domestic polity due to the success of nationalist constructs of the moral community to which we are bound, the cosmopolitan challenge consists of spatially unbounding this sense of solidarity in order to make it applicable to humankind in general. In fact, when foregrounding the principle of equal worth of every person in the world, the redistributive favouring of compatriots over foreigners is exposed as a type of arbitrary discrimination that cannot be impartially legitimated (Singer 2002). As post-Rawlsian cosmopolitan theorists (Beitz 1999, Pogge 2002) have indicated, the restriction of norms of justice to a community composed of fellow citizens of one's nation-state is morally and logically flawed, effectively ignoring socio-economic duties to inhabitants of the rest of the planet. A much stronger case can be made for the generalization of the social contractualist framework through the lens of global economic justice, in order to tackle the egregious maldistribution of material and symbolic power transnationally. A global social contract is based on the dynamics of transnational economic integration and interdependence between regions of the world, which have created social bonds and moral responsibilities towards distant strangers that are akin to those among national populations. Redistribution is further justified by the fact that the global economy is an asymmetrical system from which inhabitants of the rich world structurally extract disproportionate and unearned benefits, whereas persons and groups elsewhere are subjected to involuntary participation in it due to their subordinate standing and the uneven capacities of poorer nation-states to set the operating rules of this system (Pogge 2002). Consequently, redistributive legitimation is found in a cosmopolitan variant of Rawls' 'difference principle' (Rawls 1971), according to which the only acceptable socio-economic inequalities are those which are to the greatest benefit of the least advantaged sections of the global population.

However, a critical approach to global economic justice cannot limit itself to redistributive matters while leaving unattended the transnational structures and relations of domination and exploitation that underpin massive distributive inequalities (Forst 2001). On the contrary, it must put forth principles of organization of economic activity that correspond to egalitarian and democratic norms, such as Fraser's notion of 'participatory parity'—which can be applied to design economic arrangements in which all persons can participate on a par with others in the world (Fraser 2008). Hence, critical cosmopolitanism can put forth demands for alternative models of organizing of production, ranging from anti-capitalist self-management and collective ownership of the means of production to the regulation of markets through cosmopolitan democratic law (Held 1995). Additionally, it can push for the founding of an infrastructure of global economic governance that, unlike the current institutional order (represented by the World Bank, the IMF and the WTO), is neither intrinsically neoliberal nor even capitalist in design; such an infrastructure would enable various forms of economic activity and ownership to emerge, prioritize the meeting of the needs of all human beings, and introduce policies that would break with the reproduction of mass poverty in the global South (debt cancellation, fair trade, import substitution, etc.).

The formal cultural facet of critical cosmopolitanism is directed towards the elaboration of an interculturally—and dialogically—produced universalism. As such, it obviously eschews nativism and civilizational chauvinism, which inherently privilege familiar or indigenous modes of thought and action because of what is presumed to be their inherent superiority over other ways of thinking and acting. Similarly, it is wary of the ethnocentric universalization of Euro-American values and practices, which have conventionally been assumed to be diffused, imposed or emulated in the rest of the world (e.g. in modernization theory and Eurocentric discourses about the uniquely Western origins or nature of cosmopolitan principles). At the same time, critical cosmopolitanism steers clear of the most frequent response to the peril of ethnocentric universalization, an absolute cultural relativism coupling contextual determinism (the discreteness of evaluative criteria for a society's moral system) with assumed cross-cultural incommensurability (the necessary incompatibility between different societies' moral systems).

Rather, a stance of critical cosmopolitanism underscores the possibility of generating an overlapping consensus or fusion of horizons through transnational public deliberation and debate, which can lead to mutual understanding and the discursive constitution of intersecting points of agreement between parties. For instance, Kögler specifies three capabilities that are required among actors participating in the dialogical construction of cosmopolitan universalism: a post-conventional sense of normative commitment (the capacity to potentially commit oneself to norms that challenge or transcend one's own traditional socio-cultural context); interpretive perspective-taking (the capacity to understand another party's perspective from within her or his own context of meaning); and social self-reflexivity (the capacity to gain critical distance from one's self-evident background assumptions) (Kögler 2005). The kind of universalism that such a dialogical process can yield is fundamentally pluralist, since its normative substance is specified by comparatively evaluating the relative worth of various socio-cultural settings' worldviews and moral systems in relation to each other and selecting elements from them most compatible with principles of human unity and equality, rather than by attributing an intrinsic superiority to a particular setting's worldview or wholly adopting it (Parekh 1999). The resulting possibility of a provisional 'overlapping consensus' (Rawls 1993) would remain perpetually open to contestation and reformulation, yet also take shape in different iterations around the world because vernacularized, that is, filtered through and adapted to specific customs and belief-systems (Merry 2006).

However, equally significant for a critical cosmopolitanism is its grounding in more informal or banal cultural practices (Beck 2006, Diouf 2000, Kendall et al. 2009), in order to displace the widespread perception of the world being divided into territorially discrete and socially homogenous cultures (contained within spatial units binding ethnicity to nationality). By contrast, one can point to the longstanding existence of cultural syncretism as an ordinary, lived experience in many parts of the world, notably in metropolitan areas where peoples from numerous backgrounds have met, mingled and lived peacefully for centuries while generating creolized social manifestations; great centres of learning (Alexandria, Baghdad, Paris, etc.), maritime gateways for refugees and trade routes (Shanghai, Marseille, New York, etc.), and global cities shaped by diverse and large migrant communities (Los Angeles, Toronto, London, etc.) all exemplify such banal cosmopolitanism. In the contemporary world, urban life is defined by creolization, the mixing-and-matching that involves selective appropriation and creative adaptation of varied influences, ideas and modes of conduct from several parts of the globe, which result in novel intercultural practices. Likewise, far from being exceptional, globalized and hybridized musical genres borrowing and reassembling various seemingly incompatible traditions and styles (jazz, Afrobeat, bhangra, rai, etc.) illustrate the commonplace status of syncretic aesthetic forms (Gilroy 2000).

Cosmopolitan syncretism, then, is more ambitious and subversive than the multicultural ethos of cultivating and tolerating diversity, where ethno-cultural communities exist alongside each other yet remain relatively self-contained and thus characterized by mutual indifference. Indeed, syncretic dynamics deliberately transgress and blur seemingly rigid boundaries between groups and territories through acts of 'social promiscuity' (Zubaida 2004) that revel in the inauthentic and the impure as zones of transcultural creativity. A critical cosmopolitanism puts forth these sorts of hybrid amalgams as an alternative to nativist or parochial defences of the purity and authenticity of culture, and as a way to valorize cross-cultural 'contamination' (Appiah 2006) and interpenetration. The resulting model is suspicious of discourses designed to assert single dominant cultural or civilizational influences (Eurocentrism, Sinocentrism, Afrocentrism, etc.), in favour of a series of cultural formations without a core, formed out of intersecting points of contact and constantly reinvented (because incomplete and unfinished) hybrid elements.

Substantive Tensions

Lest the previous argument be misunderstood, we should note that critical cosmopolitanism is not a homogenous or unified system of thought, for it is best grasped as an intellectual field structured by a series of substantive debates and differing positions on certain key questions. Foremost among these is the matter of whether, and to what extent, identifying as a citizen of the world must be accompanied by a renunciation of patriotism and nationalistic attachments. While some cosmopolitans argue that this is precisely what is required if the attachment to humankind is to be prioritized morally (Nussbaum 2002a, Singer 2002), others claim that certain forms of patriotic attachments and rootedness in particular communities of belonging (from the local to the global) are fully compatible with a cosmopolitan worldview (Appiah 2006); in such instances, the question is less a matter of uprooting oneself than of questioning the potentially exclusionary dimensions of modes of collective belonging to open them up to alterity and thus translating them into cosmopolitan terms, and vice versa (that is to say, translating cosmopolitan discourses into more rooted and vernacularized forms). In the sphere of political activism, the more pervasive phenomenon has been one of 'rooted cosmopolitanism', with actors whose identities are nested at various scales and seek to articulate particularized and universal discourses, often by connecting localized struggles or causes to global processes and building transnational coalitions that work both inside and outside of the framework of the nation-state (Merry 2006, Tarrow 2005).

Yet, even more basically, what are the sources of human unity that bind us to each other? For some cosmopolitans, human reason plays this role, although less in the sense of sheer cognitive abilities than moral reasoning, i.e. the capacity to recognize certain basic universal norms and duties which are either discovered through reflection or constructed through mutual understanding via discourse-ethical procedures (Habermas 1990). Another cluster of cosmopolitan thought contends that empathetic moral sentiments represent a much more powerful force for the creation of human solidarity, as the act of being exposed to and imagining ourselves in the place of others experiencing suffering is what humanizes them and binds us to their fate (Rorty 1998, Laqueur 2001). The capabilities approach, for its part, problematizes conventional devices of human commonality (primarily needs in philosophical anthropology and rights in socio-political discourses) in favour of the identification of shared capabilities—understood not only in the formalistic sense of a set of aptitudes or requirements, but also as the opportunity for persons to exercise freedom in the cultivation and subjectivities (Nussbaum 2002a).[2]

When assessing the dynamics driving cosmopolitanism, critical analysts fall into three camps. The more culturally-minded among them focus on the presence

---

[2] The capabilities approach proposed by Sen and Nussbaum specifies 10 core human capabilities: life; bodily health; bodily integrity; senses, imagination and thought; emotions; practical reason; affiliation; other species; play; and control over one's environment (Nussbaum 2002b: 129–30).

of a globalized and deterritorialized 'space of flows' (Appadurai 1996), marked by the acceleration and intensification of transnational movements (of people, commodities, images, etc.) and the consequent emergence of various social imaginaries that cross borders and generate a sense of planetary interconnectedness. Other theorists highlight the existence of a set of cosmopolitanizing forces tied to the establishment of a 'world risk society', whereby the coming into prominence of several structural risks that imperil humankind in its totality (chiefly, environmental degradation, terrorism and pandemics) are necessarily leading to a growing awareness of planetary interdependence among the world's population and the search for solutions that transcend the territorial confines of the nation-state (Beck 2006). A third cluster of analysts insist on the determining role of neoliberal capitalism, whose privatizing, individualizing and deregulating logic subsumes any ethos of wordliness and instrumentalizes the latter into a device facilitating the unimpeded circulation of capital and its accumulation (Harvey 2009).

An additional area of contention within critical cosmopolitanism concerns the interpretation of nationalism. Agreement does exist about the significance of abandoning 'methodological nationalism' (Beck 2006), the tendency to take the nation-state as the self-evident unit of analysis in the social sciences (e.g. the sociological equation of a society with a certain territory demarcated by national borders).[3] However, the contributions of political nationalism to an emancipatory cosmopolitan project are vigorously debated, with many analysts viewing nationalist discourses as intrinsically drawing upon racial or ethno-cultural forms of xenophobia and chauvinism. Further, as explained above, patriotism is thereby understood as counter-cosmopolitan in its fostering of a primary devotion to one's country and insistence on equating persons' senses of moral community to national territory (Habermas 1998b, Nussbaum 2002a). A second cluster of theorists assert that critics of nationalism overlook the latter's vital historical role as a revolutionary, civic republican force with progresssive ambitions, born out of resistance to colonialism in the global South or struggle against authoritarian monarchical and religious rule in the Euro-American world. In other words, civic nationalism may be entirely compatible with—and perhaps even a necessary condition for the advent of—cosmopolitanism (Appiah 1998, Calhoun 2002, Cheah 2006). And in the contemporary world, the two realities will likely continue to co-exist simultaneously.

Finally, critical cosmopolitanism has approached the theme of human rights from numerous perspectives. From one vantage-point, the discourse of human rights is troubling, not least because its focus on relieving suffering depoliticizes many types of structurally-produced injustices and impoverishes the horizons of radical politics, whereas its liberally-tinged insistence on the primacy of individual civil-political rights fits all-too-easily with the imperatives of the capitalist market (Brown 2004, Žižek 2005). Worse still is the possible instrumentalization

---

3   Nevertheless, it should be noted that much classical and contemporary sociology was methodologically cosmopolitan *avant la lettre* (e.g. Marx on capitalism, Weber on world religions, and Durkheim and Mauss on civilizations).

of the rhetoric of human rights for imperialistic purposes, which converts them into ideological devices selectively applied to legitimate the use of military force against countries or groups perceived to threaten global Euro-American hegemony (Bartholomew and Breakspear 2004, Chandler 2003). Against these outcomes, critical cosmopolitanism seeks to explore the possibility of an emancipatory politics of human rights. The first move in this direction involves a critique of the individualistic and liberal emphasis on civil and political rights, to incorporate at the core of this politics a strong notion of socio-economic rights that would include recognition of collective struggles for self-determination and development for peoples of the global South (Cheah 2006). To this can be added a formalist dimension of human rights politics, dedicated to redesigning the institutions of global political and economic governance in a manner that would be congruent with the three dimensions of cosmopolitanism specified above. Among other measures would be the entrenchment of a multilateral regime of cosmopolitan law, a restructuring of international financial institutions, and the participation of progressive elements of global civil society in decision-making processes. Just as importantly is the informal labour of human rights, their utilization by persons and groups performing practices of resistance to injustices and inventing egalitarian projects in different areas of the world (Kurasawa 2007).

Conclusion

To sum up an essay on critical cosmopolitanism can be accomplished by reflecting on how the term 'critique' itself functions, and in particular the double meaning contained therein: as a theoretical critique of other cosmopolitan paradigms, notably the liberal counterpart against which it defines itself; and as a normative critique of the existing world order, against which it poses alternative modalities of organizing humankind's socio-cultural, economic and political relations. As such, critical cosmopolitanism is a substantivist framework, which goes beyond the formal versions of ideas of being a citizen of the world, experiencing the world as one's home, and human unity in order to support modes of political struggle that enable social actors to acquire the subjective and structural capacities to materially realize these principles. Transforming the current global order in a cosmopolitan direction, then, requires engaging in practices of global justice confronting all systemic relations of subordination while committed to establishing projects of egalitarian and pluralist universalism.

The above-mentioned tension between critical cosmopolitanism's analytical and normative aspects represents the foundation of its intellectual dynamism. On the one hand, investment in cosmopolitan ideals is driving the vast array of research on the institutional obstacles to the achievement of such ideals, the political actors opposed to or bolstering them, and the forces of cosmopolitanization more generally. On the other hand, empirically-based findings (about global warming, the ravages of transnational capitalism, or the spread of mass human rights violations, for instance) are making the commitment to cosmopolitan norms—even in their most utopian iterations—appear ever more urgent. Until these two components can be reconciled, until the present state of affairs comes to more closely resemble what it ought to be for the whole of humankind, the theoretical and practical underpinnings of critical cosmopolitanism will remain as tasks to be performed.

Bibliography

Appadurai, A. 1996. *Modernity at Large: Cultural Dimensions of Globalization*. Minneapolis: University of Minnesota Press.

Appiah, K.A. 1998. Cosmopolitan Patriots, in *Cosmopolitics: Thinking and Feeling Beyond the Nation*, edited by P. Cheah and B. Robbins. Minneapolis: University of Minnesota Press, 91–114.

Appiah, K.A. 2006. *Cosmopolitanism: Ethics in a World of Strangers*. New York: Norton.

Archibugi, D. 2008. *The Global Commonwealth of Citizens: Toward Cosmopolitan Democracy*. Princeton: Princeton University Press.

Archibugi, D., Held, D. and Köhler, M. 1998. *Re-imagining Political Community: Studies in Cosmopolitan Democracy*. Stanford: Stanford University Press.

Arendt, H. 1968. The Decline of the Nation-State and the End of the Rights of Man, in *The Origins of Totalitarianism*. New York: Harcourt Brace, 267–302.

Balibar, E. 2004. Outline of a Topography of Cruelty: Citizenship and Civility in the Era of Global Violence, in *We, the People of Europe? Reflections on Transnational Citizenship*. Princeton: Princeton University Press, 115–32.

Bartholomew, A. and Breakspear, J. 2004. Human Rights as Swords of Empire, in *Socialist Register 2004: The New Imperial Challenge*, edited by L. Panitch and C. Leys. New York: Monthly Review Press, 124–45.

Beck, U. 2006. *The Cosmopolitan Vision*. Cambridge: Polity.

Beitz, C. 1999. *Political Theory and International Relations*. Princeton: Princeton University Press.

Benhabib, S. 2002. Nous et les Autres (We and the Others): Is Universalism Ethnocentric? in *The Claims of Culture: Equality and Diversity in the Global Era*. Princeton: Princeton University Press, 24–48.

Benhabib, S. 2006. *Another Cosmopolitanism*. Oxford: Oxford University Press.

Bohman, J. and Lutz-Bachmann, M. (eds). 1997. *Perpetual Peace: Essays on Kant's Cosmopolitan Ideal*. Cambridge, MA: MIT Press.

Bourdieu, P. 1984. *Distinction: A Social Critique of the Judgement of Taste*. Cambridge, MA: Harvard University Press.

Brown, W. 2004. 'The Most We Can Hope For …': Human Rights and the Politics of Fatalism. *South Atlantic Quarterly*, 103(2/3), 451–63.

Butler, J. 2004. Violence, Mourning, Politics, in *Precarious Life: The Powers of Mourning and Violence*. London and New York: Verso, 19–49.

Calhoun, C. 2002. Constitutional Patriotism and the Public Sphere: Interests, Identity, and Solidarity in the Integration of Europe, in *Global Justice and Transnational Politics*, edited by P. De Greiff and C. Cronin. Cambridge, MA: MIT Press, 275–312.

Calhoun, C. 2003. The Class Consciousness of Frequent Travellers: Towards a Critique of Actually Existing Cosmopolitanism, in *Debating Cosmopolitics*, edited by D. Archibugi. London and New York: Verso, 86–116.

Chandler, D. 2003. International Justice, in *Debating Cosmopolitics*, edited by D. Archibugi. London and New York: Verso, 27–39.

Cheah, P. 2006. *Inhuman Conditions: On Cosmopolitanism and Human Rights*. Cambridge, MA: Harvard University Press.

Derrida, J. 2001. *On Cosmopolitanism and Forgiveness*. London and New York: Routledge.

Diouf, M. 2000. The Senegalese Murid Trade Diaspora and the Making of a Vernacular Cosmopolitanism. *Public Culture*, 12(3), 679–702.

Douzinas, C. 2007. *Human Rights and Empire: The Political Philosophy of Cosmopolitanism*. Oxford and New York: Routledge-Cavendish.

Forst, R. 2001. Towards a Critical Theory of Transnational Justice, in *Global Justice*, edited by T. Pogge, Oxford: Blackwell, 169–87.

Fraser, N. 2008. Abnormal Justice. *Critical Inquiry*, 34, 393–422.

Gilroy, P. 2000. 'Race', Cosmopolitanism, and Catastrophe, in *Between Camps: Nations, Cultures and the Allure of Race*. Harmondsworth: Penguin, 279–326.

Habermas, J. 1990. *Moral Consciousness and Communicative Action*. Cambridge, MA: MIT Press.

Habermas, J. 1998a. Kant's Idea of Perpetual Peace: At Two Hundred Years' Historical Remove, in *The Inclusion of the Other: Studies in Political Theory*. Cambridge, MA: MIT Press, 165–201.

Habermas, J. 1998b. Struggles for Recognition in the Democratic Constitutional State, in *The Inclusion of the Other: Studies in Political Theory*. Cambridge, MA: MIT Press, 203–36.

Hannerz, U. 1990. Cosmopolitans and Locals in World Culture. *Theory, Culture and Society*, 7, 237–51.

Hardt, M. and Negri, A. 2000. *Empire*. Cambridge, MA: Harvard University Press.

Harvey, D. 2009. *Cosmopolitanism and the Geographies of Freedom*. New York: Columbia University Press.

Held, D. 1995. *Democracy and the Global Order: From the Modern State to Cosmopolitan Governance*. Stanford: Stanford University Press.

Keck, M.E. and Sikkink, K. 1998. *Activists Beyond Borders: Advocacy Networks in International Politics*. Ithaca: Cornell University Press.

Kendall, G., Woodward, I. and Skrbiš, Z. 2009. *The Sociology of Cosmopolitanism: Globalization, Identity, Culture and Government*. New York: Palgrave Macmillan.

Kögler, H.-H. 2005. Constructing a Cosmopolitan Public Sphere: Hermeneutic Capabilities and Universal Values. *European Journal of Social Theory*, 8(3), 297–320.

Kumar, A., Scholte, J.A., Kaldor, M., Glasius, M., Seckinelgin, H. and Anheier, H.K. (eds). 2009. *Global Civil Society Yearbook 2009: Poverty and Activism*. London: Sage.

Kurasawa, F. 2004. *The Ethnological Imagination: A Cross-Cultural Critique of Modernity*. Minneapolis: University of Minnesota Press.

Kurasawa, F. 2007. *The Work of Global Justice: Human Rights as Practices*. Cambridge: Cambridge University Press.

Laqueur, T.W. 2001. The Moral Imagination and Human Rights, in *Human Rights as Politics and Idolatry*, edited by A. Gutman. Princeton: Princeton University Press, 127–39.

Levinas, E. 1999. The Rights of the Other Man, in *Alterity and Transcendence*. New York: Columbia University Press, 145–50.

Merry, S.E. 2006. *Human Rights and Gender Violence: Translating International Law into Local Justice*. Chicago: University of Chicago Press.

Nussbaum, M.C. 2002a. Patriotism and Cosmopolitanism, in *For Love of Country?*, edited by J. Cohen. Boston: Beacon Press, 2–17.

Nussbaum, M.C. 2002b. Capabilities and Human Rights, in *Global Justice and Transnational Politics*, edited by P. De Greiff and C. Cronin. Cambridge, MA: MIT Press, 117–49.

Parekh, B. 1999. Non-Ethnocentric Universalism, in *Human Rights in Global Politics*, edited by T. Dunne and N.J. Wheeler. Cambridge: Cambridge University Press, 128–59.

Pogge, T. 2002. *World Poverty and Human Rights*. Cambridge: Polity.

Pollock, S., Bhabha, H.K., Breckenridge, C.A. and Chakrabarty, D. 2000. Cosmopolitanisms. *Public Culture*, 12(3), 577–89.

Rawls, J. 1971. *A Theory of Justice*. Cambridge, MA: Belknap/Harvard University Press.

Rawls, J. 1993. *Political Liberalism*. New York: Columbia University Press.

Rorty, R. 1998. Human Rights, Rationality, and Sentimentality, in *Truth and Progress: Philosophical Papers, Vol. 3*. Cambridge: Cambridge University Press, 167–85.

Sen, A. 2005. *The Argumentative Indian: Writings on Indian Culture, History and Identity*. London: Penguin.

Singer, P. 2002. *One World: The Ethics of Globalization*. New Haven: Yale University Press.

Tagore, R. 1997. *Rabindranath Tagore: An Anthology*. New York: St. Martin's Press.

Tarrow, S. 2005. *The New Transnational Activism*. Cambridge: Cambridge University Press.

Žižek, S. 2005. Against Human Rights. *New Left Review*, 34, 115–31.

Zubaida, S. 2004. *Cosmopolitans, Nationalists and Fundamentalists in the Modern Middle East*. Inaugural Lecture, Birbeck College.

17

From Cosmos to Globe: Relating Cosmopolitanism, Globalization and Globality

David Inglis and Roland Robertson

Introduction

The terms cosmopolitanism and globalization are now both undoubtedly central topics within the social sciences, each being used to diagnose some of the most important and pressing issues facing the whole world today. Understanding how the terms relate to each other is an important task, precisely because they are often put to work for similar purposes, namely probing the essential characteristics of the present age, and also – especially in the case of cosmopolitanism – seeking to change the world in normatively-guided ways.

But delineating the relations that do and could pertain between cosmopolitanism and globalization is a complex task, because the terms have come to have multiple meanings – and this complexity is increased if one also takes into account the issue of diaspora which is implicated in intricate ways with both terms (Hall 2008). There has appeared in recent years a plethora of writings on cosmopolitanism (Lu 2000, Mignolo 2000, Harvey 2009), ranging from formal political and legal theories (Eckersley 2007) to accounts of multiplicitous forms of 'lived cosmopolitanism' (Pollock 2002, Nowicka and Rovisco 2009). Likewise, over the last two decades there has been a seemingly unstoppable outpouring of analyses of globalization and its consequences (Robertson and White 2003, Martell 2007). There are now multiple cosmopolitanisms in the plural (Holton 2009, Delanty 2009), just as there are today multiple understandings of globalization.

The situation is made even more complex by the general tendency to confine the study of cosmopolitanism to the Western world, such that much of East Asian history is excluded. This is particularly egregious given the vital part which that region has played in world history and also its present strategic importance. This omission excludes attention to, for example, the Japanese Enlightenment and ways in which a distinctively 'Japanese' form of elitist cosmopolitanism involved exploration of the United States and much of Europe, as well as parts of India and China (Kunitake

2009, Daikichi 1985). This kind of instrumental cosmopolitanism has been almost totally neglected in the present debate about cosmopolitanism. Ironically, this type of cosmopolitanism has some resemblance to the prescriptive, normative and methodological cosmopolitanism advocated in an arguably Eurocentric way by Ulrich Beck and his colleagues (Krossa 2009, Bhambra 2007). This is one of the reasons that led us to emphasize here the concepts of globalization, globality and glocalization, as counter-weights to overly narrow Eurocentric understandings of cosmopolitanism, for focus on such matters widens the analytic focus to the 'world as a whole', and the forms of consciousness, including putatively 'cosmopolitan' ones, to be found outside the Euro-American complex (Robertson 1995, 2007c, Holton 2009; Robertson and Krossa 2011).[1]

Nonetheless, an overview of the current cosmopolitanism literature provides a number of central connections that authors have drawn between cosmopolitanism and globalization. These are:

1. *Globalization generates conditions that are 'cosmopolitan' in nature.* Such conditions include the cosmopolitanism of the global capitalist market (for Marx's foundational account, see Renton 2001); cosmopolitan political structures and legal norms (Archibugi 2008: 85–122); cosmopolitan modes of citizenship (Turner 2002), such as 'trans-national citizenship' (Mau et al. 2008); cosmopolitan lifestyles (Calhoun 2003); cosmopolitan aesthetics (Chaney 2002); cosmopolitan cultures (Hiebert 2002); and cosmopolitan forms of consciousness (Hannerz 1990).[2] Moreover, if we look at such issues using Robertson's (1992) conception of the *global field*, we can see more clearly the cultural relativizations that produce and amplify what are today often called 'cosmopolitan' social conditions.

2. Processes conventionally labelled under the heading of 'globalization' can be understood as processes of 'cosmopolitanization', precisely insofar as these involve the problematization and undermining of boundaries both between and within nation-states (Beck 2002, Beck and Sznaider 2006). However, the degree to which nation-state boundaries are actually being broken is still very contentious. This is evident in contemporary controversies about migration (Cohen 2006, Swain 2007, Honig 2001) as well as in theses which contend that the nation-state is a central ingredient of globalization itself (Robertson 1992,

---

[1] The modern concern with cosmopolitanism arose at the same time as national consciousness was becoming particularly conspicuous, towards the end of the eighteenth century (Yoshino 1992: 54ff.). Moreover, we are becoming increasingly aware of the significance of 'world travelers' well before the European Enlightenment (for instance Colley 2007).

[2] The overwhelming concentration on connectivity in studies of globalization is enormously misleading, since global consciousness is of equal importance. One cannot be reduced to the other (Robertson 2007a, Robertson 2007b). Recent developments on the global scene – such as global awareness of climate, demographic, financial and yet other problems – demonstrate the great and increasing importance of (reflexive) global consciousness.

Holton 1998). Nation-state consolidation and assertion has been particularly evident in the present global economic crises, as well as the controversies surrounding the issues of climate change, oil exploration at the North and South Poles, and numerous other world-political phenomena. Even such an apparently transnational phenomenon as the European Union is becoming increasingly fragile and ridden by national cleavages.
3. Globalization produces needs for, and generates forms of, social science which can analyse its deepening complexity. Such forms of social science include 'cosmopolitan sociology' (Beck and Sznaider 2006) and 'global sociology' (Albrow 1990), which have the common characteristic of being furnished with cosmopolitan lenses, in the sense of having non-parochial and potentially world-encompassing foci, conceptual frameworks and research methods.
4. Globalization generates the 'need' for cosmopolitan political theories, in order to regulate or mitigate certain of the problems it throws up in its wake. Some cosmopolitan theories are explicit attempts to criticize, tame and transform conditions produced by and associated with globalization (Cheah 2006, Held 2002). In fact, globalization may well be the ultimate grounding of contemporary cosmopolitan concerns. Globalization is the ground upon, or the background against, which cosmopolitan political theories are constructed or invented. Globalization produces, and is in part constituted from, 'ecumenical sensibilities', which are the bases for more formalized 'ecumenical analytics', of which cosmopolitan political theory is one variety (Inglis and Robertson 2005).

Clearly the actual and potential relations between the terms 'cosmopolitanism' and 'globalization', and the various phenomena associated with each, are manifold. Here we will focus on what we take as the core of cosmopolitanism, namely cosmopolitan political philosophy, and its claims as to political affiliations and modes of citizenship that are somehow beyond bounded political units, be those the ancient city-state or the modern nation-state (Benhabib et al. 2007). There are certain recurring themes and motifs which have historically clustered, and still cluster, around the term 'cosmopolitanism', understood as referring to political doctrines. These are sufficiently different from the notions and symbols which tend to cluster around the term 'globalization', that despite overlaps between them, one can say that each term connotes different sets of problems and means of answering them.

Despite the present-day complexity of each term, cosmopolitanism's mainstream (or core) involves ideas about human life which are primarily 'political' in ancestry, and also synchronic and relatively static in tenor. Conversely, globalization tends to involve ideas about human life which are primarily 'historical' in nature and historiographical in ancestry, and diachronic and dynamic in orientation. This difference is already pointed to in the etymology of the terms. Cosmopolitanism comes from the Greek kosmos (cosmos) and polis (polity), and is centrally concerned with political themes, namely citizenship (being a member of some polis) and affiliation to some sort of political structure that putatively covers the whole 'cosmos'. Globalization is concerned with the 'globe' (from the Latin globus), and the dynamic, long-term historical processes that have made it ever more densely connected among its various 'parts' (however defined), such that it becomes, in certain senses, 'one place'. This condition of globality involves multiple and divergent forms of consciousness arising, which, despite their other differences, all are aware of and try to make sense of this condition, and of each other (Robertson 1992).

Thus 'cosmos' and 'globe' are the condensed symbols of two related, but nonetheless different, imaginaries. Both construe of the realm within which human life exists as in one way or another 'one place'. But for cosmopolitanism, that place – the cosmos – was always-already unified, as it refers to a conceptual space which expresses the philosophical-anthropological unity of all humankind. Globalization, by contrast, is not tied to that kind of very abstract philosophical commitment, and instead regards the construction of globality as the result of particular historical dynamics. Cosmopolitanism's primarily political-theoretical dispositions orient it to issues of citizenship. But globalization, rooted more in historiography, suggests a broader remit, which situates the political matters that concern cosmopolitanism within broader frameworks that seek to understand the intertwined political, social, economic and cultural facets of globalization and globality.[3]

Given this, globalization thinking can be seen as a necessary conceptual underpinning of cosmopolitan political theory, if the latter is to avoid over-abstraction, is to be rooted in concrete historical processes, and is to operate as a practicable set of norms rather than be purely idealistic in nature. In order to be rhetorically compelling and plausibly practicable, cosmopolitanism as political theory has to be rooted within the broader intellectual vistas furnished by globalization frames of reference. This involves moving one's field of vision from cosmos to globe.

In what follows, we will examine two central cases drawn from the history of cosmopolitan political theory, where the latter was indeed grounded within historical accounts of increasing globality:

1. Kant's cosmopolitical thought, which underpins its normative claims with an account of 'globalizing' historical processes; and
2. Durkheim's attempt to present a cosmopolitan sociological (as opposed to purely political-theoretical) position that was normatively and empirically adequate for the globalizing socio-political conditions of the late nineteenth and early twentieth century.

---

[3] We cannot explore here the broader theme of the historical-intellectual connection between cosmos and polis – as the Order of Nature and that of Society. It can simply be noted that in classical China people spoke of their country as the Celestial Kingdom, while rulers relied for their authority on the Mandate of Heaven. The same kind of relationship can be seen in ancient Babylonia, Plato's Republic, and the empire of Alexander the Great (Toulmin 1990: 67–9).

In both cases, a grounding of cosmopolitan political norms within historical analysis of developing world-conditions, meant a concretization of the former beyond pure abstractions, and so an increase in argumentative efficacy. Linking cosmopolitics to historical dynamics of (what we today call) globalization and globality, means that cosmopolitanism can avoid being seen as speculative metaphysics, as it is rooted in emerging world-conditions. Our position seeks to challenge the sometimes rather glib versions of cosmopolitanism on offer today.[4] Whereas globalization is not extensively invoked as 'a good thing' except by neoliberal evangelists, cosmopolitanism is nearly always employed in a very positive, sometimes highly utopian, way (Harvey 2009: 77–97). The millennial enthusiasm for the terms cosmopolitan and cosmopolitanism demands critical interrogation in its own right. But when cosmopolitan political theory is underpinned by more historical and sociological concerns, the risks of such utopianism are mitigated in efficacious ways.

Cosmopolis and Globality: From Plutarch to Kant

In conventional histories of cosmopolitan thought, its two great flowerings in pre-modern Western history are Greco-Roman Stoicism and eighteenth-century political theory (Heater 1996). Since Nussbaum's (1997) classic intervention, present-day cosmopolitan theory is said to take inspiration from Stoicism's focus on the universal 'brotherhood' of all persons, which leads individuals to ethical commitments to 'humanity' rather than to particular polities. The ideas of thinkers such as Cicero and Marcus Aurelius are invoked as regards their ideas of common humanity and its ethical demands, as well as their speculations about a putative 'world state' (Baldry 1965). But the history of cosmopolitan theory almost always concentrates on philosophical-anthropological and political-theoretical ideas. Another stream of Stoic-influenced thinking is ignored, namely Greek and Greco-Roman historiography which, taking its cue from the Stoic sensibilities as to the 'world as a whole', narrates how the world has become ever more interconnected among its diverse parts. Historians writing in this vein, most notably Polybius and Plutarch, have visions quite as 'global' as their philosophical counterparts, but they add to the Stoic 'ecumenical sensibilities' the 'ecumenical analytics' of studying how *historically* and *empirically* the world has come to be 'one place'. The philosophers focus on universal humanity as a general, timeless *cosmic* condition; but the historians examine the *globe*, understood as a realm characterized more and more by dense connectivity brought about by empirical political processes (Robertson and Inglis 2004, Inglis and Robertson 2004, 2005).

---

4 It should be emphasized that the vast majority of present contributors to the debate about cosmopolitanism ironically overlook its prominence in American sociology and anthropology between the 1940s to 1960s (McKinney and Loomis 1957: 12–29), Hannerz (1990) being a major exception.

Thus Plutarch (1936: 329) depicts the world-conquering activities of Alexander the Great as bringing together 'into one body all men everywhere, uniting and mixing into one great loving-cup, as it were, men's lives, their characters, their marriages, their very habits of life. He bade them all consider as their fatherland the whole inhabited earth'. Thus what Stoic political theory regards as a universal (human brotherhood) is understood by Plutarch the historian as being concretized by Alexander; and what Stoic philosophers regarded as a mere metaphor – a world-state – Plutarch claims Alexander actually constructed. The historian adds to the political-theoretical ideas an analysis of how cosmopolitan potential empirically unfolds and is embodied.

Of course, Plutarch's 'empirical' account is also highly speculative. But the point remains that ancient historiography, influenced by Stoicism, is rarely included in histories of cosmopolitan thought 'proper', even though it was a contemporaneous endeavour to add to cosmopolitan theory an empirical and concretizing dimension through reconfiguring analysis from a purely theoretical notion (cosmos) to an empirical object of analysis (globe). Our argument is that the same sort of blend of theoretical and empirical is to be found in the foundational work of Immanuel Kant (1963a, 1963b). As Williams and Booth (1996: 71) note, Kant was the 'first political philosopher of significance to emphasise the primacy of the international in understanding politics'. Kant's analytic revolution is to insist that a good and pleasant life can be lived by the citizen of a particular polity (the overwhelming focus of most previous Western political theory) only if that polity is in certain sorts of relations – of peaceful coexistence, of international cooperation – with other polities across the world. Political philosophy is regrounded upon an international and cosmopolitan basis, which derives in substantial part from Stoic notions. Since Nussbaum's (1989, 1997) influential interventions, there has been an explosion in discussions of, and attempts to refurbish for contemporary conditions, Kant's political-philosophical writings on cosmopolitanism (for instance Habermas 1997). But just as present-day authors have generally ignored the historiographical aspects of ancient thought in favour of explicitly political-philosophical themes, so too have the dimensions of Kant's thinking vis-à-vis cosmopolitanism, which are historiographical, anthropological and sociological in nature, been largely bypassed.

Kant's (1963b) programme for 'perpetual peace' among states went beyond the attempts of earlier thinkers, jurists such as Grotius and Pufendorf, to formulate basic protocols of international law. He held that republics are the best political form, as they are less bellicose than monarchies, requiring the consent of citizens to go to war, whereas monarchies can go to war wholly on the whim of the monarch (1963b: 94–5). However, he does not advocate a republican 'world state', a supranational body with authority over all states (1963b: 102). He admits that this may be the best theoretical solution to the problem of inter-state conflict (1963b: 101), but at the pragmatic level no state would accept the undermining of its own sovereign status, so the idea cannot be seriously pursued, at least currently. He also notes that this world-state could itself become despotic, overriding the rights of the particular states under its power (1963b: 113). Instead, his plan respects state sovereignty, arguing for a 'league of states', all cooperating together for the purposes of ensuring ongoing peace between themselves. He predicts that eventually all states across the world will join this league (1963b: 101). Because of his treating state sovereignty as a given, Kant's advocacy of 'world citizenship' is a restrictive one – no individual would be a citizen of a world-state. Instead, 'world citizenship' extends only as far as the condition of 'universal hospitality' – people are to be free to travel and trade where they wish, and they are not to be treated badly by the host state (1963b: 133).

Kant knew that drawing up utopian schemes of world government was impractical, as no monarch or parliament would listen to what they would regard as the fanciful outpourings of a philosopher (Friedrich 1947: 12). Kant explicitly aimed to rest his proposals for 'perpetual peace' among states on a stronger, less utopian grounding (1963b: 119). It is here that political philosophy starts to merge with historiographical considerations. Kant claimed that the ideal of which he spoke was practicable, in that human history was inevitably moving in its direction. The end-point of human societal evolution was claimed to be a condition whereby different human communities had learned to live together without conflict arising between them. The aims of the political philosopher are thus the same as those of the philosopher of history, namely to 'discover a natural purpose in this idiotic course of things human' (1963a: 12).

This position allowed Kant to take on objections from Hobbesian thinkers that human nature, inclined towards eternal dispute and dissension, would never permit a permanently pacific (that is cosmopolitan) state of affairs. Yet it was the very human orientation towards conflict itself which was the means which would drive historical development towards its eventual permanently peaceful outcome. Humans are characterized by 'unsocial sociability' – they have to live with each other, but each one constantly wants to aggrandize himself at the expense of everyone else (1963a: 15). It is this restless and ambitious aspect of human nature which drives humans onwards to ever greater achievements. It is thus Nature itself which compels human discord, but it is this discord which eventually drives humans to peaceful association with each other, first within particular states (the Hobbesian social contract), and then between states (cosmopolitan conditions). Humans would learn over time from the experience of incessant warfare that the best means of meeting their interests, individual and collective, was to engage in peaceful associations with each other, not just within particular states but in the relations between particular states too. Thus Nature eventually brings about amongst humans 'that which reason could have told them at the beginning and with far less sad experience ... to step from the lawless condition of savages into a league of nations ... [where] even the smallest state could expect security and justice ... a united power acting according to decisions reached under the laws of their united will', this 'cosmopolitan condition' pertaining throughout the world (1963a: 19, 20). Wars are means of achieving the eventual outcome of world governance, the 'last stage to which the human race must climb', the state humanity reaches when it 'works its way out of the chaotic conditions of its international relations' (1963a: 21).

There are intriguing anthropological and sociological strands in Kant's account of the development of cosmopolitan conditions, features of his writings which contemporary writers on cosmopolitan matters generally ignore. One reason as to why a cosmopolitical condition eventually arises is due to the geographical limits of the globe itself (indicating Kant's focus on globe, not cosmos). The 'right to associate', which all persons possess as a matter of natural law, comes about by virtue of every nation's 'common possession of the surface of earth, where, as a globe, they cannot infinitely disperse and hence must finally tolerate the presence of each other' (1963b: 103). The development of world history involves initial human dispersal across the planet, followed by increasing interconnection between geographically disparate parts of the world. Nature brings about eventual worldwide peaceful association through the means of inter-group conflict. It was warfare between groups which pushed some of them into even the most inhospitable icy and desert regions of the planet, such that it is 'war which Nature uses to populate the whole earth' (1963b: 110). But even in the most unfriendly terrain, from the northern tundra to Tierra del Fuego, Nature furnishes the groups so dispersed with means of gaining food, building shelter and travelling.

The next stage is that Nature, by placing 'each people near another which presses upon it', compels each group to 'form itself into a state in order to defend itself' (1963b: 111). This alone compels war, but two cultural factors also impel different nations-as-states to be hostile to each other – both 'differences of language and of religion ... involve a tendency to mutual hatred and pretexts for war'.[5] Eventually each group becomes so sickened by warfare that it feels the need to enter into the league of states. But there is another mechanism that Nature has put in place to develop eventual global harmony. Over time, international trade develops. Different states 'unite because of mutual interest. The spirit of commerce, which is incompatible with war, sooner or later gains the upper hand in every state ... states see themselves forced, without any moral urge, to promote honourable peace' (1963b: 114). The telos of world-level trading relations is that 'understanding, conventions and peaceable relations [are] established among the most distant peoples' (1963b: 110).

So the unintended consequences of geographical dispersal, warfare and trade all combine as mechanisms of generation of emerging cosmopolitan conditions. In his own time, Kant sees only the beginnings of this cosmopolitical order, but he is confident that the current situation paves 'the way for a distant international government for which there is no precedent in world history ... there is a rising feeling which each [state] has for the preservation of the whole ... [and thus] a universal cosmopolitan condition ... will come into being' (1963a: 23). He sees the beginnings of a world-level moral community, within which 'a violation of rights in one place is felt throughout the world' (1963b: 105; emphasis added). This is

---

5   Kant also briefly speculates upon the issue of intercultural influences and diffusion of practices and ideas from one culture to another – for instance he considers that certain practices at an early stage in Greek history had come there from Tibet and China (1963b: 105).

an important early anticipation of later notions of world-spanning moral culture, centred on human rights regimes. The general point is that the Kantian cosmopolitan vision roots political-philosophical notions in historical dynamics. The realization of cosmopolitical conditions involves not just a league of pacific stages, but also a world-spanning moral culture which is based around and generates sentiments of condemnation and revulsion for actions impugning globally-recognized human rights. Regardless of where those actions happen, the condemnation that follows is literally global, in that it comes from all over the world, and indeed in a certain sense it is the moral response of the whole world itself, understood as a single moral entity (1963b: 103). Here we see the significance of global consciousness as a vital ingredient of globalization. Human rights are not merely abstractly universal (level of the cosmos), but have become concretely global, at the levels of both thought and practice.

This allows Kant the grounds upon which to criticize instances whereby European states, in the processes of colonizing other parts of the world, have signally failed to observe the evolving world-level moral codes. European powers have gone to 'terrifying lengths' (1963b: 103) to subjugate other peoples, taking their lands away by cynically considering the natives as too undeveloped to be considered as the owners. Kant also criticizes the downside of international trade: its use by European powers for their own aggrandizement. In Hindustan 'under the pretence of establishing economic undertakings, they brought in foreign soldiers and used them to oppress the natives, excited widespread wars among the various states, spread famine, rebellion and perfidy, and the whole litany of evils which afflict mankind' (1963b: 104). The basis from which Kant can criticize the European powers is the emerging world-level moral culture that itself is a product of globalizing historical processes. If colonialism is a facet of globalization, so too is the planet-spanning moral culture that provides grounds for colonialism's condemnation: globalization simultaneously produces both colonialism, and the moral norms and means (for instance newspapers of global reach) for condemning it.[6]

Cosmopolitan Norms and Globality: The Case of Durkheim

In Kant, then, we find a combination of abstract claims as to cosmopolitan political and moral structures, together with historiographical endeavours to demonstrate their increasing empirical concretization and global reach. Kant is both cosmopolitan philosopher and early theorist of globalization. Cosmopolis was not just some idle dream but the emerging expression of the historical construction of an ever more densely connected world. Kant has in effect combined the figures of cosmos and globe, using the latter to explain the coming into empirical being of the former. Of course, Kant's historiography is not 'empirical' in the modern sense, for it is rooted

---

6   But for what today would be called Kant's 'racism', see Eze (1997), Robertson (2006).

in a speculative philosophy of history. However, the point remains that his overall project was a fusion of cosmopolitan ideals with historical dynamics. The same can be said of the next figure we examine, Émile Durkheim (Inglis and Robertson 2008). Durkheim's reworking of Kant at the level of epistemology is well known (Inglis 2007), but his indebtedness to, and reworking of Kant's political theoretical/historical position on cosmopolitanism, is much less attested. His *oeuvre* indicates how cosmopolitanism and globality can be theorized together, and indeed be conceived of as inseparable.

Durkheim's cosmopolitanism has been the subject of significant interest in recent years, among those seeking to defend classical sociology against charges of naively held 'methodological nationalism' (Chernilo 2006, 2007). Instead of taking the nation-state as its main unit of analysis, as some critics (for instance Beck 2000) have charged, classical sociology, especially its Durkheimian variant, is said to possess a cosmopolitan vision that Turner (2006: 133) describes as challenging the nationalist assumptions of the time (also Fine 2003: 467). Although Turner refers to Durkheim's 'cosmopolitan sociology', it would actually be better to describe the relevant features of Durkheim's thinking as the latter's cosmopolitan political philosophy, albeit a philosophy thoroughly underpinned by sociological conceptualization. The cosmopolitan political philosophy expresses some of the more Comtean and international-socialist dimensions of Durkheim's thinking. These are summed up in an address given at the Paris Universal Exposition of 1900:

> *Doubtless, we have towards the country in its present form, and of which we in fact form part, obligations that we do not have the right to cast off. But beyond this country, there is another in the process of formation, enveloping our national country: that of Europe, or humanity.* (Cited at Lukes 1973: 350)

Durkheim's central text that explores these issues derives from the series of lectures on morality and politics he gave in Bordeaux between 1890 and 1900, repeated at the Sorbonne in 1904 and 1912, and published posthumously as *Professional Ethics and Civic Morals* (Durkheim 1992). There Durkheim considers the apparently contradictory notion of 'world patriotism'. This does not involve modes of affiliation to a putative 'world state'. Like Kant, he does admit the possibility that at some future period, there could arise a situation where 'humanity in its entirety [was] organized as a [single] society'. However, he notes that 'such an idea, while not altogether beyond realization, must be set in so distant a future that we can leave it out of our present reckoning' (1992: 74). He then develops the concept of 'world patriotism', taking into account the apparently rigid realities of the contemporary international system, while attempting to raise this system to a higher moral and ethical level, strongly echoing Kant's similar efforts. Each state would encourage the highest moral sentiments among its citizens. Each national government would endeavour 'not to expand, or to lengthen its borders, but to set its own house in order and to make the widest appeal to its members for a moral life on an ever higher level' (1992: 74). Consequently 'civic duties would be only a particular form of the general obligations of humanity' (1992: 74). Durkheim here points towards some sort of 'world culture', constituted of certain – as yet unspecified – moral and ethical codes, which are both contributed to by particular nation-states and which are, when they have become part of an acknowledged 'world culture', taken on board by all of them in turn, albeit with specific national colourings, as regards the cultivation of the aspirations of their citizens.

Certain positions in present-day social thought draw inspiration from, or are akin to, Durkheim's remarks. Appiah's (1996) concept of 'cosmopolitan patriots' argues that a sense of belonging to a particular (national or local) community is necessary for actors to achieve more 'cosmopolitan' political goals. Habermas (2001) depicts 'constitutional patriotism' as a way of reconciling actors' orientations and responsibilities towards 'cosmopolitical' institutions like the UN, with their feelings of national identity. Virtuous nationalism compels respect towards the cosmopolitical moral and institutional order (Fine 2003: 462). These explicit or implicit debts to Durkheim on behalf of these scholars and others like them allows Turner (2006: 141) to claim that 'in equating what he called "true patriotism" with cosmopolitanism, Durkheim anticipated the modern debate about republicanism, patriotism and cosmopolitanism by almost a century'.

Durkheim's presentation of cosmopolitan patriotism exists primarily within political philosophy, being a series of reflections of what should be the case, rather than what currently is the case. The various European countries 'have not yet reached the point when this kind of patriotism could prevail without dissent, if indeed such a time would ever come' (Durkheim 1992: 75). But Durkheim, like Kant, wishes to root his political philosophy in an account of what he takes to be emerging world-level social conditions that could further foster cosmopolitan modes of citizenship. Turner (1990: 347) has argued that for obvious pragmatic reasons compelled by the international political situation, at the outbreak of the First World War Durkheim in part turned away from such 'cosmopolitan' reflections towards 'the idea of nationalism as a modern version of more traditional sources of the conscience collective'. This is true in part. But the onset of war did not compel Durkheim to drop the world patriotism position entirely, as it was a potent resource for anti-German sentiment. In the 1915 pamphlet 'Germany above all' (Durkheim 1915), the German state's aggressive behaviour is shown to be driven by a narrow and chauvinistic nationalism antithetical to 'world patriotism'. It is morally condemnable because it goes against the norms of – the empirically existing, if rudimentary, contemporary version of – 'world culture'. German elites of the nineteenth century were contributors to this world-level moral culture (Durkheim 1915: 4). But their subsequent instigation of the war, and their brutal treatment of combatants and civilians, meant a total failure to meet their responsibilities as members of the global moral community, making Germany a renegade state.

Durkheim seems to have thought that in order to make a convincing case for the existence of world moral culture, and to be able to condemn serious departures from it, he had to show the empirical mechanisms whereby it had come into existence, moving from political philosophy to historiography and sociology. Read in a certain way, this is precisely what the masterwork *The Elementary Forms of the*

Religious Life (Durkheim 2001 [1912]) set out to achieve. In other work (Inglis and Robertson 2008) we have demonstrated how an embryonic theory of globalization and globality is contained in its later chapters, and this underpins his views on world moral culture and political cosmopolitanism. These later chapters depart quite considerably from the strong emphasis on 'society' – a bounded, territorial unit with strong symbolic boundaries – found in the earlier chapters. What emerges is an account of the sociological (implicitly historical) reasons whereby a world-spanning moral culture can develop, and has actually developed, over time. The Australian aboriginal ethnographic material is deployed to show that 'religious universalism' – a condition whereby a particular belief system claims to have authority over, and relevance for, more than one 'national' group – is found not just in the 'world religions' but 'at the summit' of Australian aboriginal religion too. Durkheim argues that in Australia, particular gods are recognized by multiple tribes and so 'their cult is, in a sense, international' (2001 [1912]: 321; emphasis added).

Neighbouring tribes cannot over the long term avoid contact with each other. They become ever more systematically interlinked, primarily through the means of commerce on the one hand, and group inter-marriage on the other. They enter into a condition where they become ever more conscious of what aspects of life they have in common, and 'mutual [cultural] borrowings ... serve to reinforce' this sense of 'international' commonality (*ibid.*). With the increasing interpenetration of hitherto distinct tribal groups at the material level (a rudimentary form of emergent organic solidarity), the 'international gods' referred to are born. At the wholly ideational level, each tribe's idea of a god fuses with the ideas of the other tribes they are in systematic and interpenetrating contact with, and the resulting 'international god' is made manifest as an idea in the minds of all participants. Thus the 'international gods' are products of a 'hybridization' of distinct tribal ('national') traditions. The 'international gods' are above all gods of initiation ceremonies. As such they are generated through the initiation rituals held at 'intertribal assemblies'. At these assemblies 'sacred beings were ... formed that were not fixed to any geographically fixed society'. The geography they correspond to, and are produced by, is inter-tribal, that is to say 'international', does not have clear borders, and conceptually speaking is 'spread over an unlimited area'. The gods that correspond to this territory have the same character as the territory itself: 'their sphere of influence is not circumscribed; they glide above the particular tribes and above space. They are the great international gods' (Durkheim 2001 [1912]: 321, also McCoy 1980).

Durkheim's key argument in the earlier parts of *The Elementary Forms* was that a territorially-bounded 'society' produces a body of religious beliefs which express the structure of that society. Thus we would expect that 'international society' produces a body of beliefs – about, and symbolized by, the 'international gods' – which reflect its nature too. If 'national' religions are the necessary preconditions for effective social functioning within a given bounded 'society', then the functioning of 'international society' would also seem to depend on its 'religious' expressions, both in the guiding of individual actions through norms, and in the carving up of 'reality' through its cognitive lenses. One might expect that an 'international religion' does its conceptual carving up of reality in ways that are more 'cosmopolitan' than those of 'national' religions, especially given that it is, at least in some ways, a 'hybrid' entity.

From these ideas, Durkheim sought to analyse the emerging world-spanning social and cultural conditions of his day. He notes that in his time,

> *there is no people, no state, that is not involved with another society that is more or less unlimited and includes all peoples ... There is no national life that is not dominated by an inherently international collective life. As we go forward in history, these international groupings take on greater importance and scope.* (Durkheim 2001 [1912]: 322)

What Durkheim points towards here are the historical-sociological reasons for the development of a world-level moral culture, a cosmopolitan ethical condition, involving cosmopolitical forms of citizenship mediated through the citizenship structures of the nation-state. The 'globalizing' transformation of aboriginal life reveals the fundamental mechanisms of growing organic solidarity, inter-group assembly and cultural hybridization that have generated cosmopolitan moral cultures in the aboriginal past, and are producing them now and in the future at a truly global level. Just as Kant had proffered historical reasons for the generation of cosmopolitan moral culture, so too does Durkheim. His remarks on cosmopolitan moral culture are simultaneously empirical and normative, in the same manner as Kant's.[7] They both transcend boundaries between political philosophy, and historiography and sociology. The political-philosophical concern with world patriotism has been dubbed by Turner and others as 'cosmopolitan sociology'. But Durkheim's position is better described as a normatively-informed sociology of globality, for it is sociological analysis of the historical development of globality which underpins the account of cosmopolitan morality and affiliation. It is the empirical condition of expanding globality that makes possible the cosmopolitical moral order and modes of activity associated with it.

Conclusion

Too often in discussions of cosmopolitanism, matters are framed as if cosmopolitan political theories need now to be made more concrete and rooted in empirical circumstances, as if all of their early progenitors had never endeavoured to do this themselves. But following the lead of some strands in ancient historiography, two of the greatest cosmopolitan thinkers, Kant and Durkheim, had already endeavoured to do this, in manners notably similar to each other, to the extent that we may refer without too much overemphasis to Durkheim as the Kant of the early twentieth

---

7   Although Durkheim's historiography is generated from anthropological data treated in evolutionary fashion, rather than directly rooted in a philosophy of history.

century. Both endeavoured to transcend the boundaries of genre and discipline, to conjoin cosmopolitical morality with global dynamics, to transcend the abstractions of 'cosmos' by moving to the more concrete considerations of 'globe'. Today it is still too often the case that cosmopolitan political thinking remains overly relatively disconnected from understandings of globalization and globality, even though it makes sense to understand the latter as generating, or at least making possible, the former, and its embodiments in actual institutions and practices.

Reconsidering the history of cosmopolitan thinking demonstrates that connecting cosmopolitan theoretical considerations with globalizing empirical actualities was already a concern of the classical thinkers. The valuable lesson we need to learn from them is that the politics of cosmos need always to be considered in light of the empirical processes that both go on across the globe, and which render it into one distinct, but vastly multiplicitous and heterogeneous, entity. This is especially crucial if claims to global justice and aspirations to new forms of post-national citizenship are ever to be more than phantasms of the intellect.

Bibliography

Albrow, M. 1990. Introduction, in *Globalization, Knowledge and Society*, edited by M. Albrow and E. King. London: Sage/International Sociological Association, 3–16.
Appiah, K.A. 1996. Cosmopolitan patriots, in *For Love of Country: Debating the Limits of Patriotism*, edited by J. Cohen. Cambridge: Beacon, 21–9.
Archibugi, D. 2008. *The Global Commonwealth of Citizens: Toward Cosmopolitan Democracy*. Princeton: Princeton University Press.
Baldry, H.C. 1965. *The Unity of Mankind in Greek Thought*. Cambridge: Cambridge University Press.
Beck, U. 2000. *What Is Globalization?* Cambridge: Polity.
Beck, U. 2002. The cosmopolitan society and its enemies. *Theory, Culture and Society*, 19(1–2), 17–44.
Beck, U. and Sznaider, N. 2006. Unpacking cosmopolitanism for the social sciences: a research agenda. *British Journal of Sociology*, 57(1), 1–23.
Benhabib, S., Shapiro, I. and Petranovic, D. (eds). 2007. *Identities, Affiliations, and Allegiances*. Cambridge: Cambridge University Press.
Bhambra, G. 2007. *Rethinking Modernity: Postcolonialism and the Sociological Imagination*. Basingstoke: Palgrave.
Calhoun, C. 2003. The class consciousness of frequent travellers: towards a critique of actually existing cosmopolitanism, in *Debating Cosmopolitics*, edited by D. Archibugi. London: Verso, 86–116.
Chaney, D. 2002. Cosmopolitan art and cultural citizenship. *Theory, Culture, and Society*, 19(1–2), 157–74.
Cheah, P. 2006. *Inhuman Conditions: On Cosmopolitanism and Human Rights*. Cambridge, MA: Harvard University Press.

Chernilo, D. 2006. Social theory's methodological nationalism: myth and reality. *European Journal of Social Theory*, 9(5), 5–22.
Chernilo, D. 2007. A quest for universalism: re-assessing the nature of classical social theory's cosmopolitanism. *European Journal of Social Theory*, 10(1), 17–35.
Cohen, R. 2006. *Migration and its Enemies: Global Capital, Migrant Labour and the Nation State*. Aldershot: Ashgate.
Colley, L. 2007. *The Ordeal of Elizabeth Marsh: How a Remarkable Woman Crossed Seas and Empires to Become Part of World History*. London: HarperCollins.
Daikichi, I. 1985. *The Culture of the Meiji Period*. Princeton: Princeton University Press.
Delanty, G. 2009. *The Cosmopolitan Imagination: The Renewal of Critical Social Theory*. Cambridge: Cambridge University Press.
Durkheim, É. 1915. *Germany Above All: German Mentality and War*. Paris: Librairie Armand Colin.
Durkheim, É. 1992. *Professional Ethics and Civic Morals*, trans. by Cornelia Brookfield. London: Routledge.
Durkheim, É. 2001 [1912]. *The Elementary Forms of Religious Life*, trans. by Carol Gosman. New York: Oxford University Press.
Eckersley, R. 2007. From cosmopolitan nationalism to cosmopolitan democracy. *Review of International Studies*, 33, 675–92.
Eze, E. (ed.). 1997. *Race and the Enlightenment*. Oxford: Blackwell.
Fine, R. 2003. Taking the 'ism' out of cosmopolitanism: an essay in reconstruction. *European Journal of Social Theory*, 6(4), 451–70.
Friedrich, C.J. 1947. The ideology of the united nations charter and the philosophy of peace of Immanuel Kant 1795–1945. *Journal of Politics*, 9(1), 10–30.
Habermas, J. 1997. Kant's idea of perpetual peace, with the benefit of two hundred years hindsight, in *Perpetual Peace: Essays on Kant's Cosmopolitan Ideal*, edited by J. Bohman and M. Lutz-Bachmann. Cambridge, MA: MIT Press, 113–54.
Habermas, J. 2001. *The Postnational Constellation: Political Essays*. Cambridge: Polity.
Hall, S. 2008. Cosmopolitanism, globalisation and diaspora: Stuart Hall in conversation with Pnina Werbner, in *Anthropology and the New Cosmopolitanism*, edited by P. Werbner. Oxford: Berg, 345–60.
Hannerz, U. 1990. Cosmopolitans and locals in world culture, in *Global Culture*, edited by M. Featherstone. London: Sage, 237–51.
Harvey, D. 2009. *Cosmopolitanism and the Geographies of Freedom*. New York: Columbia University Press.
Heater, D. 1996. *World Citizenship and Government: Cosmopolitan Ideas in the History of Western Political Thought*. London: Macmillan.
Held, D. 2002. Culture and political community: national, global, and cosmopolitan, in *Conceiving Cosmopolitanism*, edited by S. Vertovec and R. Cohen. Oxford: Oxford University Press, 48–58.
Hiebert, D. 2002. Cosmopolitanism at the local level: the development of transnational neighbourhoods, in *Conceiving Cosmopolitanism*, edited by S. Vertovec and R. Cohen. Oxford: Oxford University Press, 209–23.
Holton, R. 1998. *Globalization and the Nation-State*. Basingstoke: Macmillan.

Holton, R. 2009. *Cosmopolitanisms: New Thinking and New Directions*. Basingstoke: Palgrave.
Honig, B. 2001. *Democracy and the Foreigner*. Princeton: Princeton University Press.
Inglis, D. 2007. The warring twins: sociology, cultural studies, alterity and sameness. *History of the Human Sciences*, 20(2), 99–122.
Inglis, D. and Robertson, R. 2004. Beyond the gates of the *polis*: reworking the classical roots of classical sociology. *Journal of Classical Sociology*, 4(2), 165–89.
Inglis, D. and Robertson, R. 2005. The ecumenical analytic: 'globalization', reflexivity and the revolution in Greek historiography. *European Journal of Social Theory*, 8(2), 99–122.
Inglis, D. and Robertson, R. 2008. The elementary forms of globality: Durkheim and the emergence and nature of global life. *Journal of Classical Sociology*, 8(1), 5–25.
Kant, I. 1963a. Idea for a universal history from a cosmopolitan point of view, in *On History*, edited by L.W. Beck. New York: Bobbs-Merrill, 11–26.
Kant, I. 1963b. Perpetual peace, in *On History*, edited by L.W. Beck. New York: Bobbs-Merrill, 85–135.
Krossa, A.S. 2009. Conceptualising European society on non-normative grounds: logic of sociation, glocalisation, and conflict. *European Journal of Social Theory*, 12(2), 249–64.
Kunitake, K. 2009. *Japan Rising: The Iwakura Embassy to the USA and Europe*. Cambridge: Cambridge University Press.
Lu, C. 2000. The one and many faces of cosmopolitanism. *The Journal of Political Philosophy*, 8(2), 244–67.
Lukes, S. 1973. *Emile Durkheim: his Life and Work. A Historical and Critical Survey*. London: Allen Lane.
McCoy, C. 1980. *When Gods Change: Hope For Theology*. Nashville: Abingdon.
McKinney, J. and Loomis, C. 1957. The application of gemeinschaft and gesellschaft as related to other typologies: the typological tradition, in *Community and Society*, edited by F. Tonnies. New York: Harper, 12–29.
Martell, L. 2007. The third wave in globalization theory. *International Studies Review*, 9(2), 173–96.
Mau, S., Mewes, J. and Zimmerman, A. 2008. Cosmopolitan attitudes through transnational social practices. *Global Networks*, 8(1), 1–24.
Mignolo, W. 2000. The many faces of cosmopolis: border thinking and critical cosmopolitanism. *Public Culture*, 12(3), 721–48.
Nowicka, M. and Rovisco, M. (eds). 2009. *Cosmopolitanism in Practice*. Farnham: Ashgate.
Nussbaum, M. 1989. Recoiling from reason. *New York Review of Books*, 36(19), www.nybooks.com/articles/archives/1989/dec/07/recoiling-from-reason.
Nussbaum, M. 1997. Kant and stoic cosmopolitanism. *Journal of Political Philosophy*, 5(1), 1–25.
Plutarch. 1936. *Moralia*, vol. III. Cambridge, MA: Loeb.
Pollock, S. 2002. Cosmopolitan and vernacular in history, in *Cosmopolitanism*, edited by C.A. Breckenridge, S. Pollock, H.K. Bhabha and D. Chakrabarty. Durham, NC: Duke University Press, 15–53.

Renton, D. 2001. *Marx on Globalization*. London: Verso.
Robertson, R. 1992. *Globalization: Social Theory and Global Culture*. London: Sage.
Robertson, R. 1995. Glocalization: time-space and homogeneity-heterogeneity, in *Global Modernities*, edited by M. Featherstone, S. Lash and R. Robertson. London: Sage, 345-66.
Robertson, R. 2006. Civilization. *Theory Culture & Society*, 23(2-3), 421-7.
Robertson, R. 2007a. Global consciousness, in *Encyclopedia of Globalization*, vol. 2, edited by R. Robertson and J.A. Scholte. New York: MTM/Routledge, 502-7.
Robertson, R. 2007b. Globality, in *Encyclopedia of Globalization*, vol. 2, edited by R. Robertson and J.A. Scholte. New York: MTM/Routledge, 524-6.
Robertson, R. 2007c. Glocalization, in *Encyclopedia of Globalization*, vol. 2, edited by R. Robertson and J.A. Scholte. New York: MTM/Routledge, 545-8.
Robertson, R. and Inglis, D. 2004. The global *animus*: in the tracks of world-consciousness. *Globalizations*, 1(1), 38-49.
Robertson, R. and Krossa, A.S. (eds) (forthcoming). *European Cosmopolitanism in Question*. Basingstoke: Palgrave Macmillan.
Robertson, R. and White, K. (eds). 2003. *Globalization: Critical Concepts in Sociology*. London: Routledge.
Swain, C. (ed.). 2007. *Debating Immigration*. Cambridge: Cambridge University Press.
Toulmin, S. 1990. *Cosmopolis: The Hidden Agenda of Modernity*. Chicago: University of Chicago Press.
Turner, B.S. 1990. The two faces of sociology: global or national. *Theory Culture & Society*, 7(3-4), 317-32.
Turner, B.S. 2002. Cosmopolitan virtue, globalization and patriotism. *Theory Culture & Society*, 19(1-2), 45-63.
Turner, B.S. 2006. Classical sociology and cosmopolitanism: a critical defence of the social. *British Journal of Sociology*, 57(1), 133-51.
Williams, M.C. and Booth, K. 1996. Kant: theorist beyond limits, in *Classical Theories in International Relations*, edited by I. Clark and I.B. Neumann. Basingstoke: Palgrave, 71-98.
Yoshino, K. 1992. *Cultural Nationalism in Contemporary Japan*. London: Routledge.

Cosmopolitanism and Postcolonial Critique

Gurminder K. Bhambra

Introduction

The paradigms of postcolonialism and cosmopolitanism have emerged in recent times offering different responses to similar questions, the most pertinent, perhaps, being: how do we, with our manifest differences, live together in the world?[1] While the two approaches have been articulated and elaborated in a number of disciplines, my concern in this chapter is with their sociological expression in the context of a global world. In work spanning the first decade of the twenty-first century, Ulrich Beck (2000, 2006) has argued that a cosmopolitan approach is necessary to engage critically with globalization. As such, cosmopolitanism, for him, is defined explicitly in terms of a global world society, separate and distinct from the age of nation-states which preceded it (and which gave rise to the intellectual tradition of cosmopolitanism he uses).

Globalization has often been regarded as a synonym for modernization or Westernization and so it is not surprising that ideas of the global have similarly been equated with the modern West. In recent years modernization theory, with its assumption of global convergence to an explicitly Western model, has been supplanted by the approach of multiple modernities (Eisenstadt 2000). Within this theory, the modern is understood as encompassing divergent paths, with the diversity of cultures in the world giving rise to a multiplicity of modernities. Beck (2006) allies his version of cosmopolitanism with the global understood as multiple modernities and so cosmopolitanism confronts the modern world as, potentially, a multicultural world. This raises the question of cosmopolitanism's relation to multiculturalism.

In what follows, I shall take issue with Beck's cosmopolitanism because of its inability to deal with issues raised by a multicultural world deriving from a

---

1   The literature on both postcolonialism and cosmopolitanism is vast. As an indicative guide, see Bhabha (1994), Gutmann (1994), Nussbaum (1996), Loomba (1998), Vertovec and Cohen (2002), Fine (2007).

'Eurocentric' definition of the cosmopolitan.[2] He is not alone in his 'Eurocentric' definition of cosmopolitanism; in fact, in this regard, as we shall see, he is typical rather than unusual. However, what does make his work distinctive is that he places his argument in the context of an embrace of the idea of 'multiple modernities' and in criticism of 'multiculturalism', both of which are central to my concerns. If we can now understand dominant approaches as Eurocentric, it is because of new voices emerging in wider political arenas and in the academy itself, which might now be regarded as beginning to emerge as a 'multicultural' space. More specifically, I argue that postcolonial scholarship, with its critique of Eurocentrism in particular, provides more adequate resources for making sense of our contemporary world (Bhambra 2007a). The demise of colonialism as an explicit political formation has given rise to understandings of postcoloniality and, perhaps ironically, an increased recognition of the role of colonialism in the formation of the modern world and its associated concepts. Scholars such as Homi Bhabha (1994) and Walter Mignolo (2000) argue for the necessity of postcolonial or decolonial understandings as integral to the opening out and questioning of the assumptions of these dominant discourses. Such recognition, I suggest, is not present in most contemporary discourses on cosmopolitanism; what is required instead is a form of provincialized cosmopolitanism.

Cosmopolitan Eurocentrism?

What appears striking in not just the sociological, but also the wider academic literature on cosmopolitanism, is the extent to which 'being cosmopolitan' (as a practice) is associated with being *in* the West and cosmopolitanism (as an idea) is seen as being *of* the West.[3] As will be discussed later in this chapter, by writing out the wider contexts within which ideas and practices are located, a particular cultural homogeneity is assumed and this becomes a standard of universal significance. Anthony Pagden, for example, writes:

> it is hard to see how any form of "cosmopolitanism" can be made to address the difficulties of the modern world if it does not in some sense begin where Kant [and the Stoics] ... began, that is with some vision of a community of "the wise" whose views must in the end triumph ... In the modern world it is equally hard to see, at least in the immediate future, that those views can be anything other than the reflection of the values of western liberal democracies. (2000: 19)

---

2   The terms 'Europe' or 'Eurocentric' are used in this chapter as continuous with central aspects of North American social and political undertakings.
3   This section is informed by arguments made in Bhambra (2010).

With this, Pagden asserts the origin of 'cosmopolitanism' – both as idea and as practice – in the history of what he claims as European, or, more generally, Western thought and draws a direct link between that history and our present – again, here, in the West. This is a parochial reading of cosmopolitanism which betrays the very ideals that the concept expresses. The issues with the claims made here are twofold. First, there is a refusal to acknowledge that there have been cosmopolitan practices and the development of cosmopolitan ideas in other parts of the world outside of European contact, in relation to European contact, and not subordinate to it (see, for example, Bhabha 1994, Pollock et al. 2000). Second, there is no engagement with the problematic tension brought to the fore when we (*if, we*) address contemporaneous European domination over much of the world as the very real negation of the idea and ideals of cosmopolitanism otherwise put forward.

Even scholars critical of the standard forms of cosmopolitanism as expressed by Pagden, often remain circumscribed to a particular geographical territory and intellectual tradition in their exposition of a critical cosmopolitanism. Muthu (2003), for example, develops a sustained argument for 'Enlightenment against Empire', the title of his monograph, in which he uses the relatively lesser known (or 'underappreciated') resources of Enlightenment thinkers to elucidate the largely unacknowledged anti-imperialist strand within their philosophies of cosmopolitanism. Fine, in turn, presents a critical engagement with modern cosmopolitanism and seeks to reinstate it within the tradition of *social* theory as distinct from the natural law tradition from which it is said to emanate (2007: 133–4).

Yet, while opening up the space to consider the standard histories of cosmopolitanism differently, these histories also reproduce what it is that they are counter to and, in many cases, what *is* reproduced – even in the work of scholars who may not wish consciously to do so – is a European genealogy. It is not that forms of universalism are peculiar to Europe, but that Europe seems to have real difficulties with the universalism it espouses. While scholars argue for the universalism of what are assumed to be European categories, they then rarely acknowledge the processes through which that universalization is enacted, processes of colonization and imperialism for the most part. Nor do they address the forms of cosmopolitanism that have emerged in non-European contexts. As a consequence, they limit the possibility of cosmopolitanism properly to be understood 'cosmopolitan-ly'.

From Modernization to (Cosmopolitan) Multiple Modernities

Beck's (2000, 2006) argument for a cosmopolitan approach is based on his critique of the contemporary state of the social sciences. He argues that disciplines such as sociology and political science have been historically bound to nation-states in their emergence and development such that they are no longer adequate to the task of dealing with the problems and processes that emerge at the level of the 'global' world that is now increasingly our common fate. He highlights the increasing number of social processes that are no longer contained within national boundaries and suggests that, as a consequence, 'world society' should now be the starting point of sociological and other research. His argument is based on a perceived transition from a process of singular 'modernization' to one giving rise to co-existing 'multiple modernities'. This shift is understood by Beck as a shift from the first age of modernity – that is, one shaped by nation-states – to a second, global cosmopolitan, age.

Increasing recognition of the global context of sociology is evident in recent arguments against the supposed methodological nationalism of the past (although, see Chernilo 2007, for a qualification of this interpretation applied to past sociological discourse). This view is supported by a shift within sociology more generally towards the paradigm of multiple modernities as a more adequate frame within which to understand global, and globalizing, processes. Key to this development has been the work of Shmuel Eisenstadt (2000, 2001) in conjunction with a core group of European historical sociologists such as Johann Arnason (2000, 2003), Bjorn Wittrock (1998) and Peter Wagner (2001).[4] In essence, they have argued that the problem with earlier modernization theory was that it understood modernization as a singular, unidirectional process that emerged in the West and, in its diffusion globally, brought other societies and cultures into line with its own presuppositions. Modernization was believed to have initiated a process of convergence and homogenization globally such that the rest of the world would, one day, become modernized, that is, Westernized. However, towards the latter part of the twentieth century there has been a growing realization that modernization was not coming to pass as had been expected in the heyday of modernization theory (Eisenstadt and Schluchter 1998).

The emergence of multiple modernities, then, came in the context of scholars beginning to appreciate that the differences manifest in the world were not, as had previously been believed, simply archaic differences that would disappear through gradual modernization. Instead, there was an appreciation that societies could modernize differently and that these differences, for theorists of multiple modernity, now represented the different ways in which societies adapted to processes of modernization. There was still a belief that modernity was, in its origins, a European phenomenon, but now, the argument is that in its diffusion outwards it interacted with the different traditions of different cultures and societies and brought into being a multiplicity of modernities. These modernities are defined in terms of a central institutional core that was taken from the European experience and the particular cultural inflections of that core as it was interpreted through the cultures present in other places. Beck concurs with this analysis by arguing that 'the Western claim to a monopoly on modernity is broken and the history and

---

[4] See the two special issues of *Daedalus*: 'Early Modernities', *Daedalus* 127 (1998) and 'Multiple Modernities', *Daedalus* 129 (2000). For further details on the sociological debates on modernization and the shift to multiple modernities, see chapter 3 of my *Rethinking Modernity: Postcolonialism and the Sociological Imagination* (Bhambra 2007a).

situation of diverging modernities in all parts of the world come into view' (2000: 87). The global age, then, is necessarily perceived as being a *multicultural* age, given that multiple modernities are said to be the expression of cultural differences.

Beck (2006) follows the multiple modernities paradigm in its general analysis, but his call for a *second age* of modernity, and what follows from this, is distinct and, I will argue, contradictory. In this age, he argues, not only is modernity now multiple, but the concepts which had been in use in developing sociological understandings in the first age are no longer adequate to the task. This is primarily a consequence of the fact that the standard concepts of the social sciences, according to Beck, were developed to understand a world of nation-states and now that we are in a global world, these concepts are no longer appropriate. What is needed is a new set of categories and concepts that would emerge from reflection upon this new cosmopolitan second age of modernity. While I have also argued that sociological concepts are inappropriately bounded – specifically, that they are 'methodologically Eurocentric',[5] rather than methodologically nationalistic – this is not something that is *only now* becoming problematic as a supposedly 'first modernity' has given way to a contemporary now-globalized world.

Such an approach, I suggest, is as limited as the state-centred approaches under criticism as it is based on the idea that the concepts of the first age of modernity were appropriate to that age and that the only problem is with the application of those concepts to the present and the future (for discussion, see Chernilo 2007, Fine 2007). At a minimum, however, the 'first age of modernity' is as much characterized by empires as by nation-states and so the concepts of that age would be, by that token, as inadequate in their own time as they are claimed to be today. There is little acknowledgement in Beck's work that if certain understandings are seen as problematic today then there is also an issue of whether they were not also problematic in the past and have, in fact, led to misunderstandings of the nature of the present in terms of how it has arisen from that past (for discussion, see Holmwood 1997). As such, the concepts of first age modernity require a more thorough overhaul than Beck proposes in his simple shift to a cosmopolitan second age.

Another significant problem with Beck's call for more appropriate sociological concepts is that his version of cosmopolitanism is at odds with the global age he describes. To the extent that multiple modernities, as the contemporary condition of the global world, are predicated on cultural inflections of modernity, then the world has to be understood as a multicultural world. Beck's version of cosmopolitanism, however, is set out in both explicit and implicit opposition, if not downright hostility, to understandings of multiculturalism. These issues will be discussed in further detail in the following section.

---

5   I owe the coining of this term to Peo Hansen.

Cosmopolitanism and Multiculturalism

While Beck argues for the singular Western claim on modernity to have been broken and suggests that it is necessary to engage with divergent modernities, the place of Others within his new cosmopolitan paradigm is not straightforward. Cosmopolitanism, for him (Beck and Grande 2007), is something if not already achieved in Europe is nonetheless defined by the European experience. Its intellectual genealogy is seen to be European as is its political practice. In particular, Beck (2003) argues that the project of a 'peace-loving' Europe, which emerged in the wake of the Second World War, was a cosmopolitan project and one that was the political antithesis of the destructive nationalism that had culminated in the Holocaust. Europe, he suggests, was now to be 'motivated by clear ideas of inviolable human dignity, and of the moral duty to relieve the suffering of others' (Beck 2003). This duty appears not to apply, however, when those Others exist outside of commonly acknowledged European frontiers, or commonly accepted understandings of 'being European' (see Weber 1995, Ehrkamp and Leitner 2003, Saharso 2007). Quite apart from other anti-colonial struggles involving European states, as Hansen argues, not even a war fought *within Europe* – the Algerian–French War, 1954–62, which resulted in the deaths of over a million people and engaged approximately half a million French troops – 'has been able to impinge on the notion of European integration as a symbol of peace' (2002: 488); or as a symbol of cosmopolitanism in practice.

In the contemporary context, there appears to be little recognition of the potential discrimination against those subject to the face veil ban being proposed in France and other European countries (see BBC 2010). What purchase does the idea of 'Europe' and its supposedly distinctive civic traditions have on cosmopolitanism when a number of states seek to repress the exercise of religious freedom of some of its citizens through an over-zealous attention to the clothes that women choose to wear? The political debates regarding 'banning the burkha' (see Saharso 2007), call into question the depth of the cosmopolitan commitment within Europe that is otherwise, for Beck, seen to be one of its defining features. The issue, as I will go on to suggest, is that Beck's cosmopolitanism is a cosmopolitanism of similarly constituted individuals that is unable to accommodate Others within its conceptual or political frameworks. In fact, Beck addresses the issue of multiculturalism by pointing to its inherent incompatibility with the idea of cosmopolitanism.[6] He sets up the difference between the two in the following terms.

Multiculturalism, according to Beck, asserts a world of variety and plurality while at the same time presenting humanity as a collectivity divided on cultural grounds. Individuals within this conception, he continues, are seen as the product of their own languages, traditions, customs and landscapes and have an attachment to their homeland which 'is regarded as a closed, self-sufficient and sacrosanct unity' (2002: 36–7). This entails a defence of that homeland 'naturally' against

---

[6] For a discussion of the relationship between cosmopolitanism and multiculturalism, see Stevenson (2002); see also Gutmann (1994).

imperialism, but also, he suggests, against 'miscegenation, internationalization, and cosmopolitanism' (2002: 37).[7] This then leads to the conclusion, again without any substantiation, that 'multiculturalism is at loggerheads with individualization' and that, within multiculturalism, 'the individual does not exist', being simply an 'epiphenomenon of his culture' (2002: 37). Cosmopolitanism, however, Beck suggests, 'argues the reverse and *presupposes* individualization' (2002: 37). However, Beck does not elaborate on how a cosmopolitanism of individuals is accommodated within a vision of the world as otherwise structured by different cultures. The concept of 'multiple modernities', as suggested earlier, expresses a form of global multiculturalism; cosmopolitanism, then, must also be a cultural issue, and one that, for Beck, is the expression of European culture. In this way, Beck's cosmopolitan version of multiple modernities is more thorough-going in its Eurocentrism than the simple version embodied in multiple modernities.

In a subsequent article, Beck and Grande develop the cosmopolitan perspective by arguing that 'it is vital to perceive others [both] as different and as the same', but without lapsing into postmodern particularism (2007: 71). In other words, the active cosmopolitan tolerance of Others has to be balanced by 'a certain amount of commonly shared universal norms' (Beck and Grande 2007: 71). It is this, they suggest, that enables cosmopolitanism 'to regulate its dealings with otherness so as not *to endanger the integrity of a community*' (2007: 71, emphasis added). Where cosmopolitanism had initially been defined, against multiculturalism, as being presupposed by the individual, it is now being defended as an expression of a particular community *threatened* by others. As Beck and Grande go on to argue, 'the *legitimate* interests of Others' ought to be taken into consideration in the 'calculation of one's own interests' (2007: 71, emphasis added), but there is little discussion on what basis 'legitimacy' is to be established or how those Others are constituted separately from oneself in a way different than within the premises of multiculturalism. What is clear is that the prescription for a cosmopolitan Europe 'united in diversity' takes little account of the diversity within Europe as constituted by its minorities within states.[8]

Beck's failure to address the place of Others internal to Europe – except obliquely, as mentioned, via a reference to 'cosmopolitan society and its enemies' (2002) – is exacerbated by the way in which he discusses the issue of Others explicitly seen as external to Europe and the West. Not only does he not recognize cosmopolitanism as also having a provenance beyond the European intellectual tradition, he is loath to discuss cosmopolitan practices in other places. Engagement with Others, in this new cosmopolitan age, seems to follow a pattern also prevalent in the previous

---

7 This attribution is ironic not least because the term 'cosmopolitan' was used in European discourse to indicate the 'de-racinated' foreigner – frequently, the 'Jew' – whose allegiance to national state formations and political communities could not be guaranteed.
8 The problematic place of Turkey within a cosmopolitan Europe is another issue within this debate. For discussion, see Ahiska (2003), Baban and Keyman (2008) and Parker (2009).

age: condescension. This is nowhere better illustrated than in Beck's statement that: 'the West should listen to non-Western countries *when they have something to say* about the following experiences' (2000: 89, my emphasis).[9] He then lists four main themes:

1. the possibilities for co-existence in multi-religious, multi-ethnic and multi-cultural societies;
2. the question of tolerance in a confined space where cultural differences are prone to lead to violence;
3. 'highly developed' legal and judicial pluralism in non-Western countries (his use of scare quotes);
4. experience of dealing with multiple sovereignties (such as are a consequence of empire, although this word is not used).

The implication is that, when non-Western countries are not speaking about these issues, it is not necessary for the West to listen. This appears to be less a form of cosmopolitan engagement, new and distinct from the nation-state hierarchies of the first age, and more like 'business as usual'.

Beyond the simple arrogance of listing areas where 'we' should listen to 'them', there is also much to comment on in the substance of the list itself. Not least, the aspect that the West and the non-West are presented as two internally homogenous blocs confronting each other as 'actors' in a world that is not recognized to have been structured by historically constituted hierarchical relations. Beck's (2002) argument, that he is not interested in the memory of the global past, but simply in how a vision of a cosmopolitan future could have an impact on the politics of the present, is disingenuous at best. He appears to think that it is possible to discuss 'the present implications of a globally shaped future' (2002: 27) without addressing the legacies of the past on the shaping of the present. He simply brushes away the historically inherited inequalities arising from the legacies of European imperialism and slavery and moves on to imagine a world separate from the resolution of these inequalities. Any theory that seeks to address the question of 'how we live in the world' cannot treat as irrelevant the historical construction of that world (for discussion, see Trouillot 1995).

Beck (2000: 89) continues to ignore the presence of Others on the global stage with his assumption that the European 'social settlement' presents the apex of negotiating the contradictions of the modern world order. There is little discussion of other constructions of social solidarity that have existed such as the Universal Negro Improvement Association (UNIA) which, as Shilliam argues, 'stretched across 800 chapters in 40 countries on four continents' (2006: 379). Further, where there is some acknowledgement of 'development' in other places it is relativized through the use of scare quotes. The implication is that legal and judicial pluralism is only necessary in otherwise complex and developed Western societies because

---

9   The following paragraphs in this section are informed by arguments made in Bhambra (2010).

of the migration of populations to them from places that have such pluralism due to the presence of ethnic and religious differences (for discussion, see Amin 2004). This is then compounded by Beck's subsequent list of areas in which the West is 'beginning to adopt non-Western standards of reality and normality *which do not bode well*' (2000: 89, my emphasis). Presumably, the point is that they do not bode well *for the West* since, in his own terms, they are the everyday conditions of existence for the non-West – on which there is no comment. In particular, Beck identifies the de-regulation of the labour market in the West as leading to the 'abandonment of the co-operatively organized employee society that froze the class conflict between work and capital' (2000: 89). This is an expression of methodological nationalism, given that he does not comment on the conditions of the international division of labour, and the hierarchies between the global North and South, which were themselves a condition of this 'frozen' settlement.[10]

In another, again un-reflexive, example, Beck uses the image of a sandpit to address the current world situation. He argues that the first age of modernity involved capital, labour and state 'making sand cakes in the sandpit' (where the sandpit is the national community), and attempting 'to knock the other's sand cake off the spade in accordance with the rules of institutionalized conflict' (2000: 89). The situation in the second age of modernity is akin to business having been given a mechanical digger which is being used to empty out the whole sandpit (2000: 89). The metaphor is peculiarly inept given the association of infancy with the sandpit and the use of adult-child metaphors to understand colonial relations and responsibilities from a Western perspective. What is clear is that Beck's construction is itself an example of the methodological nationalism he opposes. He appears ignorant of the processes of colonialism, imperialism and slavery, which 'emptied out' from the sandpit of the colonized, not only mineral resources, but also human bodies, and did so not 'according to rules of institutionalized conflict', but through naked appropriation.

In one rare attempt to address the issue of cosmopolitanism 'from below', Beck substitutes the term 'transnationality' for cosmopolitanism and writes that this 'characterizes not only the globalization elites, but the poor exploited immigrants as well. They are treated as "excluded others" in the United States, but Haitians, Filipino or Indian immigrants are at the same time active in sustaining "their" households overseas *and* engaging in political struggles against corrupt regimes [back home]' (2002: 33, emphasis in original). While Beck does not say 'back home' this is the clear implication at the end of that sentence (in that I don't think he means corrupt regimes in the 'West'); his emphasis on 'and' is also telling – the implication being that it should be of some surprise that these immigrants can be active in sustaining households overseas (as opposed to 'back home') as well as engaging in politics elsewhere. His refusal to ascribe the notion of 'cosmopolitanism' to the 'poor exploited immigrants' makes them 'excluded Others' from his framework

---

10   For a discussion of the development of the UK welfare state in the context of the 'postcolonial' demise of a system of Commonwealth preferences and re-orientation to the EU, see Holmwood (2000).

and locates them in nationalistic particularity without providing any information on why this must be case. Further, there is little explanation about what makes global elites specifically *cosmopolitan* while these immigrants are only *transnational*. Beck's patronizing attitude towards these 'poor immigrants' continues a few lines along when he says that: 'it is not only the global players who are learning the de-territorialized game of power and putting it to the test, but also some *ethnic minorities*' (2002: 33). 'Global players' are not, in Beck's understanding, 'ethnic minorities' and 'ethnic minorities' are not 'global players'; the Eurocentrism implicit in the identification of 'global players' is apparent.

Beck's (2000, 2006) argument for cosmopolitanism is part of a long line of social theory that takes Western perspectives as the focus of global processes, and Europe as the origin of a modernity which is subsequently globalized, whether in convergent or divergent forms. Beck's cosmopolitanism is not a cosmopolitanism inclusive of Others who, in his terms, are different in some potentially radical way. He is not interested in what he can learn from them in their own terms.

Cosmopolitanism Provincialized

A 'provincialized' cosmopolitanism, as Pollock et al. (2000) argue, would be made up of dialogues among a series of local perspectives on cosmopolitanism, with no unifying centre. If, as they argue, we were to take cosmopolitanism as *a way of looking at the world*, this would require us to take the perspective *of the world* in our considerations; that is, we would need to be cosmopolitan in our very practices in understanding what it was and is to be cosmopolitan. Cosmopolitanism, as a sociological or historical category, they continue, should be considered as open and not pre-given in form or content: it 'is not some known entity existing in the world, with a clear genealogy from the Stoics to Immanuel Kant, that simply awaits more detailed description at the hands of scholarship' (2000: 577). Rather, they suggest, we should look at 'how people have thought and acted beyond the local' (2000: 586) in different places and across time to generate new descriptions of cosmopolitanism.[11] These would suggest new practices, which in turn 'may offer a better understanding of the theory and history of cosmopolitanism' (2000: 578).

The primary argument made by Pollock and others is that the very phenomenon of cosmopolitanism is threatened by the work of purification that insists on regarding it as the product of one culture, emerging from a centre and diffusing outwards. If we wish an inclusive cosmopolitanism, it would have to be one outside a centred universalism. Mignolo, in putting forward an argument for a

---

11 See Lamont and Aksartova (2002) for one example in which this has been successfully undertaken. Acknowledging that much of the literature on cosmopolitanism is either implicitly or explicitly associated with elites, they seek 'to explore ordinary cosmopolitanisms, defined as the strategies used by ordinary people to bridge boundaries with people who are different from them' (2002: 1).

'critical cosmopolitanism', similarly argues against the idea of a 'cosmopolitanism that only connects from the centre of the large circle outwards' (2000: 745). His argument for decolonial understandings resonates with Chakrabarty's (2000) call to provincialize Europe, that is, to decentre Europe in our considerations. At the same time, we would need to recognize contributions made in connections of which Europe had no part, as well as connections suppressed in representing the history of European uniqueness. Contra Pagden (2000), we do need to think of cosmopolitanism as something other than the values emerging from a reflection on Western liberal democracy (though, this is not to say that there is nothing to be learned from such reflection). The task now is a provincialized cosmopolitanism that can learn from others where we recognize that what they contribute is *not a confirmation of what we already know*, but the bringing into being of new understandings relevant to the worlds we inhabit together. These new understandings both reconfigure our existing perceptions *of the world*, as well as inform the ways in which we live *in the world*.

Some of what is required is captured in Homi Bhabha's earlier work on postcolonialism. The starting point for Bhabha's (1994) explication of postcolonial theory is a history adequate to the political conditions of the present. Those conditions are not simply informed by understandings of 'globalization', but more specifically by an understanding of the postcolonial global conditions which are rarely the starting point for sociological analyses (see Bhambra 2007b). As Seidman remarks, sociology's emergence coincided with the high point of Western imperialism, and yet, 'the dynamics of empire were not incorporated into the basic categories, models of explanation, and narratives of social development of the classical sociologists' (1996: 314). The potential contribution to the sociological paradigm of events outside the West (and the experiences of non-Western 'Others') has not often been considered (see Chakrabarty 2000, Bhambra 2007a). This is, in part, a consequence of the erasures that are implicit when the remit of sociology is understood to be 'modern societies' – that is, societies engaged in processes of modernization – where the 'postcolonial' is necessarily associated with 'pre-modern' societies, societies that have traditionally fallen to anthropology, or to the interdisciplinary area of development studies. The association of cosmopolitanism with an intellectual genealogy that begins with the ancient Greeks and is located in the modern West similarly prevents any meaningful discussion of cosmopolitanism in a postcolonial context. As Bhabha argues, however, shifting the frame through which we view the events of 'modernity', or cosmopolitanism, forces us to consider the question of subaltern agency and ask: 'what is this "now" of modernity? Who defines this present from which we speak?' (1994: 244).

This is not a version of multiple modernities, in that it does not offer an alternative other modernity to be placed alongside those already seen to be existing. Rather, it calls on us to interrogate the conceptual paradigm of modernity, as it has commonly been understood, from the perspectives of those Others usually relegated to the margins, if included at all. These Others, constituted 'otherwise than modernity' Bhabha argues, exist both in the global South and the global North (1994: 6). Their perspectives are now taken to be central to understanding modernity conceptually. The task, as Bhabha puts it, is to take responsibility for the unspoken, unrepresented pasts within our cosmopolitan present and, in their renewal, to interrupt, refigure and re-create present understandings adequate to that past (1994: 7). One aspect of this would be for the metropolitan centres of the West to confront their postcolonial histories whereby the 'influx of postwar migrants and refugees' would be constituted as part of 'an indigenous or native narrative *internal to [their] national identity*' (1994: 6, emphasis added; see also Amin 2004). It is not only by movement across 'borders' that migrants might be argued to express cosmopolitanism, but also in their very understanding of how those borders came to be constituted and their involvement in reconceptualizing understandings of citizenship and belonging, that is, as cosmopolitan subjects within nation-state boundaries.[12] This reconsideration of modernity does not relegate difference simply to cultural expression, but calls upon that difference to make a difference to the narratives already in place.

For Bhabha, as for Edward Said (1978) before him, the social expression of 'difference' is to be contextualized with the historical 'emergence of community envisaged as a project', that is 'at once a vision and a construction' (1994: 3). As such, the question of difference is not to be addressed simply through its multiple expressions, but by problematizing 'the unity of the "us" and the otherness of the "other"' that *produces* these differences in an interconnected and interdependent world (Gupta and Ferguson 1992: 14). This is to be understood not in terms of a community of individuals who happen perchance to live in an age of cosmopolitanism – that is, individuals who, in Beck's terms, exemplify the cosmopolitan age because they 'shop internationally, work internationally, love internationally, marry internationally, research internationally, grow up and are educated internationally (that is, multi-lingually), live and think transnationally' (2000: 80). Rather, they are a cosmopolitan community because of the postcolonial history that brought them into being – they are economic and other migrants, refugees, asylum seekers, temporary workers. Their cosmopolitanism is inextricably linked to their (post) colonial past, present and future. The cosmopolitanism of 'now' within the West, then, has to be recognized as the outcome of a history that was colonial and then postcolonial; a history to which Others have always contributed whether willingly or not. While there have been few voices identifying a specifically 'postcolonial' Europe (see Hansen 2002, 2004, Bhambra 2009), there has been an increasing focus on the seeming diversity and hybridity of European cultural constellations that moves us beyond the stale binaries of much of the literature in this area (see Gilroy 1993, 2003, Stevenson 2006).

---

12   Thus, long before the 'rediscovery' of cosmopolitanism in Western discourse, minorities within Western populations were expressing cosmopolitan aspirations in their engagement with wider anti-colonial struggles. For example, Black American citizens were cosmopolitan in their pan-African engagements, while their fellow citizens were engaged with national expressions of citizenship (see Singh 2004). For a discussion of the limits of cosmopolitanism in addressing the situation of refugees and asylum seekers as they attempt to challenge nation-state border controls, see Morris (2009).

Cosmopolitanism, of course, is not simply at issue in colonial and postcolonial migration to the West (see Yeğenoğlu 2005). The exercise of coloniality itself, as Mignolo (2000) has argued, needs to be considered as an important locus of cosmopolitanism, both in intent as well as practice. Mignolo begins his articulation of a critical cosmopolitanism, not from the Greeks, but in the commercial circuits that brought together 'the Spanish Crown with capitalist entrepreneurs from Genoa, with Christian missionaries, with Amerindian elites, and with African slaves' (2000: 725). He presents a philosophical consideration of cosmopolitanism that engages with European thinkers, but does so from the perspective of the historical debates on the Spanish engagement with the Amerindians in the sixteenth century. By bringing attention to otherwise 'silenced and marginalized voices' (2000: 736) within contemporary discussions of cosmopolitanism, Mignolo enriches the debate and opens up productive avenues for further exploring the question of how we live with and across differences. As he argues, critical cosmopolitanism must be truly dialogic where 'everyone participates instead of "being participated"' (2000: 744); that is, he is not arguing for the inclusion of Others in our conversations, but rather, for a recognition of their already existing participation, if only we could listen (see Back 2009).

Beck's version of cosmopolitanism is an expression of cultural Eurocentrism masquerading as potential global inclusivity. As has been demonstrated, however, this inclusivity is dependent upon Them being included in Our designs. It is not an inclusivity that recognizes the Other as already constitutive of, if marginalized within, the frameworks of understanding. Further, while Beck uses the approach of multiple modernities to present the distinctiveness of the present age over preceding ones, he does not deal with the contradiction this poses for his commitment to his version of cosmopolitanism. Multiple modernities are predicated on an understanding of different cultures such that their vision of the global is constituted as a form of global multiculturalism. To the extent that Beck sets up cosmopolitanism in opposition to multiculturalism he denies the basis for the very global age he describes. Concluding an article on 'Understanding the Real Europe', Beck writes that '[m]ore than anywhere else in the world, Europe *shows* ... Europe *teaches* ... The catchphrase for the future might be Move over America – Europe is back' (2003: n.p., my emphasis). Perhaps what is also needed, however, is for Europe to listen, and to learn, for Europe and the United States, alike, to move over. A cosmopolitan sociology that was open to different voices would be one that *provincialized* European understandings, not one based on the perpetuation of 'triumphalist' ideas of Europe's singular contribution to world society.

Provincializing cosmopolitanism would require both a decentring of dominant understandings of cosmopolitanism as well as an acknowledgement of understandings of cosmopolitanism outside of the otherwise canonical frame of reference exemplified by European thought and practice. This would need to be done through an address of global histories and interconnected experiences that requires 'both critique and the production of a different archive of knowledge' (Featherstone and Venn 2006: 4). New understandings of such conceptual issues, however, cannot simply be added to already existing ones without in some way calling into question the legitimacy and validity of the previously accepted parameters – both historical and ethical. As such, a more thorough-going critique is needed, one which goes beyond *decentring* to *transforming*. The provincializing of cosmopolitanism is not just a different interpretation of the *same* ideas, but the bringing into being of *new* understandings.

Bibliography

Ahiska, M. 2003. Occidentalism: The Historical Fantasy of the Modern. *The South Atlantic Quarterly*, 102(2–3), 351–79.
Amin, A. 2004. Multi-Ethnicity and the Idea of Europe. *Theory, Culture and Society*, 21(2), 1–24.
Arnason, J.P. 2000. Communism and Modernity. *Daedalus: Multiple Modernities*, 129(1), 61–90.
Arnason, J.P. 2003. Entangled Communisms: Imperial Revolutions in Russia and China. *European Journal of Social Theory*, 6(3), 307–25.
Baban, F. and Keyman, F. 2008. Turkey and Postnational Europe: Challenges for the Cosmopolitan. *European Journal of Social Theory*, 11(1), 107–24.
Back, L. 2009. Global Attentiveness and the Sociological Ear. *Sociological Research Online*, 14(4), www.socresonline.org.uk/14/4/14.html.
BBC 2010. France MPs' Report Backs Muslim Face Veil Ban, http://news.bbc.co.uk/1/hi/world/europe/8480161.stm.
Beck, U. 2000. The Cosmopolitan Perspective: Sociology of the Second Age of Modernity. *British Journal of Sociology*, 51(1), 79–105.
Beck, U. 2002. The Cosmopolitan Society and its Enemies. *Theory Culture Society*, 19(1–2), 17–44.
Beck, U. 2003. Understanding the Real Europe. *Dissent*, 32–8.
Beck, U. 2006. *Cosmopolitan Vision*. Cambridge: Polity Press.
Beck, U. and Grande, E. 2007. Cosmopolitanism: Europe's Way Out of Crisis. *European Journal of Social Theory*, 10(1), 67–85.
Beck, U. and Sznaider, N. 2006. Unpacking Cosmopolitanism for the Social Sciences: A Research Agenda. *The British Journal of Sociology*, 57(1), 1–23.
Bhabha, H.K. 1994. *The Location of Culture*. London: Routledge.
Bhambra, G.K. 2007a. *Rethinking Modernity: Postcolonialism and the Sociological Imagination*. Basingstoke: Palgrave Macmillan.
Bhambra, G.K. 2007b. Sociology and Postcolonialism: Another 'Missing' Revolution? *Sociology*, 41(5), 871–84.
Bhambra, G.K. 2009. Postcolonial Europe: Or, Understanding Europe in Times of the Postcolonial, in *Sage Handbook of European Studies*, edited by Chris Rumford. London: Sage.
Bhambra, G.K. 2010. Sociology after Postcolonialism: Provincialized Cosmopolitanism and Connected Sociologies, in *Decolonizing European Sociology:*

Trans-disciplinary Approaches, edited by M. Boatcă, S. Costa and E. Gutiérrez-Rodríguez. Aldershot: Ashgate, 33–48.
Chakrabarty, D. 2000. *Provincializing Europe: Postcolonial Thought and Historical Difference.* Princeton: Princeton University Press.
Chernilo, D. 2007. *A Social Theory of the Nation-State: Beyond Methodological Nationalism.* London: Routledge.
Daedalus. 1998. Special Issue on 'Early Modernities', 127(3).
Daedalus. 2000. Special Issue on 'Multiple Modernities', 129(1).
Ehrkamp, P. and Leitner, H. 2003. Beyond National Citizenship: Turkish Immigrants and the (Re)Construction of Citizenship in Germany. *Urban Geography,* 24(2), 127–46.
Eisenstadt, S.N. 2000. Multiple Modernities. *Daedalus: Multiple Modernities,* 129(1), 1–29.
Eisenstadt, S.N. 2001. The Civilizational Dimension of Modernity: Modernity as a Distinct Civilization. *International Sociology,* 16(3), 320–40.
Eisenstadt, S.N. and Schluchter, W. 1998. Introduction: Paths to Early Modernities – A Comparative View. *Daedalus: Early Modernities,* 127(3), 1–18.
Featherstone, M. and Venn, C. 2006. Problematizing Global Knowledge and the New Encyclopaedia Project: An Introduction. *Theory, Culture, and Society,* 23(2–3), 1–20.
Fine, R. 2007. *Cosmopolitanism.* London: Routledge.
Gilroy, P. 1993. *The Black Atlantic: Modernity and Double Consciousness.* Cambridge, MA: Harvard University Press.
Gilroy, P. 2003. 'Where Ignorant Armies Clash by Night': Homogenous Community and the Planetary Aspect. *International Journal of Cultural Studies,* 6(3), 261–76.
Gupta, A. and Ferguson, J. 1992. Beyond 'Culture': Space, Identity, and the Politics of Difference. *Cultural Anthropology,* 7(1), 6–23.
Gutmann, A. (ed.). 1994. *Multiculturalism: Examining the Politics of Recognition.* Princeton: Princeton University Press.
Hansen, P. 2002. European Integration, European Identity and the Colonial Connection. *European Journal of Social Theory,* 5(4), 483–98.
Hansen, P. 2004. In the Name of Europe. *Race and Class,* 45(3), 49–62.
Holmwood, J. 1997. Postmodernity, Citizenship and Inequality: Social Theory in 'the New Consumer Society', in *Constructing the New Consumer Society,* edited by P. Sulkunen, J. Holmwood, H. Radner and G. Schulze, London: Macmillan, 58–78.
Holmwood, J. 2000. Europe and the 'Americanization' of British Social Policy. *European Societies,* 2(4), 453–82.
Lamont, M. and Aksartova, S. 2002. Ordinary Cosmopolitanisms: Strategies for Bridging Racial Boundaries among Working-Class Men. *Theory, Culture and Society,* 19(4), 1–25.
Loomba, A. 1998. *Colonialism/Postcolonialism.* London: Routledge.
Mignolo, W.D. 2000. The Many Faces of Cosmo-Polis: Border Thinking and Critical Cosmopolitanism. *Public Culture,* 12(3), 721–48.

Morris, L. 2009. An Emergent Cosmopolitan Paradigm? Asylum, Welfare and Human Rights. *British Journal of Sociology*, 60(2), 215–35.

Muthu, S. 2003. *Enlightenment against Empire*. Princeton: Princeton University Press.

Nussbaum, M. (ed.). 1996. *For Love of Country: Debating the Limits of Patriotism*. Boston: Beacon Press.

Pagden, A. 2000. Stoicism, Cosmopolitanism, and the Legacy of European Imperialism. *Constellations*, 7(1), 3–22.

Parker, O. 2009. 'Cosmopolitan Europe' and the EU-Turkey Question: The Politics of a 'Common Destiny'. *Journal of European Public Policy*, 16(7), 1085–101.

Pollock, S., Bhabha, H.K., Breckenridge, C.A. and Chakrabarty, D. 2000. Cosmopolitanisms. *Public Culture*, 12(3), 577–89.

Saharso, S. 2007. Headscarves: A Comparison of Public Thought and Public Policy in Germany and the Netherlands. *Critical Review of International Social and Political Philosophy*, 10(4), 513–30.

Said, E.W. 1978. *Orientalism: Western Conceptions of the Orient*. London: Routledge and Kegan Paul Ltd.

Seidman, S. 1996. Empire and Knowledge: More Troubles, New Opportunities for Sociology. *Contemporary Sociology*, 25(3), 313–16.

Shilliam, R. 2006. What about Marcus Garvey? Race and the Transformation of Sovereignty Debate. *Review of International Studies*, 32(3), 379–400.

Singh, N. 2004. *Black is a Country: Race and the Unfinished Struggle for Democracy*. Cambridge, MA: Harvard University Press.

Stevenson, N. 2002. Cosmopolitanism, Multiculturalism and Citizenship. *Sociological Research Online*, 7(1), www.socresonline.org.uk/7/1/stevenson.html

Stevenson, N. 2006. European Cosmopolitan Solidarity: Questions of Citizenship, Difference, and Post-Materialism. *European Journal of Social Theory*, 9(4), 485–500.

Trouillot, M.-R. 1995. *Silencing the Past: Power and the Production of History*. Boston: Beacon Press.

Vertovec, S. and Cohen R. (eds). 2002. *Conceiving Cosmopolitanism: Theory, Context, and Practice*. Oxford: Oxford University Press.

Wagner, P. 2001. *Theorizing Modernity: Inescapability and Attainability in Social Theory*. London: Sage.

Weber, B. 1995. Immigration and Politics in Germany. *The Journal of the International Institute*, 2(3), www.umich.edu/~iinet/journal/vol2no3/ozdemir.html.

Wittrock, B. 1998. Early Modernities: Varieties and Transitions. *Daedalus: Early Modernities*, 127(3), 19–40.

Yeğenoğlu, M. 2005. Cosmopolitanism and Nationalism in a Globalized World. *Ethnic and Racial Studies*, 28(1), 103–31.

19

Border Thinking, Decolonial Cosmopolitanism and Dialogues Among Civilizations

Walter D. Mignolo

Introduction

Cosmopolitanism and Eurocentrism

Cosmopolitanism is Eurocentered from its inception. By describing cosmopolitanism as "Eurocentered" I mean what Carl Schmitt meant by the use of the word in reference to the second *nomos* of the earth. The second *nomos* that emerged toward 1500 brought together "global linear thinking" (his expression) and the *Ius Publicum Europaeum* (that is, international law) and contributed to decolonial responses on the other side of the line, so to speak. How to turn decolonial responses into decolonial cosmopolitanism is the question my argument addresses. Any cosmopolitan project today has to be evaluated by whether or not it takes into account imperial and colonial differences, that is, dependencies and hierarchies of the world order (for instance, developed and underdeveloped countries, emerging and fully fledged economies, the memories of the First/Second/Third World division), and the clash/dialogues/alliances of civilizations. Consequently, a cosmopolitan world order that is dictated from above has all the features of global imperial designs where a set of institutions or country determines the rules to be followed. Decolonial cosmopolitanism proposes another vision and has other ambitions.

However, since the current world order is organized around unequal power relations and hierarchies among civilizations and cultures, and such unequal world order is a consequence of coloniality (the darker side of Western modernity), decolonial cosmopolitanism shall be based on border rather than on territorial global linear thinking which was precisely the result of global designs and the creation of borders between *humanitas* and *anthropos*, between the West and the

Rest.[1] This dichotomy is not mine: it is a fundamental aspect of the rhetoric of modernity and, hence, of the logic of coloniality. It is one thing to say that it is necessary to avoid dichotomies and another not to recognize that dichotomies shape the discursive ontology of modernity. Moreover, the current world order demands that border thinkers and decolonial intellectuals and scholars confront the imperial and colonial differences to which Western cosmopolitanism (*à la* Kant) contributed to create and that are still with us. Like Japan, Chinese were classified—not by themselves, but from Western enunciation and management of knowledge—as the "yellow race." The imperial difference applies here although racialization is common to both colonial and imperial differences. China and Japan were not colonized but did not escape racialization—hence, the imperial rather than the colonial difference placed the "Orient" in relation to the West. In fact, "orientalism" was mainly the articulation of the imperial difference. On the other hand, indigenous people of the world from the Americas to Australia and New Zealand, Africans and enslaved Africans transported to the Americas, as well as South Asians, were colonized and the colonial difference was infringed upon them. Nevertheless, imperial and colonial differences are strategies of classification and hence of discursive ontologies, hegemonic or dominant, that make believe that the world is built on two poles, the negative and the positive. Decolonial cosmopolitanism has to deal and surmount both imperial and colonial differences. And border thinking is one way to do it.

To understand how border thinking confronts and at the same time attempts to delink from imperial and colonial differences, and how it could contribute to global futures, we need to take a detour exploring some aspects of the present world order. Border thinking and decolonial cosmopolitanism need to build histories-other rather than other histories. Histories-others are written and told, lived and embodied by people who have been defined as not having histories. People without histories is an invention dated in the sixteenth century. It implied that people without histories were people without alphabetic writing (Mignolo 1992). Today, people without histories are not only writing their own but writing the imperial histories of the West. It is in that terrain that border thinking and critical cosmopolitanism need to, and are building, histories-others in the double sense: histories written by those who were made others and the histories of Western expansion seen from the receiving end of globalization. For decolonial cosmopolitan projects, the history that counts is the one of the sixteenth century, the emergence of the Atlantic commercial circuit, the genocide of the Indians, the

---

1   I am borrowing these categories from the insightful article by Nishitani Osamu (2006) where he correctly argued that *humanitas and anthropos* are two Western categories invented by those who considered themselves *humanitas*. It may be surprising for some that a Japanese scholar coincides in his argument with many indigenous, Afro and people of European descent in the Americas (particularly Latin). But after a second thought, one realizes that "being yellow" one is less human, perhaps a little bit more than Indians and blacks, but not as human as *humanitas*.

massive appropriation and expropriation of land by European monarchies and the massive slave trade and exploitation of labor.

Since the logic of coloniality that originated then is still alive and well today, the need to delink from Kantian legacies that maintain the rhetoric of modernity and hide the logic of coloniality, is necessary and desirable. For cosmopolitanism cannot be a homogeneous world order based on hierarchies or in a universal voice recognizing the differences but still believing that universal cosmopolitanism is not only possible but, worse, desirable. These ideals are precisely what neoliberal globalization attempted to do and now (2010) we are witnessing its failure. Any universal cosmopolitan project would be outright imperial, which confront us with the need to advance on decolonization of universal cosmopolitanism and to advance pluriversal and decolonial cosmopolitan projects. Paradoxically, the most recent stage of a globalizing process that started in the sixteenth century (following Schmitt), intensified the cracks of imperial and colonial differences and generated the project of de-Westernization at the level of the state (e.g. China) and of decoloniality mainly at the level of the political society, with the exception of the process of decolonizing the state in Bolivia under Evo Morales.

To be decolonial, any cosmopolitan project couldn't be proposed as a *new* universal alternative to past and existing universal or global designs (Mignolo 2000a). Such a project would not be decolonial but neo-Kantian. Modernity and postmodernity are based on the celebration of *newness* while decoloniality is based on the undoing of the rhetoric of modernity and postmodernity that maintains and hides the logic of coloniality. It is therefore imperative to delink from imperial and colonial differences upon which the current world order has been mapped and remapped, instead of proposing a "new" cosmopolitanism that recognizes imperial and colonial differences but feels comfortable with maintaining them. That would be one difference between postcolonial and decolonial conceptions of cosmopolitan futures. Before Kant, in the sixteenth century global projects were initiatives of what we call today "the West," which was then at its inception. Global linear thinking coupled with the origination of international law (de Vitoria, Grotius) was the first attempt at making the world a Christian *orbis*, which Kant translated into a secular global *polis*. By the second half of the eighteenth century, *cosmopolitanism* became the ambition and the vision of secular philosophy and left a legacy from which decolonial thinkers are detaching and building decolonial cosmopolitan options.[2] Decolonial options do not require a chair person or CEO directing the traffic in a pyramidal model. Or, better yet, decolonial options bend to the rule of "mandar obedeciendo" (ruling and obeying simultaneously). Decolonial cosmopolitanism should in fact aim at creating decentered networks, and de-centered networks are the very foundations of cosmopolitan localism. The Zapatistas' dictum "mandar obedeciendo" could be extended to imagine international relations, which is where decolonial cosmopolitanism has its function and distinguishes itself from liberal conceptions where the focus is the cosmopolitan individual who was born in Africa, studied in England and teaches in the United States.

---

2   I explored some of these issues in a previous article on the subject (see Mignolo 2009a).

Thus neoliberal globalization, on the one hand, and liberal as well as Marxist cosmopolitanisms (while apparently the latter confronting the former) on the other, both have a common enemy: the nation/state. The common enemy placed both projects in the same camp, pursuing their efforts to build a global world without frontiers that, apparently for some, was much better than a world divided by nation-states. Defenders of globalization and postmodern intellectuals coincided in celebrating a world without borders. Border thinkers did not buy into it. Consequently decolonial cosmopolitanism began to be built as an option to this particular structure of the imperial equation: global linear thinking that traced the borders, global capitalism that erased the borders and liberal and Marxist cosmopolitanism that dreamt with a world without borders, although organized differently.

Decolonial Cosmopolitanism and Dialogues among Civilizations

Liberal versions of cosmopolitanism could easily be brought into (when they are not already) the company of dialogues among civilizations.[3] There is plenty of compatibility between both projects. But how could then decolonial cosmopolitanism relate to the project of dialogue among civilizations? And how may decolonial cosmopolitanism and decolonial conversations among actors and institutions of different civilizations look as options to current debates on cosmopolitanism, on the one hand, and to dialogue among civilizations on the other? Where do dialogues among civilizations take place, or should take place? Among the state, among civil societies or among corporations? Beyond this canonical model, dialogues among civilizations are already taking place in the sphere of the emerging global political society (e.g. the sector of the civil society that is taken its destiny in its own hands and is not waiting for the state, God or the corporations to decide for them).

Cosmopolitanism as a project of global conviviality in the modern/colonial world is attributed, as we know and I already mentioned, to Immanuel Kant.[4] For Kant all non-European civilizations (even the South of Europe) were deficient in relation to the standards set by France, England and Germany. That was the world order in which Kant ambitioned cosmopolitan conviviality and perpetual peace. The main problem with Kant's cosmopolitan legacies is that cosmopolitanism is

---

3   Activities in this area have been underway in the past 10 years at the UNESCO (Academy de la Latinit'e) and at the UN (Alliance of Civilization). Scholarly debates and publications are already present in the field of international relations and philosophy of the social sciences and humanities. See EDUCAM (2007) and Michael and Petito (2009). These are also "cosmopolitan" projects based on the idea of "urbis civitas" rather than "cosmo polis."

4   I am referring mainly to Immanuel Kant (1784).

and continues to be a European-based problem (while "alliance" and "dialogue" of civilizations involve states outside and at the margins of former Western Europe, now the European Union), even if we can find scholars and intellectuals in the United States or beyond Europe who may be interested in such cosmopolitan conceptions, while "dialogue of civilizations" (Khatami, Havel) and "alliance of civilizations" (Zapatero, Erdogan) are projects put forward from the perspective of the non-Western (Iran and Turkey) world and from the margins of the European Union (Czechoslovakia and Spain). The politics of Eurocentered cosmopolitanism is not different from the politics of banks and corporations: they have the good solution for you, your family, your life and the future of all. You have just to sign and follow the rules, to be saved and developed. The question is then how are imperial cosmopolitan legacies taken up in the non-European world? Who in and from the non-European world would be invested in promoting Eurocentered cosmopolitan visions? Are they signing up to cosmopolitanism and endorsing, without being pronounced, all "development plans" since the 1960s mutated into "globalization and development" since the 1990s?

"Dialogue among civilizations" was proposed by the Iranian scholar, politician (and president of Iran between 1997 and 2005), Mohammad Khatami (2000) in response to Samuel Huntington's (1993) analysis or forecast of the "clash of civilizations."[5] His proposal was submitted to the UN while he was still president of Iran. The first interesting aspect to notice, although it is obvious, is the following: the fact that it was a Western political theorist who was predicting the clash of civilizations while an Islamic president, scholar and politician was instead calling for "dialogue among civilizations." It is a good indication of who wants war and who wants peace. From a Western perspective the "clash of civilizations" was forecast (or promoted) while from a non-Western perspective the call for "dialogue among civilizations" was put on the table. The Kantian call toward perpetual peace was taken up and appropriated and twisted, indeed, by people whom Kant was listing well below the English, French and Germans (e.g. the *anthropos*) and that were the object of the civilizing mission and cosmopolitan projects. For I do not think that will be easy to argue that Khatami was indeed updating and

---

5   For a detailed analysis of the role of both "dialogue among" and "alliance of" civilizations," see Michael and Petito (2009) and Petito (2007). In April of 2007 former President of Portugal, Jorge Sampaio, was appointed as the High Representative for the AoC by Ban Ki-moon, General Secretary of the United Nations. The logic continues: Turkey is a non-Western country historically but also by the European Union lack of enthusiasm of Turkey becoming one of them. Spain and Portugal are the South of Europe in the geopolitics of Kant and Hegel. The next meeting of the Alliance of Civilization will take place in Rio de Janeiro. Lula da Silva, Ban Ki-moon, Tayyip Erdogan, José Luis Zapatero and Jorge Sampaio are in the opening session: www/imapc/prg/cpmtemt/view/63/79/lang.english. Alliances as well as dialogue of civilization are proposing a cosmopolitan world order at the level of the states. They may or may not be beneficial for the civil and political society; and these projects may or may not be effective with re-orienting the predatory "corporate world order" based on competition rather than cosmopolitan conviviality.

enacting Kantian legacies. If you look at this situation carefully, you would realize that the role has been inverted, the geography of reasoning has shifted: here the "barbarians" are calling for dialogue while the "civilized" are pre-announcing a clash. And if you look more carefully, you would notice that in Khatami's call we have on the one hand a call to dialogue that presupposes border thinking (Khatami needs to acknowledge Western calls while the West can ignore what the non-West thinks or care about), and a call (or expectation that it will happen) for war that operates under an imperial and territorial epistemology where "dialogue" is possible only if the rest accepts the conditions of the West. Territorial epistemology (which undergirds post-Kantian cosmopolitanism, although with good intentions) doesn't recognize reason and rational options beyond the universality of a Western one. Within the clash of civilization no dialogue is necessary or desirable. In the case of Khatami, his call comes from a subject who is dwelling in the borders (who is not just border crossing), who is dwelling and sensing the humiliation infringed by imperial and colonial differences and territorial epistemology but who has to recognize that the West is in all of us. These are the necessary conditons of border thinking. In the case of Khatami, we are listening to someone who has behind him not the memories of Greece but the memories of Persia. Persians were never directly colonized but, through the nineteenth century, two of the three Islamic Sultanates (Safavid and Ottoman) began to be intervened by England and France: Iran was detached from the Safavid and Iraq from the Ottoman Sultanates. In other words, although different from Africans and Indians, Islamic regions also felt the "colonial" wound although at a different scale. Well, "dialogue among civilizations" emerges from that history, sensing and experience. And if you push the argument further, you would see that Khatami's call is indeed a call for decolonial cosmopolitanism in the sphere of state organizations.

Furthermore, although Huntington was clear about the challenge of Islam, he was also aware of the Chinese menace. And of course, China and East Asia are important players in a future possible decolonial cosmopolitanism toward dialogue among civilizations. Huntington divided the world among nine civilizations. And it was obvious by the end of the 1990s that "Chinese civilization" was also a menace, although of a different kind: economic at that time; no longer just economic by 2010. Huntington's argument hides the economic under the language of civilization. He must have been aware (giving his career in Washington, during the years of Walter Kissinger), that the clash with Islamic civilization was related to the wealth of oil that have been uncovered in the early twentieth century in Iran and Iraq, through the joint mandate of England and France.

In a nutshell, what was already becoming apparent toward the end of the 1990s with the rapid economic growth and global impact of Chinese economy, on the one hand, was accentuated on the other hand, by the collapse of the physical building of the World Trade Center (attributed to Islamic extremists), and its global symbolic effect and consequences. What was also becoming apparent was that behind China's economic growth there was a long lasting civilization that was directly interfered with in the process of the expansion of Western civilization in 1848. Behind the collapse of the Twin Towers, and the alleged interference of Islamic civilization in Western civilization, was a forgotten historical episode. These are crucial issues for decolonial cosmopolitan projects and they should be also for any other cosmopolitan ambition.

Does dialogue among civilizations proposed by Mohammed Khatami in 2000 and followed up by the Alliance of Civilizations proposed by José Luis Zapatero and Recep Tayyip Erdogan in 2005, contribute to build convivial cosmopolitan futures? The differential in economic wealth goes hand-in-hand with racialization of differences (everyone is ready today to recognize that there are differences, and all of us know that what matter are not differences but the differential of power, colonial or imperial, grounded on global racism), and both are foundational for Western capitalist civilization as it carries over to non-Western ones that have recently become capitalist. However, global capitalist economy doesn't mean either that capitalism is universal or that only the West has today the right to call the shots of international relations and global trades.

On the contrary, if dialogue among civilizations and decolonial cosmopolitanism have a purpose it will be to value and celebrate life and pluriversal co-existence rather than value and celebrate the number of billionaires or to make believe that the "war" in Afghanistan will take us to paradise behind the Taliban's mountains. Territorial epistemology promotes death in the name of peace and prosperity. When Frantz Fanon insisted that decolonization means to decolonize both the colonizer and the colonized, he meant that the colonized are also prisoners of the lifestyle and subjectivity celebrated by Western civilization and capitalism and today adapted to state capitalism in non-Western civilizations. For that reason, the G7, G8 and G20 have become builders and defenders of a fortress of "democracy." Global conviviality cannot be attained by maintaining war predicated over eternal peace. One of the tasks of decolonial cosmopolitanism is to uncouple "democracy" and "cosmopolitanism" from the private liberal and neoliberal domains (complemented by the same logic with the different content of the European and global left) and to open it up to the non-hierarchical and non-dependent pluriversality of all existing civilizations.

The Colonial Matrix of Power: Difficulties and Challenges that Decolonial Cosmopolitanism and Dialogues among Civilizations will have to Surmount

In the middle of the Cold War, Carl Schmitt traced three possible futures scenarios to imagine what the new *nomos* of the earth would look like. Schmitt traces the history of the *second nomos of the earth*, from 1500 to World War I and its agony extended to World War II. Europe entered at that time in a mode of *global linear thinking* and international law was created, precisely, to justify the division of the globe to the benefit of European Atlantic monarchies (Schmitt 1952). Of the three future scenarios that Schmitt infers based on his own history of the *second nomos of the earth*, the first scenario was that one in which the two contenders, the United States and the Soviet Union, would prevail and establish a global order based on their global designs. The second scenario forecasted an alliance between the United States and Britain, the previous world power and that would prevail over its contender. The third scenario would be a global order based on a plurality of territorial domains. From today's vantage point it would look like Schmitt was acknowledging the end of Western management of the world order (from 1500 to 2000) and that a "new nomos" would emerge of which Western civilization would no longer be the sole manager. I would say that the signs of the closing really emerged around 2000. But Schmitt was no longer with us to speculate on the new turn of events.

Schmitt's foresight on the idea of global linear thinking was based—naturally—on the history he constructed: global linear thinking and the partition of the world among European powers (and the United States with its "Western Hemisphere" since 1500).[6] Huntington's vision of a multi-polar world was based on the end of the US hegemony (not on the end of the Eurocentered *nomos* [Schmitt's expression] of the earth) and a history he located in the North–South line dividing Christian Europe from Christian Russia and from Islamdom. Huntington's was a map that anticipated the clash between Western Christianity and South Eastern Islam, when the United States needed a new enemy to justify expenses on national security after the collapse of the Soviet Union. But for the future, Huntington based his forecast on the "World Civilizations Post-1990." Huntington's map of the global order after 1990 is somewhat arbitrary, but it served the orientation of his argument. As the reader will recall, he identified nine civilizations. Whether arbitrary or not, dialogue among civilizations requires that we know which are the civilizations entering into the dialogue. The UN was not clear about it. Huntington's classification identifies civilizations based on religions (Sinic, Hindu, Buddhist, orthodox); on continent and sub-continents (Africa and Latin America, respectively); one country (Japan) and one sector of the globe, Western civilization that includes North America—(except Mexico), Canada, Greenland, Australia, New Zealand, and the Federal Constitutional Monarchy and parliamentary Democracy of Papua New Guinea. Beyond the Borgesian logic of this classification (well known after Michel Foucault rehearsed it in *Les Mots et les Choses*, 1966), any attentive reader would soon see the power relations among these civilizations. And differential in power relations is not just economic—it is epistemic. Without control of knowledge it would be difficult to manage and control the economy. Therefore, any project promoting dialogues among civilizations and any cosmopolitan project, including decolonial cosmopolitanism, cannot go very far if it doesn't acknowledge from the very beginning that modernity goes hand-in-hand with coloniality and that coloniality, through 500 years of imperial Western civilization, created an unequal world order and differential of power among civilizations.

---

6   For the idea of the Western Hemisphere in the colonial horizon of modernity see Mignolo (2001).

BORDER THINKING, DECOLONIAL COSMOPOLITANISM AND DIALOGUES

Huntington's classification and hierarchies (rather than dialogue or alliances) of civilizations may be fine to imagine a multi-polar world in which multi-polarity means economic relations between corporations and states regulated by international law and relations. How would cosmopolitanism and dialogue among civilizations look in such multi-polar world crossed by differential power relations grounded in colonial (cf. the ex-Third World and the former Eastern Europe) and imperial differences (Islam, China, Japan, Russia)? For Kant the prospectus was easier to imagine: Western civilization was marching to civilize the world, and cosmopolitanism was its creed. It may look a little bit messy at the first sight to envision a cosmopolitan world crossing the economic and political interests of each of the nine civilizations while one can surmise that dialogues among the nine civilizations (since we cannot reduce dialogue of civilizations to Islam and the West) would be necessary for a cosmopolitan world order. Now, if cosmopolitanism shall be maintained as a set of projects toward global conviviality, it is no longer the Kantian universal cosmopolitanism that shall offer us the guidelines but decolonial cosmopolitanism (which also means de-Westernization). We all in the planet are enacting or experiencing (or going through without knowing it) a drastic turning point, an epistemic shift indeed and delinking from Western cosmopolitan vision. Decolonial cosmopolitanism shall be understood as cosmopolitan localism (see below), although not every cosmopolitan local project has to be decolonial, but has to be pluriversal. That simply means that any universal cosmopolitanism is globally unacceptable. In this view, decolonial cosmopolitanism is predicated on localism (decolonial cosmopolitanism is tantamount to cosmopolitan localism) and grounded on decolonial border thinking confronting, and delinking, from the imperial and colonial differences upon which the current territorial (or linear in Schmitt's terms) epistemology and the global order is managed. That means that dialogue among civilizations and cosmopolitan localism are two different projects. Dialogue among civilizations has been construed in the sphere of the states and of international relations, while cosmopolitan localism evinces the growing presence and participation of the political society, delinking from state managerial designs and building decolonial conceptions of life and communal futures. Many will say that this is impossible. It is only impossible if you do not want to do it because you are more interested in success, domination, leadership and "being number one." Cosmopolitan localism (whether decolonial or dialogue among civilizations as proposed by Khatami) promotes pluriversality while Kant's legacies are still entrenched in the dream of a renewed (and good) universalism.[7]

So then a multi-polar world could be imagined and built through universal cosmopolitanism and global linear thinking (Kant's and Schmitt's logic) or through border thinking (the logic of decolonial cosmopolitanism and dialogue of civilizations). In the latter, the aim is pluriversality rather than a new universality which, in the best possible scenario, would be distributed among a limited numbers of capitalist centers. Pluriversality and border thinking traces a desired horizon

---

7   On this matter see Eduardo Mendieta's (2009) very insightful and at the same time well informed mapping of the process from imperial to dialogical cosmopolitans.

of decolonial cosmopolitanism or what is the same of cosmopolitan localism. The emerging global political society is delinking from the liberal cosmopolitan ideals as well as from the Marxist conceptions of the common. The communal is part and parcel of the decolonial option (Mignolo 2009b). Cosmopolitan localism points toward the re-investment of the communal, that is, non-capitalist socio-economic organization. However, not the communal as a new abstract universal, but the communal as would be enacted in all local histories who want to organize themselves re-inscribing the non-capitalist principles that were ruled out by Western civilization. This is what I mean by cosmopolitan (decolonial) localism and border thinking as the necessary epistemology. I am speaking about non-capitalist rather than pre-capitalist economies. Pre-capitalists means that whatever was there before capitalist ended and as superseded by capitalism, while non-capitalist economies reminds you that capitalism is, on the one hand, an option and not the irrevocable unfolding of history and, on the other, that those economies that are non-capitalist co-exist with capitalism and that non-capitalist economies will come about in the future. "Pre-" capitalism belongs to the imperial rhetoric of modernity. Non-capitalist economies existed before capitalism, for sure, but, more important, existed all along the 500 years of Western capitalism and are being re-invigorated today by the emerging global political society. It is here precisely where border thinking and decolonial cosmopolitanism find their *raison d'être* and field of operation. Not everything shall be oriented toward the state and even less to corporate values of excellence, success and success understood in terms of material possession and ego-celebration.

The Colonial Matrix of Power and Imperial Cosmopolitanism

Western civilization—the first in Huntington's list—was founded on a new structure of management and control—the colonial matrix of power. Put in place in the Atlantic, it undergirded the formation of modern Europe—before the Renaissance what is today Europe was the land of Western Christians.[8] It was at the historical junction that Europe became the geopolitical manager of knowledge and the actors and institutions under which such management took place, defined themselves as *humanitas*—the point of arrival and universal model of *human history* and the point of reference to created epistemic and ontological differences with pagans, Saracens, Indians, blacks, women, homosexuals, primitives, communists and the like—in one word, the *anthropos*. From the perspective of the non-Western world where the *anthropos* inhabits (and now migrations from the North to the South are relocating the *anthropos* in the land of *humanitas*), modernity goes hand-in-hand with coloniality—the invention

---

8   *The Clash of Civilizations* (Huntington 1993).

and endurance of the *anthropos* (that is, of racism) is one of the consequences of coloniality. The history of modernity/coloniality is therefore the history of social and global order transformed in its surface and maintained in its deep structure by the colonial matrix of power (coloniality for short).

A new economic horizon emerged, which consisted of producing commodities for a global market and in dismantling existing economic formations (in the Andes and Mesoamerica first, in Asia and Africa later on). That type of economy, before the industrial revolution, needed land and labor. The separation of Man and Nature like in the eighteenth century the separation of Church and the state, are foundational pillars of Western civilization. The first pillar established the foundations for the control of the economy. And the second, preceded by a "separation" of Christian Theology from Judaic and Islamic Theologies, established the foundation for the control of authority. Christian Theology was the form of authority that established itself in the New World while dismantling Aztec and Inca forms of governance. "Nature" that is, life, was put at risk when the industrial revolution needed "natural resources." Thus, the capitalist economy based on extraction (gold and silver) or harvest and regeneration (cotton, sugar, tobacco, etc.), was transformed into an economy based on natural resources to nourish the machine that, at their turn, transformed the economy of harvest and regeneration.

Next to the sphere of the economy and of authority, the colonial matrix was established by means of the control of knowledge. The Western businessman doesn't know what the Chinese man knows: the Chinese man knows that the white man makes him yellow while the white man doesn't have to worry about being white, because after all it is whiteness that was presupposed in the epistemic formation and management of Western knowledge. The colonial matrix works at two simultaneous levels: its own self-legitimation chanting the rhetoric of modernity and the disavowal (logic of coloniality) and discredit of all that doesn't fit into its rhetoric. In this scenario, both decolonial cosmopolitanism and dialogues among civilizations would have to start from there: the epistemic foundation of the modern/colonial world (its racial and patriarchal pillars) rather than from an arbitrary division of world civilization or from an ideal cosmo-polis in a far distant and ancient Greece revamped by Immanuel Kant in the European Enlightenment.

Now we can understand that if there are some points in common between dialogues among civilizations and decolonial cosmopolitanism, there are also significant differences. Decolonial cosmopolitanism operates mainly, and currently, at the level of the political society while dialogue among civilizations operates at the level of existing institutions. On the one hand, decolonial cosmopolitanism has its point of reference in the colonial matrix of power, a structure of control and management that emerged together with the emergence of global linear thinking, in the sixteenth century. On the other hand, the concept of dialogue among and alliances of civilizations operates on a different horizon: the horizon of "civilizations" as defined in Western economy of thoughts, where the concept of civilization is already ingrained in the rhetoric of modernity that places Western civilization (like in Huntington) on top of all others. Decolonial cosmopolitanism instead starts from the underlying logic of "modernity" and "civilization" and focuses on the rhetoric of modernity that constructed the idea and the logic of coloniality that justified the need of such invention: that is, the civilizing mission. The modern idea of "civilization" is daughter of the "civilizing mission" and Huntington's "clash" the realization that the civilizing mission did not work and that the "not-civilized" have their own opinion about how they shall live their lives.

Possible Alliances between Decolonial Cosmopolitanism and Dialogues among Civilizations

"Western civilization" was a latecomer, but since 1500 it began to build itself with global ambitions. Western Christianity was behind those designs. Defining itself as "civilization" the rhetoric of Western modernity was able to define the other as such, but ranking them below the Western model, the point of arrival in time and the center of space (Europe). That is why to remain within the Kantian legacies would mean to endorse imperial cosmopolitanism (Mendieta 2009). And since cosmopolitanism in the modern colonial world (in its Christian legacy of the *orbis terrarum Christianus* or in its secular Kantian version revamping of the Greek *Kosmopolis*) has been the empire's companion (as Spanish grammarian and philosopher, Elio Antonio de Nebrija, described his first grammar of Castilian language), critical cosmopolitanism shall be decolonial. Otherwise, it would remain within the same rules and cosmology of Western modernity. Decolonial cosmopolitanism means, then, that the days of imperial cosmopolitanism (Christian, liberal, or Marxist, modern or postmodern) are over and that a convivial world would have to deal with capitalism as the global economy and social racial hierarchies supporting it.

The fact is that Western civilization turned, toward the end of the twentieth century, to a market-driven society instead of maintaining the priority of social organization in which the market is a sector of it. Thus, both any Western-guided cosmopolitan project and dialogues among civilizations are heavily undercut by an economy based not only on competition and on *success* and on *competitive leadership* rather than on *cooperative leadership* and non-material compensations. A common goal of liberal and Marxist cosmopolitans and dialogue of civilizations could be to re-orient the economy and the capitalist overflow.[9] At that moment, it could be a productive collaboration between critical versions of Western cosmopolitanism, on the one hand, and decolonial cosmopolitanism on the other. From this perspective, Sinic, Islamic, and Western civilizations in Huntington's chart are today connected by an economy that prevents any kind of dialogue between civilizations beyond political and economic talks between competitors. By the same token, cosmopolitan

---

9   For a Marxist perspective on cosmopolitanism see Harvey (2000); for a liberal take on cosmopolitanism see Martha Nussbaum's celebrated article (1994) and, more recently, the celebrated book by Kwame Anthony Appiah (2006).

projects would be stopped by the prevalence of competition and success (by persons, by institutions, by countries, and so on); competition and success of which advocates of modern forms of cosmopolitanism may not be able to avoid, could find themselves "competing" to come ahead with their own universal and abstract version of a cosmopolitan world order.

If cosmopolitanism, in general, could be the empire's companion and also the companion of a multi-polar and capitalist world (although no longer ruled by (neo-)liberal designs) and therefore promote global designs and competition in the name of cosmopolitanism managed from above, decolonial cosmopolitanism shall promote cooperation over competition, communal (different versions, the Marxist common as well as liberal common good) pluriversal organization rather than social organization based on one universal model promoting individual success with good conscience. Thus, decolonial cosmopolitanism as argued here shall be twofold: one is the critical understanding of the avatars of the colonial matrix of power (cf. coloniality), its formation, transformations between 1500 and 2000 in the hands of Western civilization institutions and actors, to the first half of the twenty-first century. There is here a double implication: Western civilization is both the generator and the result of coloniality. That is why coloniality is the darker side of Western modernity and that is why the triumphal narrative of modernity has to hide the logic of coloniality. Understanding the formation and constant transformations of the rhetoric of modernity (progress, economic growth, and well-being based on consumerism and individual success) as well as understanding the changing faces of the logic of coloniality, are the necessary conditions for decolonial cosmopolitan goals and border thinking. Why border thinking? Because what has been disavowed by the rhetoric of modernity (barbarians, primitives, traditions, etc.) has to be re-inscribed in order to disrupt the totalitarian impulses and global designs of Western modernity recognizing, at the same time, the emancipating ideals that modernity brought to global conviviality. Where modernity went wrong was to believe that emancipation justifies imperialism. And that emancipation goes hand-in-hand with free enterprise and predatory economic organization that needs the logic of coloniality to be disguised under the rhetoric of modernity (progress, development, civilization, freedom, and consumerism). Modernity is the theodicy of Western civilization as discourse; coloniality is its curse. On the second fold, decolonial cosmopolitanism(s) are projects delinking from the mirage of modernity and the hidden logic of coloniality. By so doing, decolonial projects, and cosmopolitanism among them, establish lines of demarcation to the indeterminacy of coloniality. Contested at the level of its content, coloniality operates in an open field, since contesting the content leaves its logic intact. And that is the problem with liberal and Marxist cosmopolitan projects. For that reason, again, the Kantian cosmopolitan legacy and Marxist internationalism ran their course and cannot offer plausible roads toward decolonial global futures. Now we get to the point where border thinking or border epistemology become the necessary method of any decolonial project.

To understand what border epistemology is means in essence to understand and explain how territorial epistemology appropriates concepts introduced from the perspective of border epistemology. The United Nations, for instance, has appropriated the concept of "interculturality" and the concept of "sumak kawsay" introduced by indigenous leaders in the Andean regions of South America in clear and distinctive decolonial goals (UN Volunteers 1999; UNESCO n.d.) to claim epistemic rights and cooperation in building a pluri-national Ecuadorian state, predicated in the basic principles of doing business in a world without borders.[10] The "Alliance of Civilizations" of the United Nations has a chapter on "Business Coalition for Intercultural Dialogue and Cooperation."

The announcement states the following:

> *It is also based on recommendations of the joint Alliance of Civilizations-Global-Compact publications entitled "Doing Business in a Multicultural World: Challenges and Opportunities":*

> *In partnership with the United Nations Global Compact Office, the UN Alliance of Civilizations is committed to engaging the business community, recognizing the crucial role that business can play in establishing dialogue and improving understanding and cooperative relations among nations and peoples across cultures and religions. (AoC 2010)*

For decolonial intellectuals this rhetoric is half of the story. Decolonial cosmopolitanism appears as an option and a contribution to several existing options to unveil the false promises of the rhetoric of modernity and the hidden logic of coloniality that engenders all type of counter-violence and prevents dialogue of civilizations based on critical and decolonial cosmopolitanism rather than on the continual updating of the rhetoric of modernity.

Border Thinking and Cosmopolitan Localism

The decolonial option is the connector, the spine of decolonial cosmopolitanism, the links between the commonality of colonial experiences of people with uncommon local histories—Indians in India and indigenous populations in America, New Zealand and Australia; Chinese struck by the Opium War and by neoliberalism and the legacies of Maoism in struggles of liberation. In sum, decolonial cosmopolitanism is the cosmopolitanism that emerges from the decolonial option and cuts across— at the same time as respecting—identities in life and politics: all human beings confronting—at different scales—the consequences of modern/colonial racism and patriarchy have something in common, beyond their religious, ethnic, gender,

---

10 For a clear denunciation of the twisted politics of the UN and UNESCO (as well as the PNUD) in the Andes, and the appropriation of border thinking concepts and their managements within territorial epistemology, see Walsh (2009). An interview, in English, is forthcoming (see Walsh and Mignolo 2010).

sexuality, nationalities, languages. Frantz Fanon had a name for them/us: *les damnés de la terre*. The decolonial option materializes in multiple trajectories where identities emerge. But, beyond identities, the commonality that identify peoples and communities for being "not quite human," runs like a thread across identities, connecting (rather than uniting) many projects and trajectories in a global process of decolonial cosmopolitanism; toward the horizon of pluriversality as a universal project.

Mehrzad Boroujerdi (1996) distinguished "Orientalism in reverse" from "Nativism."[11] In the first case subjects that became oriental objects in Western knowledge, responded by making the West the other. By so doing, "Orientalism in reverse" accepts the rules of the game and attempts to change the content—not the terms—of the conversation. "Nativism" in Boroujerdi's conceptualization is something different. The term "nativism" here may surprise members of the cosmopolitan club.

> *Nativism stands in the same relation to Orientalism in reverse as Eurocentrism does to Orientalism proper. Both Nativism and Eurocentrism provide an ontological and epistemological umbrella under which it becomes possible to develop a theory of history and a political platform. Whereas Eurocentrism does advocate such ideas as the uniqueness and superiority of the West and its unequivocal manifest destiny, Nativism champions the cause of abandoning, subverting, and reversing these same meta-narratives and master codes. Nativism was born of the lamentable circumstance of colonialism and the agonizing milieu of the post-World War II period of decolonization. It represents a cultural reflex on the part of many Third World intellectuals from Southeast Asia to the Caribbean eager to assert their newly found identities.* (1996: 14)

The reader may suspect that we are here confronting another essentialist proposal. The interesting aspect of the proposal is that Frantz Fanon comes up, for an Iranian intellectual, as the paradigmatic example of "Nativism." Boroujerdi doesn't offer any specific reference or quotation as to why Fanon would be a paradigmatic example of "Nativism." I suspect that he has in mind statements like this one:

> *I am ready to concede that on the plane of factual being the past existence of an Aztec civilization does not change anything very much in the diet of the Mexican peasant of today ... But it has been remarked several times that this passionate search for a national culture which existed before the colonial era finds its legitimate reason in the anxiety shared by native intellectuals to shrink away from that Western culture in which they all risk being swamped.*

---

11 Being of Iranian descent and embodied in the legacies of Persian civilizations, his sensibility goes beyond his expertise in Iranian matters. The idea of "Nativism," I submit, owes more to his sensibility than to his professional expertise in political science and in Iran.

> *Because they realize they are in danger of losing their lives and thus becoming lost to their people, these men, hotheaded and with anger in their hearts, relentlessly determine to renew contact once more with the oldest and most pre-colonial springs of life of their people. (Fanon 1963: 209–10)*

Let's then translate "Nativism" into "Localism" and be clear that locals have been conformed by the formation and transformation of the colonial matrix of power. The point is then that Localism emerges because the advent of a powerful intellectual and political elite, some of them still linked to Europe through Marxism but in the colonies, and some plainly already decolonial. Localism, crossed and conformed by historical forces (in this case, Persia, Islam, the Western creation of the Middle East as a region and the Middle East becoming part of the Third World) then emerges as a pluriversal response and confrontation with universal Eurocentrism.

Eurocentrism, in the last analysis, is Western localism (or perhaps "nativism" is a good name for Eurocentrism) with a global design that became synonymous with universalism. Thus, Kant's cosmopolitanism and its legacy propose the universalization of Western Nativism/Localism. And the Marxist left, for better or worst, belongs to that world. This is a serious challenge for cosmopolitanism. On the contrary, non-Western localism is plural, since there are many multiple memories and colonial wounds infringed by racism, ways of life, languages, beliefs, experiences connected to the West but at the same time not subsumable to it. Localism (which shall not be confused with "national fundamentalisms" or "Nativism from the right") should be pluriversal and therefore decolonial. Since Localism originated "from the lamentable circumstance of colonialism," or better yet, of the logic of coloniality common to different Western imperial/colonial expansion (Spain, France, England) and its surrogates after the sixteenth century (Imperial Russia, Soviet Union, Japan), a trademark of localism is the decolonial thread that connects and makes of pluriversality a global project. Decolonial localism is global or if you wish cosmo-political. Thus we arrive at the paradoxical conclusion that if cosmopolitanism shall be preserved in the humanities goal toward the future it should be "cosmopolitan localism," an oxymoron no doubt, but the Kantian project of one localism being the universal is untenable today. "Cosmopolitan localism" is another expression for pluriversality as a global project. Kantian's legacies shall be reduced to its proper localism and stripped of its imperial/global pretensions. Recognizing the "idea" doesn't mean accepting its implementation. Cosmopolitanism can only work if there is no master global design, but a global agreement in which no one will rule without being ruled.

Tough call for those who believe that his/her party, religion or ideology is the best for everybody and has to be imposed for the well-being of all and for universal peace. Tough but realistic call now that the global political society is growing and is on its feet; it is aware that the era of being ruled and obeying, or being repressed for disobeying, is reaching its limit.

Coda: Border Thinking and Decolonial Cosmopolitanism Join Decolonial Dialogue Among Civilizations

The pending question was: would it be possible to have a decolonial vision in the dialogue among civilizations that could work in tandem with decolonial cosmopolitanism? If that cooperation is possible, then border thinking shall be the point of encounter between both.

Thus de-Westernization and decoloniality share the colonial wound, be it infringed upon colonized and enslaved people as well as upon regions and people that had not been colonized but that, through the Western control of knowledge, became in their mono-topic discourses inferior beings—whether the Ottoman or the Mughal Sultanates, the Chinese Dynasties, the Kingdom of Africa or the Incanate, they all were devaluated or disarticulated by the razor of the colonial and imperial differences inflicting the colonial wound. Although de-Westernization doesn't question capitalism while decoloniality does, decolonial cosmopolitanism may then find a common ground with decolonial dialogue of civilizations as far as dialogue of civilizations engage in a critical distance of any similar project that doesn't question today global economy based on the presupposition that economic growth will make us all happy and self-denying that economic growth cannot and shall not be the only justification of human life and action. And dialogue among civilizations remains part of the rhetoric of modernity, progress and growth and hides the logic of coloniality in which progress means increasing poverty and growth means the destruction of natural balance and life on the planet.

Thus, decolonial border thinking, on the other hand, asserts that an economy of accumulation and growth, based on exploitation, land appropriation and poisoning of the planet and of people, cannot by its very nature allow or support decolonial cosmopolitan projects and/or decolonial dialogue among civilizations.[12] The bottom line is that the decolonial option in the two versions argued here, cosmopolitan and dialogue among civilizations, shall be based on a fundamental principle that changes the horizon of life and vision of the future: life, of the planet and therefore of human beings (since you cannot save human lives if you destroy life), shall be the final horizon of a world in which many worlds shall co-exist (as the Zapatistas have it). Institutions shall come second and be at the service of life. It is really hypocrisy to fight to save capitalism and democracy when indeed capitalism and democracy have taken us to the world we are living in today and that developed countries and the media serving them have created and continue to endorse.

---

12   See Stephen Leahy, "Violenta ofensiva contra cientificos del clima," *TIERRAMERICA*, March 13, 2010, www.tierramerica.info/nota.php?lang=esp&idnews=3561; the bad news is that there is tendency in higher education to increase the corporate values at the univesity, see my "At the end of the university as we know it," May 7, 2009, www.waltermignolo.com/2009/05/07/at-the-end-of-the-university-as-we-know-it-world-epistemic-fora-toward-communal-futures-and-de-colonial-horizons-of-life.

Bibliography

AoC. 2010. *Business Coalition for Intercultural Dialogue and Cooperation* (Online: United Nations Alliance of Civilizations). Available at www.unaoc.org/content/view/430/284/lang,english.

Appiah, K.A. 2006. *Cosmopolitanism. Ethics in a World of Strangers*. New York: W.W. Norton and Co.

Beck, U. 2004. The truth of others. A cosmopolitan approach. *Common Knowledge*, 10(3), 430–49.

Boroujerdi, M. 1996. *Iranian Intellectuals and the West. The Tormented Triumph of Nativism*. Syracuse: Syracuse University Press.

Chatterjee, P. 2004. *The Politics of the Governed. Reflections on Popular Politics in Most of the World*. New York: Columbia University Press.

EDUCAM. 2007. *Alianca das Civilizaçoes, Interculturalismo e Direitos Humanos*. Rio de Janeiro: EDUCAM.

Fanon, F. 1963. *The Wretched of the Earth*. Translated from the French by Richard Philcox. New York: Gove Press.

Fine, R. 2007. Kant's theory of cosmopolitanism and Hegel's critique. Philosophy and social criticism. in *Philosophy and Social Criticism*, 29(6), 609–30.

Harvey, D. 2000. Cosmopolitanism and the banality of geographical evil. *Public Culture*, 12(2), 529–64.

Huntington, S. 1993. The clash of civilizations? *Foreign Affairs*, 72(3), 22–49.

Kant, I. 1784. *Idea of Universal History from a Cosmopolitan Point of View*. Translated by Carl J. Friedrich. In *Basic Writing of Kant*, edited and with an introduction by Allen W. Wood. New York: The Modern Library, 2001.

Khatami, M. 2000. *Dialogue among Civilizations* [Online: United Nations, New York, September 18]. Available at: www.unesco.org/dialogue/en/khatami.htm. [accessed: 2001].

Latour, B. 2004. Whose cosmos, which cosmopolitics? Comments on the peace terms of Ulrich Beck. *Common Knowledge*, 10(3), 461.

Mahbubani, K. 2008. *The New Asian Hemisphere. The Irresistible Shift of Global Power to the East*. New York: Public Affairs.

Mendieta, E. 2009. From imperial to dialogic cosmopolitanism? *Ethics and Global Politics*, 2(3), 241–58.

Michael, M.S. and Petito, F. 2009. *Civilizational Dialogue and World Order. The Other Politics of Cultures, Religions and Civilizations in International Relations*. London: Palgrave.

Mignolo, W. 1992. The darker side of the Renaissance: colonization and the discontinuity of the classical tradition. *Renaissance Quarterly*, www.jstor.org/pss/2862638.

Mignolo, W. 2000a. *Local Histories/Global Designs: Coloniality, Border Thinking and Subaltern Knowledges*. Princeton: Princeton University Press.

Mignolo, W. 2000b. The many faces of cosmo-polis: border thinking and critical cosmpolitanism. *Public Culture*, 12(3), 721–48.

Mignolo, W. 2001. Coloniality at large: the western hemisphere in the colonial horizon of modernity. *CR: The New Centennial Review*, 1(2), 19–54.

Mignolo, W. 2009a. Cosmopolitanism and the decolonial option. *Studies in the Philosophy of Education*, 29(2), 111–27.

Mignolo, W. 2009b. The communal and the decolonial. *Turbulence, Ideas in Movement*, 5, http://turbulence.org.uk/turbulence-5/decolonial.

Nussbaum, Martha. 1994. Patriotism and Cosmopolitanism. *Boston Review*, 19(5).

Osamu, N. 2006. Anthropos and humanitas: two western concepts of "human beings," in *Translation, Biopolitics, Colonial Difference*, edited by Naoki Sakai and Jon Solomon. Hong Kong: Hong Kong University Press, 259–74.

Petito, F. 2007. The Global Political Discourse of Dialogue among Civilizations: Mohammed Khatami and Václav Have, in *Peace and Security*, 19(2), 103–126.

Schmitt, C. 1952. *The nomos of the Earth in the International Law of the Jus Publicum Europaeum*. Translated and Annotated by G.L. Ulmen (2003). New York: Telos Press.

UN Volunteers. 1999. Caminando al Sumak Kawsay—English Summary.www.unv.org/en/what-we-do/thematic-areas/culture-sports/doc/caminando-al-sumak-kawsay.html.

UNESCO. n.d. Diversity and interculturality. http://portal.unesco.org/geography/en/ev.php-URL_ID=9127&URL_DO=DO_TOPIC&URL_SECTION=201.html.

Walsh, C. 2009. *Interculturalidad, Estado, sociedad. Luchas (de)coloniales de nuestra época*. Quito: Universidad Andina Simón Bolívar/Abya Yala.

Walsh, C. and Mignolo, W. 2010. De-coloniality. Decolonial thinking and doing in the Andes: a conversation by Walter Mignolo with Catherine Walsh: a propos of her book *Interculturalidad, Estado, sociedad. Luchas (de)coloniales de nuestra época/ Interculturalism, State, Society. (De)Colonial Struggles of Our Times*. In Reartikulacija, www.reartikulacija.org/?tag=walter-mignolo.

Cosmopolitanism and Mobilities

Mimi Sheller

Mobility is the essence of cosmopolitanism. And cosmopolitanism owes everything to the mobilities of people, cultures, and ideas around the world. The two concepts, it would seem, go hand-in-hand. Yet both ideas also have contested histories that draw them together in a more negative light (Beck and Cronin 2007 [2004]: 1–3). In Europe the term cosmopolitanism was "frequently employed in an anti-Semitic context in both Nazi Germany and Stalinist Russia," according to Paul Overy, "while nomadism [was employed] … to denigrate 'rootless' cosmopolitan left-wing—and by implication Jewish—intellectuals" (Overy 2005: 56). Emmanuel Levinas (1997 [1961]), in contrast, reflected on Yuri Gagarin's orbit of the earth in 1961 in his essay "Heidegger, Gagarin and us" as symbolizing the choice between "enlightened uprootedness" (*enracinement éclairé*) and the "earthly attachment" (*attachement terrestre*) of nationalist place-based ideologies of dwelling. Cosmopolitanism has also been used to describe the "creolized" cultures of the Caribbean, yet only thinly veils a *frisson* of exotic allure in the possibilities of racial and sexual miscegenation suggested by the term (Sheller 2003a, 2003b). Thus the concept functions as precisely the kind of "North Atlantic Universal" that anthropologist Michel-Rolph Trouillot takes to task for seducing us by their "ability to project transhistorical relevance while hiding the particularities of their marks and origins, including their affective load" (Trouillot 2003: 36).

Insofar as recent European social theory seeks to explore the relation between cosmopolitanization and mobilities in new ways, it may still be necessary to ask whether it has adequately addressed and overcome these problematic historical nuances and debates. How do theories of cosmopolitanism and of mobilities address Europe's past histories of nationalism, xenophobia, colonialism, and racism, which rest on the very idea of "roots" for some who belong to the soil, and "routes" for others—a kind of forced mobility for those who do not belong, those who are expelled, and those who are not let in? And how might ideas of cosmopolitanism and understandings of (im)mobility and dwelling arising from non-European locations contribute to the debate? If cosmopolitan creolization is theorized as a Caribbean condition that now informs the world as a whole (Hannerz 1996), what are we to make of the contemporary turn to cosmopolitan mobilities as a solution to the dilemma of an ethical modernity for Europe?

Both cosmopolitanism and mobilities are today key theoretical terms identified with emerging branches of European social theory over the last decade. When the *British Journal of Sociology* published a special 60th anniversary edition, reprinting significant articles representing each decade along with new commentaries on them, the two agenda-setting articles selected for the latest decade were John Urry's "Mobile sociology" (Urry 2010 [2001]) and Ulrich Beck and Natan Sznaider's "Unpacking cosmopolitanism for the social sciences: a research agenda" (Beck and Sznaider 2010 [2006]). Beck has also made a significant effort to understand the relation between the two perspectives in his 2008 piece "Mobility and the cosmopolitan perspective." A number of younger scholars have also tried to bridge the divide between the two schools of thought (Canzler et al. 2008), yet there remain a number of unresolved differences between these two influential approaches and they each bear a slightly different relation to the historical legacies alluded to above.

I want to examine the commonalities and differences between Beck's version of "cosmopolitan realism" and Urry's approach to mobilities research in terms of their theoretical, methodological, and normative projects, as well as comparing the parallel critiques of both approaches. I examine these debates in the context of wider currents of postcolonial, feminist, and anthropological thought, which have addressed related issues of mobility, circulation, and differential access to movement, yet are not always cited as influential currents in recent social theory. My aim is to highlight some of the misunderstandings that have plagued a constructive dialogue across these competing critical approaches to mobilities and cosmopolitanization in the contemporary world, while also bringing back into play the more critical dimensions of alternative theoretical approaches which have emphasized "cosmopolitanism-from-below" situated beyond Europe and grounded in postcolonial histories of racial, ethnic, gender, and sexual formations. Once these dimensions are addressed, the way is then cleared to assess what the actual key philosophical differences are between the two approaches.

Comparing Cosmopolitan Realism and the New Mobilities Paradigm

Beck's work is philosophically situated in a continental European tradition of critiques of modernization that hold onto the reflexivity that is seen as the hallmark of Enlightenment modernity, rejecting the (mainly French) post-structuralist turn towards language in favor of a realist approach to communicative action. Urry's work, in contrast, builds on more Anglo-American approaches to post-Marxist historical materialism that take a post-humanist turn, as described below. While differing in their philosophical and empirical orientations, both Beck and Urry begin from a crucial critique of "methodological nationalism," "which subsumes society under the nation-state" according to Beck and Sznaider, and reinforces a "sedentary" view of social life, according to Urry (see Sheller and Urry 2006, Hannam et al. 2006, Urry 2007 for further elaborations). Mobilities theorists, like theorists of cosmopolitanism, resist the traditional sociological image of the social world as an array of bounded entities or sedentary containers with separate "societies" and "cultures," fixed ethnic populations, stable national identities, and associated racial projects.[1] Thus both perspectives agree, as Beck puts it, that "fundamental dualisms—the national and the international, we and the others, inside and outside, fixity and motion—collapse; [and therefore] the social sciences face an epistemological crisis because they lose their subject of inquiry (see, for example, Urry 2000: 18–20)" (Beck 2008: 26). And because of this, both would agree, an entirely reconfigured realm of the empirical is emerging (Büscher and Urry 2009).

Yet, while Beck's "cosmopolitan realism" and Urry's "mobile sociology" share these common starting points, there is much that divides them in practice. Beck (2008) himself characterizes the difference as being between a post-modernist approach and his preference for a "second-modern" approach, stating that post-modernists such as Urry (2000) "underestimate the importance and contradiction of 'boundary management' in a world of flows and networks" (Beck 2008: 33). Yet when he goes on to point toward the "powerful infrastructures and machines that enable individuals, groups, companies, and whole nations to be connected with other places and spaces around the world," he might as well be citing Urry's own arguments. "Together with complex systems of IT infrastructures and the Internet," Beck argues (echoing Urry 2007 almost word for word), "these networks of mobility (such as airports, road systems, the worldwide system of vessels and ports and so on) build the backbone of the cosmopolitan society and the process of globalization" (Beck 2008: 33). So if both indeed address "a specific constellation of 'fixity and motion' (David Harvey) and the dialectics of (im)mobility and a strained relationship between moorings and flows" (*ibid.*)—as they both claim to—then what is it that really sets them apart?

Over the past decade the "new mobilities paradigm" (Sheller and Urry 2006) has promoted more interdisciplinary study of the intertwined practices of many different systems of contemporary mobility and immobility, including public and private transport systems; tourism, migration, and border studies; mobile communications and software-supported infrastructures; automobility, aeromobility, velomobility, and various kinds of passengering; children's mobility, elderly mobility, and studies of gendered mobility; walking, climbing, dancing, and other forms of trained bodily movement; and studies of the regulation, governance, and legal structures pertaining to all of these. It arguably engages in precisely the kind of methodological cosmopolitanization that Beck calls for, but

---

1   The Chicago School studies of urbanism at the beginning of the twentieth century, for example, assumed that sedentary forms of life were the norm, and were preferable to the abnormally peripatetic life of the vagabond, the displacement experienced by the immigrant, and the over-stimulus and anomie of the rapidly growing city, into which immigrants required "assimilation," "acculturation," and "integration."

does so by scaling research not only up toward the transnational level, but also down toward the sub-national level of everyday mobilities. Mobilities research equally recognizes crucial aspects of cosmopolitan realism, such as the importance of "motility," the "politics of scale," the "active relationship of actors to space and place," and "the power techniques and the strategies of boundary management that define and construct places and scapes" (Beck 2008: 32–4).

There is also another unexpected resemblance between the two theoretical approaches in that critics have framed both as being specifically *European* social theories that ignore gendered, racial, and colonial power relations by re-centering the European masculine subject. This is despite the fact that both Beck and Urry are often at pains *not* to do this. Yet, undeniably, their work does at times marginalize the scholarship within the fields of postcolonial and feminist theory that has directly contributed to the very cosmopolitanization of the world that is at stake. In what follows I want to clear up both the misunderstandings between the two approaches, as seen in Beck's critiques of Urry for ignoring boundaries and immobilities—when in fact this is precisely Urry's argument; and shift the debate to a more pertinent question of the mobilities of theory and the cosmopolitanization of academic schools of thought. By this I mean to address the disjunctures between the location of cosmopolitan theory in European networks of knowledge-production versus the view of cosmopolitanism that arises from other locations, itineraries, or circuits of meaning. When we ask who is experiencing cosmopolitanization, who is imagined as cosmopolitan, and who is being mobilized or demobilized, then the disjunctive temporalities of what James Clifford called "discrepant modernities" come to play a crucial part.

Common Critiques of Cosmopolitanism and Mobilities Theory

Both cosmopolitan realism and mobilities theory posit that at the beginning of the twenty-first century "we are witnessing a global transformation of modernity which calls for a re-thinking of the humanities and the social sciences" (Beck and Sznaider 2010: 381). The agenda-setting programs in both cases involve an overlapping set of ontological, epistemological, methodological, and normative claims. Beck and Sznaider refer to four different aspects of the concept of cosmopolitanism by noting that it is simultaneously a description of the world, a basis of social theory, a research agenda, and a normative guide. The same could be said for Urry's theory, which oscillates between a description of the contemporary world as more mobile than in the past; a basis for social theorizing that puts mobility at its center; a research agenda around the study of various complex systems of mobility; and at times a normative move toward addressing the future of mobility in relation to ecological sustainability. Thus we have two ambitious agendas for social theory and research, both premised on a notion of post-national social and cultural interconnectivity.

Yet each has also attracted a very similar set of critical responses, grounded in issues of power and difference.

In her response piece in the *British Journal of Sociology*, Nina Glick Schiller judges that Beck and Sznaider's article "seems simultaneously strangely dated, somewhat innocent, and refreshingly visionary" (Glick Schiller 2010: 414), much like European social theory is generally judged in the empirically-driven US social sciences. In terms of a description of the contemporary world, she dismissed Beck and Sznaider's binary contrast between the cosmopolitan present and an allegedly nation-centered past, which echoes Mike Savage's critique of the "epochal claims" that are made in contemporary (especially British) social theory, including Urry's (Savage 2009). The basis of these criticisms is not simply that earlier eras were also mobile and cosmopolitan (such that the bounded nation-state was never a good organizing principle for social analysis), but also that in some situations historical actors also *reflexively* understood themselves as partaking in a high degree of mobility or cosmopolitanism. Previous eras have debated these terms and gone through many iterations of identification with place, locality, or nation versus movement, connectivity, or universality. To claim that the present epoch is *newly* mobile or cosmopolitanized asserts a situated European perspective that symptomatically ignores the experiences of the colonized world, which has arguably long been mobile and cosmopolitan at least since the seventeenth century. Thus by launching his analysis out of the ashes of Auschwitz and claiming that cosmopolitanism "is a vital theme of European civilization and European consciousness and beyond that of global experience," Beck inadvertently relegates the "global experience" to a predicate of Europe (Beck and Cronin 2007 [2004]: 2).

The critical response to this kind of European theory arises out of extensive studies of migration, diasporas, and transnational citizenship, which offer trenchant critiques of the bounded and static categories of nation, ethnicity, community, and state within much social science (Basch et al. 1994, Brah 1996, Chow 1993, Clifford 1997, Gilroy 1993, Glick Schiller and Fouron 2001, Ifekwunigwe 1999, Joseph 1999, Ong 1999, Ong and Nonini 1997, Van der Veer 1995). These works highlight dislocation, displacement, disjuncture, and dialogism—the sine qua non of cosmopolitanism—as widespread conditions of migrant subjectivity in the world today *and in the past* for many colonial subjects. From the ships, sea routes, and interconnectivity of the Black Atlantic (Gilroy 1993) to the complex mobilities of diasporas and transnational migrants in the modern world (Cohen 2008), postcolonial anthropology and cultural studies already pay great attention to the interplay of "routes and roots" (Clifford 1997), "scapes" and "flows" (Appadurai 1996), and transnational connections (Hannerz 1996). All of these antecedents must be encompassed in any approach to contemporary cosmopolitanism or theorization of mobilities, yet seem to be insufficiently acknowledged by Eurocentric theorists who begin from the assumption that the world today is empirically more mobile or cosmopolitan than ever before.

Second, as a basis for social theory, Glick Schiller critiques Beck and Sznaider's "decentered approach to a world of interdependent networks [because it] fails to capture the politics of wealth extraction and political and military oppression," thus failing to analyze power (Glick Schiller 2010: 417). The same critique is leveled against Urry's work by those who charge that, "Mobility and control over mobility both reflect and reinforce power. Mobility is a resource to which not everyone has an equal relationship" (Skeggs 2004: 49). As a research agenda, both the cosmopolitan perspective and the mobilities paradigm have been decried for lacking an analysis of structures of domination, of actors, and agency. As Glick Schiller puts it, "Contemporary social analysis must direct our attention to the actors and unequal relationships that shape and respond to struggles against injustice and deprivation" (2010: 419), which she sees as being more effectively carried out through studies of "subaltern and every day forms of cosmopolitanism" such as labor movements, Pan-Africanism, anti-colonialism, and transnational feminism.

Thus we have a whole range of alternative terms: James Clifford's notion of "discrepant cosmopolitanism" which "gives us a way of perceiving, and valuing, different forms of encounter, negotiation, and multiple affiliations" (Clifford 1998: 365); Homi Bhabha's "vernacular cosmopolitanisms" (Bhabha 2001 [1996], 2000); Partha Mitter's notion of the "'virtual cosmopolitan' who was a native of the peripheries, but who intellectually engaged with the knowledge system of the metropolis" (Mitter 2005: 39); and Kobena Mercer's understanding of the "critically cosmopolitan" and his discussion of "what could be called a 'cosmopolitanism-from-below,' in which perspectives on mass migration, exile, asylum, and border-crossing feature prominently" (Mercer 2005: 11). Srinivas Aravamudan even coins the word "tropicopolitan," combining "the idea of *tropic* with that of *cosmopolitan*" in order to create "a name for the colonized subject who exists both as fictive construct of colonial tropology *and* actual resident of tropical space, object of representation *and* agent of resistance" (Aravamudan 1999: 4). These overlooked figures (such as Olaudah Equiano or Toussaint Louverture) "challenge the developing privilege of Enlightenment cosmopolitans" (*ibid.*: 4) in a way that Beck's work remains deaf to. These postcolonial theorists all provide important counter-weights to Beck's cosmopolitanism, which claims reflexivity yet fails to reflect on its relation to European colonial history or its relation to European social theory that systematically erases "peripheral" scholarship.

Beck, of course, distinguishes between normative or "philosophical cosmopolitanism" and what he calls the "cosmopolitanization of reality," which is unintended and involuntary (Beck 2008: 26–7). Nevertheless, not only is the historical relation between ideas of cosmopolitanism and symbolic meanings of mobility fraught with a troubled history, but certain recent appropriations of the term have not sufficiently acknowledged the preceding work of postcolonial, feminist, and other "peripheral" theorists who have contributed to the genealogies of these concepts. Theorists using these concepts as if they were innocent descriptions of the present (European) moment must pay greater attention to the contested meanings of both cosmopolitanism and mobilities because they carry such a heavy freight with them. By acknowledging the work within anthropology, feminist theory, and postcolonial theory that has addressed aspects of cosmopolitanism "from below" or on "the periphery," European theorists of cosmopolitanism and mobilities would actually be able to claim a greater cosmopolitanization and mobility of knowledge, demonstrating that which they posit is taking place.

We might also compare several important feminist critiques of "nomadic theory," which point out that it is grounded in masculine subjectivities, makes assumptions about freedom of movement, and ignores the gendered production of space. Nomadic theory rests on a "romantic reading of mobility," argues Caren Kaplan, and "certain ways of seeing [that arise] as a result of this privileging of cosmopolitan mobility" (Kaplan 1996). Both Beck and Urry completely agree with this, yet they are still vulnerable to the charge. Beverley Skeggs likewise argues that the mobility paradigm could be linked to a "bourgeois masculine subjectivity" that describes itself as "cosmopolitan," and she further points out that "mobility and fixity are figured differently depending on national spaces and historical periods" (Skeggs 2004: 48). Rather than simply accepting these criticisms, I would counter that the new mobilities paradigm *does* move on from this kind of disavowal of power. It does not privilege a "mobile subjectivity," but rather tracks the power of discourses and practices of mobility in creating effects of both movement and stasis. Mobilities research in its broadest sense concerns a full politics of mobility (Adey 2009); not only physical movement, but also potential movement, blocked movement, immobilization, and forms of dwelling and place-making (Büscher and Urry 2009), all of which are also central to the sociology of cosmopolitanization, which also acknowledges the uneven and contested nature of mobility and the struggle over what Beck calls the "production of place" (Beck 2008: 33–4). Power relations are at the heart of mobility and immobility.

Issues of uneven motility and of mobility rights, ethics, and justice have become crucial to the field of critical mobilities research (Cresswell 2006, Bergmann and Sager 2008, Uteng and Cresswell 2008), thus suggesting important overlaps with the field of "cosmopolitanism-from-below" through an attention to subaltern mobilities (and immobilities), as well as recognition of the importance of uprooting, dwelling, homing, and grounding (Ahmed et al. 2003, Sheller 2003a, 2004). In sum, there is far more in common between both approaches than each recognizes of the other, and both suffer from matching forms of misrecognition or mistaken critique. Nevertheless, there are crucial blind spots in both paradigms (or, more modestly, research programs), which are indicative of the difficulties that some other fields of critical scholarship (especially in anthropology, postcolonial theory, critical race studies, feminist theory, and so on) have had in embracing either cosmopolitan realism or mobilities research. These blind spots include an ongoing sense of Eurocentrism in defining the spaces and times of cosmopolitanism and mobile modernity; a preponderant exemplification of the white, male, middle-class subject as the normative mobile or cosmopolitan subject; and a failure to engage with the academic literature produced in more marginal locations that is relevant to theorizing the contemporary cosmopolitan or mobile world. While much of the criticism is due to mutual misunderstanding on the one hand, and the power dynamics of academic field-building on the other, there nevertheless remain some actual underlying differences that need to be better described. In the following section I turn to an entirely different set of distinctions between the two approaches.

The Material Turn in Mobilities Research

One of the most crucial yet little-noted distinctions at play between cosmopolitan realism and the new mobilities paradigm, I would argue, revolves around their analytical relation to the non-human, non-representational, material and affective dimensions of social life. Unlike the study of cosmopolitanism, the post-societal (perhaps even post-sociological) study of mobilities encompasses not only human mobility, but also the mobility of objects, information, images, and capital. And it includes study of the infrastructures, vehicles, and software systems that enable physical travel and mobile communication to take place. What especially sets mobilities research apart from approaches to cosmopolitanism is the extent to which the new mobilities paradigm has taken seriously "the material turn" and "the spatial turn" in the social sciences. Influenced by social studies of science and technology, in particular actor-network theory (Law and Hassard 1999), mobilities theorists pay close attention to the infrastructures and technical objects that assist mobility (everything from shoes and bikes, to mobile phones and motor vehicles). It also highlights the in-between and liminal places at which movement is paused, slowed, or stopped: borders, airports, toll roads, hotels, motels, detention centers, refugee camps, and so on. These would appear to be concerns of little relevance to cosmopolitan realism, or even hindrances to its emphasis on reflexivity and human agency, yet they emerge as central to critical mobilities studies.

Many commentators have mistakenly equated mobilities research with earlier theoretical projects that embraced concepts such as nomadism, flow, and liquidity. For example, Knowles says of Urry's "Mobile Sociology" that

> 'flow', and the 'fluidity' underpinning it, conveys a sense of ease, a smoothness of motion that is contradicted by even cursory examination of how specific mobilities actually work. I have two objections to 'flow': it is misleading as a description of mobilities; and analytically it erases important social information in the texture of the shifting, contingent connectivity that forms mobile sociology's core business. (Knowles 2010: 374)

This entirely misses Urry's and other mobility theorists' continuous efforts to emphasize the relations between mobilities and immobilities, scapes and moorings, movement and stillness, and precisely these kinds of frictions and differential movements (for instance, Hannam et al. 2006: 3, Wood and Graham 2006). Differential mobilities are at the heart of the new mobilities paradigm, whether tracing different mobility systems and their complex relations to each other, mapping uneven rights to mobility and degrees of potential mobility, or showing the relation between mobility and immobility in specific instances. Urry argues that the *complex* character of mobility systems stems from the multiple fixities or moorings often on a substantial physical scale that enable other things to be fluid (Urry 2007). Kaufmann (2010) also observes that Urry's "Mobile Sociology" has been misunderstood, and that subsequent work such as *Mobilities* (2007) emphasizes power, inequality, and difference; concepts which are later elaborated with the concept of "network capital" (Elliott and Urry 2010).

Recent empirically-grounded interdisciplinary studies of mobility differ from earlier theories of flow or nomadism (and from some approaches to cosmopolitanism) in part because of the emphasis on the relation between mobility and immobility, between movement and infrastructural moorings, and in some cases attention to the valuation of stillness or non-mobility, or at least cultures of alternative (and often slower) mobility (Vannini 2009). Some call for the investigation of "stillness" as a positive experience, or at least one that requires greater exploration and analysis (Bissell 2007, Bissell and Fuller 2009). Recent work also often highlights the differential capacities and potential for mobility with the concept of "motility," defined as "the manner in which an individual or group appropriates the field of possibilities relative to movement and uses them" (Kaufmann and Montulet 2008: 45). By bringing together studies of exile, migration, immigration, migrant citizenship, transnationalism, and even tourism, new approaches to mobility are able to highlight the complex relation between local and global "power-geometries" (Massey 1993), showing how both the physical and symbolic aspects of human mobility—including claims to cosmopolitanism—are political projects. It thus intersects with the field of critical border studies (Cunningham and Heyman 2004), which understands borders as constituted by the regulation of mobility, that is, of how they are legally and illegally crossed by people, by goods, and by cultural flows.

Even further, the move toward complexity theory within mobilities research is suggestive of non-actor-centered processes of feedback, self-organization, and tipping points, which may shape dynamic processes in ways that are not directly caused by reflexive modern subjects and their agency. As Urry argues, "All systems are dynamic, processual and generate emergent effects and systemic contradictions, especially through positive feedback mechanisms" (Urry 2008, cf. Dennis and Urry 2008). Thus mobilities theory branches off into complex systems theory in ways that are deeply grounded in materiality, and depart from the traditions of social theory, including cosmopolitan realism, that focus on structure *in relation to* (human) agency. This is related to the post-humanist turn in some Anglo-American theory (for instance, Hayles 1999, Law and Hassard 1999), which is highly critical of Enlightenment liberalism and its theory of history as progress. Complexity theory offers recourse to unintentional causal processes and implicates causal mechanisms possibly beyond human control, quite unlike the still humanist impulses of reflexive modernization.

The claim to a new mobilities paradigm, therefore, is not simply an assertion of the novelty of mobility in the world today (although the speed and intensity of various flows may arguably be greater than ever before). As Sheller and Urry (2006) put it: "we do not insist on a new 'grand narrative' of the global condition as one of mobility, fluidity, or liquidity. The new mobilities paradigm suggests a set of questions, theories, and methodologies rather than a totalizing description of the contemporary world." It delineates the context in which both sedentary and nomadic accounts of the social world operate, and it questions how that context is itself mobilized, or performed, through ongoing socio-technical practices. Rather than celebrating mobility or advocating a masculine mobile subjectivity, research in this field is in fact highly engaged with unmasking such discourses and revealing what is at stake in debates over differentiated mobility. Within geography this more nuanced approach is especially associated with the work of Tim Cresswell on the cultural history of mobility, its modes of regulation, and the power relations associated with it—in short the politics of mobility and immobility (Cresswell 1999, 2002, 2006). The politics of (im)mobility are also a central concern in the presentation of the field by geographer Peter Adey (2009).

There are interdependent systems of immobile material worlds and especially some exceptionally immobile platforms (transmitters, roads, stations, satellite dishes, airports, docks, factories) through which mobilizations of locality, labor, and capital are performed and re-arrangements of place and scale materialized and spatially fixed (Harvey 1985). Such infrastructures are at one and the same time enhancing the motility of some, while detracting from the motility of others by leaving them in a relatively slower channel or disconnected position. This sense of the materiality of (im)mobility poses interesting problems for Beck and other theorists of cosmopolitanism, inasmuch as they operate within a realm of human agency and ideas, rather than human/non-human encounters and non-representational geographies of space and affect (Thrift 2007). Thrift, for example, counts on what he calls "a very faint view of human agency, to put it mildly":

> *The classical human subject which is transparent, rational and continuous no longer pertains. Classical ethical questions like 'What have I done?' and 'What ought I to do' become much more difficult when the 'I' in these questions is so faint, when self-transparency and narratibility are such transient features. Similarly, more modern ethical questions like what it means to be genuinely open to another human being or culture take on added layers of complexity.* (Thrift 2007: 14)

This could be said of Urry's faint account of human agency as well, in sharp contrast to Beck's, whose very project of reflexive modernization counts on the self-transparency and self-narration of the reflexive modern cosmopolitan subject. And as Thrift alludes to, the capacity to be "open" to others as cosmopolitanism normatively calls for is vexed by the complexity of disjointed subjectivities.

While the cosmopolitan realist theorist seeks to confront risk society and develop a "moral cosmopolitanism" that would mitigate human exposure to risks at an everyday level, the critical mobilities theorist remains more concerned with a relational ethics of mobility rather than a morality. Rather than assuming that we all live within a "risk society" and that we can reflect on those risks and try to act morally toward others, critical mobilities theory demands that we pay greater attention to the uneven distribution of risks, and that we understand some claims to cosmopolitan subjectivity as the conversion of mobility capital into a form of power. This leaves the normative projects of the two branches of social theory quite at odds with each other not because one is post-modern and the other second-modern, but because one casts doubt on the humanist subject of the other and throws out-of-joint the representational practices of knowledge construction. While cosmopolitan realism calls for more humanity, more civility, and more reflexivity, critical mobilities theory questions whether there can even be a human, civil, reflexive subject.

Empirical Evidence: Mobile Methods

Finally, there are also crucial methodological differences between the two fields. The new focus on mobilities has led to methodological innovation, as researchers have pushed to develop empirical tools pertinent to the new approach to the study of mobilities. One of the most important contributions of mobilities research is the lively experimentation with multiple methods, and the creation of new "mobile methods" that can both capture, perform, and even intervene in processes of movement as they happen. Over the last decade, inspired by the mobility turn in the social sciences, numerous researchers have been exploring various ways of researching and representing mobilities in all of their complexity. Sheller and Urry's article "The new mobilities paradigm" summed up the developments of this "mobility turn" and called for new research methods that would be "on the move" and would "simulate intermittent mobility" (Sheller and Urry 2006: 217). The "mobile methods" called for included: interactional and conversational analysis of people as they moved; mobile ethnography involving itinerant movement with people, following objects, and co-present immersion in various modes of movement; after the fact interviews and focus groups about mobility; the keeping of textual, pictorial, or digital time-space diaries; various methods of cyber-research, cyberethnography, and computer simulations; imaginative travel using multimedia methods attentive to the affective and atmospheric feeling of place; the tracking of affective objects that attach memories to place; and finally methods that measure the spatial structuring and temporal pulse of transfer points and places of in-between-ness in which the circulation of people and objects are slowed or stopped, as well as facilitated and speeded (Sheller and Urry 2006, and see Hannam et al. 2006, Urry 2007).

Some critics of the new mobilities paradigm posit that mobilities theory valorizes mobility as against immobility, viewing mobility as always desirable and positive, and immobility as, by default, undesirable and negative. Yet slowness, stillness, waiting, and pauses, are all part of a wider sensuous geography of movement, affect, and dwelling. Others have called for new methodologies in order to study the more ephemeral, embodied, and affective dimensions of interlocking relational (im)mobilities (see for instance Adey 2009, Hannam et al. 2006, Fincham et al. 2010). Thus there are emergent strains of mobilities research that focus on these affective and atmospheric non-representational geographies and a wide range of embodied practices, as well as a growing interest in cultures of "alternative mobility" (Vannini 2009), including biking, boating, climbing, walking, and so on.

This requires a very different kind of empirical evidence, involving everything from time-space diaries and participant observation to use of mobile video and ethnomethodology, or autobiographical narrative and immersion of the researcher in mobile activities (Fincham et al. 2010). Research on the socio-cultural dimensions of air travel and airports, for example, has generated new methodologies and theoretical questions within the subfield of "aeromobilities" research (Adey 2004a, 2004b, 2010, Adey et al. 2007, Cresswell 2006, Urry 2007, Salter 2008, Cwerner et al. 2009). Adey emphasizes the socio-technical production of airspace, the ways in which it is embodied and practiced, and its affective and experiential dimensions (Budd and Adey 2009, Adey 2010). Aeromobility is "a complex enfolding of the social and technical" and it remains "a space whose embodied, emotional and practiced geographies remain to be adequately charted" (Adey et al. 2007).

Cosmopolitan realism remains far more interested in politics at the societal level, even if that is understood as the emergent dynamics of local-global experimentation in an emergent cosmopolitan everyday. Beck and Cronin emphasize that in the era of reflexive modernity,

> *national borders and differences are dissolving and must be renegotiated in accordance with the logic of a 'politics of politics'. This is why a world that has become cosmopolitan urgently demands a new standpoint, the cosmopolitan outlook, from which we can grasp the social and political realities in which we live and act.* (Beck and Cronin 2007 [2004]: 2)

This argument rests strongly on the notion that the world is one shared reality; that "we" can know that reality; and that in grasping these social and political realities we can know how best to "live and act." All of which is anathema to the post-humanist outlook on complexity, partial knowledge, and faint human agency, in which all standpoints are modest and disjointed. Büscher's work on mobile visualization and interactive design goes so far as to suggest that the very nature of the empirical is in question, as it emerges as a collaborative production (Büscher and Urry 2009).

The concerns of mobilities research may appear as shallow or banal from the cosmopolitan perspective, yet this difference in both politics and empirical agenda reflects a true philosophical difference. For mobilities research is driven in part by a turn toward complexity theory, which recognizes that out of the multitude of iterations of small background actions, larger social changes may happen. The argument for "tipping points," for "normal accidents," and for self-adjusting feedback loops all take attention away from the historical social actors of the sociological tradition. Such social actors remain present within theories of cosmopolitanization, and this leads toward very different normative projects vis-à-vis the contemporary environmental crisis of risk society. For Beck, it would seem that there is a possibility for concerted reflexivity and the advancement of cosmopolitanization in ways that will help to mitigate risk and preserve the human species. Urry, on the other hand, has taken a far more agnostic view toward the ability of humans to take action against the systems that are driving us toward our own planetary destruction. If changes in complex mobility systems are to take place, it is likely to be driven by phenomena such as climate change, peak oil, and environmental catastrophe, which will make cosmopolitanization a moot point.

To return to the beginning, in conclusion, there are strong parallels between the origins of cosmopolitan realism and mobilities research in terms of both the history of the concepts and their theoretical starting points; yet there are also great differences in their empirical and reflexive projects. Rather than wrestle over mistaken criticisms concerning their alleged embrace of metaphors of flow and forms of mobile subjectivity that are viewed as masculine and Eurocentric (since both schools of thought have moved far beyond such simplistic positions) more compelling would be to thoroughly interrogate the relation of each to alternative critical and philosophical discourses. First, we need to better understand how each school is positioned with regard to postcolonial and feminist theory, and how European theorists of cosmopolitan mobilities might more effectively enter into dialogues with these critical approaches. Second, we need to unearth the critical histories of racialization and colonial formation that are implicated in contemporary European social theory, yet are largely silenced. This also demands a cross-disciplinary dialogue with contemporary anthropology and its critical reflexive positioning. Finally, as we further investigate the intersections of cosmopolitan realism and mobilities research, we need to understand that what is at stake politically are the fundamental conceptualizations of human agency that are the basis of social scientific thought and a key legacy of the European Enlightenment.

Bibliography

Adey, P. 2004a. Secured and sorted mobilities: examples from the airport. *Surveillance and Society*, 1, 500–19.

Adey, P. 2004b. Surveillance at the airport: surveilling mobility/mobilising surveillance. *Environment and Planning A*, 36, 1365–80.

Adey, P. 2006. Airports and air-mindedness: spacing, timing and using Liverpool Airport, 1929–39. *Social and Cultural Geography*, 7(3), 343–63.

Adey, P. 2009. *Mobility*. London and New York: Routledge.

Adey. P. 2010. *Aerial Life: Spaces, Mobilities, Affects*. Oxford: Wiley-Blackwell.

Adey, P., Budd, L. and Hubbard, P. 2007. Flying lessons: exploring the social and cultural geographies of global air travel. *Progress in Human Geography*, 31(6), 773–91.

Ahmed, S., Castaneda, C., Fortier, A. and Sheller, M. (eds). 2003. *Uprootings/ Regroundings: Questions of Home and Migration*. Oxford: Berg.

Appadurai, A. 1996. *Modernity at Large: Cultural Dimensions of Globalization*. Minneapolis: University of Minnesota Press.

Aravamudan, S. 1999. *Tropicopolitans: Colonialism and Agency, 1688–804*. Durham, NC and London: Duke University Press.

Basch, L., Glick Schiller, N. and Szanton Blanc, C. 1994. *Nations Unbound: Transnational Projects, Postcolonial Predicaments, and Deterritorialized Nation-States*. Amsterdam: Gordon and Breach.

Beck, U. 2008. Mobility and the cosmopolitan perspective, in *Tracing Mobilities: Towards a Cosmopolitan Perspective*, edited by W. Canzler, V. Kaufmann, and S. Kesselring. Aldershot: Ashgate, 25–35.

Beck, U. and Cronin, C. 2007 [2004]. *The Cosmopolitan Vision*. Cambridge: Polity.

Beck, U. and Sznaider, N. 2010 [2006]. Unpacking cosmopolitanism for the social sciences: a research agenda. *The British Journal of Sociology – The BJS: Shaping Sociology Over 60 Years*, 61, 381–403. [Originally published in 2006 *British Journal of Sociology*, 57(1), 1–23.]

Bergmann, S. and Sager, T. (eds). 2008. *The Ethics of Mobilities: Rethinking Place, Exclusion, Freedom and Environment*. Aldershot: Ashgate.

Bhabha, H. 2001 [1996]. Unsatisfied: notes on vernacular cosmopolitanism, in *Postcolonial Discourses: An Anthology*, edited by G. Castle. Oxford: Blackwell, 39–52.

Bhabha, H., Breckenridge, C.A., Pollock, S. and Chakrabarty, D. 2000. Cosmopolitanisms. *Public Culture*, 12(3), 577–89.

Bissell, D. 2007. Animating suspension: waiting for mobilities. *Mobilities*, 2(2), 277–98.

Bissell, D. and Fuller, G. (eds). 2009. The revenge of the still. *M/C Journal*, 12(1). Online, available at: http://journal.media-culture.org.au/index.php/mcjournal/article/viewArticle/136/0.

Brah, A. 1996. *Cartographies of Diaspora: Contesting Identities*. London: Routledge.

Budd, L. and Adey, P. 2009. The software–simulated airworld: anticipatory code and affective aeromobilities. *Environment and Planning A*, 41(6), 1366–85.

Büscher, M. and Urry, J. 2009. Mobile methods and the empirical. *European Journal of Social Theory*, 12(1), 99–116.

Canzler, W., Kaufmann V. and Kesselring, S. (eds). 2008. *Tracing Mobilities: Towards a Cosmopolitan Perspective*. Farnham and Burlington: Ashgate.

Chow, R. 1993. *Writing Diaspora: Tactics of Intervention in Contemporary Cultural Studies*. Bloomington: Indiana University Press.

Clifford, J. 1997. *Routes: Travel and Translation in the Late Twentieth Century*. Cambridge, MA: Harvard University Press.

Clifford, J. 1998. Mixed feelings, in *Cosmopolitics: Thinking and Feeling Beyond the Nation*, edited by P. Cheah and B. Robbins. Minneapolis: University of Minnesota Press, 362–71.

Cohen, R. 2008. *Global Diasporas: An Introduction*. London and New York: Routledge.

Cresswell, T. 1999. Embodiment, power and the politics of mobility: the case of female tramps and hobos. *Transactions of the Institute of British Geographers*, 24(2), 175–92.

Cresswell, T. 2002. Introduction: theorizing place, in *Mobilizing Place, Placing Mobility*, edited by G. Verstraete and T. Cresswell. Amsterdam: Rodopi, 11–32.

Cresswell, T. 2006. *On the Move: Mobility in the Modern Western World*. London: Routledge.

Cunningham, H. and Heyman, J. 2004. Introduction: mobilities and enclosures at borders. *Identities: Global Studies in Culture and Power*, 11(3), 289–302.

Cwerner, S., Kesselring, S. and Urry, J. (eds). 2009. *Aeromobilities*. London: Routledge.

Dennis, K. and Urry, J. 2008. *After the Car*. Cambridge: Polity.

Elliott, A. and Urry, J. 2010. *Mobile Lives*. New York and London: Routledge.

Fincham, B., McGuinness, M. and Murray, L. (eds). 2010. *Mobile Methodologies*. Aldershot: Ashgate.

Gilroy, P. 1993. *The Black Atlantic: Modernity and Double Consciousness*. London and New York: Verso.

Glick Schiller, N. 2010. Old baggage and missing luggage: a commentary on Beck and Sznaider's "Unpacking cosmopolitanism for the social sciences: a research agenda." *British Journal of Sociology – The BJS: Shaping Sociology Over 60 Years*, 61, 413–20.

Glick Schiller, N. and Fouron, G. 2001. *Georges Woke up Laughing: Long Distance Nationalism and the Search for Home*. Durham, NC: Duke University Press.

Hannam, K., Sheller, M. and Urry, J. 2006. Mobilities, Immobilities, and Moorings. *Mobilities*, 1(1), 1–22.

Hannerz, U. 1996. *Transnational Connections*. London: Routledge.

Harvey, D. 1985. The geopolitics of capitalism, in *Social Relations and Spatial Structures*, edited by D. Gregory and J. Urry. London: Macmillan, 128–63.

Hayles, N. Katherine 1999. *How We Became Posthuman: Virtual Bodies in Cybernetics, Literature, and Informatics*. Chicago: University of Chicago Press.

Ifekwunigwe, J. 1999. *Scattered Belongings: Cultural Paradoxes of "Race," Nation and Gender*. London: Routledge.

Joseph, M. 1999. *Nomadic Identities: The Performance of Citizenship*. Minneapolis: University of Minnesota Press.

Kaplan, C. 1996. *Questions of Travel: Postmodern Discourses of Displacement*. Durham, NC: Duke University Press.

Kaufmann, V. 2010. Mobile social science: creating a dialogue among the sociologies. *British Journal of Sociology*, 61(1), 367–72.

Kaufmann, V. and Montulet, B. 2008. Between social and spatial mobilities: the issue of social fluidity, in *Tracing Mobilities: Towards a Cosmopolitan Perspective*, edited by W. Canzler, V. Kaufmann, and S. Kesselring. Farnham and Burlington: Ashgate, 37–56.

Knowles, C. 2010. Mobile sociology. *British Journal of Sociology*, 61(1), 371–9.

Law, John and Hassard, John (eds). 1999. *Actor Network Theory and After*. Oxford and Keele: Blackwell and the Sociological Review.

Levinas, E. 1997 [1961]. Heidegger, Gagarin and us, in *Difficult Freedom: Essays on Judaism*, trans. Seán Hand. Baltimore: Johns Hopkins.

Massey, D. 1993. Power-geometry and a progressive sense of place, in *Mapping the Futures: Local Cultures, Global Change*, edited by J. Bird, B. Curtis, T. Putnam, and G. Robertson. London and New York: Routledge, 59–69.

Mercer, K. (ed.). 2005. *Cosmopolitan Modernisms*. Cambridge and London: The MIT Press.

Mitter, P. 2005. Reflections on modern art and national identity in India: an interview, in *Cosmopolitan Modernisms*, edited by K. Mercer. Cambridge and London: The MIT Press, 24–49.

Ong, A. 1999. *Flexible Citizenship: The Cultural Logics of Transnationality*. Durham, NC: Duke University Press.

Ong, A. and Nonini, D. (eds). 1997. *Ungrounded Empires: The Cultural Politics of Modern Chinese Transnationalism*. London: Routledge.

Overy, P. 2005. White walls, white skins: cosmopolitanism and colonialism in inter-war modernist architecture, in *Cosmopolitan Modernisms*, edited by Kobena Mercer. Cambridge and London: The MIT Press, 50–67.

Salter, M. (ed.). 2008. *Politics at the Airport*. Minneapolis: University of Minnesota Press.

Savage, M. 2009. Against epochalism: an analysis of conceptions of change in British sociology, *Cultural Sociology*, 3(2), 203–16.

Sheller, M. 2003a. *Consuming the Caribbean: From Arawaks to Zombies*. London and New York: Routledge.

Sheller, M. 2003b. Creolization in global culture, in *Uprootings/Regroundings: Questions of Home and Migration*, edited by S. Ahmed, C. Castaneda, A. Fortier, and M. Sheller. Oxford: Berg, 273–94.

Sheller, M. 2004. Demobilizing and remobilizing the Caribbean, in *Tourism Mobilities: Places to Play, Places in Play*, edited by M. Sheller and J. Urry. London and New York: Routledge, 13–21.

Sheller, M. and Urry, J. 2003. Mobile transformations of "public" and "private" life. *Theory, Culture and Society*, 20(3), 107–25.

Sheller, M. and Urry, J. (eds). 2004. *Tourism Mobilities: Places to Play, Places in Play*. London and New York: Routledge.

Sheller, M. and Urry, J. 2006. The new mobilities paradigm. *Environment and Planning A*, 38, 207–26.

Skeggs, B. 2004. *Class, Self, Culture*. London: Routledge.

Thrift, N. 2007. *Non-representational Theory: Space, Politics, Affect*. London: Routledge.

Trouillot, M.R. 2003. *Global Transformations: Anthropology and the Modern World*. New York: Palgrave Macmillan.

Urry, J. 2000. *Sociology Beyond Societies: Mobilities for the Twenty-first Century*. London: Routledge.

Urry, J. 2007. *Mobilities*. London: Polity.

Urry, J. 2008. Climate change, travel and complex futures. *British Journal of Sociology*, 59, 261–79.

Urry, J. 2010 [2001]. Mobile sociology. *The British Journal of Sociology – The BJS: Shaping Sociology Over 60 Years*, 61, 347–66.

Uteng, T.P. and Cresswell, T. (eds). 2008. *Gendered Mobilities*. Aldershot: Ashgate.

Van der Veer, P. 1995. *Nation and Migration: The Politics of Space in the South Asian Diaspora*. Philadelphia: University of Pennsylvania Press.

Vannini, P (ed.). 2009. *The Cultures of Alternative Mobilities: Routes Less Travelled*. Farnham: Ashgate.

Wood, D. and Graham, S. 2006. Permeable boundaries in the software-sorted society: surveillance and the differentiation of mobility, in *Mobile Technologies of the City*, edited by M. Sheller and J. Urry. London: Routledge, 177–91.

Cosmopolitanism and Feminism[1]

Niamh Reilly

Introduction

Globalizing trends and forces, especially in a post-Cold War and post-September 11 world, raise major questions about the nature and scope of justice, democracy, and citizenship and their application both within and beyond sovereign states. Recognition of the pressing need to respond to global issues from ongoing economic and financial crises and deepening global inequalities, to mass migration, escalating trafficking in persons, HIV/AIDS, and environmental catastrophes has fostered renewed interest in cosmopolitan discourse and its relevance to twenty-first-century governance. This ongoing re-evaluation of cosmopolitan ideas also takes place against a backdrop of rising religious fundamentalisms (across all religions and regions) and other neoconservative movements, which explicitly reject human rights discourse as western, a threat to national sovereignty, individualist, and/or "anti-family." At the same time, contemporary forms of conflict, including the "war on terror" and its promotion of the securitization of everyday life, pose profound challenges to proponents of cosmopolitanism; it is increasingly difficult to articulate and defend the normative importance of international law and norms in the face of unequal global power dynamics, democratic deficits throughout UN institutions, and the cynical use of international standards by dominant powers.

The model of cosmopolitan feminism outlined here is fully cognizant of the new global context; it rejects the western-centric, false universalization and undemocratic imposition of narrowly defined understandings of human rights. At the same time, it contests relativist and communitarian claims over individually-held human rights when they are used to conceal violations against women in the name of the cultural and religious integrity of the community (Rao 1995, Okin 1999, Shaheed 2004). In doing so, cosmopolitan feminism retains a commitment to critically reinterpreted universal human rights in the context of democratically grounded, emancipatory political projects.[2] In traditional feminist political theory, the interest in cosmopolitanism is reflected in attempts to theorize global feminism

---

1   This chapter is a revised version of an earlier article by the author (Reilly 2007a).
2   This theorization of human rights, as integrally linked to transformative political

and transnational advocacy, especially in relation to "women's rights as human rights" (Okin 2000, Jaggar 2000, Ackerly and Okin 1999). This global turn, which is partly a response to anti-universalist and cultural relativist intellectual currents in feminist thinking, is relatively recent. Until the 1990s, the bulk of feminist political theory presupposed a territorially-bounded, western, liberal "developed" state as its empirical frame of reference. A number of factors have combined to draw the attention of such feminist political theorizing to the global arena and the prospects for the feminist solidarity and gender justice beyond the liberal democratic state. These include: the rising influence of anti-racist, "Third World," and post-colonial feminist theorizing from different philosophical perspectives (for example, hooks 1984, Spivak 1988, Mohanty et al. 1991); the surge in transnational feminist organizing sparked by the UN Decade on Women (1975–85) and extended throughout the 1990s to the present (Antrobus 2004, Fraser and Tinker 2004, Moghadam 2005, Ferree and Tripp 2006, Reilly 2009); and a growing recognition within feminism of the need to address the gendered impacts of globalization and refocus attention on the interplay between economic, social, and political arenas (Mohanty 2003, Moghadam 2005).[3]

Beyond feminist scholarship, the literature on cosmopolitanism as a political project is primarily concerned with the implications of globalizing trends for how politics are conceived and implemented and how to "democratize" the global arena. Within this literature, neo-liberal globalization poses unprecedented policy challenges in the form of mass migration, disease pandemics and health crises, environmental destruction, and transnational crime, which raise questions about the efficacy of the sovereign state as the principal locus of policy-making and governance. These developments also reinforce concerns about the suitability of states—democratic and otherwise—as the primary guardians of human rights in a globalizing age. However, the leading proponents of cosmopolitanism rarely highlight the gendered power dynamics at play in globalization and the global issues that their cosmopolitan visions seek to address (Archibugi et al. 1998, Archibugi 2003, Falk 2004), nor are feminist analyses brought to bear in the elaboration of models of cosmopolitan democracy. This account of cosmopolitan feminism, therefore, builds on recent feminist analyses of the global women's human rights movement noted above and responds to the gender blindness of mainstream political cosmopolitan scholarship. It is also linked to a relatively recent international relations literature on "global civil society" (for example, Keck and Sikkink 1998, Edwards and Gaventa 2001) insofar as it addresses the role of women's non-governmental organizations (NGOs) and networks as transnational actors in global forums and considers the ways in which their activities can be understood as constituting new forms of "cosmopolitan citizenship" and as part of a shift to "cosmopolitan democracy." At the same time, however, the model of

---

engagement, is most developed in writing by Kothari and Sethi (1989), Baxi (2002), and Sen (2004).

[3] See in particular the special edition of the *Indiana Journal of Global Legal Studies* on feminism and globalization (1996–7).

cosmopolitan feminism elaborated here gives equal billing to bottom-up processes to claim and define (women's) human rights in local contexts. Similar to Levitt and Merry (2009) who talk about such processes as the "vernacularization" of global norms I suggest that, viewed through a feminist cosmopolitan lens, such bottom-up processes should be seen as constitutive of a counter-hegemonic vision of human rights and not only as the translation of global values into meaningful local forms.

It is important to note that cosmopolitan feminism does not assume that women are united by a common gender identity or common experience of patriarchal oppression across regions and other boundaries. Instead, I posit cosmopolitan feminist as a process-oriented framework wherein the direction and content of feminist practice is determined in cross-boundaries dialogue within and across women's movements. Before proceeding to a fuller elaboration of the constitutive elements of this framework, the next section sets out the main tenets of contemporary approaches to cosmopolitanism and signals how cosmopolitan feminism builds on these and departs from problematic aspects of mainstream approaches.

Approaches to Cosmopolitanism

While cosmopolitan thinking takes many forms, Carol Gould's distinction between moral and political cosmopolitanism is a useful one (Gould 2004: 166). The former refers to accounts that retain a commitment to treating all human beings with equal concern within a global frame. This is most cogently expressed in the idea of universal human rights, which underpin human freedom (variously defined) and are independent of legal or political status (Habermas 2001, Okin 2000, Nussbaum 1999). Kant is the principal originator of cosmopolitanism in modern political thought. In *Perpetual Peace: A Philosophical Essay* (1795), he advances cosmopolitanism to promote peace among nations and foster mutual respect among individuals by virtue of their common humanity. This includes the idea of "cosmopolitan right" resonant in contemporary accounts of cosmopolitanism that embrace some form of discourse ethics (Held 2002, Linklater 1998). Cosmopolitan right entails a universal entitlement and duty to engage in free and open dialogue with others from different cultures and contexts, enabled by the human capacity to "present one self and be heard within and across political communities" (Held 2002: 310). Such Kantian cosmopolitan values flow from the idea that all persons are equal moral, reasoning, and autonomous beings and, as such, are entitled to, and have a duty to treat all others with, equal concern and not as means to ends. This philosophical grounding of cosmopolitan claims in a particular form of human rationality and ontology is questionable. Nonetheless, a moral assertion of the equality of all human beings, and the idea that the well-being of persons is paramount in the pursuit of justice, remain at the heart of all contemporary cosmopolitan positions, including the account of cosmopolitan feminism set out in this chapter.

The critiques of traditional universalist accounts of human rights are well established. From communitarian and post-colonial standpoints, they are seen as inimical to cultural integrity or as vehicles for the global imposition of western liberal values (An-Na'im 1992, Matua 2002). Feminist critics have exposed how the supposedly universal human attributes posited in liberal political theory, which in turn shapes human rights discourse, in fact are examples of false universalization from particular, dominant, male, standpoints. While these critiques are well-taken, I argue that it is vital to challenge examples of false universalization in concrete ways through emancipatory political projects and not solely in the realm of metaphysics or deconstructive analyses. The global women's human rights movement exemplifies such a project in its refusal to accept discriminatory practices and structural and intersectional forms of oppression based on morally irrelevant categories of gender, race, class, and so on.

Proponents of political cosmopolitanism build on moral cosmopolitanism but are also concerned with specifying the legal, political, and institutional loci of cosmopolitan political practice (Held 2002, Archibugi 2003, Falk 2004). David Held, for example, defines cosmopolitanism as "the ethical and political space which sets out the terms of reference for the recognition of people's equal moral worth, their active agency, and what is required for their autonomy and development" (Held 2002: 313). Advocates of political cosmopolitanism often argue that international law and organizations are already primary loci for cosmopolitan governance, while acknowledging the need to build democratic legitimacy and deepen democratic practice at the global level. In particular, they point to international human rights law (Beetham 1999, Pogge 2005) and the International Criminal Court (Held 2002, Falk 2004) as important ingredients in formulating global governance that is more accountable. Most ambitiously, some envisage a form of world government, underpinned by international law (Held 1995, Falk 2004). In tandem with discussions of cosmopolitan democracy, others explore evolving modes of global citizenship, often with particular reference to the role of social movements and non-governmental organization (NGOs) in cosmopolitan practice (Edwards and Gaventa 2001, Khagram et al. 2002).

In contrast, skeptics flag various democratic deficits and problems of legitimacy associated with such "cosmopolitical" visions. These include: the potential emergence of a tyrannical world power (Urbinati 2003); the absence of democratic, participatory "bottom-up" channels of decision-making (Gould 2004: 170); the ways in which the composition of "global civil society" mirrors wider political, economic, cultural, and gender power imbalances (Robinson 2003: 169); and the impossibility of facilitating "the ethical-political self-understanding of citizens of a particular democratic life" in a "community of world citizens" supported by a relatively weak "cosmopolitan solidarity" (Habermas 2001: 107). These are all valid concerns and in the absence of a global, broad-based movement, I am profoundly skeptical about cosmopolitan proposals for a constitutional world government. However, I agree with proponents of political cosmopolitanism that international law and UN forums—if they are approached from a critical, bottom-up, transformative perspective—can be key elements in the realization of emancipatory cosmopolitanism. The following framework sets out the conditions under which such a vision of cosmopolitanism might be realized.

Cosmopolitan Feminism

My account of cosmopolitan feminism entails six mutually constitutive moments. It is important to emphasize that the different elements need to be taken together to understand "cosmopolitan feminism" as a transformative political framework. These are:

1. A critical engagement with public international law, especially human rights.
2. A global feminist consciousness that challenges the systemic interplay of oppressive patriarchal, capitalist, and racist power relations.
3. Recognition of the intersectionality of women's identities and experiences across diverse categories and a commitment to cross-boundaries dialogue that such recognition demands.
4. The development of collaborative advocacy networks and strategies above and below the state around concrete issues, aimed at transforming conditions inimical to the realization of human rights.
5. Ongoing engagement in global forums as sites of cosmopolitan solidarity and "citizenship."
6. A renewed and sustained commitment to democratic governance, accountability, and participation, from the local to the global levels, including constitutional democracy at state level.

A critical engagement with public international law and global norms

In keeping with other articulations of cosmopolitanism, cosmopolitan feminism expresses a commitment to public international law,[4] particularly international human rights. Fully recognizing the "limits" of established international law— as a "progressive narrative" and "liberal conception" with a "state-centric focus" (Crawford and Marks 1998), cosmopolitan feminist projects are characterized by a critical, practical engagement with legal discourse and a radical critique of public/private configurations in international law. In addition to the 1990s global campaign for women's human rights, other significant examples of such engagement include efforts to ensure the inclusion of feminist analyses and gender perspectives in the International Criminal Court statute and the adoption of UN Security Council

---

[4] Public International Law encompasses binding intergovernmental treaties and comments by treaty bodies, as well as non-binding declarations and programs of action produced by intergovernmental conferences.

Resolution 1325, which addresses women's roles in peace-building and post-conflict reconstruction.

The paradigm of international human rights is generally understood in legalistic terms as a body of law to be interpreted by experts or as a system of intergovernmental institutions and procedures charged with implementing human rights standards. Cosmopolitan feminism unsettles this legalist bias and seeks instead to integrate the moral, legal, and political elements of human rights into a framework of critical, global civic action to achieve what Charlotte Bunch calls the "feminist transformation of human rights" (1990). The act of "claiming rights," therefore, is central to this conception in which international human rights ideas and standards are subject to an ongoing process of contestation, (re-)interpretation, and (re-)definition. This is very different, however, from saying that the content of rights is decided in a relativist vacuum because the struggle to contest the meaning of human rights is always with reference to established human rights standards (Bronner 2004: 147). Consequently, a participative, dialogic process—grounded in the idea that the substantive content of universal human rights must resonate with the concerns of, and be defined by and with concrete, situated women—is integral to advancing women's human rights claims. This understanding also relies on a variation of feminist standpoint theory insofar as it strongly values, although not exclusively, critical perspectives articulated from marginalized and counter-hegemonic positions.

The 1990s global campaign for women's human rights is a particularly strong example of this approach (Reilly 2009).[5] In the late 1980s, there was a growing recognition within and across women's movements around the world that violence against women was a universal phenomenon that affected women in every region, even though the form it took differed from place to place (Carrillo 1991). An unprecedented mobilization of women's networks and feminist advocates around the issue of violence against women was pivotal in the emergence of a far reaching challenge to mainstream human rights concepts and practice. When plans for a UN world conference on human rights were underway in the early 1990s, many questioned the failure of international human rights standards and advocacy to address women's experiences. This meant asking why abuses primarily affecting women, such as domestic violence, trafficking, and forced pregnancy, had not been taken seriously as human rights issues (Bunch 1990).

With the exception of the UN Convention on the Elimination of All Forms of Discrimination Against Women (CEDAW) (1979), which attempts to deepen the definition and scope of sex-based discrimination as a human rights issue, women's rights have been viewed very narrowly in terms of legal equality with men and are generally invisible or marginalized within the wider human rights machinery. The global campaign highlighted the gendered ways in which traditional approaches

---

5   This is not to say that aspects of the campaign have not been subjected to criticism, for example, in relation to the inaccessibility of UN forums to some women's movements (Dutt 2000) or the disproportionate structural privilege enjoyed by US and other western NGOs (Romany 1995, Grewal 1999).

to human rights privileged male-defined aspects of civil and political rights in situations where violations are carried out by the state. This includes, for example, denials of freedom of expression, arbitrary arrest, torture in detention, and the death penalty. While not discounting the gravity of these issues, Hilary Charlesworth argues that the emphasis on state perpetrated acts reflects a deep gender bias wherein human rights are primarily defined according to the criterion of "what men fear will happen to them" in their relationship with the state, society, and other men (Charlesworth 1994: 71). The global campaign, especially through the use of popular tribunals organized alongside major UN forums, demonstrated how this gender bias has served to close off recognition of the human rights dimensions of harmful and often fatal forms of gender based violence, because they occur in "private" contexts of family or community and are generally perpetrated by non-state actors such as spouses and family members (Bunch and Reilly 1994).

As a result of the campaign, many significant gains were achieved in the form of new international human rights standards in a relatively short period of time. For example, violence against women was recognized as a violation of human rights in the 1993 Vienna Declaration and Programme of Action and in the UN General Assembly Declaration on the Elimination of Violence Against Women. In 1992 the committee monitoring compliance with the Women's Convention (CEDAW) defined VAW as a form of gender-based discrimination.[6] In 1999 new complaints and investigation procedures further strengthened CEDAW as an avenue of redress. In 1994, a UN Special Rapporteur on Violence Against Women was appointed to investigate the issue and encourage effective governmental, regional, and UN remedial measures. Finally, in 1995, the Beijing Platform for Action (BPfA), which is still considered by many to be a comprehensive "blueprint" for women's human rights, was adopted by 189 countries. Above all else, therefore, the "women's rights as human rights" movement is associated with achieving recognition of violence against women as a global, human rights issue.

More recent examples of cosmopolitan feminist engagement with international law build on this recognition. The ICC NGO Women's Caucus for Gender Justice effectively mobilized the support of women's networks internationally in its campaign to ensure the incorporation of gender perspectives and feminist analyses in the Rome statute of the International Criminal Court (Copelon 2000). For the first time in international law, the ICC criminalizes sexual and gender violence as war crimes and crimes against humanity. The Caucus also sought to redress the gendered impact of the adversarial character of traditional legal practices, including rules of procedure and evidence that afford particular protections for victims of sexual violence. Some feminist scholars have expressed concern that such measures cannot alter the inherently abusive dynamics of adversarial criminal legal systems, which are fundamentally inhospitable to the pursuit of justice in relation to sexual violence (Mertus 2004). Nonetheless, I argue, the act of seeking gender-sensitive legal practice is an important intervention if it unsettles the gendered exercise of power in legal discourses and establishes principles and precedents that can be

---

6   General Recommendation No. 19.

invoked to advance women's human rights in other "safer" contexts (Reilly 2007b). For example, the strategic use of popular tribunals by feminist movements, which are framed in terms of international human rights law and draw on the expertise and support of sympathetic legal practitioners, demonstrates a critical engagement with international law that epitomizes cosmopolitan feminist practice. In addition to the Vienna (1993) and Beijing (1995) tribunals of the global campaign for women's human rights (Bunch and Reilly 1994, Reilly 1996), more recent examples include the Tokyo Women's International War Crimes Tribunal on Japanese Military Sexual Slavery (Chinkin 2001) and the International Initiative for Justice in Gujarat 2002 (Cockburn 2005, 2007).

Another example of cosmopolitan feminism is the "PeaceWomen" project, which links "women, peace and security" NGOs around the world.[7] This initiative, which secured the adoption of Security Council Resolution 1325 (SCR 1325) in 2000, coordinates NGO efforts to ensure its implementation and remains very active at the time of writing as the 10th anniversary of the adoption of SCR 1325 approaches. SCR 1325 is significant because it signals the first time that the Security Council turned its "full attention" to the subject of women and conflict situations.[8] Previously, women were dealt with peripherally as victims and as a "vulnerable group" (Cohn 2004). The "PeaceWomen" initiative is an important example because the Security Council is the most graphic symbol of masculine power politics and the most powerful decision-making body in the UN system. Unlike many UN agreements, its resolutions are legally binding (albeit selectively implemented or ignored). Just as the global campaign for women's human rights sought the feminist transformation of traditional human rights discourse, and the ICC NGO Gender Caucus extended this to international criminal law, the ongoing campaign to implement SCR 1325 entails a critical engagement with international law aimed at achieving the feminist transformation of peace and security discourses.

A global feminist consciousness

A global feminist consciousness that challenges the systemic interplay of patriarchal, capitalist, and racist power relations is integral to contesting false universalization and neo-imperialist manifestations of supposedly cosmopolitan values. Such a consciousness has antecedents in Charlotte Bunch's account of global feminism which she defined as: a "transformational feminist politics that is global in perspective [where] … the particular issues and forms of struggle for women in different locations will vary [and activists] … strive to understand

---

7   See the PeaceWomen website at: www.peacewomen.org.
8   Resolution 1325 recognizes the disproportionate and gender-specific impact of conflict on women and children. Additionally, it calls for women's "full and equal" participation at all decision-making levels in "prevention, management, and resolution of conflict" and for all participants in peacekeeping operations and peace-building processes to "adopt a gender perspective."

and expand the commonality and solidarity of that struggle" (Bunch 1987: 303). My understanding of global feminist consciousness also borrows from Chandra Mohanty (1991). Just as she argues that a coherent "Third World Feminism" can be located, despite the multiplicity of identities and locations occupied by Third World women, a global feminist standpoint is possible without requiring homogeneity of identity or experience or even an ongoing consensus among women across a range of issues. From this perspective, the global arena is understood in terms of interconnected patterns of domination and resistance along geo-political and geo-economic lines, as well as, in terms of gender, "race," class, and other categories. In particular, a global feminist consciousness contests the false dichotomies that pervade understanding of the international arena—especially in the western "developed" world. Powerful hierarchical binaries of north/south, Christianity/Islam, secular/fundamentalist, First World/Third World, freedom/authoritarianism are implicated in the construction of harmful stereotypes and the invisibility of inequalities along lines of gender, race, class and other categories. For example, poverty and inequality are major features of the so-called First World; Islam is not synonymous with fundamentalism, terrorism, and anti-democratic values; Christian fundamentalism is pervasive in all regions, undermines democratic values, and potentially promotes terrorism (for instance, attacks on abortion clinics); and free-market privatization is not equivalent to democratization.

More concretely, a global feminist consciousness brings the gendered dimensions of globalization and related global issues sharply into focus and underlines the necessity of bringing feminist analyses to bear in the formulation of cosmopolitan political responses. For example, worldwide, women constitute half of an estimated 33 million people living with HIV/AIDS, in Sub-Saharan Africa, women constitute 59 percent of all people living with HIV/AIDS, and among young people aged 15–24, the HIV prevalence rate for young women is almost three times that of young men (Foundation for AIDS Research 2009). This pattern is explained in large part by the persistence of various forms of gender violence, sex-based discrimination, women's disproportionate poverty, and the marginalization of poorer countries on the global stage. Women represent half of the world's migrant population and in some countries make up 70 or 80 percent of the total (International Labour Organization 2008). While migration is inextricably linked to profound economic disparities between countries, women experience migration in gender-specific racialized ways that leave them more vulnerable than male counterparts and non-migrant women to violence and exploitative employment, including work in the sex industry. More generally, there is recognition of the unequal, gendered impact of globalization (Streeten 2001). On balance, while offering new opportunities to some women for economic independence, globalization has made most women more vulnerable to poverty, involuntary migration, economic and sexual exploitation, and related forms of violence against women.[9] While proponents of

---

9 For analyses of gender, globalization and trade and related issues, visit the websites of Women in Development Europe (www.wide-network.org) and Development Alternatives with Women for a New Era (www.dawnnet.org/index.php).

cosmopolitanism effectively argue that current global problems cannot be "solved" without a cosmopolitan approach, women's experiences equally underscore the need for a feminist cosmopolitan response to globalization. More positively, a global feminist consciousness also recognizes new opportunities for collaboration among groups and individuals in seeking to advance social justice internationally. The model of cosmopolitan feminism posited here reflects such an optimistic response.

Recognition of intersectionality and a commitment to cross-boundaries dialogue

Feminist cosmopolitanism has as its driving process a commitment to action-oriented networking among women across boundaries of class, race, ethnicity, religious/cultural identity, sexual orientation, and so on — both within states and across geo-political divides. More than three decades of internal critiques of "second wave" feminism have underlined the message that any feminist project, academic or practical, cannot be based on an assumption of women as a monolithic group with a "natural" common agenda. This demands a strongly anti-essentialist standpoint, which recognizes that even as gendered power dynamics generally work to the disadvantage of women and girls, gendered disadvantage is experienced differently according to other aspects of identity and location, especially with respect to class, race, sexuality, (dis)ability, and so on. This recognition of the intersectionality of women's experience (Crenshaw 1997, Brah and Phoenix 2004, Yuval-Davis 2006) means that feminist practice must address the complex and often contradictory ways in which women's multiple identities and locations interplay in context-specific ways to produce patterns of "multiple discrimination" in some situations and cumulative advantage in others. It follows that the priorities of feminist cosmopolitan projects can only be determined through ongoing cross-boundaries networking and dialogue in specific contexts where agendas are always open to review and amendment.

The centrality of cross-boundaries dialogue in this process of negotiating the nexus of universal principles and particular claims resonates with the emphasis on discourse ethics in the mainstream cosmopolitan scholarship (Held 2002, Linklater 1998). However it departs from classic accounts of discourse ethics in significant ways. Feminist criticism has challenged the latter's reliance on "impartialist reasoning" (Held 2002: 312) as well as the very idea that open "authentic dialogue" is attainable wherein participants question their own "truths" and are moved only "by the force of the better argument" (Linklater 1998: 92). Such a vision, while appearing to be radically democratic, fails to comprehend the reality of occupying marginalized subject and social positions within complex, gendered relations of power that silence and subtly coerce. In contrast, the methodology of cross-boundaries dialogue and networking that underpins feminist cosmopolitanism acknowledges that inequalities necessitate the creation of safe "public" dialogic spaces within and across feminist communities, which may warrant the exclusion of some (Jaggar 2000). This qualified dialogic approach is more accurately captured by the idea of "feminist social criticism" (FSC) posited by Ackerly and Okin (1999: 136). Cast as a "formula for working toward social change," FSC entails three interrelated elements: deliberative inquiry and skeptical scrutiny anchored by guiding criteria. Okin and Ackerly persuasively use the strategies of the global campaign, and especially popular tribunals, as prime examples of deliberative inquiry and skeptical scrutiny in practice. They also argue that within the campaign these dialogic practices were anchored by the guiding criterion that "all human beings, female and male, are of equal worth" (136). I would argue, however, that a richer concept of indivisible human rights,[10] recognizing the intersectional and structural dimensions of gender inequalities in global perspective, must constitute the "guiding criteria" in South–North dialogue that hopes to produce genuinely collaborative strategies.

Collaborative advocacy strategies around concrete issues

Cosmopolitan feminism is ultimately an account of emancipatory feminist practice. As such it only becomes coherent in the context of struggles linked to concrete issues and events. As already noted, in the case of the global campaign for women's human rights, violence against women emerged as a pivotal unifying issue that galvanized a far-reaching cosmopolitan feminist project. Similarly, the transnational feminist advocacy to address gender justice in the ICC statute was directly linked to the wider mobilization of women's movements against war rapes in the Balkans conflict of the 1990s, and a longer-running campaign for recognition of the human rights of 200,000 "comfort women" who were subjected to sexual slavery by Japan during World War II.

In the late 1980s, the reality and threat of violence came into focus as a common factor in women's lives in every region, and a growing body of research demonstrated that it cut across all socio-economic and cultural categories (Pietilä and Vickers 1990: 142–8). While women in North America and Europe set up refuges and shelters for victims of domestic violence, in Africa they challenged customary practices that permitted the dispossession of widows and the practice of female genital mutilation. In Asia, groups organized against female infanticide, dowry-related abuse and killings, and trafficking in women. As the global campaign for women's human rights took shape in the early 1990s, the issue of gender-based violence emerged as an obvious focus given the vitality of organizing in every region. An important aspect of the issue of violence was that no region could claim immunity and "developed" western countries could not evade the issue as one that only occurred in "less developed" countries. This recognition of violence against women, as a global phenomenon that takes different forms in different contexts,

---

10 Indivisibility means that all rights—civil, political, economic, social, and cultural—are viewed as interdependent, inseparable and interrelated. This idea is pivotal to any claim that seeks to tackle substantive inequality as a human rights issue.

was crucial in underpinning a call for accountability to human rights standards across all regions and cultural contexts and rejecting any defense of such violence on the basis of "cultural" differences.

The emergence of violence against women as a unifying issue at global level, therefore, reflected the priorities of local organizations and networks. Importantly, as campaign participants collaborated to develop global campaign strategies, they did so on the understanding that local strategies to counter domestic violence, dowry abuse, female infanticide, and so on, would be context specific. This standpoint accommodates a wide range of experiences of violence against women. It includes, for example, male violence in the home as well harmful traditional practices that are carried out by women. This context-sensitive approach contrasts with previous South–North feminist encounters, for example, at world conferences during the UN Decade on Women (1975–85). During this period efforts by US and European feminists to target female genital mutilation for condemnation were (usually correctly) perceived as neo-imperialist and prompted some African women to defend the practice in cultural relativist terms (Joachim 1999: 145).

Utilization of global forums as sites of cosmopolitan solidarity and "citizenship"

A growing body of scholarship argues that patterns of increased NGO activity around UN forums over recent decades signal the emergence of a global civil society and a shift away from the nation-state as the primary locus of political power. Women's transnational NGO networks are frequently cited as playing a pivotal role in this process (Dickensen 1997, Keck and Sikkink 1998, Joachim 1999, Brown Thompson 2002). Lending support to this point, the global campaign for women's human rights targeted a series of UN world conferences beginning with the World Conference on Human Rights (Vienna 1993) and culminating with the Fourth World Conference on Women (Beijing 1995). It utilized these global forums to promote public awareness, develop the campaign, and secure concrete commitments to women's human rights. Through a combination of strategies that create opportunities for bottom-up participation (popular tribunals, petition drives, and so on) the global campaign and similar cosmopolitan projects also fostered intensive lobbying at local, national, and regional levels. In doing so, participants acquired the knowledge and skills needed to be active "cosmopolitan citizens" and participate in multilevel governance processes. The new women's human rights measures achieved in the 1990s, therefore, attest to the success of transnational feminist advocacy and the possibility of local non-governmental actors playing an increasingly visible and effective role in shaping international law and policy.

Addressing women's transnational organizing around the fourth world conference on women (Beijing 1995), Dickensen suggested it marked a "global feminist transformation of liberal democracy" wherein the "possibilities of self-determination, long denied at the nation-state level, may be realized by circumventing the nation-state from above or below" (Dickensen 1997: 110).

This very optimistic understanding of NGO activity at UN sites fits with a vision articulated by David Held of evolving "cosmopolitan democracy" wherein the nation state and civic identity are unlinked and "People can enjoy membership in the diverse communities which significantly affect them ... and ... [c]itizenship would extend, in principle to membership in cross-cutting political communities from the local to the global" (Held 1995: 272).

Post-September 11, however, such optimistic accounts of the prospects for cosmopolitan citizenship are less evident and the focus on law has intensified in academic cosmopolitan discourses. More recently, Held stresses that the post-World War II "rule based multilateral order" is "fragile, vulnerable and full of limitations" (Held 2005: 15). He talks less about new forms of cosmopolitan political participation and more about the importance of sustaining progress toward a "truly internationalist or cosmopolitan framework of global law" (10). This emphasis on law reflects an understandable sense of urgency that egregious acts of international terrorism should not be accompanied by a retreat into national particularism or security policies that potentially erode the foundations of human rights and democracy.

It is also important, however, to consider the gender dimensions of this "backslide" (Chinkin and Charlesworth 2002). Well before September 11, women's human rights gains had become the subject of intense backlash in UN, regional, and national policy as conservative governments and NGOs mobilized to contest gains secured under the rubric of women's human rights.[11] This backlash is linked to the rising influence of politicized religious fundamentalist movements and a burgeoning neo-liberal resistance to rights-based approaches that are seen as a threat to the advance of economic innovation and growth. Also, following September 11, the resurgence of a masculinist military security paradigm at the expense of critical human security and human rights discourses, makes it even more difficult to articulate women's human rights concerns. Once more such concerns appear trivial in comparison to more important "global security" issues. Consequently, instead of advancing implementation of hard-won global agreements, feminist advocates are expending much energy simply keeping women's human rights on key UN agendas, for example, in relation to the Millennium Development Goals.[12] These events underline the critical importance of sustained cosmopolitan feminist practice that engages with global political, legal, and economic arenas in the struggle to keep a focus on women's human rights issues at the macro level. Held's call for strengthened "global law" and emphasis on connecting economic globalization to "manifest principles of social justice" (14) are key elements in any post-September 11 cosmopolitan framework. However, it is also important to keep a focus on opening up opportunities for bottom-up cosmopolitan political participation—especially in relation to claiming human rights and reinforcing the legitimacy of human rights standards from local to global levels.

---

11 For discussions of the backlash see Sen and Corrêa (2000), Neuhold (2000), and CWGL and WEDO (2000).
12 See, for example, Gender Monitoring Group of the World Summit (2005).

A commitment to democratic governance and accountability from the local to the global levels

As noted, contemporary cosmopolitan discourse begins with the observation that globalization trends of the late twentieth and early twenty-first century call into question the continued centrality of the territorial nation-state. Hence, while always implied, the commitment of cosmopolitan thinkers to democratic governance at state and sub-state level is often understated. Indeed, neoconservative critics capitalize on this when they construct cosmopolitan and "globalist" perspectives as the antithesis of constitutionalism and state level democracy (Drolet 2010) and inimical to the principal "democratic" check on the exercise of power internationally that neoconservatives recognize—the primacy of state sovereignty. From a feminist point of view, state level democracy remains an unfinished agenda for most women in most societies, whether in the global North or South (Paxton and Hughes 2007). While Dickenson suggested that women's broad based civic participation in transnational forums could be viewed as a solution of sorts to their persistent exclusion from power at state level, this optimistic view runs into difficulty on the level of implementation of global commitments to women. While transnational feminist advocacy of the 1990s produced a raft of very significant intergovernmental commitments to advance gender equality and women's human rights, progress by governments to implement these gains has been extremely slow and uneven (UN Division for the Advancement of Women 2010). For example, implementing the provisions of the Beijing Platform for Action or the Convention on the Elimination of All Forms of Discrimination against Women relies overwhelmingly on the sustained commitment of political leaders and governments at national level to do so. Arguably, ensuring the political will and resources necessary to realize global commitments to women requires a critical mass of leaders and decision-makers at national level who are committed to such a transformative agenda. Strong and active civil society organizations pressing for such implementation are also vital but not sufficient. For this reason, cosmopolitan feminism, understood as transformative emancipatory practice, necessarily demands a sustained commitment to bottom-up democratic governance and accountability at state level and a renewed commitment to ensuring women's full and equal participation in policy decision-making at every level.

Conclusion

The account of cosmopolitan feminism developed here recognizes the significance of vibrant transnational feminist advocacy over the past three decades, especially targeting UN forums. While skeptical of the prospects for a constitutional "world government," I have argued that the example of feminist transnational human rights advocacy fits with cosmopolitan readings of an emerging "global civil society." As such, it flags new forms of de-centered cosmopolitan solidarity and citizenship above and below the state, underpinned by a critical commitment to universal human rights. It also draws attention to the gendered impact of globalization and related global issues, which are generally ignored in mainstream cosmopolitan literature.

In terms of feminist theory, the embrace of "universal" human rights values by diverse women's movements presents a quandary. In much feminist scholarship, universalist discourses have come to be viewed as oppressive, totalizing narratives or discredited vehicles of white, male, and western domination. In addition, the very basis of "the feminist project" appears to be undermined in the imperative to reject essentialism and recognize the diversity of women's experiences and identities. My account of cosmopolitan feminism attempts to specify the conditions under which it possible to maintain a constructive tension between endorsing universal values—such as human rights—and what it means to enjoy human rights from the standpoint of particular marginalized experiences and identities. In doing so, cosmopolitan feminism retains a principled commitment to critically reinterpreted "universal" values including the rule of law, human rights, and constitutional, secular democratic politics at national level.

This cosmopolitan feminist approach resonates in the practice of countless feminist activists, NGOs, and networks in every region, but perhaps most particularly in the advocacy of Third World feminists. Such advocates are fully cognizant of abuses of "universal" values (most recently in the wars on Afghanistan and Iraq). But nonetheless they seek to (re-)articulate and claim their radical promise. This is especially evident in women's movements that have been on the frontline of resisting fundamentalism and intolerance in every region (Abeyeskera 2001). It is not a coincidence that women's movements resisting fundamentalism have been most vocal in the call for "moderation and adherence to principles of international human rights and humanitarian law and standards" in dealing with the September 11 attacks (*ibid.*). However, this cosmopolitan feminist commitment to international law is qualified by an equally strong commitment to the critical (re-)interpretation of such international norms to ensure that they take account of women's lives and facilitate the pursuit of gender justice.

Further, cosmopolitan feminism demands recognition of the gendered impacts of neo-liberal globalization and contests the many exploitive hierarchies that structure international politics. To date, however, the women's human rights movement has been most successful in achieving the recognition of violence against women as a violation of human rights—whether in the home or in conflict situations. Arguably, the struggle to achieve recognition of women's wider economic and social rights has lagged behind the feminist challenge to the public–private divide—at least in relation to the issue of violence. At the same time, the legitimacy of the international human rights regime is facing profound challenges in a post-September 11 global context. Against this backdrop, the task of deepening and extending the reach of cosmopolitan feminism and using international human rights to challenge the gender dimensions of socio-economic inequalities and abuses is a major ongoing challenge.

In sum, I have presented cosmopolitan feminism as a model of emancipatory political practice. In particular, I argue that critically reinterpreted human rights offer enormous potential in meeting current global challenges. In making this argument however, I fully recognize that the false universalization of human rights—from privileged, male, neo-liberal, western, and state-centric perspectives—continues to undermine the radical promise of human rights. And, at the same time, the intersectionality of different forms of oppression, across economic, social, cultural, and political domains, must be fully taken into account by any feminist project. However, these problems of false universalization and exclusion are political ones and need to be tackled through emancipatory political projects that expose previously hidden abuses of power and give expression to previously excluded and marginalized voices. Cosmopolitan feminism offers a way of conceptualizing such projects from women's diverse perspectives in a globalizing era.

Bibliography

Abeyeskera, S. 2001. *Paying the Price for Ignoring Women's Calls against Fundamentalism*. Online, available at: www.wluml.org/english/newsfulltxt.shtml?cmd%5B157%5D=x-157-3422 (accessed November 11, 2010).

Ackerly, B. and Okin, S. 1999. Feminist social criticism and the international movement for women's human rights, in *Democracy's Edges*, edited by I. Shapiro and C. Hacker-Cordon. Cambridge: Cambridge University Press, 134–62.

An-Na'im, A. 1992. Toward a cross-cultural approach to defining international standards of human rights: the meaning of cruel, inhuman, or degrading treatment or punishment, in *Human Rights in Cross-Cultural Perspectives: A Quest for Consensus*, edited by A. An-Na'im. Philadelphia: University of Pennsylvania Press, 19–43.

Antrobus, P. 2004. *The Global Women's Movement: Origins, Issues Strategies*. London: Zed Books.

Archibugi, D. (ed.). 2003. *Debating Cosmopolitics*. London: Verso.

Archibugi, D., Held, D. and Köhler, M. (eds). 1998. *Re-Imagining Political Community*. Stanford: Stanford University Press.

Baxi, U. 2002. *The Future of Human Rights*. New Delhi: Oxford University Press.

Beetham, D. 1999. Human rights as a model for cosmopolitan democracy, in *Democracy and Human Rights*, edited by D. Beetham. Cambridge: Polity, 136–47.

Brah, A. and Phoenix, A. 2004. Ain't I a woman? Revisiting intersectionality. *Journal of International Women's Studies*, 5(3), 75–86.

Bronner, S. 2004. *Reclaiming the Enlightenment: Toward a Politics of Radical Engagement*. New York: Columbia University Press.

Brown Thompson, K. 2002. Women's rights are human rights, in *Restructuring World Politics: Transnational Social Movements, Networks and Norms*, edited by S. Khagram, J.V. Riker, and K. Sikkink. Minneapolis: University of Minnesota Press, 96–122.

Bunch, C. 1987. Global feminism, in *Passionate Politics: Feminist Theory in Action*. New York: St. Martin's Press, 269–362.

Bunch, C. 1990. Women's rights as human rights: towards a re-vision of human rights. *Human Rights Quarterly*, 12, 486–98.

Bunch, C. and Reilly, N. 1994. *Demanding Accountability: The Global Campaign and Vienna Tribunal for Women's Human Rights*. New York: UNIFEM.

Carrillo, R. 1991. *Violence Against Women: An Obstacle To Development*. New Brunswick: Center for Women's Global Leadership.

Charlesworth, H. 1994. What are women's international human rights? in *Human Rights of Women: National and International Perspectives*, edited by R. Cook. Philadelphia: University of Pennsylvania Press, 58–84.

Chinkin, C. 2001. Women's international tribunal on Japanese military sexual slavery. *American Journal of International Law*, 95(2), 335–41.

Chinkin, C. and Charlesworth, H. 2002. Sex, gender, and September 11. *American Journal of International Law*, 96(3), 600–5.

Cockburn, C. 2005. *War against Women: A Feminist Response to Genocide in Gujarat*. Online, available at: http://cynthiacockburn.typepad.com//Gujaratblog.pdf (accessed November 11, 2010).

Cockburn, C. 2007. *From Where We Stand: War, Women's Activism and Feminist Analysis*. London: Zed Books.

Cohn, C. 2004. Feminist peacemaking: in Resolution 1325 the UN requires the inclusion of women in all peace planning and negotiation. *Women's Review of Books*, February.

Copelon, R. 2000. Gender crimes as war crimes: integrating crimes against women into international criminal law. *McGill Law Journal*, 46, 217–41.

Crawford, J. and Marks, S. 1998. The global democracy deficit: an essay in international law and its limits, in *Re-Imagining Political Community*, edited by D. Archibugi, D. Held, and M. Köhler. Stanford: Stanford University Press, 72–90.

Crenshaw, K. 1997. Intersectionality and identity politics: learning from violence against women of color, in *Reconstructing Political Theory*, edited by M.L. Shanley and U. Narayan. London: Polity.

CWGL and WEDO. 2000. Beijing +5 review process. Center for Women's Global Leadership and Women's Environment and Development Organization, July. Online, available at: www.cwgl.rutgers.edu/globalcenter/policy/beijing5reflections.html (accessed November 11, 2010).

Dickensen, D. 1997. Counting women in: globalization, democratization and the women's movement, in *The Transformation of Democracy*, edited by A. McGrew. Cambridge: Polity Press, 97–120.

Drolet, J.-F. 2010. Containing Kantian revolutions: a theoretical analysis of the neo-conservative critique of global liberal governance. *Review of International Studies*, 36(3), 533–60.

Dutt, M. 2000. Some reflections on United States women of color and the United Nations Fourth World Conference on Women and NGO Forum in Beijing, China, in *Global Feminisms since 1945*, edited by B. Smith. London: Routledge, 305–12.

Edwards, M. and Gaventa, J. (eds). 2001. *Global Civic Action*. Boulder: Lynne Rienner Publishers.

Falk, R. 2004. *The Declining World Order*. New York: Routledge.

Ferree, M.M. and Tripp, A.M. 2006. *Global Feminism: Transnational Women's Activism, Organizing and Human Rights*. New York: New York University Press.

Foundation for AIDS Research. 2009. Statistics: women and HIV/AIDS. Online, available at: www.amfar.org/abouthiv/article.aspx?id=3594 (accessed November 11, 2010).

Fraser, A. and Tinker, I. (eds). 2004. *Developing Power: How Women Transformed International Development*. New York: The Feminist Press at CUNY.

Gender Monitoring Group of the World Summit. 2005. United Nations 2005 World Summit Outcomes: Gains on Gender Equality, Mixed Results on Poverty, Peace, and Human Rights. A report prepared by a coalition of women's NGOs (Center for Women's Global Leadership (CWGL), Development Alternatives with Women for a New Era (DAWN), Family Care International, United Methodist UN Office, and the Women's Environment and Development Organization (WEDO)). October 12. Online, available at: www.cwgl.rutgers.edu/globalcenter/policy/millsummit/reportbackOct12.pdf (accessed November 11, 2010).

Gould, C. 2004. *Globalizing Democracy and Human Rights*. Cambridge: Cambridge University Press.

Grewal, I. 1999. "Women's rights as human rights": Feminist practices, global feminism and human rights regimes in transnationality. *Citizenship Studies*, 3(3), 337–54.

Habermas, J. 2001. *The Postnational Constellation*. Cambridge: Polity Press.

Held, D. 1995. *Democracy and Global Order: From the Modern State to Cosmopolitan Governance*. Cambridge: Polity Press.

Held, D. 2002. Cosmopolitanism: ideas, realities and deficits, in *Governing Globalization: Power, Authority and Global Governance*, edited by D. Held and A. McGrew. Cambridge: Polity Press, 305–24.

Held, D. 2005. Globalization, International Law and Human Rights. Lecture presented on September 20 at the Human Rights Center, University of Connecticut.

hooks, b. 1984. *Feminist Theory from Margin to Center*. Boston: South End Press.

International Labour Organization. 2008. Gender issues in labour migration governance. Online, available at: www.ilo.org/public/english/protection/migrant/areas/gender.htm (accessed November 11, 2010).

Jaggar, A. 2000. Globalizing feminist ethics, in *Decentering the Center: Philosophy for a Multicultural, Postcolonial and Feminist World*, edited by U. Narayan and S. Harding. Bloomington: Indiana University Press, 1–25.

Joachim, J. 1999. Shaping the human rights agenda: the case of violence against women, in *Gender Politics in Global Governance*, edited by M.K. Meyer and E. Prügl. Lanham: Rowman & Littlefield, 142–60.

Keck, M. and Sikkink, K. 1998. *Activists Beyond Borders: Advocacy Networks in International Politics*. Ithaca: Cornell University Press.

Khagram, S., Riker, J.V. and Sikkink, K. (eds). 2002. *Restructuring World Politics: Transnational Social Movements, Networks and Norms*. Minneapolis: University of Minnesota Press.

Kothari, S. and Sethi, H. 1989. *Rethinking Human Rights*. New York: New Horizons Press.

Levitt, P. and Merry, S. 2009. Vernacularization on the ground: local uses of global women's rights in Peru, China, India and the United States. *Global Networks*, 9(4), 441–61.

Linklater, A. 1998. *The Transformation of Political Community*. Columbia: University of South Carolina Press.

Matua, M. 2002. *Human Rights: A Political and Cultural Critique*. Philadelphia: University of Pennsylvania Press.

Mertus, J. 2004. Shouting from the bottom of the well: the impact of international trials for wartime rape on women's agency. *International Journal of Feminist Politics*, 6(1), 110–28.

Moghadam, V. 2005. *Globalizing Women: Transnational Feminist Networks*. Baltimore: Johns Hopkins Press.

Mohanty, C.T. 1991. Under Western eyes: feminist scholarship and colonial discourses, in *Third World Women and the Politics of Feminism*, edited by C.T. Mohanty, A. Russo, and L. Torres. Bloomington: Indiana University Press, 51–80.

Mohanty, C.T. 2003. *Feminism Without Borders: Decolonizing Theory, Practicing Solidarity*. Durham, NC: Duke University Press.

Mohanty, C.T., Russo, A. and Torres, L. (eds). 1991. *Third World Women and the Politics of Feminism*. Bloomington: Indiana University Press.

Neuhold, B. 2000. WIDE briefing paper on the UN General Assembly Special Session: Women 2000: Gender Equality, Development, and Peace for the 21st Century. WIDE: Brussels.

Nussbaum, M. 1999. *Sex and Social Justice*. Oxford: Oxford University Press.

Okin, S.M. 1999. *Is Multiculturalism Bad for Women?* Princeton: Princeton University Press.

Okin, S.M. 2000. Feminism, women's human rights and cultural differences, in *Decentering the Center: Philosophy for a Multicultural, Postcolonial and Feminist World*, edited by U. Narayan and S. Harding. Bloomington: Indiana University Press, 26–46.

Paxton, P. and Hughes, M.M. 2007. *Women, Politics and Power: A Global Perspective*. Los Angeles: Pine Forge Press.

Pietilä, H. and Vickers, J. 1990. *Making Women Matter: The Role of the United Nations*. London: Zed Books.

Pogge, T. 2005. Real world justice. *The Journal of Ethics*, 9(1–2), 29–53.

Rao, A. 1995. The politics of gender and culture in international human rights discourse, in *Women's Rights, Human Rights*, edited by J. Peters and A. Wolper. London: Routledge, 167–75.

Reilly, N. (ed.). 1996. *Without Reservation: The Beijing Tribunal on Accountability for Women's Human Rights*. New Brunswick: Center for Women's Global Leadership.

Reilly, N. 2007a. Cosmopolitan feminism and human rights. *Hypatia: A Journal of Feminist Philosophy*, 22(4), 180–98.

Reilly, N. 2007b. Seeking gender justice in post-conflict transitions: towards a transformative women's human rights approach. *International Journal of Law in Context*, 3, 155–72.

Reilly, N. 2009. *Women's Human Rights: Seeking Gender Justice in a Globalising Age*. London: Polity.

Robinson, F. 2003. Human rights and the global politics of resistance: feminist perspectives. *Review of International Studies*, 29, 161–80.

Romany, C. 1995. On surrendering privilege: diversity in feminist redefinition of human rights law, in *From Basic Needs to Basic Rights: Women's Claim to Human Rights*, edited by M. Schuler. Washington, DC: Women Law and Development International, 543–54.

Sen, A. 2004. Elements of a theory of human rights. *Philosophy and Public Affairs*, 32(4), 315–56.

Sen, G. and Corrêa, S.O. 2000. Gender justice and economic justice: reflections on the Five-Year Reviews of the UN conferences of the 1990s, paper prepared for UNIFEM in preparation for the Five-Year Review of the Beijing Platform for Action, DAWN Informs.

Shaheed, F. 2004. Dossier 26: constructing identities—culture, women's agency and the Muslim world. Online, available at: www.wluml.org/node/478 (accessed November 11, 2010).

Spivak, G. 1988. Can the subaltern speak? in *Marxism and the Interpretation of Culture*, edited by C. Nelson and L. Grossberg. Urbana: University of Illinois Press, 271–313.

Streeten P. 2001. *Globalisation: Threat and Opportunity?* Copenhagen: Copenhagen Business School Press.

UN Division for the Advancement of Women. 2010. *Beijing at 15: Gender Equality, Development and Peace*. Online, available at: www.un.org/womenwatch/daw/beijing15/media/Beijing15_Backgrounder_FINAL.pdf (accessed November 11, 2010).

Urbinati, N. 2003. Can cosmopolitical democracy be democratic? In *Debating Cosmopolitics*, edited by D. Archibugi. London: Verso, 67–85.

Yuval-Davis, N. 2006. Intersectionality and feminist politics. *European Journal of Women's Studies*, 13(3), 193–209.

Cosmopolitanism and the Humanist Myopia

Harry Kunneman and Caroline Suransky

Introduction

In view of the many pressing problems facing humanity in the new century, the idea of cosmopolitanism seems to have a higher relevance and greater urgency than ever before. In reality however, present-day world society is far removed from a cosmopolis. Both on the level of individual orientations and on the level of worldwide institutional structures, global developments point as much to the dominance of disrupting economic forces and to the increasing political significance of national, religious, and ethnic conflicts, as to a political framework and economic practices which are oriented toward a cosmopolitan ethos and more just world-society. As Jürgen Habermas, one of the staunch defenders of the project of a cosmopolitan world society, says: "It is an open question whether we will succeed in overcoming the atavistic condition of the social-Darwinist 'catch as catch can,' still dominant today in international relations, to the point at which capitalism, globally unleashed and run wild, can be tamed and channeled in socially acceptable ways" (Habermas and Mendieta 2007). The urgency to address this question is enhanced by the fact that in our times the development of a cosmo-political world-society not only asks for "socially acceptable" but also for "ecologically acceptable," sustainable relations. In view of this tension between the great relevance and urgency of a cosmopolitan ethos on the one hand and the worrisome practical situation of our planet and its inhabitants on the other hand, it seems that the cosmopolitan project is in need of new horizons of inspiration. In search for such a horizon, we will focus on the relation between humanism and cosmopolitanism, more in particular on the consequences for the cosmopolitan project of what we have termed the "humanist myopia." This nearsightedness springs from the belief that "deep down" all human beings are oriented primarily toward benevolent, empathic, and dialogical forms of bonding with others. This leads to a systematic neglect of the propensities and capabilities of human beings for indifferent, malevolent, and violent forms of relating to others. Moreover this myopia is connected with a view on politics as a dialogical and deliberative endeavor and with a perspective on science and technology as neutral and objective resources, thus neglecting the crucial function fulfilled by political institutions and technological practices in organizing and legitimating networks of economic exploitation and political subjugation.

In view of the negative consequences of these manifestations of the humanist myopia for the cosmopolitan project, we will argue in favor of a *critical* humanism, holding on to a cosmopolitan vision of a more just and sustainable world society, but also critical with regard to the different manifestations of the humanist myopia. As backdrop for the argument, we start with an example of the humanist myopia and its consequences for the cosmopolitan project.

This example concerns a classical formulation of the idea of cosmopolitism: the circle model of identity formulated by the Stoic philosopher Hierocles in the second century AD. As a late Stoic, his work strongly resonates the general tenets of Stoic cosmology and their roots in the Cynic philosophy of Diogenes and Zeno (Long 2001). To the question where he came from, Diogenes famously answered "I am a kosmopolites." This answer not only signaled his disdain for local laws and conventions, but also his conviction that human nature in general and human reason in particular transcend all existing forms of political community and its concomitant laws. As A.A. Long reminds us, this view was normative rather than descriptive: Diogenes's worldwide city "should be regarded as the community of the wise, an ideal of enlightened persons united not by local or relational ties but by the common values they share—a group that understands what human nature needs in order to perfect itself" (Long 2008). According to Long "in light of the hundreds of individual Greek city-states, highly jealous of their autonomy" this idea must have seemed quite improbable to most contemporaries of Diogenes, although they were also "Panhellenic in many of their customs and collective sense of superiority to the 'barbarians'" (Long 2008). Writing almost five centuries later, Hierocles could build on the spread of Hellenistic culture after the conquests of Alexander the Great, on the unifying influence of the Roman Empire and of course on the work of illustrious philosophical precursors, notably Cicero and Seneca (Schofield 1999). Hierocles elaborated upon the powerful metaphor of concentric circles, coined by Cicero to articulate the ideal of cosmopolitanism. Whereas Cicero distinguished three expanding communities—the family, political societies, and the community of all humans—Hierocles placed the individual in the center of these concentric circles. His central concept is oikeiosis: lovingly making something one's own, appropriating something. This process starts with the appropriation of and reconciliation with oneself, the love of oneself to which reason leads us. This loving appropriation of self find its complement in the loving appropriation of others, "syngenike," starting with one's close family and extending to more distant relatives, to political communities and finally to all human beings. As Elisabeth Asmis says:

> *By placing the individual at the center, Hierocles shows that the growth of society is the continuation of the process of oikeiosis that begins with the individual. Self-appropriation goes hand in hand with social appropriation. In social development we not only make things our 'own,' but also make them*

'common.' Hierocles term 'syngenike' suggests that there is a recognition of ever wider groups of 'kin' or family, extending as far as kinship with the whole human race. (Asmis 1996)

This idea of extension of empathy to wider circles of human beings, strongly echoes Cicero's cosmopolitan vision of ever widening circles of connection, starting with oneself and one's next of kin. According to Hierocles, this extension can be accomplished by drawing in the widest circles toward the center in a series of steps, in which the next circle is treated as the most nearby, for instance by designating people situated one circle further also as "brother." Building upon Diogenes, Zeno, and Cicero, Hierocles thus provides a classical articulation of an idea central to most subsequent forms of humanism. All human beings are deemed able to develop an empathic, understanding relation with themselves and extend this relation to other nearby human beings. The close bonds which thus emerge can subsequently be extended to ever wider circles of human beings, up to a worldwide political community.

This classical formulation of a core humanist conviction also show the concomitant myopia. The deep disdain of the Greeks for "barbarians," the crucial role of military power and strategic superiority in the unifying projects of Alexander the Great and of the Roman emperors, and last but not least the asymmetric streams of labor, goods, and cultural representations of the world at large between the periphery and the center of these forms of political community, all disappear out of sight in the humanist focus on a loving appropriation of self and others as the basis for the eventual development of a truly human cosmopolis (Wallerstein 1974, 2004). In the work of influential postmodern, poststructuralist, and feminist thinkers, the critical analysis of the humanist belief in the empathic capabilities of human beings and the concomitant nearsightedness, lead to a radical disqualification of humanism and of humanist hopes for a cosmopolitan world society (Foucault 1979, Lyotard 1988, Braidotti 1991, Rose, 1996). In our eyes, however, such a disqualification engenders a complementary "postmodern nearsightedness" for the empathic and dialogical capabilities of human beings and their potential significance for the cosmopolitan project. Instead of totally debunking humanist hopes for a cosmopolitan world society, we think with Edward Said (2003) that one can be critical of humanism in the name of humanism itself, and thus strive for a rejuvenation of the cosmopolitan project with the help of a self-critical humanism.

In the remainder of our argument we will sketch three pointers toward such a critical humanism, beyond the humanist myopia which emerged from our research and teaching at the University for Humanistic Studies in Utrecht during the past two decades. The first pointer concerns the limits of the modern notion of autonomy and the importance of peaceful containment. The second pointer concerns the role of economic, technological, and cultural power relations on a worldwide scale and the importance of a global civil society. The third pointer refers to new forms of critical reflexivity concerning the role of economic and political interests shaping scientific and technological developments at a worldwide scale.

The Case of Humanistics

The University for Humanistic Studies is a small university which is connected with the (quite influential) humanist movement in the Netherlands, one of the most secularized countries in the world, and is fully financed by the Dutch state. Teaching and research at our university are explicitly guided by "humane values," as articulated primarily within humanist philosophical traditions and the critical social sciences, but also within literary traditions and within the great spiritual traditions. However our research is also informed by the practice of humanist counseling and of related professions, and by the experiences and feedback from clients in social domains where humanist counselors are employed, such as hospitals, prisons, the army, and homes for the elderly, but also in educational institutions and in the business world dealing with for instance social responsibility programs.

Thus, from the start the humanist perspective which dominated our research and teaching has been shaped by two different perspectives. On the one hand, a perspective that is firmly rooted in modern humanism, especially in the notions of autonomy, rationality, and solidarity, as articulated in Kantian ethics, in humanistic psychology, and in the work of contemporary critical thinkers like Jürgen Habermas. On the other hand it has also been shaped by another influence, which corrected up to a point the humanist myopia that we "inherited" from modern humanism. This countervailing influence stems from the specific questions and challenges that confront humanist counselors in their work with clients.

Slow questions

Humanist counseling developed in the Netherlands from the 1950s onwards, starting in prisons and different branches of the Dutch army, spreading from there to (mental) hospitals, homes for the elderly, and educational institutions. Thus, as a profession, humanist counseling is bound to the panoptical institutions and the "governmental" forms of power explicitly addressed by Foucault and his followers (Foucault 1979, 1998, Rose 1990). Within these institutions, however, they are positioned at the margin of the official power structures and work in "free spaces" allowing for countervailing influences to the panoptical forms of power dominant there. These oppositional influences stem from the specific character of the existential questions which are dealt with by humanist counselors and their clients. These questions can be metaphorically characterized as "slow questions" and can be grouped around two focal points (Kunneman 2005). First, they are connected with the fragility of human bodies and the vulnerability of the human psyche which manifest themselves primarily in experiences of sorrow, finitude and loss of control, connected for instance with extreme poverty, with injuries, with illness and with the prospect of death. On the other hand, slow questions can also be connected with experiences of indifference, maltreatment, and violence, either committed by others or by ourselves. We call such questions "slow questions" for two related reasons. First, because they have accompanied humanity from the beginning of our history and have not changed that much in the long course of human civilization. Second, we speak of slow questions because they cannot be adequately addressed with the help of "fast" technical interventions. Such "fast" remedies often leave existential and moral "residues," which cannot be absorbed by technical means and expert knowledge. An example would be a diagnosis of breast cancer and the decision to amputate a breast and to apply chemo-therapeutic treatment of the cancer. Even if this would lead to a fast healing process in the somatic register, it would nevertheless also engender slow questions, connected for instance with worries about return of the cancer, the mourning of lost beauty and tensions and readjustments on the level of erotic relations. The same goes for painful experiences of indifference or violence from other persons; but also for feelings of failed responsibility and guilt for our own acts of violence or lack of care for others. A first defining characteristic of slow questions is thus the confrontation with the limits of fast, technical solutions and the necessity to "muddle through," to apply oneself to the "labor of mourning," to try and re-write one's life history to a certain extent and envisage alternative ways to lead a meaningful life. A second defining characteristic of slow questions is the entanglement of existential questions and moral dilemmas. In many cases slow questions of one person generally imply moral challenges and dilemmas for others, because they foreground questions of care and responsibility, or indifference and desertion.

Faced with such slow questions at the side of their clients in hospitals, homes for the elderly, prisons, and the army, humanist counselors have not much to offer in the way of fast remedies or technical expertise. In a reflection on her work as humanist counselor in a big hospital, Elly Hoogeveen formulates the bottom line of her work as follows:

> *You should not abandon a client; not even when the other communicates that everybody should go away. As counselor you can feel desperate with someone like this, because you receive nothing back. Still, it is important also in this situation to perform the quality of staying with the other—right through your own fear of being rejected. The other can then feel my relating to the total impasse she finds herself in, where I could also be. This form of relating can possibly help the other.* (Hoogeveen and Jorna 1997)

In some cases the acceptance of the "total impasse" clients find themselves in and the offer to stay with the other in their effort to muddle through and find "real words" for their situation, can lead to the emergence of new meaning and even to a certain healing. Hoogeveen describes this emergence as follows: "To my surprise, with wonder and admiration, I see how people suddenly admit something to themselves, that life also has another side to it than only this grotesque and disgusting side they are confronted with in their situation. And then you see the emergence of a certain healing. Every time you see this, it is almost art" (Hoogeveen and Jorna 1997).

In our eyes such confrontations with slow questions also have a critical potential, because they show the limits of the dominant individualistic and rationalist worldview, which projects our world as a field of unlimited technological control in the service of autonomously defined values of free and independent individuals. The confrontation with slow questions entails the realization that one cannot choose freely, that one's fate in life in the last resort cannot be controlled with technological means and, moreover, that one is *deeply dependent* upon others to try and wrestle meaning from the situation one finds oneself in. Along these lines, this confrontation also points to the limits of modern humanism, especially its one-sided focus on individual liberty, autonomy, and personal development on the basis of scientific progress and technological control.

We undo each other

Our reflection on the nature and critical implications of slow questions was further stimulated by the work of Judith Butler, especially her book *Precarious Life* (Butler 2004). One of the most important goals of her book is to clarify a dimension of political life "that has to do with our exposure to violence and our complicity in it, with our vulnerability to loss and the task of mourning" (Butler 2004). According to Butler, it is precisely in these conditions for political life that a new foundation for communality could be found. To that end she sketches the possibility of a new political theory, no longer based on the idea of autonomous individuals, but based on the precarious character of their emotional and existential ties with others. This new political theory does not give up on the idea of autonomy and individual political rights, but tries to clarify their inherent limitations as descriptions of what we are as human beings.

According to Butler we are socially constituted bodies, which are not only attached to others and therefore at risk of losing others, but also "exposed to others [and] at risk of violence by virtue of that exposure" (Butler 2004). Butler analyzes the special character of those ties in view of two ways in which the constitutive character of our ties with others hits us with great force: in mourning and in longing. In the loss and the mourning that inevitably goes with it, we experience that there is something bigger than our own conscious plan, our own project, our own knowing, and choosing. At such moments, there no longer is an "I," existing independently from a "you" situated somewhere opposite that "I." Instead, through the loss of an important other we experience a form of loss of the self as well. The grief over the loss of another human being shows the constitutive character of our ties with others. Our "management" of our own life is disrupted, Butler says, and the notion that we are autonomous and have everything under control becomes doubtful. However, this absence of control over "our" ties with others should not be understood as a risk, to be averted at all costs. On the contrary, as Butler writes in a fascinating phrase: "Let's face it. We're undone by each other. And if we're not, we're missing something" (Butler 2004).

Along these lines a shift occurs in the center of gravity of modern humanism: central to it are no longer the autonomous subject and its freedom of choice, but the constitutive ties and the mutual involvement between individuals stemming from their entanglement as fragile and longing beings and all slow questions flowing from this entanglement. A further elucidation of this relational complexity which was of great help for us in overcoming the humanist myopia for the central role of power and aggression in relations between human beings, can be found in the work of Jessica Benjamin, who connects the tradition of psychoanalytical and feminist thinking with insights from critical and postmodern theory.

Peaceful containment

Benjamin's point of departure is provided by the Freudian idea that human subjects are unable to leave other persons alone. According to Benjamin, "the subject ... constantly assimilates what is outside itself. The ego cannot leave the other to be an independent outside entity ... because it is always incorporating the other, or demanding that the other be like the self" (Benjamin 1998). By way of mutual projections and identifications subjects try to neutralize the loss and the lack of control, which ensue from the fact that others do not automatically satisfy their demands. Benjamin interprets the difficulties we encounter in bearing the independence of other persons in terms of the desire for omnipotence over important others as a deep emotional sub-layer of human contact:

> *By omnipotence, we mean not merely a wish but a mental state. In this state we are unable to take in that the other person does not want what we want, do what we say. Violence is the outer perimeter of the less dramatic tendency of the subject to force the other to either be or want what it wants, to assimilate the other to itself, or to make it a threat.* (Benjamin 1998)

Following Donald Winnicott, she interprets this pursuit of omnipotence as a form of destruction of the difference embodied by the other. This difference is hard to bear; its reality is frightening: after all, to accept it means giving up our omnipotence and autonomy.

At this point, Benjamin introduces a sharp distinction between, on the one hand, the intra-psychic constructions of the persons involved, which destroy the other's difference, and on the other hand the inter-subjectivity that might emerge when they are able to acknowledge the uncontrollable difference of the other. In a conceptual move which in our eyes is of decisive importance for a critical humanism, Benjamin finds the starting point for this inter-subjectivity in aggression and negativity! The experience of inter-subjectivity can only emerge, when in the exchange between the Ego and Alter, the latter contains the aggressive projections and identifications of the Ego toward Alter in a peaceful manner. The core of this peaceful containment is that Alter stands up for her right to differ from those projections and identifications, and explicitly rejects them, but at the same time indicates that she values the relationship with the other, and wishes to continue it. The decisive question is then of course whether Ego is capable of "taking back" his or her omnipotence, and accept Alter's offer to continue the relationship on the basis of the recognition of the other's difference. Looked at this way, the emergence of inter-subjectivity cannot be controlled or directed by either one of them: it is the result of a process of co-creation that breaks through the confinement of an individual's own intra-psychic constructions, allowing the other to become visible as being genuinely different:

> *The other's difference must exist outside. Only the externality of the other that survives destruction allows a representation of the other as simultaneously outside control and non-threatening ... only the outside other can be loved. It is ultimately this pleasure in the discovery of somebody to love that compensates the breakup of identity. (Benjamin 1998)*

Our reflection on the experiences of humanist counselors with slow questions, combined with insights from Judith Butler and Jessica Benjamin, provide us with a first pointer in the direction of a critical humanism and to a possible renewal of the cosmopolitan ethos. Their analyses point beyond the humanist myopia, without falling prey to a complementary "postmodern nearsightedness." The idea that "deep down" all human beings are oriented primarily toward benevolent, empathic, and dialogical forms of bonding with others is replaced with the idea that we can hardly bear difference, that we cannot leave each other alone, that we necessarily undo each other. But this aggressive potential also provides an impetus for peaceful containment of omnipotence, not only on the level of personal relations, but also on the level of political conflicts.

In conclusion of this paragraph we want to illustrate this crucial point by the interventions of Edward Said in a political conflict which, in its bitter repetitiveness, perhaps more than any other of the many violent clashes of our times, runs counter to the hopes underlying the cosmopolitan project: the ongoing conflict between Israel and Palestine. Everything Said has written on this controversial subject can plausibly be interpreted as a sincere effort to *peacefully* contain manifestations of Israeli omnipotence, which he encountered for the first time in 1948 when his family was driven into exile from Palestine (Said 1979, 1994, 2003). Instead of joining the equally omnipotent choirs of hateful Israel-bashers, Said holds on to the idea of a "bi-national state in which Israel and Palestine are parts, rather than antagonists of each other's history and underlying reality" (Said 2003). In his subtle lecture on "Freud and the Non-European," Said focuses on Freud's insistence that Moses was himself a "non-European," an Egyptian. Thus in the person of its founding father, "Jewish identity" is characterized from the beginning by an *internal* difference, a "constitutive fissure" as Said says, which seems to be sadly absent from present-day Israeli legislation: "Quite differently from the spirit of Freud's deliberately provocative reminders that Judaism's founder was a non-Jew, and that Judaism begins in the realm of Egyptian, non-Jewish monotheism, Israeli legislation countervenes, represses and even cancels Freud's carefully maintained opening out of Jewish identity towards its non-Jewish background" (Said 2003: 44). In Freud's critical analysis of "the man Moses," Said thus discerns an idea which in his eyes has a profound cosmopolitan relevance, namely the "irremediably diasporic, unhoused character of identities" (Said 2003). The differences embodied by the other, we could perhaps say, cannot be kept outside of us, neither outside of our personal identities nor outside of our communities. According to Said "in our age of vast population transfers, of refuges, exiles, expatriates, and immigrants," this "needn't be seen as only a Jewish characteristic … it can also be identified in the diasporic, wandering, unresolved, cosmopolitan consciousness of someone who is both inside and outside his or her community" (Said 2003: 53). This analysis of the relation between a cosmopolitan consciousness and the ability to de-identify with, and criticize, powerful, unitary identities, strongly resonates with Benjamin's analysis of our structural dependence on *others* for the containment of our omnipotence. The acknowledgement of the aggressive potential of human beings and of the difficulties we have in respecting differences, thus provides a first pointer beyond the humanist myopia and toward a critical humanism. While acknowledging this aggressive potential such a critical humanism also keeps open the possibility of a—albeit fragile—inter-subjectivity which can emerge out of the peaceful containment of omnipotence.

Post-Colonial Insights

The views of Edward Said provide a bridge to the second pointer toward a critical humanism which we want to sketch. Our awareness of this second pointer was furthered by our practical involvement with another humanist organization in the Netherlands, *Hivos*: the Humanist Institute for Cooperation with Developing Countries. Hivos is especially concerned with human rights and with the development of strong civil societies in the South (www.Hivos.nl). With support from Hivos, the University for Humanistic Studies founded the Kosmopolis Institute in 2004, dedicated to research and education concerning the possibilities and impediments for the development of cosmopolitanism. In 2007 this institute initiated together with Hivos an international "Knowledge Program" on *Promoting Pluralism*. Against the background of worldwide discussions and controversies concerning human rights and the role of a vital civil society with regard to the supposed treats of "fundamentalism," this knowledge program brings together academics, civil society based development professionals, and activists from India, Indonesia, Uganda, and the Netherlands. They generate and share knowledge on different, often contested, forms of diversity, coexistence, and conflict in local communities and their interdependence with economic and political developments at national and international levels.

Our experiences in this "knowledge program" helped us to realize that the second manifestation of the humanist myopia—the nearsightedness for global forms of economical, technological, and cultural power—is even more difficult to overcome than the first. On the basis of a comparison between China and Europe, Francois Jullien warns us that two pitfalls need to be avoided in this respect: "the first is 'easy humanism', our humanism, built on the belief in universal categories; the second is 'lazy relativism' that thinks each culture has its own peculiarities, which runs the risk of enclosing it within its identity" (Jullien 2003: 17). Our experiences in the knowledge program made us realize that the idea of "pluralism" could easily be absorbed into a lazy humanism and the concomitant uncritical belief in the universal validity of one's deepest convictions.

Significantly, the Promoting Pluralism Knowledge Program started out with the Dutch-initiated title of "Resisting Fundamentalisms." However, this name was contested by participants from post-colonial locations. They argued that in the aftermath of 9/11, the use of the term "fundamentalism" had become heavily criticized since it was often used in the Western public debate to describe extreme positions taken in the name of Islam and all too quickly associated with terrorism. "Fundamentalism" as a label for the knowledge program was thus rejected as it was likely to preclude real dialogue with those whom could be considered "different" and thereby countering the core objective of the program. The rejection of the term "fundamentalism" meant a serious confrontation with our "easy" humanist thinking about universalism and "otherness" and our taking for granted a lot of the economic and political structures that organize and manage "difference" on a worldwide scale on the basis of fundamentally asymmetrical relations. From the onset, it thus became apparent that many key concepts in the program, which all carried assumptions about democracy, could not be considered to be "neutral" or "universal" notions. Hence, while "promoting pluralism" may have started out on the basis of a presumably universal conception of "the good life," its universalist assumptions turned out to be problematic in a complex global political context.

A salient example of such a problematic universalist assumption is provided by the idea that modernization and secularization are inseparably connected. Local research projects in the pluralism program, especially in Indonesia and India, showed that the idea of secularism is challenged, as a contemporary concern of how politics and religion are fundamentally related and how the sacred and the secular connect in the public and private lives of people (Manschot and Suransky 2009).

In a seminar on the role of the secular state, Kakarala, coordinator of the pluralism program in India, drew from the work of Nandy (Nandy 2007) when he argued:

> *if the problem with the secular is, firstly, to be understood as part and parcel of the problem modernity is identified with, and, secondly, the secular is always something that is associated with the state as a category, it is interesting to consider that some postcolonial scholars believe that to be the central problem. For Nandy, for instance, the religious conflict in India cannot be sufficiently addressed and/or substantially resolved unless one dissociates from the predominant view that the state alone should provide the solution. In other words, if secularism, similar to the French concept of laïcité, is state-centric,*

then the state is expected to be pro-active in being socially non-partisan and to deploy its neutral forces to effectively mitigate inter-religious violence. However, what happens to that normativity, if over a long and persistent time, the state does not act in the way that it ought to? I think that is a puzzling question for all of those who live in postcolonial societies. (Kakarala 2009)

The critical dialogues with participants from the South in this knowledge program and their "peaceful containment" of easy forms of humanism, provided us with a small scale manifestation of the globalized civil society pictured by one of the most famous humanist scholars of our times, Jürgen Habermas, as a necessary countervailing power to the worldwide influence of global capitalism. In his earlier work Habermas more or less equated societies with national states and concentrated on the strengthening of communicative and deliberative processes in the context of national states (Habermas 1975, 1984, 1987). In his later work, from the 1990s onward, he is increasingly impressed (and depressed up to a point) by the diminishing influence of nation-states and the ever growing power of global market forces, operating at a transnational level on the basis of their own, overpowering logic of unlimited accumulation of shareholder value (Borradori 2003, Habermas 2001). As a consequence, Habermas has been paying increasing attention to the necessity of a "countervailing power" equally operating at a worldwide scale. In critical discussion with Kant's cosmopolitan vision of a world society governed by universal laws based on the rational capacities of autonomous individual, Habermas advocates the gradual extension of national civil societies as a widening social context for peaceful deliberation and argumentation. Building upon his theory of communicative action, Seyla Benhabib has analyzed civil societies as deliberative networks

in which all affected can have the right to articulate their point of view ... It is through the interlocking net of these multiple forms of associations, networks and organizations that an anonymous 'public conversation' results. It is central to the model of deliberative democracy that it privileges such a public sphere of mutually interlocking and overlapping networks and associations of deliberation, contestation and argumentation. (Benhabib 1996)

In the eyes of Habermas, the gradual emergence of a transnational civil society within the European Community, however fragile and contested it may be, provides a concrete example pointing to the possible emergence of a plural civil society encompassing the globe (Benhabib et al. 2006, Habermas and Mendieta 2007).

In our eyes, this notion of a global civil society functioning as a countervailing power to the influence of a global capitalist market economy provides a second important pointer toward a critical humanism. The further development of a global civil society is not only furthered by transnational forms of cooperation between critical secular and spiritual movements, but also by the new global risks and the concomitant forms of interdependence facing humanity in the twenty-first century. These global risks can be seen as possible containing forces on the level of international relations. In this vein, Ulrich Beck states in his book *Cosmopolitan Vision*:

> *The everyday experience of cosmopolitan interdependence is not a love affair of everyone with everyone. It arises in a climate of heightened global threats, which create an unavoidable pressure to cooperate. With the conceptualization and recognition of threats on a cosmopolitan scale, a shared space of responsibility and agency, bridging all national frontiers and divides is created that can (though it need not) found political action among strangers in ways analogous to national politics. (Beck 2006: 23)*

A Third Mode of Knowledge

Beck's reference to new global threats on a "cosmopolitan scale" and the pressure to cooperate which flows from these threats, provide a bridge to the third pointer to a critical humanism which we want to sketch. This pointer critically addresses the humanist myopia with regard to the *politically* loaded content of the dominant perspective on scientific knowledge and technological progress, especially the blindness for the active contribution of science and technology to the threats at a cosmopolitan scale envisaged by Beck. In this respect, the history of modern humanism is characterized by a continuous tension between a *rationalistic* current, focusing on scientific rationality and technological progress as the prime vehicles for human progress, and a *humanistic* current focusing on cultural traditions, values and hermeneutic understanding. Fifty years ago, C.P. Snow famously analyzed the tensions between these two currents as a split between two cultures (Snow 1998). Although many humanistic scholars deplore this split, by and large they tend to see a fundamental difference between objective causal explanation in the "hard sciences" on the one hand and value-oriented hermeneutic understanding in the "soft sciences" on the other. In this way, however, they also run the risk of accepting the view dominating of the "hard" sciences, namely that scientific knowledge has a neutral, objective, and universal character and is somehow "above" or beyond politics. In the framework of research at the University for Humanistic Studies into social and political aspects of biotechnology (Derkx and Kunneman 2011), we critically analyze this supposed neutrality, building among others on the distinction between two modes of knowledge production introduced by Gibbons, Nowotny, and Scott (Gibbons et al. 1994, Nowotny et al. 2001). The first mode of knowledge production, designated as Mode 1, is oriented to questions and problems which are defined within specific academic disciplines, which act as sole arbiter on the quality of proposed answers. In contrast Mode 2 knowledge production is oriented toward the solution of *practical* problems, connected with social needs and with economical and political priorities, such as the development of new medicines, faster computer chips or more "effective" weapon systems. Mode 2 science is characterized by its trans-disciplinary character and by the dynamic and heterogeneous character of the research communities involved. Most importantly it is "monitored" by a multiplicity of different stakeholders who define the adequacy of possible solutions for the practical problems at stake from different perspectives, involving diverging interests and values. According to Gibbons et al., the majority of scientific work has shifted from Mode 1 to Mode 2: it is oriented toward the solution of practical problems, has an inter- and trans-disciplinary character and is characterized by mixed forms of quality control which reflect (often) conflicting interests and values (Nowotny et al. 2001, Nowotny et al. 2005).

According to these authors, the increasing importance of economic and political interests in shaping the development of Mode 2 science, provokes new forms of social reflexivity regarding the development of science and technology. In our eyes such new forms of social reflexivity are of primary importance for the cosmopolitan project. In present-day world society the actual development of scientific research and technological innovations are shaped more by economic and political interests oriented to the maximization of profits and the safeguarding of narrow national interests, than by concerns for different forms of social exclusion, injustice, and ecological degradation confronting us at a worldwide scale. Although pressure "from the outside," for instance through critical interventions by civil society based organizations and social movements, to this one-sided situation are necessary and important, we believe that a cosmopolitan ethos has to be strengthened *within* the sciences themselves. To stimulate this development we have introduced the idea of a third form of knowledge production, critically supplementing the two modes of knowledge production analyzed by Gibbons et al. (Kunneman 2005, 2010). Mode 3 knowledge concerns meaningful professional responses to the *moral* challenges which confront scientists and engineers, but also managers and civil servants, within the context of Mode 2 knowledge production. Of central importance to the idea of Mode 3 knowledge is the link between moral and political considerations and the *content* of technological solutions and organizational arrangements. A good example of the importance of such direct links is provided by critical initiatives in the domain of agro-biotechnology. A lot of research by big international corporations in this field is aimed at increased productivity and resistance of food crops against pesticides, but also to a smoother integration in global production chains by genetic engineering of local crops. According to Guido Ruivenkamp, a researcher at Wageningen University with whom we cooperate closely, products are developed within present-day agro-biotechnology such as new enzymes, "which enable farmers to adapt the agricultural produce to those globally organized food conservation methods which reinforce the uncoupling of agricultural produce from local food consumption ... by linking them to the international market through which, subsequently the agro- and food produce are reconnected to the local context" (Ruivenkamp and Jongerden 2011). In critical response to this exclusively profit-driven form of Mode 2 knowledge production, local networks of scientists and farmers have emerged which critically oppose this development. Their *"location-specific networks"* as Ruivenkamp says,

> *aim at developing seeds which reconnect the seeds to the territorial potentialities for development … by re-establishing the relation between local crop development and local food production and consumption. An example is the development of the zinc and iron enrichment of local cowpea and maize varieties in Ghana, for which also specific supporting measures have been taken to relate the local cultivation of these crops to the local consumption of national dishes such as waakye and kenkey stimulated by a national school feeding program. (Ruivenkamp and Jongerden 2011)*

This example nicely illustrates the direct link between moral and political considerations on the one hand and the *content* of technological solutions and organizational arrangements on the other. Just as new enzymes facilitating specific forms of food conservation materially embody the dependency of local farmers from international corporations and global markets, the cooperative thrust, social commitment, and ecological sensitivity characterizing the location-specific networks highlighted by Ruivenkamp are materially *embodied* in the development of pest-resistant potato varieties based on local races. In our eyes it is of great importance for the rejuvenation of the cosmopolitan project to rethink the notion of "the political" connected with the idea of a cosmopolis, and include the political content of scientific and technological developments into the domain of cosmo-politics. Within present-day world society, a cosmopolitan ethos should not only be developed and strengthened in the context of a global civil society but also and even especially within the sciences and within the many professional domains in which the global risks which confront us on a cosmopolitan scale have to be dealt with in humane ways.

Conclusion

The point of departure for our argument was provided by the humanist myopia flowing from the idea that all human beings are able to develop an empathic relation with themselves and with nearby others and can extend this relation to ever wider circles of human beings, up to a worldwide political community. In our days it is becoming increasingly clear that the cosmopolitan project has to mobilize more complex resources than the empathic and dialogical capabilities of human beings which up until now have formed the backbone of the cosmopolitan ethos. In our eyes this ethos also has to include the courage to face—instead of repress—slow questions, to contain inevitable manifestations of the desire for omnipotence and last but not least to accept the peaceful containment of our own omnipotence. To this end we have sketched three pointers beyond the humanist myopia, based on our experiences at the University for Humanistic Studies and anchored in feminist psychoanalysis, in post-colonial thinking, and in the idea of a global civil society, complemented by the development of Mode 3 knowledge. By further exploring the direction indicated by these three pointers, we hope to contribute to a critical humanism, which can creatively renew a cosmopolitan vision of a more just, more humane, and sustainable world society, because it "owns" instead of disavows its own involvement in relations of power.

Bibliography

Asmis, E. 1996. The stoic on women, in *Feminism and Ancient Philosophy*, edited by J.K. Ward. New York: Routledge, 68–95.
Beck, U. 2006. *Cosmopolitan Vision*. Cambridge: Polity Press.
Benhabib, S. 1996. *Democracy and Difference*. Princeton: Princeton University Press.
Benhabib, S., Honig, B., Kymlicka, W. and Waldron, J. (eds). 2006. *Another Cosmopolitanism: Hospitality, Sovereignty and Democratic Iterations*. Oxford: Oxford University Press.
Benjamin, J. 1998. *Shadow of the Other. Intersubjectivity and Gender in Psychoanalysis*. New York: Routledge.
Borradori, G. 2003. *Philosophy in a Time of Terror: Dialogues with Jürgen Habermas and Jacques Derrida*. Chicago: University of Chicago Press.
Braidotti, R. 1991. *Patterns of Dissonance: A Study of Women in Contemporary Philosophy*. Oxford: Polity.
Butler, J. 2004. *Precarious Life: The Power of Mourning and Violence*. Verso Books.
Derkx, P. and Kunneman, H. (eds). (forthcoming 2011). *Towards a Lingua Democratica for Genomics*. Amsterdam and New York: Rodopi.
Foucault, M. 1979. *Discipline and Punish: The Birth of the Prison*. Harmondsworth: Penguin.
Foucault, M. 1998 (1976). *The History of Sexuality, Volume 1: The Will to Knowledge*. London: Penguin.
Gibbons, M., Limoges, C., Nowotny, H., Schwartzman, S., Scott, P. and Trow, M. 1994. *The New Production of Knowledge. The Dynamics of Science and Research in Contemporary Societies*. London, Thousand Oaks, New Delhi: Sage Publications.
Habermas, J. 1975. *Legitimation Crisis*. Boston: Beacon Press.
Habermas, J. 1984. *The Theory of Communicative Action, Volume 1: Reason and the Rationalization of Society*. Cambridge: Polity Press.
Habermas, J. 1987. *The Theory of Communicative Action, Volume 2: The Critique of Functionalist Reason*. Boston: Beacon Press.
Habermas, J. 2001. *The Postnational Constellation*. Cambridge, MA: The MIT Press.
Habermas, J. and Mendieta, E. 2007. A Postsecular Worldsociety? An Interview with Jürgen Habermas. Available at: http://mrzine.monthlyreview.org/2010/habermas210310.html (accessed January 24, 2011).
Hoogeveen, E. and Jorna, T. 1997. Samenvallen met leven. ton jorna in gespek met elly hoogeveen, in *Door eenvoud verbonden*, edited by T. Jorna. Utrecht: Kwadraat, 28–44.
Jullien, F. 2003. China as philosophical tool. François Jullien in conversation with Thierry Zarcone. *Diogenes*, 50(4), 15–21.

Kakarala, S. 2009. Rethinking the secular: possibilities and challenges—a response to Abdullahi Ahmed An-Na'im. *Pluralism Working Papers Series, Paper no. 1.* Available at: http://www.uvh.nl/uvh.nl/up/ZkwquzkIO_PWP_no_1_2009_Rethinking_the_Secular.pdf.

Kunneman, H. 2005. *Voorbij het dikke-ik*. Amsterdam: SWP/Humanistics University Press.

Kunneman, H. 2010. Viable alternatives for commercialized science: the case of humanistics, in *The Commodification of Scientific Research. Science and the Modern University*, edited by H. Radder. Pittsburgh: University of Pittsburgh Press, 307–36.

Long, A.A. 2001. *Stoic Studies*. Berkeley: University of California Press.

Long, A.A. 2008. The concept of the cosmopolitan in Greek and Roman thought. *Daedalus*, 50–8.

Lyotard, J. 1988. *The Differend: Phrases in Dispute*. Minneapolis: University of Minnesota Press.

Manschot, H. and Suransky, C. 2009. The hidden dimension of the secular: rethinking humanism in an age of religious revitalism. *Pluralism Working Papers Series, Paper no. 2.* Available at: http://www.uvh.nl/uvh.nl/up/ZkwquzkIQ_PWP_no_2_2009_The_Hidden_Dimension_of_the_Secular_1_.pdf.

Nandy, A. 2007. Closing the debates on secularism, in *Crisis of Secularism in India*, edited by A. Needham, R. Rajan, and S. Rajan. Durham, NC: Duke University Press, 107–12.

Nowotny, H., Scott, P.K. and Gibbons, M. 2001. *Re-Thinking Science: Knowledge and the Public in an Age of Uncertainty*. Cambridge: Polity.

Nowotny, H., Pestre, D., Schmidt-Aßmann E., Schulze-Fielitz, H. and Trute, H.-H. 2005. *The Public Nature of Science Under Assault: Politics, Markets, Science and the Law*. Berlin: Springer.

Rose, N.S. 1990. *Governing the Soul: The Shaping of the Private Self*. London and New York: Free Association Books.

Rose, N.S. 1996. *Inventing our Selves: Psychology, Power, and Personhood*. Cambridge: Cambridge University Press.

Ruivenkamp, G. and Jongerden, J. (forthcoming 2011). From prescription to reconstruction: opportunities for subpolitical choices in biotechnological and genomics research, in *Towards a Lingua Democratica for Genomics*, edited by P. Derkx and H. Kunneman. Amsterdam and New York: Rodopi, 272–91.

Said, E. 1979. *The Question of Palestine*. New York: Times Books.

Said, E. 1994. *The Politics of Dispossession*. New York: Vintage Books.

Said, E. 2003. *Freud and the Non-European*. London and New York: Verso.

Schofield, M. 1999. *The Stoic Idea of the City* (enlarged edition). Chicago: The University of Chicago Press.

Snow, C.P. 1998 (1959). *The Two Cultures*. Cambridge: Cambridge University Press.

Wallerstein, I.M. 1974. *The Modern World-System*. New York: Academic Press.

Wallerstein, I.M. 2004. *World-Systems Analysis: An Introduction*. Durham, NC: Duke University Press.

The Capabilities Approach and Ethical Cosmopolitanism: The Challenge of Political Liberalism[1]

Martha Nussbaum

In a world filled with unjust inequalities, it is fitting that theorists should be turning their attention to the ethical ideal known as "cosmopolitanism," a view that holds that our loyalties and our ethical duties ought to transcend the local and even the national, focusing on the needs of human beings everywhere. In a world in which reasonable people differ about religious and secular values, however, this new theoretical attention will prove productive for the practical political debate only if we insist on the distinction between cosmopolitanism, the comprehensive ethical doctrine, and a set of basic political principles for a minimally just and decent world.

Cosmopolitanism and Political Liberalism

Cosmopolitanism, as I understand it, is an overall ethical doctrine about how people should organize their loyalties in a world where we have many types of local attachment, and in which strangers at a distance also seem to demand our ethical concern. I have written relatively little on this ethical doctrine: the very brief essay in

---

[1] This chapter originated as an invited critical response (Nussbaum 2007b) to Noah Feldman's review (2007) of my book *Frontiers of Justice* (Nussbaum 2006a). I am grateful to the editors of the present collection for their suggestions, and to the Yale editors for permission to reprint. I have retained many, though not all, references to Feldman's arguments, because I think they help to bring out some of the issues with which we are both concerned.

the volume *For Love of Country* (Nussbaum 1996),[2] a later introduction to the revised edition of that same book (Nussbaum 2002), and a much fuller development of my ideas in an article entitled "Compassion and terror" (Nussbaum 2003a, 2003b)[3] are the only relevant sources. "Compassion and terror," indeed, is my only academic publication dedicated to that topic.

Because I have long been persuaded by the arguments of John Rawls in *Political Liberalism* (1986), I believe that a doctrine of basic political entitlements should not be based on any comprehensive ethical doctrine.[4] All modern societies contain a plurality of reasonable religious and secular comprehensive doctrines, and political principles must show respect to citizens by not biasing the account of political principles in favor of any particular such doctrine. Political principles, therefore, ought to be justified by an argument that does not presuppose the acceptance of any particular comprehensive ethical doctrine. Political principles must and should have an ethical content, but the way I think of this content is similar to Rawls's way: namely, the moral content is not comprehensive, and thus people with different comprehensive doctrines can attach it to the rest of their comprehensive doctrines. The political is a place of "overlapping consensus," meaning that people who otherwise differ (with doctrines both religious and secular) can agree in affirming the political principles and the argument for them. They could not arrive at such a consensus if the argument presupposed one particular comprehensive doctrine. That is why Rawls describes the desired arguments as "freestanding" – not resting on any controversial metaphysical, epistemological, or religious foundation (such ideas were around before Rawls: the framers of the Universal Declaration of Human Rights also saw the list of rights as a political doctrine that people from different parts of the world and different backgrounds could all affirm, while differing on many other things).

Thus my capabilities approach, as I have developed it in two books and numerous articles,[5] is not and could not be a form of cosmopolitanism. It could be at most a part of cosmopolitanism – as it is hoped that it could be a part of Roman Catholicism, and Judaism, and Utilitarianism, and a variety of other comprehensive doctrines. It is in the sense, and for that reason, that someone whose comprehensive ethical doctrine is cosmopolitanism can endorse the political principles contained in the capabilities approach: it is a part of her own comprehensive doctrine. But so, too, could many people endorse the capabilities approach who reject my form of cosmopolitanism as too demanding, or as not demanding enough. Or so I hope. The capabilities approach is a doctrine concerning a social minimum, deliberately agnostic about how we treat inequalities above a rather ample threshold; thus, it does not state that we should always think of loyalty to humanity as our primary loyalty. In keeping with my philosophical commitments, I have tried to develop

---

2   My short lead essay in this volume is discussed by Feldman (2007) in his review article.
3   Feldman does not mention this publication.
4   My views about political liberalism are stated in Nussbaum 2006a and 2000. The fullest account of my position is forthcoming.
5   A third book will shortly appear (Nussbaum 2011a).

the capabilities approach without any reference to cosmopolitanism: like Rawls's arguments in *Political Liberalism*, mine are intended to be "freestanding," not relying on any materials from the comprehensive doctrines, apart from shared ethical ideas that can be the object of an overlapping consensus. Of course, as a separate matter, I could always develop a dialogue between my own comprehensive doctrine – or the rather different doctrine of cosmopolitanism (see below), or any other reasonable comprehensive doctrine – and the political principles, but that but that is not the project in which I am engaged in *Frontiers of Justice*. My arguments in its favor deal, instead, with a notion of basic human dignity and what is required in order for people to live a life in a manner worthy of their human dignity. The notion of dignity is deliberately "freestanding" in Rawls's sense, not articulated in terms of controversial metaphysical ideas such as the idea of the soul.

My views have often been compared with those of Anthony Appiah (2006, 2007) in his books on cosmopolitanism. But it is actually very difficult to compare my two books on capabilities with Appiah's book on cosmopolitanism: it is rather like comparing apples and oranges (see also Nussbaum 2006b). Appiah does not propose a doctrine of basic political entitlements; he focuses on ethical requirements. I do not propose a comprehensive ethical doctrine, for the reasons I gave: I focus on political principles. (Appiah does not make the mistake of comparing his ethical doctrine with my political doctrine: he refers to my ethical writing, as he should.) Of course, as I said, the capabilities doctrine ought to be one part of the ethical doctrine of cosmopolitanism, as I also hope it can be seen as one part of Roman Catholicism, Judaism, Utilitarianism, and many other comprehensive doctrines. But naturally, all the subtlety and detail of the ethical doctrine would be deliberately left out, since I am seeking a political consensus on some basic political principles. Thus Feldman's remark that Appiah's book is "more fine-grained and subtle than Nussbaum's," though accurate, is not pertinent as a criticism of what I am attempting, since I am deliberately prescinding from subtleties and fine-grained details that would divide people along the lines of their different comprehensive doctrines.

If one were to ask what my own comprehensive ethical doctrine is, one really could not make much progress on the basis of the very brief newspaper article that ultimately appeared in the popular book *For Love of Country*. My more detailed academic presentation of my ideas in "Compassion and terror" (Nussbaum 2008) makes it clear that I envisage a complicated dialogue between local attachments and loyalty to humanity. I have since developed these ideas in writing about a globally sensitive patriotism. In "Compassion and terror," I spend a lot of time on the extreme Stoic version of cosmopolitanism and argue that it is profoundly flawed. Among the arguments I bring forward against the Stoic view, the most pertinent for our purposes is that it does not give real human beings sufficient basis to go on living. Love of the near and dear, I argue, is an essential ingredient in a meaningful life. So I argue that we ought to retain our local attachments, or at least many of them, but that we also should consider what we owe to people at a distance, and try to constrain our local attachments by a commitment to fostering dignified lives for people everywhere. I don't think that my views are significantly different from Appiah's. Feldman thinks that we differ, but that is in large part because he does not discuss this article, the major statement I make on ethical cosmopolitanism. (I believe that the article does not contradict anything I say in *For Love of Country*, but I say very little there.)

It will by now be evident how this ethical doctrine links up with my political doctrine: one of the tenets of my ethical doctrine is the obligation to support something like the political doctrine. That, however, is only one of the tenets of my ethical view, which also contains statements about love of family and locality that are not part of the political doctrine. The political doctrine, as I have stated, is also compatible with many other ethical views, including extreme Stoic cosmopolitanism, which I reject.

The Capabilities Approach

My book *Frontiers of Justice*, then, is not about cosmopolitanism, but about the political doctrine that I call the "capabilities approach." Put very briefly, this view states that the key question to ask about a nation is not a question about opulence or the satisfaction of desire, but rather a question about a set of key human opportunities or "capabilities." I argue that any minimally just society will make available to all citizens a threshold level of 10 central capabilities, as core political entitlements. These 10, I claim, are inherent in the idea of a life worthy of human dignity. These capabilities are envisaged as entitlements that could be protected by a nation's constitution (see Nussbaum 2007a). The current list:

1. *Life*. Being able to live to the end of a human life of normal length; not dying prematurely, or before one's life is so reduced as to be not worth living.
2. *Bodily Health*. Being able to have good health, including reproductive health; to be adequately nourished; to have adequate shelter.
3. *Bodily Integrity*. Being able to move freely from place to place; to be secure against violent assault, including sexual assault and domestic violence; having opportunities for sexual satisfaction and for choice in matters of reproduction.
4. *Senses, Imagination, and Thought*. Being able to use the senses, to imagine, think, and reason – and to do these things in a "truly human" way, a way informed and cultivated by an adequate education, including, but by no means limited to, literacy and basic mathematical and scientific training. Being able to use imagination and thought in connection with experiencing and producing works and events of one's own choice, religious, literary, musical, and so forth. Being able to use one's mind in ways protected by guarantees of freedom of expression with respect to both political and artistic speech, and freedom of religious exercise. Being able to have pleasurable experiences and to avoid non-beneficial pain.

5. *Emotions.* Being able to have attachments to things and people outside ourselves; to love those who love and care for us, to grieve at their absence; in general, to love, to grieve, to experience longing, gratitude, and justified anger. Not having one's emotional development blighted by fear and anxiety. (Supporting this capability means supporting forms of human association that can be shown to be crucial in their development.)
6. *Practical Reason.* Being able to form a conception of the good and to engage in critical reflection about the planning of one's life. (This entails protection for the liberty of conscience and religious observance.)
7. *Affiliation: A.* Being able to live with and toward others, to recognize and show concern for other human beings, to engage in various forms of social interaction; to be able to imagine the situation of another. (Protecting this capability means protecting institutions that constitute and nourish such forms of affiliation, and also protecting the freedom of assembly and political speech.); *B.* Having the social bases of self-respect and non-humiliation; being able to be treated as a dignified being whose worth is equal to that of others. This entails provisions of non-discrimination on the basis of race, sex, sexual orientation, ethnicity, caste, religion, national origin.
8. *Other Species.* Being able to live with concern for and in relation to animals, plants, and the world of nature.
9. *Play.* Being able to laugh, to play, to enjoy recreational activities.
10. *Control Over One's Environment: A. Political.* Being able to participate effectively in political choices that govern one's life; having the right of political participation, protections of free speech and association; *B. Material.* Being able to hold property (both land and movable goods), and having *property rights on an equal basis with others; having the right to seek employment on an* equal basis with others; having the freedom from unwarranted search and seizure. In work, being able to work as a human being, exercising practical reason and entering into meaningful relationships of mutual recognition with other workers.

Three corrections to Feldman's account of my views are in order, and these corrections are of general interest, since they represent widespread misunderstanding of the capabilities approach. First, Feldman declares that the central capabilities are "universal capacities of everyone everywhere." If by this claim Feldman means that all people have all the capabilities, he is wrong. Indeed, I would venture to say that very few people anywhere have all 10 of them. They are political goals, quite ambitious ones, such as having adequate health care, having adequate free public education, having sufficient protection for one's bodily integrity; and it is a good bet that most of the world's people do not have the whole list, if, indeed, they have any of them. I do argue that without a threshold level of all 10 one cannot live a life worthy of human dignity. But what I think is that most of the world's people have not been given the conditions of a life worthy of human dignity. Second, Feldman says "she wants everyone everywhere to be entitled to all the capabilities on her list." Besides being inconsistent with the earlier statement I cited (which ascribes to me the view that everyone everywhere already has all the capabilities), it is inaccurate: what I say is, that in virtue of their equal human dignity all human beings are already entitled to those 10 capabilities. They don't have them, but they are entitled to them. That is why their failure to have them is a problem of justice. Third, Feldman describes my view as "consequentialist." I do call it "outcome-oriented" in order to contrast the view with the Rawlsian procedural approach to justice, but it is quite important that the view is not a form of consequentialism, since consequentialism, as philosophers standardly define it, is a comprehensive ethical doctrine that proposes an overall test for all ethical choices (namely, that the right choice in all situations is the one that promotes the best overall consequences).

Briefly put, my view of political justification parallels Rawls's view, as he announces it in *A Theory of Justice* (1971): we work through the major theoretical views known to us in the philosophical tradition, holding them up against our considered judgments of justice and trying to achieve the best overall coherence and fit. We go on doing this until we achieve what Rawls calls "reflective equilibrium." In *Women and Human Development* (Nussbaum 2000) I executed one part of this task, holding my view up against preference-based utilitarian views and arguing that my view fits better with our considered judgments of justice. In *Frontiers of Justice* I then take the next step, confronting my view with a much more subtle opponent, the classical doctrine of the social contract.

Although I spend some time on Locke and Kant in *Frontiers*, I choose to focus on Rawls's theory because I believe that it is the strongest and most appealing form of the social contract doctrine that we have. Thus Feldman's remark that I focus on Rawls but am "after even bigger game" expresses his view of the relative rankings of this list of philosophers, not mine.

I argue that Rawls was correct when he stated that his own theory would have difficulty dealing with three problems: the entitlements of people with disabilities, the entitlements of animals, and justice across national boundaries. These three problems are the "frontiers" of my title. What they all have in common is that there is a great asymmetry of power among the parties, who cannot without gross distortion be imagined as roughly equal in physical and mental capacities. Thus it is quite important that the book is not solely or even primarily about justice across national boundaries. It is about a philosophical problem: justice in situations of asymmetrical power. The three specific problems must be seen as instances of this more general philosophical question, since it is in dealing with asymmetrical power that I locate the weakness of the social contract doctrine. The book argues that wherever this asymmetry obtains, the classical doctrine of the social contract will not produce good results, since it begins by assuming a rough equality of power among the parties, and it argues that in this situation of rough equality of power, a contract will be to the mutual advantage of the parties. What I am trying to show is that in order to find a workable account of justice in asymmetrical situations, we must give up the assumption of rough equality and the associated goal of mutual advantage. Most of this argumentative work is done in chapters 1 and 2 of the book, and is thus more or less complete, in outline at least, before we turn to the question of justice between nations. A focus merely on chapters 4 and 5 cannot, then, give a very accurate sense of what my project is or how I argue.

Where international justice is concerned, one consequence of my general line of argument is that I greatly prefer the approach of Charles Beitz (1999) and Thomas Pogge (1989) to the Rawlsian (1999) approach. Rawls envisages the international contract as being made between nations, or representatives of nations; Pogge and Beitz argue that we ought to envisage, instead, an Original Position that includes all the world's people. Only this, they believe, can do justice, in the end, to the large inequalities that obtain between people within nations guarantee that all individuals receive a decent level of support. Like my approach, then, theirs focuses on the entitlements of individuals; and I argue that under my capabilities approach justice has not been done unless and until all the world's individuals enjoy a threshold level of the 10 capabilities on my list. Feldman says that I "[b]racke[t] the possibility that the social contract should exist among all persons regardless of their states," but that is incorrect, as his later allusion to my longish section dealing with Beitz and Pogge makes clear. It is not right, moreover, that my "main criticism of them relate to their vagueness." For, while I do hold that Pogge's view has some unfortunate areas of vagueness, I argue that the main problem for both Beitz and Pogge is the individual people of the world are not rough equals in power even when considered as individuals (rather than members of nations), since differences in nutrition, education, and so forth, create great asymmetries in basic power at the level of the person. People are not equal even before birth, since differences in maternal nutrition, exposure to the HIV virus, and other such things make the individuals of the world grossly unequal in power even before they come into the world. That is my main worry about Beitz and Pogge, but I continue to see large areas of convergence.

As for practical and legal consequences, I do state, and offer a preliminary argument for, 10 practical proposals for global governance (Feldman does not comment on these proposals, and I would like to know his response to them). On one issue, however, I want to insist firmly: my reason for opposing the creation of a monolithic world state has to do with my defense of national sovereignty and with my argument that the nation-state is the largest unit we have yet seen that is decently responsive to people and their voices. It is thus, at least at present, a necessary vehicle for the entitlement of people to give themselves laws of their own choosing. That is why I think that any coercive structure over and above the nations ought to remain thin and decentralized.

The question of justice across national boundaries is one of the thorniest currently facing political philosophy. Like the questions of entitlement for people with disabilities and the question of animal entitlements, it is one of the "frontiers" of the field of political philosophy, and future work should focus on these issues, whatever else it also pursues. These hard questions, however, are not productively addressed by conflating a political doctrine of global justice with the comprehensive ethical doctrine of cosmopolitanism. Cosmopolitans can, and should, support the principles of global justice for which I argue, but so should the holders of many other reasonable comprehensive doctrines. And it is only when political principles are framed so as to be acceptable to all these reasonable citizens that they are sufficiently respectful of their dignity and their freedom.

Bibliography

Appiah, A. 2006. *Cosmopolitanism*. New York: Norton.
Appiah, A. 2007. *The Ethics of Identity*. Princeton: Princeton University Press.
Beitz, C. 1999. *Political Theory and International Relations*. Princeton: Princeton University Press.
Feldman, N. 2007. Cosmopolitan law. *Yale Law Journal*, 116, 1022–70.
Nussbaum, M. 1996. *For Love of Country: A Debate on Patriotism and Cosmopolitanism*. Boston: Beacon Press.
Nussbaum, M. 2000. *Women and Human Development: The Capabilities Approach*. Cambridge: Cambridge University Press.
Nussbaum, M. 2002. *For Love of Country: A Debate on Patriotism and Cosmopolitanism*. Boston: Beacon Press.
Nussbaum, M. 2003a. Compassion and terror. *Daedalus Winter*, 10–26.
Nussbaum, M. 2003b. Compassion and terror, in *Terrorism and International Justice*, edited by J. Sterba. New York: Oxford University Press, 229–52.
Nussbaum, M. 2006a. *Frontiers of Justice*. Cambridge, MA: Harvard University Press.
Nussbaum, M. 2006b. Political soul-making and the imminent demise of liberal education. *Journal of Social Philosophy*, 37, 301–13.
Nussbaum, M. 2007a. Constitutions and capabilities. *Harvard Law Review*, 121, 4–97.
Nussbaum, M.C. 2007b. *The Capabilities Approach and Ethical Cosmopolitanism: A Response to Noah Feldman*, 117 Yale L.J. Pocket Part 123. Available at: www.yalelawjournal.org/the-yale-law-journal-pocket-part/international-law/the-capabilities-approach-and-ethical-cosmopolitanism:-a-response-to-noah-feldman (last accessed: November 18, 2010).
Nussbaum, M. 2008. Toward a globally sensitive patriotism. *Daedalus Summer*, 78–93.
Nussbaum, M. 2011a. *Creating Capabilities: The Human Development Approach*. Cambridge, MA: Harvard University Press.
Nussbaum, M. 2011b. Perfectionist liberalism and political liberalism. *Philosophy and Public Affairs*, 39, 3–45.
Pogge, T. 1989. *Realizing Rawls*. Ithaca: Cornell University Press.
Rawls, J. 1971. *A Theory of Justice*. Cambridge, MA: Harvard University Press.
Rawls, J. 1986. *Political Liberalism*. New York: Columbia University Press.
Rawls, J. 1999. *The Law of Peoples*. Cambridge, MA: Harvard University Press.

Index

Page numbers followed by 'n' refer to a footnote; those in bold type refer to Tables.

9/3 Mémoire d'un territoire (Benguigui) 97–8
11 September 2001 attacks 206, 207, 262, 334, 381

aboriginal culture, Australia 306, 307
Ackerly, B. 377
active agency (principle of cosmopolitanism) 166
activism 8, 220, 223, 284–5
    see also social movements
actor-network theory 356
Adey, Peter 358
Adorno, Theodor 148
aeromobility 351, 360
aesthetic cosmopolitanism 34–5
affiliation (Nussbaum's capabilities) 407
Afghanistan 335
Africa:
    consumers' adoption of European culture 41
    diaspora 129, 131, 132
    female genital mutilation 377, 378
    HIV/AIDS 47, 48, 375
African Americans 140, 324n12
Afro-Caribbean culture 128–9
agency 166, 228–31, 235, 238–9, 358
agro-biotechnology 399–400
Ahmad, Aijaz 110–11
AIDS 47, 48, 375
Akenson, Donald 132–3, 134
Akhtar, Javed 120

Aksartova, S. 54
Albrow, Martin 26, 297
Alexander the Great 298n3, 300, 388, 389
Algerian-French War (1954–62) 318
Alter 393–4
Amerindians 325
Amnesty International 171, 176
'anchoring points' 262
Anderson, Benedict 111–12, 202
animals 407, 408
anthropology 246
anthropos 329, 333, 338–9
anti-colonialism 217
anti-globalization movement 182, 182n5
anti-Semitism 349
    see also Jews
anticosmopolitanism 125, 189
    and diaspora 138–9, 141
Appadurai, Arjun 26, 34, 37, 113, 127, 219
    on fetishism 46, 47
Appiah, Kwame Anthony 109, 112, 226, 226n1, 245, 305, 340n9, 405, 406
Aravamudan, Srinivas 354
Arendt, Hannah 245, 246–7, 280
Armenian diaspora 114, 132
Arnason, Johann 316
art, tribal/aboriginal 102
Asia:
    diaspora 108, 114–15, 119–20
    fashion 44
    violence against women 377

Asmis, Elisabeth 388–9
assimilation 103, 134, 136, 138, 141, 351n1
attachment 60
Australia 88
    aboriginal culture 306, 307
avoidance of serious harm (principle of cosmopolitanism) 167
Aztec civilization 339

Bakhtin, Mikhail 127, 133
Bakrania, Falu 130
Balibar, Etienne 255, 256, 263, 268–9
Balkans, war crimes against women 377
Ball, John Clement 90
banal cosmopolitanism 36, 40, 46, 287
banal nationalism 36
banlieus (Paris) 93
Bartov, Omer 247
Bauman, Zygmunt 247, 248, 250, 261
beauty industry 42
Beck, Ulrich 2, 5, 10, 17–30, 36, 39, 46, 49, 197, 221, 249–50, 256, 287, 296, 324, 350, 351, 354, 355, 360, 398
    Bhambra's critique of 313–14, 315–16, 316–17, 318–22, 325
    on borders 261, 262, 269–70
    Glick Schiller's critique of 352–4
Beijing Platform for Action (BPfA) 373, 374, 380
Beitz, Charles 185, 409
belonging 60, 207–8, 261–2
Benguigui, Yamina 97–8
Benhabib, Seyla 397
Benjamin, Jessica 393, 395
Besnier, N. 41
Bhabha, Homi K. 112, 126–7, 128, 129, 139, 314, 323–4, 354
Bhambra, Gurminder K. 10, 313–26
BIE (Bureau of International Expositions) 74
Billig, M. 36
Binnie, J. 38, 39, 89, 90
Black Atlantic (Gilroy) 26, 27, 129, 353
Black Bazar (Mabanckou) 99, 100
black cultural studies 130

British 125, 128–9, 141
Bleu-Blanc-Rouge (Mabanckou) 99–100
bodily health (Nussbaum's capabilities) 406
Boer, Inge E. 266, 269, 273
Bollywood 108, 110, 118–20
Bombay cinema *see* Bollywood
Bono 47
Booth, K. 300
borders 10, **26**, 28, 261–2, 324, 356, 360
    border thinking 329–30, 332, 334, 337–8, 341–2, 345
    and cosmopolitan localism 342–4
    critical 11, 357
    borderwork 262, 264, 265, 270, 273
    Calais case study 272–3
    changing nature of 263–4
    cosmopolitan 264–5
    Melton Mowbray case study 270–1
    and networks 266–9
    re-orienting 269–70
    see also boundaries
Boroujerdi, Mehrzad 343
boundaries 352
    see also borders
Bourdieu, Pierre 21, 58, 63, 64, 254–5, 256
Boyarin, Daniel 132
Boyarin, Jonathan 132
boycotts 47
Braudel, F. 56–7
Brazil:
    and climate change 22
    Sem Terra Movement 223
Brennan, Timothy 39, 110, 111
Briggs, C.S. 110
Brock, Gillian 8, 179–91
Bunch, Charlotte 372, 374–5
burkhas, banning of 318
Büscher, M. 360
Butler, Judith 392

Cabral, Amilcar 216, 217
Calais case study 272–3
Calhoun, Craig 45, 207–8, 254
Canada 76, 79, 88

capabilities approach (Nussbaum) 11, 404–5, 406–10
capitalism 23, 38, 39, 345
 non-capitalist and pre-capitalist economies 338
Caribbean 141, 349
 Afro-Caribbean culture 128–9, 135
 Indian labor diaspora 134–5
cartoon controversy, Denmark 19
Casanova, Pascale 91–2
Castells, Manuel 267
'causumerism' 47
CEDAW *see* Convention on the Elimination of All Forms of Discrimination Against Women
Chakrabarty, D. 323
Chaney, D. 58
Charlesworth, Hilary 373
Cheah, Pheng 9, 39, 211–23
Chicago School 351n1
China 40, 216, 252, 298n3, 330, 396
 Chinese diaspora 113, 132
 and climate change 22
 media consumption 41
 as threat to the West 334
Chinatown, London 95, 96
Chirac, President Jacques 102
Christianity 115, 133, 182, 331, 336, 338, 339, 375
 Roman Catholicism 404, 405
 see also religion
Cicero 299, 388, 389
cinema, Bollywood 108, 110, 118–20
 see also film
circle model of identity 388–9
'Cité Nationale de l'Histoire de l'Immigration', Paris 101
cities 6
 cosmopolitan 80
 branding as 38, 95–6, 102–3
 Paris case study 87–103
 global 26, **26**, 89–90, 218–19, 287
'citizen-detective' 268
citizenship 169–70, 245
 cosmopolitan 243–57
 world 70, 72, 72n3, 88, 153, 170, 179–80, 191, 212, 231–4, 279, 280–1, 288, 301, 370
civil society 82, 395
 global 284–5, 368, 370, 380, 397–8
civilizations:
 'clash of civilizations' 333
 dialogues among 332–5, 339–42, 345
 difficulties and challenges 335–8
 Huntingdon's classification of 334, 336–7
class 21, 23, 37, 59
 and cosmopolitanism 42–3
Clifford, James 112, 127, 130–1, 132, 352, 353, 354
climate change 22–3, 24
CND (Campaign for Nuclear Disarmament) 248
code-switching/code-mixing 140
Cohen, Robin 1, 90, 132, 137, 138, 139, 353
Cold War 198, 199, 206, 248, 252, 335
collective decision-making (principle of cosmopolitanism) 167
collective memory *see* memory
colonialism 217, 303, 314, 321, 324, 329–31
 colonial matrix of power 335–40
 see also postcolonialism
coloniality 329, 330, 331, 339, 341, 344
commodification 39
common sense, cosmopolitan 201, 249–50
communal, the 338
community-building 25
compassion 205
 'compassionate consumerism' 47, 48
'Compassion and terror' (Nussbaum) 404, 405
compensation 24
complexity theory 357, 360
connectivity 264–5, 266, 271, 272, 296n2
Connell, Raewyn 251
consent (principle of cosmopolitanism) 167
constitutional patriotism 109, 254, 305
consumer-citizenship 44–8, 47
consumerism:
 'ethical' 47, 48

and tourism 78
consumers, fetishism of 46, 47
consumption, and cosmopolitanism 7,
 33–49, 56–9, 62–5
contact studies 64–5
control over environment (Nussbaum's
 capabilities) 407
Convention on the Elimination of All
 Forms of Discrimination Against
 Women (CEDAW) 372–3, 380
Cook, Thomas 79
Cooper, Anthony 9–10, 261–273
Copenhagen Climate Summit 2009 22
cosmetics *see* beauty industry
'cosmo-multiculturalism' 63
'cosmocrats' 42–3
cosmopolitan borders 264–5
cosmopolitan citizenship 243–57, 379
cosmopolitan common sense 201, 249–50
cosmopolitan consciousness 238–40
cosmopolitan diaspora 125, 136–7, 141–2
cosmopolitan education 54
cosmopolitan feminism *see* feminism
cosmopolitan global order 173–6
cosmopolitan justice 184–8
cosmopolitan law 152, 169–73
cosmopolitan localism 337–8
 and border thinking 342–4
cosmopolitan memory 195, 197, 201
'cosmopolitan omnivorousness' 43, 58, 59
cosmopolitan openness 7, 53–5, 59–60
 attachment and belonging 60
 as a concept 65–6
 consumption and cultural flows 62
 cultural/political consequences 63–5
 ethics and reflexivity 61
 mobility 60–1
 socio-cultural contexts 55–9
cosmopolitan patriotism 109, 304–5
cosmopolitan political theory 297–9
cosmopolitan polity 174–5
cosmopolitan publics, European 253–6
cosmopolitan realism 350–2, 360
 Glick Schiller's critique of 352–4
cosmopolitan sociology 297, 298, 304

cosmopolitanism 19, 163, 369–71
 aesthetic 34–5
 analytic 69, 70, 71, 73, 81
 anticosmopolitanism 125, 138–9, 141,
  189
 banal 36, 40, 46, 287
 concept of 70–3
 and consumption 7, 33–49, 56–8, 62–5
 context of 164–5
 cosmopolitan global order 173–6
 cosmopolitan law 152, 169–73
 critical *see* critical cosmopolitanism
 cultural 4, 5, 6
 as cultural orientation 34–7
 decolonial 329–42, 345
 definition 33, 53, 279–80, 370
 deformed 49
 and diaspora 125–42
 ethical 4, 11, 403–6
 and Eurocentrism 10, 314–15, 317, 319,
  329–32, 333, 343, 344
 and feminism 367–82
 and global justice 179–91
 and globalization 136–7, 217–23,
  295–308
 hermeneutic 9, 225–40
 history of 54, 299–303, 315
 and humanism 387–401
 limitations of 10
 and mega-events 69–75, 81–2
  cultural forms and historical
   developments 75–81
 methodological 2, 5, 17, 23, 25–9, **26**
 and mobilities 349–61
 in modern European philosophy 212–14
 modernist 77–8
 moral 4, 182–3, 369–70
 and multiculturalism 63, 281–2, 313–14,
  317, 318–22, 325
 and nationalism 214–17
 negative or minimalistic 72
 and neoliberalism 251–3
 normative 69, 70–1, 71–2, 74–5, 81–2
 and postcolonialism 313–26
 principles of 165–9

Index

proletarian 216–17
provincialized 322–6
'superficial' versus 'authentic' 44–8
'thick' and 'thin' 168–9
touristic 77, 78–81
weak versus strong 183–4
cosmopolitanization 17, 20
cosmopolitans 5, 34–5, 37, 58, 261–2
   the virtual cosmopolitan 354
cosmopolitics 9, 370–1
   of consumption 48–9
   the cosmopolitical 211–23, 284–5
cosmos 298
counseling, humanist 390–1
creolization 6, 128–30, 133, 139, 140, 141, 286, 349
Cresswell, Tim 358
crimes against humanity 247, 373
   see also war crimes
critical border thinking 11, 357
critical cosmopolitanism 5, 10, 42–3, 265, 279–82, 290, 323
   cultural aspect 286–7
   economic aspect 285–6
   political aspect 284–5
   tensions in 288–9
   theoretical frames 282–4
critical theory 249
Cronin, C. 360
cultural ambidexterity 6, 139–41
cultural appropriation 63
cultural capital 58
cultural consumption 7, 58–9, 62–4
cultural cosmopolitanism 4, 5, 6
cultural globalization 37–8
cultural orientation, and cosmopolitanism 34–7
cultural studies:
   black 130
      British 125, 128–9, 141
'cultural wounds' 22

D'Alembert, J.L.R. 212
de-localization, and global risk 24
de-Westernization 331, 337, 345

decision-making, collective (principle of cosmopolitanism) 167
decolonial cosmopolitanism 329–30, 331, 332
   and dialogues among civilizations 332–5, 339–42, 345
   difficulties and challenges 335–8
decolonization 217
deformed cosmopolitanism 49
Dekker, Thomas 56–7
Delanty, G. 270
democracy 245, 335
   cosmopolitan 8
   democratic rights 187
   and feminism 380
Denmark, cartoon controversy 19
Derrida, Jacques 127, 133
dervishes 117
Dharwadker, Vinay 6, 125–42
dialogue 227, 228–31, 238–40
   among civilizations 332–5, 339–42, 345
      difficulties and challenges 335–8
   cultural capabilities for 234–8
diaspora 6, 26, 295, 353, 395
   African 129, 131, 132
   anticosmopolitan 138–9, 141
   Armenian 114, 132
   and Bollywood 119
   Chinese 113, 132
   complex 114–15
   cosmopolitan 125, 136–7, 141–2
   and creolization 128–30, 141
   definition of 130–1
   Greek 114
   Indian 132
      Indian labor 125, 134–6
   Irish 132
   Jewish 6, 114, 125, 131–4
   migration and hybridity 126–8, 141–2
   religious 138–9
   South Asian 108, 114–15, 119–20
Dickensen, D. 378, 380
difference:
   difference principle 185, 187, 285
   homogeneity versus heterogeneity 37–40

dignity, human 405, 406, 408
Dikeç, Mustafa 93
Diogenes 53, 54, 279n1, 388, 389
disability 408, 409
discourse ethics 9, 283, 369, 376
distinction 40–4, 58
distributive justice 181, 183–4, 185, 190, 285–6
domestic violence *see* women, violence against
domination, structures of 11
double consciousness 139, 140
Du Bois, W.E.B. 139, 140
Durkheim, Emile 18, 298, 304–8

East Asia, history 295
Eastern Europe 119, 243, 255
economics 29
    and critical cosmopolitanism 285–6
economies 233
    non-capitalist and pre-capitalist 338
education 233, 406
    cosmopolitan 54
    and mega-events 74
    and world citizenship 191
Ego 393–4
Egypt, *mulid* festivals 116
Eichmann, Adolf 247
Eisenstadt, Shmuel 316
Elden, Stuart 266–7
Elementary Forms of the Religious Life, The (Durkheim) 305–6
elites 5, 7, 89, 112, 137, 262, 281, 283, 322
embedding the national 26, **26**, 28–9
emotions (Nussbaum's capabilities) 407
employment 407
END (European Nuclear Disarmament) 248
endangerment 25
Engels, Friedrich 38, 216
Enlightenment:
    European 70, 72, 148, 212, 245–6, 257, 315
    Japanese 295
environmental issues 170–1
equal worth and dignity (principle of cosmopolitanism) 166

equality 190–1
    Fair Equality of Opportunity Principle 185
    Global Equality of Opportunity 187
equivalence principle 172
Erdogan, Recep Tayyip 333, 333n5, 335
ethics 61
    ethical consumerism 47, 63
    ethical cosmopolitanism 4, 11
    and political liberalism 403–6
'ethnic' restaurants 43
ethnicity 37, 138–9
EU *see* European Union
Eurocentrism 10, 314–15, 317, 319, 325, 329–32, 333, 343, 344, 353, 355, 361
Europe 396
    cosmopolitan citizenship 243–53, 256–7
    cosmopolitan publics 253–6
    and cosmopolitanism 212–14
    culture 41, 319
    Eastern Europe 119, 243, 255
    Enlightenment 70, 72, 148, 212, 245–6, 257, 315
    history 71, 71–3, 335–6, 338
    imperialism 154, 251, 303
    mega-events 6, 69–75, 81–2
        cultural forms and historical developments 75–81
    nationalism 215
    social movements 255
    sociology 18
European Convention for the Protection of Human Rights and Fundamental Freedoms 165
European Union (EU) 19, 29, 71, 72, 72n3, 164, 165, 221, 244, 245, 254, 257, 297, 397
    and borders 264, 270
    and climate change 22
    Protected Geographical Indication (PGI) status 270–1
Eurostar 263, 268
exclusion, versus inclusion 40–4
expos 6, 69, 70–1, 74, 75–82
    see also mega-events

Fadzillah, I. 42
Fair Equality of Opportunity Principle 185
fair trade 47
Fanon, Franz 216, 244, 335, 343–4
fashion 43–4, 56–7
    ethical 47
Federation of Nations *see* League of Nations
Feldman, Noah 403n1, 405, 406, 407–8, 409
female genital mutilation 377, 378
feminism 11, 37, 352, 355, 361
    cosmopolitan feminism 5, 11, 367–9, 371, 380–2
        collaborative advocacy strategies 377–8
        global feminist consciousness 375–7
        and global forums 378–9
        intersectionality and cross-boundary dialogue 376–7
        and public international law 371–4
    see also women
Ferguson, J.G. 41–2
fetishism 46
Fichte, Johann Gottlieb 216
Fiji 135–6
film 96–9
    Bollywood 108, 110, 118–20
Fine, Robert 8, 31, 147–60
First World War 305
Florida, Richard 95
flows 127, 289, 353, 357
food 36, 43, 45, 64, 65
    food sovereignty 223
    hunger 249
For Love of Country (Nussbaum) 404, 405
foreign-induced endangerment 25
forgetting 203
    see also memory
forgiveness 204
Forsdick, Charles 91, 100
Foucault, Michel 127, 336, 390
Fourth World Conference on Women 378
France 138
    immigrant communities 88, 97–100, 101–2, 318
    and mega-events 75, 76
    postcolonial studies 91–2
    see also Paris case study
Freud, Sigmund 394–5
Friedmann, J. 89
Frontiers of Justice (Nussbaum) 403n1, 406–9
FSC (feminist social criticism) 377
fundamentalism 107, 379, 381, 396

Gandhi, Leela 129
gay urban spaces 39
gender 37
    and globalization 375–6, 381
    see also feminism; masculinity; women
gentrification 90, 94, 103
geography 358, 359
George, Susan 256
Germany 305
Gibbons, M. 399
Giddens, Anthony 257
Gierke, Otto 150
Gilroy, Paul 26, **26**, 27, 129, 353
'*girmit* ideology' 135–6
Glick Schiller, Nina **26**, 27–8, 353–4
global challenges 170–3
global cities 26, **26**, 89–90, 218–19, 287
global citizenship *see* world citizenship
global civil society 284–5, 368, 370, 380, 397–8
global consciousness 297n2
Global Difference Principle 185, 187
Global Equality of Opportunity 187
global forums, and feminism 378–9
Global Fund 47
global governance *see* world government
global justice 179–84, 188–91
    distributive justice 181, 183–4, 185, 190, 285–6
    and Rawls' *Law of Peoples* 184–8
Global Justice Movements 180–1
global linear thinking 329, 331, 332, 335, 336, 337, 339
global media 40–1, 60, 195, 221, 236n2, 238, 248
global order 164
    cosmopolitan 173–6

global public goods 172–3
global sociology 297
globality 10, 298
globalization 10, 18, 19, 22, 28–9, 34, 55, 164, 171, 175, 249, 251, 313, 331, 332, 368
   anti-globalization movement 182, 182n5
   and cosmopolitanism 136–7, 217–23, 295–308
   cultural 37–8
   gendered dimensions of 375–6, 381
   and global justice 180–2
   and global media images 205–6
   and the nation-state 218
   and values 229
globe 298
Globo-Indians 42
Gorz, Andre 251–2
Gould, Carol 369
Goutte d'Or, Paris 93–4
   La Goutte d'Or: vivre ensemble (Lemesle) 96–7
government, world 8, 9, 183, 213, 243, 247, 282–3, 300–1, 304, 370, 409
Grande, E. 26, **26**, 28, 319
Gray, John 257
Greece, Greek diaspora 114
Greenhalgh, P. 79–80
Gypsies 131

Habermas, Jürgen 9, 148–9, 170, 220–2, 254, 256, 305, 387, 390, 397
Hage, G. 43, 45, 63–4
Halbwachs, Maurice 196
Hall, Stuart 58, 128
Hannerz, Ulf 5, 33, 34–5, 37, 40, 48, 89, 112, 113, 353
Hargreaves, A. 91
harm, avoidance of (principle of cosmopolitanism) 167
Harvey, David 245–6, 251, 252, 253, 340n9, 351
health (Nussbaum's capabilities) 406
Hebdige, D. 35
Hegel, G. 148, 157, 159
Held, David 8, 163–76, 370, 379

Heldke, L. 45
hermeneutic cosmopolitanism 9, 225–40
heterogeneity:
   homogenized 39
   versus homogeneity 37–40
Hierocles 388–9
Hindus:
   and Bollywood 118
   and Sufi pilgrimages 115–16
Hindustan, colonialism in 303
historical studies:
   and cosmopolitanism 10
   and transnational historiography 28
histories-other 330
history:
   and memory 201–2
   and natural law 155–8
HIV/AIDS 47, 48, 375
Hivos: the Humanist Institute for Cooperation with Developing Countries 395
Hmong diaspora 40
Hobbes, T. 150, 207
Holocaust 195, 199, 200, 247, 248, 318
homogeneity:
   homogenized heterogeneity 39
   versus heterogeneity 37–40
Hong Kong 41
Hoogeveen, Elly 391
hooks, b. 38
Horvath, Christina 6, 87–103
hospitality 54, 154, 169, 213, 283
human dignity 405, 406, 408
human rights 8–9, 21, 165, 187, 191, 213, 220, 244, 247, 250, 284, 289–90, 395
   Human Rights Regime 195, 198, 198n1, 199, 205, 206, 207
   and memory 195, 197–201, 204
   Universal Declaration of Human Rights 199, 404
   women's 11, 367–8, 370, 372, 373, 378, 379, 381
humanism, and humanist myopia 387–9, 400–1
   case of humanistics 390–5

post-colonial insights 395–8
   third mode of knowledge 398–400
humanitas 329, 338
hunger 249
   see also food
Huntingdon, Samuel 333, 334
hybridity 6, 39, 139–40, 141–2
   and migration 126–8

ICC *see* International Criminal Court
identity 180
   circle model of 388–9
   self-identity 234–5, 238
IGOs (inter/international governmental organizations) 171, 173
IMF (International Monetary Fund) 252, 284, 286
immigrants *see* migrants
immobility 351, 355, 356, 357, 358
imperial cosmopolitanism 338–40
imperialism 217, 246, 321, 329–31
   Europe 154
   United States 250
Inca civilization 339
incalculableness, and global risk 24
inclusion, versus exclusion 40–4
inclusiveness and subsidiarity (principle of cosmopolitanism) 167
indentured labor, Indian 134–6
India 395, 396–7
   beauty culture 42
   and climate change 22
   diaspora 6, 125, 132, 134–6
   vernacular cosmopolitanism 107–8
individualization thesis (Beck) 21
Indonesia 395
industrial revolution 339
infrastructures of mobility 356, 358
Inglis, David 10, 295–308
institutional cosmopolitanism 182–3
integrity, bodily (Nussbaum's capabilities) 406
interconnectedness 19, 25
interculturality 128, 342
international borrowing privilege 186

International Criminal Court (ICC) 164, 165, 284, 370
   and feminism 371, 377
      Women's Caucus for Gender Justice 373, 374
international government organizations *see* IGOs
International Initiative for Justice in Gujarat 374
international justice 408, 409
international law 152–3, 165, 284, 370, 381
   public 371n4
   and feminism 371–4
international resource privilege 186
international trade 302, 303
Internet 56
intersectionality, and feminism 376–7
IOC (International Olympic Committee) 74
   see also Olympic Games
Iran 333, 334
Iraq 334
   Iraq War 221, 222, 253
Islam 107–8, 115–17, 118, 336, 339, 340, 344, 375, 396, 375
   Islamic regions 333, 334
   see also Muslims; religion
isolationism 20
Israel 394
   see also Jews
Italy, Senegalese Mouride community 113

Jameson, Frederic 110–11
Japan 295–6, 330
   sexual slavery war crimes 374, 377
Jews 349, 394–5
   Jewish diaspora 6, 114, 125, 131–4
   Judaism 404, 405
   see also Holocaust
Jones, C. 37, 39, 43, 44
Jullien, Francois 396
justice:
   cosmopolitan 184–8
   distributive 181, 183–4, 185, 285–6
   global 179–84, 188–91

international 408, 409
see also law

Kakarala, S. 396–7
Kaldor, Mary 248
Kant, Immanuel, and cosmopolitanism 4, 8, 54, 72n3, 74n11, 169, 212–15, 216, 245–6, 298, 300–4, 307–8, 332–3, 337, 344, 369, 397
   natural law 147–50, 155–60
   neo-Kantian theory 282–3, 331
   system of right 150–4, 369
Kaplan, Caren 355
Kaufmann, V. 356
Kaul, I. 172
Kern, R.M. 58, 59
Khair, Tabish 118
Khatami, Mohammad 333–4, 335
Khomeini, Ayatollah 107–8, 126
Klapish, Cédric 98–9
knowledge:
   control of 339
   Promoting Pluralism Knowledge Program 395, 396–7
   third mode of 398–400
Knowles, C. 356
Kögler, Hans-Herbert 9, 225–40, 286
Kosmopolis Institute 395
Kosnick, Kira 95
Kotkin, Joel 137
Kunneman, Harry 11, 387–401
Kurasawa, Fuyuki 10, 279–90

Lamont, M. 54
landmarks, in Paris 100–2
language, and Bollywood 118–19
Larsen, J. 270
Lasch, Christopher 137
law 151–3
   cosmopolitan 152, 169–73
   see also international law; natural law
Law of Peoples, The (Rawls) 181, 185–8
League of Nations:
   in Kant's philosophy 153, 156, 157, 301
   the organization 199

Lemesle, Bruno 96–7
Leshkowich, A.M. 37, 39, 43, 44
Levinas, Emmanuel 283, 349
Levy, Daniel 8, **26**, 28, 195–208
liberal democracy 243, 250
liberalism:
   neoliberalism 243, 251–3, 254–5, 256, 283–4, 289, 331, 332, 368, 379
   political, and ethical cosmopolitanism 403–6
life (Nussbaum's capabilities) 406
'Life-Savers' 268
Lisbon Treaty 256
literature 99–100, 126
   literary culture 91–2
   and vernacular cosmopolitanism 110–12
localism, cosmopolitan 337–8, 342–4
locality, as a fetish 46
locals 34–5, 37
London 92, 102–3, 218, 268
   2012 Olympics 95
   consumer culture 36–7, 43, 57
   multicultural communities 95, 96, 100–1
   postcolonial 90, 91
   size of 92
Long, A.A. 388
Loomba, Ania 129
Louvre, Paris 102

Mabanckou, Alain 99–100
McClaurin, Irma 132
McLeod, John 90
Madrid, size of 92
Mahfouz, Naguib 110
Make Poverty History 47
Manifesto of the Communist Party (Marx and Engels) 216
Mann, Michael 252
Marcus Aurelius 299
Marx, Karl 38, 56, 216–17
   neo-Marxist theory 283–4
masculinity 37, 47, 352, 355, 358, 361, 374, 379
   see also gender

Massey, Doreen 95
material turn, in mobilities research 356–9
Mazzini, Guiseppe 215–16
media:
    cosmopolitan 205–6
    global 40–1, 60, 195, 221, 236n2, 238, 248
    UK 40–1
mega-events and cosmopolitanism 6, 69–75, 81–2
    cultural forms and historical developments 75–81
Melton Mowbray case study 270–1
memory:
    cosmopolitan 195, 197, 201
    fragmentation and decontextualization of memory culture 201–5
    and human rights 197–201
Mercer, Kobena 128, 354
methodological cosmopolitanism 2, 5, 17, 23, 25–9, **26**
methodological nationalism 17, 18–19, 25, 26, 28, 29, 249, 304, 316, 321, 350
Midnight's Children (Rushdie) 108
Mignolo, Walter D. 11, 265, 314, 322–3, 325, 329–45
migrants 321–2
    illegal 268, 272–3
    Paris 93–4
migration 21, 296, 324, 354
    history of 101
    and hybridity 126–8
    transnational 26, **26**, 27–8, 219, 221
    and women 375
military power 250
minority status 138–9
Mishra, Vijay 135–6
Mitter, Partha 354
mixité sociale 93, 94
mobilities 10–11, 55–6, 60–1, 89–90, 262, 263, 267, 268, 289
    and cosmopolitanism 349–52
        critiques of 352–5
        material turn in mobilities research 356–9
        mobile methods 359–61

modernity 20, 323–4, 330, 331, 340, 341
    second-modern approach 351
modernization theory 18, 313, 315–17, 350
Mohanty, Chandra 375
Molz, Jennie Germann 7, 33–49
'mongrelization' 128
moral cosmopolitanism 4, 182–3, 369–70
moral culture, world 302–3, 305–6, 307
Morrison, Toni 102
Mosse, George L. 246
motility 352, 355, 357, 358
Mouffe, Chantal 250, 253
mourning 391, 392
multiculturalism 39, 88, 137, 138
    and cosmopolitanism 63, 281–2, 313–14, 317, 318–22, 325
multiple modernities 314, 315–17, 319, 325
mundane consumption 7
mundane cosmopolitanism 35, 57
Munshi, S. 42
Murphy, David 91, 100
music 58, 287
Muslims 107–8
    and Bollywood 118
    and Sufi pilgrimages 115–16
    see also Islam
Muthu, Sankar 148, 154, 315

Nagor-e-Sharif, Tamil Nadu 116
Nandy, A. 396–7
nation-states 8, 18, 19, 21, 23, 71, 148, 215, 315–16, 317, 397, 409
    and borders 263, 264, 265, 269–70
    and citizenship 243, 280–1
    and globalization 218, 296–7
    and memory 201
    and national culture 196, 197, 202
    and the public sphere 232–4
    relationship to transnational structures 28
    as units of research 25, 26–9, 289
'national outlook' 18
nationalism 170, 200, 201, 218, 256, 289, 305
    banal 36
    and cosmopolitanism 214–17

methodological 17, 18–19, 25, 26, 28, 29, 249, 304, 316, 321, 350
   origins of 202–3
'Nativism' 343–4
natural law theory, and Kant 147–60
Nava, M. 36–7, 43, 57
'negative utilitarianism' 72
Negri, A. 253
neo-Kantian theory 282–3, 331
neo-Marxist theory 283–4
neocolonialism 217
neoliberalism 243, 254–5, 256, 283–4, 289, 331, 332, 368, 379
   and cosmopolitanism 251–3
Netherlands 395
   humanist counseling 390–1
networks, and borders 266–9
New York 218, 252
NGOs (non-governmental organizations) 171, 219, 221, 222, 284–5, 370
   women's 368, 378–9
Nigeria:
   literature 112
   women 37
No Borders 273
Noli me Tangere (Rizal) 111–12
nomadism 355, 356, 357
non-capitalist economies 338
non-compensability, and global risk 24
Nora, Pierre 100
Nowicka, Magdalena 1–11
nuclear disarmament 248
Nussbaum, Martha 4, 11, 54, 112, 180, 191, 299, 300, 340n9, 403–10

oil 334
Okin, S. 377
Old Testament 133
Olympic Games 69, 74, 75
   2012 Olympics 95–6
   see also mega-events
omnipotence 393–4
Ong, Aihwa 41, 42, 113
openness *see* cosmopolitan openness
orientalism 33

'Orientalism in reverse' 343
other species (Nussbaum's capabilities) 407
Overy, Paul 349
Oxfam 171, 176

Pagden, Anthony 314–15, 323
Palestine 394
Papadopoulos, D. 269, 272
Parekh, Bhikhu 246
Paris case study 87–92, 102–3
   branding as cosmopolitan 95–6
   commemorative landmarks 100–2
   emerging mongrel Paris 96–100
   multicultural communities 92–4
   see also France
Paris (Klapish) 99
Parsons, Talcott 18
patriotism 154, 170, 189, 254, 288, 289, 405
   cosmopolitan 3–7, 109, 304–5
peace 54, 301–2, 333, 369
   peace movement 248
PeaceWomen project 374
Persia 334
personal responsibility and accountability (principle of cosmopolitanism) 166–7
Peterson, R.A. 58, 59
Pettigrew, T.F. 64–5
PGI (Protected Geographical Indication) status 270–1
Philippines, literature 111–12
'pick and choose' behaviour 63–4
pilgrimages, Sufi 108, 115–18
Pinçon, Michel 93–4, 96
Pinçon-Charlot, Monique 93–4, 96
play (Nussbaum's capabilities) 407
pluralization 58
Plutarch 299–300
Pogge, Thomas 182–3, 185, 186, 409
political liberalism, and ethical cosmopolitanism 403–6
Political Liberalism (Rawls) 404, 405
politics 29
   and cosmopolitanism 33, 48

political cosmopolitanism 4, 7–10, 370–1
polity, cosmopolitan 174–5
Pollock, S. 322
Polybius 299
polysemy 263
pork pies 270–1
postcolonialism 6, 90–1, 129, 141, 219, 323, 352, 354, 361
   and cosmopolitanism 5, 37, 313–26
   and humanism 395–8
   postcolonial nations 22, 88, 222
   see also colonialism
postmodernism 331, 332, 351
power 354
   colonial matrix of 335–40
practical reason (Nussbaum's capabilities) 407
pre-capitalist economies 338
Precarious Life (Butler) 392
private law 151, 152
Product (RED) 47–8
production fetishism 46
Professional Ethics and Civic Morals (Durkheim) 304
proletarian cosmopolitanism 216–17
Promoting Pluralism Knowledge Program 395, 396–7
property rights 407
Protected Geographical Indication (PGI) status 270–1
provincialized cosmopolitanism 322–6
public goods, global 172–3
public law 151, 152
public sphere:
   cosmopolitan 9, 225–40
   global 249
publics, European cosmopolitan 253–6

Quai Branly Museum, Paris 101–2
'quilting points' 262, 273

race 37, 244
racism 246–7, 252, 255, 339
Ramraj, Victor 134–5
range 26
Rawls, John 4–5, 181, 184–8, 285, 404, 408–9
reconciliation 204
redistribution 181, 183–4, 185, 285–6
reflexivity 61
refugees 247, 324
regulation, global 28
Reilly, Niamh 11, 367–82
religion 506–7
   religious diasporas 138–9
   religious freedom 318
   religious fundamentalism 379
   see also Christianity; Islam; Sufism
remembrance 203
   see also memory
'remote control' of borders 268
replacing the national 26, **26**, 27–8
republicanism 156–8
republics 300
research 5
   shifts in 2–3
   unit of 25–9, **26**
responsibility 180
   personal (principle of cosmopolitanism) 166–7
right 155–6, 159
   system of 149, 150–4
Right-wing political parties 256
risk:
   global 17, 22, 24
   world risk society 23–5, 221, 289, 358, 398
Rizal, José 111–12
Robertson, Roland 10, 295–308
Roche, Maurice 6, 69–82
role-playing 235
Roman Catholicism 404, 405
Rousseau, J.-J. 212
Rovisco, Maria 1–11
Ruivenkamp, Guido 399–400
Rumford, Chris 9–10, 261–273
Rushdie, Salman 107–8, 110, 126, 127, 128

Safran, William 130–1, 133, 134, 136, 138
Said, Edward 324, 389, 394–5

Saiyed, A.R. 117
Sales, Rosemary 96
sampling 62
sandpit analogy 321
Sangatte 272
Sarna-Wojcicki, M. 47, 48
Sartre, Jean-Paul 244
Sassen, Saskia 26, **26**, 28, 218–19
Satanic Verses, The (Rushdie) 107–8, 126
Savage, Mike 353
Save the Children 171
scapes (Appadurai) 26, 34, 353
Schein, L. 40, 41, 42
Schielke, S. 116
Schmitt, Carl 329, 335–6
scientific knowledge 398–400
Second Modernity 20
second-modern approach 351
secularism 396
self-identity 234–5, 238
self-induced endangerment 25
Selfridge's department store, London 36–7, 43, 57
Sem Terra Movement 223
Sen, Amartya 187
Seneca 388
Senegalese Mourides 109, 113
senses, imagination and thought (Nussbaum's capabilities) 406
sexual slavery 374, 377
sexuality 37
    as cultural difference 39
Sheffer, Gabriel 138
Sheller, Mimi 10–11, 349–61
ships in motion **26**, 27
shrines *see* pilgrimages
Shriver, Bobby 47
Simmell, Georg 271
Skeggs, Beverley 38, 39, 63, 64, 355
Skrbiš, Zlatko 7, 53–66
slavery 102, 129, 156, 158, 184, 250, 251, 320, 321, 325, 330, 331, 345
    sexual 374, 377
slowness 359
    slow questions 390–2

smart borders 262
Smith, Michael Peter 90
Snow, C.P. 398
social class 23
social democracy 251, 252
social inequality 17, 21–3
social movements 8, 256, 284–5, 370
    Europe 255
    global 8, 220, 223
social vulnerability 22
socialism 243
sociology 29, 323
    cosmopolitan 297, 298, 304
        paradigm shift in 5, 17–30
    European 18
South Africa, and climate change 22
South Asia, diaspora 7, 108, 114–15, 119–20
sovereignty 195, 197–201, 213, 300–1, 368
Soviet Union 252, 336, 344
Spain 325, 333n5
Spivak, Gayatri 139, 246
starvation 249
    see also food
state *see* nation-states; sovereignty
Stevenson, Nick 9–10, 47, 243–57
stillness 356, 357, 359
Stoics 180, 244, 279n1, 299–300, 322, 388–9, 405
Subaltern Studies 131
subsidiarity (principle of cosmopolitanism) 167
Sufism 108, 115–18
    see also religion
Suleiman, Hajji 117, 118
'sumak kawsay' 342
Sun Yat-sen 216
supply chain capitalism **26**, 27
Suransky, Caroline 11, 387–401
sustainability (principle of cosmopolitanism) 167
syncretism 128, 129, 130, 134, 135, 136
    cosmopolitan 287
Szerszynski, B. 40–1
Sznaider, Natan 8, 10, 28, 195–208, 249–50, 297, 350

Index

Glick Schiller's critique of 352–4

Tamil quarter, Paris 93–4
television 97–9
   see also media
terrorism 243, 268, 379
   and human rights 206–7
Thailand, and Western culture 42
Theory of Justice, A. (Rawls) 184–5
There Ain't No Black in the Union Jack (Gilroy) 129
Third Space of Enunciation 127
Third World novels 110–11
Thompson, E.P. 248
Thrift, N. 358
Todorov, Tzvetan 248, 250, 257
Tokyo 218
   Tokyo Women's International War Crimes Tribunal on Japanese Military Sexual Slavery 374
Tonga 42
Toulmin, Stephen 149
tourism 35
   sociology of 79n14
   touristic cosmopolitanism 77, 78–81
trade:
   European 255
   global 45–6, 213–14
   international 302, 303
transnational cities 90–1
transnational policy regimes **26**, 28
transnational states 19
transnational structures 26, 27–9
transnational urbanism 90
transnationalism 90–1, 218
transnationalization 26
'tropicopolitan' 354
Tropp, L.R. 64–5
Trouillot, Michel-Rolph 349
truck drivers 268
Tsing, Anna **26**, 27
Turkey 333

U2 47
Uganda 395

UK:
   borders 262, 263, 268
   Calais case study 272–3
   media 40–1
   mega-events 75, 76, 79, 80
   South Asian diaspora 114
UNIA (Universal Negro Improvement Association) 320
United Nations (UN) 164, 171, 174, 191, 199, 219, 221, 249, 250, 284, 342
   Alliance of Civilizations 333, 333n5, 335, 342
   Convention on the Elimination of All Forms of Discrimination Against Women (CEDAW) 372–3, 380
   Decade on Women 368, 378
   General Assembly Declaration on the Elimination of Violence Against Women 373
   Security Council Resolution (1325) 371–2, 374
United States 336
   Asian-American population 220
   and climate change 22
   imperialism 250, 252–3
   invasion of Iraq 221, 222
   and mega-events 75, 76, 79, 80
   and neoliberalism 252
Universal Declaration of Human Rights 199, 404
   see also human rights
Universal Negro Improvement Association (UNIA) 320
universalism 286–7
University of Humanistics, Utrecht 388, 389, 395, 398, 400
urban renewal 38
urban spaces 6
   gay 39
urban studies 95
Urdu:
   and Bollywood 118–19
   literature 110–11
Urry, John 34–5, 37, 40–1, 44–5, 46–7, 267, 359, 360–1

'Mobile sociology' 350, 351, 352, 353, 354, 355, 356–7, 358
Utilitarianism 404, 405

values 227, 228–31, 238
Van der Veer, Peter 115
Van Eijck, K. 58
Van Hear, Nicholas 129, 137
Vaughan-Williams, Nick 268, 269
VAW (violence against women) 372–4, 375, 377–8, 381
vernacular cosmopolitanism 7, 36, 107–10, 114–18, 262, 264–5, 354
　and Bollywood 118–20
　popular versus elite forms 110–13
Vertovec, Steven 1, 132
Vienna Declaration and Programme of Action (violence against women) 373, 374
violence 392
　against women 372–4, 375, 377–8, 381
virtual cosmopolitan 354
vulnerability, social 22

Wagner, Peter 316
Wallerstein, Immanuel 253
war 152–3, 157, 245, 301–2, 334
　war crimes 199
　　against women 373, 374, 377
　　see also crimes against humanity
　war on terror 243
Washington Consensus 173
Weber, Max 18, 23
welfare state 222
Werbner, Pnina 7, 107–20
Western civilization 246, 334–5, 336, 337, 338–9, 340, 341
　de-Westernization 331, 337, 345
Western culture 41–2
Westphalia, Treaty of 159

When the Cat's Away (Klapish) 98–9
Williams, M.C. 300
Wittrock, Bjorn 316
Wolff, K. 89
women:
　burkhas 318
　and consumer culture 42, 43–4
　human rights 11, 367–8, 370, 372, 373, 378, 379, 381
　femal genital mutilation 377, 378
　Nigerian 37
　violence against 372–4, 375, 377–8, 381
　see also feminism
Women and Human Development (Nussbaum) 408
Woodward, Ian 7, 53–66
World Bank 252, 284, 286
world citizenship 44–5, 70, 72, 72n3, 88, 153, 170, 179–80, 191, 212, 231–4, 279, 280–1, 288, 301, 370
World Conference on Human Rights 378
world culture 305
world government 8, 9, 183, 213, 243, 247, 282–3, 300–1, 304, 370, 409
World Health Organization 171
World Music 58
world patriotism 3–7, 304–5
world risk society 23–5, 221, 289, 358, 398
World Social Forum 180–1, 223
World Trade Center *see* 11 September 2001 attacks
worldliness 279, 280
World's Fairs *see* expos
WTO (World Trade Organization) 252, 284, 286

Zapatero, José Luis Rodriguez 333, 333n5, 335
Zeno 388, 389
Žižek, S. 39, 262